THIS WAS MY AFRICA
Living with changes

JUNE KASHITA

Born in Yorkshire, flame-haired June Kashita read avidly from the age of four, finding herself captivated by tales of the far-flung places to be found in such books as The Man-Eaters of Tsavo (Kenya) and Living Among Cannibals (Papua New Guinea). As a newly qualified primary school teacher and all set for an English life, June met a man who was to become her future husband and as a black African, the cause of an almost irreconcilable rift between June and her parents. Consequently, risking all to follow her dreams and aspirations, June departed for a new life in the racial hot-bed of Northern Rhodesia as one of the impossibly few crusaders for mixed-race marriage. Her Yorkshire genes stood her in good stead to weather the storm as Zambia slowly arose from the fire of racial segregation, facing censure and deprivations with a clear and reasoned eye and, as this book will reveal - a good dollop of humour.

This Was My Africa
Living with Changes and a Return

JUNE KASHITA

EXMOOR
NEWS

For Ceri and Simon

With grateful thanks to
Tony and Ceri
for all their support.

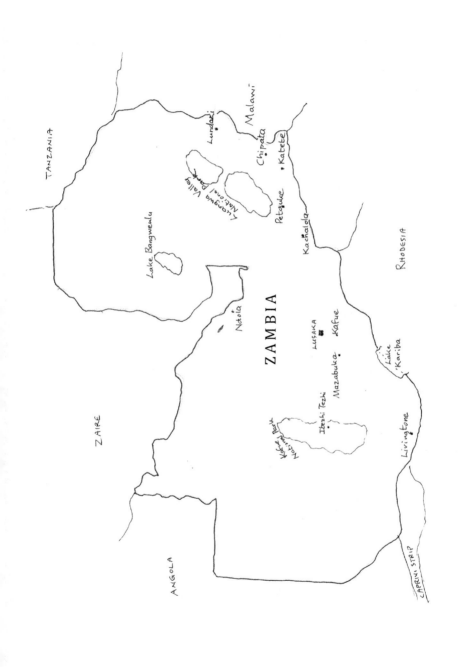

Contents

INTRODUCTION

It seems a long time since I began to write down my memories and impressions of my time in Northern Rhodesia/Zambia... Recently I began to read them again.

How very long ago it all seems. And it strikes me now that anyone else reading it, will be reminded how much society and people have changed. When I was young I was very much influenced by my parents and the thought of disagreeing openly or disobeying them was extremely difficult. Talking to friends of the same age, I am relieved to have it confirmed that it wasn't just me!

We were afraid of rebelling in the 1950's in a way that the younger generation now will find difficult to comprehend.

Racism however, is still around - albeit changed.

Initially I began by writing my memories of our life in Northern Rhodesia/Zambia from 1962 to 1978 and it was chiefly personal family memories. Later I spent some time in the British Library Newspaper section in Colindale, where I read copies of The Northern News, African Mail and Central African Post for that period. And was pleased with the fairly accurate dating of my account – and of course, reading the newspapers, reminded me of some other incidents I had almost forgotten, some of which had bearing on my story. But being a personal account for family, accurate dating has not been the be-all and end-all.

It seems to be quite fashionable today to criticise the Colonial era – it is always easier to be wiser after the event. But I believe there needs to be a recognition of the work and aspirations of some of those long gone 'servants of the Empire', who went off to little known areas, to work and live in isolated areas and had a genuine belief that they were working for the good of the common man and for the future of that country. Many, if not most, were of good intent; what politicians' intentions were – as now – open to debate.

In the great scheme of things the colonial civil service and the settlers didn't have very long before the 'winds of change' swept across Africa bringing about swift changes – often by people who had little or no experience or understanding of what had preceded them. And it has been all too easy to lay the blame on any failings of newly independent countries on the 'Colonial masters' - who had had only a few years to try to weld a nation together and install road and rail and an infrastructure. And we should also remember the hopes and intentions of the man in the field was not always the same as his political masters.

And so I lived through the period of change – from the end of the Colonial era in Northern Rhodesia to the newly independent Zambia and some subsequent changes.

CHAPTER 1
Where It Began In 1960

'I don't know what you're thinking of,' said my mother. 'I just don't know what you're thinking of.'

'She's not thinking at all,' said my father. 'That's the trouble, she never thinks.'

'I don't know what you're thinking of,' said my mother yet again. 'Why, it's ... it's nearly as bad as marrying a German.'

At which point there seemed very little I could say. I had expected a mixture of blank incomprehension and total resistance to my news and I certainly had it. My mother could not understand why I should contemplate such a step and my father would not try to understand. What more was there to say?

The dull wet November weather matched my mood as I sat and waited for my parents to continue the conversation. There was nothing more for me to say. I wanted to get married, they could not and would not consider the idea and so the heavy silence continued. I watched the flames flicker in the fireplace as we sat there and I wondered vaguely what it was like if one broke the news of an engagement and everyone reacted with delight and congratulations and good humour all round. The silence hung between us like a heavy blanket.

'I just don't know what you're thinking of,' repeated my mother for what seemed like the hundredth time. She got up slowly and walked over to the door. I felt sick with guilt as I watched her bowed shoulders and then listened to her slow footsteps going up the stairs.

My father got up suddenly and banged the door shut, he turned and thrust his face close to mine.

'You realise you're breaking your mother's heart, don't you?' he asked. 'Or don't you care? You are only thinking of yourself aren't you? Do you know what you are doing to your mother? You go ahead with this and ... and ... I don't know what I'll do. You are breaking her heart.'

I sat on, frozen by the fire, while he argued and threatened. There was nothing more I could do or say. My silence seemed to anger him even more, but when I tried to say what I felt he overrode my first words.

'You just bloody well don't care,' he said.

The word 'bloody' from my father who never swore, was a measure of his anger. All my life I had been the adored daughter, doubly treasured after the loss of their first daughter. And now set upon – to them – a totally unacceptable course.

I don't remember how or when I went to bed that night. I suppose we all did and we slept in some way or another, worn out by the repeated words which beat against each other until none of us knew what we meant.

I think I went back to my flat the next day, or perhaps I stayed on for the rest of the weekend. I really do not remember. I remember the dull wet November day, the bare trees and the grey skies.

Travelling back to Leeds on the bus I felt for the ring which I had kept in my handbag and slipped it on my finger. I would not hide it any more. The further from home the bus travelled and the nearer we drew to Leeds and my small flat, the more my spirits lightened. It had not been easy breaking the news to my parents but now it was done, I felt as though a heavy load was easier on my shoulders.

Once back in the flat I looked at the photo of Andrew, his dark gentle face looked thoughtfully back at me. I reread the small cramped handwriting in the corner 'All my love darling, Andrew'. And told myself we were on our own, the two of us together in the life to come.

However, once back it was not long before I went to see my friends the Divechas, to have a coffee and tell them my news. Dinesh and Shalini Divecha were an Indian couple who lived nearby and Shalini in particular, with her traditional outlook, expressed concern as to what I should do next - as the idea of going ahead with a marriage without family approval was something she could not understand.

'But she is your mother,' she kept saying. 'You are her daughter, you must listen to your mother. Oh June, what are you going to do?'

What June was going to do – was go ahead. Feeling more confident back with friends, I hoped my parents would come round to the idea and I also knew that Andrew and I would go ahead with the wedding we had planned for the following summer. Perhaps by then they might even feel more approving and the wedding could take place in a friendly atmosphere.

Looking back at that period I do not recall any doubts about my love for Andrew and our plans for a future together. I had known for some time that my parents did not approve of my being more than casually friendly with 'foreign' students. Perhaps they had foreseen the possibility of my falling in love with a 'foreign' student. And in no way could they approve of such an idea. On the other hand, I had not been swept off my feet in a whirlwind romance; in fact I had broken off the relationship at one point feeling that it was more serious than I could cope with.

More than sixty years later it may seem strange to young people today - strange that I was so apprehensive of my parents' reaction - strange that my parents were so wary of 'foreign' friends – the 1950's were just a completely different world.

In my second year at teacher training college in Scarborough I shared a room with another student, Kathleen, who was rather quiet and a regular church goer. I was not so committed but the local Methodist church was only a short walk from the college and the Minister and his wife were more than welcoming to students. So, most Sunday evenings found me walking down to South Cliff Methodist church with Kathleen.

One particular Sunday Kathleen asked if I were going to church, adding that she had met the Minister's wife in town who had said there would be some overseas students there on a visit and they, the Cummings, were anxious that as many young people as possible were there for supper after the service.

So, there we were on Sunday evening, down to South Cliff and over to the manse afterwards. It always seemed chilly in the bedroom where we left our coats but there was a large fire and generous snacks in the sitting room. Not to mention a warm welcome from the Cummings. It was a small group of about twelve 'young people' and the two young men, who were introduced as students from Leeds University. Michael Wearing was the son of a local Minister and was intending to become a Minister himself. His friend Andrew Kashita was an engineering student and clearly the 'overseas' student from Africa

Both Michael and Andrew made a humorous story about their holiday at Michael's home and being waylaid by Rev Cummings to talk to 'our young folk'. No doubt the Cummings had the best of intentions but it increasingly felt as though we had all been gently hoodwinked. Andrew and Michael had gone to help with the young people, who had gone to support the overseas student who had come to give a talk ...

However, the coffee and sandwiches were good and we were out of college and in different company. Andrew was soon drawn to talk about his impressions of England and regaled us with some amusing reminiscences about his schooldays in Northern Rhodesia. Local missionaries had been a great influence on his life, in particular those at Johnson Falls primary school. He said that the Scottish missionaries made such an impact and impression on most people in that area that New Year was a far more important occasion and the Christmas festival passed almost unremarked.

He gave us a brief description of his time at Munali Secondary school – at that time the only secondary school for African boys in the country. He had earned enough money for his school fees there by staying on and working as a 'garden boy' in the holidays. He appeared to have had a reputation of being a bright boy as he was there in his early teens and working alongside young men who had just managed to scrape together the fees and necessary qualifications. The Principal, Mr Clifford Little, had been a strict man with a clear set of rules. For example, the boys would often come from their outdoor activities with dusty legs and it was quicker to wash them under a garden tap on their way into class, rather than going all the way back to the dormitories. This was forbidden, the punishment for which was being made to dig a large hole and then fill it in again. Andrew's large dark eyes shone and his wide open smile became a broad grin as he cheerfully admitted to having dug many holes for that particular misdemeanour - and for having jumped over the low hedges, also punishable.

Then, at long last, after many battles with the officials in the Ministry of African Education, he had won a scholarship to travel to England to study for the Higher School Certificate. At that time (1950's) Africans could not take the Higher School Certificate in Northern Rhodesia. As Andrew had set his sights on being a mechanical engineer he had a long argument with officialdom who did not consider that Africans were 'ready' for such a profession. He added that when he was eventually granted permission to study abroad he was given a most earnest piece of advice from one of the missionaries.

'You must buy a hat.'

Apparently Andrew remembered this advice and carefully selected a hat before sailing from Cape Town but noting that no one appeared to be wearing headgear when he arrived in Britain, it was consigned to the nearest dustbin.

'But my,' he added. 'Your country! You do not know how beautiful it is! So green! I have never seen such greenness. I stood at the ship's rail and stared and stared. It is so green!'

Well, the evening passed pleasantly enough and as we were getting our coats and making our farewells I glanced across and noticed that the two young men looking rather abandoned. On the spur of the moment I invited them both to tea the next day. Kathleen looked rather scandalised, this was NOT the usual pattern. Michael and Andrew, exchanging amused glances, said they would be at college promptly at four o'clock. All the way back to college Kathleen worried about the invitation, the fact that we had nothing to eat in the cupboard and that we had never had anyone to tea before during the week. Even in the late 1950's colleges were much stricter and we were only allowed visitors between 4pm and 6pm during the week - and that had

7

to be downstairs in the Common Room! At the weekend there were wild excesses - friends were allowed in the building from 10am and could actually be entertained upstairs in one's room between 2pm and 6pm!

After inspecting our sparse cupboard and our even sparser purses on Monday lunchtime I dashed down to the local store and invested in a packet of biscuits. Promptly at 4 o'clock Michael and Andrew arrived in a very cheerful mood and, to our astonishment, the latter clutched a large guitar. This he proceeded to play throughout most of our conversation every once in a while smiling at me and asking if I recognised the tune. A most embarrassing situation as every tune sounded the same and to this day I do not know whether it was because he played so badly or because I have very little ear for music. Probably the latter. Kathleen was no help at all, being taken very much with Michael's conversation. Whenever I managed to catch her eye and beg for help in this seemingly endless serenade she gave me a jolly-well-serves-you-right look. I had never thought I would be so pleased to hear the bell ring for Prayer and Dinner - which was also the signal for friends to quit the college grounds. I remember them departing to the strains of what I had been gently informed was Old Man River.

'You knew that one of course,' was his arch parting shot, which left me in a state of bewilderment for the rest of the evening. It was only months later that I discovered Andrew nurtured the delusion that he could give a most effective rendering of his idol Paul Robeson.

Later that week there was a letter from Andrew saying how much he had enjoyed his visit to 'the ladies establishment' and would I ever be in Leeds? This coincided nicely with Kathleen and I, as committee members, going to the annual SCM meeting at Leeds University the following week. Talk about fortuitous timing!

Andrew and Michael had offered to meet us at the bus station but we missed each other – giving rise to a permanent arrangement for future meetings that I would always stand still in one place and wait – 'You know I will always find you!'

So, we skipped the afternoon session – being at Devonshire Hall (their Hall of residence) listening to Andrew play that infernal guitar in his room, while Michael made the most revolting coffee with condensed milk that we had ever drunk. The rules in their Hall were nowhere near as strict as those in our college and we stayed well into the evening.

Later we walked down the road in the twilight to the bus stop and I was taken by surprise when Andrew suddenly pulled me aside into a gateway to kiss me gently. Unexpected but very pleasant. For the rest of the term we went at different times to Leeds but Kathleen's romance soon wavered and died, while I was increasingly attracted to this lively and yet quiet young man who could, and did, talk for hours about his home and his country and his friends. He had already arranged to spend Christmas in Wensleydale with a University friend. I went home. Once back in the Spring term we resumed our relationship and tripped to and fro between Leeds and Scarborough at regular intervals.

Half term was looming and when Elizabeth Bates said she was staying on in college to be near her boyfriend Bob who worked in Scarborough I decided that would solve all my problems. I did not want to spend a week at home if I could not invite Andrew to visit me. I didn't think the situation through in any depth. I just knew that my parents would not approve of my being very friendly with a 'foreign' student and on the other hand I couldn't invite him home and ask him to be a casual friend.

Elizabeth's fiancé was the proud owner of a battered black Austin he had bought for the princely sum of £20. Even at that time it was a period piece with its yellow mica windows but it was a reliable means of transport. So we had planned I would prepare lunch for the four of us while Bob and Liz were at church after which we would all go for a drive together on Sunday afternoon. Andrew arrived. Lunch was ready. But no Liz and Bob.

Eventually we decided to go ahead with lunch and the afternoon was wearing on very pleasantly when we had a message to report to the Principal's office. Bob and Liz had driven straight into a lamp post after leaving church and were now in hospital with minor injuries. I hoped then that we could make our escape but the Principal, Miss Edna Madge, insisted we have tea with her. I was acutely embarrassed but Andrew appeared to find the whole situation highly amusing as he nibbled round tiny sandwiches and made small talk on the political activities in developing countries.

Many years later recalling that afternoon, Edna said she was always very aware that as the age of consent was 21 she had a serious responsibility for the welfare of her students. And I was stepping outside the norm.

1959 Andrew   *1959 June*

It was some time after Easter that I began to have doubts about whether I was ready for a very serious commitment and we agreed to stop seeing each other and we parted on friendly terms. The rest of the summer term was spent first with Brian and then with Peter, both of whom had their attractions but as soon as I felt they were getting serious I felt myself withdrawing. Brian was a blind date arranged by Jill and was a tall fair chap who blushed easily. On our first date he produced tickets for the

Theatre in the Round and off we went to see The Glass Menagerie. The Theatre in the Round was a very new idea introduced by Stephen Joseph. It was a most entertaining evening. Brian was delightful company and managed to stop blushing every time I looked at him. Unfortunately he had presented me with HUGE box of Black Magic chocolates as soon as we sat down and to my dismay insisted I eat one after another, looking so disappointed when I refused yet another one that I had far too many. At the end of the play with about half the box weighing down my uneasy stomach, my only thought was to get back to college before I was sick.

Brian was the typical 'nice' English boy of the period. As we walked up the college drive his footsteps slowed and with the all too familiar crimson tide advancing upwards, he coughed and murmured

'There is something I would like to ask you.'

'Of course,' I said, thinking longingly of the college door, a short flight of steps, turn left, there's a bathroom on the right...

Brian coughed again, carefully lifted his neatly folded overcoat from his left arm and laid it neatly over the right arm. He adjusted his tie slightly and checked the middle button of his jacket.

'I hope you don't mind my asking, please may I kiss you goodnight?'

He was a wonderful chap. Quiet and dependable, thoughtful and kind, amusing company. Why then did I refuse his invitation to tea one weekend to meet his parents? We had enjoyed each other's company but a formal invitation to meet his parents, made me decide to break off the friendship, rather than hurt his feelings even more later.

Peter blew into my life a little later. Tall and dark with a sulky handsomeness, he was the exact opposite of Brian. No more quiet walks or theatre trips. Peter would roar up in his red sports car and we would be off to race through the country lanes. One weekend he insisted we watch the motor cycle racing on Oliver's Mount nearby.

'You will love it,' he assured me.

Deafened by the roar of engines and buffeted by the wind I wondered if this was to be a regular event. My lack of enthusiasm clearly disappointed him but after a couple of drinks he was convinced I would grow to like it. I kept quiet. One evening he picked me up at college and we went for a long drive. It was a beautiful evening and we travelled quite a long way down the coast before stopping for a drink. What with one thing and another we did not keep an eye on the time, realising suddenly there was barely time to get back to college before checking in time. (As I said earlier, colleges were more restrictive then and ours was probably one of the extremes - we had to be in our rooms by 10.30pm and a tutor patrolled the corridors to check all lights were out by 11pm).

Racing back through the dusk we ran into police signs, an accident had blocked the road. The long diversion meant I would definitely be late so at the next call box I phoned the tutor on duty. Thanking me for my consideration, she warned us not to speed. Of course we took this literally and made several stops to pick bluebells by the car headlights. My arrival in college after midnight with an arm full of bluebells caused an envious stir for half an hour.

However, life was not all bluebells.

July arrived and the end of yet another friendship. Peter delivered as his parting shot, how good he had been about not letting me know how repugnant he had found the idea of my having been friendly with a 'coloured'. I found this such an astonishing statement that words failed me. But afterwards thanked my lucky stars he had said that. I had no regrets about having hurt his feelings.

In the September of 1958 I started my first teaching job at a primary school in the small market town Selby, not far from the village where my parents lived. I thoroughly enjoyed myself at Selby Abbey Primary, being fortunate in having an experienced Head, Miss Vera Storr, who taught me the real practicalities of infant teaching, which stood me in good stead throughout my teaching career. The only problem was, to be at school in time,

I had to catch an early morning train which got me into Selby by eight o'clock. Arriving so early and having time to prepare leisurely for the day is a habit which has stuck with me through the years.

My first experience of part time fostering also began that autumn. Part of our college training had been working for a short period in a children's Home and it left me with a desire to do a little more in that field. So once I was settled in my first job I applied to Leeds Social Services to foster a child part time. After an interview I was asked to take an interest in Kathleen, aged five years in a Children's Home in Pudsey.

Blonde and blue eyed, Kathleen looked a sweet little girl but proved to be a handful as she chattered incessantly. I was often driven to wonder if she ever had time to hear what anyone else said. As I was what was known as a part time foster Aunt the arrangements were somewhat fluid and were between the person running the Home and myself. Sheila Wilson was a dedicated woman who ran the Home with 10 children largely single handed. She gave me sterling advice on how to handle my new responsibility. I was told the times I took Kathleen out for a film, visit to a funfair, picnic in the park and gave her my undivided attention helped her to relate to other people. After a short time we learned with great pleasure that she was to be adopted and would have the opportunity of a more normal family life.

Sheila, at that point, asked me if I were interested in taking on another child and when I agreed, suggested a brother and sister, Douglas and Denise Mason. They were five and six years old at that time and an engaging couple. Douglas was the quieter and more serious of the two, Denise was a bouncy vivacious little girl, quite sure the world loved her as much as she loved it. Their father had disappeared long ago and their mother had put them into care when Douglas was barely two and Denise merely a baby. She had not been seen since.

Usually, on Sheila's advice, I took them out separately to give each more individual attention. But occasionally it was both

together. A Saturday outing would mean a film or a picnic in Roundhay Park or a tour of all the big stores in Leeds city centre riding up and down all the escalator and lifts before a meal out. The end of the day was always the same - a visit to the pet shop in the Grand Arcade not far from the bus stop on Vicar Lane. The outings must have been enjoyable because they always tried to prolong it and manufactured many ruses to ensure we missed the bus. And I well recall one dark wet evening when we finally boarded a bus and Denise announced she would sing the carol recently learned at school. The bus, packed with weary and laden Christmas shoppers, endured the first line of
'We will rock you, rock you, rock you ...' for nearly half an hour – and she only knew the first two lines.

At the same time I was happily settled in my new job and into the routine of travelling early and enjoying the quiet market town in its quieter period before the streets were filled with shoppers and strollers. So much so that one bright and sunny morning in Spring I felt so full of joie de vivre that I wanted to share it and stepping into a convenient call box, phoned Andrew.

He was somewhat taken aback at being called to the phone in the porters lodge at Devonshire Hall at that hour in the morning only to have me inform him that the sun was shining and wasn't it a lovely day? To his eternal credit he made a very good recovery and suggested we celebrate the sunshine and my new job with a meal at the weekend. And, he added, he would tell me about the trip he had just made back to his home in Northern Rhodesia the previous summer.

And so my troubles really began, while it had been easy to see Andrew when I was at college and not mention our friendship often to my family, it now became apparent that something would have to be done. As the days and weeks went by I knew that I was more than serious about Andrew and was sure he felt the same way. Previously I had thought that if we were not serious there was not much point in saying much about him. Now that I did feel serious, I dreaded my parents' reaction.

It was still easy for some time to drift along, nobody was

surprised that I would go off to Leeds every weekend 'to meet friends'... clearly there was more to do in Leeds than back home in a little village. I made a point of talking about my friends including Andrew, but it was all very casual and my parents didn't seem at all interested in meeting any of them. The weekends in themselves were quite innocent. I would arrive at Devonshire Hall and we would shop locally for the bits and pieces for a mixed grill and after trying our hands at cooking on the rather primitive cooking facilities, we would sit over coffee and talk and talk and talk. We would walk in local parks and talk and talk and talk. We would have a meal in a Chinese restaurant – heady days of meals at 2/6 d each! And talk and talk and talk. What did we talk about?

A lot of lover's nonsense I suspect.

But I was also fascinated by Andrew's descriptions of his life back in Northern Rhodesia. It opened up a vision of a completely new world where things I had taken for granted all my life now assumed different values. The most obvious one, of course, being education. Where I had sailed through my school days more or less without a thought, 'everyone went to school' and it was merely a part of one's living pattern, now I saw that it was for some people a cherished privilege to be fought for and agonised over. Andrew's father had with great foresight made sure that all his nine children attended the local primary school – local being several miles away – and when the boys showed sufficient ability and won coveted places at the only secondary school for African boys - he made sure that they got there, although the costs were high.

Andrew had enjoyed and appreciated the education he had had at Munali and was full of praise for the Principal, W. C. Little. He and Rob Moffat, (Secretary in African Affairs) had given pupils like Andrew every encouragement and assistance. When Andrew had expressed the intention of being a mechanical engineer they had approved of the idea and were most supportive when Andrew met with a point blank refusal by officials in Government circles. A Mr Gorman, who at that time was in charge of MSD

(Mechanical Services Department), pointed out that Africans could not be engineers. They were, quite simply, not capable of achieving such status. After all, it had taken Europeans many centuries to develop engineering skills, now how could an African hope to achieve such heights?

I stared at Andrew the first time I heard this story, unable to follow the reasoning. He laughed at my expression and tried to explain how Europeans in Northern Rhodesia - and indeed in other developing countries - had this attitude towards 'the native'. If for example, the African had not discovered the wheel for himself before the arrival of the European, then, they reasoned, he was not capable of using and developing the wheel. A line of reasoning I continue to fail to comprehend.

However, Andrew had persevered with his intention of training as an engineer with the support of Clifford Little and Rob Moffat. After leaving school he had worked with a fellow Munali student Titus Mukope as census takers in the rural areas of Kawambwa while the battle for permission to study overseas continued.

'Supplied with yellow Government bicycles, we were regarded as very important fellows in the villages,' he laughed.

Andrew at Devonshire Hall

In due course Andrew arrived in England and after taking his A levels in Leicester he had then won a place to study mechanical engineering at Leeds University. When we were catching up with each other's news that summer he told me that he had been amused that there had been such a negative reaction to his progress on his visit back to N Rhodesia earlier in the year . 'Gorman told me that there was no likelihood of my getting an engineer's job in MSD when I return home,' he said.

I, in my naivety, had thought Andrew's progress would have aroused interest in the various engineering departments. He laughed. 'Of course not,' he said. 'They don't want me there as an example of what an African can do. But I shall go back and if they don't give me a job, I shall work something out.'

He showed me pictures of his home in the village in Kawambwa, a small brown brick built house. I had not known what to expect. A thatched hut? Like one saw in books? Andrew said the Bemba people in his area built their houses with mud bricks (I didn't quite understand why they didn't dissolve in heavy rains). I thought it looked dry and bare, but then I wasn't expecting a house in a village in the middle of Africa to resemble a 3 bedroom semi in an English suburb.

He talked about his elder brothers, who had taught him to swim by taking him out in a canoe on the river and dropping him overboard. He talked about his grandmother to whom he would run when he was a small boy and in trouble for some naughtiness at home. He talked about the difficulties Africans had in their daily lives waiting to be served outside a store, through the natives hatch in the wall. Being addressed as 'boy' when one was an adult; perhaps even a respected man of 50 would be called 'boy!' by a small white child. Not being allowed to enter hotels and restaurants which were for Europeans only.

He talked about the Central African Federation – also known as the Federation of Rhodesia and Nyasaland. This was the semi-independent federation of the three territories – S. Rhodesia had been self-governing while N. Rhodesia and Nyasaland had been British Protectorates. The CA Federation was established in 1953 but by now there was a growing African demand for the end of colonial white rule. Sir Roy Welensky, Prime Minister of the Federation, was proud of boasting that as a boy he had swum bare arsed in the river with the local African children – this bond had not extended to a desire to improve the lot of Africans once he was a politician.

Listening to Andrew I felt ashamed of my fellow Europeans and was relieved to discover how he could, on the whole, talk of these situations without too much bitterness or resentment. Of course he must have felt that, but it had not coloured his attitude to all whites.

Croquet at Devonshire Hall

With all this talking and listening, Spring had cantered into the long hot summer of 1959. One of those long hot English summers which are remembered because they are so rare. I would pick a small basket of strawberries from the back garden before taking the early morning train to Leeds where Andrew would meet me at the University bus stop with a single carnation and each week was more and more enjoyable. He spent the summer vacation at Devonshire Hall and we played croquet on the parched lawns and chatted over coffee with other students also spending summer in Hall.

I tried to find a flat in Selby where I was teaching but there was nothing, nothing at all to be had. So I decided that I should have to teach elsewhere, far enough to warrant living away from home. My parents reacted to this news of moving school with some disappointment but said that after all it was natural that I should want to be independent.

I had the idea that once I was away from home I could break the news about Andrew and our deepening relationship. And deepening it was. So 1959 moved into 1960 and I applied for a teaching post in Leeds and started searching for a furnished flat, finding one near the University and on the bus route to my new school, Saint Luke's Primary in Beeston. Andrew would be leaving university soon and Leeds was a fairly central place where we had many friends. Once I had the job and flat lined up I began to talk even more about some of my friends who were not English. The parents were not very approving but it was generally assumed that there was safety in numbers and 'after all, one must be liberal'. I wondered sometime later whether my insular parents had notions of white slave traffickers!

But just before the end of summer term 1959 any doubts I had about leaving home were swept away by a very embarrassing evening. One of our friends, a medical student from Ceylon, Percy Gunesana, was planning a party when something unexpected cropped up and he had to postpone it. So with casual friendliness Percy decided to drive over and leave a message at my home, having no phone number. He found the house and was invited in. As my mother's first words were, as soon as the door closed behind him, 'Well, I suppose you are Andrew?' delivered in such frosty tones that he said afterwards that he knew instantly that he had sadly blundered.

In great embarrassment he explained he was not Andrew and about the party being postponed after which he asked for directions to my school, thinking he had better tell me what he had done. I was standing on the station platform in Selby when Percy appeared and in great agitation began the saga of the afternoon. At this point I spotted my father walking on to the platform - we often caught the same train home. I thought that it never rained but it poured and now that the deluge was upon us, I might as well make the best of a bad job. In a way I suppose I felt a certain sense of relief that Percy had unwittingly forced the situation out into the open, but now my parents would be forced to admit that there was nothing alarming about my 'foreign' friends.

I walked over to my father to ask if he would like a lift home with us and to my utter horror he hissed,

'How dare you embarrass me like this? Who is that? What do you mean going home? If you go home with him, don't bring him into the house.' And he turned his back.

Oh well, there could not be much more embarrassment to come so off I went with Percy, who drove slowly along explaining over and over again that he had had no idea that my parents did not approve of Andrew, he should have guessed etc etc. Percy had an English girlfriend too but her parents had got over the shock long ago and they were all very good friends.

Poor Percy. He was so very upset over the uproar he had caused and felt he should come indoors to 'explain' all over again. But he looked most relieved when I said he should drive off and leave me to lighten the atmosphere. It was an evening to end all evenings and when I saw how my parents really could not accept my friendship with 'foreigners' my heart sank at the thought of telling them that I was seriously attracted to Andrew. And in sheer apprehension decided I could not say anything at all until I had actually left home.

I continued spending my weekends in Leeds and now had to face a continual criticism about my choice of company. There was the constant refrain 'what will the neighbours say?' – a comment and thought I sadly only understood many years later when I learnt more of my parents personal histories. But at the time – who cared what the neighbours thought? And so selfishly (or not, depending how one viewed it) I pursued my own way.

Percy did have the infamous party later and as I always had to go home, Andrew insisted on seeing me to the last train. The fates really were hotting it up for me, as we reached a compartment about halfway along the train a beaming neighbour waved her hand. I know she would delightedly tell my mother she had seen us. And of course my mother reacted with predictable panic when I related the incident.

One must make sure that the neighbour understood that it was kind of the foreign student to escort me safely to the train, but oh dear, oh dear, why couldn't it have been a foreign student with a white face?

Why not indeed? I was getting thoroughly sick of the topic by now. One minute foreigners were all very well in their way - but their way was not our way - of course we should be friendly because after all we had a duty to the Empire or Colonies or whatever - but being friendly and having a duty did not mean being actually seen in their company ... more and more I felt that my parents and I did not speak the same language.

As I describe this period of my life I think so many young people today will find it laughable that I was so apprehensive. They cannot understand how antagonistic so many people were against non-whites even though they had not met any. My parents' generation very much held the view that daughters would live at home when they started work and would live by their rules. It is even more laughable when I remember how very innocent our parties were - especially in comparison with many held by teenagers or young adults today. I never saw anyone drunk or more than mild displays of affection. Sex, excessive drinking and drugs never crossed our minds. Shortage of funds and no birth control pills probably had a lot to do with it! But the end result was the same. Bill Haley and his Comets were about to streak across the horizon but flower power and hippies were a long way ahead in the future.

In July I left Selby Abbey Primary and took a post at Saint Luke's Primary in Beeston, Leeds. And then I moved into the small flat in Leeds – flat? A glorified bed-sit really. It was a large ground floor room of what had originally been a vicarage. My father helped me move cases and boxes over a weekend. I thought everything was going fairly amicably in spite of a somewhat perfunctory conversation until he muttered, 'No! I don't like your flat. I know why you're moving here - not because it's convenient for the town centre and your school. It's just to be near all your university friends. Isn't it? Don't think I haven't realised what's going on.'

I hated seeing the pain on his face but turned away, knowing that I was increasingly being pushed into a position of making a choice. At least here I could have some peace. At home, if the conversation was not bordering on an argument, it was strained and stilted, always hovering on the edges of what was almost a forbidden topic - but one uppermost in our minds.

65 Clarendon Road, a large detached house set in a large neglected garden and surrounded by a high wall. My room had a huge bay window overlooking the rear garden. The first time I pulled the curtains across I nearly fell over backwards in surprise. Two enormous winged horses sprang across the window and a strong smell of cigar smoke drifted across the room. Afterwards I discovered that the landlord had bought the old curtains from the Odeon cinema and cut them to fit several rooms – I had the Pegasus corners, which many of my generation may remember, leaping across the screen at the start and end of every performance.

It was a wonderful Autumn, heady in its peace and freedom. Andrew came as often as he could at weekends, he was now working at Massey Ferguson and moved from Peterborough to Kilmarnock to Coventry to Stoneleigh and wherever he went, I spent some weekends. And if it was a half term and he was working, I would wander the towns sketching in churches, sightseeing and absorbing local colour.

I found a pencil sketch the other day, fan vaulting in Peterborough Cathedral. I went to watch Andrew playing hockey and disgraced myself by sitting in someone's car to escape the rain, reading a book and missing his winning goal.

Returning from a weekend away with Andrew always had the same strange ending. Arriving back at Leeds station late at night I would take a taxi home.

'65 Clarendon Road,' I would say as I climbed into the taxi with my case and off we would go - only for the driver to draw up outside number 63. As the dark and gloomy entrances to both houses were rather far apart I got more and more irritated. At last came the evening when we went through the usual routine and it was raining cats and dogs and my case was heavy.

'Number 65,' I said in cross tones.

'It's all right love,' said the cheerful driver. 'Get out here, you don't want to carry that case too far.'

'Precisely,' I said with pardonable asperity, 'so please move up to 65 will you?'

The driver turned round. 'It's all right love, you get out here, you don't want to go carrying that case far in your condition.'

Then he looked at my blank face.

'Do you really want 65?'

Which of us was mad? It was only then that I found that number 63 was a Home for unmarried mothers in their final days of waiting to go round the corner to the Maternity hospital in Clarendon Place! Local taxi drivers were quite used to delivering young ladies with suitcases, who would often ask to be dropped at 65 in the vain hope of arriving discreetly. The fashionable loose coats had certainly not suited me that evening.

Andrew arranged to come one weekend early in November and I felt the weekend would be a special one. I knew nothing at all about cooking and made it up as I went along. If only there had been the convenience foods of today! However, I invested in a tiny chicken which I actually got roasting in the Baby Belling oven in the curtained off corner that was my kitchen (or kitchenette as the landlord grandly called it). Perched on top of the cooker on its two tiny rings were two pans of vegetables jostling for space and heat. Puddings were beyond me - and the facilities - so fruit and cheese were standing by. Once the meal was organised I ran upstairs to the bathroom I shared with the three other tenants, only remembering as I stepped into the bath that I had let the Yale lock close on my room door behind me.

Peter, another tenant, was very forbearing about going to phone the landlord as I was clad merely in a towel and dressing gown. The landlord was not quite so polite when he arrived hot from his dinner on the opposite side of town.

Eventually though, there we were eating a dinner I had actually cooked and which did not appear to have suffered over much by its neglect. Andrew suddenly became very solemn and after talking very carefully about how he felt, went down on one knee and proposed in what he said he thought was the traditional manner. I had known what he was going to say and side by side with the happiness I felt was the whispering thought,

'Now how will you tell your parents?'

We talked this over. Andrew knew that I would not really be influenced by their attitude. Now we had come to a formal decision I felt braver and more positive than before. The next morning we went out to buy the ring. And great was Andrew's relief when, after looking at the horrific prices in jewellers windows along Briggate, I pointed out that I preferred the old rings I had seen in an antique shop behind Leeds Town Hall. Andrew also admired the rings and so I had an old Victorian ring set with pearls and garnets for the princely sum of £12!

The following weekend I went home to break the news to my parents.

'It's nearly as bad as marrying a German,' said my mother.

Christmas 1960

Andrew spent Christmas with his friend John Hodgson in Wensleydale as usual and I went home knowing it would be the last time I would spend Christmas with my parents. Unable to talk about Andrew he hung there in the air between us, colouring the conversation and influencing every thought expressed. My mother's pain and distress was like a garment and I was aware that she grasped at any word which might suggest that I might change my mind or even that it really just was not true and happening at all. My father was more in control but I knew that he watched her every word and glance, blaming me for the anguish in her face. His very silence was like a continual blow hammering away at me. My head and heart ached at their distress which I could not ease; my mother knew this was the last Christmas we would be together but tried to pretend that all was as usual. We were all living through a play with superficial conversation which did not convey what we were trying to say to each other. We were all clinging to the routine of Christmas, as though by so doing we could prolong it and put off the moment of my departure back to Leeds.

Once away from them I felt easier and the routine of school and planning the wedding kept me from brooding with guilt. Somehow I still clung to the hope that at the last moment my parents would put a good face on things and agree to attend the wedding.

After Christmas I heard from Percy that there would be vacant rooms in the house where he lived, 10 Mount Preston was a three storey mid terrace just behind the university, not quite so grand as 65 Clarendon Road. He had to return to Ceylon, having failed his exams yet again. Jock Miles, a Scottish medical student had qualified and was moving on and a third student on the ground floor was moving too. As their rent was only £5 a month compared to the £12 I was paying at Clarendon Road it seemed like a good move. I went into a ground floor room next to John Settle, yet another medical student. Margaret Ellerby, who taught with me, fled her family and moved upstairs into Jock's room on the first floor. Masaud Malik, a medic from Pakistan, next to Margaret. On the top floor were Dinesh Divecha, an architect student from India, and his wife Shalini and their baby son Sunil. My mother came for coffee one day after we had been shopping and I suggested she come upstairs to meet Shalini and the baby. Shalini made us coffee and Sunil was his usual charming cooing self and I believed the visit had been a huge success. After this, I thought, she will find it easier to meet Andrew.

How naïve can you get? Once we were safely back in my room with the door closed my mother began her usual theme song.

'What was I thinking of?'

'How could I bear the smell upstairs?'

It was no good saying that not only did I like the smell of the tiny incense stick which Shalini often had burning on her mantelpiece and the spicy smell of her curries which lingered on the top floor, I was so used to them that I hardly noticed. There was no point in trying to take my mother in to share my life. We had no point of contact at all. Anything that was different or 'foreign' was immediately suspect or wrong.

Now that Andrew and I were engaged and were quite definite in our plans for our future I was happier and more relaxed, the worries about my family sank into the background. I think I consciously decided that if they would not try to meet me halfway then I was going ahead with what I wanted and Andrew would come first in my thoughts and care.

Now I was all set to enjoy as much as possible my last summer in England for we were quite determined to make our lives together in Northern Rhodesia.

I decided to book myself in for some ballroom dancing lessons knowing how fond Andrew was of dancing and how unmusical I am. The class was held in an upstairs room just off Boar Lane and a poor man more than earned his fee as he tried, oh how he tried, to get me to waltz around the room but I could not recognise the 1,2,3 much less get my feet to do the same. Finally, as much in compassion for him as acceptance for me, I cancelled after a few sessions. Explaining this to Andrew, it was a relief to hear it didn't matter. And of course in the early days it didn't, there was neither time nor money nor the opportunity.

The sun seemed to shine a lot and life was a whirl with friends and the heady excitement of being in love, friends passing exams and finding jobs, friends marrying and parties. 10 Mount Preston was close behind the university and near most of our friends. Geoff Anteson from Ghana lived just down the road and Mary Allison, a lively Irish girl who worked in admin at the university, lived at the top of the hill. Jock and Pat Miles were not far away and Festina Georges from Sierra Leone was in the next street.

Teachers wages were then about £30 a month. At the beginning of the month when we were affluent, Margaret and I would leave school and indulge in a large meal at a Chinese restaurant – about 2/6 d – and then on to the Odeon for another 2/-. Nearer the end of the month we knew we would be living on spaghetti on toast – fourpence ha'penny a tin!! Thank goodness for school dinners – free, because we ate with the children.

My room at Mount Preston was smaller but there was a separate kitchen this time although it did not do much to improve my culinary interests or abilities. Our landlord had been a student at the university and only came back once a year to inspect the property. Early in the Spring I wrote to him to ask if we could decorate the rooms. He not only agreed but told us to deduct the cost of the paint from our already negligible rents. So cheerful coats of emulsion were splashed over walls and the general appearance of the place was much lighter. When it came to the front door and railings running down the steps, we all agreed on the brightest scarlet possible. Number 10 glowed like a beacon halfway down the street. We thought it warm and welcoming but for some reason the landlord was most distressed on his annual visit, pointing out we had made his house the most conspicuous on the street.

I spent many evenings chatting with Shalini and putting Sunil to bed and then staying on for a meal. Shalini said how relieved she was to have some help with the baby but savouring her curries, I knew I had the best of the deal. Shalini had not been long in England; Dinesh had gone back home to India to marry her in what had been an arranged marriage. At first she had found England cold and grey and depressing; there were still times when she cried for the colour and warmth of India and her family. I think the loneliness of her life was the hardest part to bear, isolated both by language and the tiny flat on the third floor with Dinesh out at work all day. As her English improved and their circle of friends widened she became happier and more outgoing, she ventured out to shop alone but was baffled by the reluctance or inability of local shopkeepers to bargain.

Dinesh and Shalini were Hindu and Masaud was a Moslem; it was a constant joke that while he could smoke and drink alcohol with ease he could not bear the thought of eating pork. I only discovered how strongly he felt this when he had breakfast with me one morning. Having risen early (for him) in the mistaken belief he had an early lecture, he came back into the house as I began making breakfast and offered him some. He sat at the table eating a slice of toast and laughing about his mistake, but came to a sudden halt as I carried in plates of bacon and egg for me and two eggs for him.

'Had I cooked his eggs in the same pan as my bacon?'

I admitted I had thoughtlessly done so. He was angry with himself for not being able to eat his eggs. Bacon on my plate was no problem but the fact that his eggs had shared a pan was. It seemed to puzzle and infuriate him that he had overcome the taboo against alcohol and tobacco but he could not accept any contact with pork.

I was still maintaining my contact as foster aunt to Douglas and Denise, now both at primary school, they thought my tiny flat was a perfect place and were never happier than when they were shopping at the little corner shop for the meal we would prepare together. They would breeze their way around the students union with Andrew and me when we were meeting friends there. One highlight was the university Rag Week and after watching the Parade on the Saturday we sampled everything at the Fair. Dirty and exhausted we finally returned to the Children's Home with an enormous painted dragon from one of the floats.

Sometimes Andrew and I would spend a weekend in London where I met other Northern Rhodesian students. I recall Patrick Chuula, a law student who had married an English girl, Rosemary. Edward Shamwana, another law student with his English girl-friend Stella, a sister at the Middlesex Hospital. Bruce Manyama and Mainza Chona, law students again. It was Mainza who also worked in the UNIP (United National Independence Party) office at 200 Gower Street and who dramatically leapt from a first floor window when the basement office for the Anti-

Apartheid Movement was fire bombed. And there was Gwen Konie, studying to be a social worker. Mabel Mutale, training as a nurse in Northampton. Names who later became so well-known after N Rhodesia became the independent Zambia.

We went to parties held by the Northern Rhodesian Students Association. We went to the UNIP office on Gower Street where the heady atmosphere created by those involved in the fight for independence was so infectious. After getting up to date with the news we would go round the corner to eat at Shahs Indian restaurant.

I clearly remember walking into Shahs one day and Andrew introducing me to the great man himself - Kenneth Kaunda! And next to him, Simon Kapwepwe. And of course Mainza Chona, whom I had already met.

That was the first time I met the men who achieved so much. Kenneth Kaunda of course was the leader of UNIP and in due course was elected President of Zambia. Simon Kapwepwe was for a long time his right hand man.

Margaret often went home at weekends and offered Andrew the use of her room whenever he came to Leeds, this helped with our saving for the wedding. We were saving hard knowing there would be no family support. For a while we considered having a small quiet wedding - but only for a short time. If we were to marry without parental approval - then we would invite everyone who did approve. And so the guest list grew. We used to go to services at Wrangthorne church in Hyde Park, Leeds and arranged to have the wedding there. The reception would be at Devonshire Hall, Andrew's old Hall.

Ordering the wedding invitations was a strange experience because I had to dispense with the conventional

Mr and Mrs.......

request the pleasure of.......

The assistant in the shop was unsure how to express his sympathy, obviously under the impression that I was a totally orphaned orphan with nary a relative to my name. Michael Wearing, who had introduced us, agreed to give me away, although he was quite sure that he would not be called upon at the last minute. Andrew insisted that the date should be 12th August - or the Glorious Twelfth as he frequently phrased it. Then we planned a fortnight's honeymoon touring Scotland.

After Andrew had written to his family, I decided that I too should write and introduce myself. Later I received a letter dated 12 June

Dear June Spalton

    This is the first time of writing you that missive as your father in law.

I was very surprised when I received your letter dated 19th April 1961. And what was quoted in were comprehensived and well understood. There was a question you asked me, that I didn't think of you as daughter in law ? because you are an English lady? NO! in fact, I can only say you are my daughter in law. Because within Northern Rhodesia we have struggled for the burying of TRIBILISM in the interest of the African.

At the same time if it comes to Christianity there is no Jew or a Gentile because we were made by Jehovah as all and we are human beings. And this is the time we should put ourselves in communication with other races on earth.

As you know that N Rhodesia is running to total march to victory. Therefore we inhabitants of the territory we are in need of so many white who please to come and live with us,

About your wedding. Never be worried that I am here! No! for in the place of those who are there – in my place, whatever will happen will happen for me.

But as soon as you are wedded, please send me the pictures also the message concerning the sacrament of your wedding. So that I can prove what sort of wedding it was.

You informed me, you shall come to Lusaka in January 1962 as you will be stationed at Chilanga. Please do not forget to notify me the time you will be shifted from up there. Pass my greetings to your parents. As well as to Mr Andrew. You're greeted by your mother in law as well as sisters in law.

Yours sincerely,
Andrew Lunkoto

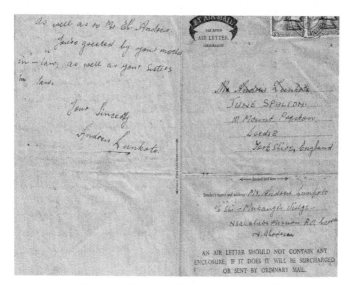

Letter from Andrew Lunkoto, Andrew's father

One could ask no more, I thought. The old man was taking the unusual news in his stride and whatever misgivings he and his family were entertaining, they were being politely kept to themselves.

But why the Andrew Lunkoto name? why wasn't he Andrew Kashita or why wasn't my Andrew named Lunkoto like his father? Andrew explained that in Bemba tradition sons were given an uncle's name but either couldn't say, or didn't think it relevant to explain, which uncle he had been named after. I asked if we had sons, which uncle ... but he said such traditions were dying out.

As the plans went ahead I found myself increasingly detached from my family and less upset by the distress I was causing. I handed in my notice at school and had a few words of advice from the Head, Mr Lumley, who was under the misapprehension that N Rhodesia was part of South Africa and that we were obviously heading for troubled times. Once I had convinced him that they were two separate countries and that N Rhodesia was still a British Protected Colony he looked a bit relieved and wished me well. It was a constant surprise to me how few people knew anything at all about N Rhodesia and, in fact, any of the British Colonies. It seemed as though the general British public were content to know that such places existed and that they were being taken care of – by some One or some Body, who doubtless knew what they were doing for the good of the locals. A fellow teacher once advised me, after cautiously skirting round the topic for some time, that I really ought to check on what kind of housing I was heading for - '... some people still live in ... those you know... grass huts ...' once reassured on that point (I did not mention that mud brick houses were all the rage in the Bemba villages in Northern Province) she visibly relaxed but added, 'Of course, I still think you ought to have your own bank account, you never know when you will need a little money of your own. Not much, but you do need to know you have something of your own.' Dear Miss Garrett, was that her advice to every would-be bride, or did she foresee problems in the jungle?

I must confess that I had a somewhat skimpy idea of what kind of life style I was heading for, in spite of Andrew's descriptions of 'home'. It all sounded so different and in its way exciting that I had more or less decided not to anticipate but let it happen in its own good time. Looking back I believe that was entirely the right attitude. I was constantly surprised and occasionally disappointed but having no strongly preconceived ideas I found it fairly easy to accept and adjust – and sometimes reject.

One evening the doorbell rang and on opening the door I found two men on the doorstep, who introduced themselves as friends of Andrew. Henry Shikopa and Andrew Sardanis insisted on taking me out for a meal and talking about Northern Rhodesia. Andrew Sardanis appeared a little concerned about my ignorance of local customs and I remember him describing how I should accept anything offered.

'You must always take it with two hands held together,' he said. 'It is considered impolite to receive something with only one hand. Look, this is how you should cup the hands together, even if you are being offered something quite small.'

It all sounded innocuous to me and if the local custom decreed that this was a polite thing to do, I thought I would be able to remember a small thing like that and rise to the occasion. They also talked about how a man inherited his brother's wife, should the brother die; while this was clearly a practical solution in village life with no state support for a widow and children, I did not think it would be particularly relevant to me. I did not plan on embracing local customs quite so closely.

On the whole it was quite an enjoyable evening and I was impressed that these two friends had taken it upon themselves to be so welcoming and helpful when they were in the area. To my surprise Andrew did not appear to be so happy about their visit and said that he thought they had spent far too much time talking about irrelevant trivialities.

I recall Andrew Sardanis asking me if I had any idea about the reaction there would be in Lusaka to our mixed marriage. I replied that I had gathered it was not common but no doubt it would be a seven days wonder. Both Henry and Andrew were at pains to let me know that it was more than uncommon – it was in fact illegal and I would be the first white woman married to an African in that part of the world. They added that I should expect some strong opposition. Having faced some strong reactions from my parents I thought nothing else could have much more effect on me.

(And after all, I thought, Seretse and Ruth Khama had set tongues wagging once. Andrew and I would merely be an addition to that number. The Khamas who married in England were actually banned from returning to his home land Bechuanaland by the British Government for a while, even though he was a traditional ruler).

Back at school the Head took it upon himself now that he knew I was no longer in any danger by being in South Africa, to go to the other extreme and gravely pointed out that in fact we would be much closer to the Congo, which at that time was reeling in its own bloodbath as Belgians prepared to pull out.

When I agreed that yes we would be closer to the Congo and added that in fact I was at that time fundraising with my class to help the starving children in the Congo, he shook his head and wandered sadly away murmuring

'Oh my dear girl, my dear girl ...'

Douglas and Denise were now seven and six years old and I asked the Authority if they could be page and bridesmaid. Permission was granted and I took Denise off with me to the Bridal House to be fitted for our dresses. Douglas maintained he was NOT going to be a page boy with everyone looking at him. However, housemother Sheila with her usual diplomacy, won him over to 'dress up' a little bit. Denise had no such inhibitions and thoroughly enjoyed our fitting sessions. A pair of frilly knickers had her, for once, speechless.

The 12th of August 1961
A bright and sunny Saturday.
I hurried off to have my hair done early in the morning and

was amused to meet Andrew as I came back. He cheerily called across the street

'We are not supposed to see each other before the wedding. So I am not here, you understand?'

And we passed each other with faces averted and broad grins to the mystification of a bystander. Back at number 10 all was quiet. There was nothing to do much except drink some coffee and hope we had not forgotten anything. I was enjoying the peace before my friends Mary and Jean were due to arrive, when the doorbell rang and there was my mother.

For a few brief moments I thought there had been a change of heart but I was soon disillusioned. She had come to see if even now I would reconsider, would I not cancel the wedding? It was not yet too late. She would take care of all the details. Here was some money from her handbag, here, take it and go, go anywhere you want. 'I will see to all the cancellations'.

This was worse than I had ever expected. Although I was hurt and angry, I also ached for her distress and desperation. I don't remember how we parted or what I finally said to make her finally go but at last she left and I closed the door. Although I had managed to keep calm enough now I needed some comfort and fled up to Masaud's room and rushed in. Poor Masaud, deeply embarrassed, hopped around half in and half out of his trousers and fended me off. When I told him what had happened he mopped my face and said all the right things.

I had just got back downstairs and back to thinking rationally when the doorbell rang again and in came my mother once more. 'I just could not go without begging you to think it over just once more,' she began.

At which point Masaud appeared and started easing her towards the door. If I had not been so distraught the sight of my mother's 5'2" fluttering against Masaud's broad 6' frame it might have struck me as amusing.

Very gently but very firmly he steered my mother back to the front door, repeating over and over again that June must know what she was doing by now and that such scenes were not going to change matters. And then she was gone.

Poor Masaud. Although I thanked him I do not know whether he knew what a tower of strength he was that day. Wherever you are, Masaud Malik, thank you once again. Jean and Mary appeared shortly afterwards to help me dress and check my hair. Michael was there to take me to church. The car was at the door and we were off.

Sheila had Douglas and Denise waiting at the church door and after a quick hug she took Douglas inside. Denise was bursting with pride and happiness, clutching her basket of flowers at all impossible angles. Michael held my hand tightly as we walked into the church and began the long walk up the aisle. Andrew was standing very straight – he had had his hair cut very short, shorn like a lamb. Masaud was in the front pew, he said afterwards he thought he had better be at hand if my mother reappeared.

Denise waiting for Michael and me at Wrangthorne Church

The service began. I remember Douglas looking very sadly on, Denise beaming with happiness and Andrew, warm and comfortable beside me. The awful long, long pause when ' ... or forever hold his peace... '

Surely now I would have peace?

Then we were in the vestry and my aunt, the only relative there, refusing to sign the register, whispering to me 'I dare not, you know ... your father ...'

Thank you, Aunt Clare, for being brave enough to come.

Devonshire Hall - Sheila with Douglas, Denise and Tony
(who lived in the Home with Douglas and Denise)

Outside the church, the surprise of seeing some parents and children from school, who had travelled across Leeds to wish us well.

Up to Devonshire Hall for the reception and the sheer exhilarating relief, tension gone and happiness.

So many friends and so much laughter.

Wedding group at Devonshire Hall

Photographs and more photographs. Groups here and groups there, everybody crowding together. Andrew's friends from the Dales, his university friends, my college friends, N Rhodesian students up from London ... Edward Lubinda looking very preoccupied – we discovered later that he had borrowed a camera from the BBC where he was on a course and it had been stolen from the car.

Denise showing all and sundry her frilly knickers.

The difference between English and African customs – while we were upstairs changing at the end of the reception - Pat Chuula expressed his concern that there had not been the usual long extended African speeches extolling Andrew's virtues and he was most anxious to rectify this omission. Edward and Stella Shamwana successfully held him back and convinced him that it was not necessary – although I long suspected he has always entertained misgivings.

Mary and Shalini with Sunil

Finally off in the car and out of Leeds and heading north towards Barnard Castle. The sudden silence - and the odd feeling that this was a total stranger beside me. What a relief years later to hear friends say they had experienced the same reaction!

Barnard Castle where we carried off the old married look so well until the following morning, when the receptionist suggested we clean off the treacle and confetti from the car roof before the sun hardened it.

On, up to Edinburgh where we were to spend a week and watch the Edinburgh Tattoo. Knocks on the bedroom door late one night, finding the manager and a policeman there. Instant panic picture of my parents, what could they do now? But it was only a damaged car in the car park, mistakenly identified as ours.

When would I be free of fear that I had hurt them into some final desperate act?

We drove on further north. Sunlight and freedom, pleasure in each other's company and total understanding of each other's moods.

Once back in Leeds we hurried on with the packing of our wedding presents and everything that was to go ahead of us by sea. Andrew was still battling with the Northern Rhodesian Government and the Colonial Office. Now that they had a black graduate engineer they were in no hurry to have him back in the country proving what black Africans could achieve. To all their suggestions that he consider another degree or stay on in UK on some research project or other, Andrew had only one response. 'Now I am qualified I want to help my country.'

A place had eventually been found for him in the Ministry of Agriculture, although it was hastily added that he was more than welcome to stay on in UK and gain some more experience ...

But by September it was finally agreed that we would spend a month in Coventry with Massey Ferguson and then go to Wrest Park Lodge, the Agriculture Research Station in Silsoe, Bedfordshire. And finally in December 1961 we would set off for Northern Rhodesia.

Once he had won the battle of being offered a job and his fare paid back home, Andrew raised the matter of his wife's fare. But in spite of all the arguments we could muster, the Colonial Office were quite adamant that if Kashita had chosen to get married in UK then it was up to Kashita to get his wife out to N. Rhodesia.

Now that Andrew had been offered a post as a mechanical engineer at Mount Makulu Research Station at Chilanga, ten miles from Lusaka we could begin the massive operation of moving our goods and chattels there. For some reason I cannot for the life of me remember, we decided to make a start on the books, of which we both had an extraordinary number. Again for reasons now lost in the mists of time, we decided to send them out in job lots and twice a week I parcelled up twelve paperbacks or four hard backs in brown paper to be dispatched from the local post office. I believe Andrew had worked out that book post by sea was the cheapest option. As the book shelves began to look rather depleted I began to believe we really were going to N. Rhodesia. It was not a dream.

As there was no rush, indeed no one appeared keen to hasten our arrival there, we decided to travel by sea and accordingly made our plans to travel by Lloyd Triestino down the east coast of Africa. Our worldly possessions were taken from us by the packers and with only one bulging suitcase each we headed down to the Hughenden Hotel in Coventry. We lived there for a month and while Andrew worked at Massey Ferguson, I explored the town and helped his boss' wife with her voluntary work with a pensioners group. Commander Ellis and his wife were friendly and welcoming throughout that month and we kept in touch for many years.

Relaxing at Hughendon Hotel, Coventry

One week a couple with two young children arrived at the hotel, the children were fascinated by their first sight of Andrew in the dining room and their forks could hardly make contact with their mouths, they were so bemused. Andrew and I found this highly entertaining but their parents were clearly uncomfortable and must have had words with the children because after that they made a conscious effort not to stare. A few days passed and then to our amusement the children wandered into the lounge where we were reading the newspapers. For a few moments they stood there, nudging each other and edging slowly forward. As last Andrew raised his eyes from the paper and said,

'Yes?'

More nudges and shy giggles.

Then 'He wants to know.'

'Yes?'

'He wants to know something.'

'Yes?'

'He wants to know – canwetouchyourhair?' all in one breath.

Andrew gravely bowed his head forward and said, 'Yes, why not?'

Two small hands came slowly forward and stroked Andrew's head and off they ran shrieking

"We did it, we did it!"

We just fell about in helpless laughter but their parents arrived shortly afterwards, red with embarrassment, to apologise and it took us some time to convince them that we were not offended. They explained that they came from a small Scottish town and that ... well ... it was the children's first time to ... to see a black face.

From Coventry we moved on to Wrest Park Lodge, Silsoe, Bedfordshire. Here we lived in a hostel for men on the agricultural courses and while they were prepared to accommodate me as a special concession there was nothing to do all day and no midday meal for me, which the men had in a works canteen. For a brief period I was able to do some supply teaching at a local school but otherwise time dragged. We were on a very tight budget so for some days I made do with coffee and a biscuit and reading piles of old Punch magazines I had found heaped in a deserted lounge.

Andrew then worried that I was not having a midday meal and ordered me to take the bus into Luton every day and have a meal. I inspected Luton from one end to the other on foot and then I began to read along the library shelves. I ate in a Chinese restaurant at 2/- a time. And then one day I saw in a shop window a leather toilet case, just the thing for Andrew's Christmas present, but the price was too high. However, if one added up the cost of Chinese lunches for the next few weeks ... and it was back to coffee and a biscuit. I forget the exact price of the toilet case but it was in use for many years and Andrew's appreciation when he knew what I had done made it all so very worthwhile.

In the evenings we watched TV in a communal lounge with the various men on the course or who worked there permanently. There was one man who eventually aroused my interest, he always smiled amiably when we met but never responded to my Hello or How are you? One day we learned that he had been a prisoner of war and had been sent to work as a labourer at Wrest Park, time passed and the war ended. The chap did not wish to be repatriated. More time passed. Staff changed. And slowly it was realised that no one could remember the man's details – nor could he give any – he had stopped speaking altogether – if he ever had. No one could remember his nationality, he was believed to be German or Polish but when a student arrived who spoke both languages, the man could make no response. He appeared to have forgotten any language. So he stayed on, seemingly content to work, be fed and housed and presumably paid in cash? He would watch TV every evening quite happily. I wonder now what happened as he aged.

And then in November another step forward – I got my Residence Permit. Number 11310 for the Federation of Rhodesia and Nyasaland stamped by the British Immigrants Selection Board – I was authorized to enter the Federation.

G.P. & S.—5732—200-100B—4-6-59.   Form 2 (S.)

FEDERATION OF RHODESIA AND NYASALAND

RESIDENCE
PERMIT   N⁰   11310   **B**

File No. ....1577........

Year ....1961........

The undernoted person (and dependants named below) is/are authorized to enter the Federation of Rhodesia and Nyasaland not later than ....1.6.MAY.1962... and to reside in the Federation subject to compliance with the provisions of the Immigration Act, 1954, as amended.

1. ....

2. (Wife) .... KASHITA :   June Rose

3. (Child under 18 years) ....

4. (Child under 18 years) ....

5. (Child under 18 years) ....

6. (Child under 18 years) ....

A valid Passport (not a Tourist Passport) is essential in addition to this Permit.

This permit is granted on the condition that the holder shall follow the occupation of ....

in the Federation for a period of not less than two years from the date of his arrival in the Federation. It may be cancelled if during that period the holder, without the permission of the British Immigrants Selection Board, Salisbury, Rhodesia and Nyasaland, engages in any other occupation or fails to engage in that occupation.

This permit will cease to be valid if the holder departs from and resides outside the Federation with the intention of making his home outside the Federation or is absent from the Federation for a period of six months before he has acquired domicile. The Board may extend the period of six months.

....
Secretary,
British Immigrants Selection Board.

Residence Permit

It was about this time that Andrew was engaged in exchanging long letters with the District Commissioner in his father's area back home, his father had been arrested and was in prison. But when Andrew demanded to know on what charges the old man was released.

'Now I suppose he will call himself a freedom fighter! But all that seems to have happened is that there have been some UNIP

43

meetings in the area, which as headman, he is supposed to have been able to prevent.'

In December we paid a fleeting visit to Leeds where at last we had a meal with my parents and an uneasy truce was declared. Then down to London where we set about the final arrangements. It was bitterly cold and we stayed with John and Margaret Mwanakatwe. He was then the Assistant Secretary in the Northern Rhodesia Office. It was one of those old Victorian mid terrace houses and had the highest ceilings and coldest rooms imaginable.

There I met Titus Mukope from the African Mail, who later wrote a short article about us for his newspaper with a photo of us standing with John and Margaret, chilled and shivering in their bare London garden.

Clifford Little was in London and invited us to lunch – an early Christmas dinner he called it. I was impressed with his humorous personality. No wonder Munali had turned out such independent students with tolerant and adventurous minds

SETTING OFF   December 1961

Stella Shamwana saw us off at Victoria station and with great glee I thrust my umbrella into her hand with the insane idea that I would not require it in Africa - the land of eternal sunshine. Stella thought I was mad.

'But after all dear, an extra umbrella is always useful.'

I looked at the last English policeman on duty at Dover and had a sudden pang at leaving England – would I ever come back?

Then we were on the train to Paris where we stayed a couple of days before travelling to Venice. Paris was fun but humiliating when my schoolgirl French let me down repeatedly. Venice was bright in the winter sun and almost empty of tourists. We wandered round, endlessly sightseeing and savouring the feeling that at last we were on our way. The last few months in England had seemed very much like a filling in stage, hanging around waiting for the action to begin. Now at last we were heading home – already I thought of the unknown ahead as 'home'. We took photos in San Marco Square with the pigeons in the very best tourist manner and sent postcards to Douglas and Denise. We were travelling on the Europa, Lloyd Triestino line. My first real intimation of the reactions I should now expect came when we embarked and met up with the steward who was allocating tables in the dining room. He glanced up from his list, froze for a moment, double checked his list running his pencil up and down. There appeared to be many people not yet allocated tables but his pencil wandered to and fro until at last with obvious relief he crossed out three names and put them beside ours.

'I've put you with the White Fathers,' he said. 'I'm sure they won't mind - I mean you don't mind sharing a table with the Fathers?' I realised that it was a perfect solution to what he saw as a problem although I did not believe that anyone would have made more than a token objection to sitting with us - but then I was not aware that as the Europa's final destination was Cape Town, there was bound to be a large number of Afrikaaners on board. I said earlier that I was naïve, there must be a stronger word to describe for what I was at that time!

I suppose, looking back, that Andrew was the only non-white passenger on board that ship but I did not think about it at all at the time. As the days unfolded and little incidents occurred I always reacted with slow surprise and then amusement. No matter how often one is told about racism and colour prejudice, it takes a long time before one can anticipate a reaction. At least, I never pre-thought a situation - which was why each incident took me unawares.

The White Fathers, bless them, rose to the occasion admirably and were the most amusing and charming of companions. The tall Dutch Father and the Italian, Father Charles Talone, who was returning to a parish in Ndola kept us company throughout the voyage – the third White Father excused himself, saying he had been invited to join another table. (Now, I wonder ...?) They reminisced with Andrew about places they knew in common and I listened, fascinated by their descriptions of places which were as yet merely names on a map. Father Talone was a jolly man who enjoyed the good things in life and was making the most of his trip on the boat with its excellent chefs. At our first dinner together as the boat left Venice, he unfolded his napkin, regarded the menu with a practised eye and announced that he would follow his usual method. This consisted of eating his way through as many of the dishes as he could - I watched with awe as he steadily ate through the evening. At last he put down his wine glass, twinkled at me and said,

'Do not worry. Tomorrow I eat only lettuce.'

His method, which he followed throughout the three week voyage, was to alternate daily between eating everything he could and the next day confining himself to lettuce and black coffee. And his twenty laps round the deck after breakfast.

Our cabin, being one of the cheapest, was a tiny one hidden in the bowels of the ship. At first I had thought I might find it claustrophobic but as we spent very little time in it, that was not the case. Most of the time was spent on deck where it was remarkable that we were spending so much time in close proximity to so many people, with whom, in fact, we had so very little contact.

The Europa was to stop at Brindisi, Port Said, Mombasa, Dar es Salaam and Beira - where we would disembark - and then it proceeded to Cape Town. That being so there were a large number of South Africans and Afrikaaners on board. We were not their favourite people.

On the whole we were avoided, but as we were still fairly newly married and very much wrapped up in each other, much of the social disapproval washed over us unnoticed. One young man, a South African doctor, I seem to recall, took us aside one day into a laundry room off one of the corridors and furtively explained that he thought we were doing a wonderful thing. He really admired our courage, it was people like us who would actually break the apartheid system. Andrew beamed at him and with a wicked gleam in his eye, thanked him most sincerely.

'Now how about a drink at the bar?' he asked. 'Let's celebrate this hope for the future.'

The poor man turned pale and glancing once more out into the corridor said hurriedly,

'Oh no! oh no! I dare not. I wish I could. But you see ... '

Poor chap, we did see. We were not hurt or offended, I think we both pitied him. If only he had stood up to be counted, others may have had the courage to join him too. It seemed to me that there were some people who expressed sympathy or approval but only in a corner and never in front of their peers.

Before we left the laundry room, the doctor said that he had had to talk to us so that we would know he was not like all the others on board who were so angry at our presence. He was somewhat surprised that we had not noticed the simmering anger we were causing and the ostracism which was in force by 'everyone'. This was food for thought. I suppose the crew were polite and helpful, the White Fathers good dining companions and for the rest of the time we were wrapped up in each other. Andrew must have been more aware of it and would have known how to interpret some glances. My sheer ignorance may have helped him in that we certainly not spending our time fretting over not making new friends. After this secretive meeting however, I began to look round me with a more practised eye, I began to notice who avoided looking at me altogether, or glanced at us and then looked quickly away. When I saw a group at the bar and heads turned, I felt sure they were discussing us.

As for the doctor, he too somehow was never looking at us or walking in our direction after our brief conversation. But we respected his fear.

What the hell! We had been on board for some days now and there could not be much more left to comment on. I realised later of course that that would have been the exact opposite as we were a permanent sore in their midst and there is no end to the talk about what should be done with cheeky kaffirs. What precisely they would have done about me I can't imagine. Perhaps even they were at a loss. The idea of a black man marrying a white woman was not unknown, Seretse and Ruth Khama had hit the headlines earlier, but we were probably – if not certainly – their first direct experience of a mixed marriage. Seretse Khama went to England for a year at Balliol College Oxford, moving on to study to become a barrister in London where he met Ruth, an English girl and after a year he married her in 1948. The inter-racial marriage sparked a furore at home, South Africa and back in Bechuanaland among the tribal elders. After a long exile they were allowed to return to Bechuanaland in 1956 - only five years before we set off.

Some had their own ways of dealing with the situation. A dear little grandmotherly looking soul, South African or Afrikaaner - I could not always tell - eventually made a point of coming to sit beside me on deck and initiated a conversation. We sipped our coffee and watched some deck games. I thought in my innocence that she had come to accept the situation. But no, after a little talk about where I was going and where I had come from, she seriously told me that I was doing a very wrong thing as I was not really married.

I wondered if she was under the illusion that we had had a register office wedding and that this had offended some religious belief or hers, so I assured her that we had been well and truly married in a church, by a Minister of the Church and that we actually had a marriage certificate. All this she swept aside as completely irrelevant.

'No, no,' she said. 'You aren't really married - you can't marry One of Them and of course you can't have children.'

Yet another misapprehension. I assured her that as far as I knew I was more than capable of having children and what was more, fully intended having them. In fact I rather fancied the idea of having four.

She visibly reeled at this but rallied.

'But my dear, you can't do that. You don't want to have bastards.'

I began to wonder whether she had taken in any of the preceding conversation. Patiently I went back over the ... we were married ... in a church to boot ... any, nay, all of the children we intended having most certainly would not be bastards....

'Of course they will dear, all babies like that are bastards.'

Whereupon this dear little old lady tottered off on her way, having failed to make me understand the enormity of what I was doing and to no doubt further scandalise the Afrikaaner contingent with our conversation.

Well, life on board ship in no way resembled what I had seen on Hollywood films where there were jolly games and romances on deck in the moonlight.

There were highlights of course, crossing the line which was as funny as I had expected (but we had the sense not to try to participate) and evenings when we walked on deck and listened to the soft swish of the sea and it seemed as though we would sail on forever, wrapped in our own little cocoon of discord.

Christmas came with a cable delivered in the middle of the night - Happy Christmas -Hurley and Horsman, two of my tutors at college.

We exchanged presents in the early hours in Andrew's bunk and wished each other many more happy Christmases together.

Christmas Greetings

As with the New Year later, the Fathers were good companions in the dining room but no one else invited us to share in a celebratory drink and we were wise enough not to press anyone else to join us. The mutual truce of apparent courtesies continued only because we kept our distance. I wonder now whether the good officers of the good ship Europa had held their breaths when we boarded and anticipated possible open conflict. Now I was much more aware of what racial tension was all about but there was not much time to think about it because there was the thrill of my first time to sample so many new places and experiences.

In leisure moments I tried to settle down with a book of Bemba grammar and useful phrases which Andrew's friend, Goodwin Mutale, had sent me earlier (Goodwin was working as a District Officer while his wife Mabel trained as a nurse in Northampton). I had hopes and intentions of arriving in Northern Rhodesia with a useful smattering of Andrew's language at my fingertips. As the words were pronounced phonetically I had no problems on that score but I did wonder at the mentality of the author, while I could see the need to list simple instructions which would help me to communicate with the servants, they would be of very little use in conversations with Andrew. But when I got to the translation for 'the fierce rabbit' my patience wore thin and I thought it would be better to rely on some simple conversation with Andrew. We made very little progress - or rather my progress was so slow we did not pursue it seriously enough. This dilatory start was bad enough but when we finally arrived in Lusaka and I realised how many local languages were used in the capital alone I lost interest. It was a very great mistake on my part, I should have persevered with Bemba.

Some memories.

We sailed through the Suez Canal and everyone on deck was highly amused when at one point when we were between two high banks with nothing to suggest any nearby life, two men appeared clad in swimming trunks and waving a casual towel, they sauntered down to the water's edge.

The weather of course got steadily hotter and hotter.

Port Said was terribly hot with smelly sewers and camels lying in the streets, despite the hazardous walking conditions I loved it. I was actually on my way and England was far behind.

Mombasa was hotter still. We took a local bus into town and

wandered down the wide streets. We sent postcards to Douglas and Denise and hoped they were following our progress as they received cards from each stopping point. I really was in Africa now with all its colour and sounds and smells. The hot sun beat down on my head and I found the glare hard to adjust to (instead of giving away my umbrella, why hadn't it occurred to me to invest in some good sunglasses?). Never mind. The streets were alive with such variety of language and dress it was hard to absorb it all. The contrast of poverty and riches side by side was startling, barefoot ragged people side by side with large expensive cars and their occupants. The main road into town was arched by huge elephant tusks and everywhere flamboyant colours and scents of unknown flowers.

Dar es Salaam – which seemed a quieter version of Mombasa - and where a man, one leg swollen by elephantiasis, dragged his weary way. Queueing at a post office to buy stamps for postcards to Denise and Douglas, we found ourselves standing behind a man whose body odour was more than over powering. I thought as I tried to face the other away as I inhaled, that such poverty was sad. Andrew, as we got the stamps and left the crowded place, sounded angry, saying there was no excuse for that, the man should wash. But I wasn't sure if he were angry or embarrassed ... I was puzzled.

We left the ship at Beira, disembarking early in the morning and where we would have to wait until the evening for our connecting train. It was appallingly hot and humid. Two Italians, who had managed to exchange some civilities with us at the very end of the voyage, suggested that we spend the day on the verandah of a local hotel by the sea where at least we should catch some cooling breeze. It was a Sunday and everywhere had a shuttered look, the sun beat down on my head and cicada beetles shrilled until I thought my head would split.

This was Portuguese East Africa so our presence did not cause much comment when we arrived at the hotel and we sat through most of the day, sipping cold drinks on a wide cool verandah overlooking the sea.

It was a relief to board the train in the evening where we had a compartment to ourselves. There were four bunks in dark green leather and a neat little washing contrivance in one corner. As soon as the bunks were let down and the beds made up we stretched out with the cool night air blowing in through the mosquito gauze on the windows. I lay and listened to the regular chug of the steam engine which would pull us several thousand feet above sea level and watched the stars appear in the dark sky. This was the last stage of the journey.

There were a few stares when we entered the dining car next morning but I was beginning to take this as part of the local scenery by now. Back in our compartment it was exciting to watch the African countryside unfold, lush and green as we left the coast and climbed towards Southern Rhodesia. Once we saw a sable antelope poised among the tall grasses but otherwise there was little animal life to be seen.

Suddenly the door slid back and two girls looked in.

'Excuse me, can we come in?'

They slid the door closed behind them and pulled down the blinds on the corridor windows.

'We are from South Africa and we wanted to talk to you. Where are you going? And is it true that you are ... really ... married? and what did they say to you last night?'

It was only then that we discovered that our joining the train had not gone unremarked by the Afrikaaners around. One man in the saloon car had become so incensed that he had declared no kaffir was going to share a compartment with a white woman on any train on which he was travelling. He had set off with the intention of bodily heaving Andrew off the train but fortunately someone had called the guard. In the end the poor man had been locked in a first class compartment and kept out of our way.

'Didn't you hear the uproar?'

But no, we had slept through all the upheaval and were completely unaware of the storms which had raged up and down the train while we slept. The two girls did not stay long, afraid they would be seen leaving our compartment. They wished us well and said that if only more people could do what we were doing the world, especially South Africa, would be a better place.

So, people wished us well and gave us secret support, but they were all afraid to stand up and be counted.

That night we double checked our door was locked.

Early the next morning we arrived in Bulawayo, where we were to take the 8am train to Lusaka. To our annoyance the guard denied we had a booking and refused to allow us on the train. We trekked across the station to the booking office where the clerk there agreed there had been a mistake but assured us that we would be able to travel on the next train which left in 12 hours' time at 8pm. We knew full well that the guard had refused to have us on his train – perhaps our contentious friend was heading north too and it was thought advisable to keep us apart?

However, there we were at Bulawayo, very early in the morning with nothing to do and nowhere to go. We bought coffees and newspapers and sat down on a bench. Later we could deposit our luggage and take a walk round town. The station was large and deserted now the train had left. We read on.

Footsteps. They stopped in front of us. I looked over my paper to see an enormous pair of black boots and puttees. I looked up to see a hefty pair of tanned hairy legs, I raised my eyes further. Rigidly starched khaki shorts. Topped by a typical – as I was to discover - muscular broad white Southern Rhodesian policeman. He stood there tapping his cane on his leg.

'Good morning.'

'Good morning', we replied.

The police officer looked uncomfortable, we felt a mixture of apprehension and amusement.

"Staying in Bulawayo?"

"No, waiting for the evening train."

"Ah! You're going to Northern Rhodesia?"

'Yes.'

The police officer noticeably relaxed.

'Well now, what are you going to do during the day?'

Andrew smiled. 'We had thought of taking a walk round the town, have a look at Bulawayo you know. Anything to pass the time.'

'Hmmm, well now, there's nothing much to see in Bulawayo you know. You are going to find it very hot too ... and this is not the north you know, things are not quite the same down here. You'll be all right up north but the people are not quite so up to date down here. Know what I mean? Look, I've got a suggestion to make. Come along to my office.'

We followed him along the station concourse to a small police office where he suggested we spend the day.

'I'm not saying you must spend the day here, you understand? But there isn't much to do in town. And you might find things a bit uncomfortable at times. Know what I mean? Now, I am not making you stay here. But I am suggesting you have the use of my office and make yourselves comfortable.'

I think the same thought crossed our minds simultaneously. We were short of cash and knew that we would spend the day sightseeing on foot and it would be a long hot day.

We hesitated.

'We were going to have lunch in town of course,' said Andrew.

'It's a very kind offer,' I said. 'But what could we do here all day? Have you anything I could read after I've finished the paper?'

The officer knew we had reached an agreement and nothing was too much trouble. Nothing! Nothing at all.

The chairs were comfortable enough surely? He would have a coffee tray delivered at once from the station buffet, he would send along a selection of reading matter and after that he would arrange for lunch at the station restaurant.

Faced with such cooperation and knowing that there could well be some concrete opposition if we did not show similar consideration for the peace of Bulawayo's population, we agreed. The police officer was by now all smiles and marched off to arrange everything for our welfare. A well supplied coffee tray appeared as if by magic, followed shortly afterwards by armfuls of papers and magazines - all for free. We sat back - relaxed and smiled at each other.

'Coffee?' I asked, raising the pot and my eyebrows at the by now perspiring man.

Once he was sure of cooperation, he relaxed even more and asked Andrew where he was going in N Rhodesia and where we had come from; his patent relief that we were going to be out of S Rhodesia by the next morning was quite transparent. Over and over again he assured us that 'it's different up there'. He then disappeared for the rest of the morning and we savoured the steaming coffee, biscuits, new papers to read in comfortable armchairs, with our personal police toilet to hand. The morning passed pleasantly enough in the cool office and the police officer was back to escort us to lunch. I had given no thought to the effect we were having on the station staff but once we walked into the restaurant all the by now familiar signs were there. Rigid staff and bristling local whites. The officer took us to a reserved table in the corner and nodded to the manager as he walked out.

There was a dead silence as an African waiter produced a menu and stood with an expressionless face at our table, only his uneasy sidelong glances betrayed him occasionally. We read the menu and ordered a meal. The dead silence continued as we sipped a cold drink which arrived without being ordered.

'Courtesy of the officer, and the meal will be too of course.'

We wished we had ordered a larger meal.

The windows of the restaurant looked out on to one of Bulawayo's main streets and we began to realise that it was a very busy town, especially near the station. A constant stream of Africans were walking along and glancing into the restaurant; it was not long before we realised that many of them were going past for the second, third, fourth ... nay, even fifth time! The humour of what was happening hit us both at the same time. The unheard of novelty of a mixed couple sitting and eating together in a white restaurant, seated at the same table no less ... 'Oh brother! Come and see this one'.

Our fellow diners hit upon the same interpretation shortly afterwards and the desultory conversations they had endeavoured to nurture lapsed into an icy silence once more. Andrew and I looked at each other and smiled. If one is providing a talking point, a small light diversion and so on at no expense or discomfort, why not prolong the episode? We had a very leisurely lunch, nodded to the silent room and strolled back to our sanctuary.

The train of the fascinated and curious continued past the police office window. No one dare approach the doors so at one point Andrew stood in the doorway to admire the platform. After a while a taxi driver came along and asked if we were under arrest, finding we were not he offered to take us for a drive round Bulawayo.

'Everyone wants to see you,' he added.

We thought discretion was the better part of valour and pointed out that an uneasy truce existed. He nodded, unsurprised and went off saying there would be plenty of people wanting a trip to the station to see us. By now the whole day had assumed a slightly lunatic quality. By keeping us at the station the police officer had hoped to keep our presence very low key, unfortunately for him, the news had spread even faster, with the added spice that no one was sure whether or not we were under arrest.

And so the procession of the curious continued and the European staff looked more and more harassed as they were unable to deny anyone the right to walk through the station, check through our open door and window that it really was true and out at the other end of the station, to either repeat the performance or to rush off to spread the word.

A bountiful tea tray arrived with even more magazines and a slightly weary looking officer.

'Your bookings for tonight are all confirmed, no problem tonight. You will be off to night, no problem at all. And it is different up there.'

The train was in the station well before eight o'clock and off we went to find our compartment and load our luggage. Time then to stand and look out of the door, wondering what the town of Bulawayo really was like and whether we would see it one day. Other passengers were arriving, friends were being bade farewell ... when we saw that a few folk had come to say goodbye to us.

Several people came up to the window to say that they had heard about us and they had come to thank us - it was this repetition of thanks which struck me as curious. We answered questions about going to N Rhodesia and confirmed that yes, we were married (married!), in England, Andrew had graduated and was to work as an engineer. Our crowd of new friends grew and there were backward glances over shoulders which we understood better when we were reminded that there was a ban on public gatherings in force. In fact, by having so many Africans crowding around us we were all flagrantly breaking the law.

While the railway authorities and the police officers walked by at regular intervals, they had clearly decided that it would be better to have the train depart on time and wash their hands of the whole affair. It was different up north after all, and if they were insane enough to grant permission for a black to return home with a better education than most whites and with a white wife too - let them get on with it, but the Southern Rhodesian police wanted nothing to do with it at all.

The train departed on time and we waved goodbye to a crowd of over fifty who had wrung our hands until they ached.

Years later I was introduced to David Phiri's father who had come to visit him in Lusaka - David's father lived in Bulawayo. As we shook hands he smiled and said, 'Ah, but we have met before.' He had been among the crowd on Bulawayo station that evening. The train chugged slowly on up into N Rhodesia. Crossing the tiny bridge spanning the Zambezi River at Victoria Falls - not such a tiny bridge really but miniature in its majestic setting, I marvelled at the spectacular beauty of the Falls. What was it that David Livingstone had written when he first saw them?

'Scenes so lively must have been gazed upon by angels in their flight.'

Andrew told me that the local name for the Falls was Musi o Tunya which meant The Smoke that Thunders, it seemed a far more fitting name than that of a far away and long dead British monarch.

 At the end of the third day we were now heading for Lusaka, on the home stretch as it were and I watched the passing scenery with renewed interest. Being the rainy season the countryside was lush and green, endless savannah country and a far cry from the dry deserts and steamy jungle which often spring to mind when thinking of Africa.

CHAPTER 2
MOUNT MAKULU
January 1962

We arrived in Lusaka about seven in the evening as the sun was setting, the air dark and cool. Andrew had told me that Lusaka now boasted a new and modern station so I had expected something along the lines of Bulawayo and definitely something rather grander than a long bare platform and a small building. Even more curious was the fact that we had arrived at an apparently anonymous station, there being no name board. It was in fact there, but was hidden by tall grasses at the spot where the trains used to stop many yards away and where people had had to jump down from the train on to the track side.

I had read that Lusaka only came into being with the arrival of the railway in 1905, was gazetted as a village in 1913, was made capital in 1935 and here we were less than 30 years later.

I have read (Lusaka Management Board minutes 1933) that it had been difficult in the early 1930's so far from ordinary radio to fix the time accurately. The Lusaka Management Board thought the clock in the Railway station was the most accurate but the Government thought the Post Office clock should be taken as Lusaka time. After a discussion it was decided that a signal gun would be fired by the police. This idea was never finalised as no ammunition could be found. So until the coming of radio, Post Office time was fixed as Lusaka Time with the police blowing a bugle at noon each day. Both railway station and post office had new buildings in the late 1950's.

But here we were at last in January 1962! and we began to climb down from the train. Elijah Mudenda was meeting us and would take us to Mount Makulu Research Station where we were to live. As we looked around for Elijah we were approached by two white men in crisp white shirt and shorts, who introduced themselves to us as Government Information Officers and asked Andrew for an interview. He looked somewhat taken aback but they pointed out that an African graduate engineer was a newsworthy event and that if they had all the details for a press release we would be spared any further visitations by the press. It was not a bad idea so the train departure was delayed while back we climbed on to the train so that photographs could be taken of us arriving and having our first look at Lusaka. Then off the train once more and into the small station building for Andrew to answer questions about his student days in UK and what he hoped to achieve now that he was home.

While they were talking I made a polite and somewhat perfunctory conversation with the younger information officer. It was not a long interview but in that short period I managed with my usual lack of tact to say quite the wrong thing to the young man's clear mortification and my bewilderment. He seemed to have run out of questions for me so trying to help the conversation along, I asked how long he had been in N Rhodesia. 'Five years.'

'Oh, so you are quite a native of the place then?'

Andrew said afterwards that he realised there was an appalled silence at our side of the table but I could not think what had caused it. When I repeated the conversation, he roared with laughter at my poor choice of phrase.

The interview was at an end shortly after that and Elijah drove us off to Mount Makulu. Leaving Lusaka station we turned into Cairo Road where I was impressed by the wide dual carriageway, well-lit shop windows and a set of traffic lights - great place! It was of course already dark and the street largely deserted but I had the impression it could be a busy town centre.

What I did not know then was that Cairo Road was less than quarter of a mile long and was basically the centre of the city with two minor parallel shopping streets. I was impressed with the wide street - wide like all early main streets in Africa because ox carts had to be able to turn in them when towns were first developing and no one was going to attempt a three point turn with one of those, especially if there was a span of twenty oxen. As for the traffic lights which had suggested a bustling metropolis, there were still only two other sets of lights for many years, one near the Anglican Cathedral and the other at the hospital crossroads.

Cairo Road, Lusaka

At the end of Cairo Road was a roundabout and then we were out of town heading ten miles south to Mount Makulu. Elijah's wife Zeenie was warm and welcoming; we were to stay with them until our house was ready to move into. Elijah was from the Tonga tribe who lived in the Southern Province, his very large eyes and slow gap toothed smile gave him an air of childlike surprise and innocence. Zeenie, a Xhosa from South Africa, was as plump as he was slim and bustled about the house urging the servant to hurry with the dinner and ushering me into the bedroom and thence to the bathroom. In spite of all her small talk there was an underlying shyness and I wondered how she felt about having a white guest.

As we sat over dinner Elijah, who worked as a plant breeder, told us how they had only recently been allocated a Europeans officers' house. Before that they had had to live in the African compound with the farm hands, office orderlies, house servants etc. This despite the fact that Elijah had graduated from Cambridge with exactly the same degree as the English man, now also at Mount Makulu and recruited at the same time - but of course he warranted Officer status immediately. He was white. Elijah had met Zeenie, when he was studying in South Africa; she had come from a country where apartheid was the official policy to a country where it was practised to a lesser degree. I was to discover so many sections of life in N Rhodesia were segregated on racial lines - schools, hospitals, residential and shopping areas etc but more of that anon.

Mount Makulu then was a spread out station covering many acres of gently rolling land. There were about thirteen houses set in a circle – these were for the European Officers and were spacious bungalows with 2 or 3 bedrooms and with corrugated iron roofs, which I found incredibly ugly at first. They were all furnished with very basic Government furniture and were surrounded by large and pleasant gardens. The Head of the station lived some distance away in dignified solitude and the four bachelors were accommodated in the bachelor quarters overlooking the club house and swimming pool. The compound for other workers ie drivers, servants, clerical officers, lab assistants, messengers etc was huddled at the base of the small steep hill from which the station derived its name.

Mount Makulu Admin Block

The next day Andrew went off to the offices with Elijah and soon returned with a set of keys for the house we had been allocated. Zeenie, her small daughter Janie and I walked over to inspect it. We walked along a narrow track wide enough for one which wound its way behind the houses between grasses taller than myself and past a clump of tall blue gums. This winding path was largely used by servants coming to work via the back gardens or taking messages from house to house. The sun was hot and there was a smell of rich soil and bursting juicy growth. A large blue headed lizard ran across my path, startling me for a moment.

The white painted house had been standing empty for some time and looked forlorn and dusty. Windows, iron framed and fitted with mosquito gauzes looked out on to a bare garden, green grassed but with no flower beds or fruit trees. There were two bedrooms with fitted wardrobes and clumsy wooden beds of differing heights and solid chests of drawers. Sitting room and dining room sported a heavy table, four solid chairs, a drinks cupboard and a set of two wooden arm chairs and a settee. These latter had adjustable reclining backs and wide flat arms on which to rest your glass. Cushions there were none and the criss-cross strap bases looked uninviting. Standard Government issue I learnt.

The kitchen sported a black Dover wood burning stove, a sink with running water, some fitted cupboards and a meat safe - this was fitted with gauze to protect food from flies - was in the ironing room, which had also a solid wood table.

Hot water was provided by a Rhodesian boiler, this was a tall slim boiler set in the outside of the kitchen wall and heated by a wood fire below.

Artistically arranged on the sitting room floor were piles of books, still in their brown paper wrappings, which I had despatched so long ago, but all with a torn corner where the stamps had been. What an odd postal service I thought as I looked them over, only to discover later that an avid stamp collector on the station had happily helped himself as the parcels arrived.

The floors throughout the house were bare red cement. Zeenie clicked her tongue over these.

'You are going to have to have these polished and polished and polished! You are going to need the largest tin of COBRA.'

I soon became very knowledgeable on the subject of Cobra polish. Red in particular. It was the bane of my life for some time to come. The floors of all Government houses and many private houses too, were plain smooth concrete, which sounds pretty Spartan and dull but in actual fact was a cheap and practical floor. They were smooth and easy to clean and polish and were delightfully cool in hot weather. They were also disaster with a capital D to anything dropped. Once the floor was laid in a new house it was stained with a red dye and thereafter polished weekly with red Cobra polish. It looked both warm and inviting as it glowed with a dull red gleam and yet it was cool. However, the polish was particularly penetrating, clinging and all pervasive. The soles of ones feet and the feet of all furniture all had a red tidemark and, as I discovered later, when the baby started to crawl, she was destined to have pink tinged nappies. Many people used the red polish year after year and lived with the red tidemark quite happily. I went to the other camp who said to hell with the look of the place and we used white Cobra polish. This gave the desired shine but the red stain soon receded along the main thoroughfares of the house so that one had a gleaming grey-pink path surrounded by deep red borders. In my early innocence I accepted Zeenie's advice and dived into the red sea with enthusiasm.

The house was painted white inside and out and it was all topped with the green corrugated iron roof. It was a long time before I got used to these roofs, they looked so ugly and harsh. But they were of course highly practical, being easy to build and maintain. However, in a heavy storm the rain bounced off them with the sound of rolling drums and if one were unlucky enough to have a leak between two sheets then you were fated for eternal misery. The rains would start and there was the leak. The workmen arrived from the workshop on the station and a long session commenced with men in, on and under the roof for days. They chatted loudly and cheerfully with each other and any passers-by, finally departing with the assurance that all was in order. Come the next storm, back came the leak. This would happen with monotonous regularity for some weeks until the foreman was pressured and browbeaten into admitting that yes, you did need a new roof but did you want half your roof removed in the middle of the rainy season?

A compromise would be reached until the advent of the dry season when long and laborious days were spent in renewing roof sheets. Of course by now it was the dry season and one had no idea how well fitted the sheets were until the next rains.

And so Andrew and I moved into an AK2 – AK was the type of house and 2 referred to the number of bedrooms. At first I felt a trifle disappointed in my surroundings ... it was all very green and on the opposite side of the road from the house a herd of Jersey cows browsed in the lush green grass! Very soon I appreciated their fresh milk which Andrew would bring up at midday from the office. But ... Africa and Jersey cows? It was a bit of a let down.

I spent a couple of days at the house with two young men Elijah had found for me saying he thought they would make very good house servants when trained. The last phrase was the telling one. I had no idea that it meant starting from below the very basics with two young lads who knew not one word of English, so it was an achievement that the house was prepared at all.

I had spent a frustrating and unbelievable amount of time in trying to have a table moved from the sitting room to one of the bedrooms. It had seemed a simple request but I had never reckoned with the fact that my two willing helpers would pick up the table and try to walk through the doorway with it. After a while I came out of the bedroom to find why they had not arrived with the table and found them still in the sitting room trying to carry a 4 ' wide table straight through a 3'6" doorway. As I stood open mouthed they put the table down, agreed that it was not possible and after due deliberation they solemnly picked up the table, turned it round and attacked the doorway with the opposite end of the table. Mission impossible. A pause. They then picked up the table and tried it long ways on which was obviously even more impossible. By now I was so fascinated I could not bear to interfere. At about which point they became aware of me waiting down the corridor.

So up with the table again and they approached the doorway with the narrow end once more but this time, to show their determination, they pushed vigorously. But the table did not yield and neither did the door frame.

At the next pause I tried to explain that if the table were placed on its side and it was slid sideways through, two legs first ... half of this idea got across. They crashed the table on to its side and tried to push it straight through.

Fearing for my sanity I seized the table legs and began to heave it into position and with a wiggle here and a wiggle there the table slid sideways through the doorway and into the bedroom. I glanced at the two young chaps, convinced they had been ham acting but no, they were rubbing their hands and congratulating each other on a job well done.

I could not begin to describe our antics with the simple operations involving mops, buckets, soap and water and later the infamous Cobra polish. But move into the house we did and Of course, we were there in the house but our goods and chattels were not.

They had been sent ahead in late August 1961 and this was now January 1962 and where were our crates? Still sitting on a ship off the coast of Beira we were told, monsoons having delayed everything. (I did not recall having seen a monsoon as we passed that way but doubtless they picked their moments - or their ships). We could not stay with the Mudendas ad infinitum nor could we afford to buy even the basics for the house so we were lent the station safari box, which was used by officers going on a long inspection tour in remoter areas. This was literally a huge wooden box which contained two of everything from kitchen utensils to bed linen, but only two! So when Elijah and Zeenie came to see us, two of us would have coffee in cups and two would have cold drinks in glasses.

The Mudendas took us into town that first week to shop and Zeenie and I set off round Greatermans store. I needed everything and Zeenie was pointing out that it was more economical to buy the largest size of everything when the men returned from their trip to the bank.

We knew we had arrived on Lusaka platform with 6 English pennies, a sousa (sixpence) and two Rhodesian tickeys (silver threepenny pieces) in our pockets but Andrew had now found to our surprise that we had miscalculated and that we actually had £20 transferred from the UK account. While the expected overdraft was not there as we had feared perhaps buying the largest sizes was not a wise move just yet. Zeenie and I began changing items and discussing the merits of various brands new to me and the men were sauntering after us.

A white man kept reaching for things on the same shelf as me, in fact everything I wanted, he wanted too and it began to be awkward as I apologised yet again for bumping into him. At last, as we collided yet again and I was thinking what an oaf he was as I said 'Sorry' once more when he suddenly turned his head, spat in my face and snarled,

'You! You! What are you doing this for?'

And he motioned with his head towards Zeenie and the men. Then he slammed down the tin he was holding and stamped off towards the door, leaving behind his basket of goods.

I never knew who he was, whether he recognised Andrew and me from the article about our arrival which had been spread across the front page of the Northern Rhodesian News or whether he just objected to a white person shopping with Africans.

We had had to indulge in some other shopping. Andrew had to buy at least two pairs of shorts – men wore shorts as a matter of course. They were very practical in that climate and I quite envied him. It didn't take me long to ditch the stockings (tights had not yet arrived) during the day but somehow women in shorts for everyday wear just hadn't taken off. It did take me a while though to get used to six foot tall schoolboys sauntering through town in short shorts and school tie. But I was more than happy with Andrew, sleeves rolled up and baring his knees all day.

By now of course, I was beginning to look for people's reactions - although there would be many occasions when I would still be taken by surprise because I would forget what we represented to the bigoted many - it was not a bigoted few. So many who declare themselves liberal in their ideas and beliefs are not and eventually give themselves away.

The Head of the station, Alec Prentice, had gave a sundowner party on our second evening, it was mainly for people on the station although there were some people from Lusaka there too. Prentice probably thought it would be a chance for us to be formally welcomed and introduced, at the same time it would break the ice for what many people would find an awkward, and to some, actually an offensive situation. I think that I was always aware that some people were offended by what we had done and if they had lived all their lives with one set of values and attitude then I did not expect that our mere presence was going to work a miraculous change overnight.

At the sundowner we were introduced around and Andrew was soon chatting with some men about the work on the station, although there was a clear division between those who were introduced and drifted away not to exchange another word and those who initiated and continued conversations. Talking it over later we saw that it was often the men who were not professionally qualified who were the most resentful. Regrettable but understandable in a country where so many held a position by virtue of white skin alone.

Most of the women also found it difficult to accept me but we battled on. This clear division of the sexes at parties I found to be a novelty and was disappointed to find it widespread. Jopie and Anneke Vogt, a Dutch couple, were friendly. A Dutchman Bill Verboom and his wife made a point of coming to stand beside me and talking at great length, for which I was very grateful.

There had just been a short exchange of overheard remarks which were not at all complimentary. I can't remember who the women were or if they were even based on the station but for some reason I felt very hurt, partly because this was supposed to be a gathering of people who were linked by work and partly feeling that some of them were united against me.

Zeenie had not been at the party and when I described the episode she said,

'That is why I never like going to parties on the station. But you looked very smart and I was sure you could stand up to it all. It is easier for the men, they talk about work. But the women are difficult and I could not tell you before you went. Anyway, I was sure you could cope. You dress well and you can talk.'

If only Zeenie had known what a shy and shaky person was underneath that cocky flippant exterior!

We soon settled into the routine of living with the safari box and life on Mount Makulu. Andrew was busy down at the offices every day - or at least trying to be busy. To his astonishment and frustration Alec Prentice had informed him that there was no hurry for him to proceed with any particular project of work. 'Look around and read around ' he was told, and anyway, no money had been allocated for an agricultural engineer this year! So Andrew read and looked and thought and wrote reports and fumed. I rattled around the sparsely furnished house trying to find things to do. We had by now taken on a cook, Kapitu, who dealt efficiently with the housework and cooking and a school leaver David to work in the garden. Kapitu was a blessing in another way, I was beginning to find the altitude of 4000 feet and hot weather a bit of a trial and to my chagrin I often fell asleep on the bed after lunch - I, who had always ridiculed the notion of siestas. So life was settling into a routine – Kapitu would arrive to make breakfast for 7 o'clock after which Andrew would depart for the office. Then there was the hustle and bustle which was Kapitu sweeping through the house and then 'shining' – which meant he stood on two large oval brushes which had canvas straps which fitted over his bare feet and he literally danced a

69

shine on to the floors. Dusting did not appeal, much less raising the eyes up to see any cobwebs on the ceilings. The laundry was done in the bath with much beating and sighing, then hung out to dry in the eternal sunshine – and no, it wasn't sunshine every day all day - just felt like it after the cold grey English winter I had so recently left behind. It all ran like clockwork and the only hiccup I recall was the time a yellow duster inadvertently went in the bath with the white sheets. A matter for much sorrow at the time but as the sun bleached the sheets every time they were washed, the yellow glow gradually faded – just as well as we couldn't afford any more.

Not having passed my driving test and not having a car meant I was restricted to being in the house and walking across the station to have a coffee with Zeenie – invitations from a couple of other wives came very gradually. Not having much in the way of household goods meant there was not much to occupy me - few tools and the heat meant I would do even less in the garden. We had only been in the house for a short while when there was a knock at the door one afternoon and I found a young woman introducing herself as a reporter from the Central African Post, could she have an interview? I pointed out that the information Department had all the details and that the Northern News had already run a story about us.

'We thought there might be an interesting story in how you are finding life in N Rhodesia and ask you to give a more personal interview now that you have been here a while, your impressions of Lusaka and so on.'

We sat over coffee for a while and while I willingly answered her questions I was aware of a growing sense of frustration on her part. At last came the comment,

'You are just like everyone else aren't you?'

At which I could not help laughing. 'Did you expect me to have two heads?'

These are the reports which featured in the Central African Post

'Wednesday 17 January 1962

African Engineer Back Home With White Wife

An African returning to N Rhodesia with an English wife has taken up a post with the Ministry of African Agriculture as its first qualified African engineering officer. He is 29 year old Mr Andrew Kashita, a graduate member of the Institute of Mechanical Engineers (Grad 1 Mech 1) and he has a second class Honours degree in engineering. Mr Kashita is employed as an agricultural engineering officer on a salary scale rising from £1,150 to £2,435 a year. He went to Britain in 1953 on a Government bursary and by the end of 1955 qualified for entrance to Leeds University where he obtained a B Sc degree.

PROBLEMS

His duties with the NR Government include the investigation of problems of mechanisation and the instruction of African farmers and organising workshop facilities.

Mr and Mrs Kashita, who arrived in Lusaka last week, are now living at the Government Mount Makulu Research Station near Lusaka. He is the first African in the Territory with a white wife ... '

One would have thought that that covered the story but no, after the personal story the poor public were then subjected to a repeat of the photo taken at the station when we first arrived and

'... Mr Andrew Kashita the NR African and his white bride, newly arrived in the territory ... Mr Kashita is seen helping his wife off the train at Lusaka station. They travelled by sea from Europe to Beira and from there by train to Lusaka. For interview see page 7.'

If one had not had enough by then one could read the 'personal' interview.

Being young and foolish I had chatted quite freely with the reporter, not thinking she would use every word I uttered and even place her interpretation on some things.

'JUNE AND ANDREW KASHITA meet with stares, curiosity and good wishes.

'We want two children, four if we can afford it', said the red haired young white girl from Leeds, newly arrived at Mount Makulu ...

ATTRACTIVE

She is attractive Mrs June Kashita who arrived in the Territory last

week with her 29 year old husband ...

Already Andrew and June are being met with stares as they walk down the street together. Sometimes Africans they do not know come up to them, introduce themselves and wish them luck, but white people tend to hang back more, although a few have spoken similarly to them ...

On one occasion during the train journey a white woman came four times to the Kashita's compartment, just to look at them.

'Eventually I said Hello? And she did not come back'. Mrs Kashita said she felt people expected to see something quite out of the ordinary when they looked at them.

'When they find we are just ordinary people, they seem quite surprised, 'she said.

Proudly she showed me her wedding photograph, she looked lovely in her long stylish wedding gown standing next to her smiling husband. How did she meet her husband? It was after church at the Minister's home ...

Mrs Kashita, who was setting her home in order when I called on her, has black and white neighbours. 'My neighbours have been very friendly,' she said. '

One thing I was sensible enough to do, was not to talk about unfriendly or aggressive reactions we had encountered. I would not give such people the satisfaction of publicity.

On the same page as this report was

CHILD WAITS AND WONDERS

'Monique Stephenson, Congo born Belgian girl staying with Mr and Mrs Rundle of Kingfisher Farm 10 miles from Lusaka is attending the Dominican Convent School. Her parents returned to Elizabethville to salvage what they could of their business and personal possessions after their garage was commandeered by the United Nations. There has been no news for a month and the Red Cross cannot trace them.

Monique was sent to school in Lusaka immediately after the Congo Independence, she would have had to go to the new multi-racial schools and sit side by side with African children in the same standard but nearly twice her age.'

I often wondered what her parents thought on their return (they were traced shortly after this report) if they had read that next to their report was the one about a white woman marrying a black man, not just sitting next to him.

Only two days later I opened the door to a chap who had come all the way from Johannesburg to write a report for his magazine Drum. Charming though he was, I could not produce a startling character for him to write about and in fact had begun to dislike reading about myself. Andrew and I had to go into Lusaka that afternoon and the young man followed us around, a 'mixed' couple doing anything was apparently newsworthy. How true that was we did not realise until we bought a copy of the magazine and found that even Andrew's slippers by the fireplace warranted a comment!

PHOTO DRUM MAGAZINE

Back then our reading ranged from The Northern News to the Central African Post and the Central African Mail with an airmail weekly copy of the Guardian from UK. The African Mail edited originally by Richard (Dick) Hall had a very independent voice.

In January 1962 the Mail criticised Voice of UNIP for saying the killers of Mrs Lilian Burton were heroes. (The murder of Mrs Burton in 1961 had shocked the population. Driving on the Copperbelt her car was attacked by frustrated UNIP activists after leaving a meeting. Today it would be said she was in the wrong place at the wrong time. No comfort to her family and friends). The Mail stated that the editor of Voice of UNIP, Sikota Wina, disgraced himself for publishing wrong-headed nonsense. 'The fight for African rights is not a matter of throwing petrol over women, white or black'. The following month later Titus Mukupo took over as editor and Dick became editor of The Northern News, later The Times of Zambia. Dick's wife, Barbara Hall, ran the agony page Tell Me Josephine in the African Mail where the readers' letters had a wholly new slant on lovers or the young and confused dilemmas. 'The father of my dream girl is asking for twenty cows as lobola (bride price) but ...'

Picking a pawpaw at Mount Makulu with
Bashful the boxer from next door

A very enjoyable encounter was the arrival of Bill and Josephine Mackerill one Sunday morning. They arrived with a huge pawpaw – a new experience for me – and I watched as Josephine sliced open the large golden fruit. It was about 15 inches long.

She cut four fat slices and scooping out the black seeds, she squeezed lemon juice over with a liberal hand. My first thought was that the texture was rather soapy but the combination of smooth delicate sweetness combined with the sharp lemon juice grew to be one of my favourite breakfast dishes.

Bill was an Englishman who had taken the unwarranted step of marrying an African woman and he too had faced many difficulties. They could not be married in N. Rhodesia of course so they had gone down to S. Rhodesia to be married. This being one of the anomalies of the legal system in the Federation of the Rhodesias and Nyasaland at that time.

Once back in N. Rhodesia they could not live in the white section of town so Bill bought a plot of land at Makeni about 8 miles south of Lusaka. But then of course they were not eligible for a mortgage because they were outside the town boundaries. Undeterred Bill hired labour and built his own house of corrugated iron sheets on a simple cement block foundation.

They were a startling couple. Bill looked so quiet and meek and mild that I often wondered how he had had the courage to stand up to all the ostracism they had had to face, it would have been quite acceptable and understandable for him to have a black mistress on the side but he had persevered and married his Josephine. She had a generous and lively personality, a wonderful contrast to Bill's quietness.

Their house may have been rough and ready but we had many enjoyable afternoons there. After one of Josephine's inspired dinners cooked on a wood stove we would laze under the tall blue gums and when the heat became too much we would dive into the 'pool'. This was their water tank and main source of water. A windmill pumped water into a tank for drinking water and the overflow ran down into the large circular concrete tank Bill had built. It was about 4 feet deep - deep and cool enough for us to splash about in. Excess water from our efforts ran down a small ditch to a vegetable garden.

Another of our first visitors were Safeli and Martha Chileshe, a charming older couple, who arrived one evening in the traditional manner complete with a live chicken. I looked at the protesting bird with some misgivings. WHAT was I supposed to do with such a large and cross bird in the evening? Martha explained that traditionally one should arrive with a chicken so that one's hosts would not be embarrassed if food were short. A sort of 'I've come to dinner with my dinner' approach. But this contribution was more likely to run around under the table than sit on it.

'Aha,' said Martha. 'There is no fridge in the village so this sort of chicken will stay fresh until you want to eat it.'

Safeli had an unusually quiet and slow and dignified manner of speaking, which leant a solemn and learned air to his simplest observations. They regaled us with the hilarious account of Martha's difficulties when taking her driving test.

'The examiner said he could not fault me but he would have to fail me because the sight of an African woman behind the wheel would be bound to cause someone else to have an accident.'

One offer of friendship I did not pursue and later regretted, was from a white police officer, who arrived at the house one morning causing my stomach to lurch for a moment. Looking back now I wonder why. I can only think that the antagonism we had met had made me a little apprehensive. He had come to say welcome and would I like to meet his wife, who could not come herself being confined to a wheelchair. They lived at Chilanga police station at the turn off from Mount Makulu on the main road. I never followed this up because Andrew showed a marked lack of enthusiasm for the idea. Anything connected with the police was suspect, looking back I think he was biased and I gave in to his decisions far too easily. And at that point I couldn't drive myself.

We had known before we set sail that we would not be popular with many white people and the journey out had emphasised that knowledge. So I made a very conscious decision that I would not be offended or hurt when I met any ostracism, just try to take it in my stride. But it did make me value any overtures of friendship – even if, as in that case, I had not been able to pursue it.

One such was at a PWD (Public Works Dept) or MSD (Mechanical Services Dept) sundowner - and I can't for the life of me recall why we had such an invitation - especially as Andrew would not have been employable by either Dept at that time. Suffice it to say there we were, and as usual at such events, there were a majority of white faces, many of whom were looking affronted, or just the other way. I clutched my drink and smiled sweetly at anyone looking my way, usually one could be sure of a chap making a little desultory conversation - they coped better than women for some reason. And then, out of the blue, a couple approached us and not only spoke to us, but seemed quite happy to get involved in conversation. In fact we chatted quite animatedly for some time. They were Madge and Tommy Slinger, he was employed as an upholsterer in PWD (or MSD?) and had been in Lusaka for some years. Sadly I now forget the details and they are long gone but I do remember Madge telling me how hard it had been initially – they had gone out to N Rhodesia after the war in the 1940's and for some reason they had had to live in a tent in what was later the Northmead (or Thorn Park?) area of Lusaka but back then was still largely bush. But eventually were allocated a Government house in Northmead when the area was developed. It is no exaggeration to say it was quite brave of them to openly extend the hand of friendship - Tommy had a lowly post and they could both have suffered some backlash. We were friends for some years and December 1963 they arrived at our house bearing a very swish child size blue leather armchair for our first born, which Tommy had made - but I jump ahead.

Tommy used to come home from work every evening, greet Madge and go sit in the garden to read the newspaper and have a beer. Madge would call when dinner was ready. One evening years later he did not respond, he had died in his chair, his beer half drunk. 'A good way to go' she said. We lost touch when she moved south with daughter and son in law.

It was a period of change. Political moves were afoot for the break-up of the Federation. But while it may have appeared rapid to those who had lived there for a long time or indeed all their lives, to me coming from UK it was not!

To cheer us up, Edward Shamwana, our old friend from England arrived in February, to take up a post with Ellis and Co (I think) and was our first African barrister at law in Lusaka if not the whole of Zambia. He rented a house in Kabwata and invested in a large ginger cat duly christened Marmalade while he waited for Stella's arrival.

It was at that time Taxima Kalulu, the 7 year old daughter of Soloman Kalulu, chairman of UNIP, was admitted to the Dominican Convent School. The first African child to be admitted to a European school - as far as I could discover. The good Sisters were well to the forefront of race relations.

Not so the person who wrote to the Central African Post shortly afterwards on the topic of the Build A Nation campaign then gathering momentum with European politicians at that time

'... let me add it won't be multi-racial alone in church. It will be multi-racial at games and pleasure - where there are women, wine and song there will be other things.

Here in Africa the Bantu are our peasants, just as Europe has her peasants. The Bantu morals are not our morals'.

Nor was Think Again of Mumbwa alone in his beliefs. Moves to integrate the races by politicians or town councillors were not welcomed by many whites.

In May the same newspaper carried the following article.

'Despite official statements to the contrary it is believed attendances at Lusaka Municipal Swimming Pool have slumped alarmingly since the announcement that rate payers of all races can use the pool. Membership of Lusaka Otters Amateur Swimming Club dropped by a third to just over 200 ... Mr Johan Jones spoke out forcibly against multi-racial swimming. 'I've not been near the pool since it became multi-racial,' he said. 'I'm all for multi racialism provided it's in Jamaica or the US.'

One city woman, who had paid £20 to make her daughters members, said,

'I won't have them swimming with Africans. In any case, my

children refuse to go to the baths now.'

Reading these reports I smiled, what a funny place I had come to live in. And decided I could join in the fray. Recently I found tucked in a book two cuttings from either The Central African Post or The Northern News, I really cannot remember after all these years - two letters I wrote under pseudonyms.

In the longer one I puzzled over Build A Nation campaign started by Sir Edgar Whitehead of the Federal United Party in S. Rhodesia and in the short pithy comment I queried one Sir Roy Welensky's statements. I did not get much response and decided I either had no journalistic talent or everyone was set in their opinions anyway.

Several weekends were spent at UNIP rallies where huge crowds would wait patiently in the hot sun to hear Kenneth Kaunda address them on the fight for independence - not that there was much actual physical fighting in Northern Rhodesia. Nothing on the scale of the violence which erupted in the Belgian Congo. On the platform with him were of course, Simon Kapwepwe and Mainza Chona.

I remember sitting on the roof of a Land Rover with Dick and Barbara Hall – he edited The African Mail – near the back of a huge crowd on the waste ground near the roundabout at the

Letters to newspaper 1962

south end of Cairo Road. White police watched on the side but it was all very peaceful and at the end they drove off in their black police Land Rovers as the huge crowd slowly dispersed.

The stir caused by our arrival had died a natural death by now and we felt as though we had been at Mount Makulu for a long time. One day Andrew came home and said that someone in the office was looking for a home for some kittens and produced from behind his back a small black and white kitten.

'No special food for this cat, it's going to live on the same food as we do. It's not going to be a pampered animal which gets more attention than I do.'

This was obviously a reference to a friend on the station who put the welfare of her cats before that of her husband - or so Andrew thought. Certainly she talked more about them. So our kitten was known as Scraps, although it was certainly not content with just the scraps from our meals and very soon was paying Andrew very marked attention as he could be relied upon to give just that little extra – 'he looks a bit peckish'.

It was left to me to check for fleas. As Scraps decided to live up to his name as he grew older and was often reported to be throwing his weight around down in the compound, it was a very necessary check.

Our neighbours Dick and Joan Ballantyne had four cats, to whom they were devoted. For so long their cats had had two gardens to themselves, Scraps was the interloper. No sooner would I be asleep on the bed after lunch than two of them would meet - usually below my window. The first intimation would be a low growl which would steadily increase to a high yoo-oo-oo-oo-oo, after a long time this would end in an ear splitting shriek and scream. By which time I would be leaping off the bed and trying to stuff my feet into slippers before rushing off to either rescue or kill both of them. The latter was a great temptation! My bursting on to the verandah was the signal for both cats to vanish round the corner under the orange trees in the Ballantyne's garden.

We had been in Mount Makulu for a while before we had an invitation for Andrew to give a talk to the students at Munali,

(Andrew's old school) I was invited along and the Principal Hedley Roberts and his wife Mary made us very welcome. Andrew gave a cheerful talk to the gathered students in the hall and at the end invited questions. They appeared to have enjoyed the talk and perhaps been inspired to listen to an old boy, who had surmounted many difficulties and returned a qualified engineer. One boy put his hand up to ask, what was Andrew's favourite memory of his time in England? I don't think any of the boys believed, or even understood, his description of being invited to spend holidays with a fellow student on the family farm in the Yorkshire Dales - the best bit of which was - lending a hand with the muck spreading. After explaining what he meant by muck spreading there was a deathly silence. Hedley and Mary laughed as we walked back to their house ... 'Obviously none of the students could envisage enjoying muck spreading ... that is not for the educated elite! You have really opened their eyes.'

At this time Andrew had the use of the station Land Rover for visits to other agricultural stations and I was delighted to find that I could accompany him on many of these trips. It was an excellent way to see the country and meet people. Officers' wives on isolated stations always looked forward to the arrival of touring officers. One such trip we made was down to Mapangazia about 10 miles from Mazabuka, which was about 100 miles south of Lusaka.

There we found Ifor and Jill Edwards and their three children. Jill was a trained infant teacher so we had a common bond and while the men were out touring the station she showed me how she was teaching her two girls, Menna and Marion, at home. The Ministry of Education sent fortnightly lessons to families who lived in isolated areas and mothers had to cope with the first three years schooling at home. After the first few years, children were sent to board in various Government boarding schools. This service was of course only for Europeans. While the two girls worked at their lessons on a verandah with a fantastic view across miles of African bush to a range of distant blue hills and the baby boy David had his morning nap, Jill showed me round the homestead. All cooking was done on a wood stove of course and lighting was by oil lamps. In her spare time Jill ran classes for the labourer's wives on what was called the Badge Scheme.

'It is rather ridiculous,' she commented. 'These women have to be able to roast a chicken to earn one of the badges, but it is far more nutritious the way they cook it traditionally with vegetables as a stew. And certainly easier for them to do!'

I think this was the first time I had heard a European say that an African had a better way of doing something. It was a startling statement in its time.

Another of Andrew's visits took him down to Mazabuka and we were invited to stay with Barry and Ingilby Coxe some miles from Mazabuka ... another long dirt road, which led us to a charming house built as two large rondavels joined with a square living area and all thatched. The thatch was of deep interest to their peacocks, who were inclined to perch on the ridge pole and scrabble until they could peer through to watch us at dinner. Barry could talk about his work and plans for the farm ad infinitum while Ingilby appeared to be equally knowledgeable and enthusiastic. She was also of an extremely hardy disposition. Years later when medical facilities were not at their best - to put it diplomatically - she broke her arm, decided it would be quicker and more reliable to insert her arm into a cardboard bottle holder and fly to UK for medical attention. They also became good friends and we visited each other over the years as their children Charles and Sarah became firm friends with our children.

Peter and Annette Miller invited us over to their farm at Lilayi, I was fascinated by their stories of the Miller family history. Peter's father having arrived in N. Rhodesia in the early 1900's, he bought the land in Lilayi in 1912 and built the house in 1924. It was the period of travel by ox carts and the early railway on the Cape to Cairo route – a catch phrase coined by Edwin Arnold, editor of the Daily Telegraph in 1874. The ambitious idea was taken up by Cecil Rhodes but sadly not completed. The bridge over the Victoria Falls was only completed in 1905.

At long last in April our crates arrived and we unpacked things we had forgotten we owned. Wedding presents which had been looked at and then immediately repacked were now unpacked to be exclaimed over and used. The floor was strewn with straw as we rejoiced in our long lost friends. Oh, for a variety of sheets and towels! More than one knife each! and cups and glasses a-plenty! Even pictures on the walls!

Not only had we spare sheets and towels, dishes and glasses, pictures and ornaments, pots and pans ... we had at last been able to invest in a second hand fridge which loomed large in the ironing room, which led off the kitchen. It was an ancient model which chugged ominously and sounded perpetually on the verge of breaking down but did in fact last us many years. A fridge meant that foodstuffs would keep longer of course - an essential in the heat. A car was also a necessity and after inspecting what seemed like every second hand car in town we bought a dark green Morris Traveller, a solid little vehicle which proved to be worth its weight in gold. B3439 travelled anywhere and everywhere taking all roads and weather conditions in its stride without a murmur.

CHAPTER 3
PETAUKE
April 1962

No sooner had we the luxuries of life and the means of independent transport than we had to leave Mount Makulu.

Andrew was not altogether happy with his life of look around and think what might be done one day in the future but we were taken by surprise one Sunday morning when a car stopped at the entrance to the drive and the Director of Agriculture, a Mr Halcrow, leaned out of the window and beckoned to Andrew, who was investigating B349's insides.

A few minutes later Halcrow drove off and Andrew walked back across the garden with a grim face.

'We are to go to Petauke, I'm being posted there.'

'Great - now I'll see a bit more of N Rhodesia....where IS Petauke?'

'It's in Eastern Province, but never mind where it is. I'm to go there and 'look around' some more and also test a peanut sheller - run some field trials on the thing.'

He did not look terribly enthusiastic; I think it was a mixture of resentment that once more he was being kept busy doing nothing very concrete, which was further aggravated by Halcrow's beckoning him across the garden ('as though he was gesturing to the garden boy' snorted Andrew) and saying,

'I have decided you are to go to Petauke - the reason is quite secondary - it's very good for everyone to have a spell in the bush.'

While the last reason may have sounded vague and perhaps a little irrational, I have always been glad we had a spell in the bush and it was an experience I would not have missed for the world.

In the meantime of course there were various minor details. The car was in good working order but we had only had it a couple of days and Andrew would rather have had time to give it a thorough service. We had just acquired the fridge which would be useless on a bush station where there was no electricity and we most certainly could not afford now to buy a paraffin fridge – even second or third hand.

However, you cannot argue with the boss and so we packed up the house, planning to take only the barest essentials with us - after all, we were only going for three months. And I was going to live way out in the bush in Petauke Boma, which seemed more exotic than Lusaka with its street lights and a zebra crossing. A Boma, I had read, referred originally to an enclosure for the protection of livestock, usually of thorn bush fences. Another explanation I've heard was British Overseas for Military Administration - which did not link up with my reading of Man Eaters of Tsavo many years earlier.

At the end of April we set off for Petauke. I had never been along the Great East Road and was looking forward to a whole new range of scenery. Some boxes had been sent ahead with Carter Patterson. Kapitu and his wife had bus tickets and would arrive shortly after us, together with their katundu (luggage). We had the car loaded up with immediate needs and breakables, some food - and the cat.

I read that while Fort Jameson had been linked to Lusaka in 1928, the road was only open to motor traffic in 1929 and 'like the footpaths it replaced, the road deviated round every large tree and ant hill'.

The Morris Minor Traveller is a great little car but it is not the roomiest of vehicles and by the time we reached Petauke we were on very close and dusty terms indeed. The Great East Road ran eastwards of course from Lusaka to Fort Jameson on the Nyasaland border – Petauke was about 300 miles from Lusaka. I had hoped for some changes in scenery but was destined to be disappointed. As it was now April the rains had ended and the countryside was rapidly drying out - it would not rain again until November. The road wound its way across endless miles of open savannah or bush – both words appear synonymous. It was a narrow road, it was a dirt road and the surface was corrugated in varying degrees so that as soon as you became accustomed to one series of bounces and jounces, the lie of the road altered slightly and the jarring attacked your seat from another angle. Clouds of dust flew up behind us and there was no hope of seeing anything in the rear view mirror. There was practically no traffic so any car or lorry ahead was visible for miles - or at least its cloud of dust was. As we were not in a fast car and were also well loaded anyone who was going in the same direction overtook us in clouds of choking red dust.

On this, my very first really long car journey, I was amazed at the seemingly endless space in Africa. Mile after mile, hour after hour of almost unchanging scenery. At that time of the year the lush green of the rainy season was moving into the bleached faded yellows and oranges ... low scrubby trees .... a distant collection of low thatched huts clustered in a village .... occasionally a low hill.

The cat decided immediately he was not going to travel in a box and escaped with ease in a few seconds every time I put him back. We bowed to the inevitable and after prowling over and through every bit of luggage and several times over us, he settled down between my feet wailing incessantly for the first two hours until he fell into an exhausted sleep. I would dearly have loved to follow his example. By midday we had our first puncture, it happened near a cluster of huts by the roadside.

Andrew decided to repair the tyre once he had put on the spare. The cat actually decided to sleep on in the car and I sat in the shade of a tree near a patch of cotton plants watching Andrew wrestle with the tyres and inner tubes. It was unbearably hot and the glare of the sun beat down like a hammer. Stretching my legs I wandered over to look more closely at the cotton plants and their fluffy white bolls and then over to the nearest hut and as there seemed to be no one about, I peered in through the open door. The mud floor was smooth with wear, one or two boxes and pots stood in the shadows, a shirt hung on a nail on the wall. A tiny mirror hung beside it. A homemade wooden chair was near the door and one or two enamel mugs and plates were just outside on a sort of platform. They were upside down but I didn't like the look of the flies which crawled over them from time to time. The mud walls were plastered thickly enough over the poles so I supposed it was weatherproof enough, especially as the thatch hung down in a long shaggy fringe. Apart from a few chickens scratching under some banana trees, the whole place was quiet, deserted.

'I suppose everyone is working in the fields?' I asked Andrew. He nodded.

Tyre repaired at last we set off, the cat insisting now that he would only travel on my lap. After more endless miles of apparently endless bush it was a relief to start the descent into the Luangwa valley. The escarpment road was one way traffic only for set hours of the day and we had had to time our journey accordingly. The escarpment road gave fantastic views across the valley, if only one could tear one's eyes away from the drop at the side of the road. The little car bounced and skidded its way over the corrugations down to the river and bridge. We stopped here to eat on the banks of the Luangwa and the sight of the water was cooling.

Stiffness and aches eased as we walked about on the banks watching the wide river slowly flowing past, the banks were well wooded here and I reflected this was probably the closest I should ever get to the 'jungles' of Africa.

Thatched hut Eastern Province

We set off again, climbing out of the valley, somewhere along the road another puncture. Another hot and dusty stop while we changed the tyre and the cat protested bitterly at his confinement but I knew if he was allowed out and wandered far it could be impossible to get him back.

The road wound on over and round small almost imperceptible hills. At times we would surmount a slight rise and find the road stretching out in front of us, a thin orangey brown ribbon reaching towards the horizon; perhaps several miles ahead a cloud of dust indicated a moving vehicle. A dirt road doesn't sound too bad until you take into account the corrugations. As we travelled I found the regular - and irregular - corrugations jarred my poor bottom almost into numbness. Once or twice we met a grader and I could well understand the story about a newcomer, who is supposed to have asked why graders were used to put the corrugations into the surface of the roads. Certainly there was little sign of improvement after you had passed a grader, waving to the man high up on the machine – an unenviable task – scraping the road surface into comparative evenness.

We saw villages in the distance, round huts with long shaggy thatch, bare swept earth and all apparently deserted.

It was dark long before we reached Petauke and as we turned off the Great East Road to drive down the even smaller road to the Boma - only a few more miles - I felt as though I would never be able to climb out of the car. Every bone in my body ached with the constant pounding and my teeth were gritty with dust.

We knew Jim and Anne Alexander were expecting us to stay with them for the first night and had been told they were 'the fifth house on the left'. As far as I could see there were six houses on the left and two on the right.

Jim Alexander was a tall rangy Scot with a broad accent and the largest dog I had ever seen. While Jim threw open the car doors rolling his rrrs and exuding boisterous hospitality, the dog showed an overwhelming desire to climb in the car and make a close friendship with Scraps, who did not share his enthusiasm. We shook off clouds of Eastern Province topsoil, deposited the spitting cat in a store room with food and water and found we were to sit down to a formal meal with several people, who were in Petauke for a cricket weekend. Anne Alexander produced a marvellous meal - or her cook had - but everything tasted of mud that first night and I was sure my teeth were being ground away on the all-pervasive gritty dust which no amount of brushing and spitting seemed to disperse.

Standard Government furniture certainly made you feel at home wherever you went and I saw with delight that there were electric light switches on the walls. I was surprised to see that the Alexanders were using paraffin lamps, or was it for a party atmosphere? Jim roared with laughter as he pumped up the Tilly lamp again,

'The switches and electric fittings are for when the electricity comes to Petauke - if it ever does!'

Petauke and our trusty B3439 having a tyre pumped up yet again

Next morning I found that there were actually twelve houses on the Boma, we had an N2 on the opposite side of the road, not so big or well planned as the AK2 but it would be fine for three months.

It was the usual small Boma so it didn't take long to know who did what, although as the men were often away on tour it took a little time to get to know them well.

Aileen Hepworth helped me to remember them recently, the few people responsible for a large area of Eastern province – the Mitchells – Colin was an agricultural officer, the Hepworths

– Johnny was the mechanic at PCMU (Petauke Cooperative Marketing Union), a builder (?), the Alexanders – Jim was an agricultural officer, DC Ian Breingan, DA Peter Smith, the police officer(?) … and on the opposite side of the road – ourselves, nurse Mariette, an accountant(?)and finally Sven, who appeared to do a bit of everything.

And then there was the Rest House. I was told the Rest Houses, scattered across the country, were originally built for visiting civil servants not staying with the DC.

The men were out touring or busy down in the Boma offices, which were fairly close to our house so I could easily stroll down to watch the Boma messengers on early morning parade. Like the police they too took pride in their uniforms which looked starched until they were as stiff as cardboard. With their slouch hats, dark blue shirts with dark red edging, dark blue shorts and all finished off with neatly bound puttees and gleaming black boots – they were a colourful sight. Our house had been further from the Mount Makulu offices and so I saw less of the messengers there.

Meanwhile the wives wrestled with housekeeping in the African bush and servants of varying degrees of ability. But it was never dull, from the stories of the people's experiences in the local area to my little 'school' and the occasional extra social event. Such as when Peter Smith's fiancée Mary flew out from England and we were invited to their wedding in Fort Jameson. Even more exciting was the aftermath when we heard that in fact she had eloped to marry her Peter and while her father was not in actual hot pursuit, his angry communications with the District Commissioner were the main topic for a few days.

Oil lamps became the bane of my life when Andrew was travelling and I was left alone. I never turned one off at night without fearing that I would never be able to light it again in the middle of the night (where I thought I would be going with an oil lamp in the middle of the night I have no idea).

No electricity meant a woodstove of course and I looked at the small black object huddled in the corner of the kitchen with misgivings, it was even more primitive than the one we had left at Mount Makulu. Kapitu pulled open the door with a bit of wire - the door knobs had long since disappeared.

'Wood in here, dinner in here, ash in here,' he explained.

Reflecting that it would all be ash if it were up to me, I thankfully left it to him.

He was not so accommodating about the iron and even he regarded the charcoal iron with a gloomy face. I had never seen such an object before and had no idea how he would use it - in fact would barely have recognised it for an iron. Kapitu cheered up at the prospect of teaching the Dona something new and impressing her with his knowledge and efficiency.

It was large iron, no not large, it was huge. The top had massive hinges and swung back to reveal a large open space into which hot charcoal was put. You then wiped the iron carefully with a cloth and began to iron. After a couple of garments the iron was getting cool so you went out into the garden where you had room to swing a cat - or in this case an iron. And you swung it to and fro until the charcoal glowed red again. Back to the ironing and as like as not you had forgotten to wipe the iron with a cloth, so back to the wash went another shirt smeared with charcoal ... Domesticity had never appealed to me and faced with such medieval equipment I knew Kapitu was worth his wages and more. He took charge of all the household chores, a gardener was not necessary because the rains had stopped and no way was the grass going to grow any taller on that thin laterite soil. There was no point in starting a vegetable garden, we would be off - back to Lusaka and civilisation - before anything grew big enough to eat.

When we moved in both Anne Alexander and Aileen Hepworth warned me to spray for cockroaches and I duly invested in a spray. But it really was a waste of money as I told them both - I never saw a cockroach. But then one evening after dinner when Kapitu had washed up and gone home, I went through to the kitchen to find something. I was shaken to find that as I set the oil lamp down on the table the whole surface rippled with scampering roaches.

The Boma offices were on the roadside, a small neat white building topped with the inevitable corrugated iron roof, in front of which the Messengers would parade for inspection each morning. I often paused by the lantana hedge in front of the Boma offices to watch them.

The shopping facilities were simple. Halfway along the Boma road on the way back to the main road were two small Indian stores. The first one was known as Mollywollers - as no one could ever pronounce his name correctly. This was the equivalent of the village store back home in UK. Mollywoller stocked everything you might conceivably require and more besides.

We were hundreds of miles from the coast and I was amazed to see a clutch of children's seaside buckets dangling from the rafters. Perhaps he had seen a child with one on the beach at Lake Nyasa, I never did find out. When I once asked him he smiled broadly and pointed out that I had no children so why was I interested? I never went to Mollywollers without browsing around, always finding something new I had not noticed on an earlier visit. His range included the exotic tins of caviar and jars of stuffed olives but as he had no cold storage the only butter available was tinned and tasted foul. Browsing around, inhaling the strange mix of spices, paraffin, dust and unidentifiable smells I could always be sure of discovering something I hadn't noticed before. His greatest asset was his innocent seeming salesmanship. No matter how often you went in there with a specific list in mind or on paper, his never ending patter and 'What next please?' midway in the conversation resulted in everyone I knew coming out of the store with at least one or two unwanted items.

Outside on the verandah an African tailor pedalled away at an old Singer sewing machine making dresses and shirts for local villagers. There were always a few people about, standing in the shade of the verandah or sitting on the steps examining and comparing purchases. A dog or two would be lying under a mango tree and small children would cling to their mothers' skirts waiting for the long walk back to the village.

Vegetables were brought to our kitchen door by villagers, usually in a box on the back of a bicycle. And eggs were available from the local Mission, Minga.

Meat could be bought once a week when an ox was slaughtered on the station. I was told to give Kapitu a list and send him down on a Wednesday morning with a bowl or a bucket. As I had little to occupy my time I decided one day to collect my own meat. The 'butchers' was a small brick building tucked away at the back of the Boma. Outside was a group of women with an assortment of paper wrapped bloody bundles which they were balancing on their heads together with the odd bunch of green bananas or cloth wrapped bundle. Tucking their babies on their backs they exchanged cheerful banter and set off in groups of twos and threes along the narrow paths which wound apparently aimlessly through the long grasses. Dogs were scratching in the dust as I pushed open the tattered mesh door, the tiny room was crowded with more buyers haggling over lumps of unidentifiable lumps of meat piled indiscriminately on a bloody bench. Meat was picked up and tossed aside as the women ridiculed the prices; standing on the floor was an assortment of bowls and buckets topped with paper labels on which were scrawled D.C. .... Hepworth....... Mitchell and containing paper wrapped bundles through which the blood was already soaking and over it all was a thick cloud of flies which rose up in the air as they were disturbed by the women sorting or the occasional flick of a dog's tail. Changing my mind I handed over my list and a pound note to one of the men, smiled, nodded and stepped outside again where I drew breath once more.

'I told you not to go down there,' said Aileen virtuously. 'That mesh door keeps more flies in than out. Mind you, you've got to admit the beef here has far more flavour than the beef back in UK'

'Tough as old boot leather though.'

'Now you can't have everything and where else are you going to get a large piece of sirloin for five shillings?'

Aileen and Johnny Hepworth proved to be stout friends. Living in the cold wastes of the north of England, Johnnie had one day seen an advertisement for a mechanic in N. Rhodesia. Sun! at last!

They were none too sure where N Rhodesia might be so they consulted an atlas, which not only revealed its whereabouts but also gave Petauke's position.

'There you are,' declared Johnnie with admirable logic. 'Not only is it on a main road but it must be a pretty big place to be on the map at all.'

Armed with such knowledge they set off for N. Rhodesia and their descriptions of their early days were hilarious. Theirs was the generation of 'lets get up and go somewhere different' with little thought for prepaid passages, gratuities and the like. Nor did they pack up and go home when they saw the conditions in which they were to live and work. The country owed a great deal to people like them.

Aileen still laughs over the memory of their first two days in Lusaka when they stayed at the Lusaka Hotel. Gillian, aged two, had just begun to associate the sound of a bell with an ice cream man so whenever the waiter walked down the corridor ringing a bell for a dinner, Gillian would rush out of their room but on meeting a black face - the first in her life - she would burst into piercing shrieks of horror.

Gillian was now six years old and her brother Peter, aged three, had been born at Fort Jameson 200 miles away. When I said at a coffee morning in my first week there that I was an infant teacher I was astonished at the attention I received from Aileen and Maddo, the District Commissioner's wife. Clad in robes of scarlet and riding on a white charger I could have warranted no more rapt attention.

Aileen was battling with the correspondence lessons teaching Gillian. The following morning Gillian and Amanda Breingan appeared at my front door for their first taste of school!

Aileen handed over all the lesson notes for Gillian with her blessings and heartfelt thanks with obvious relief. Amanda was not due to start school until the following January but as Maddo said, 'This is too good an opportunity to miss.'

Gillian and Amanda took their 'school' very seriously and were always on time, walking down the dusty road together. We had lessons in the dining room but used the verandah for painting - thanks to Mollywoller who had risen to the occasion. PE was usually ball games, with the cat joining in. School was from 8am to midday when they went reluctantly home and I dropped on the bed from sheer exhaustion.

Aileen did suggest I start a nursery class for three year old Peter and Mark, Amanda's brother, but I managed to wriggle out of that one.

And in any case, I thought Mark had quite enough on his plate. Ian, his father was a Scot and his mother Maddo was Swiss and they had decided that they would speak French in the home to encourage the children to grow up bilingual. Ian had been District Commissioner in Mwinilunga before Petauke and their eldest son had stayed on there at boarding school, Maddo making the long, long journey of over 780miles each term to collect him on the inevitable dirt roads.

Before the end of term we were asked if we would like to go to watch the Sports day at the local village primary school. Alongside the track were a row of chairs for the guests - the Europeans from the Boma and a few of their visitors and we sat in style to watch the events. Race after race and excited cheering children on the side lines as is usual. Usual, with the exception of the girls' bottle race when girls ran (ran!) while balancing empty Fanta bottles on their heads. Allowing for African women's ability to balance loads of all descriptions on their heads I still thought it a pretty remarkable race. What was even less usual was the European woman (not from Petauke) who had brought her large Alsatian. As excited children gradually edged further and further on to the track she became irritated that her view was blocked and sent her dog 'at' the children who fled back in fear. The dog only barked and ran at the children and it had the desired effect but I couldn't join in the laughter when she said she had trained her dog 'to chase natives'.

I was finding more to do here and could still travel with Andrew if an interesting trip were lined up - school could always have a short holiday.

Together we toured many parts of Eastern Province and we even got up to Lake Nyasa for a long weekend. It was yet another long and dusty and bouncy journey but by now I was well used to them. So from Petauke and along the Great East Road to cross the border into Nyasaland and yet more dirt road. One could only wonder at the endless ribbons of dirt roads – red, orange, brown and all shades between – and all guaranteed to be thick with dust and all with the corrugations, those bum jarring corrugations created by traffic, smoothed out by graders, only to form again. All these dirt and gravel – and in the rainy seasons, muddy - endless miles of road, cleared through the bush when? And who by?

Main shop in Fort Jameson - the main shopping centre in Eastern Province

I would have loved to have been around when the first roads were officially opened up – replacing ox cart tracks through the bush.

Travelling through Nyasaland one was struck by the denser concentration of population and the large numbers of goats browsing everywhere.

97

Coming down to the lake and seeing the vast expanse of water stretching out in front of us, was breath taking. This was indeed an inland sea. We stayed at a small hotel on the lake side. The bedrooms were individual rondavels painted white with thatched roofs, which meant they were always cool even at midday. They were barely furnished but the beds were equipped with mosquito nets. From the hotel you walked down a steep path to the sandy beach. Not being the greatest of swimmers I watched as Andrew ran in and swam further out than I would ever dare.

'Come on in, the water's lovely.'

I shook my head and called, 'Not as far out as that, you know I'm not a good swimmer.'

At which he stood up and revealed that the water, even as far out as that, was only knee deep. This was exactly my kind of holiday, warm water with only the tiniest of waves and shallow enough for me to float out a long way with confidence.

Morning coffee and afternoon tea were brought down to the beach by waiters deftly balancing trays as they walked down the steep path and across the burning sands. As they carefully set down the trays on tables under the thatched umbrellas I wondered how they could bear to stand still on the burning sand, even allowing for the fact that their soles would be toughened after usually walking barefoot.

At midday and the evenings we were called to the dining room by a waiter, who sat on the steps beating out his own rhythm on a large drum. Fish featured largely on the menu, caught each day by fishermen in dugout canoes. I tasted roast goat here for the first time. It was a wonderful break and I wished the lake were nearer Lusaka - there we could only swim in the Municipal pool. Aileen told me that they had taken Gillian and Peter to the lake and realised that they would be within reach of a railway line for the first time since Peter was born. As steam engines featured largely in story books this was a trip not to be missed. They had the sense to realise that two children used to living on a quiet bush station might find their first experience of a steam engine more than daunting so they explained at great length how large and noisy it would be and even had practice sessions of who could make the loudest engine chuff chuffs. It was a wholly wasted exercise as the smallest service locomotive they had ever seen chugged gently into Salima station. As that was the only train due for some days the whole event went rather flat.

After Lake Nyasa our next most interesting trip was to Lundazi Castle. I was told this was a real castle but took the whole story with a pinch of salt. I knew we were to stay at a place called Lundazi Castle which was a Government Rest House at Lundazi Boma. The long and dusty journey was more irksome than usual because the dry season was well advanced by now and the soil as we grew nearer Lundazi grew sandier and sandier, at times the car slid sideways in the soft drifts.

Finally we rounded the last bend and drove up the narrow road and through the trees I glimpsed a castle, brick built with towers and turrets and battlements, my jaw dropped as Andrew laughed, 'I've kept telling you it is a castle.'

Lundazi Castle

Apparently when the Government rest house was being built the District Commissioner Errol Button, drew up his own plans on the back of a cigarette packet (if that seems a somewhat tall story, bear in mind that smokers normally carried a flat box of thirty in their shirt pockets). Then he set his labourers to work. As the building progressed they could not imagine what it would look like as it grew in a very different way from anything they knew. Hence this large rest house was completed far more quickly than any other rest house in the Territory - or so the story goes.

I also heard that the DC thinking that as the local labour was far more used to building a traditional round hut, decided to utilise their ability and as far as possible base much of the building on round shapes. Whatever the reason, the castle was an impressive place and well sited on a slight rise above a dam and was a deservedly a popular place to stay with Government officers and tourists on their way to the Luangwa Valley Game Reserve.

Also staying at the at the rest house the same weekend were Dennis and Renate Proctor with their six month old daughter Suzanne, who had the most expressive face of any small child I had ever met. We met over breakfast where Suzanne kept us well entertained with her murmurs and gurgles and beaming smiles. They were easy to talk to and became life-long friends. Dennis was touring the country looking at and advising on the storage of seeds for the small farmer so he and Andrew had a mutual interest in agricultural development.

As people gathered in the bar in the evenings there were many tales told of visiting dignitaries and tourists. The one I enjoyed most was the one of the American and his wife, who were on safari with Norman Carr, the well-known big game hunter.

The American was an insatiable photographer and hunter but not particularly skilled in either. At each and every kill there was a long delay while photos were taken by both the hunter and his long suffering wife.

At last they were on the trail of a buffalo. The American took aim, fired but unfortunately the animal was only wounded and made off into the tall grasses. Carr placed the couple in safety on a tall ant hill with strict instructions not to move until he had finished off the wounded buffalo. There then ensued a weary and tense stalking session in the tall grass ending with a confrontation between Carr and the beast. At that moment the American hove into view, having descended from his ant hill and asking for yet another shot, 'Let me finish him off!' in ringing tones.

The enraged buffalo turned and charged him as Carr, with calculated skill, shot the animal before it could fall upon the now immobile tourist. The buffalo crashed to the ground literally at the feet of the open mouthed man and as Carr wiped the sweat from his brow, the American turned to his wife and yelled,

'Did ya film that honey?'

Needless to say the camera was still dangling from her nerveless fingers.

We heard that story, sipping our drinks, at the bar behind which hung row upon row of tie ends. Traditionally all newcomers had the ends of their ties cut off to add to the collection and we were regaled by their owners' histories (Andrew, forewarned, was in open necked bush shirt that evening.

One weekend we left Petauke at first light, about 5am, and drove over to Katete for the Agricultural Show where I met for the first time Goodwin Mutale, who had sent me my first Bemba grammar and I tried out the little Bemba I had learned. The Show was very much like any other agricultural show except that it was the first time I had walked ankle deep in chewed up and spat out sugar cane. Everyone, from toddlers to elders, walked along chewing at the long sticks and spitting out the masticated pulp. I tried a section of cane but thought it disappointingly unsweet.

These ox carts were a frequent sight on Eastern Province roads, trundling slowly along they seemed to blend into the landscape far better than the cars creating sand and dust storms in their wake. (Katundu meaning luggage/baggage).

Katete - a katundu ox cart

Goodwin (or Goodie as he was always known) was based at Chadiza Boma and suggested we pay him a visit there as soon as possible. He painted such a plaintive picture of his lonely life, Mabel his wife still training as a nurse in Northampton, we could not resist.

It was there that we met farmers, George and Flora Osborne and their lively brood of attractive children. George and Flora were 'Coloureds' but as far as farming went they were 'European'. As we walked round the farm George told us why he was one of the very last large scale farmers left in the area.

With the changing political situation some bright fundi (expert) in Salisbury, Southern Rhodesia, had conceived the bright idea of resettling all 'European' farmers from Eastern Province (ie efficient large scale farmers) along the line of rail in Central and Southern Provinces and thus making it easier to split Northern Rhodesia into two sections. The rich copper and farming North and Central Provinces could then be annexed to Southern Rhodesia and the comparatively poor Eastern Province would then be joined with Nyasaland. Many European farmers took the opportunity to move, with Government aid, from Eastern Province leaving George and only a handful of others.

Nothing further actually came of the plan to split the country but as George said, it was a great temptation when all expenses were to be paid. His story certainly linked in with a report earlier in the year when Kenneth Kaunda said that Sandys (UK Foreign Secretary) had a plan for the fragmentation of N Rhodesia. He claimed that NW Province would be joined to Katanga, Northern and Luapula and Barotseland would be independent. Eastern Province would be joined to Nyasaland. And the rich Central and Southern provinces would be annexed by Southern Rhodesia.

On all our field trips we were constantly advised to be sure to try a lunch at 'the Portuguese pub on the border' (with Portuguese East Africa) and at long last we found ourselves in the area. After all the big build up it was irritating after a long hot drive to find it was the one day when meals were not being served - the owner and chef being away on urgent business. After all the anticipation we stood in a bare and dusty bar, had a cold drink and wondered if we would ever make the journey again, was the place really as good as its reputation claimed, perhaps we would never find out for ourselves.

Before long we got chatting to an Italian drinking alone and who took pity on our plight and invited us to go back to the road camp where he was based, to lunch with him and his friend - 'a great Italian cook, you like spaghetti?'

His friend assured us it was no bother when we arrived and they both plied us with drinks - bottles of beer for the men and sticky sweet Fanta orange for me. Lunch soon arrived with huge mounds of spaghetti and enormous dishes of meat sauces, such vast quantities of food on top of the sickly orange I had been sipping did nothing for my protesting pregnant stomach but I tried to be bright and sociable and hoped my small appetite would go unnoticed as the men exchanged political views.

Halfway through lunch a long haired cat made its appearance and came to sit cosily by me, very soon to stealthily crawl across on to my lap. Glad of a distraction I stroked it, it was an odd sort of cat, it was all lumpy and bumpy. I glance down as my fingers casually parted the fur and there were the most gigantic ticks I have ever or would ever wish to see. Bloated with blood they had sucked from the poor cat, they hung like so many grapes; how I hung on to the spaghetti I'll never know.

A newcomer appeared in Petauke while we were there but I regret I don't recall which Ministry he was connected with nor his actual posting. However, it was great to meet a new face and we went down to the Government rest house to meet Sammy Mutone. The rest house was a few minutes' walk to our right and Sammy was to live there until he was allocated a house. A few days later he invited us to dine with him at the rest house and promised he would treat us to a roast chicken dinner - courtesy of the rest house cook of course. It was a hilarious meal.

Petauke Rest House

First of all Sammy declared he was not very adept at carving, would Andrew do the honours? Andrew declared he was a guest and as such could not, nay would not, carve ... during the impasse I worried that it would be cold roast chicken all round. Matters were sorted and one of them carved and dinner began. Sammy then regaled us with an account of his first trip to UK - he had been sent on some training course. On his very first morning in London he set out to buy a newspaper and was dismayed to find an array of Sunday newspapers. Faced with such a choice, he hesitated and then - a flash of inspiration - The News Of The World would surely have the widest range of news. Andrew and I fell into peals of laughter as Sammy, looking extremely embarrassed, said, 'Such stories! I didn't know such things could happen! And in England! Could they really be true?'

An interesting reflection of the way so many Africans had grown up believing Europeans were so much better educated and far more moral.

April led to May and on into June and naturally July followed. What was not following was the testing of the Slattery groundnut sheller. It was still in Lusaka - or perhaps somewhere along the road. No one seemed quite sure. In the meantime the farmers were beginning to harvest their groundnut crops which were destined for marketing in Lusaka.

There was a small African hospital based at Petauke and when the Sister in charge (Mariette) married and left the station, Anne Alexander was asked to run the clinic for some time. A doctor came to the hospital once a month on a day's visit.

But what was to be done with baby John Alexander?

Baby John came to June's crèche in the mornings as school was now on official holiday. He slept most of the time, which was just as well because by this time I was about four months pregnant and was most put out to find that all the old wives tales of morning sickness were not old wives tales at all.

Anne came home with a marvellous story one day. Messengers had arrived at the clinic that morning asking for some Dettol for the chief, Chief Kalindowalo, but they refused to say why he required it. Anne offered them a small bottle but this was shrugged aside with the comment that it was too small. With increasing annoyance Anne offered larger and larger bottles of Dettol which were steadily spurned until one of the messengers spotted a large drum of Dettol. That was more like it!

At this point Anne dug in her heels. That was more than a month's supply for the hospital and chief or no chief, she had to know why it was needed. With great delicacy she eventually prised the story from them. There had been a beer drink the night before in the village when all and sundry got very merry. Late in the evening the chief went to answer a call of nature and took himself off to the chimbuzi (latrine), but being somewhat unsteady, overbalanced and fell down into it. His calls for help went unnoticed in the jollity of the evening until at last his wife noticed he was missing and went to investigate. On trying to pull him out, being equally unsteady, she fell in beside him. It was some time before they were rescued. And so a very large bottle of Dettol was required for the chief and his wife.

One weekend Johnnie and Aileen asked us to go for a picnic with them to 'Sesari gold mine'.

After Lundazi castle I was a bit more wary of dismissing place names as airily as I had done. But a gold mine? It was indeed a gold mine, but long since abandoned. We all went together in Johnnie's Land Rover along a winding - what else? And dusty - what's new? road which ran between tall grasses - why not? And from clump to clump of trees so that we ran from sun to shade to sun with sick making regularity. Arriving at the mine Johnnie indicated the elephant droppings which were fairly fresh and advised we should take a good look round and keep our ears open - 'Although they can move as quietly as cats when they want to' he added comfortingly. We did not see any elephant on that trip but we thoroughly enjoyed the outing. Walking inside the entrance to the mine filled one with speculation as to who had tried their luck and why, there in that remote spot and how much gold had actually been mined. Not enough to make it a viable proposition obviously.

There was a tiny club house at Petauke which was not used very much during the week and there I found 'the library'- a few shelves of dusty books, probably abandoned by families as they packed up at the end of a tour and left the station. It had a large section of Dennis Wheatley and I frightened myself silly one week when Andrew was away on tour by reading one black magic saga after another by the light of the oil lamp which I then feared to extinguish.

This all came to an abrupt halt one night when I had read into the early hours in bed and then turned down the wick with cold fingers. For the rest of the night I was convinced I could hear sounds in the house and lay with my eyes riveted on the bedroom door waiting for I knew not what spectres. With the dawn of course I laughed at myself and walked down to the kitchen and fell over a bundled up body. I fled with chittering teeth back to the bedroom and waited until I heard Kapitu unlocking the kitchen door.

A Boma messenger was soon at the house to escort the woman away.

She was 'mad' was the comforting explanation. Harmless but quite mad, thought she lived in the house and would come back from time to time ' to wait'.

I wondered later why a poor village woman would have the delusion that she had ever lived in a European house. How had she got in? she must have had a key? If so, who gave her it? Who was she waiting for? One could have woven some long sad and tragic Somerset Maugham story around her ...

I kept meeting people who prompted the beginnings of stories in my mind or about whom I wondered why? And when? ... odd little incidents scattered around the back areas of N. Rhodesia, an isolated grave here and a lonely abandoned building there. Or merely people who were a little different and original.

Like the Welsh agricultural officer's wife who sat quietly playing an enormous Welsh harp after dinner. It had travelled all over the country with them and was the most unexpected after dinner entertainment one could have envisaged in the middle of the African bush.

The two little old men, we passed on a dirt road miles from anywhere. Neither of them could have been over 5 feet tall, they were both very, very old and wrinkled. And clad in ancient tattered jackets and trousers the colour of the soil, they were amiably strolling along the centre of the road hand in hand. Andrew slowed down to a crawl, the old men beamed and raised a feeble hand. We drove carefully round them as they stood still and watched us pass and then tottered on their way. I was quite concerned about them being out on their own but Andrew only laughed at me.

It was my turn to laugh when we drove round a bend one day

and he almost turned the car over - walking towards us was a tall young man stark naked except for a navy peaked cap and a short stick in one hand. As we passed he negligently touched the peak of his cap with the stick, nodded gravely and carried on his way.

Thankfully we were in Eastern Province. Driving in the Luapula Province was not so safe at that time, a large lion had developed the habit of chasing cars on a lonely stretch of the road about 15 miles from Kawambwa. The first report came from a Government driver, who said it had leaped up and grabbed at his arm resting on the open window, then a bus inspector watched it pursue his bus. The lion was very fit - the Provincial Commissioner G F Tredwell saw it in his rear view mirror and had to speed up to leave it behind. I never found out whether it was enraged by passing traffic in its territory or....? Thankfully we saw no lions, friendly or otherwise on our travels.

When I think of Petauke I remember the orange brown dusty road and the cold sharp mornings and the jacarandas just bursting into bloom, the tall graceful trees bowing down with masses of purple blue blossom, bluer than the piercing blue of the high dazzling sky, and the bright turquoise birds with pink breasts which flew from tree to tree ahead of me as I walked up the road to have coffee with Aileen.

She could always be relied upon to be cheerful - making me laugh with her descriptions of looking out of her sitting room window one day down to the dirt road below and seeing a man cycling sedately home. It was 'meat day' at the Boma, on the back of his bike sat his wife with a large enamel bowl on her head - a common sight. What was not common was the fact that the bowl contained a whole ox head complete with horns.

And the time she was sewing while Gillian (5) and Peter (2) played outside on the verandah. All was quiet until Gillian bustled in to announce in shocked tones, 'Peter's eating a chongololo'.

(Chongololos are huge black centipedes, often twelve inches long and correspondingly fat).

Only once did I find Aileen in a cross mood. As I walked in she held up some material from the sewing machine and wailed, 'Look at that! The third time I've done it!' Peering at the half sewn garment I said it looked OK to me, clearly short trousers for Peter?

'Can't you SEE? I've sewed the right front to the left back AGAIN!'

Aileen! With your never ending sessions at the sewing machine and stories of your sisters back home in UK and whom you missed so much, your dread of Gillian being sent off to boarding school at the age of seven and never a complaint of being 'at the back of beyond' with so few visits to town.

At least the Kees boxes were reliable, you said.

Kees boxes?

Aileen explained, Kees (later to become CBC) was the large department store in Lusaka and they ran a most efficient box service to bush stations. Each month a box of ordered groceries arrived on the bus and last month's empty box went back with next month's order. Not only did groceries arrive, Aileen bought her sewing patterns and materials, small garments and even the children's shoes in this way.

As long as Aileen could run her kitchen and home as she wished she was usually happy but the woodstove was a never ending source of frustration, having a malignant way of ruining the most important meals.

The whole Boma shared in her excitement when Johnnie managed at last to buy a gas cooker fitted with a Calor gas cylinder. The installation of which was a noteworthy event but once it was in situ and in working order, Johnnie departed for his workshop. Aileen's house servant was sent round the houses with the message 'It Has Arrived'. And the women of the station arrived like homing pigeons. We sat around the cooker and admired the gleaming whiteness of it all; after our black leaded monsters we knew a good cooker when we saw one.

Aileen had already mixed up a sponge cake and this was carefully placed in the oven and we admired it through a GLASS DOOR. She served us all coffee while we sat around to savour the delight of watching a cake bake at the flick of a switch and a match. No wisps of smoke. Or piles of wood to dirty the hands.

Years later when we were reminiscing, Aileen admitted to me that if anyone had given her a ticket she would have been on the next plane out of the country. Coming from a large and close family she had found the isolation on a bush station hard to accept.

'It was all very well for the men,' she said. 'They enjoyed their work and the challenge. But the challenge of running a home in such different conditions was hard, added to which Johnny could be called away at any time to help someone who had broken down on the Great East Road. I would have no idea how far he would have to go, when he would be back or even who or how many people he might bring back with him to offer a meal and bed for the night.'

(We complain about the modern addiction to mobile phones but they have their advantages).

And Aileen was living on a bush station with several other European families - we both remember Alan (geologist) and Cecile Drysdall living in a tent down in the Luangwa Valley. Like Aileen, Ciss would have grabbed any ticket out offered at the time. But as is usual, now they look back with great affection to their years in the bush.

Ciss has often entertained me with her descriptions of meals cooked in a hole in the ground, her son Peter being tethered with a length of rope to a tent peg to stop him crawling out of the camp and her explanations of why she often thinks aloud even now – 'Alan would be away from camp for weeks at a time and none of the staff left with me spoke any English – so I talked to myself to hear some English'.

While we were in the bush, political events continued their momentum towards independence and as Andrew had been asked to help with the writing of the UNIP (United Independence Party) party manifesto we had gone back to Lusaka for a couple of weekends. Although we did not say much to the Europeans on the station about why we were going there, there were jokes about us missing the city life at which we just smiled as if in vague agreement. The first time we went to one of the meetings Elias Chipimo from Fort Jameson had been asked to attend too so he offered to pick us up on his way through. He arrived at Petauke late at night and we set off early the next morning on one of the most hair-raising rides I have ever had. Elias drove with his foot on the accelerator and the window wide open until he was a few yards behind a lorry, whereupon he would swing out into the cloud of red dust and overtake, in complete but terrifying confidence. We arrived in Lusaka in record time but Andrew was as red haired as me.

Slight though Andrew's connections were with UNIP they must have gone unnoticed for one day Harry Franklin of the Liberal Party made a stopover in Petauke and approached Andrew, would he stand for the Liberals? It took quite a while to convince him that Andrew really meant it when he said he was interested in politics - but only as a bystander. Andrew told me Franklin, in the Colonial Service, had gained fame when he had been given the job of starting an information service, radio being part of that initiative, broadcasting at low power, in the 1940's. But there were few African listeners, the cheapest radio being about £45. In 1948 while on leave Franklin met the chairman of Ever Ready and proposed cheap radios could be sold at cost, profit being made from the sale of batteries. The prototype had indeed been built in an aluminium saucepan. They sold for £5, (batteries extra). Ever after Harry Franklin was well known for the saucepan radio.

July moved into August and at long last the Slattery groundnut sheller arrived; enough bags of nuts had been retained for Andrew to run the trials.

The Slattery was then returned to Lusaka. And so did we.

Kapitu had long since wearied of life in the bush and had returned to the bright lights of city life; we had taken on William, who was a far better cook anyway and more than willing to go to Lusaka with us. Once more the old Morris was loaded up and the cat was tentatively introduced to a box but we gave in to his protests and he travelled free.

We said our farewells to Petauke with light hearts and set off early one morning with the cat's penetrating wails as accompaniment. We had decided to make an overnight stop at Kachalola Rest House which would break the journey nicely.

The cat was in fine fettle after a shorter journey and was obviously well rested as early morning tea arrived with the shattering of crockery as he pounced on the bare toes of the waiter. The tray was thrown to the heavens as he fled from the room.

The Great East Road was increasingly familiar by this time and almost an old friend especially as we were heading back to Lusaka for the last time. However the tyres had taken quite a pounding and were not going to release us from Eastern Province quite that easily. In spite of Andrew repairing each puncture as it happened the day dragged on and on, we were about 50 miles from Lusaka when we had yet another puncture and Andrew admitted there was nothing he could do as we were down to three tyres and no patches.

In the distance was a small farmhouse and he set off to ask if he could use a phone to reach a garage in town. The white man looked at Andrew suspiciously and said that he had no phone, although the wires clearly ran from the road to the house. We wondered whether to leave the car if there were the chance of a lift but it was full of our belongings - and the cat.

After some time a lorry appeared in the distance and we waved it down. The driver cheerfully agreed to take Andrew into town, he climbed on to the back with the spare wheel and sat with a crowd of farm workers. He told me afterwards that as they drove along one of the men asked who was the Dona, left in the car. When he told them it was his wife they laughed with appreciation at his sense of humour and he didn't manage to convince them otherwise.

Meantime I sat on in the car with the cat, watching the sky darken. The road and surrounding bush were silent and I knew that there probably would not be another vehicle passing until Andrew managed to get a lift back.

CHAPTER 4
BACK TO MOUNT MAKULU
September 1962

We limped into Mount Makulu very late in the evening and after dropping our possessions on the floor we fell into bed.

It was now September and the weather was very warm, I unpacked the house again and hoped we would stay put for a while. William, his wife and son Chembe arrived promptly by bus and seemed very pleased with their quarters in the compound. Chembe managed to get a place in the African primary school in Chilanga and joined the crowd of children on the long walk daily up to the main road and into Chilanga.

Mount Makulu and William and his first snake

William reported to me one day with a snake he had killed in the back garden as he came in to work. Impressed, I took his photo. And sent a copy to my parents. Even more impressed, my mother wrote back enclosing a ten shilling note for him as a thank you gesture. Which had the unfortunate result for a time of William disappearing unexpectedly, he could be found walking round the garden, stick in hand, checking for any more snakes

William considered himself much superior to Kapitu and insisted his status be recognised - this took the form of wearing 'whites'. I had supplied him with the usual two pairs of khaki uniforms but now we were in town (albeit 10 miles from Lusaka) he informed me that he should have a pair of whites to wear in the evenings while serving dinner. As he was a better worker all round I told Andrew we should have to change for dinner to keep up with the cook. That, I thought, would be that. But William had his own notion of what comprised the well turned out cook and the first night he appeared in all his glory - gleaming 'whites' topped by what looked like a large white halo. He had walked up to the Indian store at Chilanga, and invested in a 'cook's hat'. Made of white drill it fitted snugly round the head and the top opened out like - a huge halo! This was later alternated with a red fez complete with large black tassel, which would dangle rakishly over one eye.

I remember William also for producing a variation on an omelette. I always ordered breakfast the night before – and often forgot what I'd said. So was totally unprepared for a fluffy meringue omelette which I'd never met before and have never seen since. The white was so light and fluffy I think it was only the surrounding yellow omelette which kept it anchored on the plate.

Petauke had been a valuable and interesting experience but I had to admit that it was wonderful to be back with electricity at the click of a switch, tarmac roads and shops - a whole range of shops along Cairo Road, Livingstone Road which ran parallel and then Stanley Road parallel to that. Admittedly money was still tight but at least they were there and I could make a weekly shopping list.

After Petauke it was quite exciting to drive the ten miles to town and crossing the south end roundabout see Cairo Road in all its glory! It was dual carriageway to the north end roundabout - a 15 to 20 minute stroll if one were in a walking mood - and the centre was shaded by double rows of flame trees under which sat the curio sellers and their wares. Most of their goods were wood carvings with some ivory carvings - the latter were quite acceptable at the time as there were vast herds of elephant and more than enough room for animals and humans together. The escalation of poaching and wholesale slaughter of these magnificent beasts could not have been foreseen as the demand for ivory increased when personal wealth increased in China. A large tusk often carved with a series of elephants in decreasing sizes would be for sale for £20 - a large amount to us at the time. We would park after the first garage, walk past the butchery and a fabric shop and go into Kees, a supermarket with several small departments. Jameson Street ran at right angles where we could indulge in a Fanta (sticky sweet orange drink) at a café next to the cinema.

Continuing along Cairo Road was Greatermans supermarket which disappeared fairly early becoming a more expensive general store Zambiri. Then Barclays bank set back a little from the road and entered up a small flight of steps. Barclays where Andrew refused to have an account remembering how Africans had had to queue outside at a hatch in the wall. And so we banked at National and Grindlays. Then Goodmans store, an expensive department store where I ventured to yearn - but years later found a trouser suit I could afford in a colour which matched my auburn hair perfectly and was drip dry and creaseless after countless washes. Outside Goodmans sat a blind beggar reading a large Braille Bible with a tin bowl beside him. Late afternoon a small boy would appear to guide him home. Another man stood by the wall not far away. He stood. He just stood, gazing into space, dressed in a motley collection of rags and hair long and matted. He never seemed to move or speak and one day he was gone. Barclays bank relocated to the corner, a much larger and swish building faced with marble slabs and a huge mosaic designed by Gabriel Ellison, a well-known local artist.

Apart from the two beggars I've just described, the streets had many young boys selling vegetables from cardboard boxes which they carried endlessly to and fro. All were clad in the most miserable collections of torn and tattered shirts and shorts. One stays in my memory for some reason - a collar and the seams of the shirt with a few fluttering tatters above a pair of shorts which revealed more than they concealed. But all with beaming smiles and hopeful eyes.

Rhodes Street ran at right angles where we found a small greengrocers and Dels baby wear shop. But continuing along Cairo Road, Lusaka Hotel on the corner ... Kingstons stationers (they relocated to the opposite side of Cairo Road)... Codrington Street was the next side street where I think Lipschilds art shop was on the left. Opposite was Lusaka library and (joy of joys) Overseas bakery where an Austrian produced indescribable cakes of mouth-watering deliciousness. Antoinettes hairdresser and Milady, a swish dress shop owned by the Austins.

Klaus Rygaard was on the corner followed by Kingstons book and stationers (which later relocated to the opposite side of Cairo Road), Holdsworths chemist, Treasures shoe shop, Margots dress shop, Behrens electrical store, Revells dress shop, Royal Art Studio ...

An arcade connected Cairo Road to Livingstone Road and had Winstons opticians, Guttmans toy shop and a café and doctors surgery.

Across the next side street to a second hand furniture store ... Tarrys for tools and farm implements and eventually Lusaka Book Shop where I browsed endlessly for my children's first books.

Oh, what variety!

On the other side of the road the National Milling Company with their tall grain silos and the Farmers Coop opposite the Post Office imposing with its six floors ... and all this before we walked down the other side of Cairo Road from the Post Office to the Rendez Vous café, Modern Fabrics, National and Grindlays bank, the Education Offices in Grindlays House ... but there wasn't much development on that side when we first went there. That side of Cairo Road ended with a small white Police Museum opposite Kees store.

Most of my shopping was done in Kees, later CBC, where I could stock up on most groceries in the early days. Back in 1962 there was a wide range of goods – though I could never understand who would want to buy TINS of potatoes, carrots and green beans when fresh fruit and vegetables were in abundance and cheap all year round. Flour was the one difficulty at first until I managed to accept that all flour had tiny tiny black ? - weevils/insects/crawlies of some description. After a while I just accepted that all flour would be sieved and sifted before use. Were the silos infested? The packing place? No one seemed to know or care. Kees also sported clothing, china, materials, toys – my first Elna sewing machine included three free sewing lessons.

And all this before we ventured down Livingstone and Stanley Roads (parallel to Cairo Road) which were mainly Indian stores and the large Mistrys, the central market and Limbadas ... Limbadas was a treasure trove and deserves a whole chapter to itself to do merit to the range and variety of goods so more of it later. The market was fascinating with its rows of small stalls and wide range of fruit and vegetables, many owned and run by Afrikaaner farmers. After the Second World War shops in UK were slow to stock a wide range of goods so I was delighted to see such wide ranges of fruit and vegetables, some I'd never seen before – sweet potato, avocados, pawpaws, guavas, mangoes, egg fruit (aubergines), lychees, a range of peppers, corn on the cob, water melons ...

By now I was not the only white woman married to an African in N. Rhodesia; Pat and Rosemary Chuula had arrived while we were in Petauke. Pat had qualified as a lawyer in London and now had a job with Ellis and Company (?). They were renting a house in Kabwata, an African township. Rosemary was making an effort to learn Tonga, Pat's language, and even had vocabulary lists pinned up all over the house. We could not practise with each other and if we had had any sense at all we would both have agreed to learn Nyanja which is generally spoken in the Lusaka area. One is always wiser after the event! The Chuulas had one daughter, Malele, a delightfully pretty little girl with dark curling hair and skin like honey. I hoped for a daughter like Malele.

Into October and it was 'suicide month' - as everyone called it. It certainly did grow hotter than I had ever imagined but as the climate was so dry - no rain since March - it was not unbearable. Once the cat had settled down in the house we decided to have a dog and went off to the RSPCA pound. There was a range of abandoned hounds and it was hard to choose one but we eventually settled on a black and tan sort of mongrel. Once home and washed he proved to be black and white and, after an initial fear and wariness, proved himself to be a dog of an unquenchable bouncy nature. Micky was our constant companion for twelve long years and was a dog of character. We were never sure whether he was just quarrelsome or whether he had an inferiority complex and had to prove himself top dog - but he just had to take on all comers, especially larger dogs.

Andrew at Mount Makulu dambo (dam) with Micky

On his collar was his dog tag, everyone had to pay a dog tax for which you had to produce a valid rabies certificate, the dog tags had the year embossed on them and changed colour yearly.

A very simple, but wise arrangement, which ensured that the majority of dogs were vaccinated and were quickly identifiable. If not vaccinated in a rabies outbreak, they would promptly be shot.

November saw the arrival of the rains and after the recent long hot dry weeks it was a heady relief. The weather would get oppressively hot and it would build up to a magnificent storm with purple skies lying almost within reach, brilliant flashes of lightning and crashes of thunder which out-rivalled anything I had ever imagined. Then the rain fell in solid sheets. I loved the drama of it all and the clear freshness it left behind. There were days of grey steady drizzle of course, and days of rain-washed sunshine. Overnight the bare brown landscape turned green again and the grass grew even as you stood and watched it. Everything grew rapidly and the air was heady with new scents. There is nothing to beat the smell of rain on land after months of dry heat – the heady choking smell filling the nostrils, I could almost taste the smell.

We had begun developing the garden when we heard that the Brockingtons were moving to Nyasaland, they were only two houses away but had a magnificent well-established garden so we soon had permission to move. Joan gave me such long and detailed instructions about how to care for the roses until I was sure I would let standards fall. A popular phrase of the day – 'we must maintain standards', used constantly whenever there were discussions of independence and Africanisation of jobs. We were sorry to see the Brockingtons leave and I did not envy them their long journey through Eastern Province and into Nyasaland with their four cats on the back seat - even if they did have proper cat baskets.

But it was great to have a garden with established pawpaw trees - and oranges and lemons and guavas and bananas. There was a large patch of Himalayan raspberries by the garage wall, which I thought to have moved until Joan pointed out that they were above the septic tank soak away and therefore well-manured. The lemon trees produced the largest lemons I have ever seen with thick crinkly skins; the sharp tangy smell of lemons was all round the garden and I grieved over the large numbers rotting on the ground, but everyone had far more lemons than they knew what to do with. The garden was enclosed by a tall mulberry hedge at the side and back and the dark purple berries were thick among the large leaves. At the back we installed the chickens and began our first vegetable garden – anything and everything grew in great abundance in the rainy season and pretty well in the dry season courtesy of the gardener's diligence with hosepipes.

At the front was a six foot high hedge of hibiscus bushes with bright scarlet flowers - and where at times I would find a group of African women, babies on their backs, picking off the new leaf shoots 'for relish' - a vegetable side dish for the traditional nsima (the staple food, maize meal porridge).

Poinsettias taller than me grew down one side of the house and by our bedroom window was the most pretty and graceful shrub with small maple like leaves and delicate yellow bells veined with red - my first abutilon. It was not long before I saw that it attracted tiny birds which hovered with fast beating wings to probe the bells with long thin curved beaks.

Next door lived Bill and Ita Shepherd with their boxer dog Bashful, an ingratiating animal who would wag the stump of her tail so enthusiastically around Micky until she would overbalance in a quivering heap to his constant embarrassment. Ita suffered with repeated asthma attacks and spent much of her time wheezing on the verandah. I would go over many mornings and sit knitting for the baby due in January while she chain smoked, leafing through piles of magazines and wheezing until midday. Then we flapped towels to clear the air in the hopes she could convince Bill that she had not smoked more than one or two cigarettes.

Sometimes I would go over to the Mudendas and take Janie for a walk, pointing out flowers and insects, lizards and birds to each other. There were invitations to the Vogts next door to Mudendas. They were a hardworking couple who gave so much to the development of N. Rhodesia and it was tragic later to see their hurt when the new independent Government no longer wanted 'old' expatriates who had an extensive knowledge of the country and really knew what could and needed to be done. But this was all some way off in the future. In the meantime they were friendly and helpful and had none of the racial prejudice which we still sometimes met

Coffee mornings may sound a very barren way of spending the morning but apart from being welcomed by some people I did also pick up some useful information. Coffee mornings introduced me to red ants and putzi flies and the eternal topic of cockroaches. Red ants, I discovered later, really were as vicious as they were made out to be. It was at a coffee morning with Barbara Angus that I heard how their pet rabbits had had a visitation of red ants overnight. Only a pathetic heap of bones remained when the hutch was opened the next morning.

Putzi flies I was told were a real menace in the rainy season when the fly laid its eggs on the ground where dogs and cats would then lie and pick up the eggs. Even worse, the flies would lay their eggs on washing hung out to dry, which was why EVERYTHING must be ironed. Anne had told me in Petauke how her sheets had not been thoroughly ironed and she later found she was infested with putzi grubs all down one side. Barbara said she had had putzi grubs on her bottom when her pants had not been ironed with a hot enough iron. Both women agreed that the tickling of the developing grub was bad enough but it was the thought of a live grub developing under one's skin which was revolting.

'And you have to leave them there to fully develop before you can 'pop' them out.'

I later saw the havoc putzi flies could cause when our pet rabbits were infected and their paws were swollen with the growing grub. Once 'ripe' and popped open the grub could be destroyed and the hole healed over with no apparent after effects. Seeing the large white maggot as it was eased out of the hole had such an effect on me that I still ironed every garment and even towels meticulously, even after some years back in UK.

Inswa were of course another matter. I did not find out about them at a coffee morning though! Early in the rainy season Andrew and I were driving in town and under every lamp standard were groups of boys, each clutching a tin and collecting something from the ground.

Andrew explained that when the rains came, a certain type of large ant grew wings and took to the air at night, attracted to bright lights they would flutter round it, mate, lose their wings and fall to the ground. 'They are very tasty roasted,' he added.

Thinking of the tiny ants back in UK and the tiny black ants which would process through the house in search of sugar I thought that no matter how many ants one collected, it would only result in a teaspoonful.

That night Andrew left the verandah light on and put a large bowl of water under it.

'When the ants fall in, the wings will float away and the ants will be easier to collect.'

We waited. Later in the evening there were ants floating in the bowl. And they were big, over an inch long fat monster ants! We fried them lightly in oil and very tasty they were too. I heard some time later that chocolate coated ants were all the rage in America. And years later, in 2015, we have had reports of how nutritious insects can be ...

What I never did try were dried caterpillars. No matter how tasty Andrew said they were, I could not bring myself to try them. Perhaps if I had prepared my own it would have been different but the sight of the mounds of black dried up caterpillars in the market with flies buzzing around did not appeal.

I believe the caterpillars could be prepared in a different way, I only ever saw the ones dried in the sun. But I did read that they could be washed and boiled in clay pots and then pounded with groundnut butter, this mixture should then be roasted and made into a relish to eat with nsima, the maize meal porridge.

Andrew also told me that sugar cane rats were considered a delicacy but I never saw any on the markets. Nor did I ever see smoked and preserved frogs known as machesi, in Eastern Province. But I did like the dried salty small fish kapenta, rather like whitebait.

Shopping for normal goods in normal shops had its own surprises. In Kees department store one day I saw very large tins bearing the label Cooked Chicken, I looked at them and wondered who one earth would want to buy such a thing. Walked on and then thought actually what a good idea to have one of those as a standby emergency meal when a wood stove would mean slow going. So I bought a couple - they were extraordinarily cheap. Cheaper than buying a fresh chicken actually. Once home and stowing away the shopping I put the tins out of the way on a top shelf ... then noticed as I lifted the first one up another label. Actually stamped in large back letters on the metal base ... US AID TO THE CONGO.

I think my very first experience of corrupt officials and how well intentioned aid does not always reach its destination.

We had found on our return to Mount Makulu that Alec Prentice, the Head of the station, had retired and departed to farm in the Mazoe valley in Southern Rhodesia. He was replaced by Dick Ballantyne. So in December 1962 when Andrew was to attend a meeting in Salisbury we accepted an invitation from the Prentices to stay at their farm. Driving down to Salisbury was a very different kettle of fish from Eastern Province. A tarmac road all the way! Granted it was a strip road for long stretches, it was still tarmac and you only had to get your nearside wheels off the tarmac when passing another vehicle. Usually this was a simple courtesy but we soon found there were the foolhardy - or arrogant - few who played chicken by keeping all four wheels firmly on the tarmac until the last moment. Then swerving off, if your nerve held.

The Prentice's farm was perched high on a hillside and had marvellous views across the valley. Andrew was busy at meetings in town and I was dropped off to do some shopping. Salisbury was far more developed than Lusaka and I enjoyed the large stores and bustling atmosphere. I bought some baby clothes and then sat in Meikles Hotel to relax over a coffee. Andrew had arranged to pick me up at midday and we were aware of frozen looks as he walked in to collect me. It was a whites only hotel and I did not improve the shining hour by automatically standing up as he arrived and kissing him on the cheek. (He could not sit down and have a coffee of course and the watchers had probably assumed at first that he was my driver).

Driving back to Lusaka was an amusing trip. For some reason travelling down had been uneventful but the return journey was not so quiet. Being eight months pregnant I needed to go to the toilet fairly often; it was accepted on a long journey you just had to hop out of the car and squat behind the nearest bush or clump of tall grass. However, on the return journey every time I wanted to stop there seemed to be a car approaching or overtaking and I would stand in extreme discomfort at the road side while I convinced braking motorists

'Yes, I really was OK'.

'No, he wasn't giving me any trouble.'

The immediate assumption being of course that Andrew was my driver. The funniest part was when we stopped on the escarpment to let the engine cool down. Andrew had his head under the bonnet and I was stretching my legs on the roadside. A lorry chugged slowly up the incline, picked up speed as it neared the summit and the driver was preparing to roar away when he did a quick rethink and slammed on his brakes. He reversed backwards towards us with some difficulty and stuck his head out of the cab.

'You OK?'

'Yes, fine thank you,' I replied.

'You sure?'

Andrew stood upright, wiping his hands on a cloth.

'Just letting the engine cool down,' he said cheerfully.

The man stared at him in disbelief.

Then he turned to me.

'Sure you're OK? Don't let him get cheeky now. And you - speak when you're spoken to. Sure you're going to manage?'

With great reluctance he went on his way, while I suggested to Andrew that we might have a less interrupted trip if he invested in a driver's cap and remembered not to speak. It was a relief to return to Lusaka and settle down among people who were getting used to seeing us.

Until we embarked upon some Christmas shopping.

We had decided to open an account with Kees store in town and after some initial surprise and caution by the manager, Andrew had done this. We had not actually used the account until it was nearly Christmas. But, in town one day, we went our separate ways to buy presents. I began in Kees where I bought a few items and charged them to the account. Later when I met Andrew he was pacing up and down fuming. He had just emerged from Kees, where he had planned to buy a tie for Bill Astle, who was due to spend Christmas with us. But the assistant had refused to charge the goods to his account, saying that 'Blacks don't have accounts'.

On being asked to check, he had refused and told Andrew to pay cash or leave the store.

I could not imagine why Andrew was standing there being angry. I marched back into the store with Andrew at my side muttering, 'What's the use?'

To my delight it was the very same man at the men's wear department who had served me earlier. The man was in a very abject state after I had showed that he had credited my goods and never queried what was clearly an African name and then had refused Andrew on those very grounds. I insisted on also seeing the manager and saying what I thought of a store with such racial and inconsistent attitudes.

A pleasant beginning to the season of goodwill.

Life was very confusing, one minute Andrew was being told that Africans did not have charge accounts and the next minute one could read the news that Mr Kenneth Kaunda and his family had moved into 8 Prospect Hill former home of Rodney Malcomson when he was Member of the Northern Rhodesia Government, 'Mr Kaunda is the Minister of Local Government and Social

Welfare and shortly after the family moved in the children could be seen playing cricket on the lawn ...'

I suppose the fact that his children were playing such a good old English game as cricket was a point in favour, one could just imagine the comments over the coffee cups '... and now there are blacks next door, my dear. But of course, they are quite nice really and one sees the children playing cricket ...'

But it did seem odd that while it was clear that the country was moving steadily towards independence so many whites tried to ignore its coming. Did they really think they would not have to change their attitudes, at least in public?

I wondered sometimes how people would behave in a couple of years' time, but did not worry over much. There were - to me - far more important things to be concerned about.

The baby was due in late January 1963 and with a pram and cot bought from the second hand furniture dealer on Cairo Road and the clothes I had made we thought we were all prepared for the coming event. Ante natal classes were non-existent, I seem to remember an occasional check up with a doctor Doctor Lootit at the hospital. One day I decided to wash the new nappies and was standing in the sunshine, enjoying a premature maternal feeling as I pegged a row of whiter than white nappies on the line when I felt red hot needles being jabbed into my feet and legs. Looking down I saw large ants were swarming up my legs, behind them was a thick line of ants marching across the garden. My first experience of red ants! I beat them off and retreated into the house thinking of the pet rabbits which had been eaten alive. Fortunately these ants did not turn into the hen run, why I can't imagine.

As we approached zero day Andrew was sent to Uganda for a week. His consoling remark as he left was,

'Be sure to have a bag packed and I've told the Shepherds if they hear a knock in the night that it's probably you wanting a lift to the hospital.'

Reflecting that if I managed to wake Bill and Ita in the middle of the night I would more than likely be bowled over by their dog

Bashful and squashed in the bed of canna lilies by the verandah. I thought I'd pack a case and cross both my fingers and my legs. The baby got the message and dutifully held off until late January, and Andrew's return from Uganda. While he was away I had thought to look out some books I had sent for to UK about pre-natal exercises and natural childbirth. I should have given them more than a cursory glance when I had first received them as I now realised I should have been doing the exercises for some time. I lay on the bed with the book propped on the huge mound of my belly, did as the first chapter advised and thought that it more or less amounted to think beautiful thoughts and breathe deeply. It was all an over-rated business and I put the book back on the shelf and forgot all about it.

Early one morning I woke to a vague feeling of unease and thought, 'I should have read that book to the end.'

I poked Andrew and suggested he got the car out of the garage and went off to have a bath and reread that chapter about breathing deeply. Andrew not only got into some clothes and the car out in less than two minutes, he also threw a fit outside the bathroom door where I was beginning to entertain some regrets about having started all this. It was all very well I reflected as we raced along the road in the faithful Morris, but I was in no hurry at all never having read the last chapter.

Well, here we were – about to create yet another first without thinking about it beforehand. Andrew drove me to the European hospital where I was admitted to the maternity ward under the keen eye of Sister Betty Keith. A diminutive Scot, she was a renowned martinet but there was a visible relaxation in her manner when I gave her greetings from Anne Alexander back in Petauke. They had nursed together and I was on firm ground now that I could give her fresh news of them and baby John.

'And has she still got that great hound Skipper?'

'Yes although he was in disgrace some time ago when Jim had to keep taking him all the way to the vet in Fort Jameson - he had picked up VD from some bitches in the village.'

Sister Keith clicked her tongue in disapproval and bustled off.

This giving birth was a very long process I reflected as Thursday dragged on and Friday dawned with very little change. I had had the sense to keep a fresh book in reserve for my stay in hospital and every time I relinquished my hold on the gas and air mask I took my mind off things by reading a few more pages of Gone With The Wind until Sister Keith took the book away saying perhaps We would all do better if We concentrated.

I was not so sure. Ceridwen Mwape eventually made her arrival via a Caesarean after I was suddenly whisked down a corridor to the operating theatre. Ceridwen the Welsh name meaning beloved and pure. Mwape for her maternal grandmother.

Andrew looked ten feet tall at visiting time. I was lucky in being the only patient in a two bed ward and was able to rest and read to my heart's content - although I have never cared much for Gone With The Wind since then. The babies were all out of ear shot in a little nursery and only made their appearance at feeding times. Sister Keith was of the opinion that mothers needed their rest. I quite agreed.

Andrew came back from visiting the nursery one day smiling broadly. He had chatted to a sad looking Indian chap standing by the cots in which were three tiny babies - all his. Andrew had naturally admired the babies and congratulated the man. Looking even sadder the man commented, 'Triplets! All girls! And we have four more daughters at home already.'

'Thinking of dowries, what could I say?' said Andrew.

(I said it was the European hospital – Asians rated as Europeans at the hospital. Just as Asian and Coloured schools came under the European Education Ministry).

One of the staff, a nursing assistant, a pretty Coloured girl Dawn Abrahams, brought in a sheaf of what looked like privet and said they were from her mother and I would enjoy their smell. They smelt of nothing at all as far as I could tell but I thanked her for the thought. Come the evening though I knew what she meant, even though the flowers were removed from the wards and put on the corridor the rich sweet smell of Queen of the Night hung in cloying eddies throughout the entire maternity wing. Next day

Andrew was firmly asked to take them home. We subsequently planted a cutting from the original bush and the scent was heady on the night air - out in the garden it was wonderful!

Ceri, as she was known, was a bouncing eight pounder with straight dark hair, blue eyes and a clear white skin, much to my surprise and the complete consternation of many people, who gave Andrew and me curious sidelong glances. But while she thrived I felt increasingly lethargic which did not please Sister Keith who demanded the doctor have a blood test done. The very low result proved her right but then we faced a delay O Rhesus negative was not in stock and we had to wait for a donor on the hospital list to be contacted and called in from a distant bush station.

Elijah and Zeenie were some of my first visitors and Elijah, leaning enthusiastically and uncomfortably over the end of the bed, rocking the bag of blood which was slowly dripping into my right arm, told me that now, according to custom, I really was recognised as a woman. It was hard to concentrate on my new found status while I was apprehensively watching the rocking bag. It was bad enough having it drip in at what appeared to be an icy temperature without feeling that the whole caboodle was in imminent danger of flying across the ward.

Mary Roberts from Munali was an early visitor, bearing a white sleeping bag for Ceri which would convert into a dressing gown as she grew older. We chatted for a while and then she leapt to her feet saying she had to get back to roll the grass on the tennis courts. I could only gaze in admiration at the tiny figure as she cheerily waved goodbye, thinking the roller was probably as high as her shoulders. A couple of pints worked wonders and Ceri and I went home after two weeks as Andrew and I reflected that this was one of the quietest firsts we had had, the first baby born to a mixed couple in the European hospital and there had been no comment or difficulty we congratulated ourselves, not knowing until much later that an English nurse out on contract from UK had refused to attend me and was promptly reassigned to another ward by Sister Keith.

We should not have been so complacent of course.

When I went back for the post-natal check it was decided to admit me for a minor operation; as Ceri was being breast fed she was to be admitted on to the children's ward and brought to me at feeding times. This all seemed very straightforward. Andrew drove me to the hospital early in the morning and left us at the Duty Room with the Sister on duty.

A nurse whisked Ceri off and I was taken through to a four bed ward. There is always a hesitant silence when a newcomer goes through the undress-and-get-into-bed stage, but after that the three women were chatty and very sympathetic when they heard my baby was on the children's ward.

Midday and a nurse brought Ceri for a feed, instantly she was the centre of attention with sympathetic coos and clucks round the ward.

Lunch and enforced siesta.

Two thirty and visiting time. Andrew walked jauntily into the ward. Conversation stopped dead as he bent and kissed me. He sat down by the bed and began to ask about Ceri as our eyes signalled 'Here we go again'.

At this point other husbands arrived, going rapidly from shocked silence to infuriated growls and stomping off to the nurses' Duty Room. I suppose I had been put in a ward with three Afrikaaners quite by chance. And there was nothing they or their husbands could do to change the hospital's stand, that I had every right to be in that hospital and that Andrew had every right to visit me. After all, it was only a year since the Government had decided to allow fee paying African patients - judging by the atmosphere when I was there, there could not have been many actually admitted.

I had to endure total ostracism and was never spoken to again by the good ladies and had to listen to offensive conversations about kaffirs and munts aimed at hurting me. But it was only words after all. There were of course, no more sympathetic coos over Ceri, after all, 'it was clear that that was a kaffir bastard'.

On the other hand, they had to endure my constant presence

and apparent good humour and cheerful conversations with a few of the nurses, my apparent calm ('keep your cool June, and don't let them see you are hurt'). In a way it was worse for them, after all they had to endure the humiliating indignity of a black, a kaffir, a munt, sitting daily in the room where they lay in bed. Sheets were pulled tight up to chins and three beefy Afrikaaner men sat in suppressed rage every visiting hour. As I say, I guess it was harder for them in the long run. But it was lonely after Andrew left when the conversations were always more barbed. However, as I stayed there for two weeks I saw them out with a determined cheerfulness and their replacements were easier.

Andrew with Ceri   *June with Ceri*

Shortly after Ceri was born I read a statement in the paper by Harry Nkumbula, then Minister for African Education, which made me wonder how some people were going to cope in the coming months. Nkumbula said that once independence was achieved he planned to introduce compulsory and integrated primary education for children of all races.

'This will come about with the break-up of the Federation,'

he said. 'I will not allow segregation in education. We want all children to grow together from infancy. If N Rhodesia is to develop as a society where all races live in harmony it must start at the beginning - with children before they develop prejudices.' Bully for you Harry, I thought, but let's start a bit earlier! Let's start when they are born. Once I was back home Andrew and I had gone to register Ceri's birth at the Boma. A huge register was produced and the details of Ceri's name and date of birth were taken but when it came to us signing we found that the pages for the parents' signatures were divided into   FATHER European   Asian   Coloured

But there was no column for Father   African

The registrar, Alistair (?), looked uncomfortable but tried to pass the situation off in a jocular manner. I seem to remember Andrew wrote his name in the margin and wrote AFRICAN above, in bold capitals.

As this would have been in February 1963 I wondered what happened a few months later when the Lusaka City Council supported the proposal by the Municipal Association of Rhodesia and Nyasaland that legislation should be introduced making compulsory the registration of all births in the Territory. Did the margin get amended into a column for Africans? Or did the various Councils invest in a whole set of new registers?

A welcome to us and to Ceri in particular came from unexpected quarters. We bought our meat from Lusaka Meat Supplies on Livingstone Road (now Cha Cha Cha Road), the European chap who always served me was always most pleasant and hadn't batted an eye lid when I once walked in with Andrew and introduced him as my husband. The first time I went in after Ceri's birth and clearly no longer pregnant, he asked if it had been a boy or a girl. On being told a girl and she was out in the car with Andrew he shot out of the door to congratulate us both, admire Ceri and then asked if he could follow the old English custom and offer Ceri a silver sousa (sixpence). I had almost forgotten the custom and smiled yes as I explained to Andrew if her fingers grasped the coin she would be blessed with plenty.

She did. (As all small babies grasp anything offered it's a sure winner). But we remembered it as a kind and sincere welcome to Ceri and approval and acceptance of us.

But it was good to be home and well enough to walk Ceri in her pram round the station attended by the faithful Micky, who never left the pram if Ceri were in it. A neighbour once offered to have Ceri for an afternoon while I got on with some sewing. I left Micky in the house when I wheeled the sleeping baby over, knowing their dog would not relish his company. Back home I sewed away not knowing the garden boy had let the dog out into the garden. To my surprise when I went over to collect Ceri a couple of hours later, there was Micky lying watchfully by the pram.

'He came tearing along the road nose to the ground about twenty minutes after you left and has not moved from that spot.'

It was about this time I think that Andrew Sardanis paid us a visit from the Copperbelt to introduce his new wife Danae. I don't think we had met since he had paid that fleeting visit back in Leeds so it was good to catch up with news. The Sardanis' later moved to Lusaka and we maintained a friendship over the years – when the men would be deep in political discussions.

I had written home with news of Ceri's arrival and not long afterwards a small parcel arrived containing the old christening gown which my brothers and sister and I had worn. I handled the old silk with gentle fingers and thought that at last my parents were trying to accept developments. William brought in the afternoon tea tray and I showed him the gown, explaining it was the one I had worn.

He shook his head sadly.

'A-a-a, Madam, so sorry.'

I raised my eyebrows.

'So sorry, Madam, so sorry. Miss Ceri she not have a new dress.'

The baptism had been arranged to take place in the Anglican Church on Church Road, later to become the offices for the Zambian Youth Service. Alan and Pat Jarvis and Gwen Konie were godparents and many friends crowded to the service. Ceri did not think much of the events and her howls were so penetrating that at last Rev Fielding asked me to take her outside while the service continued without her. Back home tea was delayed while William tried to sober up, having paid a hurried visit to the beerhall in the compound to celebrate the occasion.

At this time Alan Jarvis was teaching at Chalimbana Teacher Training College near Lusaka. We had met at a party at Martin Kaunda's, a teacher at Munali School and on exchanging news found that Alan had gone to school with Michael Wearing in Scarborough. Gwen was working as an Assistant Officer in the Department of Social Services. Later she was appointed to the Legislative Council (LegCo) and was the first African woman there. When interviewed, she said that she hoped many more African women would be given the chance to serve on the Council. At first she had no special assignment and it may have been this which prompted the Opposition leader John Roberts to query her appointment. All these speculations were ended when the Acting Governor Ricard Luyt announced that Gwen was appointed a specially nominated Member because with her qualifications she would be an asset - as anyone who had any personal knowledge of Gwen's forthright Bemba character and wide interests would agree.

Ceri with godparents Gwen Konie, Alan and Pat Jarvis

Ceri - christening group. Bill and Josephine Mackerill behind me.
Dawn Thompson at my left shoulder. Edward Shamwana far right.

Ceri was born in January and within a couple months we were driving out to the airport with Edward to welcome Stella and their two small sons, Edward and Malcolm. They stayed with us a few days before moving into a rented house in Kabwata not far from Pat and Rosemary Chuula.

We were able to live among Europeans in 'European' houses because we were on the research station out of town. The Shamwanas and Chuulas had to live in Kabwata because the law still made it illegal for them to live in a 'European' area in town. The houses were fine but the irritation and frustration of being prevented from choosing where to live rankled. I think they both rented houses from a Dr Konoso, a doctor who had qualified and practised, but was also restricted to living and working in the African township, Kabwata.

At times I felt as though progress was both forwards and backwards. While Gwen was being appointed to LegCo letters were appearing in the Press from African State Registered Nurses. They accused the Anglo American Corporation and Rhodesian Selection Trust of 'flagrant discrimination in employment - based on colour - aimed at exploiting the nursing profession'

One SRN had her application for a nursing post turned down - 'Instead I was offered a job as a hostel supervisor - looking after the hospital maids in training. I was told quite frankly that the

135

mines had no fixed salary scales for African qualified nurses. I was taken on as a Group 8 at £27.10 a month.' Another SRN was offered £15 a month, the same as hospital maids and yet some European 'nurses' who had never been inside a training school were getting £60 a month.

This seemed to be more than contradictory when one looked at the situation at Roan Antelope Mine where some African employees were being promoted to jobs in what used to be 'Europeans only' category and were also being moved into houses in the Luanshya 'European' township. They were the second mine in the RST Group to provide senior African employees with housing in 'European' areas, the first was in Mufulira.

For some months I took Ceri to the European baby clinic in Lusaka until she had all the necessary vaccinations - I think it was DWT, polio, smallpox and yellow fever. By now her skin was slowly darkening and one mother asked if I were not afraid of my baby being sunburnt if I let her start sunbathing too early. All these stories of 'knowing a Coloured' and being able to 'recognise a touch of the tar brush' were a bit overdone I thought. The nurse, knowing my name, gave me a conspiratorial smile. And perhaps it was best we said nothing - after all our babies were using the same scales.

Now my days were fuller with Ceri growing and beginning to assert her personality on the household. Having come adrift over the relaxation exercises I immersed myself in an array of baby books and magazine articles on baby care, most of it seemed plain common sense - especially the bit about not picking up a baby every time it cried.

So when Ceri was fed and winded and should have her nap, down she went in the pram or cot to have her nap. And no way was I going to be an over indulgent mother who picked her baby up on its every cry. Ceri did not share this view and was a persistent child, not one to sleep by the clock but I thought it was all a matter of training. And I knew I had won the day when, on the third day of the new regime, she cried for a while and then there was peace, perfect peace. I glanced out into the garden in satisfaction. And there was William sitting on the grass, patiently rocking the pram. More books went on the shelf, never to be opened again. Red Cobra polish went out of the household not long after this when Ceri started to crawl and I could no longer face the pink tinged nappies. Apart from insisting she would not sleep by the clock, Ceri was a most adaptable child and travelled many dusty miles in her carry cot on the back seat of the Morris and later sprawled out on a blanket spread out on the put-down back seat. With a few toys she could wake up and crawl around as she wished. Seat belts were way off in the future! We even ventured to the drive-in cinema on the Kafue road with Ceri sleeping in her carry cot on the back seat.

With Bill and Josephine Mackerill

And of course, there were trips over to the Mackerills for barbecues by the 'pool' and Ceri watching our splashing with interest.

Out to Chalimbana to the Jarvises for the weekend, down to Mazabuka and over to Mapangazia, Ceri slept and crawled. She slept on the back seat of the car while we were at parties given at that time by Europeans, who seemed to be quite genuine in their wish to meet Africans and we would feel that with so much goodwill the races would integrate more easily than some predicted. I still met from time to time European - especially wives - who would say plaintively,

'Of course, I have never met any Africans. I'm sure some of them are all right. It is easy for you (!) but where do I meet ... you know... NICE Africans. Educated Africans.' I was quite intrigued by this desire to meet 'nice educated Africans'. But for the life of me I could not understand quite what they were getting at. It took some time for me to realise they wished only to 'meet' Africans with whom they could socialise. As I was not, and am still not, particularly interested in meeting anyone 'socially' I often felt adrift.

All these witless women (mostly wives out with husbands on contracts in the Civil Service, or with various professional firms etc) had ample opportunity to meet 'nice' Africans if they had bothered to invite home any of their husbands' work colleagues, there was growing integration in the workplace. And they all had one or two or more servants. The fact that these men servants for example - it usually was a man - had put traditional life on one side, had learnt more than a smattering of English, (few of these women knew more than a couple of words in a greeting in a local language), had learnt to run a house on unfamiliar Western lines showed that the 'uneducated native' at the kitchen sink was capable of some intelligent exchange.

It was quite beyond their comprehension that there was a person with something to offer. The few women who seemed to know more than their servants' names were settlers' wives and many of them adopted the paternalistic attitude which resulted in the servant behaving in the expected submissive manner, which did not show the real personality. I knew a number of couples who had decided to give a servant a Western name as they could not get to grips with pronouncing and remembering a tribal name ... so Johns abounded. I found this offensive. Surely if you can pronounce Tchaikovsky or Cholmondeley, you could have a go at Chikwanda?

Coupled with the many Johns were servants who rejoiced in such names as Handlebar and Sixpence, where their parents had chosen a newly acquired word and wanted to show off their

138

familiarity with the new language.

I remember being invited out to dinner, our hosts had eight of us round the table, Andrew being the only non-white. During conversation we were carefully allowed to know how very non-racial our hosts were. The illusion was sadly shattered at the end of the main course when the cook came to clear the dishes. Our host carefully carved three thin slices of beef, moved them slightly to the side of the meat dish, saying to the cook, 'And those are for you. You may take those '– and turning to us he kindly observed –' I think it's only right he can eat the same food as us sometimes'. More than my toes curled in embarrassment as I avoided looking at the cook.

Slightly different from the story we heard from some South African Africans who told us that at last they, as educated blacks, were occasionally invited to dine at the homes of university lecturers back in SA. But, they said, we know, we KNOW that they have a separate set of crockery which is smashed after we leave.

I suppose the social event of the year where many races mingled, was the wedding of Sikota Wina and Glenda McCoo. Sikota, a Lozi, was at the time Parliamentary Secretary to the Minister of Local Government and Social Welfare. Glenda was an extraordinarily beautiful black woman from Los Angeles. The wedding got off to a good start when Rev Merfyn Temple was reported to have said that he would conduct an illegal ceremony.

'I am prepared to give them a Christian marriage because they have asked to take Christian vows - despite the fact that Sikota Wina is debarred by law from marrying anyone other than a N Rhodesian African'. But in a hastily amended statement Rev Temple added that the marriage would be legal as far as it was registered under customary native law. 'But this does not give them the legal security they would have under the Marriage Ordinance'. He added that he was mistaken in saying Mr Wina was debarred by law from marrying anyone other than a N Rhodesian African. 'I should have said Mr Wina was barred by law from marrying anyone other than a person with indigenous blood.'

How long would it take to change all these laws I wondered. A Race Relations Committee had been formed but there was little it could do until laws were changed. They could of course publicise such incidents as the Lusaka barbers and hope that common sense would prevail. Lusaka barbers? An Indian from Salisbury tried to have a haircut in Lusaka and ran into problems when he wanted to patronise a European barber. Messrs Bolton, Howarth and Minnie took the line that they were employed by a customer to cut his hair and, they said, there was nothing to force them to accept employment from anybody unless they wanted to.

'We sell our trade,' said Mr Minnie. 'And we sell it to whom we want to. After all, I'd lose 75% of my customers if I started cutting non Europeans hair.'

(Did he object to cutting non Europeans hair or the prospect of losing most of his customers?)

The incident made headlines and gave food for thought because it was not long before we heard that another European barber had opened a multi-racial barbers shop - NEXT DOOR, the only 'European only' premises to meet the needs of Africa, Asian and Coloured customers. They even went to the lengths of employing an African to cater for African customers.

'We hope to have an Asian barber soon,' said Mr Baylis. 'We feel we need men of each race because they have had the experience of dealing with their own people' and he added firmly that he and his partner Giardino did not feel that they were capable of dealing themselves with people of other races ...

How I laughed when I read this. I begged Andrew to join in the debate and reminded him how he had told me that when he first went to Leeds and walked into a barber's shop there, the barber had apologised and said he could not cut Africans hair 'because he had never done it before'. It was said in such a way that Andrew laughed and said he was willing to be a guinea pig as he was sure the man could cope – 'after all, it is just hair like any other'.

140

The barber had begun with some trepidation but of course finished the job very well, he was then so elated he put a notice in the window saying that he could cut 'other types of hair'.

It was about this time that Myrna Blumberg interviewed Betty Kaunda for the Guardian and the article was reprinted in The Northern News. Mrs Kaunda had interviewed as a quiet, shy person, who had related with some amusement that she had been quite used to being addressed as 'Nanny' in the shops. (Just as an African male of any age would be addressed as 'Boy', the African woman would be hailed as 'Nanny' by many, if not most whites at that time). Now soon to be First Lady in the land, the memory must have caused her some wry amusement. Not one to dwell on the past however, Mrs Kaunda went on to describe how she had taken a quick course in domestic science at a College of Further Education in Oxford in order to polish up, among other things, her knowledge of English cooking - to enable her to cater for visitors from abroad and put them at ease.

Ironically at the same time the Woman's Page in the same paper dealt with Western fashions and in its Personal column related the gripping news that a Mr and Mrs Burns had left Nkana by train for Cape Town (I guessed he was a mine manager perhaps). There did not appear to be any interest in discovering and describing local African news or customs. I knew that if I had asked why the answer would have been that 'the reader' was not interested. How odd that people could live in a newly evolving integrated world and choose to ignore it and also assume that no Africans read the newspapers - and so I read and wondered - when I had the time. Life was busier now that Ceri had arrived and our circle of friends was slowly expanding. We met up with Alan and Pat Jarvis again when his mother came out from UK on a visit and we all trooped off to Munda Wanga for a day. Munda Wanga had started originally as a private garden but as the owner Sanders got more and more carried away, so the garden expanded until it covered more than forty acres just south of Chilanga and he decided to open to the general public. The variety of trees, shrubs and flowers was endlessly fascinating and after wandering and admiring we could then settle in some secluded spot to enjoy a picnic. In later years Munda Wanga grew even larger, included a small animal section and a swimming pool ... and eventually was sold to the State as a popular tourist attraction.

Early that year we had the surprise of meeting up with 'old' university friends of Andrew's. Ken and Pam Harkness had set about tracing Andrew as soon as they arrived in Lusaka and dropped in for a drink soon afterwards. Pam said she had taken a job at Lusaka Boys School.

'I don't know why you don't teach too now,' she said. 'The extra money is always useful, if you are anything like us, and with all the help in the house there is nothing much to do all day. It's 'morning only' teaching, remember.'

While Pam rattled on about the joys of being usefully employed again and the uses they could find for the extra money, I sat on feeling a growing anger building up inside me. I had been trying to get a teaching post for some time. When we had first arrived in the country I had applied to the European Dept of Education but there had been no vacancies in Lusaka at that time. There was no point in applying to the African Dept of Education because children in primary schools were taught in the vernacular. After that, I had written to the Dominican Convent but they had no vacancies either.

The arrival of Ceri had called a halt to teaching plans for a while but once she was four months old I had again put in a request for a teaching post with negative results. The Dept would be in touch if ...

The last letter was dated only a week or two earlier.

Pam rattled on until I could contain my annoyance no longer. She was horrified.

'But I was told of at least three jobs, all of them in primary schools. I took this one at the Boys School but there are other jobs. One of them is at the Infants School. That would suit you very well because you like infants. At the Boys School I shall have more opportunity to work with juniors. Oh June, I am sorry I didn't even think you had been trying for a job or I would not have gone on for so long telling you what you ought to be doing. But you really ought to go in again and ask about vacancies because there are some. In fact the man I saw was saying how difficult it is right now to find infant teachers.'

I was feeling angry and overnight the anger continued. I thought I would be well advised to go to the office next day and find out if there really were the vacancies Pam had quoted. But at long last I was getting my act together.

Andrew dropped me off on Cairo Road and went off to do some business at the Dept of Agriculture.

I walked into the office for European Education which was in Finlay House on Cairo Road, two young African men were busy behind a long counter, filing papers and typing. A young European man came out of the small back office and asked if he could help me.

'I am a primary trained teacher and wonder if there are any posts available in Lusaka. I have taught infants so far but I am also trained for juniors.'

And I slid my teaching certificate, probationary year certificate and two references from Miss Storr and Mr Lumley across the counter.

The young man read them, smiled and turned to consult a senior officer in the back office. He returned in a few minutes.

'Yes indeed, we have some vacancies. There is a form to complete. You could do it now or bring it in later if you wish.'

'I might as well complete it now.'

We beamed at each other.

It was not a long form and I handed it back to the officer.

He set off for the inner office, glanced down at the form, stopped and looked again.

He turned back.

'Your ... er ... name here. It's not the same as the one on your teaching certificate.'

'That's right,' I said cheerfully with a confidence I didn't feel. 'The one on my teaching certificate is my maiden name. The one on the form is my married name.'

'I see. Just a moment.'

He disappeared into the office and there was a quiet murmur and a quick look over a shoulder at me. I smiled sweetly back.

The young officer returned.

'Yes. Well. Now we have your papers we shall let you know as soon as there is a vacancy.'

'Isn't there a post available now? I thought you needed some primary teachers.'

'Yes indeed. But there is no actual vacancy just at this moment. But as soon as there is anything available we shall let you know.' At which point I blew.

Having red hair and a reputation for a quick temper in my childhood I had learned to control myself, at least in front of others. But I think all the petty frustrations and little pinpricks of the last year or so all came to a head that morning in the Dept of Education. The final straw was knowing that there was at least one vacancy and that with my maiden name I would have had the job there and then. I banged my hands on the counter and shouted,

'This is not good enough! Five minutes ago you were offering me a job! Now there isn't one!'

The typewriter came to a dead halt and two startled African clerks stared at me.

The young white officer had the grace to look slightly abashed.

'I am so sorry. There is a mistake. There was a vacancy some time ago ... but it was filled ... we will let you know as soon as ...'

I slapped my hands on the counter again, sending papers flying in all directions. A messenger walked in at this point with a tea tray and stood mesmerised beside the two clerks.

'You will not get in touch with me! There is a vacancy now and you offered it to me until you saw I have an African name.'

The three Africans began to understand what all the uproar was about and settled back to enjoy this one.

'Yes, well, I am sorry. It really is a mistake. I have said I am sorry and I can't say more than that can I ? we will be ...'

144

'There is a job available! You know it! And I know it! And I want that job!'

By now I was well away, I had not lost my temper for years but now I was more than making up for lost time - or making a 'right exhibition ' of myself as my grandmother would have said.

One of the clerks came slowly forward and bent to retrieve the scattered papers, he put them slowly on the counter and withdrew into the wings. I piled them up neatly, slapped them down on the counter in front of the officer.

'I am qualified. I have had experience. You have a vacant post in a primary school. I want that job.'

The poor young man turned to the inner office.

'Mr Joubert?'

Mr Joubert, who had been getting redder and redder in the face, came out and in a strong South African accent - wouldn't you know it? - said,

'The young man is correct. There is no vacancy right now. We will be ... '

'There is no need to be in touch. You will give me the job now.'

'I repeat, there is no vacancy. I wish there were. You say you know there is a vacancy but ...'

'There is one at the Boys School and there is one at the Infants School, there may be more of course but you would know more about that than I do.'

Mr Joubert and his assistant were beginning to flag.

I warmed to my argument.

'It is only because I have an African name and you have realised I am married to an African that you are refusing to employ me. Well, that is not going to wash anymore.'

They were on a sticky wicket, they knew it and I knew it. They knew I knew. And I knew they knew.

This was where the fences really were going to start coming down. The British Government were actually discussing independence for Northern Rhodesia and the writing was on the wall, even for those who would not read it. Mr Joubert knew that this was a delicate moment and would obviously have

145

given anything to restart the day. My knowing where the jobs actually were available had somewhat spiked his guns and he was now unsure how much else I might know or who had given me the information. He weighed up the alternatives of political embarrassment against a departmental potential trouble spot and capitulated.

He insisted the post at Lusaka Infants School had just been filled … but … ah yes, there was a vacancy at Thorn Park School.

I didn't care two brass buttons which school I was posted to, as long as I won the right to teach in the Dept of European Education. Was it a coincidence that I was posted to Thorn Park Primary - for Coloured children? Was a teacher rapidly moved to the Infants School from Thorn Park?

While Asian and Coloured schools were in the Dept of European Education, the pupils were kept strictly segregated and I was being posted to the school for Coloured children in the 'Coloured quarter'. Residential areas of towns had been segregated just as in South Africa and only now were their boundaries being broken.

But right now I had a job.

I walked back to meet Andrew hoping that the sick shaking inside me was not too obvious on the outside.

All this took place before July 23 when it was reported that Ndola Convent School had admitted its first African pupil, five year old Patricia Matsie. While the report was non -committal it was also necessary to add a comment from the Headmistress, Sister Mary de Sales, 'What is so striking is that the little girl is so completely at home with the other children'. And she added that little Patricia was the daughter of an African secondary headmaster and she spoke fluent English. The latter statement clearly intended to allay some of the worst fears of some white parents, whose attitude to integrated schooling was always that it led to a deterioration of standards because of language and culture clashes.

There was no mention of whether the other five year old white children felt quite at home with the new black girl in their midst.

Pam had said that she had found a place for her daughter Mandy in a nearby crèche. I had seen a sign for the Lady Rennie Nursery just off the roundabout at the south end of Cairo Road and decided that would be most convenient, passing it as I came into town.

I went there and introduced myself to a Mrs Stephenson, an energetic and friendly Scot, she had room for a baby for mornings only. It was all going so smoothly now but I thought I should be prepared for hiccups in the system and filled Mrs Stephenson in on the details before we agreed and signed any papers. She was, quite sensibly, honest and open in her reactions.

'It makes no difference to me whether your wee baby is white or brown - or sky blue pink for that matter - but I'm being quite honest with you, I am in charge of the nursery but I'm only an employee. The nursery is run by a Committee and I'll have to put it to them. It is a European nursery, opened originally for mothers who came in from the bush to have somewhere to leave their children while they shopped (remember mothers in from the bush would be stocking up on more than a month's supply and most likely tracking down spare parts for farm machinery etc). Now of course we take children whose mothers go to work.'

The question of Ceri's admission was put before the Committee and no objection was raised - that I heard of.

Stevie - as she was universally known - ran a happy and efficient nursery with the help of several African nannies and two young Afrikaaner women. It should be put on record that these two young ladies were completely devoted to the children in their care and were totally indifferent to the colour of their charges. After Ceri, the daughter of an Indian couple, also teachers, was admitted. Then gradually Coloured and African children were admitted and it mattered not a jot to the Misses Oosthuizens. They thoroughly spoilt the babies in particular and no protesting baby was ever left to cry in its cot - but was lifted out and cuddled and talked to until it either fell asleep or was content to go back in its cot and watch the world go by. Ceri fell in love with both the Misses Oosthuizens - as did her brother later; in fact they would go to them so cheerfully in the mornings that I would feel a jealous pang.

THORN PARK PRIMARY 1963

So, Ceri had a nursery place and I was to teach Grade 1 at Thorn Park. I went to visit the school and introduce myself to the Head, a Mr Gordon Swan. Thorn Park had six classes, Grades 1 to 6, all the children were Coloured and all the staff with the exception of Miss Sissing were white. Miss Sissing was a tiny lady, very near retiring age and a Cape Coloured from South Africa - all these labels meant very little to me but I was beginning to accept them as part of the local everyday vocabulary.

Miss Sissing was a great help to me as I tried to settle into the school. She lived in a small Government house opposite the school and over very milky and sweet tea filled me in on local history. She was very critical of many local Coloureds, saying they had no pride in themselves and that they could achieve so much more in life if only they would make the effort. When I puzzled over the number of babies born to unmarried girls, she informed me in acid tones that far too many of the local girls had so little self- respect that they tried to get pregnant by a white man to make sure that their first baby would be whiter than themselves, after which they were content to marry another Coloured man. An interesting theory which I was never able to prove or disprove.

Thorn Park was the area bordering the railway line at the north end of Cairo Road and was designated the Coloured quarter. Here were the houses for the Coloured community and their primary school, a church and a hostel for coloured boys from out of town run by Father Walsjak, a man with a gentle disposition and eternal optimism.

My Grade 1 class consisted of over forty boys and girls aged between five and six and all of 'mixed race'. There the collective nouns ended.

Victoria could have been a strikingly beautiful Spanish girl .

Rafik could have been a long limbed curly haired Indian.

Michael could have been an African.

Lorraine must surely be Scandinavian with those bright blue eyes, long blonde hair and white skin?

But no, all these children and all the shades of colour in between were 'Coloureds'.

Someone once asked me why I had not pressed right up to the end to be placed immediately in an all-white school, but the colour of the children did not matter, not even to prove a point - political or racial. I had won my battle to be recognised and employed by the Dept of European Education. And anyway, once at Thorn Park I didn't want to move.

The school year ended in December and in those few months I learnt a lot! You listened to people who talked in depth about how race relations had affected them once they realised you were truly interested, you listened and you watched people preaching one thing and believing another, you saw what racial segregation meant to people who had lived with it over a long period and had their own set of prejudices. ... but most telling of all were the children who had grown up absorbing those prejudices.

Now that independence was no longer a mad theory by 'those Communists or long haired intellectuals who have no stake in the country', changes were actually taking place. By August it was announced that school fees were to be introduced in former Federal schools (the European, Asian and Coloured schools). The fee was to be £30 primary and £45 secondary. There was an outcry from many Europeans saying they could not afford it, others pleading for the continuation of single sex secondary schools foreseeing integration problems there.

For the next year the schools were to be desegregated where places were available. I was astounded at the number of older junior girls chatting to me who disapproved of this move.

'It's not going to be the same if they allow Africans into our school.'

'Do you think you should be allowed to go to white schools?' I asked.

'Oh yes! It's a good thing for the schools to be open to everybody.'
'So it will be a good thing when SOME Africans come to this school?' I teased.

'Ah no, Mrs Kashita! That's different!'

It was interesting to note that while we were gearing ourselves up to the idea that the next January election to bring Northern Rhodesia internal self-government would be held under a new 'one man one vote' Constitution, which would provide for a limited number of reserved seats for Europeans and while we were trying to adjust to the notion of integrated schools - at the same time integration of schools in some parts of the United States was just beginning (in Birmingham, Alabama!)

In the January 1964 election African and European voters were to be divided into two rolls on a racial basis and would not be allowed to vote for candidates on each other's rolls. The main roll was for Africans and the reserved roll for Europeans. Coloureds and Asians could choose which roll on which to vote! I was reminded of these charming racial arrangements when some African children DID enrol in our school. As far as I could see, down at the infant end of the school, integration was quite smooth. Until it came to the Ministry lists. At regular intervals we had to complete forms devised by some fundi (expert) at the Ministry to check on how many of what had integrated where. No doubt a well-meaning exercise but it was not worth the uproar it caused in my room. At first I tactfully tried to discover into which category a child fitted - being still very ignorant of what constituted what. But the children would have none of this on-the-side tactful consultation and revelled in acrimonious debates around my desk.

I well recall,

'And Philip?' (black as the ace of spades- as the saying used to be - and therefore surely to be entered under Boy - African column).

'Coloured, Mrs Kashita.'

As my pen touched paper -

'No! you not be Coloured. You be black same like me!'

'I Coloured, sure Mrs Kashita. Grandmother she has mother, she

Coloured. So me, I am Coloured.'

Well, if some adults were allowed to choose their electoral race ...

European, Asia, Coloured, African, Purple, Martian ... what the hell? Anybody who wished to be Coloured - or any other colour for that matter - could have it at a stroke of the pen in my room. I often wondered since if some officer at the Ministry congratulated himself on how well integration in schools was progressing, particularly in Grade 1 Thorn Park.

Racial integration in the staffroom at break time was not quite so smooth. The Head, Gordon Swan, grew quite boring with his pacing to and fro, coffee cup in hand, pontificating upon the disasters soon to befall us. Standards would fall, that was not only obvious but inevitable. None of us would be safe in our beds as the crime rate would soar. Your home would no longer be your own, why, he had friends in (Kenya? Uganda? - some already independent country) where 'The locals just walk into your garden and help themselves to fruit and vegetables as they wish - you can't complain'.

(I thought of the women from the compound helping themselves to the new leafy shoots on my hibiscus hedge).

We endured sagas of how to battle for the best financial settlements as the British Government was apparently intent on 'selling us down the river'. On and on he ranted, every morning break was a Swan soliloquy.

Not only was it boring, so boring it was not even offensive to me, it was highly irrelevant to me in my situation. So I took to staying in my classroom at break time for peace and quiet but this offended him and he would seek me out, asking me not to boycott the social break times altogether. What a muddled little man.

Poor chap, his world of the white masters was falling down around his ears. He was out of teaching as fast as he could make it. But the tough competition back in grey UK held no attractions either because for many years afterwards I heard he clung to a 'management' post on the Nakambala Sugar estate down near Mazabuka. I heard comment that the financial conditions coupled with assistance towards his children's boarding school fees in the UK made up for the 'falling standards' all around us. Very soon we had more non-white staff appointed to the school, the writing on the wall was writ larger with the passing weeks. Tom Ravenor, a Rhodesian Coloured, came into the juniors - an attractive and well turned out young man, who suffered acute distress the whole of one morning when he inadvertently made an ink spot on his otherwise immaculate white shirt.

A Mr Surtie, a South African Coloured, moved into top juniors. An Indian Head, Mr Patel, replaced Gordon Swan. He was a gentle and well-meaning man but totally unsuited for coping with the domineering Surtie. The latter would have been far more suited to Swan's day as he too was a mine of inside information on all that was happening - usually inaccurate.

He knew of impending disasters and troop movements to combat these. Thus the day that the police - or was it the army? - had been testing some new helicopters which had circled above our school to the delight and irritation of pupils and teachers respectively we heard

'... the Government's expecting trouble, man, could be riots! They can't make it public yet, man ... And the area's to be evacuated! ... They have troops standing by, man ... There's no need to worry, the Government is prepared, man ...'

All this had me in stitches but to my surprise it had another new teacher more than a little concerned. She would have been even more concerned if she had known that Surtie had confidentially told us all on the day after her arrival that he 'knew her parents, man, no more white than I am. No, man, I know her father well, He's a Coloured just like I am ...' (but not as boring I hoped). 'Of course, her husband has met the parents but he's English, man, he won't be able to tell like we can!'

Even if his information was correct - and I never bothered to try and find out - my only reaction was to think how sad. If it were true, how sad for someone to 'pass for white', in a country where it did not matter anymore. But perhaps racial aspirations were long ingrained?

But enough of the adults, what of the children? Just as delightful as children everywhere.

Hilary Zebron left us at the end of the year and went to the previously all-white Lusaka Boys School where, as Pam Harkness, later informed me, he had come first in all of the end of year tests. Many white parents had been upset by the proof in their midst that white superiority was not as invincible as they had believed.

Other names which spring to mind – Victoria Findlay, Stanley Jordan, Stephen Mee, Freda Phiri, Douglas Williams, Valerie Phiri, Golden McTribuoy, Mona Lisa Maery, Anna Visagie...

Anna Visagie, who gave me one of the most humiliating - and deservedly so - moments of my career. In my second week (second note you) at this school I had started to teach some number jingles -

'Five little mice came out to play

Gathering crumbs along the way......'

And as the children joined in I showed them how to move their fingers to make the mice creep along

Anna did not join in the finger play

'Come on, Anna, hold up your hands like this.'

No response.

'Anna?'

Slowly the hands came up.

 Minus fingers.

I had been in that class for a couple of weeks and had not noticed that Anna did everything with the stumps of where her fingers should have been! It was no excuse whatsoever to add that Anna had been turning out immaculate pictures and writing, had removed and replaced sandals, fastened buttons etc.

Anna took her disability so matter of factly and coped so well that I think she would be astonished to know how often I have described her determination to succeed and be on an equal level with her peers. She has been held up as an example to so many children I have taught in subsequent years.

153

Father Walszak, the elderly Roman Catholic priest, was a regular visitor to the school. He was generous to a fault with his time and concern. He was well to the fore in organising fetes to raise funds for the school, money from which helped to buy the brown wholemeal bread and milk for needy children at break time. He would often appear when this was being served and exhort the children not to tell their parents that they were on his 'milk list'. He smiled sadly at me and said,

'Otherwise the parents will not give them any breakfast because I am feeding them.'

In those 'good old days' when 'standards were still being maintained' tapes and films were still available from the Audio Visual Services; we made good use of the facilities. One day when the children were sitting in a group on the floor listening to a music tape I had borrowed, I felt the cupboard near me begin to shake. I looked around to see who was kicking the furniture. No one.

The shaking continued and now the air seemed to be vibrating too as I suddenly saw the class across the way spill out of their classroom onto the paved area.

My first earth tremor. Lake Kariba was taking a long time to settle and these minor earth tremors continued for some time, but not as long as the political vibrations.

Lake Kariba was a massive undertaking and it was at the time the largest man-made lake in Africa. A great deal of political capital was made out of the plight of the Tonga people dispossessed from their traditional farming and burial grounds and their later hungry state when they were abruptly moved to unfamiliar territory. The greatest scandal being of course that the rescue of wild life, known as Operation Noah, caught the world's imagination and funds poured in to help in the rescue of marooned animals while the desolation of the Tonga tribe was ignored.

Talking of Audio Visual services. Miss Sissing did not like operating the film projector so we combined our two classes and I dealt with the mechanics. One week I had ordered a film on the life cycle of the frog and as the film progressed I noted that Miss Sissing was taking a keen interest in the life cycle of frogs. She leaned forward watching intently. Suddenly her hand shot forward completely masking the lens and blotting out the picture on the screen. Children's heads began to turn but almost as quickly her hand was lowered and she sat back, relaxed. I stared.

'If I had realised that you had ordered THAT film, dear, about the frog I would have warned you, there's a bit that's not very nice.'

'Is there?' I wondered.

'Oh yes, they actually show the frogs, you know... doing ... you know! Not very nice at all.'

Perhaps two frogs clasped in close embrace are 'not very nice' viewing for children but as the film appeared to have been shot from a great distance through a water logged lens I doubt if anyone - apart from Miss Sissing - would have taken much offence.

One day I found a large chameleon on a bush in the garden and took it into school the next day in a large box. As a subject for a mini topic chameleons are ideal. They don't smell or make loud noises, they move slowly so are unlikely to disappear under a heavy cupboard evading capture etc. On the other hand they will obligingly grasp a stout twig and swivel their eyes around while you talk about their ability, offered a grasshopper they will gaze long enough to grasp every child's attention and then whoops! out comes the tongue! My chameleon was a hit! And the children drew and wrote with enthusiasm.

I was a bit surprised how interested they had been but that was explained on the way home. That day Andrew had driven me in and picked me up at midday. On the way home I felt a twitching on my skirt and as I looked down the chameleon heaved itself up on to my knee.

'Oh bother,' I commented. 'It's escaped from the box, but we're nearly home so it doesn't matter.'

At which point Andrew glanced down and nearly swerved the car off the road.

'Put it back in the box!' he ordered abruptly.

It was only then that I discovered that the chameleon was regarded with great suspicion, if not fear, by most Africans.

It was wonderful to be back at school again and the extra money was a great help. Ceri was enjoying the nursery and the company of other children. Andrew was working harder now and actually had projects at work into which he could sink his teeth.

No one could really ignore the topic of African Independence. Ghana had led the way and the wave of nationalism was sweeping the continent. I remember reading that the Northern Rhodesian population at the end of 1962 was recorded as 2,580,000 of which 77,000 were Europeans, 2,490,000 were Africans and 10,500 were Asian or Coloured.

This was corrected in August 1963 to an African population of 3,410,000 much higher than previously estimated. The figures could be explained by the fact that this had been the first actual African census. I was puzzled that no official census of the African population had been taken before - merely estimated. However, it was obvious that one man one vote was going to initiate vast changes. And I wondered what had happened to the Gov. census Andrew and Titus Mukope had undertaken in the 1950's.

I remember being at the home of an American couple in November, there was quite a crowd of us and during the evening the results of the local elections were announced. Our host made a point of switching on the radio as the results came through, UNIP swept the board. There were a few cheerful comments but by and large the various conversations continued. Eventually the host said in disappointed tones that he had expected a much more enthusiastic response. Laughingly he was told that it was no surprise to anyone - 'Just what we expected'.

While I followed the political events with interest - something I had not done in UK where one was far removed from the people involved in decision making - I was also fascinated by the human interest stories which appeared from time to time.

A Mr Chikwanda went into the registration office in Fort Jameson to register as a voter. He was an elderly man and as Africans did not have birth certificates, he had to give some details to try to verify his age and possible date of birth. Mr Chikwanda said he was freed from slavery by David Livingstone when he was ten years old. When the village headman had heard the Arabs were trading cloth for people he was one of the first to be given away. On the way to the coast, walking in a long line of slaves they met David Livingstone. And the rest, as they say, is history.

Another man Nkoloso was quoted with great delight in some white circles - for all the wrong reasons unfortunately. He had announced with great solemnity that he was organising the building of the first spaceship in Africa, which would be launched at the Independence celebrations. Nkoloso gave the Press a field day on more than one occasion - his wild appearance and even wilder claims were solemnly photo'd and reported. While our African friends laughed gently at this frivolous caper, recognising his mental difficulties, it served only too well to fuel the cruel laughter of whites, who were busy packing their bags as they prophesied what was to come.

Not that many of them left with credit. The staff of an animal clinic, in Luanshya, were rushed off their feet, rescuing pets which were abandoned daily. Their letters to the Press were vitriolic, and Luanshya was not alone with this problem.

Most people seemed to be heading for Australia - while one could understand them heading for sunny climes I also wondered whether the statement by Scotland Yard was a deciding factor.

'UK,' said a spokesman from Scotland Yard, 'is not yet ready for non-white bobbies ... but their future recruitment is being considered.' One could imagine certain types heading for sun and a whites only policy after this. Kenneth Kaunda sought to allay their fears. As leader of UNIP and probable first black Prime Minister he pledged that there would be no legislation against political opposition to create a One Party State after independence. This was in response to charges and fears in some quarters that UNIP would stifle legitimate opposition. (I believe that at the time he was quite sincere in this statement, but the future is hidden from us).

Together with Harry Nkumbula, leader of ANC (African National Congress), he appealed to supporters to stop any violence - the increasing number of crimes ranged from arson to stonings.

On January 1st 1964 the Federal Broadcasting Company ceased to exist and Donald Lightfoot introduced the Northern Rhodesian Broadcasting Company. This smooth change over somehow indicated a promise of things to come. And although one read that 6530 Europeans left Northern Rhodesia in 1963 - mostly in October and November - 2410 Europeans had arrived during that period. Perhaps we had lost some experienced personnel but they were clearly being replaced. And perhaps some of those leaving - if not many - were the very ones we could most manage without.

Sikota Wina's wife Glenda (the glamorous American) addressing the Lions Club in Luanshya showed one of the changes in attitude in the new regime. She said one of the greatest evils of colonialism was well-meaning paternalism. For example, she said, the tradition of paying a servant £7.10.00 wage plus a food allowance was widespread, just because people believed servants did not know how to budget. I could well see her point of view but also wondered whether a man would be good at budgeting when he had not been used to handling money and would be faced with new temptations in towns. And perhaps some employers had started off on that well-meant route as an initial introduction in teaching a man how to budget ... then never got round to the next step of paying the man his wages in full once a month.

As a point of interest, we always asked our servants if they wished to be paid in full at the month end or so much plus weekly ration money – they always opted for the latter.

There was also a clear attempt in the Press to encourage Africans to be proud of themselves as Africans. For a long time lighter skin and straight hair had been admired and many women resorted to skin lightening creams and beauty aids of doubtful make. When Hazel Maoni in Kitwe decided to style African women's hair in her husband's barber shop, she had short shrift from

UNIP supporters and in particular from Alexander Chikwanda, the UNIP regional youth secretary. He was quoted in the Press as saying, '... we advised them in a friendly manner the contribution his wife planned to make to the country was not one the Africans wanted. After all, beauty is best admired in its original form. And the geography books definition of African is : dark skin, flat nose, thick lips, kinky hair. Artificial beauty costs more time and money to maintain, and to interfere with the hair of our women might inspire a feeling it is of inferior quality...'

Mrs Makoni, who had qualified after a six month course in the United States, wisely decided to turn her talents to the hair of European and Asian ladies - although the newspaper in question never did a follow up story on how many clients Mrs Makoni managed to attract. I doubt she would have found it easy at that period but I could well be wrong.

The polling days on 20th and 21st of January went off quietly, the only problems appearing to have been at five polling stations in Luapula, which were only accessible by canoe and required carriers to get the equipment in.

One woman in Kalalushi made her own problems, thinking the ballot box should open, she ripped out the rivets from the box lid! The polling officer, hearing the noise and going in after she had departed, managed to reseal the box and polling continued. As was expected Kaunda swept through on the Main Roll but lost all ten Reserved seats and he took the oath of allegiance to the Queen before the Governor Sir Evelyn Hone at Government House. But the quietness of the polls and the atmosphere generally was marred by reports of riots in Mufulira, where more than 1000 incidents of rioting, fighting and intimidation were reported and dealt with - all this within four days of the polls.

One day we took the whole school out on to Burma Road (now renamed Independence Avenue) and waited for the procession of cars carrying Kaunda and his colleagues, back from England with the proclamation for independence. The children waved their flags and cheered and talked about The Paper they had actually seen being waved aloft. Independence was a-coming and it was a-coming fast.

Africans were being promoted to positions of responsibility and some were understudying top civil servant posts. One of the first appointments however, went to James Skinner (a long serving European supporter of Kaunda and UNIP) who was given the Parliamentary Secretaryship to the Minister of Justice on 28 January. Andrew had to move from Mount Makulu to help set up a Natural Resources College, which was going to train young people and retrain farmers in modern agricultural methods and revolutionise farming in rural areas. Classes were initially to start at the former Hodgson Technical School just off Independence Avenue while the college was being built on - where else? - the Great East Road. We seemed to be continually pulled in the direction of that road.

As a temporary measure we were allocated a Government house near the Civic Centre on Wallace Road, at the end of which was a little graveyard. Once we were settled in I walked down one evening with the dog and opened the small gate which was stiff with disuse, although someone clearly cut the grass occasionally. There were only a few headstones but almost every one recorded death from Blackwater fever. These were the early settlers who had braved life in Africa without the benefits of modern vaccinations and medicines.

Leaving Mount Makulu meant we had to rent a post box at the Post Office in Lusaka, an impressive six storey building on Cairo Road, we were allocated PO box 1358, on the first floor. A novelty for me, drive into town to shop and pop into the post office, run up a flight of stairs and walk along the bank of green metal boxes and insert the key. What excitement to see post, especially if it included some thin blue aerogrammes. I never thought to explain post to Ceri and was amused one day when we had gone daily to collect Christmas mail – once the box was open we could look through and down into the sorting office. Looking at the busy men below Ceri said, 'He's very kind.'

'Who?' I asked.

'The man in the post office who gives us all the pretty cards.'

Peter Hepworth collecting post at Lusaka Post Office

Staff houses were to be built on the college site eventually but in the meantime we could be living on Wallace Road for a year or more. It was typical two bedroom house with what was optimistically known as 'shared servants quarters' to the rear. This meant that there was only one room and a lavatory for our servant to share with the servant next door. Fortunately for us, our next door neighbours were South Africans who would not allow their servant to live on the premises, so William and his wife and son had somewhere to live, although it was far from ideal. (And I suspect our neighbours were not delighted with both our arrival next door as well as the servant's quarters being occupied but managed to put on a smile whenever our paths crossed).

Another irritation was that we were not on main sewage system and our septic tanks were not capable of coping in that low lying area. Which meant that, for some reason I could never discover, every Saturday about lunchtime the septic tank lorry arrived and after opening up the manhole - directly outside the dining room window - a large pipe was lowered into the septic tank for a noisome emptying process, not at all conducive to a good digestion.

I looked around and considered other possibilities. House prices were falling rapidly as whites left the country and I begged Andrew to consider buying a house of our own. I think it was only to humour me, that he agreed and I set about reading the For Sales columns with a careful eye. Very soon I found a house for sale in Chelston, only a few miles from the college site. I went off one afternoon with Ceri in the car seat in the back of the car and had a look at the house and the area. It was perfect and such was my enthusiasm that Andrew came and saw and was conquered.

We had no money of course but there were not many buyers around in those precarious pre independence days so the building society accommodatingly accepted Andrew's life insurance policy as a deposit.

The house was a brick built bungalow with a TILED roof – no more ugly corrugated iron sheets! The house was painted white and stood among large trees on an acre of ground. There were three large bedrooms and a bathroom, a large lounge/diner and a large kitchen and even a small study. There was a parquet floor in the lounge and cement floors elsewhere, but these were a dull yellow colour – no red Cobra polish in sight.

There was a separate garage and servants' quarters. There was a small swimming pool set charmingly under the largest tree - to catch the maximum number of leaves and tree frogs as we were later to discover. There was a small orchard of guavas, oranges, lemons, naajies(tangerines), pawpaws, mangoes and bananas amongst which was a tiny playhouse for children, complete with its thatched roof.

There were also a number of thick stick-like things in the front garden which I vowed to get rid of as soon as possible. Just as well there never seemed to be time ... one day the thick sticks produced the tips of dark green leaves ... and then ! oh wonders the glorious frangipani flowers . The thick creamy tinged with pink and yellow petals - one of my favourite flowers. Years later when a friend visited from UK I waxed lyrical about frangipanis

... she looked at the dull stick like things and said, 'Mmmm if you say so'.

Another surprise was a fairly innocuous tree with thin dark green leaves which sported red waxy flowers, and which produced eventually pomegranates. Hurrah for a house of our own and all this for the magnificent sum of £4,000!

CHAPTER 5
CHELSTON

Our first house in Chelston

How marvellous to have a house of our own – but that meant having some furniture of our own. All we possessed was a double bed, bought when we found that the Government only supplied single beds and they were always of varying heights, a fridge and Ceri's cot. The bedrooms had built in wardrobes and the people selling were willing to sell their dining suite and desk in the study and the cooker. So off we went to the second hand dealer on Cairo Road and invested in a chest of drawers and two rocking arm chairs . We were all organised.

Everything was set in motion for the move - so off Andrew went on a work trip to England. With William's help I packed everything into cardboard boxes and it was loaded onto a lorry loaned by the college early one morning and we headed to Chelston. It was quite a merry little cavalcade ... first went Ceri and I in the Morris with the protesting dog and cat and some boxes of glasses and records. Next came the lorry loaded with our boxes and William and his family and their katundu (luggage) and the chickens with their rolls of wire netting and chicken house. Sepo Lishomwa brought up the rear in her car; she had come to help - or see the fun as she termed it.

The men quickly unloaded our few possessions into the house and after helping William set up a temporary chicken run, they were off. The few bits of furniture arrived from the dealers and we were fully established in our own home. By the evening William had the basics out in the kitchen and rustled up a simple meal, which he served with great ceremony on our own dining table as Ceri and I sat on our own chairs!

I decided to leave unpacking the rest of the boxes and cases until the following day. As it was a strange new house I thought Ceri would sleep better in my bed for the first night. She did not. Neither did I.

Every hour, on the hour, Ceri woke up and insisted on checking the whereabouts of her toys.

'Teddy is in this box ... Panda in that box ... where's Pooh Bear?'

Dawn saw a reassured and sleeping Ceri and a rather shattered Mum. Having so few possessions meant that we were unpacked and well organised on Andrew's return. So much so that he reasoned he should be away for any future move as everything went so well in his absence.

The sitting room had an impressive stone fireplace which was almost ceiling height, a recess contained a strip light. All very impressive until we decided the cold season warranted a fire. It was laid and lit with great ceremony and smoke billowed round the room in ever increasing clouds. Trial and error gradually revealed that the actual chimney was sited in one corner so fires had to be lit in the back left corner of the huge hearth to avoid asphyxiating all present.

We also had the doubtful joy of our first phone line - doubtful because it was a party line and while we soon got used to recognising our own 'ring' of two long and three short rings it was distracting to have to endure everyone else's rings. Plus the occasional knowledge that someone had picked up their phone when I was mid call and was eavesdropping.

The Chelston area was not fully developed at that time - mid 1964 - and was a small friendly community. A Colonel Earl-Spurr had bought a large area of bush which he later sub divided and was selling off in one acre building lots. He had had roads bulldozed, winding through the trees in an apparently haphazard fashion which gave the whole area a casual air. As the acre next door to us was still vacant we were able later to raise the £500 to purchase it.

Ken and Pam Harkness were living at the other end of Chelston in a company house. Almost next door to us were Don and Phyllis Fluck, who bred Great Danes and Bassets which they would walk along the road in the cool of the evening, much to Micky's initial annoyance.

We had moved in April and we were now in the cold season with the naajies (tangerines) ripe on the trees and on cold nights we had wood fires burning in the large open fireplace in the lounge. Ceri soon learned to explore the garden with the devoted Micky at her side, the swimming pool was fenced off with a low grass fence and as we had by now taken on Lax as 'garden boy' there was always someone to keep an extra eye on her.

Ceri aged about 18 months and Micky

One day she did disappear and as Lax searched the gardens I began to look along the road. She had wandered past our boundary and then sat down to examine some stones a little way off the road side. Micky was beside her.

Ken and Pam Harkness were regular visitors and one day suggested a picnic out on the road to Kasisi. The weather could always be relied upon unlike UK and it wasn't long before we had driven down the dirt road and found the spot Ken had raved about. To be honest I can't describe the view, the day sticks in my memory for what happened at the end. After eating Ken and Andrew went for a short walk while Pam and I stayed amusing our small daughters Ceri and Mandy at the picnic site. The men returned laughing having seen a couple walking in the bush hand in hand – amused because it was a white woman with a black man and clearly wishing not to be identified they had about turned and made off in the opposite direction. We stayed a little longer and then set off home, Ken and Pam driving off first. Once we were driving Andrew spotted a car in the rear view mirror – was it the shy couple? As Andrew picked up speed or slowed down, the following car did the same. He put his foot down and we raced ahead and then after breasting a small rise he braked quite sharply – the following car appeared over the rise - too late to stop the driver raced by, his passenger shielding her face. But Andrew had noted the car registration and within a few days we shook our heads – a friend – a married friend. No wonder she hadn't wished to be seen.

Chelston and the donkey

Where did the donkey come from? it wandered in, stayed a few hours and then set off at a purposeful trot down towards the valley and we never saw it again.

As the temperatures rose towards the hot season the swimming pool came into its own. Stella Shamwana came out one memorable day with her sons Edward and Malcolm and they plunged into the pool with Ceri. We stood and watched and chatted. Until I noticed Malcolm had been swimming on the bottom of the pool for quite some time.

'Is he all right?' I asked nervously not wanting to leap in to the rescue.

Stella looked down, thought for a moment.

'Edward! Pick your brother up.'

'Why?'

'Never mind why - just pick him up.'

Edward looked uncooperative but after a second look at Stella he leaned down, seized Malcolm by the hair and dragged him unceremoniously to the surface, The spluttering and purple faced Malcolm smiled happily, took a deep breath and went back to swimming below. I was a nervous wreck by the time they left.

Andrew tries to teach Ceri the rudiments of hockey

Andrew had the idea of encouraging Ceri to take an interest in hockey - he played for a club in Lusaka for a while. But she would seize the ball and run away.

Independence Day was set for 24th October and apart from all the official plans and announcements, scaremongering and anti-black jokes abounded. The figures quoted of the European police officers, teachers and postal workers etc leaving were enough to fuel rumour and counter rumour as to how the country would be able to run efficiently in a year or two. Also of great concern was the number of farmers in the Lusaka, Mazabuka and Broken Hill areas who had abandoned their farms ... Would we be importing more food?

And yet such was the euphoria of the period, we could not feel pessimistic - we would be independent and we would more than manage! We had several very pleasant picnics with friends on a deserted citrus farm. It had been abandoned by a white farmer who, it was said, drove into Lusaka one morning and bought the paper which gave the date for independence for the first time. He read the paper, checked that the story was correct, drove home, packed his family into the car and went south. To where the white man would still rule. Counter rumour had it that the man owed far more money than he could ever hope to repay and so used this as an excuse to default.

Whatever the truth was, we had the most enjoyable barbecues in the overgrown gardens and filled the car boot with fruit, regretting the amount of fruit rotting on the ground under the trees. Once I walked up to the house and peered in at the windows, a variety of personal items lay around giving credence to the story that the family had left at very short notice. The servants' quarters were bare and abandoned - not an item left behind there!

A sad air hung over the whole place with the flower beds already choked with weeds and the grass shaggy and unkempt. Wandering along the area at the side of the house I stopped by huge frangipani trees covered in thick creamy clusters of flowers. Under them were two headstones and barely legible were the names of a couple who had first opened up this area of bush, creating a home and farm with the hopes and fears one could only imagine. A little way to the side of them, almost covered in tall grasses, was a small headstone for a child of only a few years. Tears filled my eyes as I wondered when and how the couple had first arrived and what life had been like as they developed the land. The dates were so long ago that they may well have travelled by ox cart when Lusaka was still a railway siding - or earlier. Was the farmer who had just left their son? grandson? Or had he bought the farm at a later date? In either case it all seemed very sad. If it were a descendant of the original owner, how sad that he left all that they had worked for and what a loss that he felt he had no future here. If it were a man who had recently bought the farm, what a pity he had taken the easy way out and not given the new regime a chance. I could never find out any more about the place and its owners and when we tried it find it in later years, we could never even find the farm track leading there so I wondered if it had been totally forgotten and overgrown.

About that time - in June 1964 - we saw the first pictures of the new Zambian flag and very soon a joke did the rounds and which has been misquoted at times.

The original joke tells the tale of the servant and his employer (usually said to be a white Afrikaaner - the joke was usually told in heavy accent), the servant asks his employer to explain the meaning of the new flag.

'Well,' said the employer. 'It's like this. The green represents the land, the black represents the African people, the orange represents the copper, the red represents the blood shed in the fight for freedom and the eagle represents the spirit of Zambia surmounting all adversities.'

'But Bwana, what about the white man?'

'The white man is represented by the white flag pole, holding up the whole bloody thing!'

And there the joke ended. I heard many Zambians laugh at the tale. They laughed because they could now laugh at jokes intended to hurt them because now the white man was beaten.

It is not true - as written in Michael Nicholson's book Across The Limpopo - that all the flagpoles were repainted black by Government order.

There was at this time a feeling of cheerful optimism and amused forbearance for the pessimistic whites. The date for independence had been set and we felt that there were very positive steps being made for the future.

Northern Rhodesia was rich in its copper mines, agriculture could and would flourish, there were many educated Africans - not enough it is true but more than any other newly independent states had had - the fight for independence had not been too long, and certainly not too bloody. With good will and intent on both sides the future looked promising. As for the unconverted pessimists - why, they could leave and we would all be better off. Early in the year Northern Rhodesia's own airline was born and was named Zambia Airways - I remember William beaming with pride when I pointed out the news item in the paper. Within two months of that work started on extending the turning circle at Lusaka airport after a VC10 made a test landing. Soon we would be able to jet around the world in our own VC10's. True the airport was a tiny place with small arched buildings made of the usual corrugated iron sheets covered in riots of pink and purple bougainvillea - not quite international standard.

Work began on the Independence Stadium just outside town on the Great North Road. Very sensibly one stand was to be built in permanent materials so that later the site could be used for a sports stadium.

The Church too appeared to be making positive steps to encourage racial harmony, for the first time Africans and Europeans were confirmed together at a service in Chingola. The Most Reverend Francis Oliver Green–Wilkinson, Arch Bishop of Central Africa, was at the service making it a memorable one for all those present. Coincidentally this service was held three months to the day after Kaunda had condemned certain mine clubs which had refused to accept Africans as members - and he added that his remarks also applied to one or two churches which would not allow Africans in. Although there I believe he was particularly referring to the Dutch Reformed Church. Such was Kaunda's influence then that already, after the day of this announcement, the mine clubs voted to accept African members. If all this seems racially backward and slow progress, it should

172

be remembered that at the end of 1963 Scotland Yard were still saying that UK was not ready for non-white 'bobbies'. In May 1964 two West Indians were the first non-white milkmen on a round at Aldershot and only 3 out of the 900 housewives on the round complained. So who was right? Scotland Yard, wary of upsetting the public, or the housewives, who by and large saw black milkmen as acceptable? But would they have accepted a parking ticket or a summons from a black hand as easily as a pint of milk?

But we were not in UK and a multi-racial society was 'the thing', it was 'in' - and we had the initial stages going well. By June, 38 African 'shadows' were attached to senior civil servants. Three of them we knew well. Lish Lishomwa was attached to the Ministry of Finance, Elias Chipimo to the Ministry of Transport and Communications and James Mapoma to the Registrar of Cooperatives. Safeli Chileshe was made Mayor of Lusaka and a more dignified figure could not have been found.

All was not running smoothly of course. Suddenly one read that four mobile units/platoons (?!) and police reinforcements were confronting more than 1,000 tribesmen at Kameko village near Chinsali. The supporters of Alice Lenshina, the prophetess who claimed to have risen from the dead, were up in arms. Never before in the history of the country had a religious sect challenged the authority of the Government. This was at the end of June and soon we were reading reports that followers of Lenshina had taken to the bush after a pitched battle. The police were ambushed by followers armed with spears and axes and after they - the police - entered the village to negotiate the re-arrest of five men, a cry of 'Jericho' - apparently a pre- arranged signal - brought forth a horde of attackers.

By July 27th twenty one men were killed as a police mobile unit took the Lenshina stockaded village, including Derek Smith, a European Assistant Inspector and Chansa, an African police constable, who were speared in the ambush.

Troops were poured into the area and rumour had it that more than 800 had arrived the following day. As the Chinsali area covered several thousand square miles this did not seem a very large number of troops to me. The District Commissioner, John Hannah, had already made visits attempting to persuade villagers to lay down their arms. Police Inspector Peter Jordan was killed and the Prime Minister flew in as the NR Government assumed special powers.

I had never heard of Alice Lenshina before and scoured the papers to try to discover who and what she was. All I could learn was that she had claimed to have died in childbirth and returned to life three days later. She had formed her religious sect as an off shoot of the Church of Scotland and allowed witchcraft to enter the church at a later date.

Whatever her claims, she had certainly gained a large following and the news continued to be bleak. By the end of July refugees from villages in the area were fleeing to the White Fathers Mission at Mulanga and the troops were poised for a dawn raid. The Territorials were called to help at Chinsali. While police guarded over 200 refugees at the Mission at least 60 spearmen were launching 10 consecutive attacks against the troops armed with automatic weapons. The odds against them did not appear to affect their religious ardour and a further 150 Lumpas were killed in Lundazi . After which a mob of over 200, intent on revenge, rampaged through Lundazi Province, sacking 18 villages and killing at least 150, three of whom were Asian storekeepers. The newspapers carried photos of Alice Lenshina with the caption Wanted Dead or Alive.

Of course, the simply armed Lenshina supporters were no real match for troops armed with modern weapons and the uprising was soon put down. Reading a report by Colin Morris one felt it was all a strange mixture of religion and politics topped with a strong measure of local culture. Alice Lenshina had certainly come into her own strength when Federation was imposed and she felt let down by the European church, and although she began by attacking witchcraft it was not long before it became an element in her own church. Her genius for composing hymns and songs set to African music and expressing an African cast of thought would certainly hold a strong appeal for the local people.

While we had a great feeling of optimism now that independence was approaching, the Lenshina affair marred the atmosphere for some time.

I would read reports by Colonel Critchley, the President of the Wild Life Conservation Society of NR and feel rumblings of disquiet. In one report he stated that game was being grossly over slaughtered, much of it for sale in the Copperbelt townships. It was said that buffalo killed on the Kafue Flats were sold for £10 and would then sell for £80 on the Copperbelt. Skins and ivory were in great demand - this was by the white expatriates.

I waited to see what outcry and demands for action would be made by the up and coming African politicians and leaders of the day; but no comment seemed to be forthcoming.

On the other hand I could laugh at the continuing stories about Mukuka Nkoloso who was appointed director general of Scientific Executive Board of the National Academy of Science, Space Research and Philosophy - self-appointed it should be added!! He announced that he had put off plans to blast off several rockets for the Independence celebrations. He said they would cause terrifying earth tremors but because he was busy with his Academy helping with the Independence Day preparations further statements would be made later.

Clearly a harmless eccentric, but although one laughed it gave me a feeling of disquiet to see these reports side by side with official and serious news items.

I found myself looking at situations and feeling myself seeing both points of view and knowing that I myself did not quite know where my loyalties or support would be in a similar situation. About that time President Kenyatta denounced South African farmers in Kenya and demanded they denounce South Africa or leave Kenya. Some of them refused to do this, they had lived and worked in Kenya for many years. A chap called Roets had actually arrived on the historic trek in 1908 with the original 50 families. He said that Kenyatta had gone against everything he had told the farmers before Uhuru. He – Kenyatta - had said that he wanted them to stay and promised them encouragement and protection. Now that rumour had it that they were to be asked to sign a paper condemning South African racialist policies, many felt betrayed. I did not discuss this report with Andrew as I knew what his response would be - if they wanted to stay in Kenya, then their loyalties should be there and in fact they should repudiate the South African policies.

Part of me agreed with this, but I also knew that while I might disagree with some policies in UK and would feel free to criticise them, I could not see myself making a formal condemnation. Nor would I feel I should be asked to do so if I were not actually resident there ... I began to wonder where my loyalties lay and where I felt I belonged. The answer seemed to be nowhere and yet both but neither... I put it all to one side.

But it made me wonder whether what Sir John Moffat hoped for, would be possible to achieve. He wrote in the Journal of the Church of Scotland that Kenneth Kaunda wanted one nation - but in order to create that, said Sir John, he must first create one loyalty, without one loyalty there would be tribal break up. Reflecting how difficult I found the pull between the loyalty for my new home and England, I wondered how easy it would be to weld so many tribes - many with a long history of conflict - into one nation with one loyalty.

Politics apart, one could ignore the Nkolosos of the country because they were more than counter balanced by people like John Nyalumo, who had the only store in the chiefdom of Chiawa 70 miles from Lusaka in the extreme south east of Lusaka Rural District. His shop was inaccessible by road for most of the year, so three or four times a year, Nyalumo employed two villagers to paddle canoes up the Zambezi to Chirundu, where he caught a bus to Lusaka, purchased his goods, transported them by bus back to Chirundu from where they paddled back home.

If people were willing to work like this, the future looked good. This determination was tapped on Ubushiku Bwa Kwafwana - the Day of helping Ourselves. In one area the schoolchildren managed to raise four shillings each and 150 schools raised £13000 - no mean sum in those days!

In September the Freedom Cabinet was announced with 9 new appointments -

Reuben Kamanga as Vice President, Simon Kapwepwe as Minister of Foreign Affairs, Mainza China in Home Affairs, James Skinner in Justice, Sikota Wina in Local Government, his brother Arthur Wina in Finance, Aggrey Zulu in Transport and Works, Solomon Kalulu in Lands and Resources, M Sipalo in Health, our old friend John Mwanakatwe in Education.

Having met all of these and counting at least one as an actual friend gave me a feeling of confidence and hope... all good chaps and qualified and experienced...

Friends were keen to examine the names of new Ministers and others who were being promoted to high positions and analyse how well the President had balanced the tribes. It seemed to be a genuine concern that no tribe should appear to dominate.

Now that we had a date set for independence, Andrew asked his parents down from Luapula Province to join in the celebrations. This would be our first meeting and as my Bemba had not progressed, I was relieved to remember that at least his father spoke English.

Excitement mounted in the capital Lusaka as the streets were decorated with flags and bunting, rehearsals took place in the newly built Independence Stadium just outside town on the Great North Road. Newspapers carried photos of preparations and decorations ranging from stadium to streets to new bank notes to timetables and headlines such as
LUSAKA ALL GAY FOR OUR ROYAL GUEST

The Princess Royal, then aged 67, was to arrive on the 23rd of October as Kaunda put out a plea for tolerance. To get the country to rejoice as one would be Kaunda's first real test of how well he had set about creating a sense of unity. My own tolerance was about to be tested at the same time.

Independence flags on Cha Cha Cha Road (Livingstone Road)

Independence flags on Lusaka PO

Early in October Ceri went down with a nasty case of measles so I was more than apprehensive when Andrew's parents arrived with two small children from the village. I dreaded them picking up the measles bug too.

That was to be the least of my worries. The children were about three years old and had had little contact with Europeans; in fact I suspected they had been quietened with threats of 'the white man will get you' just as in the past white children had been told 'the bogey man will get you'. Whatever the cause, as soon as they saw me, if they were not within reach of Grandmother's arms, they wailed 'msungu, msungu' and fled. Msungu being loosely translated as white person was not very complimentary - they clearly had little conception of friendly whites.

Andrew's parents on the other hand were enjoying their reunion with their son who had done so well and their first visit to the capital for this special occasion. We got on very well in spite of the language difficulties. Father in law took the European customs in his stride, even when he did not altogether approve. But then, he was an educated and well - travelled man. He was now in his late seventies and could no longer be drawn to talk about his travels, although Andrew had heard all about them when he was a boy.

Long, long ago the first missionaries began to arrive in Northern Rhodesia and preach the word of the Lord.

Father in law listened and thought they were sincere, but - how did he know for sure that they were right?

From the Good Book of course.

Then would the missionaries teach him to read the Good Book?

For whatever reason the missionaries would not or could not.

But there was a Mission School over in Nyasaland where one could learn to read. It cost money of course.

Now how could a mere villager earn this thing called money?

So father in law left his village (and his wife) and walked down to Bulawayo in Southern Rhodesia where he had heard they were building a railroad (the famous Cape to Cairo route - never completed). He worked on the railroad as it moved north from Bulawayo to Lusaka, by which time he had saved enough money and then he walked over into Nyasaland to enrol at the Mission

School where he set about learning to read in English.

After which, he was given - or bought - a Bible and he walked back home to Luapula where he sat down and read it.

What his wife had to say about his long absence has never been repeated as far as I could discover. To my great disappointment any attempts to get him to reminisce about that period of his life was met with,

'Of what interest is all this now? That was long ago and now it is all finished.'

Grandmother was more interested in this odd new daughter in law. One who ate eggs - not only ate them but ate them every morning! She shook her head in disapproval. No wonder I had produced only one child in three years of marriage; everyone knew that for a woman, eating eggs was sure to prevent a pregnancy.

In fact European food held no charms for her and she was dismayed to find that the old man was happy to sit with us and eat 'white food'. It did not take long to reach a compromise with William's wife cooking traditional dishes, which we ate occasionally too. The old man wavered contentedly between the two. As it was also not customary for the mother to eat with the daughter in law, we ate together or not as the fancy took Grandmother.

Grandfather was an easy guest although I think he had one disappointment. He and Andrew would sit and chat in the evenings and one day he laughed and shook his head. I hadn't noticed but the conversation had been switching from English to Bemba and back again. Then he laughed, shaking his head and pointed out that he believed Andrew could no longer think in Bemba – he said Andrew was mentally translating all the time. Was he? Andrew, looking surprised, said he actually didn't know, wasn't aware he was doing so.

One weekend Edward and Stella Shamwana came to visit with their two sons, Edward three and Malcolm two. Our three children played together while the two children from the village watched from a distance or followed them about - clearly still not at ease enough to join in. We elders sat around making polite conversation with frequent pauses for translation - Edward being Ila not Bemba. Grandmother was obviously taking careful note of this yet another white daughter in law and most probably wondering what her counterpart in a far off Ila village made of the whole thing too. Andrew's father had something else on his mind. A little later in the afternoon he invited Edward to take a stroll round the garden with him and soon the pair were deep in conversation. When they returned to the house Edward was in a very jocular mood, he nudged Andrew in the ribs and whispered, 'Your father spent some time beating about the bush, umming and aahing, but when he got to the point, guess what he wants?' Andrew, Stella and I raised our eyebrows.

'As I am your very good friend Andrew, he wonders why I don't tell you what medicine I use to make sure of producing dark babies. Ceri is much too light.'

We looked at the two Shamwana boys, who were darker than Ceri, then we looked at each other.

'What did you tell him?'

'I said I would tell you, but really it is up to you to decide what to do.'

The 23rd of October soon arrived, we had tickets for the great evening at the Stadium; the children were left behind with William and his wife. Perched high above the arena we had a good view of the march past, the bands, the army manoeuvres, the tribal dancing ... until at last came the great moment when the Union Jack was to be hauled down for the last time and the new Zambian flag raised for the first time.

President Kaunda and the Princess Royal stepped forward and I think there were many lumps in many throats at that moment for different but no less poignant reasons.

As the Zambian flag fluttered proudly for the first time in the spotlight we heard the new anthem Stand And Sing Of Zambia Proud And Free to the tune of Nkosi Sikeli Afrika, the universally popular African tune. Adopted as the national anthem in 5 countries it was a hymn originally composed in 1897 by a Xhosa clergyman at a Methodist Mission School. He based the melody on the hymn tune Aberystwyth by Joseph Parry.

Then the firework display started, explosion after explosion of colour lit the dark sky as the crowds oohed and aahed ... all except for one old man. He was shaking his head.

'Independence is not all this fuss. All this money for nothing. Aa aa aa I have seen enough now.'

And so we stood up and left for home. Father in law had seen the Union Jack come down and the Zambian flag go up. That was all he needed to see.

I wondered what he would have said, had he known that the fireworks he had dismissed had cost £5000, that 10,000 pounds of hippo, elephant, lechwe and buffalo meat had been distributed from animals shot by the Game Department 'for cropping purposes' – the meat and trophies valued at £6000. I had my doubts about the official phrase 'cropping purposes' but kept my thoughts to myself.

I wondered what he would have said if he had attended the reception at State House, where the great and the famous, the diplomats and the well-connected and the politicians gathered together to express all their confidence in the future (about which some were already entertaining some private misgivings). There was all the outward confidence and bonhomie with undercurrents flowing fast and free if you cared to dip in deep enough. I think father in law would have seen through all the official sham. Independence was being able to say what you liked, where you liked, more clinics and schools. And being able to live and work where you chose, not where the laws made by foreigners said.

But these occasions are all the same, with the same ostentatious trappings and probably all the same pitfalls to come already clear on the horizon.

We were not politicians, nor well-connected, nor famous but we actually had an invitation to State House for that event. I think it was because any Zambian with a university degree was still something of a national asset to be shown off. And also, of course, because Andrew was an ex Leeds University man. The Princess Royal was Chancellor of Leeds University and someone somewhere had the bright idea that all ex Leeds students should be presented. They were a small bunch, but it was a touch which Ken Harkness, John Tattersfield and Andrew appreciated. Whether or not the Princess Royal felt the same way is not quite clear, the hot October weather and round of official duties had probably taken their toll and she looked a very tired old lady. But true to British Royal tradition she looked interested and appreciative, managing to hold an animated conversation for some minutes in spite of her clear fatigue. In the circumstances Pam, Judy and I felt our swift and cursory curtseys probably more than met the occasion.

Before the Princess Royal left she laid twin foundation stones for the new Zambian Parliament building with Kaunda on 27 October and on the following day he laid the foundation stone for the Natural Resources College where Andrew was destined to work. Within two weeks the College was advertising courses, which included a two year agricultural diploma course based on the needs of the Dept of Agriculture, subjects included agricultural engineering.

With such exciting social events it was amusing to read the Woman's Page in the daily paper - it dwelt at length on whether chunky or stiletto heels were 'in', a recipe for chicken fricassee and the hidden dangers of nylon ... no forecasts of State House fashions or etiquette with Royal dignitaries which I had expected. While visiting dignitaries were treated with respect and courtesy in Lusaka the same could not be guaranteed when they left the capital. A visit to that part of Africa is not complete without a trip to Victoria Falls so a couple of days after Independence Day 60 honoured guests were taken by coach to see the Falls. To do the job thoroughly one should see the Falls from both sides of the river and the trip had been planned accordingly. Unfortunately when the coach came to cross the border the Southern Rhodesian immigration officials said,
'All blacks out.'

Golda Meir, then Israel's Minister of Foreign Affairs, with the direct honesty for which she was much loved, said,
'If that's your order, we will all get out.'
And so they did.
Normally formalities were minimal and in fact passports were often not even stamped if groups were just going to see the Falls. I wonder if this was the first recorded nit picky occasion between Southern Rhodesia and Zambia.
It was a very hot October. The two children from the village still regarded me with misgivings, Ceri was recovered from the measles but was still a bit run down and life was very tiring. I did not feel well and at last at school one morning I gave in to the misery and phoned Andrew to take me home. Well, of course, if you are going to run a high temperature in Africa it must be malaria, mustn't it?
Pam Harkness came to see me one evening, looking worried as sweat ran off my face soaking the pillow and asked how long malaria lasted. It did not make much progress, I lay in bed and sweated and held my aching head. The children raced around the house and garden now that they would not meet me and the doctor came regularly, tut tutting over my lack of progress.
Until the day when I presented him with a couple of samples of dark brown urine that even I thought boded more than malaria. It would not have been so bad being in an isolation ward if it had not been slap bang next to the mortuary, not the most cheerful of outlooks! To raise my spirits as he drove me to hospital, Andrew bought me a glamorous new nightdress. It was a wonderful thought but neither of us realised how the black lacy garment would look against my rapidly orange - turning complexion as the jaundice ran its course.
It was a long spell in hospital completely isolated in that one small room, not even trips to the bathroom were allowed as the only one within reach was used by the children's ward. Andrew would bring Ceri to the window to wave, friends brought books and conversation that way. I lay in bed reading and reading and avoiding looking out of the window when the mortuary was in

use.

While I was tucked away Andrew's parents said they had come to see Independence and Independence they had seen. Now they could tell the people back home in the village all about it, moreover the rains would be starting and the seeds were to be planted. I could not see them to say goodbye but Andrew described how he had tried to add an extra item to their experiences by taking them to have a meal at a café before they went to the station. He got them there all right but they did not think much of the idea when he explained they were to eat a meal before catching the train. Mother in law was frankly disapproving about eating in public. She then asked why so many people were without a home in the capital when they looked so prosperous.

'Why else should people be here to eat?'

'They like to eat here.'

'You mean they have a home where they could eat?'

'But they like to come here and it's not expensive.'

This was too much for either of his parents, not only did these town people eat in public places, but Andrew proposed spending good money in this way! They went to the station in quiet disapproval - not even the idea of eating in a café which previously would have been for whites only had any attraction I was sorry I had not been able to say goodbye to the old couple and sorry also that there had not been the time to talk about their history - even if I had been able to draw the old man out more. The language barrier certainly had slowed things up and overcoming the cultural differences would have taken time. But they would come again and hopefully Andrew would be able to spare the time to take me up to the village. Eventually I would get to know them better. The miserable listlessness caused by the jaundice had not helped either. For the moment I was glad they had gone and taken the two children who had not adapted to staying with us, even up to the end they had refused to use the toilet. At first I had not realised what they were doing. And I had found it very embarrassing when Ken Harkness, leaving one evening and switching on his car headlights, abruptly illuminated Grandmother walking across the garden with one of the children, at that hour in the evening she was incongruously carrying a hoe.

'Going gardening now?' asked Ken incredulously.

Andrew gave a short laugh.

'You know how it is with these people from the village - the children won't use the toilet so she takes them out and digs a hole for them.'

I had not known how it was either and felt as uncomfortable as Ken looked on. Chelston was still sparsely populated at that time and there were still empty bush plots opposite but I could imagine what local whites would make of this.

'What will the neighbours say?' - I gave myself an abrupt mental shake!

Once the in laws had departed it was easy to forget that incident and I am sure that Ken had far more pressing matters on his mind.

I had been allowed home from hospital but was under strict instructions to remain in bed on a fat and alcohol free diet. All this resting resulted in my waking even earlier than usual and as our bedroom window was so low I could lie in bed and watch a small herd of duiker which crossed through Chelston every morning. I saw them many times flitting through the trees, high stepping through the tall grasses. To my constant surprise I never heard a dog bark as they passed. Even more surprising was that several times I watched them cross at a much later hour, about 8.30 in the morning when the township was quiet. Most people had left for town in their cars and the servants were busy with their various tasks.

Andrew took Ceri to nursery most mornings and I looked forward to the afternoons when she would sit on my bed and chat and bring her toys for us to play with among the sheets. It was a long slow recovery - but I was fortunate. There had been a number of cases of jaundice in the Lusaka area, a few had not recovered.

When I was fully recovered we thought it was time for Ceri to have a new pet. Scraps had sadly had to be put to sleep, frequent fights had left him with an infection which never fully healed. Fortunately Rosemary Chuula's cat had had kittens. They now lived in Woodlands but we hadn't visited for some time. So off we set one sunny morning in search of a kitten. Rosemary greeted us with delight and asked if we only wanted one - the reason for that was quite clear when we stepped outside her back door and kittens of all ages and colours and sizes bounced from under some banana trees.

Rosemary explained, in her gentle way, that she hadn't liked to take the cat to be spayed while she was nursing a litter of kittens ... 'And do you know, June, she has got pregnant three times - each time while still feeding a litter. What am I to do?'

I wasn't sure, but was sure that we only needed ONE. Ceri chose an all grey kitten, which grew to look very much like a British Blue. She was named, originally, Puss.

Rosemary's dilemma was solved sometime later when she went on leave and her husband Pat paid the vet a long visit.

Zambia was now weeks old, months old and very small rumblings arose. One of the first changes was the removal of the statue on the roundabout at the top of the renamed Independence Avenue. In a country decidedly short on statues or any public displays of art - European or African - I had always enjoyed driving up the road and seeing the horse and its rider outlined against the sky at the summit of the hill. The statue named Physical Energy was a memorial to Cecil Rhodes and had been presented to Northern Rhodesia in 1960 by the British South Africa Company.

The sculptor George Watts said that it was a symbol of that restless physical impulse to seek the still unachieved in the domain of material things.

Unfortunately it also reminded Zambians of the statement by Lord Malvern that 'the Federation is a partnership'. As they felt that the

Federation was not in their best interests it was a mere hop, skip and jump to the horse and rider statue being linked with the notion of partnership - with the European as the rider and the African as the horse. And so by December it was formally announced that the statue was to be returned to the BSA.

I could well understand the resentment caused by the Federation being imposed upon the population - many Europeans had not approved either - but from the purely aesthetic point of view, I was very sorry to see the statue go. I was less interested in the politics of the argument than the loss - to me - of the lines of the rider's arm and the horse's neck outlined against the sky, and the different effects one saw with the changes in the seasons and the sky's colour and mood. Wisely I kept these thoughts to myself.

Now Independence had arrived reporters delved around for stories of interest and if these related to our new President, so much the better. So we read in November about one Fredericka van Niekerk, 74 years old and living and working at the Dutch Reformed Mission 12 miles outside Fort Jameson. She came to Broken Hill originally in 1917 and then walked to Fort Jameson with 6 other missionaries and 200 carriers, the 300 miles taking 24 days. In the interview she stated that 'The Boss' (the President) was one of her ex pupils. Miss Niekerk had devoted her life to the teaching of Africans.

Now that the fight for independence was won there were many minor, and sometimes petty, officials with too little to occupy their minds. I have never been much interested in beauty competitions as such so had not followed the build up to the election of a Miss Zambia 1964. But I think a lot of people took more notice when two UNIP officials walked around the floor in Charter Hall shouting 'shameful' and 'nonsense' because Henrietta Monteiro won the title and was not wearing Zambian national dress. As the rules had stated evening or national dress could be worn one could be forgiven for wondering whether it really was a question of dress or the fact the Miss Monteiro was a Coloured and not black Zambian. And as the so-called

Zambian national dress had only made its' debut shortly before independence, there did not seem to be all that much wide spread pride in wearing it.

When I had first arrived in Northern Rhodesia I had been very disappointed to find there was no real national dress or dish - there seemed to be a cultural void which could perhaps be explained by the fact that there were so many different tribes and a comparatively short period of actual settled residence in this part of the Continent. The only evidence of a national dress was the citenge - a two metre length of cotton cloth that the women wound sarong style around their waist. Perhaps it was part of the lack of national identity and unity which had concerned Sir John Moffat.

Whatever it was, the UNIP officials were certainly miffed enough to announce within a couple of days that they were going to organise a 'competition of our own' and it was only a matter of a few more days before Miss Montereiro announced that she was going to give up the title anyway. This may have appeased the UNIP officials, who added their own footnote by stating that only a black girl should qualify anyway.

So much for equality.

What would be next I wondered? I had no doubt at that time that this incident did not reflect the President's - or his Government's - views but clearly mob rule was going to prevail. At the moment in minor matters, but what next? How much would the will of the 'common man' over ride common sense and experience of its elected peers?

But then - how much different would this be from the way other countries were run?

But it was Christmas 1964 and Ceri was nearly two years old. I turned my hand to carpentry - thank you Mr Inman back in college days and his training with saw and hammer. I doubt if he would have been much impressed with my primitive efforts but at least the doll's house was large and solid, outlasting Ceri's childhood and many hours of vigorous play.

Christmas morning dawned early as children's Christmas

mornings always do and Ceri was soon headfirst in the doll's house. Mid-morning saw the arrival of a crowd of local villagers who danced and drummed on the lawn in front of the verandah. Ceri watched through a window but could not be persuaded to venture out on to the verandah, the masked faces clearly frightening her. We distributed bonselas (gifts) sweets to the children and money to the adults and watched as they danced their way to the next house.

Christmas day dancers in Chelston

Ceri slept for the rest of the day after that, we put it down to the day's excitement but that night she developed a high temperature and began to talk wildly about things we could not see. This was her first attack of tonsillitis, after this they came with no warning and were a frequent problem as she grew increasingly resistant to the drugs. But doctors said we would have to persevere until she grew out of it, as most children did - or until she was old enough to have her tonsils out.

In the New Year of 1965 the Yugoslav company invited us to accompany Zivanovitch to inspect the Kafue Race Tunnel and have lunch with the works team. I found the trip down the tunnel interesting but a bit frightening - to be so far underground and wonder at the strength and magnitude of the tunnel as we drove along. The Yugoslav staff were friendly and enthusiastic and talk over lunch was positive about the developments, the proposed new hydro-electric power plant. Zambia seemed to be developing in all directions at once, there was always a feeling of excitement in the air as people talked about new developments. At some point when we lived in Chelston we met new friends, Irene and Map Mapulanga an older couple who arrived after independence. I really cannot recall Map's first name - he always used Map. They had met in England when Map was working there ... they met .... fell in love and the rest, as they say, is history. And as our friendship progressed so their story unfolded. Map had returned to Zambia to settle into his job, Irene followed not long after and was met at the airport with the news that they were to live temporarily in Longacres - the Government hostel where many new arrivals were first housed. That was fine but she was surprised to see a bicycle leaning on the wall. Map riding a bicycle? He explained it was his son's. And that was the first intimation she had two teen age step children, Victoria and Hopwood.

Teenagers are one thing, step children can be another. It is to all their credits that it all eventually worked out well. Of course we invited them to dinner which caused a mini hiccup. Faced with a standard sort of roast dinner Irene had to confess she didn't eat chicken - she said later she was mortified to admit this to 'the boss's wife'. I was frantically trying to find an alternative and it had to be a tin of something. But no matter, the next dinner I made sure we had a pork dish. But sadly Irene didn't eat pork. Ditto lamb. Irene only ate beef. After several meals and attempts to find alternatives whatever we had was rechristened 'Game'... It went down a treat and my conscience didn't prick at all.

And this is in no way a complaint - we were great friends for many years. And I just think Irene liked the idea of game or venison. They lived in a Government house in Woodlands before buying their own home in Kabulonga.

At some point, when we lived in Chelston, we had a visit from Oliver, a nephew of Andrew's. Now I don't recall just where he fitted into the family - whether he was a nephew as in son of one of his brothers or sisters or whether part of the extended family. It didn't really matter. Oliver wished to come and stay and get to know his uncle. He was studying in secondary school, I remember that much. And as the days passed he clearly had a great opinion of himself. He was there. And he didn't seem to do much. He didn't seem chatty or interested in what we were doing.

One weekend Andrew was busy in the garden, Oliver was languishing in a chair. When Andrew came in and suggested Oliver should join him in some gardening he met with a severe rebuff. Oliver was a student, students did not work in gardens. One of the few times I actually saw Andrew at a loss for words. Later I was not at a loss for words but had the sense and courtesy not to indulge myself. Instead I took myself off to Andrew on the quiet to say that I took a very dim view of Oliver helping himself to my books. I had noticed gaps appearing on the shelves and after a quiet recce found that the books were neatly packed in one of Oliver's cases. I would not have minded at all if he had asked or even taken a book to read, indeed would have encouraged him, asked his opinion etc. But not wanting to cause family rifts and also wary of culture differences, especially after a lunch with Charles White, I thought I'd consult with Andrew. He was shocked to find Oliver was making free - Andrew's expression - and there was a bit of a confrontation that evening.

Oliver said that he had taken books which he thought 'looked good'... and anyway, we had plenty of money and could buy some more. Andrew's patience had been wearing a bit thin after the gardening incident so now he said that he thought Oliver had stayed long enough, we had all got to know each other and perhaps it was time for Oliver to return home and get on with his studies. And he, Andrew, would like to give him a bonsela (gift) on his departure. We both had to resist the temptation to laugh the following day when Oliver presented Andrew with a list. It started off with 2 pairs trousers, 4 shirts, 2 pairs of shoes and continued on in this vein for several inches down the page.

Torn between anger and laughter Andrew managed politely to explain that even if he wished, he really just could not afford it. As a gesture he would buy Oliver a couple of shirts. It was obvious that Oliver did not believe him, but sitting there in a large 'European' house with servants, a car ... who could blame him? It was a strained parting.

I mentioned above 'after a lunch with Charles White' ... Charles was an elderly long serving Colonial civil servant, a bachelor and with extensive knowledge of Zambia's bird life. Before a lunch in our early days he had asked me if I had an interest in birds - well, I had an amateur's knowledge and interest. Taking that as a definite interest he turned to a large cabinet in the corner of the dining room and opened shallow drawer after shallow drawer, each lined with small stuffed birds, each neatly labelled as to species, habitat and date. He was, I believe, one of the greatest authorities on N Rhodesia's birds.

But my reason for mentioning him was the moment after lunch when we were all still sitting at the table in the pleasant aftermath of good food and wine. There were about ten of us, a mixed group, mostly African. One chap stood up and said he had to leave early, there were murmured goodbyes and as he walked across the dining room he paused at the drinks cabinet, removed a bottle of Scotch and a bottle of wine, tucked them under his arm and carried on out through the door.

Afterwards I commented to Andrew that it had surprised me. He said it was African custom, in the village a visitor was welcome to help himself to anything - and you were free to do the same when you visited him. And usually one bore this in mind and took in a thoughtful manner. Now, he added, the custom is abused when some have so much more than others - and he did not approve.

The visit from Oliver was in complete contrast to a visit from Frank, another nephew.

Frank was an interesting chap – always willing to talk on any subject and keen to ask Andrew's opinion on events and developments in the country. He fitted into our life easily and over the years made regular visits, he was training as a primary teacher when we first met and then worked in schools for some years before transferring to Zambia Railways. I have written less about him – probably because he was such an easy person to entertain and spend time with.

LOTUS PRIMARY

1965 – our school year began again in January and I looked forward to starting off a whole new class of 40 eager 5 year olds. We had a new Head, Jack Thornicroft, a local Coloured and I liked him at first meeting.

To my acute disappointment, term was only a few days old when I was told by the Ministry to move to Lotus Primary School - Lotus was the 'Indian' school, although of course it was officially integrated by now. I was very annoyed by the transfer but there was to be no argument and off I trundled to Lotus which was of course in the 'Indian quarter', just around the corner from the mosque. (The former ways of referring to Indian quarter, African market, Coloured area etc continued for quite some time even though integration was changing the face of all towns).

Lotus was larger than Thorn Park, I think there were twelve classes when I first went there. It had probably started initially with seven classes, Grades 1 to 7, but there were four Grade 1's when I arrived and the school was due to expand accordingly. I was given a Grade 1 class of 40 boys and girls, all Indian. There were no Africans in my class, although there were some higher up the school. By and large, African parents were keen to place their children in what had been all white schools; the Asian and Coloured schools ranked a very poor second in their opinion. Seeing the hard work and good standards in both schools I thought they were making a mistake, although I could understand their reasons - nothing but the best and the whites will have had that for themselves.

40 Indian boys and girls dressed in their blue dresses and grey shirt and shorts uniforms looked far more alike than 40 Coloured children had done and it took me a bit longer to recognise each

child by face and name. We were still using the familiar Janet and John readers though and we battled on with 'Come John come' in the same old way although with a different accent and intonation. We may have battled on with the same readers but one thing was very different - at break they produced small steel shiny tins all of which were filled with various assortments of what they referred to as Chevra (my spelling). This, they said, their mothers made at home and they nibbled this while they chatted before going out to play. I knew of Bombay Mix but there the resemblance ended. Seeing my interest one day Jaykrishna asked if I would 'like to try?' On my nodding he tipped a small heap on a clean sheet of paper on my desk. It was delicious. After that there was a competition every morning to tip a sample on to my desk - I hoped my praise was relayed to their mothers.

The Staff were a more assorted bunch and far more lively than at Thorn Park. The Head, Mr Patel, had opened the first school for Asians in Lusaka and had done much for the Indian community. He was a neat and dapper man, always smiling and always with a small rosebud fresh in his buttonhole every morning.

'My wife puts it there each morning as I leave the house. She has never forgotten. And as I turn my head and catch its perfume, I think of her throughout the day.'

Mr Patel headmaster Lotus Primary and teacher Mrs Vinu Patel

There were three other Indian men on the staff, who were friendly but kept their distance at break times, they would sit in splendid isolation in one of the classrooms, usually cross legged on the desks. One of them, Mr Vyas, the deputy Head, was a gentle poetic soul who carefully made sure that we all knew he was a Brahmin –'which just happens to be the highest caste, you know' - deprecating cough and shy smile. It was Mr Vyas, who had not much faith in mother love as a natural and strong instinct, after having seen a Rhesus monkey marooned with its baby in a tree. As the flood waters rose higher the monkey placed its baby on the topmost branch and stepped on it to be high above the water. There were tears in his eyes as he recounted the story. Gentle Mr Vyas, who wanted to write the histories of the tribes in Zambia and their folk lore, anxious that none of this should be lost to succeeding generations. He asked if Andrew would at some stage help him to verify some details of the Bemba funeral ceremonies, the Chitimukulu and the embalming of the chief. Mr Vyas who liked everyone and was interested in everything and was blown into a very nasty mess by a parcel bomb outside Lusaka Post Office, where he had just collected his mail, a few years later.

Rumour had it that the bomb had been intended for another Mr Vyas, who was reputed to be a fortune teller with Presidential influence.

The women on the staff all congregated in the tiny staffroom squashing together in easy companionship. Chris Stone from England. Pat Bruce from Scotland. Older Mrs Quested from South Africa and so wrinkled from long exposure to the sun. Annie Simmons, an outspoken Scot, with a long spell in the Northern Rhodesian teaching service and lively tales of wild parties on the Copperbelt in her younger days. Peggy Burness, a South African Coloured, who spoke out against racialism with great eloquence but once said sadly to me, 'At the end of it all, June, no matter how things change, we aren't one thing or another. I really don't think we should have been born.' I trust she has long since changed her mind. Devvi Pakkiri, an Indian from South Africa, who was one of the modern generation, and was thrown into a panic when expecting her mother in law on an extended visit. 'She will expect me to wear a traditional piece of jewellery she gave me when we married. I never bother to wear it and now I can't find it'. We all rejoiced with her when it was finally found - after some soul searching she and her husband had searched the servant's quarters on her day off - not only did they find the missing item - they also found linen, cutlery and many other household items and pieces of clothing they had forgotten about or thought were temporarily mislaid. Vinu Patel who spent hours coaching girls in their dances for Diwali in the break times and who talked about getting up extra early to prepare the curries her husband loved before coming to school at 7 o'clock every day.

And Val Whittaker, the secretary, who joined us at break times and was one of the leading lights in initiating the Dinner Evenings. This was to be an all-women group and any husband had to vacate the house while his wife hosted the Dinner. On the appointed evening everyone appeared with a national dish whilst the hostess provided the drinks. It was a great culinary, cultural and gossip session which we all thoroughly enjoyed. And there was Tina Roberts, fresh out from England, who looked at me in great surprise when I remarked as we crossed the spacious school grounds together,

'Aren't these children lucky to have such large grounds? Remember the tiny tarmac playgrounds back in UK? And when we were children half the space was taken up by the air raid shelters...'

Tina stopped dead in her tracks and stared,

'Were you alive and at school during the war?'

It was said with such awe it made me feel about ninety!

Although we were of different ages and backgrounds we all mixed together easily and particularly once the dinner nights were established, found it easy to discuss our beliefs and differences. One of the most interesting I recall being a discussion about arranged marriages. One of the greatest supporters of the tradition being a plump and rather plain little Indian lady, who emphasised that while she would never be able to leave her husband and go back to her family, she had been able to turn down quite a few men produced by her father for consideration, before deciding upon her husband.

'I knew my parents wanted the best for me,' she said. 'And I also knew that once I accepted a man they had introduced to me, I could not admit the marriage was a mistake. I must make it work.'

There are different ways of getting to know people and it's not always done over the dinner table. Now that Zambia was independent we had opened a High Commission in London and the High Commissioner Simon Katilungu reported that, although he had known about the natural reticence of the British native, he was amazed how easy it was to get to know people. 'Once I could take a walk,' he said, 'and talk to no one. Now I have bought a Corgi and everyone I meet, when I walk it in the park, stops to talk.' While Katilungu was trying to understand the traditional reserve of the British, some people in Zambia had other changes to make.

John Mwanakatwe, now the Minister of Education, announced that after the Easter holidays the Gilbert and Jean Rennie Secondary Schools (previously the secondary schools for white pupils in Lusaka and named after an earlier Governor and his wife) were to be renamed the Kabulonga School for Boys and Girls respectively. He was quoted as saying 'the names are reminiscent of the Colonial era and are now unacceptable'.

Again I found myself in the confused state of understanding why he had made that decision but at the same time thinking what a pity it was that we could not retain such 'vestiges of the Colonial era' and make a determined effort to build some MORE secondary schools with appropriate names and as an example of how we were making concrete progress in education. That way we could recognise and accept the past, while paving a new road. (Changing a name was all too easy - but it did not erase history).

Changing mere name boards had its more positive moments

such as when the Deputy Mayor of Lusaka decided that it was taking too long to replace the names on the public lavatories outside the central town market on Livingstone Road - sorry, Cha Cha Cha Road (all these had changed). The Town Council had decided in May to remove the discriminatory signs on the lavatories but the weeks had passed with no action being taken. At last in July, the Deputy Mayor Mr Sibongo, armed with a pot of paint and a brush, climbed a ladder himself and painted out European Type   African Type   Asian Type from above the various doorways. One could only applaud such a move.

Sadly about the same time one could read discriminatory letters in the Press - such as the one from a Mr Mushongo, 'Europeans rarely go back to UK with an African wife but Africans studying in Europe often return with a white wife. They create grave dangers for their children who will not be required in Europe and their position in Africa is not a good one.'

Inter-racial marriages were not welcomed by many Zambians. When Bert Pomfret announced his intention to marry an African girl he was warned by the Youth Organisation to call off the wedding or leave the country. I was pleased to see that they went ahead and by 1965 were announcing the birth of their first daughter.

Perhaps the outlook would be better when this young generation grew up? The University of Zambia was in its infancy too and one hoped that by the time our children were enrolling as students all this would be an interesting but distant bit of history.

Our old friend W. C. Little was now Secretary of the Association of Friends of the University of Zambia and in an entertaining article he recounted how fundraising was progressing.

'....in parts of the country where a subsistence economy limits the amount of cash available for any purpose, donations are accepted in kind. Besides cattle there have been gifts of fowl and fish - dried fish is more popular with collectors as the disposal of fresh fish presents problems! Bags of peanuts and maize, bales of tobacco, a treasured ancient muzzle loading gun has been offered for sale on the University's behalf ...'

While one smiles at the mental pictures this conjures, it was surely an effective way of both making people feel the University belonged to them and of raising money. By September of that year the President was able to announce that £368,000 had been raised in a year.

Our cook William had by this time returned to Eastern Province, we had agreed to part company when we found him and his wife brewing beer in our paraffin drums in the garage.

Bentley had moved in and taken charge. Which described him very well! Bentley had been a cook at Lilayi Police Training Camp and he was somewhat coy about his reasons for leaving but his references were complimentary and the man soon proved that he could cook.

He appeared to be a man of many interests, joining the local football team and he was often out training with his friends - or so we were led to believe. Came the night when a deputation of serious men arrived on the verandah to ask for a word with Bentley. As it was his evening off we were surprised he was not having a drink or training session with them. They walked off with a determined air.

Andrew chuckled, 'I hope Bentley does not come home just yet; they look as though they mean business.'

Later that night we heard some uproar in the neighbourhood but when we asked Bentley about his black eye and swollen face the next day he said he had tripped in the dark.

While Bentley may not have been averse to consoling wives whose husbands were still on duty - and some cooks and house servants regularly worked very late hours - he was not able to cope with all the propositions he received. He was still a keen footballer and always jogged conscientiously round Chelston in the afternoons. One day he returned in a state of extreme anxiety and insisted on an indaba (meeting) at the kitchen door. In a roundabout way he indicated that he was a good cook and he played a game of football and that we knew he ran every afternoon for training and that was all he did these days since ... especially since ... delicate cough ... and that if the Dona down the road came to the house, he was not here and that he had not done anything and most certainly not that, although it was said ...

It took quite some time before I unravelled the fact that poor Bentley had been propositioned by a white woman who had little to occupy her mind or her time and spent her days ... or so it was said ... with long drinks in hand on the verandah and that her gardener did   more than garden. Be that as it may, Bentley had been hailed from the verandah as he passed the house on one of his training runs and mindful of the rumours he had switched into full speed and made for home. However, as it was unheard of for a servant to ignore a summons - albeit not from his own employer - he was equally worried that we should receive a complaint that he had been 'cheeky', a usual criticism. I managed to keep a straight face and advised him to keep on with his training but to use another route. This kept Bentley safe but may have made him more attractive as the good lady then took to visiting us - seated on the crossbar of her gardener's bicycle while the gardener cycled with a straight face as if this were the most normal afternoon activity. Andrew refused to answer the door any more after she leaned confidentially against him and as I answered the door ever afterwards, she eventually lost interest. It was clear that alcohol alone was not her only trouble. Fortunately it was not long before our neighbours went on leave and the wife stayed behind in UK 'for medical treatment'. There were many sad stories about people who could not cope with the lonely life that was often their lot - often women who had to fill long days or weeks while their husbands were absorbed in their work or travelling.

Bentley proved to be more than an adequate cook but he regarded the kitchen very much as his domain and were I rash enough to venture there I would find his huge figure blocking my path and

'What does Madam want now?' and I would be neatly diverted out.

Which was slightly better than the time I was making a shopping list and he leaned close to request he wanted rape ... all I could think was 'NOT on the kitchen floor'. Thankfully he added in the next breath, 'Three packets seeds enough, Madam.'

Our cook Bentley and gardener Lax

Just outside our bedroom window was a huge tree making that part of the garden too shady and covering the rockery with piles of leaves. The huge dry eight inch long seed pods clattering down on to the roof in the middle of the night were the last straw. Andrew decided it should come down. After giving Bentley, the cook, and Lax, the gardener (I shall not say garden boy although the term was in common usage at the time) a few casual instructions he left for the office. I did say it was rather a large tree and very close to the house and supposing ... 'These chaps are used to it,' was the casual answer as he drove off.

They may have been but I found the morning extremely stressful as they steadily chopped at the trunk. The next door neighbour told me afterwards that she stood at the window and prayed for it to fall my way and not hers. Andrew, of course, was right. The tree fell exactly where he had directed it should - and before he came home for lunch.

I was only at Lotus Primary for a few months before Andrew was due to take long leave. Being in the Civil Service he earned three days paid leave per month and while some of it could be commuted into cash, he had to take a certain amount of actual leave. These were the actual original Colonial conditions which ensured that European officers took a break from the strenuous African climate and either returned to Europe or at least went down to sea level.

It was an obvious choice to take our leave in the middle of the year, so getting the benefit of whatever warm weather there was in England and also to cover my school holiday. As I was employed as a married woman each time we went on leave I had to resign and then reapply for a teaching post on our return. As many married women were teachers, schools were in a constant state of slight disruption as women had to take their leave in accordance with husbands' contracts. Nor could they be sure of being reassigned back to the same school, the same town or even the same Province. The constant change kept everyone on their toes and made for an interesting tour of the country in some cases, though perhaps not always in the order they may have wished.

When we went to England on leave, Bentley went back home to his village to collect his wife. Lax was left in charge of the garden. Stella said she would drive out weekly, pay him his ration money and check that all was well. We left Micky with Dennis and Renate Proctor who had moved to Mount Makulu.

LEAVE IN UK 1965

We were flying to England and it was with great excitement that we arrived at the small airport for our first trip on an aeroplane, a VC10. The airport in Lusaka was a small runway JUST big enough to take a VC10 and a cluster of small arched corrugated iron sheds on the side of a small brick building. Deep red bougainvillea climbed vigorously all over the dark green sheds masking their ugliness and giving the airport a flamboyant splash of colour.

The airport was small and cosy and the runway was short, so short that it was still an event when the VC10 made its weekly appearance. People would make a trip out to watch it land and take off. For the latter it was far more exciting to drive round the bend on Kalingalinga Road and stop on the side of the road, which curved accommodatingly around the end of the runway. The VC10 took off with so little room to spare that you had a deafening and impressive view of its undercarriage as it heaved itself up into the air above you, almost, it seemed, within touching distance.

So, here we were, on our way to England, looking forward to seeing old friends and places. Ceri, at two and a half, was a relaxed traveller, sleeping most of the way.

Oh, my God, London was cold! And grey! And damp! And dirty! Not the dirt which was part of the earth and which drew you into being part of the landscape, but a grimy black which clung to everything and made you feel stale and unwashed within an hour. The air was stale, used and reused by people and machines until you ached for a good deep clean breath of fresh air. We had arranged to buy an Austin Traveller and as soon as it was loaded up we set off northwards. Fares and a car had not left much over for hotels so we had managed to rent part of a furnished house near Leeds University and from there planned to visit all our friends and take Ceri to parts of England we had not yet seen.

Looking back the holiday blurs into an impression of sun and rain and laughter with friends we had not seen for so long and Ceri thrilled by everything she saw. Postmen and dustbin men were a novelty and she thought them the most impressive and important of men. Escalators were new and we went to the top of every store and down again. Stairs were a novelty too after living in a bungalow and she would play on the stairs in preference to anywhere else, or just climb to the top and then bottom bump all the way down again. We spent time with the Hodgsons in the Yorkshire Dales where Andrew had enjoyed muck spreading on the farm all those years ago.

Ceri in a hay meadow at Lowlands farm during UK leave

With Douglas and Denise and Strudwick the porter at Devonshire Hall on UK leave

We went to see Douglas and Denise in the children's home and took them out for weekends. We stayed at the Children's Home for tea and answered endless questions from the children about Africa.

I took Ceri to my parents' home, she was their first grandchild and we stayed the night. Ceri trotted to and fro, chatting to all and as always happily adaptable to everywhere we went. The next morning she trotted backwards and forwards in the kitchen carrying things for my mother, who watched her with a smile.

'Isn't she the prettiest little girl?'

'And isn't it a pity when you think about it, that you could not have imagined yourself looking forward to this?'

'Ah well, if I could put the clock back and let this never have happened, I still would you know.'

We were never going to understand each other, how could she wish to deny the existence of my child? I think that it was at this point I really gave up trying.

The holiday was coming to an end when Andrew was told he would have to return to Zambia a little earlier than planned. The car was already on its way by sea, we had seen everyone we had hoped to see - Ceri had never slept more than three nights consecutively in the same place but had adapted very well. Even better, she had been completely free of tonsillitis. So we went down to London for the last few days and stayed in one of those large rambling sort of hotels so prolific in central London. Next morning Ceri was ready for breakfast very early but missing when we ourselves were dressed. We checked along the corridors, back into the bedroom and bathroom but no Ceri. Down in the lift for me and down via the stairs for Andrew - surely she couldn't have found her way downstairs? No Ceri in reception - nor had anyone seen a small two year old. Then a passing waiter asked if that were the little girl eating breakfast on her own? Ceri had grown impatient of waiting, made her way down in the lift and having ordered breakfast, was tucking in with a large appetite in the centre of a huge and crowded dining room. Several smiling waitresses were keeping an eye on the tiny self - possessed figure, looking all the smaller at a table for eight.

BACK TO CHELSTON

Andrew returned ahead of us and there was time for one short letter in which he said I would be surprised by the changes in Chelston. It partly prepared me for the new development I suppose but it did not lessen the disappointment at seeing that every empty plot of land had been bought by the Government and houses were being erected everywhere you looked.

The quiet of Chelston was gone for ever. I never again saw the herd of deer passing through in the early morning light.

Nor did Bentley reappear from his village (neither did my copy of Mrs Beeton) so I tried my luck at the Boma employment office where I found one Patulani Zulu with a range of satisfactory references. Zulu brought his wife Titanbenji and his daughter Tita with him. Tita was eight years old and while I hoped she would teach Ceri Nyanja as they played together it was a losing battle for, as Zulu pointed out, it was far more important that Tita learned English from Ceri. While Zulu and I debated our points of view the two girls got on with a general children's lingua franca, which seemed to be a mixture of the two.

Tita was painfully thin and kept her head averted when she

remembered, having lost an eye and being very conscious of the empty socket. Zulu said she had had the eyeball pierced by a brittle maize stalk when she was in a baby sling on her mother's back and her mother had bent forward in the maize field. The mother had later died, Zulu then marrying Titanbenji who appeared a kind enough step mother although she had no patience at all with the wet blankets Tita carried out of the servant's quarters every morning. Our early mornings were often disturbed by her wails after her mother's beatings. It was quite useless for me to explain that the child would grow out of it, particularly if she were treated kindly. Titanbenji's view was that if Tita wet the blankets then Tita would be beaten and made to wash them in cold water.

While Zulu agreed that Tita should go to school he seemed little disposed to do anything about it so one day I stopped off at the small primary school in Munali Secondary School grounds and very soon arranged a place for her. I was relieved that the headmaster agreed to take her in the morning session as it meant I could drop her off on my way to work each morning and pick her up again on the way home. Like most non fee-paying (formerly African) primary schools there were two daily sessions. The first one was usually from 7.30am to 12 midday and then the second session - with the same staff - would be from 1 to 5pm.

Zulu seemed keen and willing so when I saw an evening class for cooks advertised at the Evelyn Hone college in town I thought I'd try to boost his repertoire and confidence. It was a success of sorts – I dropped him off each evening, picking him later clutching his latest dish. I remember a chicken cooked with peanut butter and coconut soaked in chicken stock being very delicious. But sadly the tutor (a teaching colleague), confided that he had such an inflated idea of his status – now he was at a college – that he ignored much of her advice).

As for me, I had been posted back to Lotus Primary again where I was given a Grade 4 class of nine year olds in the morning session. We too now had morning and afternoon sessions in order to cope with the increasing demand for places. I said farewell to my 40 pupils at midday and watched them file out of the door, meanwhile 40 pupils and their teacher were lined up at the door on the opposite side of the classroom. Not only did we share a classroom, we had to share stock, the children had to share desks, keeping as little as possible in them. It was not an easy way of working but we were only just beginning to do what had been routine in African schools for many years. At least we did not have to teach both sessions as we were a fee paying school, where the parents were assured of better conditions. This was the oldest age group I had ever taught and while they were hard working and keen I looked forward to the day when another Grade 1 teacher would go on leave and I would have the opportunity to return to an infant class.

Junior girls practising for Diwali dances at Lotus Primary

Diwali, the Hindu festival of lights, was upon us later in the year and as a preamble there was a nine day session of continuous dancing to please Lakshmi, the goddess of wealth ... and all the goddesses of love, strength and intelligence according to the local paper. This was held at the Hindu Hall and I was invited by some of the mothers in my class. Women danced in the hall watched by other women and children; the men stood outside and chatted. I was fascinated by the dances as one followed another, the music with its unfamiliar rhythms and the brilliant flash and clash of bright saris and jewellery. Women danced until they were tired and dropped out for a rest, sitting on the floor like so many discarded flowers, and re-joining the circle when they recovered. There was a slow but steady turnover of dancers but the dancing itself never stopped and one dance began as another ended. I was asked if I would like to join in but felt too shy, already conspicuous enough being the only white face in the hall. Besides, I felt my large boned Yorkshire frame would not blend easily with the delicately graceful women.

Towards the end of the evening the music stopped and we gathered round a small altar in the corner where candles and incense had been burning all evening. I slipped off my sandals like the other women and joined in the prayers, then passing my hands through the candle flames I accepted several small sweetmeats to eat. I had appreciated the women's invitation, the whole evening and had been made to feel most welcome.

When I was describing the evening to a friend and neighbour, Margaret Collingwood, I was amazed that she was so shocked to hear that I had joined the group at the altar.

'It's just like worshipping heathen gods June! You really should not have done that! As you are teaching at the school, I suppose it was nice for you to go and watch, but you should never join in anything religious.'

I remarked that I could not have gone and behaved like a detached voyeur watching the locals and their quaint customs. I could never understand this attitude of being wary of anything foreign or different.

There was a light hearted side to 'things being different' when Andrew came back from his evening walk with the dog Micky.

'Have you looked at the building going up on the plot behind ours?' he asked.

I had not looked over the hedge for some time - sad to think that we would soon be surrounded by houses and had taken little interest in their progress. But Andrew had such a twinkle in his eye that I accompanied him across the garden, through the orchard to the hedge on the boundary. We were then standing in the corner of our plot looking over at the servant's quarters being built in the corner of the plot behind. The walls were about two feet high. It was a small house - or it would be when it was finished, but about standard size for a servant's house.

'Don't you see anything unusual about it?'

I looked again. No, it was the usual sort of thing.

'I think we should check on its progress every night.'

'What on earth for?'

'Well, I'm just curious to see how far they will continue with the walls before they think it would be better to take out the tree.'

Of course! I had a fit of the giggles

We continued to watch the progress of that little house and to our amusement the walls rose to over four feet before an inspection by the foreman brought it all to a halt and the tree growing sturdily in the centre of the house was removed.

It was about this time that Theo Bull married Mutumba Mainga in what was probably the wedding of the year - at least in our part of the world. Theo, grandson of the South African millionaire Sir Otto Beit, had graduated at Cambridge and was then publisher of the Central African Examiner, secretary of the Zambian Arts Trust and was said to speculate in the property market in Lusaka. His bride Mutumba was the daughter of a member of the Royal Court of the Litunga Paramount Chief of the Lozis and had graduated with honours in History.

I liked Theo, he was one of the few people I knew who liked tea as weak as I did and when I poured him one of my usual pale, pale teas his enthusiasm was surprising. He said he usually refused offers of a cup of tea because people made it too strong and he couldn't bear to drink it.

Perhaps mixed marriages were becoming more common; whatever the reason, there was no adverse comment in the Press about this marriage. Or perhaps any critical letters just were not published. In yet another show of inter-racial goodwill the Attorney General James Skinner was elected a Member of Parliament. This was not altogether surprising though, as he had long been associated with the struggle for freedom and had been UNIP's legal advisor before independence.

Integration was not always well organised. The new Government had decided that everyone should carry a National Registration card and one had to go along to the designated office and produce evidence of name, birth date and place of birth - all of which duly appeared on the card together with one's photograph which was done there and then. An admirable idea I thought, the small two by three inch plastic covered card could be carried easily in a wallet or pocket and as Europeans as well as Africans were to have these, the stigma of the hated situpa no longer applied. (Situpa – a former card which had to be carried by adult African males only and was linked to hated colonial regulations. I believe they had to carry a situpa as a means of identity and proof of employment).

But the organisers slipped up on one small detail with their equipment. It was found that as five people were photographed together you had to make sure that you went along with friends of the same colour. For whatever technical reason I never discovered, the camera faithfully reproduced either five black people or five white people. But it could not cope with a mixed group of blacks and whites. As white people were in a minority you had to plan more carefully - or be prepared for a long wait.

October 1965 was the first anniversary of independence and we could look back and see that we had jogged along with no major disasters, there had been some changes – some long overdue - and others which seemed a bit nit-picky but which were perhaps understandable after so many years of restrictions.

In June the plaque on the war memorial in Livingstone had been removed because while it was supposed to commemorate those who had died fighting, no African names were recorded. After some comments in the Press, Southern Province Resident Minister Mr Sakubita confirmed the plaque was to be replaced as soon as African names had been added. I thought it might have been cheaper and quicker to just add a plaque with the names of the African soldiers but then thought perhaps it was far better to have all the names united on one plaque.

But no sooner had we celebrated our first birthday than trouble loomed over the border. Ian Smith, Prime Minister of Southern Rhodesia, declared UDI - Unilateral Declaration of Independence. While we waited in vain for the British Government to intervene, life underwent some rapid changes as restrictions hit home.

Rhodesian troops dug in on the banks of the Zambezi, the border between our two countries, and President Kaunda denounced the S. Rhodesian national leaders who preferred to sit and talk in our country instead of taking more positive action. I suppose some of us thought they would eventually return home and rally support, even in the face of overwhelming odds, as this would have provoked some response from the British government. But there was no sign of response or movement from the South Rhodesian nationalist leaders, who earned themselves the title of 'chicken-in-a-basket leaders' - from their fondness for sitting on the terrace at the Ridgeway Hotel and consuming the popular dish of the day.

As most of our supplies came in from the south by rail and road, this was to be our first and most immediate problem as all our supplies would have to be rerouted. It was all very well to talk of rerouting ships to Dar es Salaam but the road connections were not good and for some time vital supplies would have to be airlifted in - with our capital's airport only just capable of taking a VC10.

By the end of the year petrol was rationed in a country where distances were great and public transport far from adequate. One took less interest in the arrival of a squadron of BRAF Javelin jet fighters than the news that Hercules would airlift copper - our main export - out to Dar es Salaam and petrol back in to us. Although a giant electricity pylon was reported blown up by saboteurs with gelignite near Luanshya, which carried vital power from Kariba to the Copperbelt, it was not long before it was back in action and we were able to take comfort in the fact that life still had its lighter moments.

Southern Rhodesia had its supply problems too. A Bulawayo farmer decided he would stockpile some petrol and bought £165 worth of petrol in drums (a lot of money in those days). He transported this back to his farm and told his African employees to dig a hole and store the petrol there. He set off for town hoping to purchase some more. On his return he was just in time to see the workers empty the last of the last drum of petrol into the hole.

UDI was declared in November 1965 and by January 1966 we had progressed to a situation where the petrol supplies were at least arriving in sufficient quantities to keep the country running. The British and Canadian airlifts could fly in 20,000 gallons a day - although one did not like to think about the cost. Ships were to unload at Beira, petrol could then be railed to Salima in Malawi, through Mozambique and after that we would have to bring it in by road via Fort Jameson. Ships were also to unload at Dar es Salaam and then lorries and tankers undertook the long haul by road.

The long roads became known as the Hell Run owing to the appalling conditions particularly in the rainy season and also the apparent casual standard of driving, which resulted in the Hell Run being lined with the wrecks of lorries in varying stages of damage. Dar es Salaam being somewhat taken unawares by its new role found it difficult to deal with the physical problems as well as the paper work. Great were the frustrations felt by business men in Zambia, knowing that their goods were sitting on the Tanzanian docks in either blazing sun or drenching rain while papers were being shunted to and fro - or merely filed away for another day.

By the end of January an individual motorist's petrol ration had been increased to 10 gallons each for the coming month and we felt that the situation was under control.

As for us, we had bought the house in Chelston near the site of Andrew's college-to-be, but there was a change of plan not long after we moved in. Andrew was no longer to work for the

Natural Resources College, he was appointed to act as under study to the Permanent Secretary in the Ministry of Transport. He began his new duties just as life was at its most complicated in the Ministry.

Meanwhile at home we had become increasingly unhappy to be living in a large and spacious house with our servants crowded into one room behind the garage and a thatched hut serving as an outside kitchen. But any attempt to borrow money to extend or improve the servants' quarters was impossible.

'But, if you wish to extend your own house we are more than willing to increase your mortgage...'

Now, there was the loophole, we could build an extension on our house and at the same time quietly extend the servants quarters. A perfectly acceptable solution. In the excitement we got somewhat carried away and the small extension became a massive overhaul. 'After all,' said the builder looking round the house with the architect, 'if you are going to do something, you want to do as much as possible all at once, not keep adding bits and pieces.'

A very valid point surely?

So... a dining room was added in the existing angle between kitchen and present lounge/diner, which then became a very large lounge. The kitchen had all its piece meal home-made cupboards ripped out and was completely refurbished. An extension was added to the other end of the house consisting of a sunken garage with two bedrooms and bathroom above and the existing garage became part of the extended servants quarters.

It all looked very simple on paper. And it has been found that the simplest exercises have a way of ending up being the most complicated, troublesome and expensive as we found out.

The builder, a Mr Andreucci, attacked the project from all angles simultaneously. One had to admire the man for his confidence and enthusiasm. The dining room walls were going up. Kitchen units were being detached from walls. And excavations had begun for the drive down into the garage.

This was his first set back. In spite of the house being surrounded by large and imposing rockeries of huge and shining quartz boulders not one of us had had the wits to ask 'whence they came?' As the workmen dug down it became painfully clear. Right here on the spot. Quartz boulders, the size of the dining table, were laboriously hauled out and the progress at that end of the house was sadly delayed. As the drive would go down into the garage a good soakaway for rainwater was essential and the digging of that nearly broke the men's spirits if not their backs. Zulu would serve me morning tea with much head shaking and murmured, 'Maningi shupa, Madam, maningi shupa' (too much trouble). But at long last the building was able to commence at that end of the house.

As we were still in the throes of petrol rationing I often wondered why Andreucci could not organise his day better; all too often he delivered his men to the site and drove off only for the foreman to come to me later requesting that the Bwana be phoned in town to come back out with some urgently needed tool or material.

Once the house was finished it would all be painted white, inside and out. I felt it gave a welcome coolness and was a good foil for the dark woods of furniture - and the bright splashes of colour when I managed to build a collection of local paintings and crafts. External white walls would also reveal the presence of white ants as they built their red earth tunnels up the walls. No matter where one built or how, white ants were everywhere, building and tunnelling and nothing short of steel seemed resistant to their champing jaws.

A Lusaka dress shop imported two large boxes of Mary Quant dresses and they were put into cargo storage behind the freight office at the airport. They had to stay there five days over Heroes and Unity public holiday weekend. When they were opened up it was found that white ants had eaten straight through the boxes and dresses. As for the consignment of metal tubes at the other side, they were fine but as all the labels had been eaten no one was quite sure whether they were radio aerials or fuel tubes or indeed where they were to be delivered.

I remembered standing beside Aileen Hepworth outside an older and empty house in Petauke and listening to the white ants eating the rafters. We were standing outside the house, the walls of which were covered with the long, wandering red earth ant tunnels, all of which disappeared under the eaves. In the afternoon's hot stillness we could distinctly hear the multitudinous chomping - like the steady ticking of a clock.

It gave me a shiver, thinking how Africa was always there, ready and waiting to devour you and leave no trace of your presence. Sometimes one would come across an abandoned hut and what was left of the wattle walls would crumble at a touch, the wood left a thin hollow shell by the ants. All too soon what had been a stout and sturdy hut sheltering a family, would be devoured and the thin shells of wood and thatch would blow away on the winds and the site would disappear under new growth in the next rains.

To make life just a little more full and entertaining, I was pregnant and contemplating bringing a new baby home with only one room relatively untouched, Andrew having decided at the last minute, to have all the bedroom floors laid with parquet to match the sitting room. He then went down with a dose of shingles, which was undoubtedly caused by stress and strain now that the work at the office was so pressured by UDI.

Ordered to bed for complete rest he did retire to bed - and surrounded himself with piles of office files, which his driver delivered daily. He got up once and made a one day flight to Salisbury for an important meeting, vowing to rub his shingles and not to wash his hands until he had shaken hands with every member of Ian Smith's Cabinet.

It was about this time also that Elijah Mudenda made a mad dash south too. Only a few years ago on Mount Makulu he had successfully bred a new groundnut, fittingly named the Makulu Red. It was large and particularly tasty nut with a distinctive dark red skin. It was discovered with some alarm that ALL the Makulu Red nuts were for some reason held in Salisbury. Elijah made a hasty rescue trip, returning triumphantly with one small bag of Makulu Reds, a few pounds of the precious nut from which our supplies could be built up again.

Our house extensions took so long and were of such a fascinating nature - due to Andreucci's original working style - that our home became an attractive focal point for any of our friends who had the petrol to spare.

One afternoon a friend and I were relaxing with a cup of tea when we heard the most odd groaning. Following the sound I tracked down Andreucci seated on the new bathroom floor cradling his head in the - unconnected - toilet bowl and groaning loudly. It transpired he had delivered the workmen earlier in the day complete with materials for the day's work. The foreman had used my phone to call him (true, I remembered) to say the connecting pipe for the toilet was too short and would the Bwana bring out a longer one. He had done so and rushed off back to town. The foreman had phoned requesting a metal saw as the pipe was too long. Andreucci had just come out yet again, sawed the pipe shorter himself ... but now it was now too short. I had heard Italian is a dramatic and emotional language. I could well believe it. No one else could have rendered such heart felt emotional drama with a length of pipe.

Goodwin and Mabel Mutale, impressed by our activities, decided to improve their servant's quarters and set about dealing with the problem. Goodwin reported with incredulous amusement the reaction of his European neighbour. Seeing Goodie out in the garden with a builder, and shortly afterwards walls beginning to rise, the neighbour made enquiries. Goodie explained his plans. The neighbour nodded.

'Mmm, it might be an idea for me to extend my servants quarters too. Then the garden boy could live in too and it would be more convenient.'

He asked Goodie about costs and then to Goodie's astonishment, he proceeded to call the young garden boy across the garden and measured him, calculating the cost at the same time.

'Don't forget the lad has some growing to do yet,' commented Goodie over the hedge.

'No need to worry about that,' was the rejoinder. 'They change jobs so fast that I'm sure to get another small one.'

The proposed room was clearly going to be the length and breadth of a boy about fourteen years old.

SIMON ANDREW LUNKOTO, BORN JULY 1966

My second baby looked as though it were hanging on waiting for the house to be completed but eventually made his appearance early in July. I think that at over ten pounds he had just been too big and too lazy to make the effort. Once born he was the only baby to fit a cot in the hospital nursery from one end to the other and looked very out of place in a room full of tiny new looking babies.

By that time of course, the European hospital was the integrated fee paying hospital and I shared a two bed ward with Esther Mulaisho, who gave birth to her first son. In the room next door was Marianne Kazoka, who had her first child, a daughter Anna Lute. Marianne was from Spain and married to John Kazoka, a lawyer.

Andrew brought Ceri at visiting time and she insisted I open my mouth so that she could see where the baby had come out. So much for me having let her watch our cat give birth to a litter of kittens!

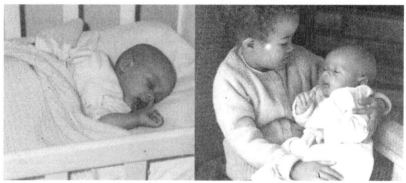

Simon - a July baby   *Ceri and Simon*

The house was finished soon after I went home and we settled down into a routine. Andrew trying to keep pace with rapidly changing events and constant pressures upon the Ministry brought about by UDI. Ceri was now going to Joyce Hamilton's nursery with her friend Fenella Redway. (Brian Redway had joined the MSD, he and his wife Margaret became great friends).

Ceri and Simon – bedtime story with Giles annual

Ceri and Fenella after Teddy Bear's Picnic at ballet class

I had the time to enjoy the new baby and take Ceri to other activities. She joined Queenie Pratts dancing class together with Fenella Redway and Suzie Proctor. We mothers endured the weekly drive to the hall, the making of costumes, the rehearsals and the concerts themselves. Our husbands were not quite so long suffering, sitting through only one concert. After which Brian Redway asked plaintively why he was paying for Fenella to learn how to lie on a stage - Fenella having missed her cue, never rose to dance with the music.

The Proctors were now stationed on Mount Makulu, where we had first lived, and as the petrol rationing improved we were able to drive over to have uproarious weekend lunches while the children played in sunlit gardens. Suzie had a younger brother Christopher and as the four children grew up they made a lively group with Suzie as an energetic leader.

Occasionally I would drive over during the week, Renate and I drinking tea while we watched the children playing in the garden. Renate was a great friend and I valued our friendship but on one small point she had me quite frustrated. We would arrive. The children would go tearing off to bedrooms and garden. Renate would say, 'Come and talk to me while I just put the kettle on.'

Just putting the kettle on also equated producing the most delicious chocolate eclairs almost before the tea was ready. I never actually saw how she did it! She would chat away as she mixed and stirred and threw a tray into the oven as she switched the kettle on ... by the time the water was boiling she would be slicing open eclairs to insert cream before she poured over melted chocolate ... and a pile of eclairs was ready as she poured the tea.

It was marvellous to be at home with time for friends and the children but I missed the thrill of seeing a class develop through the school year and the extra money would be useful. Plus I did not see myself becoming part of the superficial circle of coffee mornings and bridge afternoons, where many expatriate wives spent their time waiting for their husbands' contracts to end.

So, off to the Ministry of Education and back to Lotus Primary, where I would be having a Grade 3 class in September. I drove down to the school and reintroduced myself to Mr Patel and left feeling very happy. I knew I would enjoy being back there with some old colleagues and a few new faces.

Although I was never deeply interested in politics as such I could not help but be interested in my new country's development. Andrew's boundless enthusiasm and conviction that Zambia was off to a wonderful start, in spite of UDI, was infectious.

Arthur Wina was Minister of Finance and his claim that Zambia had the healthiest financial state of affairs in any country in Africa, except perhaps South Africa, was encouraging. According to him Zambia had a healthy economy and our reserves of foreign currency exceeded £70,000,000. That sounded fine to me, and after all, the experts should know. So what was I worried about when I sometimes accompanied Andrew on one of his informal inspections of the new International airport being built east of Lusaka, not far from where we lived in Chelston? I knew that it was supposed to be costing over £5 million but perhaps that was peanuts? or perhaps it was because it was partly being built with foreign help.

Lusaka's new International airport

Zambia certainly was moving into international standards quickly as regards public buildings. Not only was the new International airport on its way, we were also to have a spanking new National Assembly with its magnificent copper sheathing on the outer shell. Not forgetting the new University of Zambia. Of course they were all necessary and we were also to expand

221

in schools and hospitals - Lusaka was to have a new University Teaching Hospital - the list was endless. The cost of importing all the foreign expertise would be costly too – but 'we were a wealthy nation'.

It was not Zambia's fault that UDI had meant it was far more costly to export her copper nor her fault that the copper prices began to fall by the middle of 1960/1966. Neither did it help when the copper miners came out on strike shortly afterwards. I think it was because the miners demanded an immediate payment of accumulated funds in the Zaminlo pension fund before the Zambia National Provident Fund got started in October. Certainly there was also great dissatisfaction with the dual pay structure where white miners were still on a higher rate of pay and far better conditions. Whatever all the causes, production was still badly hit and in no time at all the mines were losing £1million a day. Before the end of the year the mines had to cut back production to three quarters of their normal level and calculated they lost £200,000 per day in the then current prices.

I had expected that once independence had been achieved, Zambians would throw themselves into the development of their country with a total commitment. It was disconcerting to see the lead given by His Excellency the President was not followed by the rank and file. One day publicity was given to the President picking cotton on a farm at Chombwa near Mumbwa. He did a stint on a Government farm with Ministers Grey Zulu and Elijah Mudenda, showing that not only could Zambia produce its own cotton but also that labour in the fields was not beneath his dignity. Sadly his example had little effect on the unemployed. Within a few weeks, acres of cotton in the same area had to be ploughed in as the Government could not find enough labourers to pick it.

Sikota Wina, as Minister of Local Government and Housing, took a strong line. He personally got behind the wheel of the bulldozer knocking down the infamous 'bottle houses' in Kabwata. These had been built in colonial days when the European, perhaps through ignorance, assumed that a brick built house in the traditional round shape (often known as kias or kayas) was just what the working man and his family required to make him feel well housed. What the designer or planner did not know, or care about, was that while round huts might be traditional for some tribes, living together in one small room was not. Andrew told me that in the village a family would have more than one hut so that all the adults and children did not all eat and sleep in one room.

However, there had been a long-standing dissatisfaction with the 'bottle houses' and now all that could change. Sikota personally started the bulldozing and said that the bricks themselves were of good quality and would be used on the Marrapodi Site and Service scheme where 'YOU can build your own houses. The Government has done the planning NOW IT'S UP TO YOU. This is what is meant by independence'.

Perhaps at the same time there was a positive effort to deal with the problem of the growing numbers of young unemployed, often with little or no education at all, but the majority of whom were flocking to the towns, attracted by the bright lights and plentiful supply of consumer goods.

It was decided to reform the Zambia Youth Service to run on a para military basis with three months basic army training, an agricultural course and a course on 'skills' ranging from carpentry, bricklaying to plumbing and domestic science and hygiene for the girls. The fact that the youngsters would receive pocket money while on the two year course was meant to attract the 'doubtfuls'.

It seemed that while Members of Parliament did not agree, some measures were being taken to help the young people in a meaningful manner. The MP Mr Burnside warned of a population explosion and the dangers that that could cause, but his fears were pooh poohed by Unia Mwilla, Minister for Economic Development, who prophesied that 'Zambia will soon be short of labour'.

I felt that Miss Malina Chilila, the youngest Member of the

National Assembly, was being optimistic when she thanked the President and the Government for removing much sexual prejudice from education and other fields. At the same time she took the opportunity of making a blistering attack on 'men who treat women like animals or slaves'. It stemmed, she said, from old customs and had no place in modern Zambia.

Men certainly did feel they were the dominant sex and this was painfully obvious in the case of the UNIP Youths. Girls wearing jeans or mini-skirts would be stopped in the street and have their garments slashed, or at the very least the hems would be let down there and then. The same youths would undertake a Party checking campaign and stop people without a Party card from boarding a bus or buying in a market. In these cases it was nearly always the women who suffered.

I found this kind of behaviour hard to understand especially in the face of the President's preaching about Humanism and his call for the unemployed to go back to the land to be self -supporting.

I was amused to hear our friend Patrick Chuula describe how he had waited to cross Cairo Road and found himself behind 'a young European lady whose skirt was so short one could see more than just the tops of her legs'. So he gently tapped her on the shoulder, explained he was the DPP (Director of Public Prosecutions) and he felt he must advise her that her mini skirt was such that she could be prosecuted for indecency.

I did not approve of violence but I could understand the students who rioted at the British High Commission and hurled stones through the windows and ripped down the Union Jack, tearing it to shreds. This was a demonstration against the killing of seven ZANU guerrillas in Southern Rhodesia. I did not approve, hating violence, but I could understand the young people feeling angry, depressed and frustrated at the situation so close to home. Our lives were still severely compromised by UDI and they believed the British Government by its apparent inaction condoned Ian Smith's actions.

Although goods were getting through and the petrol ration

increased there were shortages and prices had risen. The Ministry of Commerce had had to form an office for Price Control alone and appoint price inspectors. Although a statement had been issued that 'nobody may sell at a higher price than January 1966 without special authority from the Minister', we were all aware of price increases.

Life was not as peaceful as it had been and one felt there really were saboteurs at work. There was a bomb blast at Lusaka Post Office and another explosion tore a three foot hole in the bottom of an oil storage tank in Lusaka's industrial site and 100,000 gallons of diesel were lost.

Lusaka's Agricultural Show - a highlight in our small world - had to be cancelled because the RAF were being accommodated at the Showground. Reports had it that they were housed in prefab buildings imported from South Africa. Not the most comfortable of arrangements and it was not enhanced by a freak storm in May when hailstones the size of golf balls smashed windows, ripped off roofs, and swept the roof of their kitchen 100 yards away.

As usual in times of hardship, stories abounded to lighten the gloom. One of my favourites was the story of the pilot coming in to land with a load of oil and asking for permission from the control tower to land and then bellowing over the radio that he could not land 'with all those bloody cars parked on the runway'. He is supposed to have been off course and lined up to land on Cairo Road in the city centre. We loved it, repeating it over and over again.

Simon was baptised in Lusaka Cathedral. Afterwards his godparents Clifford Little and Goodwin and Mabel Mutale returned to the house with more friends for a small party. It ranked higher than a State occasion in Zulu's book and he served eats and drinks with a ramrod straight back - which may have been due to pride - or the fact that his white uniform had been starched until it crackled at every movement.

Clifford had been the Principal of Munali when Andrew was a student there, he ranked very high in Andrew's estimation and we had been honoured when he agreed to be Simon's godfather. The choice of Goodie (Goodwin) and Mabel had been equally easy. Goodie and Andrew had been friends since Munali days and we shared many happy times. I had first met Mabel in UK when she was nursing and she had been at our wedding. Goodie I first met in Petauke days when he was based in Chadiza. He was back in Lusaka and called on me for help when he had news of Mabel's return. He had recently moved into a Government house and said new curtains would be a very welcoming gesture. I was a bit dubious about helping choose another woman's curtains but we agreed to meet him in Limbadas. We inspected various rolls of material and as he narrowed down the choice I asked for a list of measurements.

'Aha,' said Goodie pulling a long length of string from a pocket, holding it up proudly, ' I remembered to measure the windows .... Now let me see. ....this knot to the second is the sitting room ... and the second knot to the fourth is our bedroom ... or was that the dining room ...?'

It didn't take long to convince him that he would have to measure up again - this time with a tape measure (which we bought on the spot in Limbadas) and a pen and paper, me reminding him that he did have to measure across for widths as well as down for length.

Much later when Mabel had arrived (and I think had chosen her own curtains) we invited them to dinner at the Woodpecker in Woodlands, a well renowned restaurant. We had been before and thought it well worth a repeat visit. Inspecting the menu Goodie opted for the Plank Steak in spite of thinking it an odd name. Andrew thought it best to say one required a large appetite, but no matter, Goodie fancied a steak. Before long the waiter was setting out the table and placed a large plank in front of Goodie, all of 18 by 12 inches I would guess. Goodie looked alarmed but he had been warned. Of course, he thought Andrew exaggerated and the look of horror on his face when a 16 by 10 inch steak appeared is indescribable.

A few invitations from us made him rather cautious, he said.

Going to see Lysistrata (the comic account of one woman's mission to end the Peloponnesian War, when Lysistrata convinced the women of Greece to withhold sexual privileges from their husbands as a means of forcing men to negotiate peace) at Lusaka Playhouse confirmed his suspicions. I KNOW he enjoyed it but wouldn't admit it and insisted women just could not ... would not ... should not be allowed ... Mabel and I looked very knowing, murmured that perhaps there was something in the idea ...

I stayed at home for a few months after Simon was born and really relished having time to spend time with both children. Ceri was very fond of the new baby, lending a hand with the bathing and feeding – but equally keen to put him down for a sleep so we could paint or read or indulge in other activities until Simon woke up – which was always with a roar of outrage at finding himself alone.

The new International Airport was opened officially in October 1966 as part of the second independence celebrations. Andrew and I were among those invited to sit on the concourse and watch the opening ceremony. The Wildlife Conservation Society had donated a life sized bronze statue of a lechwe made by the South African sculptor Coert Steynberg. It looked magnificent and I hope the nationality of the sculptor never offends someone of influence in years to come. Another donation was a piece of copper ore weighing nearly 20 tons, which had been mined at RST's Chambishi Mine. It forms a centre piece as a symbol representing the country's economy and has water cascading down it and over copper wire bars into a basin below.

I heard the final cost of the airport was estimated to be £6 million not the £5 million   originally quoted. But when one considered the changes that had taken place and the rerouting of materials and equipment, perhaps it was not surprising. It was an exciting occasion and I felt proud that Andrew had had such close associations with its building. I glanced around at the crowded concourse, smiling at friends as we exchanged a warm feeling of achievement. Then I looked over my shoulder and

227

spotted friend John with a pretty young Zambian girl. John was married to a very attractive European girl, we had been friends for some time. I nudged Andrew and whispered.

'Look at John, who is the girl with him? They look very friendly.' Andrew frowned at me.

Once the speeches were over we moved about to chat with friends and turned to John, who introduced us to his niece.

I asked where his wife was. She had flown home to visit her family.

As we left the concourse I glanced back at John and his niece, they were very animated and I felt even more uneasy. Andrew was most annoyed when I mentioned my fears.

'You women are all the same,' he said. 'You do nothing but gossip and speculate. You heard John say she was his niece, what a nasty mind you have.'

Had he really believed that I wondered, for only too soon we heard that when my friend came back from her trip she found the girl comfortably ensconced in the house and of course she was not a niece at all. To make matters worse, if that were possible, John was outraged that his wife objected and told him that the girlfriend must move out at once.

It was January 1967 ... and we were on our way. To what? Peace and prosperity with a new developing nation which had so many resources - from mineral wealth to trained manpower (in comparison to many other newly independent countries Zambia was very well endowed). All this, plus more than adequate financial reserves. What exciting times in which to live and work. Andrew was in his element with so many new ventures to start and supervise and sharing with others an unqualified optimism and complete dedication. At the beginning of the year there had been a Government reshuffle and he was now Permanent Secretary of Transport (no longer an under-study) and his Minister was Solomon Kalulu.

What other names spring to mind at that period of our lives? Edward Shamwana, long standing friend, an ex Munali boy, a lawyer now establishing his own practice and a man who liked being quietly at home with his English wife Stella, who was so outspoken and forthright.

Patrick Chuula, another lawyer, often teased for not being one of the ex Munali boys in our large group of friends. A man who was close to his village background and who liked to go home to the village as often as possible. His English wife Rosemary, so quiet and gentle with a kind word for everyone.

Lishomwa Lishomwa, an economist with an effervescent personality. Lish had had to cross the border into Malawi to marry his Shetland wife Sepo (taking, I believe, the Lozi name meaning Hope in place of Agnes) because even after independence it was still illegal to marry in Zambia - it took time to change some laws!

Goodwin Mutale with his quiet sense of humour and a desire for a daughter which amused us all and exasperated his wife Mabel until at last she produced a daughter after three sons and none of us thought Goodie would come down to earth for the rest of the year, such was his delight.

James Mapoma with his attractive wife Joyce, who had been in Eastern Province at the time of the Lenshina uprising and was speared in the arm by an infuriated (or spiritually uplifted) follower. He was transferred from Province to Province in the early days, his children having to cope with being educated in the different tribal languages.

David Phiri, a Cambridge Blue, and still a keen golfer, who married his English wife Anne in Ilkley when we were there on holiday in 1965. We bumped into David quite by chance in Leeds and were hastily invited to the wedding.

'My side of the church is going to be very bare, you know,' said David with his usual engaging wide smile. With such an invitation how could we refuse?

At the reception, Anne's parents took me on one side and asked if I had experienced 'any problems over there.' I airily answered that life had been plain sailing generally. How could one begin to explain what it really had been and still was like, standing in the middle of a quiet English lounge, all soft ... like standing in the centre of an English water colour and trying to describe the

229

hot dry colours of an African scene, in slashing oils vibrant with passions and energy.

Gwen Konie, who had trained as a social worker in Swansea and was one of the most forceful and dynamic personalities that I had ever met. She was now training as a diplomat.

John Mwanakatwe, who went on from being the Minister of Education to qualify as a lawyer and start his own practice. His wife Margaret, with her sincerity and good humour.

Emmanuel Kasonde, Geoffrey Mee, Dominic and Esther Mulaisho, Elias and Anna Chipimo, Safeli and Martha Chileshe, Aaron and Phyllis Milner ... James Skinner and Madeleine Robertson, two Europeans who had done so much during the fight for independence and who were so sadly rejected by those they had helped so shortly afterwards.

While I knew far more about Zambian politics than I had ever done about English politics and while I could share the interests and hopes of many of our friends, I have never been particularly enthralled by the power struggles and in-fighting.

I was attracted to what was happening in the schools and the shops and the developments in the towns as they affected 'the man in the street'. But these are controlled by the politicking above and the gap between the two so quickly became a chasm so that you no longer believed that the powers that be really saw - or cared - about the effects of their decisions.

The President seemed to be conscious of the casual attitude of the man in the street and he was already exhorting his people to mend their ways. He said the country was lagging spiritually and morally with an attitude of 'let's drink and be merry for tomorrow we shall die'. He had at that time, also a feeling for European sensibilities and stepped into the discussion of Lusaka City Council, which was considering the renaming of some streets after the killers Phiri and Ngebe. They had killed a Mrs Burton, a passing motorist on the Copperbelt, at the time of some pre independence unrest. It was seen by some as an act of unwarranted murder against an innocent and defenceless woman, and by others as an act of defiance for freedom.

Andrew's new Minister, Mr Kalulu, appeared to be a man of action because as soon as he read a report by Andrew that far too many of the locomotives were out of order, he made a prompt and surprise visit to the Broken Hill (now Kabwe) depot. He made a full inspection and talked to both railwaymen and the General Railway Administrator, Frank Lucarotti. His comments were particularly stinging and the railwaymen held a meeting where the Railway and Amalgamated Engineering Union discussed the allegations that certain railwaymen were deliberately not maintaining locos properly. Most of the men concerned were Rhodesian citizens who worked as mechanics and fitters and turners, they expressed concern at the inference of subtle sabotage. The fact still remained, most of the locos on which Zambia depended were broken down. Reports said that 18 out of the 27 at Broken Hill were unserviceable and 9 out of 15 in Livingstone were out of action. No wonder 18 rail trucks with 900 tons of coal for the Copperbelt and the Congo had been standing idle in Lusaka for over a week.

In a quick piece of action 12 railway officials were given a few days in which to quit Zambia and return to Rhodesia on transfer. A report released a month later said that most whites were willing to work but there was much criticism of inexperienced staff being placed in responsible posts to satisfy the Zambianisation programme. This was said by officials, leaders and the men themselves.

One could only hope that once the less desirable element had returned to Rhodesia there would be a better spirit all round and we would have no more incidents like the Allison affair.

Andrew Allison had been recently recruited as a railway fitter from UK. Shortly after his arrival he went to the Broken Hill railway club on a Sunday evening and danced with the wife of a Zambian worker. After another white insulted him over the choice of his partner he decided to leave the club and was beaten unconscious by three whites outside. He said later that new men did seem to be ostracised for mixing with Zambians.

On the other hand it appeared that some Zambians appeared

intent on taking the law into their own hands. At about this time Mrs Edna Kamanga, wife of the Vice President Reuben Kamanga, complained that she had been sold rotten meat by Longacres Butchery; the City Council ordered it closed for health reasons. We just could not resist following events as reported in the Press. Mr Ottino, the owner, was supposed to have given away 15 left-over Christmas turkeys - one of which went to Mrs Kamanga when her servant collected the meat order. It was reported that she returned it saying that it was rotten and that he was a stupid bastard. It was reported that he said that if she thought him stupid then she was as stupid as she believed him to be. The report stated that she left the shop saying that she would show him what she could do and would have the shop closed.

(It is interesting to note at this point that the word 'stupid' was usually considered more insulting than the word 'bastard' by most Zambians).

A few days later Mr Ottino received a letter from the Council saying the shop was closed for contravening health regulations. His lawyer, Mr Cunningham, said none of the reasons actually given by the Council were part of the butchery and abattoir regulations.

So when on Friday Mr Justice Ramsay granted an injunction preventing the Council from closing the shop, the stage was set. Early on Saturday morning in broad daylight 150 young men climbed out of three trucks and showered stones on Longacres butchery.

The following day the President deplored the incident and said that we must not prejudge issues and take the law into our own hands.

Within two days the Council in a meeting, attacked the Times of Zambia for describing the incident.

This was followed by Justice Ramsay ruling that the Mayor Mr W Banda and the UNIP official Mr Eustace Mumba had a case of contempt of court to answer. Mayor Banda said to the reporter Mr Soko, that anyone who defied a Council order defied the whole country and anyone, even the wife of an MP had a right to complain (we all began to wish she hadn't). And I began to get confused by the ensuing developments.

Mumba was sentenced to 12 months for contempt of court .

Banda appealed against the sentence of 6 months hard labour for contempt of court.

His lawyer Cunnningham was not in court - he was represented by a Mr Smallwood, who was not adequately briefed because Cunningham's house and office had been raided by the police and all his papers seized.

Banda won his appeal but was warned by Judge Doyle that he 'had come to the very brink of contempt'.

The Senior State Advocate said the Banda file had been returned to Cunningham in good time.

Cunningham said that was a lie.

Ian Hamilton - who I had not noticed lurking in the wings - thereupon left Zambia having been sacked as State Advocate after expressing concern in Lusaka High Court about the police raid on Cunningham's office. (I had only known Hamilton as the law student who had helped steal the Stone of Scone 17 years earlier, one of the 3 Scottish Nationalists). A detention order was made against Ottino for refusing to submit himself to an immigration examination but that was then revoked and he left for Rhodesia with his girlfriend.

And within a day or two Cunningham and his wife were also in Rhodesia, having been made prohibited immigrants in Zambia.

All this from an out of date turkey and a very young wife, who may have been inexperienced enough not to realise the consequences of her complaint. Or was it? What no one seemed interested in asking was How Many of the initial 15 left over turkeys were fit or unfit for consumption? According to the beginning of the saga, Mr Ottino had given away 15 left over Christmas turkeys - no one ever tracked down the other 14 turkeys and their recipients. There was much more to this story, there was more activity behind the scenes - and I wonder if anyone ate a gifted turkey but thought it wiser to say nothing?

But there was not much time to ponder on these events as both school and my two children took up most of my time. In addition, there were more functions to attend with Andrew.

The first American-built £82,000 diesel loco for Zambia Railways arrived and there was a special reception at Lusaka station where Vice President Kamanga and Minister of Transport Kalulu were at the controls for a ten metre drive into the station. Andrew, as Permanent Secretary, and I were among the guests of honour on the platform and we watched with pride as the sleek silver painted loco slid into the station. Stripes in the Zambian national colours of red, green, black and copper were painted along its side and it pulled 12 new Japanese waggons proudly emblazoned with ZR.

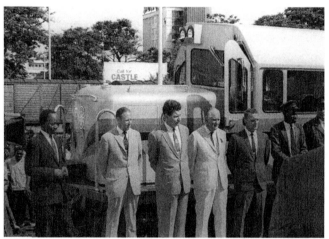

The first diesel loco arriving in Lusaka.
Andrew far left next to Frank Luccarotti

I sat with Siew Lim, wife of the general manager of Zambia Railways, Frank Luccarotti watching the ceremony. The station was gaily decked out in bunting and I watched with Ceri on my lap as Andrew performed the introductions along the line of dignitaries and thought that soon the railways would be running efficiently again when the other 25 ordered locos arrived.

Sometime later the Luccarottis invited us to dinner asking if we'd like a traditional Chinese meal. This sounded too good to miss. The starter was a melt in the mouth moment, followed by another. And yet another gastronomic delight and then another. As each course was presented we ate with enthusiasm and appreciation – absolutely wonderful. But as course followed course our appetites and commitment began to flag – but how could one let down one's hosts? At last they took pity on us and explained tradition demanded that as long as we ate they had to produce another dish.

The new Parliament building was opened with guests from a score of nations. Speaker Wesley Nyirenda welcomed President Kaunda dressed in a purple toga as tribal dancers performed on the lawns outside. The Zambia Air Force flew over and there was a 21 gun salute. In front of animal skins clad Angoni dancers and masked Nyau dancers, Kaunda gave a short speech in French - for the benefit of some VIP's I suppose - and was presented with a ceremonial key.

I had risen to the occasion in a white hat (lent by Renate) and enjoyed the ceremonial. The outside of the building was impressive with its copper sheathing on the walls, donated by Anglo Americana and RST - worth at that time £6500. Inside was well-designed and impressive. I recall huge elephant tusks arching up and over the President's seat.

Leaving home ready for the State Opening of Parliament

235

New buildings began to rise above the sky line, new office blocks proliferated until both sides of Cairo Road began to look like a real city centre and not some half developed town out in the Wild West. Some of the wonderful mature jacaranda trees vanished from the open spaces, although enough remained to give the city centre its vivid purple patches when the October heat was at its greatest. To my disappointment the tiny colonial style building, which had been the original Boma and then a Police Museum, was replaced by a multi storey department store - Mwaiseni. This store had the first escalator in Lusaka and while it was a great attraction to the young it was a great tribulation to older people or those from a village. Many have stood at its foot shaking their heads, wanting to try this new-fangled idea but hesitating to take the first step until given a helping push or pull from understanding hands. I had just hoped that the original Boma building could have been preserved as a historical site.

The library remained the same size but the block of public toilets by the market on Livingstone(sorry, Cha Cha Cha) Road were now labelled Men and Women.

No longer did we have to pause before

| European Men | Asian Men | African Men |
| European Women | Asian Women | African Women |

And remember which we were.

When integration began to be very much the topic of the day I recall a cartoon in a paper (I think the African Mail) by a schoolboy which 'solved the problem of the multi-racial toilets'. The clever lad submitted a plan for a conventional lavatory with a fitting of several seats, each conveniently labelled with sex and race - we could all now use the same lavatory but would not have to sit on the same seat.

Names were being changed as fast as possible, Cairo Road could only remain Cairo Road as it was still part of the long dreamed of Cape to Cairo route. But Livingstone Road became Cha Cha Cha Road and Stanley Road became Freedom Way. Understandable, perhaps, that some people wished to obliterate reminders of the colonial past - but I thought how sad to try to deny that Livingstone and Stanley had had links with this part of the world. I thought it would have been far better to give new names to new places or roads as they were built and so we could have reminders of our history as it had developed. And if the new developments were bigger and better than what had gone before .... then it would reflect even more to our credit.

'OK, my son, see how all these street names are from English counties/towns and are from the colonial era - and now look, here are streets we have built with the names of our indigenous flowers or trees or heroes'. Sometimes the name changes went a little astray, the Fairway by the golf course became Busuma Road, which is a literal translation. Old names and buildings began to disappear and soon little of the original central town layout will be identifiable.

But even as the city grew and expanded the African bush was not far away. In May, an armed Harry Franklin spent a night up a tree overlooking a small kraal, watching for two lions reported near Bauleni compound on the edge of Kabulonga.

As towns grew larger and the urban sprawl spread I thought how we would lose a lot of character in our lives. Bancroft Golf Club would no longer require their very individual rule whereby players were allowed to lift golf balls out of hippo spoor. On the other hand, they would be less likely to face the hazards of live crocodiles on the fairway, two golfers had to beat a six foot crocodile to death with their clubs after it attacked them on the course during this period.

Perhaps we did have a rather down to earth life style - why else would Ali Simbule, High Commissioner designate, feel free to call Britain a toothless bulldog wagging its tail in front of Ian Smith? It did little to endear him in international diplomatic circles and he was not confirmed in his appointment for quite some weeks. We did continue to have problems with thefts and burglaries which were on the increase as more unemployed flocked to the towns and found the streets were not paved with gold - many were not paved with anything at all actually. We certainly continued to have problems with UNIP youths, who were fired with political enthusiasm but had nowhere to direct their energies. As a result they constantly harassed girls for wearing mini-skirts or using skin lightening face creams (unfortunately there was still a mistaken desire to have a lighter skin and quite harmful creams were used). People were stopped and asked to produce a Party card. Failure to do so, meant being prevented from riding on a bus or buying in a shop or market. In short, the youths may have been well meaning but their energies were not well channelled.

But we could also well do without the Editorial which appeared in Britain's Daily Telegraph stating that 'a deterioration in race relations first showed in labour unrest, increased lawlessness with assault and robbery in European residential districts and victimisation of those whose presence or behaviour offended the ruling group ... spy fever is a second product of inter-racial tension ... at present 7 Europeans are in Zambian detention, 4 of whom are British. None of those held in camps are yet to be brought up in court. Access to them by the British High Commission has been difficult ...'

This referred to several Europeans held in Mumbwa prison. It was believed by early newspaper reports that they posted letters to small town newspapers in UK attacking British and Zambian policies on Rhodesia. It was believed the letters were often prepared in Rhodesia and then smuggled into Zambia to be posted.

Then it was reported that Swift, a quantity surveyor, Lt Col Arnott, a Kitwe Mines personnel manager, Nursteen, a company manager and Capt Warren, a pilot in the Mines Air Service, were accused of being members of the organisation which was alleged to have supplied information to the illegal Smith regime and to have tried to spread alarming statements inside and outside Zambia.

Then 3 self-confessed agents of spying for Rhodesia Swift, Morley and Shepherd left Zambia for UK.

Doreen Fleming, who was arrested in May, was later released

and was then deported with 14 other Europeans and declared prohibited immigrants. I never knew precisely what information they were supposed to have passed on to Rhodesia or what rumours they were supposed to have spread, but either one had to believe the Government was acting in our best interests or ... what else could one believe?

Labour unrest was to be expected when one race had enjoyed a far better style of living than another. Once independence was achieved most Africans expected to enjoy a more equal standard of living without realising that it could not happen at the stroke of a pen overnight. There were going to be more robberies in European residential districts as more people flocked to the towns and, failing to achieve their material wants by honest labour, would turn to taking from the apparently wealthy - as Europeans were in comparison. And it was a matter of comparison.

As for victimisation of those whose behaviour offended the ruling group - if that is true - it is not acceptable, but where did one draw the line between behaviour offending and behaviour likely to cause harm?

It was perhaps easy to cause offence without intent. Andrew Mutemba, Minister of State for Western Province, said that European and Asian members of UNIP must attend rallies, holding a Party card was not enough. I suppose that many of those he mentioned had bought Party cards because they thought they ought to be able to produce them when required. And perhaps they were quite prepared to contribute to the Party coffers in that way. But once Africans had won independence Europeans probably felt that they had little or no say in running the country, being in the unpopular minority. And the long drawn out political rallies would consume time they could not afford. They would not have attended long political rallies when they were in power and were likely to be even less interested now.

I doubt if any Africans really understood that gap in culture - for it was not only a political difference - Africans are content, nay, enjoy, long-winded speeches and rhetoric and the European is more desirous of saying his bit and then getting on with the job. (Now I shall be accused of a generalisation - but there is a strong element of truth there).

However, in comparison with other parts of Africa we were not doing too badly. Nigeria was in a state of emergency and Colonel Ojukwu and Biafra were tragically in the headlines. In the Congo the troops were fighting in the streets and the border between our two countries was sealed - shortly afterwards refugees began to fly in.

Our greatest problems continued to be that of getting supplies into our landlocked country. Things were not too bad but different goods were scarce from time to time and local stores would complain that they were starved of goods and were out of stock of 40% of their usual goods.

Work had begun on an oil pipeline from Dar es Salaam to Ndola and we all looked forward to the day when it was functioning. The new airport had opened and as time went on the importation of goods through the new routes would settle into a more organised routine.

We had other things to worry about at home. In 1967 Ceri was four years old and as her bouts of tonsillitis continued with depressing regularity and her resistance to penicillin increased we were advised that she should have her tonsils removed. What an ordeal for a four year old to face.

Fortunately the operation went very well and she was kept sedated for the first twenty four hours when the discomfort was at its greatest. We went in at visiting time and sat beside the sleeping child while I held back my tears. She was allowed home within a few days and while appearing quite well, did not want to eat at all - understandably. When I had mentioned giving her plenty of soft foods and ice creams I had been horrified to hear the surgeon say I should make her eat dry toast. I stared at him but he insisted that the modern view was that toast scraped the throat clean while ice cream would clog up the sore area. I could see the sense behind all this but my heart quailed at the thought of making Ceri eat dry toast. Once home she ate as little as possible and I thought we were making very slow progress. However Zulu took matters into his own hands and appeared one meal time with a plate of specially prepared chips.

'This is for the little Madam, she not eating nicely.'

He then proceeded to stand by her chair while she tried to eat a chip to please him. Once it was down her face brightened and down went another chip and another until at last she was swallowing without that look of apprehension and fear which had so wrung my heart.

Zulu left the dining room later with an empty plate and an I-told-you-so look, convinced that he alone was responsible for her recovery.

Zulu took a very personal interest in both Ceri and Simon and nothing was too much trouble where they were concerned. He was always impressed with their conversations and activities and his praise and interest were always sought by them. In his eyes the little Madam and the little Bwana could do no wrong.

Picnic at Kafue River with the Proctors

We enjoyed many weekends with our close friends the Proctors at Mount Makulu and some weekends saw us picnicking on the banks of the Kafue River, a popular spot. Andrew usually produced a newspaper at some point and he and Dennis enjoyed many discussions on agricultural developments. Renate and I will never forget walking down to the bridge where we could buy water melons etc. One memorable occasion a few years later we happily returned with huge specimens, only to be criticised for paying the princely sum of 45ngwee.

JOAN'S VISIT 1967

In August we were expecting Joan Chesher to arrive from England via Nairobi. Joan had been a fellow student at teacher training college and we were looking forward to this reunion. I answered many questions about what clothes to bring and what precautions to take with vaccines and malaria pills. My firmest and clearest advice was about clothes, no problems there. Dress as for an English summer with a cardigan because it will be the cold season. Dress as for an English summer - except there is guaranteed to be no rain. It will not rain again until November. Famous last words!

As Joan stepped off the plane one of those very rare storms which can appear from nowhere and just as rapidly vanish, swept across the runway. One of those storms which MIGHT happen just once in a dry season and it had to happen as Joan landed.

Until then my mind had been happily preoccupied with how impressive our new airport would look to Joan flying on from Nairobi which had, I knew, still the small colonial style airport. It was attractive in its way (as our little old airport had been) but it was not as sleek and modern and impressive as Lusaka airport.

I was remembering the many hours I had tramped around the site and buildings as it was built. As Andrew was Perm. Sec. in Transport and Works he had delighted in inspecting developments every Sunday morning. I had waded through many a square acre of mud and clambered over many a pile of half-completed building, weekend after weekend, and was on very intimate terms indeed with all the layout and facilities. It had been every exciting to watch the huge complex rise from a patch of bush and then commence operations.

People had come through arrivals in large and small groups, been greeted by friends and wandered off and I began to realise that the arrivals had dribbled to a halt. Had she missed the flight? But here was Joan coming through the arrivals gate at last and looking very bemused.

'You took ages,' I said. 'What on earth were you doing?'

'Having an argument with the man on immigration,' she muttered. 'He was not going to let me come into the country. He asked me how much money I had and said that it was not enough and that I would have to return to UK immediately. I argued that I would not need much money because I was staying with friends. He was very uncooperative and asked who these friends were and where did they live and started writing down your name, then he stopped and said,

'Is that Mr Andrew Kashita? WHY didn't you say so? And after that he couldn't get me through fast enough. I began to feel like a VIP.'

Then she looked down at her wet feet and began to tease me about the 'no rain until November'.

Andrew was away on business so Joan and I reminisced over college days to our hearts content. The first night Joan was talking about preconceived notions of Africa and how relieved she had been not to come across any large insects or creepy crawlies.

'And any large animals or snakes are more than likely to want to make off in the opposite direction if only you will give them the chance,' I added. Ceri, taking an active interest in the conversation, understood that Joan wanted to see some insect life, so with great consideration she moved a picture on the wall and said, 'Look Joan.'

As an enormous spider predictably sped across the wall to hide behind the next picture, Joan missed the ceiling by a very short margin which impressed Ceri no end.

'Do you want to see another one?'

Joan accepted my explanation that these particular spiders were impossible to banish and were completely harmless except to mosquitoes, for which reason I was more than happy to give them house room. She nodded understandingly but I have a strong suspicion that all the pictures in her room were removed from the wall every night. I told her about the rain spiders which were a very different kettle of fish, but which she would not see at all because, as their name suggests, they are only seen in the rainy season.

'SO? You said that it would not rain until November and look what happened when we landed at the airport today!' protested Joan rather uncharitably. 'But go on, tell me some more of the horrors I am to expect.'

Rain spiders are more revolting members of the spider family, they are large and they are hairy, they appear in the rains and they speed across the floor with long outstretched forelegs in a manner which even I found disconcerting, even a bit threatening. Joan shuddered.

'But they only run about the floor and will never climb up walls or up on to furniture, so I usually sit with my feet up in the evenings if I have seen one about – you only see them in the evenings.'

Joan's face brightened.

'At least that's what Andrew told me', I continued brutally. 'But one night when he was out playing badminton and I was tucked up in bed with a book - it was just after the jaundice - and with the mosquito net let down round the bed, I suddenly was aware that I could hear a scratching noise - '

'Don't go on!'

'And when I looked over my shoulder the biggest rain spider I had ever seen had climbed up inside the net and was advancing across the pillow.'

Joan's face was a picture.

Apart from the spiders Joan thoroughly enjoyed her visit and one of the high spots of the holiday was a trip to Livingstone. I let down the back seat to make a flat area and we packed Ceri and Simon in the back of the car with the luggage and a few toys on a spread out travelling rug - no seat belts in those days. It was my first long drive and I hoped we would have no punctures.

Just before we set off Joan asked if she should take care of the map book, looking a bit disconcerted when I said I hadn't one, we would just drive south on the road until we reached Livingstone. A mere matter of 300 miles. Joan sat back to enjoy the passing scenery and the children were quiet in the back. Too quiet. When we looked Ceri was looking at a book, Simon had pulled a toilet roll from a bag and was solemnly unrolling it. He was already festooned in swathes of pink paper. However he was quiet so we left well alone. That toilet roll kept him happy all the way to Livingstone. We had to stop for petrol a couple of times, but after leaving Lusaka early in the morning we were descending into the Zambezi Valley in the afternoon.

When we had set off Joan had asked about the route, clearly still concerned she had no map.

'We just follow the road south and turn right after the turning to Kariba.'

'And then?'

'Just follow the road until we hit Livingstone.'

We agreed navigating in Africa is much easier than in UK. On the last stages of the journey as we descended towards Livingstone we could see in the distance, before we could actually see Livingstone itself, a cloud of 'smoke' on the horizon. Although we knew it was not smoke but the spray from the Falls. Guide books said that the spray could be seen for many miles but it was still a surprise and an awesome sight.

Livingstone was all that Joan hoped for, and more. I think it always is. Visitors for the first time are always enthralled not only by its majestic panorama but also by the totally unspoilt beauty of it all. We stayed at the North Western Hotel, which was run by a Mrs Rose Hitchins and was in the town itself and was a wonderful example of old Colonial style architecture. After the drive we were glad to relax with a drink and let the children play on the verandah. Once we had all recovered we made our first visit to the Falls, as I drove down the road waited for Joan's reaction to the one and only road sign.

Quite simply it is a large black hippo on the usual yellow background.

'Oh. So we might see some hippo?'

'We might. The sign is there really to warn drivers to take care because this is one of their favourite crossing places at night when they come out of the river to feed.'

Silence and a disbelieving look.

Road sign on the way to the Falls

A few years later I sent Joan a cutting from the newspaper describing how an American man and Finnish woman had burnt to death when their car blew up following a collision with a hippo on the Victoria Falls road. The accident happened only yards from the hippo sign.

The Falls are hidden by the trees but the spray and thunder of the tumbling water is omnipresent. I parked the car under some trees. Joan watched as I meticulously wound up and locked all the windows.

'You are suspicious.'

'No, the baboons, which live here, will strip your car of every moveable item.'

We walked through the trees, past the statue of David Livingstone to stand at the water's edge. We stood in silence as everyone does at their first glimpse of this magnificent sight. The broad and mighty Zambezi, the massive volume of water falling over into the chasm below, the clouds of spray rising, falling, rising again incessantly above it - all have been described so often. There are figures available for the width of the river at this point, the number of gallons of water pouring over per second, the depth of the Falls, the height of the spray - the sheer figures are overwhelming and all irrelevant because they are totally forgotten as you stand there completely mesmerised.

It is difficult to make up your mind which is the best viewpoint - standing at the edge of the Falls, walking through the rain forest which clings to the cliffs opposite the lip of the Falls or on one of the paths which wind tortuously above the zigzag bends of the river far below. We wandered along, stopping every few yards to gaze at yet another spectacle. Ceri, for once, kept close beside us instead of dancing ahead and Simon, in my arms, grabbed at the wet sprays of leaves which brushed our shoulders.

Finally we tore ourselves away, went back to the hotel for dinner and put the children to bed. Later we sat with drinks on the verandah, Mrs Hitchins wandered over to ask if we were going to see the Falls by moonlight.

'It's a must. I'll lend you a torch and one of the 'boys' can keep an eye on the children.'

As the children slept like logs once they were asleep we had no hesitation in accepting this offer. Back down to the Falls under the black velvet sky, spangled so heavily with its brilliant stars that I would live in Africa for the night sky alone.

'Remember that hippo road sign,' whispered Joan.

'Why are you whispering?'

'Don't know. The night just makes you feel like that.'

'Thought you were afraid a hippo might hear you!'

Now we had to pick our way more cautiously along the winding paths as they were hardly indistinguishable from the grassed area, which is so bare in the dry season; we were thankful for the stones with which the paths had been laboriously edged.

The torchlight picked out the white foam masses at the edge of the Falls and shone on the wet rocks jutting above the waters. I switched off the light and we stood imagining we were the first people to wander this way. In spite of the numbers of visitors always at the Falls, it never fails to amaze me how easily you can imagine yourself completely alone. The whole area is so immense that any crowds fade into the background or are lost among the trees. And no sound can ever carry above the never ending roar and thunder, even in the early rainy season when the river is at its lowest.

We had seen it in daylight and at night. Next of course, was dawn when the river first emerges into light and the sun's first rays colour the water with rainbows.

We stayed in Livingstone a few days, going to see the museum where there were excellent displays of tribal artefacts telling much of Zambia's history. Here too was the skull of 'Broken Hill man', found near Broken Hill (now Kabwe) in 1921 and dated at between 300,000 and 125,000 years old.

We drove up the narrow winding dirt road to the look-out tree, an immense baobab where, with great inspiration, someone had built a look out platform high in the tree. From there we had a superb view of the Falls and river.

A visit to the Game Park was another 'must'. We knew it would be best to go very early in the morning so that we could hope to see the animals feeding before the heat of the day drove them into the shade of the trees and tall grasses. So, off before breakfast and into the Game Park. Almost immediately we had our first sight of a large sable antelope, which stood by the road with its head poised.

'It's posing,' whispered Joan as she rapidly focused her camera.

The sable bounded away at the first click as though indeed it had intended to give us the chance of one perfect shot.

After that I slowly followed the narrow winding dirt road, drawing to a halt each time we spotted an animal. It was growing lighter now and the sun was brightening the tops of the grasses, the fresh clear smell of dawn was fading, soon the warm smell of dust would cover all.

Joan said softly, 'Look over there. A signpost. Have we missed something?'

So I drove towards the signpost sticking up above the heavy headed grasses at the next bend in the road. As we drew nearer the 'signpost' turned and two large dark eyes looked at us in surprise, then the giraffe got awkwardly to its feet and moved off.

The car stalled as we dissolved into helpless giggles.

Not only was Joan taking photos of everything that was new and unusual she had also brought a cine camera. Back in Lusaka we drove up and down Independence Avenue several times while she filmed the 'musical policeman'. At the junction of Burma Road and Independence Avenue there is now a set of traffic lights and very necessary they are too. But in 1967 a policeman did a little duty at peak hours. One particular chap was a joy to behold. Immaculate in his stiffly starched khaki, he stood at the crossroads. Then as he went into motion he literally appeared to be poised delicately on the tips of his hefty black boots and his hands waved on or halted traffic with the most graceful of movements surely ever seen outside Saddler Wells Ballet. I say waved on or halted, but it would be more accurate to say that the traffic flowed across that junction as though wired to his white gloved finger tips. As I drove up and down Independence Avenue Joan, at first, tried to film him through the windscreen and then, fearing that she might not be doing this unique traffic control full justice, she began to hang out of the side window. We were rewarded with a particularly eloquent flow of arm and hand follow through and a hearty smile on our last trip.

After Livingstone we had to include another tourist attraction and made plans to go to Kariba Dam. This was a day trip and a blinding hot day as I recall. After UDI of course, border points were delicate areas but we thought it would be worth going down to see the dam and we had been told that we would be able to walk to the border point halfway across the dam itself. We left Ceri and Simon with Zulu and his wife and set off. It was an uneventful drive and once we had parked the car, we strolled on the top of the dam wall. Lake Kariba stretched away into the distance as far as the eye could see, as we walked in the dazzling sunlight I told Joan all I could remember about the building of the dam and 'operation Noah' when marooned wild life had been rescued in a massive operation largely manned by the army. We were nearly halfway across the dam by then, and very close to a lone Rhodesian soldier standing on guard, rifle at the ready.

Kariba dam

Suddenly there was a jeep racing down from the Rhodesian side and across the dam wall towards us. Joan and I looked at each other, we looked back at the Zambian side and how far away it seemed. The jeep screeched to a halt and a soldier leaped out, marched smartly up to the chap on guard - and handed him an ice lolly!

He leapt back into the jeep and roared back across the dam wall. The soldier leant his rifle against the parapet and sucked heartily on his lolly.

After Livingstone and Kariba, Joan enjoyed the shopping trips into Lusaka far more than I had expected.

'You have got so used to living here,' she said. 'You are taking it for granted that you will be able to park outside each store, that someone is going to pack your goods for you and carry it to the car for you - and could I keep that receipt for that meat you have just bought? No one back home is going to believe that you bought that huge piece of sirloin and the chops and all the other meat for only 17/6d. And look how many different people and life styles you see all around you all the time, and everyone is so relaxed and friendly. Nobody seems to find anyone else unusual.'

I looked around and admitted she was right.

I no longer noticed three women, babies tucked up on their backs in lengths of chitenge, sitting on the edge of the pavement surrounded by bundles of shopping, cheerfully comparing two items, a smartly dressed couple gazing into a window ... a barefoot boy carrying a box of vegetables for sale ... two women strolling along talking rapidly, one gesturing expressively and a baby suckling at one breast watching the scene with wide dark eyes .... two businessmen in dark suits and carrying briefcases crossed the road ... a woman in a brightly coloured sari got out of a car and entered an office block ... an elderly man, wrinkled and brown from long exposure to the sun, faded trousers held up by a broad leather belt and a faded trilby squarely on his head, leaned on a battered Land Rover piled high with rolls of wire netting, bags of chicken feed and fence poles, talking to one of his farm hands. A couple of white women with sun bleached hair and crisp pastel dresses came out of the store followed by an assistant with a box of groceries, one unlocked the car and gave the man a coin after he had put the box in the boot, all without pausing in the conversation. Several barefoot boys in ragged shirts and shorts strolled along scuffling their calloused feet in the dust. A man walked in front of his wife who balanced a large bundle on her head, the baby on her back was asleep, its head nodding rhythmically as it lolled from the chitenge cloth (traditional cotton print).

This was my every day scene in town and I had forgotten it would strike Joan as unusual.

Before she left we had one important job to do. She had admired a silver bracelet I wore and was keen to find another one. She did not expect me to drive her out of town into one of the shanty compounds. It was a long time since I had been there and we had to stop twice while I asked passers-by for directions. But it was not long before I found the house I was looking for. Then, to Joan's astonishment, we sat on an upturned Fanta box to watch a man finish working on a bracelet which she then bought.

'If you had told me that he worked with a small hammer, a 6 inch nail and a large flat stone I would not have believed you.'

'And if you had come next year we would not have been able to watch him, he was telling me that it is becoming difficult to obtain local silver.'

It was a pity Joan had arrived too late for the Agricultural Show. I told her how the highlight of the show that year had been Jonah the Whale. I forget now what sort of whale it was but I believe it had been caught off the South African coast and was then preserved with a chemical preservation technique with the blood exchanged for a formaldehyde solution. Quite a bit of excitement had been engendered by the news that a real whale would be at the Show and we were kept in touch with its progress as it travelled up from the south. At one point it looked as though we were going to be disappointed when the trailer carrying Jonah slipped and was overhanging the escarpment road in a perilous position 22 miles south of Chirundu, effectively blocking the road and communications between Zambia and Salisbury for some time. Fortunately all was well in the end. Our greatest laugh came when we took Zulu and his family to the Show and later asked him what he thought of the whale.

'Ah, it is no good. You could not buy any.'

Zulu had been anticipating buying a large slice of the wonder fish ... there was no point at all in catching such a super-sized fish and then NOT eating it!

All too soon Joan's holiday came to an end and she left loaded with souvenirs and many rolls of film.

I think her only disappointments had been the same ones I had felt when I first arrived in Zambia. She had expected to find a new style of cuisine and the local nsima (maize porridge) and relish held no great charms for either of us. And now Zambia sported a so called national dress but as it had made its appearance as late as independence it did not warrant much excitement either. I told her that my mother in law had said that the only genuine national dress that she could remember was the piece of bark cloth with which people used to 'dress' themselves. Nowadays we could not find anyone who could or would make bark cloth much less wear it, and the lengths of chitenge on sale for 'national dress' were imported and had Java Print firmly printed all down the edges.

LIFE GOES ON September 1967

I wondered if the building of a textile factory at Kafue would have any effect on the local market, would we get locally designed material? The contract for the building of the factory had been given to Solel Boneh, an Israeli firm, and I wondered whether it would make any difference to the local cotton market once the factory was in production. Cotton could be grown most successfully in Zambia but we had already seen the President giving an example in the cotton fields with little response. So now the Government was using valuable foreign exchange to buy cotton picking machines 'because of the shortage of labour'. This in a country where it was said that only about one twelfth of the population was in paid employment.

Later that year Andrew's parents came to visit us again, they wanted to see the new grandson. I hoped Simon would be as welcome as Ceri, although he was no darker! This time however, if father in law had any grumbles about his light skinned grandchildren, he kept them to himself.

He was not a well man and after a short while he was admitted to Lusaka hospital. As Andrew was always busy I took mother in law to the hospital in the afternoons. Our first visit was not altogether a success. We walked into the main building and checking the boards I saw that we had to go to the third floor. I urged mother in law towards the lift and pressed the button. Within moments the lift door opened and I stepped inside. Mother in law remained firmly outside. I beckoned. She shook her head. I tried to pull her in but she stepped crossly back saying something in Bemba which of course I could not understand. At which point the lift doors closed and I shot off to the third floor. Patiently I pressed the button and descended again. I stepped out to find her waiting with a cross face. Again she refused to enter the lift so we trudged up flights of stairs and made our visit. Back down all the stairs and back home.

When Andrew came home he was regaled with an animated account of our visit, after which he turned to me and said,

'Mother wants to know why you kept trying to make her go into that little empty room, she could see my father was not in there.'

I explained about the lift.

He tried to explain to his mother how the lift would have taken us up to the right floor but she could not understand the concept of a tiny room moving up and down inside a building and in fact flatly refused to believe that I had been up in it and come down again.

On later visits Andrew also tried to take her up in the lift but it was more than she could cope with. We were all quite glad when the old man was allowed home again. He was content to sit quietly in the garden watching the children playing under the watchful eye of Titanbenji, who now worked part time as a Nanny. Sometimes I took mother in law into town or to visit relatives and once I took her 'sightseeing'. As that included a visit to house number 394 Chilenje which had just been declared

254

a national monument because it was the house in which the Kaunda family had lived whilst he waged the battle for freedom, she soon declared she had had enough. She thought it was very interesting to see where the President had lived but that it was a waste for it to stand empty when another family could have been housed in it.

As always they made sure of leaving before the start of the rainy season.

It was not long since we had sat on Lusaka railway station and thought that with the arrival of the diesel locomotives transport in Zambia was entering a new era. It was. The era of how quickly and in how diverse a manner diesel locos can be wrecked. Andrew was on the Commission of Inquiry headed by Mr Justice Dole after a train was derailed between Kitwe and Ndola at an estimated cost of £100,000 but before they could make any recommendations another locomotive crashed into a steam engine train on the Kaniki siding killing seven people. The driver in the latter incident claimed his brakes had failed. I forget the excuses and reasons given in subsequent crashes, accidents and various derailments. Many were eventually reduced to a simple case of drunkenness. Simple but expensive.

We moved into 1968 with the birth of Zambia Airways on the first of January and the return of Ali Simbule as High Commissioner from London. Elias Chipimo replaced him in his post, a man renowned for his long speeches (and driving at high speed on dirt roads!) but not one likely to refer to England as a toothless bulldog .

Kaunda's concern about the apathy and laziness of the average Zambian was being echoed by other leaders. Simon Kapwepwe, the Deputy Head of State, made a hard hitting speech.

'Zambians will face unemployment in two years if this laziness continues among workers .... some Zambians refuse to accept supervision from fellow Zambians. This is, in short, a colonial mentality and irresponsibility in the first degree ... unless we work harder to increase the economic production we won't have a surplus to export to bring more money into the country. This in turn, means that we will not be able to invest in local new projects, which will demand employment of people, thereby causing unemployment.'

Solomon Kalulu, made another of his surprise visits to the railway marshalling yards in Lusaka where he found a number of workers sitting around doing nothing, prompting one of his pithy comments.

'The voice on promotions and better pay is louder than the output,'

It was reported from the mines that miners were to be found asleep on duty, drunkenness and abusive language were common and the expatriate miners were unsure when they would be Zambianised and being so frustrated, took little interest in their work.

Before we had time to register this dismal news, worse was to come. The heavy rains and constant pounding by huge lorries meant that the Hell Run, on which we relied for our fuel supplies, became a quagmire and more than lived up to its name. Suddenly the petrol was rationed to 5 gallons a month, which was depressing after supplies had been built up so well that we had actually had regular petrol derationed. Bob Yates, the transport controller in the Ministry of Transport and Works, returned to make a full report of the conditions he had experienced.

Before he could even make his report, copper production had to be slashed because of the fuel shortage. We were treated to pictures and reports of up to 500 trucks at a time bogged down in a foot of mud on the Hell Run. The Government was pressed by an unresponsive workforce, fuel shortages, falling copper prices and the concern caused by what were reported to be Portuguese air attacks on 32 villages, killing 6 people. The attacks on the Barotse villages north west of Kalabo were not reported for some time as the investigating team from Mongu had to make a 90 mile journey by canoe. It was when I read reports like this that it really sank home how difficult it was to govern a country where distances and conditions were so large and diverse.

Kaunda then, rightly or wrongly, made an attempt to end what he termed the foreign domination of Zambia's economy and invited key companies to sell at least 51% of their enterprises to the Government. In his speech at Mulungushi he referred to it as Zambia's second revolution.

Perhaps it was viewed as a revolution abroad because copper share prices in London promptly slumped even further.

I guess there were many who knew nothing at all about copper share prices and at that time cared even less. The 16th January had been Decimalisation Day and D Day had really been a day to remember. Many renamed it Q Day as queues stretched out of the banks on to the streets, everyone eager to change their money. People were keen to change shillings and sixpences for the new decimal coins with their attractively designed faces.

The 1 ngwee had the ant bear
The 2 ngwee had a fish eagle in flight
The 5 ngwee and its morning glory
The 10 ngwee coin with the hornbill
And the shiny 20 ngwee with the oribi.

No one had expected such a rush as old men from the villages turned up with sacks of dirt encrusted coins dug up from their safe hiding places. Sadly many old and bewildered people were swindled by the smart 'townies', who offered to change their money for them, assuring them that the pound was now exchanged for a kwacha - not 2 kwacha!

The straightforward 2 kwacha for 1 pound was easy enough to convert but the 200 ngwee to 240 pennies was not so easy and quite a lot of profiteering went on in the markets, where the price of small items like boxes of matches was difficult to fix, particularly when an uneducated public were grappling with the new currency.

The old folk from the villages and the uneducated were always the first to suffer in change overs and one could not see that problem disappearing for some considerable time. Not every child got into primary school and perhaps even less than a third of those would be able to continue at secondary level. There were just not enough places.

Ceri started school in January 1968, she was five years old that month and as the school year started in January this was the start of her school days. I wondered what the situation would be like when she was due to leave primary school in seven years time. Would there be education for all?

First day!

I had enrolled her at Lusaka Infants School, not wishing her to attend a school where I was teaching. Lusaka Infants had been a European school but was now of course well integrated. It was a dull collection of prefabricated buildings, seven Grade 1 classrooms built round an oblong garden, shaded at one end by an enormous tree which spread its branches over a large open air stage. All the classrooms opened onto verandahs around the garden and one had a full view of the whole Grade 1 activities from the classroom door. Seven Grade 2 classrooms were built in a long line behind. After Grade 2 the pupils separated to attend the Boys and Girls Primary schools.

Ceri's uniform was a green and white check dress which had infuriated me (still very much a novice with the sewing machine) as I struggled with the square white edged neck and the puffed sleeves. As for the buttoned bodice which ended in an unsightly gap an inch above the navel … well! I had taken that apart several times and was relieved to find every other girl similarly exposed. There was a dark green cardigan for the cold season and a dark green felt panama hat, white socks and brown Clarks shoes. The boys fared better, they wore a grey safari suit - short sleeved, open necked and the shirt hanging outside the shorts - highly practical.

Each new child was to wear a large luggage label bearing his or her name and class colour (Ceri was in Grade 1 Yellow) - a great asset to teachers when 280 five year olds arrived on the same day (no such luxuries as classroom assistants or parent helpers! 280 five year olds arrived and seven teachers took charge).

As I had to be at my school by 7.30am I took Ceri to her classroom at 7.15 and left her there in her crisp new uniform with her new pencils in her satchel, de rigeur among primary pupils. A large label

CERI KASHITA Yellow 1

was tied firmly in her top button hole. I left her like a piece of luggage waiting for her teacher to arrive.

My new class kept my mind firmly occupied all morning and I had no time to think nostalgic thoughts about my daughter's first day at school. Mr Patel was very understanding, bless him, and suggested that I leave school as soon as my class was dismissed - Grade 1 pupils finished at 12 while older children continued until 12.45 . Remembering children crying on their first day at school in UK, as I reached Lusaka Infants I wondered if Ceri had cried on her first day at school. Some children would have already been collected so she would now be watching the door for me. Ceri was not watching the door, she was busy colouring a picture. I went in and introduced myself to the teacher, Mrs Bessie Frost.

'Ceri, Mummy is here ... SUCH a good little girl and SO sensible (sotto voce) ... pack your things away now Ceri. Mummy is waiting.'

'You have come too early,' said my loving offspring. 'I was going to help Mrs Frost put away the crayons in a little while.'

Thus began my daughter's love affair with her first teacher. It was only a matter of a few days before Bessie Frost was quoted as an authority on everything and we wavered between being heartily sick of the woman's name and thankfulness that Ceri was so happy.

Her first reading book was We Look And See, in the Happy Trio reading scheme, which she proudly brought home announcing that she was to read aloud to us every night. Andrew, all unaware of infant methods, was very impressed with this piece of information and settled back in his chair, agreeing that she should read to him every night after her bath. I don't think he had expected her to start with a page of Shakespeare, in fact he said afterwards that he had expected to hear a simplified version of some fairy tale. What he was not prepared for was

Oh

Oh look.

Oh look, look, look.

Look, Sally, look.

A glazed look of disbelief spread across his face, followed by a determined struggle for self-control. After she had gone to bed, homework was delegated to my department. I suggested he take over reading Simon his bedtime story but again, that was designated my department.

CHAPTER 6
ROMA
1968

We also moved house in 1968. As Andrew was now working permanently in town we felt that it would be more convenient to live nearer town. Although he had the use of a Government Mini, the petrol rationing had made life difficult, being 10 miles from Lusaka. So, just as the Natural Resources College was about to take shape on our doorstep, we planned to move away.

Roma township (as the suburbs were called) was on the town boundary so that we would both be nearer work places but would not be living right in town. We bought an empty two acre plot.

Roma was very pretty in that it was a slightly undulating area - most welcome in that very flat part of Zambia - and was more spread out than Chelston where most people had only a one acre plot. And the Government had built their houses on half acre plots.

We found a two acre plot on Kakola Road just off the main Roma road, which was lined with cassia trees and in season we drove under a ribbon of sweet scented yellow blossom.

Our plot was an almost bare two acres with a small cluster of thorn trees, a large bohenia, a huge avocado tree and a larger fig. We decided to put the house near the thorn trees, a pool slightly behind and to the right and the servants quarters at the end of the plot where the land sloped gradually down. It was a marvellous feeling to be starting from scratch and I decided I would like to design our own house. Andrew was most agreeable once he had seen my suggestions. However, as the City Council would not accept a plan from a mere lay person we had to get an architect to make out the plans professionally. This did not detract from my pleasure at the prospect of rooms laid out in the way I wanted, electric sockets in what I thought were sensible sites, ample cupboard space and so on.

The main slab was laid before Christmas 1967 and was then left

261

while the festive season with its compulsory builders' holiday went its way. This was a very sensible arrangement - it ensured that all the people in the building trade got a holiday. Relatives could be visited in villages over Christmas and the New Year and as heavy rains usually held up building work so much the better all round.

Once the holiday was over, work began in earnest. We had decided to 'do' our own thing with a vengeance. Not only had I drawn up the plans, we engaged our own labour and were going to build our own house. Andrew had the common sense to employ a foreman recommended by a friend but we knew that we would have to visit the site every day and deal with the arrangements and problems as they arose. Fortunately the foreman was as good as his references and all in all we had no serious setbacks. In fact the only real difficulty I recall was sometimes running out of bricks when the supplier let us down. As Andrew was still travelling frequently I had my hands full at times. There were mornings when I left Chelston with Ceri and Simon at 6am to go to the plot at Roma and check with the foreman the plans for the day. Then, went on to drop Ceri at her school, across town to drop Simon at his nursery and finally was in my school by 7.10. No wonder we are all still early risers!

After school finished I would reverse my route, having collected Simon and Ceri, we would stop off at the site on the way home for lunch - and as far as I can remember my only worry was running out of bricks and wondering at the vast quantities of 'brandlings' we used. To this day I don't know if that is the correct trade description of the long lengths of wood, measuring 2" by 2". But at times I wondered if we would end up with a log cabin.

At the end of the month pay day loomed large and the list of the men's names and their wages looked vague but it all seemed to go well - I even had the right amount of small change, something which had haunted me all the preceding night.

It was while Andrew was away on one of his trips - Italy I believe - that I found a letter from the village in the post box. I did not open it because his father usually wrote in Bemba. To my surprise there was another letter postmarked Kawambwa the next week. This was so unusual I did open the letters but apart from being able to pick out odd words here and there I was no wiser. But two letters together was so odd I drove over to the Mutales for help. The letters had been written by someone in the village for mother in law. Andrew's father was very ill.

At once I got the office to send off a Telex to Rome and I worked out how to get to the village, I knew I had to cross the Congo pedicle road but after that it all seemed very vague. Goodie and Mabel were most insistent I should not attempt the drive alone. Andrew arrived on the next flight and was able to hitch a lift on a Government flight to Northern Province within a few hours. Unfortunately as we had half expected it was all too late. Andrew was somewhat comforted by his mother saying his father was quite sure to the end that Andrew would come if it were possible and had in fact thought he could be out of the country. What was also distressing was the fact that Andrew's two brothers who lived on the Copperbelt were only a couple of days drive away from the village; they arrived after Andrew.

We asked his mother if she would like to come and live with us in town but although she appreciated the offer she said she would prefer to stay in the village where she knew everyone - but she would continue to visit us. We had been sending money to them every month but now we found that sometimes the letters did not arrive. So Andrew arranged for them to go to the post office at Mwense from where they could be collected.

I had wondered at one point whether my mother in law had refused our offer of a home because she did not want to live with a msungu (white person) but on a later visit I suggested we could build a small house for her on the plot, she smiled and said that while she was grateful for the offer she just did not like the idea of living in town and that she would miss the sight of the Luapula river.

Very good reasons indeed.

The house at Roma progressed steadily and we were able to move early in the year. A bungalow again, painted white inside and out, black tiled roof and a verandah as usual along the front. Four bedrooms and two bathrooms, a small breakfast room between the kitchen and dining room which also doubled as a playroom. The cook Zulu appreciated the large kitchen with its walk in larder and ironing room, which gave him ample working space.

We had planned much larger servants' quarters than usual. There were two rooms for Zulu and two for the gardener (he might marry) and with the unheard of luxury of a shared kitchen with running water, electric lights, a hot water geyser and a small woodstove. No more heating water or cooking over an open fire outside on the ground - although I found later that Titanbenji was often to be seen stirring a pot over a small fire in front of the house.

Andrew gave Zulu some fruit trees to plant when we planted ours but they never received much attention. This was fuel for all those arguments against the bettering of the lot of workers but we both felt that we had to make the effort to improve their conditions, but did not feel we had the right to stand over them and make them water fruit trees daily. But how else could a man and his family improve their living standards if we did not give them the opportunity? we were disappointed over and over again but could not have done otherwise. When we lived at Mount Makulu we had heard how Taffy Greatrix, the farm manager, had planted fruit trees for the workers in the compound and had been disgusted to find that first they were neglected but as soon as they did grow big enough to bear fruit, they were cut down for firewood.

Moving down to Roma was a more complicated affair as not only had our possessions grown but so had our livestock. The three baby rabbits given to Ceri when Simon was born, now numbered twenty three, this in spite of being regularly culled for the pot. Scraps had died and been replaced with the grey cat who merely answered to Puss. The dog Micky was still with us and very much in charge as before.

264

Andrew busy in the garden at Roma

The chickens were as much in evidence for their panic stricken squawks and clucks whenever there was a change in routine, so being loaded onto a lorry did little for their peace of mind. The ducks were more matter of fact, squatting comfortably to await developments.

All we had to do was load everything on to the lorry loaned from the office, secure in the knowledge that we were sure of a dry day, and unload at the other end. Ceri and Simon spent most of the day on the piles of sand left behind by the builders, the dog and cat sat in sulky silence in a locked bedroom until everything was unloaded. Zulu was in raptures over the new kitchen and made regular sorties over to his quarters to tell his wife of every new discovery until I told him to take her on a guided tour of the whole house and then perhaps we could concentrate on getting the boxes unpacked.

Titanbenji then returned to her domain and harried Banda, the garden boy, into moving their belongings from A to B and back again. Although he had his own rooms, she left him in no doubt that she was really in charge and he swept and carried as she hurried him to and fro. (I said Banda was our garden boy – a term considered derogatory when used of servants, but Banda was then still but of boy of about 15 years).

Zulu and Titanbenji outside their new house in Roma

We expanded our pets in Roma, Micky was a mature dog by this time so we decided to invest in another rescue dog to keep him company and be more of a guard dog as he aged. Off to the dog pound and back with Candy, a cross Great Dane and ? unknown, who had been found living wild in the bush and who had kept body and soul together by catching and eating grasshoppers among other things, she never lost the taste for them.

Moving into a house meant there would be hopeful workers appearing at the gate from the moment our lorry turned into the drive. They ranged from out of work cooks with such glowing references that one wondered how they had avoided being snapped up, to gardeners with references which tried to highlight any asset - obviously a willing worker with little experience. And sadly, the young hopefuls who had left school with perhaps only a Grade 4 and now due to the shortage of school places were dumped on the jobs market to find any work they could. I hated to see yet another man at the door with or without his grimy papers dog-eared from much handling. On the other hand I could not bear the curt PALIBE NCITO (No Work) sign on the gate. It looked so cold and uncaring. But was it also wrong to greet each and every man and read through his references when the best I could tell him was that I did not have a job nor could I think of someone to whom I could recommend him? Perhaps the willingness to exchange a greeting and listen to his hopes lightened his heart a little on what appeared to be a daily round in the residential areas.

Having moved on to a virgin bit of land we did need more, if only temporary, labour and so for a short while we had several lads clearing ground and planting couch grass to make lawns. A boring and monotonous job but which at least put some money in their tattered pockets. Among these boys Banda was much to be envied, he had a permanent job, a place in which to live and some ground to cultivate if he wished. All at the age of 15. Banda would indeed have been a happy lad if it were not for his eye which was making no progress whatsoever, despite his trips to the clinic.

One day when Stella Shamwana came for coffee I thought to ask her to have a look at Banda's eye. Being a former Sister at the Middlesex Hospital she kept a non-committal face while talking to him but once he had gone off she advised me to get him to a specialist because she was sure it was a growth and needed more than the pills which the clinic was doling out and which looked just like aspirin.

The aspirin may well have been useless but was better than the local remedies in the Luapula Valley where one in every two hundred was blind due to a lack of vitamin A in their diet in an area infested by tsetse fly. Two common remedies there used by witch doctors were either to urinate in a hollowed out root which was then shaken and used as an eye drop or mpirimpiri - hot peppers - which were used as an eye wash.

Lusaka - and Zambia - was extraordinarily fortunate at that time to still have the services of a Mr Phillips, eye specialist at the Lusaka hospital. Phillips was the eye man to end all eye men and was reputed to be able to demand his price anywhere in the world. Fortunately for us, he had been in Zambia for many years, liked it and had no desire to go anywhere else. It did not take long for us to arrange an appointment for Banda and Phillips confirmed it was indeed a tumour which must come out before it spread to the other eye.

We did not have long to wait before Banda received his summons, knowing that he would have to have the eye removed. Andrew phoned to check that the operation had gone well and left both his office and home numbers with the Sister on duty. After a couple of days I went to see how he was progressing. He was looking very well and was glad to have some fruit and biscuits to supplement the hospital food. As I left, I checked that the Duty Room staff had our phone numbers, repeating that we would collect him as soon as he was ready to be discharged.

Andrew phoned a couple of times. Banda was progressing well but his discharge date was not known. I went in again with more food and a check on phone numbers.

So we were very surprised to find Banda at the back door one day to tell us he was back and show us his papers.

No matter how often this sort of thing happened one always felt anger and surprise, although the latter was beginning to wear thin and you began to say 'Well, what do you expect?'

But WHY couldn't the staff at the clinic have referred him to the hospital in the first place? WHY couldn't the staff on the ward have given us a phone call to tell us he was being discharged so that he did not have to walk miles home?

All the questions we asked over and over again, knowing that it was all the more depressing and disillusioning after independence when it was the Zambians themselves behaving in this way to their fellow men? After all the hurt and criticism of the colonial era it seemed as though they were set on an equally callous path.

I took Banda for his check up with Mr Phillips, who was pleased with his progress adding that while his services were free he could do nothing about an artificial eye - but no doubt if I wanted to go to the trouble and expense one of the private opticians in town would be able to help. As we were already in town I drove down to Cairo Road and took Banda to my optician Winstons in the arcade.

Not only could he do something for us, he would measure

Banda's eye socket and try an eye for size that very afternoon.

We had to wait a short time and I shuffled through a few magazines while Banda stood awkwardly in the corner of the waiting room until I told him to sit on a chair next to me, clearly uncomfortable in the 'European' environment and unable to meet the glances from the silent and offended white man waiting for his wife. We did not have to wait long.

'I won't have the perfect match of course, one never has, but we can try a few eyes for size,' said the cheerful Mr Winston.

And then he began rattling through drawers while eyes of various sizes and colours tinkled like marbles. I retreated to the pile of magazines once more, feeling that Banda might feel like a little privacy in this exercise and admitting that my stomach had become rather squeamish. It was not long before the door opened and there was Banda with a new eye in situ.

'Not only have we got the right size but I really do think that we could not get a better match! What do you think?'

I could only agree.

We both peered at Banda from various angles while he stood to attention looking embarrassed.

'But what does HE think of this? Good gracious, he must have a look at himself'.

And Banda was handed a large mirror.

It was then that I nearly disgraced myself by bursting into tears as we watched the look of amazement and sheer delight which slowly crossed Banda's face. He turned his head from side to side and was glued to his reflection.

'Well, yes, hum, I don't think we could do any better. What do you think?'

I agreed it did appear to be a very good match - in fact I think if we had tried to remove that eye from Banda we would have had a strike on our hands. So while he continued to look at himself from all angles we carried on with the details.

'While it is a very good fit now, I shall have to see him again every three months to check whether the socket has shrunk - that will take about two years altogether. But as Mr Phillips does such a good job I do not anticipate any problems.'

'How did you know Mr Phillips did the operation?' I queried. 'I never mentioned it.'

'Brilliant man, that eye has been removed so well that the muscle in the socket will still move and so will the artificial eye to some extent. Now be sure to get him to understand that he must remove the eye every night and wash it in soapy water - make sure he has Lifebuoy - and also make sure that he understands that he will never be able to see with it . Oh yes, I have had that problem before.'

The tears pricked my eyes again as we walked to the car, Banda was walking with his head held high and was looking about him with a very jaunty air. We got back home about ten o'clock and the eye seemed to have given Banda a new lease of life and confidence because he asked me for time off there and then to go visit his friends to show them his new 'face'. He said he would be back to work early in the afternoon.

What the hell I thought, you can't really celebrate a new eye and new face and come back to work early. So let's do it in style.

'Just get back in time to collect the eggs and lock up the chickens before it gets dark.'

How wonderful that we got Banda to see Mr Phillips when we did. As new contracts were arranged after independence people found themselves on new and sometimes less favourable conditions. Phillips was one of these. I forget the details but his new conditions meant that he either lost money or paid leave or some such - anyway, his conditions were not going to be so good. Although some of us argued - at high levels - that Zambia needed a man like that - in fact, should be honoured to keep such a man, the powers that be pointed out it would be cheaper to recruit a new eye specialist. And so Phillips departed and his successor was often seen sauntering along Cairo Road and was at all the 'right parties'. I suppose he was equally devoted to his work but I never actually heard mention of him professionally.

This change in qualified and EXPERIENCED personnel was one of the greatest mistakes that was made after independence

I think - and so did many others. Gradually in the late 1960's and early 70's we saw the departure of men who had served Northern Rhodesia and Zambia well. They were professional men who had been in the country 10, 15, 20 years or more. True it was cheaper to pay them off and wish them well but it was widely believed that cost was not the sole reason.

A man who had intimate working knowledge or service is more likely to know more than his political master and is more likely to stand his ground on a debateable point. Were politicians and folk at the top of the Civil Service so unable to take advice to the extent that they would remove a vast fund of experience? And bring in 'yes men'?

During this year the President had another of his reshuffles - they were a regular feature of life and I can't remember half of them. Certainly one could expect a reshuffle after he had had a holiday in the Luangwa or Kasaba Bay in the New Year. This year Andrew was moved from the Ministry of Transport to be Permanent Secretary in Agriculture.

There had been problems in Transport particularly because of UDI, there were problems in Agriculture, amongst which was trying to get the country to be fully self- sufficient. Almost anything could be grown in spite of the altitude. My mother in law grew her own rice. Wheat was being grown by a white farmer in Chilanga. Tea and coffee were viable. Sugar cane grew well, cotton flourished, cattle were possible in tsetse free areas and vegetables and fruit grew in abundance ...

But white farmers could not support all the country's needs, in fact there was a desperate need for black farmers to move from mere subsistence farming to the commercial sector. It was not happening fast enough. There were many factors.

I sometimes wondered whether actual physical fitness was ever taken into consideration when people criticised how workers performed - or did not, as the case might be.

Dr Haworth of Chainama Hills Mental Hospital said that 21% of a test group of Lusaka dagga smokers said they took it more than four times day - often to give themselves strength to do a day's work. Dr Lawless reported that 20% of Zambia's children suffered from sickle cell anaemia. These figures are alarming enough added to which one could be sure that the majority of the work force would not have a good balanced diet. The President's call for everyone to have an egg a day and a pint of milk a day was an ambitious call that was never realised.

Children who had previously been breast fed were as like as not now to be bottle fed - 'it was more civilised'. But in the absence of good hygiene they were prone to far more infections. Weaning was apt to be a thin maize gruel. A deficient diet from birth resulted in a high infant mortality rate, those who survived could well have had their mental growth stunted. What kind of work force had we inherited and were we producing?

The only indigenous people with any real energy sometimes seemed to be the UNIP youths and unfortunately, as I said, before, their energies were either undirected or often misdirected. Their greatest efforts continued to be on 'card checking' when they would harass the hapless public. Attorney General James Skinner made a formal statement saying that it was unlawful for UNIP youths to demand Party cards and prevent people using public transport. But his words had little effect, and who wished to argue with a crowd of excitable youths on a street?

As Kaunda had agreed to Axon Chalikulima's request that the youths be allowed to learn how to use minor weapons one could speculate uneasily on the future when young people had undergone Zambia Youth Service and still had no employment. (Chalikulima was Director of the ZYS).

It was argued of course that we were still under pressure from outside activities and our youth could do with some very basic military training. The Luangwa bridge was blown up in June 1968, it is only a few miles from the Mozambique border and it was clearly an attempt to frustrate our fuel supply route. The Luangwa bridge was part of the one way system over the Luangwa escarpment and although a new bridge was being built parallel to the old one it was not yet open. In the bomb attack two spans were destroyed leaving a gap of 200 feet. It was quickly decided to erect a Bailey bridge and until that was ready the tankers would have to run from Salima to Luangwa and then fuel could be pumped across in a pipe line and then transported again by tankers to Lusaka.

Oh we had problems! But we kept going!

The oil pipe line from Dar es Salaam was finally opened in September the same year and as Kaunda and Nyerere turned the valves we all looked forward to the end of the oil famine.

Apart from the oil of course, general transport was hit when the bridge was blown up. At the time we had Alan Jarvis staying with us. He was then Head of a Primary school in Fort Jameson - sorry, Chipata - and was in Lusaka on a teachers' course. He had set off with three colleagues early in the morning of the sabotage, to return home and had to turn back when they found the road closed. We agreed to put them up, as hotels would be full, and we spent an evening planning long and improbable routes round the country as the only road to Eastern Province was across the Luangwa bridge.

Alan managed to get through on the phone to his wife Pat, which did little to cheer her. He began by bawling down the phone, 'They have blown up the Luangwa bridge and we can't get back. We are thinking of driving either up to the Copperbelt and across the Congo pedicle road or round by Serenje, Mpika, Chinsali and Isoka because then we can get back down the Lundazi road ... we are completely cut off! But don't worry! We shall get back !'

Pat's comments are unprintable ... he had not thought to wonder how she would, feel cut off with the children in the Eastern Province, waiting to hear if they could circumnavigate a lengthy detour of most of Central and Eastern Zambia.

Fortunately ferries were quickly organised and Alan's journey home assumed more normal proportions.

What was not normal was my thoughtfully preparing a trolley of early morning teas and coffees for the comatose bodies littering the spare bedroom and Ceri's bedroom. After a very merry late evening with plenty of liquid refreshment none of them appeared to notice that I had absently poured tea on top of coffee. All mugs were drained.

Of course we were all used to the long distances and difficult road conditions, especially on dirt roads in the rainy season but it took something like the Luangwa bridge incident to really bring it home to one how impossible travelling could be, once one vital link was put out of action.

Another problem on the roads was possibly caused by the increased number of vehicles on the roads, many in inefficient hands. It became clear that we were losing personnel it would be hard to replace, as the number of fatal accidents rose to alarming levels. Nor was it only a problem of people being killed in accidents. Drivers, involved in fatal accidents with pedestrians, would find themselves attacked by large crowds who appeared from nowhere. A crowd of 400 beat a driver unconscious after a minor accident and stoned police, who were called to the scene. It seemed to be a mixture of idle hands plus a desire for instant justice.

We had long been aware that the gendarmes on the Congolese border were often unpaid and would therefore confiscate watches, shoes, money or any other valuables from Zambian travellers. When new currency regulations were introduced which prevented travellers carrying more than a certain amount of Zambian money, they were liable to be beaten and abused by the Congolese out of sheer frustration.

Frustration was causing more and more violence. Work was not available (or not at the rates of pay men wanted), so more men took to robbery and were now often armed. In an armed raid on the University flats Mr B Jones, a lecturer, was shot and later died in hospital.

I didn't know which was worse, the increase in robberies or the increase in violence between the two political parties, UNIP and ANC. If there was no political stability, how could we have any form of peace and progress?

The railway workers careered on their own merry way. 26 trucks loaded with coal from Livingstone hurtled off the track 25 miles south of Kafue and 3 trucks carrying copper bars jumped off the line near Lilayi but no one on the train noticed.

Perhaps the Auditor General Robert Boyd had a good description of the country in October

He revealed '... *millions of kwacha are unaccounted for* ...' he criticised in the strongest terms possible '... *Ministries and Government departments for confusion, lack of planning, unconstitutional spending, inexcusable lack of control and making a mockery of the law. Seventeen statutory books are in arrears in presenting audited accounts. Forty departments including State House, National Assembly, police and practically every Ministry spent more than K2,817,000 beyond estimates of expenditure without proper authority ... financial control has not improved. It is unlikely to do so until current attitudes and approaches to this vital matter undergo a radical change. This involves a proper understanding of the need for public accountability in all sectors of the community, a realisation that public servants of every kind are trustees of the public property of the Republic ... in September 1966 the Ministry of Transport Power and Communication spent K27,000 on a Royal Navy landing craft. A further K77,000 on making it seaworthy. It was on charter to East Africa Railway at Dar es Salaam but it is no longer required, it is not seaworthy and is being disposed of ...'*

The last item of course was of interest to me. I asked Andrew what he had been doing while he was at Transport. But it was a case of 'the lower echelons not being responsible and although one talked to these chaps, they had little idea of what was a sensible course to follow'. Which did not really answer my question.

Also in October, Clifford Little received the medal Grand Officer of the Order of Distinguished Service at the investiture ceremony at State House. I wonder if we went. Or rather, if I went? Initially I had found State House functions quite thrilling but as time progressed I became disheartened. Disheartened because these functions were held on the lawns behind State House, lovely gardens, band playing, various people smartly dressed, bars set up to the rear etc etc. But later, after attending a couple of functions where we watched as the bar was swamped by eager drinkers, who then retreated to the shade of trees with their arms full of bottles to take no further interest in the proceedings ... it all lost much of its attraction. I like to think I made the effort for Clifford.

In November Sir Mwanawina Lewanika the Third died aged 84 years, he had been the first in Central Africa to get a knighthood at Buckingham palace in 1960. In World War 1 he had led 2000 men to Luapula to deliver stores to beleaguered British troops. The end of an era.

AND INTO 1969

It had been announced in 1968 that non Zambians would not be allowed to trade in retail stores anywhere once their trading licences expired at the end of the year. Their trading would be restricted to certain areas in the centre of towns.

This move hit those in the Asian community particularly, and those who traded in the outer townships and in the rural areas, very hard indeed. Many of them had not taken Zambian nationality and although most of them had been trading in Zambia for many, many years it was believed that they continued sending large sums of money back to relatives in India. Although some now made efforts to identify positively with the country and applied for Zambian citizenship, it was not forthcoming.

One Asian who had applied for citizenship eighteen months previously, wrote a letter of protest to the newspaper in which he said, '... I came to Zambia from India twenty years ago. This is my country and I call no other home. But if it is Humanism to deprive a man and his family of his livelihood because he is not born of black parents in Zambia, then Humanism is a shame. It appears that Humanism only applies to a man if he is a UNIP member - the rest can just lie down and die'.

Although there were many applications to the trading licence authorities for business take overs, mainly in the second class trading areas for Indian shops, these moved slowly. And there were some business men who said they were willing to sell their businesses if only they could get a fair price - one man said he was offered K200 for a K5,000 concern.

Many shops remained shut because the owners could not get a trading licence nor could they find a buyer. Expatriate traders in Monze were given a week's notice by the District Governor to hand over their shops to Zambians, he said they were asking fantastic sums of money which would make a mockery of the economic reforms.

Some Asians found a loophole in the law and sold their businesses to their children, who had been born in Zambia and were entitled to Zambian nationality.

This was a most frustrating period for the Asian who found himself unable to trade and the poorer sections of the African population who relied heavily on the local Indian store. Slowly over a long period the stores began to reopen either because the owners managed to get Zambian citizenship or they sold to a Zambian, but far too many remained shuttered. The hardest hit of all of course were the Africans in the rural areas, whose only source of supply was the local Indian store.

My personal thought on the subject were that the Africans who took over Asian stores were often in for a rude awakening. I think far too many people looked at the Indian traders and assumed they were making fantastic profits and had a very comfortable life style indeed. What they did not take into consideration was the fact that the Indian storekeeper was probably living a very simple life and that he and all his family worked very hard all hours of the day. The homes I saw were always simply and basically furnished, the car was a necessity not a luxury and any free time was spent in entertainment in family surroundings. It was a sad fact that some stores taken over by Africans slipped rapidly into a state of scruffy decline. And many such were handicapped by the custom of not refusing help to relatives - many of whom then descended on the one man who had a store, expecting handouts ad infinitum.

The small stores had another problem, the Government had issued a list of 'non -essential items' and were therefore subjected to a 10% non-essential tariff. Madeleine Robertson, the European nominated Member of Parliament, took up cudgels on behalf of the common man. She bravely spoke out in Parliament against the tariff on certain items, this in spite of the fact that she was refused permission to speak by the Deputy Speaker. Sticking to her guns, Madeleine placed two tins of pilchards on the table in the Chamber the next day and said they were a valuable form of protein at 20 ngwee a pound. The Vice President, Simon Kapwepwe, agreed to suspend duty on tinned fish. I can't remember whether she had equal success with the soap and candles, which were also on the non-essential list.

For all the talk about the common man and humanism there was very little practical help for the common man at times.

One example of practical help in Lusaka was a Walk with Rev Pierre Dil in the lead. He organised the Walk With The Lusaka Nutrition Group in cooperation with the Dairy Produce Board. The aim of the Walk was to raise funds for Dzinthandizeni, the scheme run by the group to supply food at economic prices in high density areas. They would set off from the Civic Centre and walk along Independence Avenue to Woodlands, up Leopards Hill Road, along Kalingalinga Road, over to the Great East Road, finishing at the Jubilee Hall in the Showground.

Andrew walked with this group, full of support and enthusiasm, but said afterwards that he wondered how worthwhile all these well intentioned efforts were, when he saw how many people were spending their day filling themselves with chimbuku (cheap maize beer) at the beerhalls as they passed.

'Whatever they save on cheap food, will only go on beer,' he said sadly.

It was a sad fact that 4 out of every 10 Zambian children died before the age of 5, usually from malnutrition and lack of resistance to disease. Two most common complaints were marasmus, where the child had not had enough food, and kwashiorkor, where the child was not fed the right food. So many mothers who now preferred the fashionable bottle feeding, would increasingly dilute the milk powder as the supplies ran low, having no idea of food values.

Dzintandizeni as a help yourself group, gave information on nutrition as well as selling essential foodstuffs at competitive prices. Politicians paid lip service to the plight of the common man but were in fact more concerned with the conflict between the two main parties, ANC and UNIP.

On one hand we had Dingiswayo Banda, Provincial Cabinet Minister, at the time, addressing a meeting of UNIP officials

'... we shall eliminate ANC in Western Province ... ANC supporters have one month to choose between ANC and UNIP. If they remain loyal to ANC then they should pack their bags and go to other Provinces. Nor should the police give permits for ANC meetings as it provokes people ...'

All of which was more than likely to provoke UNIP youths to take the law into their own hands and harass any luckless ANC who came their way and cause unease to Europeans or any other expatriates, who had no desire for violent politics.

On the other hand we were supposed to be a democracy.

President Kaunda must have been aware of the problems because as soon as he returned from the Commonwealth Leaders Conference in London he made it clear that as far as he was concerned Zambia was NOT ready for a one party state yet.

'... not ... yet ...'

One could take solace in the NOT, but the YET was more on my mind.

Opening Parliament at that time he promised every 7 year old child would be given full primary education in the next five years and the school curriculum was to be diversified to include agriculture. Two positive plans for two of our most pressing problems.

I wished the youths could take their lead from their Leader, there was so much they could have done, but the majority of them seemed to like hanging around town checking party cards or insulting anyone wearing a mini skirt.

A Tourist Board courier, showing a group of Canadians around town, was surrounded by a gang of youths near the Luburma market. They demanded she lengthen the hem of her skirt, which was just above the knee. The Bureau protested to the Government, but the damage had already been done - a group of much needed tourists would leave the country either convinced one could be in danger in Zambia, or at the very least in danger of ridiculing and threatening behaviour.

It all seemed a bit inconsistent to me. Women walked down the streets breast feeding their babies as they walked and talked and shopped, this was quite acceptable because it was a natural function. Fair enough, although it was found embarrassing or even repugnant by some expatriates and tourists. But while they had to accept a local custom some Zambians were able to protest about the mini skirt fashion because it was Western and baring the thighs was not a Zambian tradition. I suppose the comparison between bare breasts and bare thighs was not quite a fair one, but it did seem a bit one sided. However, help was at hand.

Valentine Musakanya, Minister of State in the Vice President's Office, entered the arena.

'... *our girls are lovely to look at. When I see them walking down the street so smart, so independent and so much part of the twentieth century they make me feel so proud of them. What these girls are showing is their awareness of their independence and a pride in their freedom. They are proud of their blackness ... I am amazed at what Zambia's women have achieved in a short time. They have taken to independence much better than some men. They drive cars, hold responsible jobs and manage to look so nice. They are really enjoying their independence and that is much better than looking nostalgically to the past ... Cultural advance comes from the outrageous - if Leonardo da Vinci had not exhumed cadavers we would not have medicine as we know it today ...*'

He was further supported by Chief Justice Blagden speaking at a passing out parade at Lilayi Police Training School.

'... *to uphold the law – and there is no law against this at the present ...*'

Perhaps Lewis Changufu, Minister of Labour, was agreeing in

effect with Musakanya when he said

'... *the rate of Zambianisation may have to be slowed down, they have not accepted the responsibility ... Zambianisation has done more harm than good ...*'

But we had gone too far down the road of Zambianisation to put the clock back.

Other changes which DID need to be made were going to be held up in legislation for far too long. As early as 1969 Sefelino Mulenga was asking in Parliament for legal protection for widows against the custom whereby a deceased husband's relatives remove all possessions, leaving the widow destitute. Attorney General Patrick Chuula replied that local courts could deal with such cases. Many of us felt that the wives would get short shrift there and took some comfort from Simon Kapwepwe, who promised that a Commission would look into the customs of each tribe. It was going to be a long drawn out process knowing how many tribes there are in Zambia and how long Commissions can take to present their findings and recommendations.

The original custom had been a wise and practical solution long ago when a widow would find life hard alone, relatives would have taken her husband's possessions - but would also have been responsible for her and her children's care.

The number of tribes and their different customs would have to be brought to some mutual acceptable agreement on many things. It was all very well for some tribes to continue their circumcision rites but it was a bit tough if you were of another tribe and wandered into the area unknowingly - it was a Luvale tradition to forcibly circumcise any man who strayed into the area during the time the boys were undergoing their initiation.

But I could not get too depressed over political developments and statements. Andrew always had a reasonable and optimistic outlook, talking things over with him always made me feel more at ease.

LEAVE IN ENGLAND 1969

And what was more, we were planning another holiday. Andrew

had accumulated a large amount of paid leave so we could go to England for another holiday.

Simon would be three years old while we were there and Ceri in her second year at school. Remembering how exhausting we had found the last trip, constantly packing and moving on, we decided to rent a holiday flat by the sea to make it more of a restful holiday.

This time of course, we took off from the magnificent international airport and really felt we were travelling in style. We had planned a stop-over for a couple of days in Nairobi, naturally a day at the famous Game Park was high on the list. The first morning we hired a taxi and set off as early as possible. It seemed strange to be entering a Game Park on a tarmac road but it certainly made for comfortable viewing. As we entered the park, the driver had a short conversation with the game guards and once through the barrier he headed off down the road saying

'There is a kill this way, you will see the lions at breakfast.'

What a way to start our game viewing. The kill was not far from the tarmac, the driver swung the car expertly off the road, edging in closer over the rough grass. There was a pride of about five adults and several young around the body of a zebra. They looked up as we edged forward and the male raised his head and snarled - but not very much - as though he knew he should go through the motions. They had been at the kill for some time and the zebra was well and truly disembowelled; the lions had obviously satisfied their initial hunger and were now enjoying a leisurely munch and crunch. They were not at all bothered by our presence in the car and the driver slowly eased the window down so we could hear the rasp of tongues and crunching of bones. Andrew and I were so enthralled we could have sat there for longer, not so the children.

Taking this magnificent spectacle as a natural incident in the day, they were now whispering that we should go see something else. It was a day to be remembered as the sun rose higher in the sky and animals stood, wandered, grazed, galloped, trotted, singly and in pairs, groups and herds. Anyone who has spent time in an African game park never forgets its unique attraction. Once in England we stopped for a few days with the Proctors, who were on leave at their home in Slough. The children were pleased to be reunited while we caught up on the news. Andrew went to see Dennis' work at the Overseas Development Agency while Renate and I caught up on household chores and even more female gossip.

Sightseeing included Bekonscot model village and Windsor castle, where Simon stood glued to a fence watching a sentry go through his paces. The small figure behind the railing must have registered because at the sixth or seventh stamp, stamp, about turn just on the other side of the railing, the soldier slowly winked at Simon. After which of course, we had to wait for another five or six about turns and winks.

We had a couple of days in London when Andrew had a meeting – I think it was in connection with the proposed K24 million Indeni oil refinery.

Leaving the meeting in London

Next, over to Sonning Common for a couple of days with John and Ruth Hodgson and their three children. The weather was kind as we sat in the garden and watched the children race around. John and Andrew had much to talk about but Ruth and I found our interests had little common ground. Ruth was immersed in her family while I discovered I had been taking more interest in politics and world news than I had realised.

Next we headed for Scarborough and the holiday flat we had rented. It was ideally situated - near enough the sea for the children to enjoy days on the beach and within easy travelling distance of most of our friends. We began our stay there with an Old Students reunion at my former college where I enjoyed renewing old friendships. Fun though it was I felt a bit of an outsider. Was it just the feeling of coming back to an old place or was it feeling as though I was a bit detached, feeling a bit like a foreigner who did not really belong? I did not relate to parts of the conversations, casual 'in' jokes did not register and I had an extra dimension to which no one else related. It was a pity Joan was not there that year, I might have enjoyed it more.

We spent a few days with Grannie Hodgson at Lowlands in Askrigg. Early on 21st July we were transfixed by grainy black and white TV images of Neil Armstrong taking a first step on the surface of the moon. Typically, although we adults were fascinated, Ceri and Simon with the innocence of the young, thought it interesting but not remarkable.

The English summer was kind to us that year. Any day spent in Scarborough was spent on the beach which suited Andrew very well as he settled down with every daily newspaper printed, while I initiated the children into the English customs of building sandcastles, searching through rock pools, donkey rides and Punch and Judy. Aunt Clare, who had attended our wedding, lived in Scarborough and joined in some of our activities.

She also rashly volunteered to have the children for odd days if we wanted a day out on our own. They stood at the end of her garden, waving tea towels as our train passed, delighted at a day of independence. She took them to Peasholm Park to feed the ducks and ride on the miniature railway – her thrifty Yorkshire soul was horrified at their casual assumption that they would travel back by taxi when they missed a bus.

'Daddy just gets a taxi,' said Ceri helpfully.

'Daddy might,' was the tart reply. 'But I'm not your Daddy so you can learn what your legs are for.'

Admitting afterwards that perhaps it would have been a good idea as her old legs protested at the long walk uphill to catch a different bus and Simon dragged sadly behind.

We watched Prince Charles' investiture at Carnarvon on TV; I explained as much as I could the history and ceremony of the occasion feeling a silly sentimental lump in my throat at watching some of my cultural background - hoping the children would remember something of the occasion and feel some link. It was not likely. If we did not come to England regularly they would not feel any links with Britain, would that be the best thing? I didn't know. I felt sad at the thought of them being wholly Zambian and was not quite sure why.

Ceri, in Grade 2, was in her second year at school so her teacher, Barbara Cook, had kindly supplied me with books and work. Neither of us had taken into consideration that I would find it almost impossible to teach my own daughter. No matter how much patience I had with other people's children I found it difficult to believe that my daughter could be so slow to respond, and my impatience did not improve matters at all. I could well understand Aileen's relief in Petauke when I had been able to take over Gillian's lessons, even for that short period.

Poor Ceri, we wept bitter tears together before consigning the books to the bottom of a suitcase, agreeing that the holiday and travel were educational in themselves.

We did contact a few friends and had some happy reunions. Michael Wearing was now married to his Elizabeth Taylor and working as a Minister in the Methodist Church in Lytham St Annes.

Paul and Mary Booth and their two sons in Leeds. Dropping in to see the Divechas, we found Shalini was in the maternity hospital and headed there for visiting time. Leaving Dinesh at the door we headed down the ward towards her bed. It was a wonder that more premature babies were not born that night when her glance swept over us and then back and she let out one almighty shriek, which had staff appearing from all directions.

We went to the Children's Home to introduce Simon to Douglas and Denise. Ceri and Simon admired their older 'cousins', while Douglas and Denise enjoyed being the tolerant and doting elders.

It was good to see them again, to see how they were growing and their personalities developing. But I regretted I could not tell them that at that stage we had tried to have them out for a holiday with us in Zambia. We had made a formal request, which had been carefully considered but then turned down. I believe the Social Services Department was very conscious of their role as guardians and the possibility of some mishap while they were out of the country. While we were disappointed, we could understand the official position, nor could we tell the children of our request and the answer as this would have raised the possibility of their resentment against the Authority.

The holiday was interrupted by a phone call from the two 'girls' (Anne and Gail two of Andrew's secretaries) we had left house sitting. Candy had given birth to nine puppies, they were adorable. Adorable or not we hastily advised them to keep only two.

On leave in UK and touring Scotland

The 'summer season' would shortly be upon us - or rather the crowds upon Scarborough's beaches - and we set off for Scotland, where the children sat enthralled through an Edinburgh Tattoo rehearsal, climbed around the castle and asked to go to the zoo. What a let-down after a game park we thought, as we paid at the turnstile. Whether they were doing a child's version of being tourists or whether animals are more impressive when seen out of their natural habitat I do not know. But there seemed to be no justification whatsoever for their ecstatic shrieks,

'Oh look! Look! A lion!!'

And they raced to the railing to hang there enthralled by a moth eaten and faded specimen of the most regal of animals.

Or was it recognition of a fellow African far from home?

Andrew and I had our own thoughts of fellow Africans; the newspapers were suddenly carrying reports of disturbances in Lusaka. 'Chief Justice Skinner stood behind locked doors while thugs stormed the High Court ... hundreds of ZYS members tried to batter their way in ... Skinner leaves Lusaka amid tight security ...'

What was going on? We knew Skinner as a quiet mild mannered man, a lawyer, who had been one of Kaunda's firmest supporters and most helpful advisers.

His statement in London, '... *the present political climate in Zambia is perfectly understandable in view of the frustrations brought about by the Rhodesian and Portuguese border raids ...*' did little to enlighten us. We had to wait until our return to learn the whole story and it did not make for very pleasant reading.

For some time there had been reports of the Portuguese bombing villages in Eastern Province and in fact the Foreign Minister, Elijah Mudenda, claimed there had been at least 60 incursions in the last 3 years and Zambia was to protest to the UN.

Early in July Kaunda called upon Chief Justice Skinner for an explanation when Justice Ivor Evans said that a sentence of K2,000 each or 2 years in jail were excessive and unlawful - this had been the sentence on two soldiers in Portuguese uniform who had strolled across the border from Angola – and Justice Evans duly set the sentence aside.

In reply Skinner defended the judge saying '... *he was not motivated by political decisions ... there was nothing sinister on the part of the prisoners. They divested themselves of their weapons before entering Zambia and came openly across the border after an exchange of words with a Zambian immigration officer, who called them across. Perhaps they were foolish in so doing, but their arrest, detention and charging did not rebound to the credit of the Zambian authorities ... cannot regard these actions of a man who has divested himself of arms and strolled over the border at the invitation of an immigration officer as constituting a threat to the State.'*

The following day, newspaper headlines screamed THUGS STORM HIGH COURT and the report did not make for pretty reading.

'Chief Justice Skinner stood behind locked doors as hundreds of ZYS members in a spontaneous demonstration tried to batter their way in ... youths in khaki drill and green berets came to Lusaka in several lorries from Kafue to protest ... they lined up at Headquarters and marched to the High Court ... they stormed through corridors ... judges locked the doors ... so the youths broke furniture and pelted walls with rotten vegetables ... going out into the car park they found the Czech Press, Attache Hyneck ,and a large group beat him and tore his clothing ... banners were waved 'Away With Imperialist Judgements' and 'Zambia Faces Judicial Assassination' as they lined up on the lawns of State House, not far from the High Court ... Kaunda thanked them for their support and said he was going to arm them with sophisticated weapons ... *'each one of you will be ready to defend the nation ... I want you to be ready for the showdown with any imperialist forces ...'* He told the youths he did not consider the letter he had received from Skinner an adequate explanation of the remarks by Justice Evans.'

And then the sad comment

'Last night police guarded the Skinner's house'.

(Nowhere did I ever read or hear any comment on how this supposedly spontaneous demonstration just happened to have rotten vegetables to throw and banners to wave and lorries at their disposal... nor had I ever heard that throwing vegetables rotten or otherwise was a traditional Zambian way of protesting). The following night Skinner and his wife left for London. They arrived at the VIP lounge 35 minutes before the Nairobi flight was due to depart and 15 minutes later Kaunda arrived and went to speak to him

The two men walked across the tarmac together. Andrew Sardanis walking behind with Mrs Skinner.

What thoughts must have passed through the Skinners' minds as they walked the last yards under the soft black sky? To have worked so selflessly for the Black cause, cutting themselves off from so much of 'European society' to find that it all appeared to count for nothing. To have given so much but you were still not respected and accepted. Whatever passed between KK and Skinner is not recorded. What is recorded is KK's statement to a crowd of 1000 at State House,

'Leave it to me. I'll change the law so Zambians control the judiciary. I now instruct every UNIP member not to mention Judiciary or Skinner.'

Of the riot he is reported as saying, *'They were over enthusiastic. But I am very sorry that because I did not make myself clear, youths of the ZYS did what they did in the High Court.'*

Harry Nukumbula of the ANC stated that *'the UNIP demonstration was the end of justice in Zambia'* and he compared the Youth Service with the Nazi Gestapo in pre-war Germany.

Skinner's carefully worded release that the present political climate in Zambia was perfectly understandable, was an indication of his control and consideration for the country and President, who had rejected him at the end. And I doubt it was ever appreciated by those for whom it was done.

Coincidentally - or not - Judge Whelan announced he would be leaving at the end of the year and Judge Evans flew out the next week, bringing forward the date of his leaving. By now, the newspaper carried the explanation that it was Evans' use of the word 'trivial' when reversing the sentence which had sparked off the row.

The Financial Times commented: 'Zambia has not yet felt the

full impact of the judiciary crisis'.

That may have been true but I believe Zambia was already feeling the effect of an unsettled atmosphere - the number of tourists had dropped by 75% since 1965. I suppose a good number of tourists, pre 1965, had been from Southern Rhodesia and South Africa, who would no longer wish to holiday in an independent African country. And a good number of 'Europeans' had left Zambia and that could account for a drop when they no longer had visiting friends and relatives - but would that account for a drop of 75%? I thought not and in any case what was being done to attract tourists from elsewhere and to reassure them they would be visiting a stable state? rioting or riotous youths in the High Court - neither would indicate a peaceful and restful tourist destination.

It was interesting at this time to read that Kaunda said he regarded Skinner as a true Zambian and at the same time the Zambian African Traders Association was told by chairman Sicilongo that Zambians of European and Asian descent would no longer be regarded as Zambians. There was this constant contradiction.

This last report provoked a letter from a 'White Zambian' who objected to the statement. He claimed he was as full a Zambian as any African, his family had been there so long his grandmother could remember State House being built and he appealed to the Government to stop these provocative statements. It was heartening to read of someone who felt himself truly part of the Zambian nation, State House was first occupied in 1935. Lusaka itself was only gazetted as a township in 1930. To further encourage the tourists, Kaunda made an important speech early in August when he declared he was shaping the new Zambia.

The mineral wealth of the nation was to be nationalised in a 51% take over. Luxury cars would be heavily taxed, strikes were banned and wages frozen, income tax was increased for the high salary earners, cooperatives were to be revamped and he extended restrictions on wholesale trading licences. These were the key points in his five hour address to the UNIP National

Council and while he made the speech, units of the Zambian army and police were moved to guard vital installations.

Kaunda was at this stage making it clear that he did not approve of the increasing inefficiency and desire for high living, which was accelerating at all levels. Less than ten days later he banned crowds at the airport to welcome him, 'I want workers, not loafers,' he declared.

I think at this point Kaunda still had the right ideas and hopes but he had already lost control of a large section of the community - those in high places, who were already quick to grasp more and more power and benefits and those who had not the education or ability but preferred to be part of a crowd whatever or wherever the occasion, waving a flag or a placard was easier than going back to the land to grow food.

And the people who would have been great assets to him preferred not to do so. Four Zambians turned down jobs on the judiciary - Pat Chuula was already Attorney General and Edward Shamwana, Bruce Munyama and Lisulo, all had private practices.

Simon Kapwepwe resigned his position, saying that he knew he was unpopular and while he remained in a position of power the Bemba people as a whole would suffer. But he reaffirmed his loyalty to Kaunda. Kaunda accepted this resignation but asked him to remain until the end of August, which was the end of his term of office. The overseas Press saw this as sign of tribal disintegration. From the very beginning we had all been very aware that Kaunda had made a determined effort to balance the tribes as he appointed Ministers and other senior Government staff. And everyone I knew appreciated the intention to weld together the many tribes. Kaunda had a Government reshuffle at this point but Andrew remained as Permanent Secretary in Rural Development with Reuben Kamanga as his Minister.

At this point our lovely holiday in England came to an end - but it was good to return home again.

Back to all our commitments which now included two new puppies. The 'girls' (Ann and Gail, two of Andrew's secretaries who had house sat for us) had kept a male and female, now named Peter and Paula by Ceri and Simon - and I planned to have Candy spayed immediately and Paula as soon as she was old enough - no more litters of nine.

Andrew as usual could not wait to get back in to his office, Ceri was keen to re-join her friends at school (and I was more than happy to end our lessons together).

LUSAKA INFANTS SCHOOL

Once back home I was told to join the staff at the Lusaka Infants School in September (the school was renamed Jacaranda School some years later). I was to have a Grade 1 class while Ceri would be in her last term at the school, after Grade 2 she would move to Lusaka Girls School for Grades 3 – 7. Simon was now ready for nursery school so off he went to Joyce Hamilton's Nursery, where Ceri and Fenella had been so happy. This was a much more compact arrangement. Ceri and I at the same school with Simon just round the corner; the morning dropping off session was getting easier.

Ceri, aged 6, was having a much softer option than many of her African counterparts. I was driving her to school with me every day. Seven year olds were being left at Kamwala bus station by their parents, they were left there with a basket of food to wait for a bus to boarding school - some of them travelling the 90 odd miles to Kabwe. When the newspaper reporter went to the bus station he claimed to have talked to a seven year old, Harry Matake, who had come from Chipata (300 miles away in Eastern Province), he was waiting for a seat on a Kabwe bus. The Ministry of Education said that they were not a transport agency and a Social Welfare spokesman said they were there to help the destitutes only and would treat cases on their merits. They would not look kindly on school children who wanted extra pocket money - this was a direct reference to the unfortunate children who had been waiting at the bus station for at least four days. What chance did they have in the over-crowded conditions, orderly queues not being the norm?

I would read these reports and even allowing for media exaggeration I would find it depressing. Andrew, when consulted, would waver between agreeing how hard it was for the children and saying they would come to no harm ... 'after all, we have all had to go the same way'.

I remember reading an article on why girls abandoned their babies and the writer Mwangilwa said, '... our traditions tend to regard a child as a person not as HUMAN as an adult'. Whether I took that sentence at face value or allowed for an error in English translation, it still seemed a pretty damning statement. Mwangilwa's further comments informed us that in some tribes if a child's top teeth grew first it would be exposed to die, left handed children were despised and parents would scald the left hand to correct it, premature and light skinned babies were often not wanted. In fact, concluded Mwangilwa, '... we regard children as property to dispose of as we wish'.

At Lusaka Infants School I took over a class of 40 boys and girls from Bessie Frost who was going on leave. We had an all-female staff at the school and here are some names which stand out in my memory.

Evelyn Fernandes, the Headmistress, a small plump grey haired lady from Goa, who became more and more flurried and harassed as the Ministry introduced changes which were difficult or even impossible to implement.

Dorothy Haile, wife of a former District Commissioner, who regaled us with tales of the 'good old days' when a DC often had to tour his area on foot or bicycle (areas of many hundred square miles). We sympathised with her family's difficulties with the British nationality regulations. Because Dorothy's husband had been born in India, where his father was a serving army officer and then their own two sons had been born in Northern Rhodesia where Haile was a serving officer, his sons were not entitled to a British passport!!! This seemed to make a mockery of serving King and country.

Bessie Frost, an energetic little body, who reminisced with deep affection about life in Singapore with her meteorologist husband.

Jill Grills, who had grown up in Nigeria and whose parents were still there.

Rosemary Kirby, a locally born and educated 'white Zambian', who had a gentle and generous nature and was never seen to be ruffled; she later resigned and opened her own primary school which quickly gained a very good reputation.

Barbara Cook, out from England on contract and enjoying every moment of a wildly social life.

Jean Sandford (Sandling ?), a most quiet and gentle soul who had to cope alone one day when her horses were attacked by a swarm of bees until in pain they impaled themselves on a barbed wire fence.

May Hardie, a redoubtable red haired Scot who often wondered how the children coped not only with learning in English, but also had to cope with a diversity of accents - admitting hers was probably the strongest.

May Sharpe, a young and pretty S. Rhodesian Coloured who was married to Alfred Sharpe, a N. Rhodesian Coloured, whose two daughters became firm friends with our own two children.

Mrs Bal from India, who later moved into the room next to mine and was the most delicate and petite woman I had ever met and whose husky and amusing comments enlivened many a break time. She thoroughly enjoyed recounting the story of our first meeting.

'I was told,' she would say in her inimitable husky voice. 'to ask the teacher in the next room if I had any problems on the first day. A Mrs Kashita! Well, I thought, Mrs Kashita! What kind of a name is that? she must be a Spanish lady or perhaps a Japanese lady, she must look verrry frraagile little lady, even smaller than me.'

And then, with great glee, she would point at me and say,

'And look what I find! This grrreat big Yorkshire woman with red hair! How can this be a Mrs Kashita?'

As I said earlier all our classrooms opened out on to a verandah surrounding a large oblong garden, where the messengers would do some desultory weeding when they could no longer avoid it. We noticed after a while that after Jill joined the staff, the corner of the garden outside her classroom received constant attention from two young messengers. It did not take long to see that their eyes were glued, not to the weeds, but to the long expanse of Jill's legs as she bent over the desks. Jill, at 5'9" had long slim legs which 'went up to her armpits' as one envious member of staff phrased it. Although Zambian tradition dictated that bare thighs were unseemly there was never a word of complaint from the messengers - or much change in the weed ridden bed.

Benson was the senior messenger and he brought round the tray of teas at 9 o'clock, which was very welcome as we taught from 7.30 to 10am without a break. Round about 9am he would appear in the doorway, put down the tray, pour a steaming cup of fresh tea and silently go on his way. After I had been there about a week, he appeared in the doorway, went through the usual routine and then said, 'Excuse please, Dona, drink tea.'

I stared.

'Drink tea please, Madam. You leave too much tea in cup. Sometimes you forget to drink tea. Drink now, please Madam.'

It was also Benson who tantalised our nostrils on cold mornings in the cold season by frying onions in the messenger's kitchen. The delicious aroma would waft delicately along the verandahs and eddy by our open doors.

At break time we adjourned to a tiny staffroom where fourteen of us sat cramped together, knee to knee, in a space meant for eight - or did playground duty out on a vast expanse of sun baked grass surrounded on three sides by tall trees, where cicadas shrieked in the hottest months and children hunted for their cast off skins. When I look back I always see playground duty as hot dry period and yet the grass must have been lush and green at least in January and February.

Ceri would occasionally say hello as she passed at playtime, but most of the time she preferred to separate school and home by not acknowledging me. After half an hour's break it was back into the classrooms until midday when the Grade Ones then went to sit in a wired enclosure under the trees by the main gate, waiting to be collected. Grade twos had lessons for another half hour.

A boy being collected from the enclosure at Lusaka Infants

Ceri was delighted to be back with her friends and I was finding Lusaka Infants a most congenial work place. But Simon was showing an increased reluctance to go to nursery school - the one where Ceri had been so happy - until at length I thought I should have a word with the staff there.

'I am so glad, Mrs Kashita, that you came in. I was going to ask you to come in shortly. Have you ever thought of having Simon assessed?'

I looked at the young teacher.

'Assessed? How?'

'He does seem to be very far behind the other children in development. He has no interest in copying writing patterns and he never responds in reading lessons.'

'I should hope not,' I said with some asperity. 'I am surprised that you are expecting three year olds to sit over writing patterns and reading for any length of time.'

'Three years old? Is that all he is? He is so much bigger than many others I thought he was at least four and a half.'

Whatever the staff thought about Simon's height it did not seem to be a very good reason for sitting him down to formal work and I lost all confidence in a nursery school which did not check children's ages and even then would expect them to conform to a standard achievement. Fortunately at about that time a nursery school opened in the church hall just down the road from home in Roma and I set off that very afternoon to meet the good lady in charge.

Ann Wallace was a bright bubbly personality, who roared with laughter when I asked her at what age she would expect children to sit and copy writing patterns and read from flash cards. Her nursery school had plenty of large and small equipment, there was sand and dressing up and water play and stories and everything small children should have. Simon was to start in January. I was disappointed to find that the nursery did not open till 8am but Banda solved the problem by walking Simon down the road and collecting him at midday. It was not long before Simon persuaded him that they should go by bicycle and he rode off every morning with a bright smile sitting on a cushion strapped to the crossbar.

I warned Banda that on no account was he to allow Simon to sit on the carrier behind him, having seen a bad accident at school. A boy from another class was collected every day by the gardener and rode home on the carrier, usually waving cheerfully to his friends left behind. One day a car came tearing into the school drive and out jumped a parent calling for help. On the back seat was the sobbing boy. His foot had caught in the rear wheel spokes and the gardener had taken the cries of pain for cries of encouragement to speed on. The passing parent spotted what was happening and recognising the uniform, rushed him back to us. While she and the Head set off for the hospital I found the home address on the file and drove round to inform the parents. We got to the hospital as the doctors were requesting permission to operate on the lacerated heel.

Our classes were all over 40 now and only reached a peak because the classrooms physically could not take another desk. 'Parents come to me and when I tell them we are full, they say they will provide the desk and chair,' complained Miss Fernandes. 'I have to take them to a classroom and say Look there is no place we can put another desk. And still they come. What to do? They want to put their child on the waiting list. I say it is too long already. But still they do not want to listen. What to do?'

Poor Miss Fernandes, a thankless task indeed.

Only once was I able to give her some practical help.

'Oh, Mrs Kashita, I do not know what to do. One hour I have sat with the Minister, he wants me to take a child of a friend of his. I have showed him my lists and I have showed him the rooms are full. I cannot take another child! And it is not fair even if I have a place which I have not the child is not even on the waiting list! (all in one breath) But because it is the Minister, what to do?'

I was only half listening because this was no new story and I had 40 children wanting my attention but something made me ask, 'Which Minister is it this time?'

When she told me I smiled, for once Miss Fernandes might be left in peace.

'Listen,' I said softly. 'Go back to the office, put an application form in front of him and ask him to fill it in ...'

'But Mrs Kashita! There is no point. I have no place. If I say fill in the form he will not go away until I give a place and I have no place.'

'Ask him to complete the form,' I repeated. 'Just get out one of the forms and offer him a pen and ask him to get on with it. Believe you me, he will be out of your office like a shot. Just say, he must complete the form for you now.'

After some more 'what to do's ' Evelyn tottered off, shaking her head. In less than ten minutes she was back in my room.

'He has gone! I gave him the form and he said there was no need to write the form because he is a Minister but when I said he must complete the form he put it in his pocket and went away. Why?'

'Keep it under your hat, he cannot read and write and would be too embarrassed to ask you to fill in the form for him. Perhaps he will get someone else to do it for him, but I don't think he will be too keen on sitting in your office from now on - and if he is - just pass him a pile of papers from the Ministry and ask his opinion.'

An unfair advantage perhaps but we did need some breathing space. Nor would I have criticised the man for not being able to read, he was an able speaker in National Assembly where we assumed he had papers read to him.

Our intake was becoming more and more multi-cultural. In one class of five year olds starting in January for the first time I had Nigerians - and Biafrans - Indians from India and Indians who were third and fourth generation Zambians, Italian, Yugoslav, Ghanaian, English, Scot, Welsh, Danish, African and Coloured Zambian, Rhodesian and Japanese. Classrooms were becoming an exciting reflection of life in Zambia. Our efforts to understand each other caused some frustration and much hilarity but children being children they communicated in their own way, several languages with a smattering of English serving them very well.

I pressed ahead with a forced reading programme which gave them a fast growing working vocabulary, at the same time they were proud of their achievements in reading skills. The Janet and John reading scheme was supplemented by some Happy Trio and that was all we had for stock, so I made some class books and charts and wall newspapers, which were heavily laced with Janet and John vocabulary but which related to our daily activities. These were read avidly as I changed them every three or four days.

Conrad Nyirenda, son of the then Minister of Education Wesley Nyirenda, was greatly attached to Tokihio Tamaki, son of a Japanese diplomat, and took it upon himself to tutor Tokihiko in English. He arrived one day armed with a copy of China Reconstructs, a large and glossy magazine supplied by the Chinese Embassy to Ministries and offices in large numbers. On the cover of this particular issue was a highly coloured photo of a small Chinese boy gazing proudly at the national flag in the middle distance.

Pulling the magazine from his lunch case, Conrad waved it aloft proudly.

'Look Tokihiko! You here. Look, Japanese boy same like you,' said the proud Conrad. He was clearly about to embark upon some spirited description of what the boy was doing, but to his astonishment Tokihiko took one look at the magazine and burst into angry words.

'No! no same like me! He no same me! Me Japanese...'

'Yes' agreed Conrad happily. 'Same like you.'

'NO! me Japanese! He no same me! Me Japanese!'

And off stormed Tokihiko to his desk in high dungeon while Conrad gazed at the offending picture, shrugged his shoulders and then, catching my eye, he smiled and said

'Just same like Tokihiko' and sure that he was correct but that his friend had not quite understood, he tucked the offending magazine into his case for a later date.

He did not give up on his efforts to introduce Tokihiko to the niceties of the English language. I passed the boys toilets one day to hear a familiar voice saying

'High.....high....high....up...up...up...low...low....down....down...'

Infant teachers possess acute ESP when it comes to toilets so I walked quietly in to find Conrad giving a practical demonstration of the difference between high - up and low- down with Tokihiko an adept pupil in front of the urinals. The floor was awash but I knew that at least the full meaning of those words had been fully understood.

May Sharpe had been the first non-white member of our staff and her daughter Jennnifer was now in my class and I dreaded Open Evening as her writing grew in size and blackness in her enthusiasm until it resembled an unkempt thorny bramble hedge by the bottom of the page. But Alfred and May laughed as much as I did when I opened her books. Alfred and May moved to Roma and our children spent many happy hours together. Ceri and Jenny dominating the play while Simon and Susan trotted behind, more than willing allies.

Luipa was a new pupil too and had the problem of being a spina bifida child which necessitated him wearing a nappy and having to be changed mid-morning. Assuring his mother that it would be no problem I spoke to the class before he started school. Apart from a mild sympathy for the first two or three days the class carried on as normal while Luipa and I slipped down to the sick room to change his clothes mid-morning. However, within a week Benson, who never missed a trick, arrived at my room to inform me that he would take over this particular duty and that Luipa would do very well in his care. Once Benson had made up his mind it was pointless to argue so thereafter Benson appeared at my door shortly before 10am and beckoned to Luipa, who slipped off, with never a ripple in the classroom routine.

Looking back I marvel at the fact that I left 40 five year old children to work quietly - and they did - completely unsupervised and no one batted an eye lid or screamed health and safety.

The class was getting nicely settled in now and we were well on our way to being a close unit when the Head appeared one day with an anxious looking couple and a small boy. My heart sank because this was sure to be another 'what to do' heart felt plea for a place we had not got. But there was a difference this time.

The Grays had been told that their son, who had been at school for over a year in UK, was ESN (Educationally Sub Normal) and would never make any progress academically. In fact it was arranged that when they returned to England, Stephen would be admitted to a Special school.

'And so you see,' said Miss Fernandes. 'Mr and Mrs Gray know that Stephen will not learn anything but if he could be in school with other children it will help him settle when they return to UK and he goes away to school. You don't have to worry about teaching him anything. Just to let him play with other children.'

I looked at the small boy of six who had been told he would never learn to read and then at his anxious parents.

We squeezed him in at the end of a table and said we would try to help. Towards the end of the morning I called Stephen over to my desk and showed him some of the reading books asking if he had seen any similar at his school in England. He glanced briefly at them and then away again saying, 'I can't read.'

He insisted he had not seen any books like ours and that anyway he did not know about this business called reading because he could not read. As all the other children were proud possessors of a 'reading book' to take home each day I thought he should join in the fun. Picking up the first copy of the monotonous Happy Trio, We Look And See, I opened the first page and read to him

'Oh

Oh look.

Oh oh oh.'

And then talked about the pictures of Sally. Stephen smiled .

I pointed to the word Sally and said Sally and then at Sally on a card.

'What is that?' I asked.

Stephen looked at me in surprise and said 'Sally'.

I began to laugh while he looked at me puzzled.

'You can read! You have been pulling my leg. You read Sally.'

'Is that reading?' asked Stephen. 'But I can't read.'

And so he began to read. Every day we found a new word and talked about it in context of the pictures in the book, he found it among other words. We began to list the words on cards and read them together every day. He took them home to show his parents who were cooperative, thinking it made him feel part of the class.

Once he knew seven words of course he was able to read the first eleven pages of the book

And slowly Stephen began to admit that he could read, 'A little bit – not the real thing'.

However, once he knew sixteen words and could read each and every page 'in a real book' he started to believe he was not one of life's failures - a shocking thing for any six year old to believe. His parents, who had been holding their breath, also began to think that perhaps I was not talking off the top of my head and that perhaps Stephen was not completely uneducable. It still makes me feel good when I remember how Stephen went on to read all the way through the reading scheme and write his own news and stories until at the end of the year we felt sure that he would fit into any infant class in UK.

His confidence was wonderful to see and he rapidly forgot that he had been 'unable to read' - although his parents didn't and were over joyed that they had taken the plunge to work in 'developing Africa' for a three year contract. Coincidentally Mr Gray worked for one of the Indeco companies and was later transferred to the Copperbelt. Andrew was later made chairman of Indeco and on a visit to the Copperbelt was approached by Mr Gray, who asked if he were the husband of Mrs Kashita at Lusaka Infants School? Mr Gray related Stephen's latest success in his new school on the Copperbelt and said how delighted they were with his progress, which was a good average all round.

Andrew told me this story with some amusement, the humour of it appealing to us both. For once it was not

'Are you the wife of Mr Kashita?'

But

'Are you the husband of Mrs Kashita?'

'Now I know what you feel like,' said Andrew.

Lusaka Lusaka arrived in class one morning with his leg in plaster from the toe up to the knee. He had a broken ankle but had walked to school as usual.

'We just have to set off earlier,' said his father, who was not going to let a three mile walk to school with a plastered leg come between his son and the chance of education.

Lusaka in the swimming pool at Lusaka Infants

Some incidents were more difficult to cope with. Those were the days when children brought in things for 'Show and Tell' - I wonder if it still happens today? One morning a boy stood up, smiling widely and clutching a crumpled plastic bag. Standing next to me he described in detail how a bat had flown into his bedroom the previous night and how his father had chased it with a towel and beat it down. And! ... his father had let him bring it to school! He placed the crumpled bag on my lap, smiling expectantly. Slowly I peeled back the folds of plastic and sure enough there was the bat, not looking too battered. Cautiously I opened the bag and tried to hold the bat up in the bag but forty hopeful faces looked disappointed.

'You can take it out and hold it up?' the owner asked. (I was quite used to the intonation meaning a statement was actually a question). There was a stir of excitement so bravely I put my hand in the bag, drew out the bat and held it up by the edge of a wing. Forty little faces were definitely impressed as I talked about how bats flew by sort of radar squeaks ... and there were silent ooohs ... far more than I expected ... felt a tickle and looked down to see the dead bat was very much alive. It had slowly curled back on itself and was now trying to crawl up my arm. Startled, I released the finger-tip hold of the wing and inspired, the bat continued its ascent up my arm, which was fortunately in a sleeve, it being the cold season. But it gave the creature a better grip and I will swear it picked up speed as my mind spun from Rabies! to Never Show Fear to Children and back to Rabies! Somehow I managed to walk to the open door and waggle my arm outside and somehow the bat got the message and fluttered off to nearby trees and I told the disappointed class it would have been unkind to keep it longer.

And somehow managed not to scream throughout.

As class teachers we taught all subjects ourselves with the only exception of music, when the gifted few doubled up the classes - and we gave them support by organising audio visual programmes. And on Friday mornings Sister Pia came from the Convent to take the Catholic children for instruction. The first few weeks I dutifully lined up the few Catholic children for instruction and sent them off with Sister Pia. On the following Friday my line of Catholics at the door was much longer and I carefully checked my register, while Sister Pia waited.

'But you ... and you ... And you don't go to Sister,' I said.

'Oh yes, Mrs Kashita, we want to go to Sister.'

And then Ashley gave the game away.

'They want to come - I told them about Sister's ghost stories'.

'Ghost stories Sister?'

She looked blank for a moment and then laughed.

'The Holy Ghost.'

But we were not to be left alone to enjoy our teaching. Change and progress were the order of the day and things were afoot. The Ministry of Education was ambitious to improve primary education in Zambia. So, let us begin by setting out a Zambian primary curriculum. A most noteworthy plan but sadly, like most best laid plans of mice and men, there were hiccups. No changes can ever be made of course without a panel of experts and so we were visited by the fundis from time to time. I recall one morning very well.

A supercilious gentleman - English - and a well-built lady - English - appeared in my room one morning with the Head. They were on not a fact finding but fact imparting mission.

'Mr Ummmm and Miss Errr have been working on what is

probably a break-through in the teaching of maths,' said Miss Fernandes with a vague and somewhat preoccupied smile. The man hitched his file a little higher and looked benevolently over it at me. I smiled politely back.

The woman leaned a little closer and I retreated discreetly back from the whisky fumes.

'Yes,' she beamed. 'Language is the problem! And children without language are unable to visualise mathematical concepts. And so, this is the experimental stage you understand?' further wafts of whisky 'and so we have devised this wonderful whole New Approach.'

'Wonderful,' agreed the Head and I.

The man hitched the file until his nostril was in dire peril and smiled even more condescendingly.

'Yes,' breathed the whisky. 'It is so simple but Quite Revolutionary! Each child will have its own set of Maths Apparatus, taking the form of cards printed with number patterns with which they will see and solve the problems. For example, when you talk of 2 plus 2 it means nothing to them BUT when they can SEE 2 dots and 2 dots printed on cards and fit them together ... then we have this Complete Breakthrough in the Learning Process.'

Light dawned.

'Ah!' I said, turning to a table where some children were working. 'You mean like this?'

And I picked up the domino patterns printed on cards which I had made for the children to use as an alternative to beads and counters and bottle tops. 'My first Headmistress in UK introduced me to the idea ...'

But somehow it seemed better not to continue.

There was a slight strain in the atmosphere. An inhaling of breaths and a hitching of files and our distinguished experts departed, my home made cards ignored ... and the children's use of them totally bypassed.

In due course all the primary schools were issued with huge sheets of printed cards with domino patterns in delicate shades of blue and yellow and pink and green, which we spent hours cutting up and then sorting into individual plastic bags, one bag per child. The idea was great - my first Head had been introduced to the idea by her first Head who had ...

But I do not think it had gained in being reproduced on cards of varying sizes and colours with the result that the tiny one centimetre square dot was forever falling off tables - or being blown off by heavy breathing - and falling into cracks in the floor.

Once the reorganisation of the Maths was well on its way, the experts then tackled the reading schemes. Hurrah! Who would not welcome a change from Janet and John? And a Zambian reading scheme was a most praiseworthy idea. It was not long before Mulenga and Jelita made their appearance. As seems to be unavoidable with any reading scheme, the Zambian Primary Course devised and introduced a series of books about a brother and sister and their activities. So far, so good. But because the scheme was in its experimental stages it was done very much on the cheap. Or so it appeared.

The first books in the series consisted of just a few pages so that all the repetition of vocabulary could only be done with a blackboard and chalk and flash card work - a child could not sit and read more than a few short sentences from his book.

The second problem did not occur to me but was raised by the parents, we had decided to use the new books in conjunction with our existing books. The first set of books arrived well into the year and so my class were able to read them easily. As they had never met the books before I made it a bit of an event by talking about how exciting it was to have books about our own country and so on and so forth. I added that as the books were the first in the series and therefore the easiest we would just read the first three books through together to look at the pictures and meet Mulenga and Jelita.

'People and places in our own country!' I enthused.

We read through Mulenga. There was a silence and a definite feeling of anti-climax and then Lusaka summed it up for his fellows.

'Ah, this Mulenga! He get a ball! It is green. So?'

Hastily I pressed on with the pink book Jelita, who fared little better. The boys were not over impressed with her culinary activities and the girls felt that by virtue of being at school alone THEY would never be called upon to cook on an open fire. Not now and certainly not in the future.

Book 3 was no better. I forget what it was about - no doubt Mulenga and Jelita got together on the same page and picked up sticks for the fire.

However, I thought we should read through the books and integrate them with Janet and John - and jolly old Sally with her siblings Dick and Jane. Therefore after a Janet and John book had gone home, it would be followed by a Mulenga and Jelita – to be read to parents, who followed their children's progress with such pride and interest. If the children were disappointed with the new scheme, the parents were horrified. Very soon I had a Zambian father asking tactfully for a word.

Was his son working hard?

I assured him he certainly was.

Was his son as good as the other children?

Most certainly.

Then, ahem, was the school beginning to teach the children in a segregated manner?

I stared.

'Then, ahem, the new book my son just brought home... er ... is it just for the ... er ... Africans? I would like my son to read European books also.'

Light dawned.

I explained the introduction of the Zambia Primary Course, which, I hastened to add, was for the benefit of the whole country and so on....

I assured him that his son would not be deprived of Janet and John and the white children, would also read Mulenga and Jelita.

He relaxed and confided

'I know it is a good thing to have our own books ... but these books, they are not teaching them so well about other things. You see, our children know about cooking nsima over the fire and sleeping on the floor on a blanket. They know how it is to wash in a bowl of water on the floor because there is no bathroom (some of Mulenga and Jelita's more interesting activities) but I want them to read and learn about other ways to live. Also you know, the white children here are going to look at these books and think that all Zambian children cook over a fire. It is embarrassing for our children if their friends think they do not know anything else.'

Other teachers reported similar responses but Mulenga and Jelita were here to stay and the one dot squares from the maths scheme spread like confetti throughout the school.

The Ministry of Education then took the Zambianisation process a stage further and we were invaded by students. Until then Zambian primary teachers had been trained and worked completely separately from us. Now they were to join us. At least a selected few were. The first of these students were carefully handpicked teachers with a good number of years of experience to their credit and who were thought to have worked with some skill and showed promise.

They were carried off for further training and it was decided that they would benefit by doing some teaching practice in the hitherto banned European schools (such terms were still used although the former European schools were now integrated and were officially fee paying schools). Old habits die hard.

My first student was a young man who came in to observe for a couple of days and was then to take the class under the eye of his tutor. After a morning together he confided that he was nervous about working in such different conditions and with children whose English, in some cases, was better than his own. We went over his ideas and plans for lessons. I explained to him what I had been doing and why and what I hoped the children would achieve. He looked sadly at me, confiding,

'But we have not worked like this and we have never seen schools like this before.'

And he was filled with foreboding about the day his tutor was due to inspect his lessons.

Cursing a senseless set of tutors, who apparently did not have the gumption to crash train these chaps, I asked him if he would like some suggestions from me and we sat down to work out some fool proof lessons.

'What you really need to make the day go with a swing,' I added. 'is something to really capture the children's interest and co-operation. I tell you what, I was going to bring in a pet rabbit for the day. I'll bring it in for you and then you can have a topic you can link your lessons to.'

This struck him as a very novel idea and after I'd explained 'make the day go with a swing', we planned some work together. And I wondered what sort of practical training the students were really getting.

On the day his tutor was due all went well. The student arrived early and was introduced to the rabbit, I had chosen one of the more docile females and we went over the lesson plans again. Once the children were settled I handed them over to him and retired to the back of the classroom where I was shortly joined by the tutor.

By now we were on to The Rabbit and the animal as well as the children was impeccable in both behaviour and response. They had forgotten our presence at the back of the room and gave the student their full attention and he was responding with increasing ease and authority.

The tutor scribbled away in his file looking impressed. I began to congratulate myself that we had pulled it off and watched the children clamouring to draw pictures in their topic books. A quiet hum ensued and a general feeling of bonhomie prevailed.

'That's my red crayon you bastard,' said Ashley conversationally. The tutor's file snapped back open and the red pen was wielded with vigour. I was appalled to discover that he had expected the student to 'deal' with Ashley's choice of phrase on the spot and it was pointless for me to whisper that surely had he done so, every child in the room would have gone home rolling the expression off the tips of their tongues.

I have said that one of the joys of teaching there at that time was the range of nationalities of our children; another heady factor was the complete and satisfactory integration of so many backgrounds, diplomatic children, servants' children, office workers' children, army children, rich and poor and all levels in between made the slogan of ONE ZAMBIA ONE NATION seem an actuality not a politicians pipe dream on top of an ant hill.

We even had the President's twins in Jill's class as I well recall. Not that I remember the two children very well but I do remember the situation into which they unwittingly got us.

An exhibition of Zambian arts and crafts was being held at the Anglo American building at the end of Church Road - not too far from us - and being afire for all things Zambian four of us asked permission to take our classes. The Head was most agreeable and briefly went over the route and plans with us.

'Of course I will send a note home to the parents,' she said. 'But I think I should phone State House direct as the President is such a busy man, he will not see letters from me, but I will get permission from someone in State House office. His Excellency gave a number to ring if we ever needed to. After all, you will be taking them off the school premises.'

We nodded and forgot all about it.

When the day came we lined up our crocodiles on the drive in front of the school and repeated the usual exhortations about holding hands and behaviour-to-be-expected-at-an-exhibition. Miss Fernandes stood on the verandah beaming.

Suddenly we were deafened by a squad of motor cyclists sweeping in through the gates in tight formation.

Pandemonium.

While throttles do whatever throttles do to produce ear splitting roars a sergeant snappily saluted the Head and handed over some papers. Trying to cover both her ears at once and read the paper was impossible so she handed the papers to the nearest teacher.

We had been sent a Presidential Police Motorcycle Escort to and from the exhibition.

It was in vain to plead that a constable at the traffic lights would be a great help … an escort we had been sent and an escort we would have. Bowing to the inevitable we set off. Jill led the way, having the youngest class, and four classes of 40 children each strung out behind her with we three teachers at strategic intervals. The escort, finding that they could not travel at our pace, took it into their heads to follow a circular route to the head of the column and back again, to the great delight of the children who walked backwards most of the way to follow this manoeuvre, and to the great bewilderment and frustration of the general motoring public.

Pavements at the side of the road are a rare luxury in Zambia so we tramped through the rough grass at the side of the road, leaping over storm drain channels, thanking our lucky stars they were all small ones and not more than 2 feet across or deep.

Then another problem raised its head. Jill set off first because her class were the youngest but she did not take into account that she had the longest legs outside the London Palladium and – as she later admitted – she was desperate to get away from the roar 'of those damn bikes'. Consequently she strode ahead, the first two children valiantly trying to keep abreast but the line of 160 children strung out in ever increasing gaps. In vain I tried to shout above the roar and exhaust fumes while Jackie, naturally plump but also eight months pregnant, called plaintively behind. Mrs Bal had sensibly wrapped her sari about her face until only her two amused eyes showed and she floated far behind at the rear of our very extended crocodile.

Traffic at the crossroads traffic lights was brought to a complete standstill while we shepherded our charges through the massed ranks of escort, trying in vain to look as though this was a normal occurrence.

The exhibition itself was a haven of peace - all other visitors having rushed out to see the VIP's who had arrived 'with an escort'. I remember little of the walk back and I will not repeat what we said to the Head. But it was not an exercise to be repeated as our follow up work resulted in lurid pictures and graphic descriptions of the escort; not one child mentioned the exhibition.

In addition to being so engrossed in school in the mornings and with Ceri and Simon's activities in the afternoons, my evenings were increasingly filled with attending dinners and sundowners and official functions with Andrew. I never shared his enthusiasm for a very full social calendar, managing to bow out gracefully from quite a number of invitations, but could not do it too often.

Having sat up till all hours and then got myself to school on time I did not take too kindly to the supercilious Italian who, full of his position in Alitalia and so called social commitments, thought fit to produce his son Paolo frequently an hour or so late for school. He appeared to believe that his precious nights socialising was an excuse enough. After several of these late arrivals I saw fit to reprove the man, pointing out that his son arrived late far too often. He looked down his nose and explained once more to this half -witted teacher that he had a certain position to maintain and, for example, had had to attend a function the night before held by the Chairman of Indeco no less.

'And very pleasant it was too,' I agreed. 'But school begins at 7.30 and I am here on time and so must Paolo be.'

A blank look met my apparent irrelevancy.

'I was your hostess last night,' I pointed out.

October 1969 was the fifth anniversary of our independence. Looking around one could feel a certain satisfaction with progress being made - a University, a University Teaching Hospital, a new Parliament, the integration in schools, a bottle plant shortly to be built in Kapiri Mposhi and a cannery at Miwinilunga ... so many positive developments. But it was sad to note that while President Kaunda could say in an interview with John Leech that he wanted Skinner back as Chief Justice and that he regarded Skinner as a true Zambian, his views were not respected by officials. The Western Province Association Chairman Sicilongo told the Zambian Traders Association that Zambians of European and Asian descent would no longer be regarded as true Zambians When I pointed out this anomaly to Andrew he said, 'Ah well, who listens to these chaps anyway?' Which did not seem to be the point to me. Perhaps such 'chaps' were speaking without any real authority, but some unknowing people could be listening to them and believing it. Some of us read the reports in the Press and found it disquieting. It was hard to ignore or completely dismiss

It was even harder to ignore the growing crime rate, the continuing ANC – UNIP violence, the constant disasters on the railway and the carnage on the roads. A sad statistic in December seemed to typify the casual approach to life; the Times of Zambia stated that 19 died in road accidents in Lusaka over the weekend. And over the year there were 10,000 crashes for the 80,000 vehicles on the road. Alarming statistics indeed, especially when one considered the wide open roads and space in Zambia.

Our lives were very full at that time. I was so very involved in school, so absorbed in the rapid changes and developments that I never awoke without a feeling of anticipation. And Andrew had the air of a satisfied man; he had seen his country achieve independence and was increasingly involved in higher levels of decision making.

Our lives were completed by Ceri and Simon, expanding personalities who were a constant delight. I daily thanked God for two healthy and attractive and intelligent children. Our lives were completed by them and our relaxation with them in the home we had created in Roma.

We would wake about six in the morning to the faint clatter from the kitchen as Zulu let himself in and began preparing breakfast. Then there would be the patter of feet as Ceri and Simon went to greet him and the dog Micky, the only dog ever allowed to sleep in the house. He had a blanket on the floor of the ironing room just off the kitchen - only I never told Andrew, whenever he was away I would put Micky's blanket on the floor outside my bedroom door.

We would wash and dress while calling down the corridor to

Ceri and Simon to make a start. They would usually get to their bathroom in time for me to check on their hands and faces. Dressing was never a problem, school uniforms put a stop to any discussions on what to wear with Ceri, Simon was free to choose. Zulu would have prepared a substantial breakfast, looking back I don't know how I managed to sit down every day to cereals, cooked breakfast, toast and a pot of tea. By now the cats would be in the house and Micky trotting behind Banda as he went to feed the chickens and rabbits.

We left the house about seven o'clock, Andrew to go straight to the office where he said he would get more paper work done before the office opened at eight than all the rest of the day. Ceri and Simon would check for reading books and a biscuit and pencils – Simon liked to have a suitcase to keep up with big sister. Satchels had disappeared from the shops and small cardboard suitcases had replaced them. He would wave us off as we shot out of the house with Zulu calling what was for lunch and how many people would there be for tea?

As Ceri and I drove to school, Simon would help Banda with his jobs until it was time to ride down the hill to nursery. Zulu would make a mad dash at the washing up and the laundry so that the latter would be flapping on the line before he went down to the servants' quarters to enjoy his breakfast. Very much his own boss he would then saunter back to attack the housework, this meant making the beds to hospital tightness so we always had to fight our way into bed, polishing the parquet floors until they shone like mirrors and a cursory dust round. Any cobwebs above eye level were never seen until I made a complaint. The floors were like glass but the ceilings could resemble a cobwebby horror movie. But by the time we came home the house would be cool and shining and smelling of the fresh laundry piled high in the ironing room.

Simon with a chameleon in the Roma garden

Andrew did not always come home for lunch and if he did it was always a quiet meal as he read the paper and listened to the News on the radio perched on the corner of the table. Ceri and Simon soon learned to whisper while the News was on. Then it was into the playroom while Ceri did any homework and Simon emptied the contents of toy cupboard onto the floor. One wall was lined with a four foot high pin board and was constantly changed as their interests grew.

Many afternoons we went to visit friends or expected them to come to us. The children would play indoors or out in the garden where the dogs were always at their heels as we sat and sipped cool drinks and talked about nothing as women like to do. The couch grass had grown into good lawns, spreading right round the house, and a new mower was Banda's pride and joy. I would have liked a hibiscus hedge, remembering the one we had had at Mount Makulu. It had stood over six feet high and its large scarlet flowers were set off by the dark green glossy leaves. But remembering how the women used to walk along plucking the new leaves for relish to eat with their nsima, we thought a new hedge would take a long time to get established. So we planted a fast growing hedge with long thin leaves and yellow trumpet shaped flowers (name ? just can't remember).

Andrew relaxed at weekends with bricks and mortar, building first a fish pond and then a barbecue. We bought long treated eucalyptus poles and built the children a climbing frame. He built the rabbits super de luxe quarters with their own paved run and houses for the chickens and ducks and geese. Give Andrew a pile of bricks and mortar and you had a happy man.

At weekends Brian and Margaret Redway with their two small daughters Fenella and Veronica would arrive with Dennis and Renate Proctor, Suzanne and Christopher. Leslie and May Hardie lived in Roma and would bring Jimmy, Alistair and Laura. They would be closely followed by Alfred and May Sharpe and Jenny and Susan, who also lived in Roma.

Croquet at Roma with the Redways

With the Redways on the verandah in Roma

While the children swam or picnicked on the climbing frame or careered round the garden on their bicycles we would play wild games of croquet across the wide lawns. Wild games because Andrew was very expert after his games at University - he played a mean game sending opponents balls ricocheting into the undergrowth at the edge of the lawns. The dogs would race behind the children on their bikes until they all collapsed by the trays of food Zulu brought out and the cats would appear to sit beside the dogs, eyes large with anticipation. The geese, who would have been patrolling the hedges, would keep a sharp eyes open for crumbs and the peacocks would pace impatiently on the outer edges.

Simon and Veronica on the climbing frame

Sometimes the children would stay on for a weekend and would have to sleep sideways on mattresses laid on the floor as we ran out of beds. Malele and Mulilo Chuula would often be added to the numbers. Fortunately all the children got on very well together in spite of there being some very assertive personalities among the group.

Our children had an ideal childhood which they say they remember with much affection; so much casual outdoor life with friends and animals, sunshine and space in which to indulge their interests and energies.

Our two acres often seemed in danger of bursting at the seams. Initially I thought we had space and enough to spare. When we first moved on to the plot we had housed the chickens near the bottom of the slope near the fruit trees; the rabbits had their quarters nearer the house. When a fellow teacher Jean Sandford, was leaving I was thrilled to be offered her peacocks and hens. In our innocence we collected the birds, the cocks' magnificent tails filling the rear of our station wagon. We took them home and put them in the chicken run. They looked rather out of place and obviously felt it was rather beneath their dignity because when we returned from lunch with friends we found them stalking round the garden with an imperious air, which did not tally well with their bare backsides. Zulu said he and Banda had only noticed their escape when the dogs trotted past with mouthfuls of feathers. Sadly we removed the main flight feathers from their wings so they could not fly away over the garden fences. And wondered how long it took for their tails to grow.

Looking back it didn't seem very long because for ever after that we were plagued by the escapades of our peacocks. Within the first week we arrived at a party with Andrew looking rather dishevelled after stopping the car only a little way from home and pursuing an errant peacock along a storm drain and as he finally staggered back to the car spotting its mate sitting on next door's gate post. As Geoff had 10 foot brick pillars as gate posts it necessitated Andrew shinning up while the bird cocked a wary eye, but fortunately it took no evasive action.

However, we always forgave them as they were a magnificent sight as they paced the garden and while we soon got used to their piercing cries it initially unnerved our visitors. As their feathers grew they settled down in our garden and roosted happily in a tree or up on the barbecue. Then they became more adventurous and took to flying on to the roof ridge, we accepted the faint pitter patter of feet and the piercing shrieks above us, but the subsequent slither as they slid down the roof over the sitting room or rattled across the roof of the kitchen was always startling - and many a dish had a narrow escape.

Barry and Ingilby Cox on one of their visits from Mazabuka asked if we would like a couple of young birds if their latest clutch of peachicks survived. Happily they did and our flock of peacocks increased. But then so did their depredations.

They took to hop, skip and jump over the fence at the bottom of the garden and into a neighbour's garden to sample his lettuces. 'It's the fact that they take just one bite from each one,' complained John Simpson bitterly.

One day we were intrigued to see that our four peacocks now numbered ten but before we could make their acquaintance more intimately the Botswana High Commissioner, who lived diagonally across the road, came to ask if he could have his peacocks back! (Variation on a theme?) ours were to blame of course! We had not noticed how quickly the flight feathers had grown again and they had taken to flying across the road and landing on his roof, and then had, with raucous cries, lured his birds away. (No doubt with promises of fresh lettuce!) While we both agreed to deal with flight feathers yet again the nights were made hideous with their lovelorn shrieks until eventually flight was again possible and the love trysts began again.

When clipped feathers kept them at home they would indulge in another prank. Once in a while a peacock would decide to hop over into the chicken run and have a snack. This was perfectly agreeable to all. What was not, was his frequent desire to display his all to the chickens. A large technicoloured bird at the feed tray was fine but a flamboyant display of shaking tail feathers as he strutted and rattled the lower wing feathers was more than reserved chickens could abide. The whole flock of hens would flutter and flap over the fence and flee cackling across the garden while the peacock danced in solitary splendour. The dogs would pretend they were rounding up the hens, all the while indulging in wild barking circles and the hens protested to the heavens that no fowl should be treated thus.

A peacock displaying his all!

Micky, the dog, had gained a reputation for his willingness to tackle any dog larger than himself and had had several trips to the vet to be patched together. For a short time he would be a reformed character but then would be racing up to the gate again to insult any passing canine. One Sunday morning he came round the side of the house with a very thoughtful air and even as we watched his eyes swelled up and began to look puffy.
'Always on a Sunday,' groaned Andrew as he got the car out and I ran indoors to phone the vet George Akefekwa. By the time we got him to the surgery Micky had a frightening top heavy appearance. George took one look and confirmed
'Snake bite.'
We sat for a long time until George came out with a very sick and sorry looking dog. He had had to cut out quite a large area of dead tissue from the top of Micky's head and with heavy anti snake bite injections hoped we could save him. We drove slowly

home, the dog lying on the back seat and for once forgetting to be car sick. When I lifted him out onto the drive his eyes were mere slits in a grossly distended head and he wobbled unsteadily on widely splayed legs. But before we could carry him indoors a passing dog barked. Micky gave a feeble woof and essayed a few tottering steps in the direction of the gate.

'He will live, the fool,' said Andrew as he picked up the dog and carried him inside.

And live of course he did, to antagonise other dogs and to take up fishing. Friends asked why we had an unsightly wire mesh over the fish pond - were we expecting herons? It was of course Micky adding to his repertoire. As the peacocks grew used to him and we always kept the gate shut, Micky had to find other hobbies. He took up fishing. He would stop by the fish pond and leaning his head on the wall, which was about his shoulder height, he would take a few laps of water and gaze meditatively into the depths. Then his ears would prick forward and he would spring up onto the wall and peer down more intently. This continued for some time until the day came when his curiosity got the better of him ; he dropped down into the pond and began to follow the fish under water, coming up for occasional splutters of air.

At last a fish would be caught and he would lay it gently on the top of the wall, look at it and turn to make his second catch. Andrew tried chasing him off .... putting a large papyrus in the middle of the pond where the fish could hide ... but in the end we had to resort to wire mesh. It looked unsightly but we no longer walked across the garden to be greeted by the vision of a jaunty black tail waving amongst the papyrus fronds.

Once one began to think about the individual personalities of our assorted pets they appeared more and more eccentric. Did anyone else have, for instance, a dog who liked eating avocado pears?

Candy and Micky got on very well. They had taken an instant liking to each other and keeping an eye on her activities did distract him from the gate to some extent. But he never did understand her fondness for avocado pears. Any fruit which fell from the tree was sure to be carried around by Candy, she would stop at regular intervals to dig her snout further into the pear (we had a mature and prolific tree), the mushier the better and she would positively smack her lips over the delicacy within.

Micky, not to be outdone, tried it a few times but never developed the same craving. However, he decided the geese had a point when he found they were not only admiring the mulberry hedge but were also gorging themselves on the fat purple berries. He tried these and was frequently to be seen delicately nibbling a mulberry on the hedge with his front teeth.

He did not, thank goodness, have the same dietary problems as the geese who, having dined liberally at the hedge, would then swagger round to the front of the house and bespatter the paved areas with copious purple droppings. Banda would hose these down daily in the mulberry season and I would bewail the mess but as Andrew pointed out, we could have no better watch dogs, day or night.

Peter and Paula had none of their mother Candy's fondness for pears – nor mulberries. They were just sound sensible dogs who asked for nothing more than to follow Ceri and Simon about.

The rabbits, in comparison, were model pets. Their only problem - or rather our problem - was that they bred like rabbits are reputed to do all the year round. Contrary to all the experts books, our buck was very attached to all his offspring and moped when parted from his does and kits. For some time we admired this ideal rabbit colony until the inevitable day dawned when we had to admit we were in danger of being swamped.

'A culling operation,' said Andrew. 'After all, that is what they are for. Food! So Banda and I will see to the slaughter and you and Zulu will take care of the skinning and freezing.'

Ceri and Simon were sent tactfully off to spend the day with friends and we reluctantly chose twenty rabbits, which were neatly plastic - wrapped bundles in the freezer before the children returned home.

We had taken wholly unnecessary precautions because at Sunday lunch first one observed,

'This chicken tastes different.'

'Hmmm,' said the other. 'Is it the fluffy white one?'

Apparently their devotion lay only with the original trio and the baby rabbits while they were still in the irresistible cuddly stage. The tortoises, which we had found at different times wandering along the road, lived peacefully with the rabbits, laying an occasional egg which we assumed were infertile as none ever hatched.

The cats were perhaps the least troublesome of the livestock. Grey Puss was now about six years old and a sedate old lady who prowled around the house and garden, having mastered the dogs, she kept an interested eye on the rabbits, occasionally leaping into the enclosure to inspect the latest litter. She would sprawl in selected spots around the garden and woe betide any dog or goose who strayed too close.

Ceri began to beg for a new pet, a Siamese kitten, and thinking that Puss had settled into early retirement we agreed. We collected the cream and brown scrap one afternoon and it was finding its way around the kitchen and being offered various dainties by the solicitous children when Big Puss stalked in through the back door. Her eyebrows shot up and with fur fluffed out she was rooted to the spot. But only for a moment. As the kitten gave a plaintive miaow she stomped across, stiff legged and batted it firmly across the head. Immediate shrieks of 'Poor little thing,' from Ceri who clutched the bewildered kitten and an 'It's all right Big Puss, I love you' from Simon. From that day Wong was very firmly Ceri's cat and Puss attached herself to Simon.

In one respect the kitten's arrival changed the older cat's life style. No longer could she bear to sleep away the hours, she had to keep an eye on Wong. The Siamese was possessed of a restless and inquisitive nature and wherever she went, Big Puss was always within reach, watching with a critical or condescending eye.

Andrew added some Khaki Campbells ducks to the menagerie and then we called a halt. They added to the variety of home produced dishes but had no discernible character whatsoever.

Cats and dogs and rabbits and tortoises and hens and ducks and geese and peacocks - we knew there were limits to what we could do on two acres. Or were we merely inhibited?

When we had moved to Roma Ceri had pointed out with great envy that there were horses on a plot at the bottom of the road and there were children having riding lessons. Absently I agreed it was an ideal way to spend an afternoon. Never say 'yes dear' to a child when you are driving, you are committing yourself to all forms of the unknown.

Ceri wisely waited until we had moved into the house and, I believe, until the last box was unpacked before she began her wearing down process. However, why not encourage your children to participate in as many activities as possible? So one afternoon I parked the car outside the house on Katima Mulilo Road, heaved open the bent iron gates and walked up to the house. There was a siesta air hanging over the house and plot and as I stepped up onto the verandah I wondered whether I should call later.

There was a cough. Looking over my shoulder I saw that a couple of horses were following me up onto the verandah so I hastily knocked on the door, which immediately swung inwards as a voice shouted,

'Come in, come in, I'm in the kitchen,'

As one horse appeared intent on following me in, I quickly stepped inside, shut the door and followed the sound of the voice. I found myself in a large kitchen confronted by a wiry haired woman clutching a large and protesting dog,

'Shan't be a minute. Just worming him. He says he won't and I say he will. So just sit down for a minute.'

Obediently I looked around for a chair. A vacant chair.

There were several chairs in the large and cluttered kitchen but each one was occupied by one or more cats; there was a cat sitting on the corner of the table watching the deworming process with an interested eye. There were a couple of cats curled round each other in a basket of lemons. Two cats sat nose to nose on a window sill, outside another cat looked in.

The dog and woman slowly circled the floor, while she appeared intent on pushing her arm as far as the elbow down its throat. I glanced around again for a seat. A cat looked down from the top of the fridge and having inspected me, closed its eyes again. There were cats and cats and cats, they were all colours and sizes, everywhere I looked, there was even a cat - no, there couldn't be - but I swear there was, a cat sleeping peacefully curled up in a frying pan on top of the cooker.

The antagonists came to a halt.

'Drink?'

'Yes please.'

I followed her through to another room where piles of books competed with more cats for chairs and floor space. We settled down with a drink each and Barbara Cripps began to expound her theories on horses and people and animals - we continued this conversation for many years.

Two acres in no way deterred Barbara Cripps from doing what she felt impelled to do - living with and for animals. She took in any and all stray animals. As so many expatriates left the country at the end of their contracts and light heartedly abandoned their cats and dogs on the premise that 'someone' would take them in - or perhaps they did not even bother to justify their actions at all - Barbara was sure of many pets to be rescued. Some were found wandering in the streets, some hid in storm drains scavenging what they could and with the prospect of drowning in some sudden storm. Some, heart breakingly, stayed on guard outside vacated houses.

She kept the horses because she loved them - most of them were unwanted for some reason or another - I suspect the riding lessons were merely to give the horses exercise and help pay for their feed. It was easy to get used to several dogs wandering the grounds and the cats which were here, there and everywhere but once the children started their riding lessons I had to sit on a bench outside the ring where I was constantly unnerved by some horse sauntering up behind me and then leaning down to breath companionably in my ear. The horses were so very cosy that I felt that at any moment one would lean on its elbow - if horses have such things - on my shoulder and open up some light social conversation.

What with keeping one ear cocked for sociable horses and my eyes glued to the ring, the first few lessons were far more exhausting for me than the children. Ceri was enthusiastic and reasonably confident; Simon having decided to keep up with his sister, apparently believed that his presence was sufficient and had Mrs Cripps filled with admiration for his relaxed manner - so relaxed in fact, that one afternoon we realised that he was quietly sleeping in the saddle while the horse went through its paces.

Simon was destined for the sleepy-cowboy-rides-into-town role and was totally without ambition in the ring. So it was agreed that he would exercise the horse round the ring with a groom while Ceri moved on to greater things. I learnt to relax and smile tolerantly while Ceri progressed and not even blink when she sailed through the branches of a cassia tree to be rewarded with, 'Get back on the bloody horse. It's not going to come back and pick you up.'

Ready to go riding

Margaret Redway now took her place beside me on the bench in the afternoons as her two children started lessons. She was even more nervous than I had been. By now I had realised that Mrs Cripps' bark was far worse than her bite and that while her horses seemed possessed of as individual characters as their owner, they did in fact obey her every word. As was evidenced by the time a horse took off when Fenella lost control,

'Staaaand, you silly bugger, staaaand!'

Stand he did - almost on the spot - while Fenella slid forward to the ground in a neat somersault and was predictably told to get back on and stop messing the horse about.

Margaret and I gradually began to leave the riding to progress without us and we would quietly disappear round the corner home to fortify ourselves with tea.

Living so close it was inevitable that Ceri and Simon began to ask to ride on Saturday mornings, pointing out that they could walk down on their own. The hour long sessions grew to whole morning sessions and I wondered at Simon's interest. One lunch time I was enlightened.

'I wish we had a bathroom like Mrs Cripps,' heavy sigh.

Andrew and I looked enquiringly.

'It rained a bit this morning so Mrs Cripps took us into her house for a drink and it's LOVELY!'

I remembered the cats and smiled.

'She has all those cats! Do you know she has thirty four now? But only twenty horses. And her bathroom! Why can't we keep white rats in our bathroom?'

'What?'

'She keeps them in the bathroom because the goat is in the spare bedroom and the cats wouldn't like the rats in the kitchen ...'

'We are NOT,' interrupted Andrew, 'having ANY white rats in the bathroom or anywhere else.'

White rats in bathrooms I could take in my stride, what was really bothering me was the fact that Andrew had never heard Mrs Cripps in her impeccable Rodean accent giving her opinion of a horse - or more likely rider's performance. The inevitable happened. A Saturday lunchtime again. Having eaten an enormous helping of pudding Simon pushed his plate away and announced in ringing Rodean tones

'That was a bloody fine lunch!'

It was agreed that like white rats, such things were best left at the Cripps'.

Our friendship continued for many years and even today Ceri and Simon have very happy memories of her lessons and conversations. I don't know how old she was when we first met, she seemed one of those people who are truly ageless. There was a Mr Cripps, a charming quiet man, somewhat overshadowed by his wife's exuberant personality, who occasionally slipped into the foreground and then just as quietly slipped back again. Several pairs of brown trousers and red shirts regularly fluttered on the line and I never saw Mrs Cripps wear anything else - until I heard she was in hospital.

We had been away and out of touch with events so when I heard she was hospitalised with pneumonia - to use an Americanism - I went off to the Nursing Home on Independence Avenue bearing the conventional box of chocolates. I toured the wards twice before I recognised the little figure in a pretty flowered and frilled nightie. Despite looking so much smaller in a horizontal position the personality was much the same and, as could be expected, it was not merely a case of pneumonia.

Some time ago Mrs Cripps had taken under her wing a former police horse, which had been classified as vicious and was due to be shot. This proved the police were incompetent and the horse greatly to be pitied! Barbara was allowed to take the horse on the strict understanding that he was unmanageable and certainly unrideable. After some time, predictably, Barbara began to ride him and the horse and rider reached a mutual agreement A ride, yes. A jump, no.

Predictably again, she thought she could change his mind after a while. Hence a broken leg. Barbara's.

'All my own fault of course, bloody horse did not want to jump. Quite right of course, he has his rights.'

This was only the beginning of the saga.

Barbara then drove herself to the doctor who pooh poohed the

notion of a broken leg - 'You couldn't have driven yourself here.'
So she drove round to the vet, who agreed to X ray the leg and
confirmed it was indeed broken.

'I always said vets were a damn sight better than bloody doctors!'
I cannot now recall who put the leg in plaster but at last Barbara
was more or less immobilised for possibly the first time in her
life; she promptly went down with a dose of flu and was confined
to bed.

Not being the type to snuffle alone she held a large and
boisterous lunch party where the drinks flowed freely and after
which she fell asleep, and slept through a torrential downpour
which successfully drenched her through the open window.
Pneumonia followed and the doctor at last exercised some
influence and had her whisked off to the Nursing Home - having
found her in bed covered with some of her cats while a horse
nodded companionably in through the window.

It was not long before she was back on her feet and would never
have the horse - originator of the whole episode - criticised; he
had not wanted to jump and that was that.

I write about Barbara Cripps with great affection - and regret.
Affection for all the confidence and happiness she gave my
two children. Regret that I never got to know her better - there
was 'always tomorrow' - so many times I put off staying for a
drink and a chat. Now I shall never hear more of her history -
she was reputed to have piloted Lancaster bombers during the
war - delivering them to aerodromes. I could well believe it but
wished I had asked her to tell me more.

Ceri and Simon would spend much of their time in the garden
and I knew they were safe with the dogs and Banda busy
somewhere. They were on the whole good friends but I do
remember one disagreement which eventually made me dash
outside after hearing their voices getting louder and louder,

'I saw it first, so it's mine.'

'We can share it, it's not a very big snake anyway.'

Whose snake?

It was time for my mother in law to visit us again, this time she would travel alone by bus from Luapula, across the Katanga Pedicle and down to the Copperbelt, where she would stay for a while with Andrew's older brothers, Edward and Abner. Not the most wonderful of journeys as the Katangese soldiers on border duty were prone to confiscate money or goods from passengers to supplement their meagre - and sometimes non- existent - wages.

After a rest period on the Copperbelt with Andrew's brother Abner, she was then to travel by train and in due course we met her at Lusaka station. This time she had travelled down from the village with a present for us, a large hand of bananas. I was touched to think of the old lady struggling with this cumbersome bundle all that distance. Grandmother spent her first few days examining the new house and watching Ceri and Simon, exclaiming over how they had grown in typical grandmotherly fashion. She commented on anything which caught her interest during the day and we managed a kind of smiling communication where we spoke in Bemba and English and somehow the general gist was conveyed.

Then when Andrew came home they would have long discussions

on the day's events, although mother in law found so many of my ways strange - if not downright odd - on each visit she was less and less disapproving.

Of course, this time our newly acquired TV was a weird and wonderful novelty. Andrew tried to explain what would happen when he switched on but in no way was she prepared for the live screen. Once the picture came into focus mother in law rapidly moved away from the set and eventually came to rest on a chair very much to the side.

She was NOT going to allow 'that man' on the screen to watch her while she watched him. It took some days to convince her that she could sit nearer and in front of the screen but at last she gave up her surreptitious peeps round the back of the set to see how it was done - or how he got in.

Then her real enjoyment began. 'Cultural' programmes were loudly criticised for being too Westernised and not at all true to traditional heritage. We pointed out that the programmes were produced by local Zambians but it would not be diplomatic to repeat her comments. 'Cultural' programmes were soon ignored and she transferred her attentions to Western romances, any form of embrace was watched with disapproving but rapt attention and her greatest moment was her first screen kiss. I say her greatest moment - it was also our greatest moment in 'Watch With Grandmother'. To our huge delight, in spite of her disapproval, once the evening programmes began Grandmother would be there, making her comments, but with eyes firmly glued to the set so as not to miss one titillating moment - to be recounted at great length once back home in the village.

I regretted she had missed a programme with Alex Chanda, 'the snake man'. We first knew Alex at Munali School where he had a collection of snakes on display in an assortment of tanks under some trees. One evening he appeared on TV to show and talk about some of his snakes, I believe he had hoped to educate people and dispel some myths. He had an original way of doing so. At one point he was at pains to explain that snake venom was actually only poisonous when it entered the blood stream.

To prove this he cheerfully milked a snake into a small glass and then, smiling, drank the venom. 'You see,' he said. 'No harm done – unless I'd had an ulcer. Then it would be a different matter.' Stroking the snake gently he added thoughtfully, 'My wife doesn't like me doing it of course.'

Remembering how on an earlier visit she had asked to take some toys back to the village I suggested we weed out the toy cupboard again but met with an emphatic negative response. Grandmother had not wasted her first few days playing with Ceri and Simon. She pointed out that many of their toys were those she had seen on an earlier visit, while the toys she had taken back to the village had been broken within a few days. I could see her point but I could also see that the children back in the village would expect her to return with some goodies. The fact that care of possessions had not been part of their training was rather beside the point. Another compromise. We went to town and invested in a range of balls of varying sizes and colours. I could not resist adding a few cheap dolls although Grandmother shook her head.

Later we set off on a shopping expedition for Grandmother. She had delicately informed Andrew that my aluminium pans were a wiser buy than her enamel ones which constantly chipped. And plastic was a very useful material when one considered carrying water any distance ... so a set of pans and a large plastic water can with a screw top headed the list. After that - some dresses and lengths of chitenge material, a new blanket and some takkies (canvas shoes), which would mould themselves to Grandmother's rather comfortably spread feet.

Then we came to a dead halt. Grandmother was content to look and admire (or shake her head at town ways) but I could not draw her into making any more purchases.

What an admirable contentment with a way of life with just sufficient possessions to make life comfortable. Although by no means crowded with the good things in life, our house must have seemed full of often unnecessary objects to Grandmother. If only more of us could and would live like her, the natural resources of this world might not be danger of over exploitation - but where would employment be then? The so called civilised nations of this world are racing to their own destruction while the alternative stares them in the face.

Term began; the children and I were at school all morning but mother in law was content to sit in the garden or listen to the radio indoors. Then we had a visit from a distant relative who lived in Lusaka, he had of course to pay his respects to Grandmother. They sat for a long time working out the extended family connection and exchanging news of various kinsfolk while they enjoyed tea and biscuits. When we came home from work the next day I was surprised to find our relative there again. How kind of him to spend so much time with her, I thought. He stayed on for the afternoon and left reluctantly in the evening.

He was there again the next day and the next. The following day he was there before we had even got up ourselves and was already enjoying his breakfast when we walked through to the dining room.

While I liked Grandmother very much indeed I wished this relative far away. As I left for school in the morning he was comfortably ensconced in an armchair with a pot of tea and the radio at full blast. Arriving home at one o'clock it was shattering to find him still there with the radio on at full pitch and the cook muttering how he was all behind because he spent so much time catering to 'uncle's' whims. Having heard so much criticism about European wives not being able to fit into an African family - particularly the extended family - I bit my lip. By the second week my patience was wearing very thin and I came home one day to find he had two friends with him, all with trays of refreshments and the radio on louder than ever. After a particularly hard morning's work, my feelings got the better of me and I switched off the radio saying I wanted some peace and quiet.

This was a great insult and he took himself off on to the verandah to wait for Andrew to come home, whereupon he launched into a long criticism of me - or so I guessed - as this was all in Bemba.

Before Andrew could make any response Grandmother appeared on the scene and joined in the fray. Now I had really upset the whole family! Eventually Andrew turned and translated. Grandmother was more than leaping to my defence, the man had paid his respects and should long ago have been about his business, not creating mess and noise for me to come home to! nor should he bring all and sundry to make free in the household, as for spending time with an elder relative - he was just enjoying himself at another's expense. And THAT, she declared, was NOT 'the custom '.

Affronted relative departed, never to be seen again.

Peace settled over the household once more. Grandmother spent her mornings sitting in the sun, pottering up and down the garden with the dogs, listening to the radio and after we had come home and lunched, off we went to see 'the sights'.

Not that there was much to see in Lusaka. We went to the children's schools, the Cathedral, State House where Grandmother would have liked her photo taken by the gates but it was not allowed, round the markets and the shops.

And of course, I took her to visit friends and relatives. This was not without its lighter side. I thought I would try to be as Zambian as possible and we would just 'drop in' at Aaron Mwenya's house. All my English background said 'phone to say you will call' but no! I'll be traditional I thought.

Grandmother was looking forward to seeing her relative and we rang the doorbell with smiles on our faces at about three o'clock in the afternoon. There was a very long pause as we stood on the red polished verandah, the servants were clearly off for the afternoon but we could at last hear someone coming to the door.

A face looked through the wire mesh and Mrs Mwenya slowly opened the door, looking most uncomfortable. Delighted surprise and acute embarrassment struggled across her face. I knew I had sadly blundered but could not think where I had gone wrong. Bemba verbal greetings were being exchanged and then an awkward pause followed, something was very amiss. Then I noticed that Mrs Mwenya was not shaking Grandmother's outstretched hands and by now she was most offended.

Suddenly Grandmother rattled off what was clearly an admonishment and out came Mrs Mwenya's hands from behind her back. They were stained very black indeed.

After a split second Grandmother burst into a cackle of laughter, berating her cousin in law all the while. Mrs Mwenya turned to me and said,

'I was doing my hair.'

Grandmother was by now overcome with laughter and was making derisive gestures at Mrs Mwenya's glossy black head and her own greying hair. I think they were both relieved when I went into town to do some business; they could chat away without having to pause to translate - and I knew there was more than family news to discuss.

Sure enough that evening Andrew was treated to highly dramatized version of the afternoon's events and he translated Grandmother's opinion of townswomen somewhat unnecessarily as no one could have mistaken the disparaging tones. Oh, the village was going to be entertained for a very long time!

Driving with Grandmother could be entertaining. Driving along a quiet suburban road an African youth looked directly towards me and sauntered out across the road. I braked, slowed right down. He stopped in the middle of the road and gazed around and back at me. By this time I'd stopped. He stood, stepped forward a pace and back again. I was determined not to hoot and provoke a confrontation. He smiled. By this time Grandmother had had enough. She flung the car door open, stepped out and gave him a loud and long Bemba dressing down. Poor lad, he just was not expecting that and slunk off.

At last it was time for Grandmother to travel back, to be sure she would arrive in plenty of time before the first rains, so that she could get her garden started. Outgrown clothes from the children, shirts from Andrew and my cardigans filled one suitcase and into another went her new dresses, the lengths of chitenge, the pans and the water bottle. The balls and dolls squeezed in somehow. Our farewells were made. Edward would meet her in Ndola and see her on to the next leg of the long journey back to Kawambwa.

1970 began very sadly. Clifford Little died. We had been to see him shortly before Christmas, he was ill and his cook Aziz was very reluctant to let us in the house saying the Bwana was not well enough for visitors. It was still a shock to hear of his death; Clifford was only 56 years old but in those short years he had made a great contribution to Zambia's development from the years when he had been Principal of Munali School, Director of African Education and lastly as Head of Administrative and Technical division of the National Council for Scientific Research. The Anglican Cathedral was crowded for his funeral service and I thought sadly that Simon would now grow up not knowing his godfather but only hear stories about him.

1970 did not appear to be off to a good start at all. Zambia had been an independent country for more than five years but we did not seem to be much further ahead - or had I been too hopeful and optimistic a person? Were things going to take much longer than I expected?

There were hopeful signs for the future - Andrew was photographed at the signing of the K24million oil refinery deal between Indeco and the Italian company ENI which was to be built in Ndola by 1972.

We had paid a visit to the Kafue hydro-electric power project and while it was most exciting I had been more than nervous being driven down a huge underground tunnel to the hydro-electric power project machine hall to house turbines and generators which was 1500 feet below surface. The hall being 50 feet wide, 90 feet high and 440 feet long was a vast open space – but nonetheless deep under the ground!

New buildings were going up and new businesses developing but the average man was at a standstill. As usual it was the children I noticed most. The president had stated that his ambition was to see every Zambian eat an egg a day and drink a pint of milk a day. In a country which could be more than self-supporting agriculturally this was not too great an ambition was it? What the President did not foresee was that the man in the street (or village) would have to change his (or her) outlook and beliefs a whole lot more before we could have a fit and healthy nation.

We were already importing milk biscuits from Australia which would provide an easy way of ensuring children in particular could obtain necessary nourishment and now Australia offered to donate the baking equipment which would be installed in Mazabuka, the heart of Zambia's dairy industry. But the Government could only help so far and so many parents did not understand where their responsibilities lay. They did not seem to have moved forward with the country's developments. Dr Nalumango, the Permanent Secretary for Health, must have often wondered why the Ministry of Health opened up new areas of care. He publicly berated the parents who only took their children to hospital when it was too late. Either the children were given no treatment at all or traditional methods were tried, and only when nothing else could be done, was the child taken to hospital - where so many died. Thus fuelling the arguments that the hospitals were not any good. 40% of Zambia's children died before their fifth birthday. When Dr Nalumango announced that a new K2.5 million hospital was to be built near Independence Stadium on the North Road as soon as funds were available he must have wondered whether people would make better use of it. As Zambia was enjoying a population explosion children were being put four to a bed in the overcrowded hospital, which just about guaranteed that even if your parents had taken you to hospital early enough, you were pretty sure of incubating another disease or infection to add to the one you already had.

Ignorance played as great a part as poverty, if not more so, and sadly one learned that 88 children died of malnutrition alone in Luapula in 1969 while another 759 died from measles, smallpox and other diseases. Malnutrition in a country where there was more than enough land and a back-up service of agriculture and health and education services was already established - if not perfect, at least a working foundation.

For those children who survived their early childhood the future was still not easy. So many children had to go to boarding school, because the distances from home were so great. Once there the parents believed their children were sure of regular meals. What they may not have known or understood, was that the Government only allocated 17ngwee per day per pupil for food - and that INCLUDED the cost of transporting the food. It meant that with the best will in the world only 80% of a child's calorie needs and 95% of protein requirements could be satisfied - according to Father Pierre Dil's research.

Father Dil was the leader of the Victory Against Malnutrition Campaign and very early in the Campaign organised a charity walk led by the President and himself which raised K15,000, the President being sponsored for K2,500. But while the President supported such efforts so many of his top level people shrugged their shoulders and left the effort to someone else.

Life seemed to be held very lightly - was this because people had grown up in a culture where survival had always been a precarious business? Was this why Andrew had an acceptance of life - a belief in predestination - ' what will be will be' ?

Looking back at reports in the press and listening to Andrew when he came home railing against another instance of carelessness or crass idiocy on road or rail networks I was never sure whether to believe it was because of people's casual approach to life or an example of breakdown of discipline now that there was no longer a white bwana to exert authority. I read often that black Zambians found it harder to accept authority and discipline from a fellow black Zambian. Perhaps it was a combination of the two.

Aaron Milner as Transport Minister was clearly at his wits end when he stated that 'all dangerous drivers will be retested to cut the accident rate and the Highway Code will be updated'. This sounded helpful - but then one had to bear in mind that he did not have the man power to make this a really feasible proposition.

He tried shock tactics by sacking 10 Government drivers of GRZ vehicles after cars were found parked in townships and outside bars in direct violations of regulations. On one Saturday night alone 11 vehicles were rounded up, which included 2 Ministerial cars and 1 Police Land Rover. Government drivers were not alone in this problem of course. In 1969 there were 10,000 reported crashes for the 80,000 vehicles on the road. And on the railways Andrew continued to chair commissions of enquiry into crashes, fatal and otherwise, knowing that the recommendations would have little or no effect.

Interestingly, while drivers were frequently found to be under the influence of alcohol both on the roads and railways I never heard of an instance where they were found to be under the influence of drugs and yet a survey conducted by the Times of Zambia in Kitwe revealed that 20% of industrial workers thought that there was no harm in smoking dagga - 'it helps us work harder' appeared to be a common remark.

The use of dagga was said to be commonplace but I was never sure how much - and the use of hard drugs appeared to be non-existent then.

More of a problem, according to Grey Zulu, Minister of Home Affairs, speaking at a passing out parade at Lilayi Police Training Camp, was 'the recruitment of skilled men from Europe and elsewhere has meant the importation of some morally cheap expatriates, who have found equally morally cheap Zambians - particularly girls. Horrible rude pictures are in circulation and prostitution and VD are on the increase'.

Well, independence was bringing its benefits and problems to the country as a whole. I would read a report or look at a problem and wonder what I was doing to help and usually convinced myself that at the moment the best thing I could do was to give my utmost in school, in the hopes that in helping to educate another generation life would gradually improve for all. It is very easy to convince oneself when one is very much cushioned against the worst of the troubles. And when life is very busy with husband and children and day to day jobs, you promise yourself that 'in the future' when you are more 'free' you will get more closely involved in trying to eradicate some problems - or at least alleviate the worst of some.

I was very wrapped up in watching Andrew's career develop, although I did get VERY bored by the increasing round of 'social engagements', which seemed to me to be a very expensive and unnecessary exercise in what was essentially a poor country.

Ceri and Simon were a constant delight and my greatest enjoyment in life was being with them.

Our next door neighbour Geoff Mee did not quite share my feelings. A more relaxed and cheerful man than Geoff it would have been hard to find but even Geoff's tolerance reached a breaking point as we were to discover. Now that the garden had taken shape there was more time to stroll round together on a Sunday morning and discuss the progress of the trees we had planted and plans for the coming week. On these amiable saunters it became a habit to stop at the fence dividing the plots and chat with Geoff, who would be on a similar exercise with his gardener. One particular Sunday we stopped as usual under the cypress trees and leaned on the fence posts. The latest political events and local gossip disposed of, we chatted on for a while. But it became clear that Geoff had something on his mind and was hedging around looking for a suitable opening, until in desperation he announced that it made life much better having good neighbours, and that while we had two acre plots and so that while we were close neighbours we still had plenty of privacy and the distance between our house was such that we did not disturb each other ... we began to wonder if Geoff was finding our croquet afternoons too riotous or was he planning an all-night party?

At last,

'Would you mind if I asked you to take that bell off your son's tricycle?'

It seemed an odd request.

Geoff looked desperate.

'I don't mind him having a bell on his trike but ... COULD you stop him riding up and down outside ringing the bloody thing at 6 o'clock on a Sunday morning?'

All was now clear.

Like Geoff we appreciated a late rising on a Sunday morning but his was being marred by the cheerful early morning activities of young Simon. We knew that he woke very early and persuaded Ceri to get up and unlock the front door for him as he could not reach the lock himself. And still in pyjamas he would cycle around with the dogs trotting behind, while she went back to bed. Apparently he was riding up the drive, across the front lawns and then down the servant's path to the bottom of the plot to greet Zulu as he was preparing to come to work - and the servant's path ran alongside the fence beside Geoff's house - and the side where Geoff's bedroom was. Simon's jaunty bell ringing was not appreciated by Geoff - especially as Simon was often out and about before 6am.

We agreed to confiscate the bell until after breakfast. It was to our advantage to remain in the best possible terms with Geoff; he was an honorary game guard. And as such he was permitted to shoot a certain number of animals a year. Although it could be a doubtful honour to be one of his friends at times. With no warning at all an immense and bloody and extremely unwieldly leg of buffalo would be delivered late in the evening - usually just when the freezer was filled to capacity. More than once I gratefully and graciously accepted a hindquarter and after packing as much as possible into the deep freeze and giving some to the servants, I would have to drive round to friend May and beg her to accept a bloody hunk of buffalo.

After one hunting weekend we really appreciated the offering though. Geoff had taken his elder son Christopher with him and after spotting a buffalo, he left Chris in the Land Rover and began to follow the animal on foot. Hampered by the tall grasses Geoff found it increasingly difficult so walked back to the Land Rover hoping Chris would give him some directions. Hot and sweaty he was not amused to see Chris gesticulating and mouthing 'LION, LION!'. Irritably Geoff called out to Chris to quit fooling and help locate the buffalo. Again Chris hissed 'LION, LION' until Geoff promised himself the satisfaction of giving his son a good wallop once he reached him. But then something in Chris' face made him glance behind and there, padding along, was a lion only a few paces behind. Geoff said he had no recollection of covering the last few yards.

It says much for their mutual sangfroid that they returned with buffalo that weekend.

Our contact with Zambia's wild life was much tamer. Our friends the Proctors were due to leave Zambia within a year and would not be returning so we planned a trip to the Luangwa Valley game park in the Eastern Province. It was always sad to know friends were leaving for good so this trip was a mixture of sadness and excitement as we set off in convoy in the early morning light, down the Great East Road.

As we had all lived in Eastern Province it was an exciting and nostalgic trip. Our first stop over for a drink and to stretch our legs was at the bridge over the Luangwa river where we reminisced about 'the good old days' when we had driven on narrow dirt roads winding in and out through the bush.

Fuelling up on Great East Road

Now we motored in comparative comfort along a broad tarmac road and the distance seemed to be halved - certainly it was easier on the posterior! We could still see stretches of the old road from time to time and remembered how we had driven

343

along bouncing on the endless corrugations in the dirt roads.

We stopped at Kachalola rest house for lunch; it had not changed at all. The same narrow dusty drive up to the long low building, with the chalets to the side. While the men opened bonnets to check oil and water (always a necessity on long journeys) Renate and I busied ourselves with wet face cloths and bottles of water when she suddenly cried out, 'Where is Chris?'

He had vanished.

Christopher had covered himself in dubious glory within the first few minutes by sitting on a low wall at the edge of the car park and suddenly disappearing from view. He had leant back carelessly and descended abruptly into a bougainvillea hedge about ten feet below as the cars were parked at the edge of a steep drop. The resultant scratches and lump on his head made for a subdued Christopher and very impressed Simon.

Then on through Luangwa Valley, every bend and stretch of the road full of memories. It was dusk as we arrived and the children scurried off to explore their surroundings - until we read the notice about animals wandering about the camp at night. A little exaggerated I thought - until I had spent a night covering my ears against the sound of a hippo contentedly munching the grass just outside our window.

According to the Zambia Travel Guide published by the Zambia National Tourist Bureau in 1972,

'*What is probably the largest variety of game in Africa is packed into this 15,500 square kilometres National Park. Elephants are everywhere, it is impossible not to see them. The river lagoons are full of hippo. The black rhinoceros, though secretive, is readily seen. And so are giraffe and herds of buffalo, zebra and numerous variety of antelope, waterbuck, impala, kudu, roan and puku ... the grass is yellow, coarse, cropped short by the constant grazing of buffalo. The trees are shorn of their bark and stunted by the pressures of grazing elephants. The air is alive with bird calls and cries. You are in what several experts have called one of the finest game reserves in the world ...*'

We were staying at Mfuwe Lodge which had double room

pine chalets each with its own private bath and toilet. Once the children had eaten and were in bed we retreated to the verandah for drinks before dinner and enjoyed that early part of the evening when the heat has lifted and before the cool of the evening becomes chilly.

Mfuwe Lodge, Luangwa Valley

Once the dinner was eaten it was a case of early to bed because our friend Bill Astle - one of the Christmas tie saga - was Game Warden of the Valley and had generously offered to give of his time and knowledge. Going out just before dawn breaks to see the animals grazing as they must have been doing for thousands of years is an unforgettable experience. We would sit in silence, unable to find the words to express our appreciation of the pageant unfolding before us.

Then as the sun rose higher and the animals retreated into the shade and shadows of the trees, we returned to the camp to eat breakfast.

There was little point in driving round the park in the heat of the day so we sat by the pool and compared notes with other guests. Later as the afternoon wore on, off we set again to watch by the river or lagoons. The variety of bird life was as wide and fascinating as the brochures claimed. The next day Bill took Andrew and Dennis on foot close to a buffalo herd but Renate and I preferred to stay in the back of the Land Rover with the four children, who were loud in their disapproval of our cowardice. However, when a herd of elephant elected to cross the road almost within touching distance we noticed they were suitably impressed and needed no persuading to keep quiet and still.

Renate pounding maize meal

Norman Carr, who had been Chief Ranger in the Northern Rhodesia Game Department and who had been responsible for the creation of many game reserves and other sanctuaries including Luangwa, was at Mfuwe at the same time. He was now retired from the Game Department and ran a safari business from Chipata. I had always been impressed by stories of his ability as a hunter and a conservationist and the book he had written Return To The Wild in which he recounts the tale of how he became guardian to two male lion cubs, Big Boy and Little Boy. It is well known how he reared them and successfully returned them to the wild.

Seeing the great man in person I made a beeline for the little shop and bought his two books, The White Impala and Return To The Wild. They are both now on my bookshelves inscribed To June Kashita with very best wishes from the author Norman Carr Luangwa Valley August 1970.

It was a holiday to remember; Dennis used film after film to record every moment. Unfortunately they then had to return to

Lusaka while we were continuing on to visit friends in Chipata and go on with them to Lake Nyasa (sorry Lake Malawi).

So, early one morning we left the camp and set off up the road and across the river on a pontoon - which always felt a precarious exercise to me - and along the road to the tsetse barrier control. There of course, we had to stop and have the car sprayed inside and out to eliminate any tsetse flies which might have clung to the car. There was no chance of any tsetse clinging to me as I had vigorously swatted every one as soon as it came within range. Stopping to watch game in a car was always frustrating, if you closed the windows you suffocated and if you opened the windows tsetse flies zoomed in like homing pigeons.

What a relief to be sprayed and drive on through the barrier and feel we had left behind that area of the country where they were still a problem. We travelled through these barriers at different times and in different places while we were in Zambia and were always impressed by the very smart turn out of the men on duty. There they were, miles from anywhere in their small houses and with a tiny control room and swing pole barrier across the dirt road. As you drove up to the barrier the whole area seemed to be deserted but as the sound of the car's engine was heard, an immaculate guard would appear from nowhere and with a very snappy salute would then proceed to spray the car fore and aft meticulously. At the same time two or three small children would appear silently by the barrier to gaze and wave shyly.

The car sprayed inside and out, the guard would cheerfully salute, raise the barrier and wave you on your way. As you drove off in a cloud of dust silence descended on the guard post again until the advent of another car, perhaps some hours hence.

Once back on the turn off to the Great East Road the Proctors headed west back to Lusaka and we proceeded east to Chipata. The Jarvises made us very welcome and greeted Ceri, their god daughter, with extra affection. Their three children Carol, Huw and Kathy took Ceri and Simon off to play and Andrew and Alan were soon into their first bottle of Castle beer and a political discussion. Pat and I were more content with general chat about the children and news of friends and acquaintances - politics seemed a never ending circle sometimes best left to men.

The next day we were to drive over the border into Malawi and up to the lake. Arriving at the border however we found a scene of great confusion.

A Government regulation had just been passed forbidding anyone to carry Zambian currency outside the country. While there was doubtless some very sound reasoning behind this particular piece of legislation, its immediate implementation caused havoc. Travellers returning home on buses were having currency confiscated - naturally no receipts were being issued as that particular detail had been overlooked. So, returning passengers were refusing to continue their journeys. People crossing the border like us who wished to take Zambian currency with them in order to purchase petrol on the return journey at the weekend when the banks would be closed, were faced with returning and being unable to refuel ... and so the confusion was compounded.

Andrew and Alan entered the Customs post to try to come to some agreement with the senior officer. The poor man could see their point, but was unwilling to ignore his orders. At long last, it was agreed that we could take some Zambian money with us, authorised by him on hastily stamped bit of paper - which we hoped would be accepted on our return - and we also had a receipt for the money we left there. I felt that we were able to come to this agreement largely, if not wholly, on the strength of Andrew's position and his name being known. I felt very sorry for the poor locals returning unaware who were having their money confiscated left, right and centre. It was all very well for Andrew and Alan to say to many of them, 'Get a receipt'. How would they know where and how to claim their money back?

To his credit once we were back in Lusaka, Andrew pursued the matter with the powers that be and the ruling was changed to allow travellers to take some kwacha with them to cover initial costs on their return.

And on we went to the Lake. It was some years since we had

been there but the road was largely unchanged, perhaps the goats had eaten a bit more of the vegetation but there were no large scale road improvements and we felt that we had stepped back in time as the road wound its way over the low hills round the countless bends. The car bounced up and down the steep hills as the road ran down to the Lake - even the corrugations were as we remembered.

President Hastings Banda was well known for keeping tight control of the country – it was said to be the most authoritarian regime in Africa. Progress for the masses was slow – but it was a poor country, there were not the financial reserves to lavish on new buildings and developments as in Zambia. Political opposition was quashed before it could barely get off the ground. Life seemed to plod on very much as before.

At last the Lake was spread before us and we gazed in silence at the mighty expanse of water shimmering in the heat.

The tiny whitewashed rondavels with their thatched roofs and mosquito net hung iron beds were just the same and the friendly welcome from the staff was unchanged. Day followed day as we lazed on the hot sands and swam in the warm shallow waters. Fishermen poled in their canoes at dawn and dusk with their fresh catches, letting the children help collect the fish from the nets. Drum beats later called us in to fresh grilled fish for dinner.

Ceri and Simon watching the fishermen, Lake Malawi

The only difference this time was that we had as fellow guests some lecturers from the University of Zambia. And very poor company they made. Our children watched open mouthed at the dining room antics while we tried to stagger our meal times and avoid our fellow guests as much as possible. It had never occurred to Ceri and Simon to ask for a particular dish and then refuse to eat it and order an alternative or throw the unwanted dish across the dining room. As for not wearing your pants and then crawling across the table ...

At first we avoided the waiters' eyes in extreme embarrassment as we saw them click their tongues disapprovingly. But then with a little judicious retiming we got ourselves into meals shortly before the drummer began his beat and with the waiters' cooperation were leaving as the first of the University brigade were arriving. The young intellectuals fresh out from England to help the under privileged would have been surprised to know how they were pitied and criticised by those they had come to educate 'and civilise'.

Back to Chipata all too soon, more farewells and back to Lusaka. But on the way back we decided to drive down the Petauke turn off and make a sentimental trip to the little bush station where we had lived in 1962. There were a few new buildings but apart from that the atmosphere was the same, a little bush station sleeping in the middle of nowhere. A visit to Mollywollers store was a must and there was no apparent change here at all. The same faded building with its cracked cement verandah with surely the same man pedalling away at the same Singer? The same lounger on the steps still gazing into the distance and the same mongrel sleeping in the dust at his feet? Inside there was the same range of goods, piled up cans and tins and bundles of materials, the smell of dust and curry and hot air ... and here was Mollywoller himself.

'Yes, please?'

And then another, closer look and a beam of recognition.

We exchanged greetings and settled down to listen to him

expound the virtues of Petauke. After all, Petauke was now as modern as Lusaka - well, almost! The reason for all this delight was electricity! Which had finally arrived - and with it such modern conveniences as fridges and freezers. Now a shopping expedition to Chipata was hardly necessary, we nodded our heads and said how wonderful and we shook our heads and agreed it was not like the old days when you had to have a spirit of adventure and be prepared to drive over 100 miles for some butter!

Next a short drive along the road to see the house where we had lived but somehow it all looked very small - and it had never looked big! There was no one left there that we knew on the station and the very houses seemed to shut us out as the blank windows looked down on the empty road, deserted in the heat of the day. We felt like intruders. Andrew drove to the end of the station road near what had been the District Commissioner's house and back down again, passing the Hepworth's house and the club house and the house where we had lived for the last time. Andrew drove in silence back up on to the main road, as we turned on to it he voiced my thoughts,

'I never want to go there again.'

Back in Lusaka and back in school I enthused about the variety of game we had seen to May Hardie, who then suggested we go over to Chilanga to see the herd of red lechwe which were being kept for breeding purposes at the Game department. As we had not seen red lechwe in Luangwa, their natural habitat being the Kafue Flats, where they were in danger of becoming extinct from poaching and increased farming activities, I eagerly agreed.

On our next free afternoon May and I set off with our five children packed in the back of the car. Chilanga is about ten miles south of Lusaka and a very pleasant drive. We turned off the main road and jolted up the dirt road to a fenced area behind the Game Department farm buildings. Not only was there a small herd of red lechwe but also a mixed herd of Friesian cows, eland, zebra and a baby elephant - who were all grazing contentedly together.

351

The children hung on the fence fascinated by the mixed herd, while we were torn between watching them and the lechwe, who moved so gracefully through the tall grasses.

Quite by chance we had hit on the best time of the day. After about ten minutes a man arrived to open the gate near where we were standing.

'Milking time,' he said.

And sure enough the cows began to stroll up from the pasture, out of the gate and across the road into the opposite paddock towards the dairy, in the time honoured way of cows at milking time, who know they have an urgent appointment but are not going to be hurried.

Surprisingly the eland and zebra sauntered along with them. We looked at the game guard enquiringly. He was clearly used to this,

Game department Chilanga

'They like to go,' he said. 'They think they all the same'.

'But what do you do when they get into the dairy?' I asked.

'Oh, they walk through and go out the other door, they wait for the cows and they all come back together,' he replied.

The young elephant also took a stroll to the dairy at this time too but spotting the game guard deep in conversation, he had as silently as only elephants can, tiptoed off down the road, occasionally looking over his shoulder for all the world like a guilty schoolboy.

The children's giggles alerted the guard, who glanced down the road and shouted. The elephant glanced behind him again and gently increased his pace to a shifty shuffle, we laughed helplessly as the guard set off in pursuit, shouting all the time. He soon caught up with the truant and slapped him firmly across his baggy backside. The elephant stopped and twined his trunk round the man's neck and then delicately felt inside a jacket pocket. The man took him by the ear, turned him round and together they walked back towards us, as he neared the gate the elephant raised his trunk and - I would swear - winked.

There was a report in August 1965 that Ministry of Game and Fisheries were beginning an experiment in the domestication of selected species of Zambian wild life. The object was to allow the establishment of herds of disease resistant antelopes etc for the production of meat in rural areas where cattle could not survive. Many years later I wonder how far the scheme progressed.

Now that we had lived in Roma for a while and were over the worst of the expense we decided to invest in a small swimming pool and once again it was a case of do-it-yourself with locally recruited labour. As swimming pools go it was not all that impressive, perhaps 15 by 30 feet but it was designed in mind for children having fun. I was relieved that the deep end was only five feet deep, feeling that I would be able to leap in and rescue children at a moment's notice. As things turned out, the children were soon in a position of being more likely to rescue me - but that's by the way!

It was paved all round, then down one side was a grassed area where we could have a barbecue and we planted Queen of the Night so that evening swimming parties would be scented with our favourite bush. Down the other side was a raised flower bed in which we put easy to care for flowers and shrubs and Dutchman's Pipe. The latter proved to be a bit of a mistake. It more than flourished. In less than no time there was a vivid splash of colour across the wall and then the creeper rioted with gay abandon across the wall and threatening to take over the whole pool area. We were constantly hacking it back.

Ceri with Fenella at Roma

Simon and Andrew   *with Jennifer and Susan at Roma*

The pool was walled and gated - gated with a delicately wrought iron gate, which we had dug up when we were first developing the plot. First we had found trenches full of empty bottles and then the gates. Geoff denied all knowledge of the cache but cast suggestive looks at the house further down the road. Once the pool was completed we had a quotation from a painter to paint the pool blue. As money as once again running short and the quotation was K200 I baulked and bought some cans of paint on my way home from school and painted it myself for the grand total of K25 and a pair of rather sore knees. Once the pool was filled and in action Banda was initiated into the routine of vacuuming it daily, and then the intricacies of cleaning the filter and running the pump. At weekends Andrew took over, delighting in having a miniature pump house to play with.

Now the afternoons rang to the shrieks of splashing children and weekends found us alternating swimming and croquet

354

with barbecues. Children could not have had a more delightful childhood.

When I was a child we had spent many happy hours paddling and splashing in a local stream where we caught tiddlers and built dams but had never had the luxury of a swimming pool. On the other hand my children would not be able to have the fun I had had. We were not near a stream and I would not have allowed them to even paddle at the edge of a river. People did use rivers and lakes for water supplies and leisure activities but it was not without its dangers. From time to time one heard of crocodiles pulling people or animals into the water. One man was even seized by the leg while he was being baptised in the Kafue river by the Watch Tower sect near Mufulira. As they did not believe in modern Western medical treatment he had traditional herbal treatment. Whether it was to their credit or not, the crocodile was not killed as they did not believe that any of God's creatures should be killed.

While we had been busy building our tiny pool, great works had been going on nearby. Zambia was due to host the Non Aligned Summit Conference (also known as NAM - Non Aligned Movement) in September 1970. Members were mainly from African and Asian countries steering a middle course in the East West Cold War. The Mulungushi Village, as it became known, was built at the edge of Olympia Park, since May there had been frantic activity very close to Roma. Not only was Mulungushi Conference Hall built but also 62 Presidential Villas for visiting Heads of State and foreign ministers, complete with all mod cons in what was referred to as the Mulungushi Village.

While there was no doubt that the Yugoslav firm Zecco (Zambia Engineering and Contracting Company) had worked round the clock to complete the contract - work started on 7th May and the whole project was completed by 25th August 1970 - in 4 months! - there were more than a few rumours circulating about how it had been achieved. Earlier in the year imports of fruit from South Africa had been banned and officially we were not to buy goods from the south but it was common knowledge that the Mulungushi project could not have been completed without materials brought up from the south. It seemed somewhat of a paradox a little later to reflect that while the delegates were denouncing South Africa they were sitting perhaps in chairs from the south - and more than likely, washing their hands under South African taps.

No expense was spared for the Mulungushi Conference but we still awaited news of when there would be funds available for a new and modern hospital in Lusaka, the capital.

Was it then or later? when we had an invitation to a Banquet at Charter Hall? I have the impression it was in honour of President Tito. A Banquet! This sounded most impressive and I thought it would be a memorable event and set off with Andrew with great expectations. It was a large dinner, there were many people, we had a view of top table ... but while I hadn't really expected gold platters it was just – another dinner with speeches. And sadly no dessert, as they ran out before reaching our table.

Money was available for some schemes. The Minister of Home Affairs, Changufu, announced that the Zambia Youth Service was to be changed to a National Service and camps would be built in every district. But I did not hear of money available for more schools.

The Bank of Zambia had, in its annual report, stated that while there was a satisfactory growth rate the rural drift to urban areas needed to be watched; the Rural Development Programme was doomed unless the drift to towns was stopped. Building and staffing better schools in those rural areas would have helped and encouraged people to stay and develop the rural areas, I thought. But then, I was not a politician.

The President however was a politician and he concentrated on a matter which had been bothering him for some time and late in the year he set out the Leadership Code with the statement that *'No UNIP leader or senior public servant should be associated in any way with the practice of capitalism and other forms of exploitation ... they may not rent out a house while living in a Government house ... should not hold directorships in private*

*companies ... may not undertake in any private business ventures
...'* This was to include the wives or husbands of senior civil
servants. At the same time he announced that all major banks
and building societies were to close, expatriates were to lose
wholesale and retail licences.

It did not come as complete surprise when we heard that Harry
Nkumbula was to meet with the President over the New Year at
Kasaba Bay, where KK made his annual holiday and, apparently,
meditation. One wondered if they were discussing his statement
in May that the One Party State was on the way although it
should be created through the electorate and not by legislation.

1971 AND SIMON STARTS SCHOOL

Duly labelled Yellow 1 as Ceri had been and destined for Lusaka
Infants, Simon was quite proud of the uniform - on the first
day! But not after that. He was too used to Andrew returning
from business trips with shirts and shorts in colourful patterns,
the grey shirt and shorts uniform 'was boring'. Ceri was in her
Lusaka Girls uniform and proud of her promotion to junior
school.

Simon's first day at Lusaka Infants

The New Year in 1971, like most New Years, seemed to herald

357

changes in Zambia as the President spent his holiday break at Chinsali or Mfuwe and would emerge with, at the very least, a mini Ministerial reshuffle.

At the beginning of 1971 we started off with the introduction of the free medical scheme. The immediate effect was that the University Teaching Hospital in Lusaka was short of crockery as all patients were now entitled to the same food - and therefore presumably the same utensils. The situation must have been slightly alleviated by private doctors referring their patients to the Medical Aid Nursing Home on Independence Avenue as they themselves were now barred from treating patients in the UTH. Things had not improved much for the children as they were still two or three to a bed in the malnutrition wards.

16 million kwacha was reported to being spent on the hospital which was not yet completed and so far there did not seem to be much in the way of provision for relatives, who in accordance with custom would camp out in the hospital grounds until a patient was discharged. The new buildings going up were not enhanced by washing hanging on the perimeter fence. So much was needed at once. Later in the year there were complaints that the fridge conditions were so poor that autopsies were often performed on partially or completely decomposed bodies and therefore the findings were inconclusive.

Seventeen high ranking expatriate officers, including four colonels, were retired from the Army and Air Force; it was said to be part of the Zambianisation drive. According to Press reports the officers were summoned to the Ministry of Defence headquarters and handed two letters. The first letter was thanking the officer for his service and praising his service; the second letter stated that the appointments were to be terminated in two days and the officers had eighteen days in which to leave the country. It was understood that they were forthwith banned from the officers mess and there was an unverified rumour that they were also under house arrest.

The officers reacted with dismay and anger and disappointment but there the matter ended.

Andrew also had a few changes; now Managing Director of Indeco, he also became the executive chairman of the Corporation and also took over as Permanent Secretary in the Ministry of Trade and Industry. There was not much chance of anyone getting stale in Government service in Zambia! But as early as 1971 we saw Obote toppled by Idi Amin in Uganda, there was perhaps some wisdom in keeping everyone on their toes and no one had the chance to become too firmly entrenched and popular.

I often wondered how Andrew could maintain his enthusiasm and commitment when I looked at the problems - and of course I only saw the tip of the iceberg. Sometimes Andrew would come home and talking over dinner would sound quite disheartened but then he seemed to brace himself to look forward with conviction and belief in the path he was being forced to follow.

So often I wondered how he knew who and what to believe of the confused stories which circulated. The bakers said there was a shortage of flour and the millers said there was a shortage of wheat - I got bogged down in the details and recriminations. But all was resolved, at least temporarily, when South Africa agreed to sell us 300 tons of wheat.

At least we could feel more optimistic about some developments. In March Andrew returned from a trip to Italy where he had conducted negotiations on Zambia's behalf ... the K24 million oil refinery being built at Bwana Mukubwa near Ndola and due to be completed in December the following year, would be operated by Indeni, and Indeco and ENI would have equal shares.

It was not so encouraging to read that in May the Government felt compelled to slap a ban on the importation of millions of metres of foreign textiles by revoking more than 370 import licences. Andrew announced that as Permanent Secretary of Trade he had to protect our local textile industry - firms had been importing material available from Kafue Textiles.

I said nothing but did hope that there would be no more trouble in getting labour to harvest locally grown cotton. Sometimes I did feel as though it was one step forward and then one or two back. Andrew had arrived in N Rhodesia in January 1962, the first African mechanical engineer and with a particular interest in seeing farming being more and more mechanised. He had moved to the Natural Resources College where courses were to run to help African farmers develop along this route. So it was depressing to read as late as June 1971 that the Minister of State for Luapula was urging farmers to use ox drawn ploughs as tractors were too expensive.

No matter how I tried to take an intelligent interest in what was happening in the country, so often I knew I was not hearing the truth and to me, more importantly I had to concentrate on difficulties on the home front.

While Banda progressed from being a 'garden boy' with no skills at all to a young man with an increasing range of skills and a steady reputation, Zulu had taken a retrograde step. At first he had been a reliable cleaner and a good plain cook, but as time went on he began to drink heavily. At first these incidents had been confined to the weekend and his time off but then he began to drink more heavily and more frequently.

I began to feel any increase in pay would only disappear into the beer hall and that neither he nor his family would have any real benefit. Instead I increased his 'ration money', the weekly amount which was supposed to be for fresh vegetables and necessaries in addition to the monthly wage. But the ration money was spent on beer so then I gave him part of his wages and ration money in kind to ensure that at least his wife and daughter were sure of their food. I made the excuse that as we were so far out of town it was merely practical for me to purchase the 100 pound bag of mealie meal, sugar, tea, meat and so on and transport them. But still Zulu managed to drink heavily.

For a long time I tried ignoring it as much as possible and remonstrating reasonably when I could no longer ignore it, but then he started arriving for work on Monday mornings very much the worse for wear and this soon spread to the rest of the week. Enquiries and reproaches only produced one response in polite terms - that he drank in his own time and turned up for work at the right hour. Which was true enough. We persevered for a long time; after all, Zulu had been with us for a long time and we were fond of Titanbenji, who occasionally helped in the house and who had been Simon's nanny and their daughter Tita, who still played with Ceri sometimes.

Then he began to arrive even later for work and in more than an unfit condition.

The end finally came when Andrew was away on a business trip and Zulu had been in a very unsteady state when the Hepworths came for a meal. Watching him wobble across the plot, Aileen asked if I would be able to manage on my own.

'Don't worry,' I said, 'he will go off this evening and get completely drunk but he will be back in tomorrow with a splitting head, but he will be there.'

However on Monday morning I got up and there was no Zulu. I got the children ready for school, breakfast cooked and eaten, the dogs and cats fed and was about to depart. I was not in the best of moods when Zulu appeared in the kitchen doorway assisted by Titanbenji. He was incapable of standing upright so she carefully propped him against the wall. As calmly and politely as I could I told him he was fired.

He beamed at me benevolently.

'No matter, Madam. I am here you see? Everything she all right.'

There was no time to argue - nor would we have got anywhere with him in that condition so we departed. Lunchtime saw a quietened Zulu but I had had enough and I repeated that he was fired, finished, sacked and to go. I produced his wages for the rest of the month and the leave pay he was due and repeated that he had until the weekend to pack and leave the plot and confiscated his keys to our house.

He left in a huff but was obviously given a talking to by his wife because he came back to argue his case. But I had talked and talked and warned so often in the past that now I was adamant. Sorry as I was to cause hardship to the family there was no way I would keep on a man who was increasingly unreliable.

In fact I was so regretful that I wrote him a reference listing his qualities but avoiding giving the reason for his departure, knowing that any old hand would be able to read between the lines but that at least it gave him the chance to make a fresh start with some less knowledgeable person - probably some little expatriate wife fresh out from UK.

To the last he insisted I was being hard on him, especially as I was his 'mother and father' and that while it was true he drank too much it was quite all right ... We parted on good terms and every Christmas he appeared at the back door for news of the children and to tell me news of Tita. Then he would smile and ask for a bonsela, his Christmas present. I would give him food and money and a bottle of Castle beer in the hopes that Titanbenji would see at least some of the money.

After the departure of Patulani Zulu the house was quiet. Banda came in to clean while we were at work and I taught him to iron. But he still had not mastered the washing machine nor even any basic cooking. We jogged along for a while. I dreaded looking for another cook and scanned the Employment Wanted column in the Times of Zambia hoping to see 'Cook, recommended, employer leaving'.

But before some departing person could come to my rescue there was a knock at the kitchen door one Saturday afternoon and Andrew went to investigate.

He returned with a broad smile.

'There is a cook who used to work for Clifford Little and he says he remembers us and he says,' – chuckle – 'he says he has come to work for us .'

And so Aziz joined us. All he would ever say was that he had heard we were looking for a cook and as he remembered us lunching at Clifford's house, he thought we were quite suitable! When Clifford died Aziz had retired but for the Bwana Kashita he would work a little longer. He had bought a plot in Mutendere and built a house there with the money Clifford had left him, and his wife was loth to leave it. So we compromised that Aziz would live on our plot during the week and spend his weekends at home. He said that he would go at lunchtime on Saturday, unless we had guests on Sunday. This did not seem much of a married life to me and I asked how his wife would feel about such an arrangement.

Aziz produced one of his sweet smiles,

'Ah, ah, Madam, my wife she is all right. And we not young now, it is quite all right for me to live here during the week. And my son is a young man now and so my wife she is not afraid to stay in Mutendere.'

We agreed a trial period. It worked perfectly and if I could not avoid Sunday guests, then I made sure he left on Friday the following weekend. Servants usually worked such unsocial hours that our arrangement was considered quite reasonable, although I still felt guilty. When I voiced my thought, Andrew's reaction was predictably matter of fact, 'The man came here and said he would work here and he can leave any time he wants.'

Aziz was a delight in so many ways. One, which sounds so very trivial, was the matter of saucers in the fridge. He was the very first cook I had who did not feel compelled to fill the fridge with saucers each containing minimal amounts of left-over food. Each previous chap had been well trained to preserve any and all left-over bits of food after a meal and place them neatly in the fridge. It always took a long time to convince a new cook that we were quite happy for cook to dispose of any left-over food. I did sometimes wonder what the previous employer Madams had done with the half a tomato and three green beans and spoonful of custard.

Aziz had very definite ideas about what was proper and what was not. We realised this on his first morning when he appeared beside our bed with a neatly laid tray and two cups of tea. He was gone again before we were fully conscious; as we promptly fell asleep again the cold tea was discreetly poured away in the bathroom. After a week of this I summoned the courage to tell him that we did not really care for early morning tea. He was very disappointed.

'The Bwana Little ALWAYS had a cup of tea in the morning.'

Having thus disappointed him I went on to disillusion him on the question of 'afternoon tea'. If I was in the house I would often like a cup of tea but I did not want him to search the plot for me and wait for me to come in just for some tea. Aziz was more possessive about English customs than I was. He was also most possessive about the kitchen floor. It was a well-known fact that the majority of house servants waxed and polished floors with great enthusiasm, skill and vigour - the ceiling might be festooned with cobwebs but your floor would sparkle like diamonds. Aziz took a particular pride in his kitchen floor, the black Marley tiles shone like black mirrors reflecting every angle of the kitchen. And his pain at four o'clock when he came back on duty to find that we had WALKED to and fro across his kitchen floor was quite real. Out would come the mop and a duster and the floor would be restored to its former pristine glory while the kettle boiled for tea. Of course, with two children and frequently their friends making their way from garden to playroom and bedrooms via the kitchen the situation was unsolvable. It was in vain for me to assure Aziz that I did not mind if there were dusty footmarks on the black tiles. He did. And he tutted and mopped daily. We came to a state of acceptance until the Coxes came to stay and then Aziz all but broke.

Charles was about Ceri's age, Sarah a little younger. After the usual race round the garden, the children came in through the kitchen to the bedrooms and later back again. The mop was in and out but on the fifth trip Aziz said in admiring but angry tones,

'That Bwana Charles, he is very nice boy but he has too big feet. Why you not go see them in Mazabuka?'

And thereafter whenever I mentioned that the Coxes were coming up to town the news would be greeted with,

'Ah yes, four more for lunch and Bwana Charles with the big feet.' And his hand would reach for the mop as their Land Rover turned in at the gate.

Going down to spend a weekend with the Coxes in Mazabuka was made even more enjoyable when I could tell Aziz where we were going. And it was enjoyable for us - the four children got on together well and as usual Barry and Andrew would talk politics and agriculture endlessly. One weekend Ingilby decided we would have a barbecue - and it was one with a difference. She cooked in a plough share over a roaring fire in the most casual way I could imagine - huge pork chops were thrown into the plough share to sizzle tantalisingly before a can of pineapple chunks and juice were tossed in followed closely by a bottle of beer - after which I lost track! but a more appetising meal could not be imagined.

Visits there were always notable in some way. The most memorable included a gymkhana. Who rode what when and where are lost in the mists of time but the ending is painfully clear. As people were packing and loading etc Barry roared off with Andrew and the four children leaving me to drive back with Ingilby - towing the two horses in a rather small horsebox. The horses clearly had the same thought as me - Ingilby got one horse in but the second one was determined not to go home - at least not in that horsebox. After several efforts Ingilby decided the only alternative was to ride the horses home. Turning to me she said I could ride the quieter of the two and then, seeing my appalled face, asked if I could ride? Admitting I had never even tried I agreed to mount the beast and off we set. It was late in the afternoon and African nights descend rapidly. My inability to do more than cling on and attempt to sound cheerful meant that it was getting darker as we 'rode' (I have to use inverted commas - the only way to describe my performance) cross country back to the farm. Ingilby patiently explained how to trot but after a feeble attempt I gave up. The horse - judging by its ears - agreed that was a wise decision. Dogs in every village we passed marked our passing with loud barking and pretend attacks.

I must put it on record that Ingilby is the most kind and patient person I have ever known - she never once complained. And probably I am the only person to have blisters on my fingers after riding.

Simon and his dog Peter   *Ceri with Peter, Paula and Micky*

That was the period when we lost Micky our faithful companion of many years. He was leading a slower quieter life and one day when we came home from school at lunchtime, as usual Ceri and Simon jumped out to open the gates and as I drove through I noticed Micky was lying by the Queen of the Night bush at the front of the house. Unusually for him he did not get up to meet the car. I parked the car and walked across the lawn knowing what I would find. Only a dog. But you cry as you hoped it was peacefully in his sleep and I called Banda to dig a hole.

It was about this time that Banda's mother died. One Sunday evening he came knocking on the kitchen door and I found him standing on the steps with tears in his eyes.

'Please Madam, my mother, she die.'

Then he managed to tell me that his mother had lived in a village near Kafue and he had not seen her for some time. He had meant to take leave later in the year and visit her then, now it was too late. He had had the news from 'a brother' - which could mean any male relative, perhaps even very extended family - and so now he wanted to go to Kafue.

'Of course,' I said, hurrying off to find Andrew, feeling somewhat at a loss on how to console the young man. How little we knew about our servants. I had had no idea where his mother lived, nor that his father had died long ago, nor that Banda had not been back to the village for some years. Somehow I felt guilty.

Andrew was as usual on a Sunday evening, sitting with a pile of files beside him, working his way through the minutes of various meetings and other documents, for which there was never enough time in the office. I explained about Banda and to my surprise Andrew said,

'Well, what do you want me to do?'

'His mother has died and he wants to go to Kafue', I repeated.

'He can't go at this time of night. But of course he can go first thing in the morning. He can have the week off.'

'But aren't you going to talk to him?'

'What about?'

I felt rather angry.

'His mother for a start. Look, he is very upset and I don't know whether I am saying all the right things, perhaps you should go and say you are sorry to hear it. Man to man. And maybe there is some Zambian custom or something to say that I don't know.'

Andrew looked extremely irritated, he got up and went out to the kitchen. I heard him talk to Banda for a few minutes and he returned, sitting down to the files again.

'Yes, his mother has died and he is upset, but what do you expect?'

I went out again and attempted to find some words of consolation for Banda, who was by now sitting on the steps quietly sobbing. To this day I will never understand Andrew's apparently casual reaction, especially in a culture where grieving for the dead is taken so seriously and sympathy for the bereaved is so generously given.

I was thirty years old and Banda was probably not yet twenty. My reaction was to put my arms round him and give him a hug and say I was sorry. But I did not know whether I would offend something in his culture, somehow Andrew had failed to bridge the gap for me. I believed he should have had time to talk and listen and console, man to man – in a way that I couldn't. I stood for some time trying to say the right words and assuring him that he could leave early the next morning, I gave him money to help with the travelling and repeated that his job with us was safe ...

All our married life Andrew had had to travel frequently; first as an agricultural officer touring farms and agricultural stations and later as a civil servant, now as Managing Director of Indeco. His trips ranged from one or two days to two or three weeks, within the country and also outside. Some of the trips were planned well in advance and some were at very short notice indeed. Originally I had been able to travel with him and in fact it had really been my introduction to the country. Some of the friends I made then, I have now - the Hepworths in Petauke, the Edwards in Mapangazia, the Coxes in Mazabuka, the Proctors in Fort Jameson and Lundazi. But it is a far cry from touring within the country in a Land Rover to travelling to several countries by air. The Government quite rightly, could not afford to finance wives accompanying their husbands. In addition to which of course, I was working full time and we had two children.

So Andrew travelled frequently and usually alone. Sometimes two or three Zambians would travel together when there were some particularly important negotiations to be done and on some of these trips an occasional secretary would be taken along by the group.

'Surely you could be provided with a secretary over there?' I asked.

'And how confidential would our meetings be then? Our decisions could be leaked to the other side.'

It sounded reasonable.

And once I was delighted one trip included his secretary Ann. She had travelled on a few trips after which she tactfully introduced the subject of Andrew's raincoat. This, you must understand, was the raincoat he had had at university and to which he was passionately attached. I had suggested more than once that ... just perhaps... he could do with a new one. Shock. Horror. It was a good coat, after all he had had it for years.

Ann hinted – no, she more than hinted – it just would not do with its sadly dipping hem and rather battered appearance. She confided she thought it more than embarrassing for a person of importance representing his country to be seen in such a coat. To her delight I fully agreed and pointed out that there was no way I could lose it at home but surely it could go missing between hotels and planes Somewhere, preferably Soon.

On the very next trip the deed was done. And great was the grief when he realised he had arrived back home minus the Coat. 'I'd had it for years! Plenty of wear in it still!' Of course a new raincoat was eventually purchased – but it was never the same.

No matter how often he travelled it became no easier especially as the children were growing, they missed their father. But if he were away for more than a few days a postcard would arrive and always there were small surprises in his suitcase on his return. Ceri began her collection of dolls from other countries at this time and it ranged from France, Italy, Holland to India, Yugoslavia, the States and China. Simon formed an attachment to hats as his father brought him headgear of all descriptions.

Whenever possible we drove Andrew to the airport to wave goodbye and most certainly hoped to be able to meet him on his return. Only once were we disconcerted, when Simon was still quite young, about two. I waited with Ceri and Simon as the plane landed and taxied up to the airport buildings then we walked out of the VIP entrance and began to walk across the tarmac.

'Look, there's Daddy,' I said.

Ceri and Simon ran forward. Ceri in the right direction but Simon, in his eagerness, did not look upwards but threw his arms round the first pair of trousers he came to and shouted 'Daddy!' to the acute discomfort of a complete stranger.

'Do you think he really did not recognise me?' asked Andrew, looking very worried.

Our regular separations were a disappointment but one accepted it as part of the way of life. It had always been so in Zambia and Northern Rhodesia before that; from the days of the District Commissioner touring his district to the present day.

What I did find more of a problem was the incessant social whirl. Perhaps because it was always dark before 7pm and one cannot indulge in so many outdoor activities, because everyone had servants and thus no domestic chores, because there were only a handful of cinemas and clubs ... we had to make our own entertainment. This was the accepted way of life.

And so one was faced with the choice of clubs, and sport and bridge, the ever popular 'sundowner' or cocktail party, the dinner party, the lunch party, the braivleis or barbecue and so on. There were Bank parties, firms' parties, Ministry parties, farewell parties, promotion parties, entertaining overseas guests and visiting dignitaries ... and merely private parties. It seemed to me at times that one could go to at least one function per night indefinitely.

From the transition from the unacceptable 'mixed' couple to the wary acceptance of the 'blacks are here to rule now' to the fawning on those at the top was in fact a very short step and after the initial thrill that at last people like Andrew would, and were given, their due merit, it was not long before I found much of it very distasteful.

Andrew and I at a function

True, there was some justification for some of the social activity but most of it I found a great bore. To be honest, it would not have been so bad if Andrew had not insisted that we should accept most, if not all invitations, but also that we should arrive promptly and be among the last to depart. So, many evenings I read a story to the children in bed and then holding up my long skirts ran to where Andrew was waiting impatiently by the door and off we went to stand or sit through yet another evening almost identical to the preceding one.

Years later I was reminded of a dinner at Lusaka Hotel. In 2003 38 people were prosecuted for refusing to complete their census forms in 2001 in the UK. Among those prosecuted was the Rev. John Papworth, who was fined £120. It was reported that he once sheltered on-the-run KGB spy George Blake – clearly a character. And I remembered the dinner at the Lusaka Hotel in the 1970's when Papworth was a rural development advisor to the President.

Andrew and Danae Sardanis had invited a group of us to dinner at the Lusaka Hotel and after a few drinks we went through to the restaurant ... finding our number had grown by one. Rev. Papworth was now seated with us. Hurried whispers round the table confirmed none of us had actually asked him to join us but Andrew was unwilling to cause a scene so dinner proceeded. At intervals Papworth complained about the piped music, which was actually quiet and fairly unobtrusive. It was a merry dinner so none of us noticed the music had stopped and were taken by surprise when the manager came to complain that one of the guests at our table had gone behind the scenes and pulled the wires out of the wall and the music system was wrecked. This by an uninvited guest.

Another evening was not my favourite. We were invited to a dinner in Kabulonga by one Oliver Irwin. Walking into the house I was shocked to find it was my idea of a nightmare. Irwin must have been a keen hunter – or collector – did it matter? The floors were carpeted with animal skins, the furniture upholstered in ditto and the walls festooned with heads and horns and God knows what else, while elephant feet provided small tables ... Who was there, why we were there, I have no idea. It was a nightmare.

There were a few exceptions. One in particular stands out clearly in my mind. It was an Indeco dinner dance for some VIP American at the Woodpecker Inn in Woodlands. Andrew and I were seated beside Mr and Mrs VIP on a table of about twenty and the dinner proceeded as usual. Later as people left the table to dance, Mrs VIP and I found ourselves alone. The conversation had been superficial as usual - how do you find the weather? Is it your first trip to Africa? Will you have time to visit the Falls? or a game park? And so on and so forth.

I asked if the hotel were comfortable. Everything was 'just fine' there too - 'Of course, it does seem strange not to have a TV in the bedroom,'

I laughed and described our limited service, which still ran from 5pm to about 11.30 in black and white, and they were mostly imported programmes.

'In fact, you would probably have been watching an American programme,' I added.

On being asked what kind of American programmes were being screened I named a few and said that in my opinion one of the best at the moment was Sesame Street.

Looking at the very middle aged Mrs VIP I thought I should explain that Sesame Street was an educational programme aimed at 4 to 7 year olds.

Why did I think it was so good? It was fast, witty, light, repetitive without being boring. In fact, I told my class they should watch it for homework. I hoped I had not bored my companion. I tend to get a bit carried away once school is mentioned. I shut up. Embarrassed.

Imagine my amazement when the good woman laughed out loud and informed me that she worked behind the scenes on Sesame Street; she was on this trip to please her husband but what she really enjoyed most was her work. We talked happily of the essential ingredients for children's programmes until the end of the evening when I invited her to visit the school the next day.

Sesame Street comes to Lusaka Infants

The class were thrilled to meet someone actually involved in their favourite programme and to hear her American accent. Nor was that all. Not long afterwards I received a large parcel from the States. Inside were several large hand puppets of Sesame Street characters, a large number of finger puppets and enough postcards of the characters for each member of the class to have one each. What a thrill for Grade 1 Yellow. There was a letter from our friend too saying what a pleasure it had been to find how popular the programme was in such a faraway country. But what a thrill for my class too, long and happy thank you letters were posted to America that week.

I said earlier that our children had a delightful childhood and I often compared it with that of their counterparts in the grey cold of England and, because of Douglas and Denise, I also thought about the number of children in care in England. Andrew had explained to me that until the advent of 'civilisation' there were no old people's homes or orphanages in the African society and that all were in turn responsible for each other. An admirable part of their culture and such a pity it was too late for our Western society to emulate it. And true the thin edge of the wedge could be seen now in Zambia - there was the Kasisi orphanage run by missionaries east of Lusaka for example. The age old help-one-another culture was beginning to crack.

Even so I was taken by surprise one day when Toni Tilley phoned with an unexpected request.

'I have been asked to have a little girl for Christmas,' she said. 'Social Services say she is usually at boarding school but they have been let down in the arrangements for the holidays. But as my children are babies I don't think she would be very happy here. Your two are a bit older ... so... I hope you don't mind but I gave them your name and phone number and said you had done some fostering in UK.'

'Thank you very much Toni' - what else could I say? 'Tell me some more about the child.'

'Oh, I don't know anything except that it's a little girl. I'm sure you will hear from Social Services anyway.'

And with that Toni rang off. Social Services were most efficient, they were on the phone the very same day. I was rather surprised that I was not to be interviewed or the house inspected.

'Ah no, Mrs Kashita, it is not necessary! We all know Mr Kashita!' Reflecting that Andrew's appearance in the Press and on TV were an original reference for child care I awaited the arrival of the little girl with some interest. Andrew was most agreeable and the children were looking forward to having a little girl to stay for the holiday.

The following day a car arrived and out climbed a young Zambian woman followed by a teen age girl clutching a suitcase, no sign of a little girl.

'This is Charlotte,' introduced the Social Worker. 'We are so grateful that you can take her at such short notice. This is her bag ... what a lovely room .... I am sure you will be a good girl for Mrs Kashita ... but phone us if you have any problems,'

And she was gone.

Charlotte and I looked at each other.

'She's not a little girl,' said Simon helpfully. 'She's a very big girl.' It helped to break the ice and we showed Charlotte around the house. She seemed very quiet and I tried to think of things which interested teenagers, panic, panic. I knew nothing at all about this weird and wonderful group except that everyone said that teenagers were difficult. All my friends had small children. I had only taught infants. Panic, panic.

Fortunately Charlotte seemed only too pleased to have a home for the holiday and after school dormitory she assured me that a room of her own was bliss. I said that the servant would clean it of course but that she was free to arrange it as she wished. I then had to spend some time convincing Andrew that all teenagers covered their walls with pictures of pop stars and left half-drunk cans of Coke around and clothes scattered on the floor. We compromised pin ups were 'in' but clothes on the floor were 'out'.

My school holiday had begun too of course so I had time for Charlotte and she was happy to be part of a family for Christmas. She was a great help with shopping and preparations but I wished I had friends with teenagers. Her father was in prison, her mother was dead and as she had been sent to boarding school in another Province she knew no one in Lusaka. Except, she said, she had a sister who was working in Lusaka and was living with another family out at Makeni on the south road. It took only a few phone calls to arrange for her sister to join us for Christmas Day.

In the meantime I still had some shopping to do - with only a few days to go I left for some last minute things in town, Charlotte agreed to take care of Ceri and Simon and I was able to get back in record time. The three of them came round the end of the house to help unload the car. Ceri looked rather quiet but Simon said excitedly, 'Charlotte showed us where you put our Christmas presents.'

To say I was furious was to say the least. More angry that Ceri and Simon's surprise on Christmas Day would be muted, than I was that Charlotte had had the temerity to take the children to look through the wardrobes in my bedroom, I didn't mince my words with Charlotte.

'I didn't think about spoiling their surprise,' she said. 'I wanted to see if there was anything for me.'

Teenagers are still children.

But how it poured with rain that Christmas! I drove over to Makeni on Christmas morning and as soon as I turned off the tarmac on to the dirt road I knew I was in trouble. Makeni is a good farming area with rich red soil. The soil was a deeply rutted quagmire after a week of solid rain and the car slid from side to side. Just as I was thinking of giving up it slid obligingly into the deepest area of mud and came to rest. From there I waded to a house a few hundred yards away and found a couple of gardeners to dig me out. Why had I bothered to change before I set off?

Fortunately it was only another mile or two to where Charlotte's sister was staying and I had had the sense to come in Andrew's heavy Citroen which had better road holding power than my own car. Apart from having to present myself to total strangers clad in unbecoming mud boots the rest of the journey home was uneventful.

Apart from two things the holiday went well enough. One small difficulty arose from Charlotte's desire to wear her bikini on every occasion imaginable. I took this as part of the teenage stage and thought that it would wear off after a while but Andrew found it very embarrassing when she appeared in it for drinks on the back verandah.

'And she has not even been swimming,' he snorted.

Useless to point out that teen age girls would rather pose around than actually get wet. It amused me how prudish Andrew could be at times.

Even more difficult to understand was the attitude of Social Services. While they had decided that they knew enough about us to warrant placing a child in our care, they appeared to have no interest in whether Charlotte herself was happy. Not once did they phone her or contact her in any way. As the holiday wore on we waited to hear when she would be returning to school. I asked Charlotte if she had any idea.

'Not really, because I don't know which school I am going to,' was the surprising reply.

Apparently she had failed to secure a place for the next form at the same school and as far as she knew she had not been accepted at another. One was not automatically promoted to the next class at secondary school in Zambia; there was the form 3 examination to be passed, halfway through the course.

January was well on its way by now so I hastily made a visit to Social Services on Cha Cha Cha Road. Charlotte's file was found, no, nothing had been decided. In fact any enquiries at other schools had not been followed up. I had the impression that they had forgotten all about her.

So now I phoned the office daily, what would happen to Charlotte if a place were not found for her? How could she be left without a school place at fourteen? True enough it was an all too common plight for Zambian youngsters but Charlotte had no family to help her. At the very last minute the good Sisters at Fatima School near Ndola agreed to take her, (perhaps failing her Form 3 had made her work harder for she went on to complete her Form 5 and pass her Cambridge School certificate - O level equivalent) and as her sister married the year after she stayed with us, she then had somewhere to go in the holidays.

Andrew left all this to me - I had agreed to have Charlotte stay - but I could have done with some support. Instead Andrew was away in Livingstone, touring the Fiat assembly plant where for the first few years they would produce the 124 and 126 and 128 range and he looked at houses already being built for the workers And he reassured car dealers they would not be put out of business as they would still be able to import spare parts. And then he was on to the next Rail Commission of Inquiry where at the cost of K75,000 a driver had been found to be well over the limit with 193 mg of alcohol in his blood. Engines and rolling stock appeared to be as expendable as ever.

Having sorted out Charlotte's problems as we started 1972, we next had trouble with Simon. By the time Simon was due to start school, Ceri had left the Infants School and progressed to Lusaka Girls. Our times and routes worked even better. In the mornings Simon and I dropped Ceri off outside the Girls School and then drove round by the High Court to the Infants School, only a few minutes away.

Simon had entered Bessie Frost's class and she, poor disappointed lady, anticipating another pupil like Ceri was taken by surprise. It is never easy to follow an elder sibling - they have either been exceptionally clever and a paragon of virtue or had a reputation for misdeeds.

For a start, Simon did not have the eager-to-please and cooperative personality of Ceri, added to which he took a violent dislike to the idea of wearing a school uniform, particularly one which consisted of a grey shirt and shorts.

'School is boring enough without having to wear the same clothes every day,' he complained. I seem to recall that flower power was at its height in the 60's and so following Andrew's travels Simon had a natty selection of shirts ranging from pink flowered ones to cream brocade with equally exotic shorts and socks.

He regarded the expanse of school field with great disfavour, it was dull and bare and hot and he was not allowed to walk under the trees. School in general was a great disappointment to him.

I had not realised how great a disappointment until one day he passed through the school entrance hall on a message as I was talking to the Head.

'Ah, Simon,' she beamed. 'Enjoying school are you?'

'No, I am not,' was the short and embarrassingly cold reply as he walked on.

As time went on it became clear that he regarded the whole exercise as a dull and boring inconvenience and we searched about for an alternative. By this time I was considering giving up teaching altogether and would have time to deliver and collect children further afield. So after some consideration Simon was enrolled at the International School and Ceri's name was put down at the Dominican Convent School. The great advantage was that they would be able to continue right through primary and secondary school at both places.

The International School had no uniform and that alone was recommendation enough for Simon. It also had a free and easy

American atmosphere which he took to like the proverbial duck. There were no more grumbles but an eager and interested little boy who could not wait to get to school in the mornings. Ceri was going to have to wait for a place at the Convent so in the meantime I asked if she could start piano lessons in the afternoons.

The Head, Sister Fausta, sent me along to the Music House which stood some distance away in the school grounds - for a very good reason. There I found a diminutive Sister Georgina amid eleven pianos all going at full throttle; not only could she listen to ten children practise while she instructed the eleventh, she could also hold an animated conversation on the merits of Ceri starting the piano there and then and not waiting until she had a place at the school.

So Ceri was able to start that week, which meant dropping her off most afternoons while Simon went to afternoon sports at the International.

I handed in my resignation, determined in spite of the Head's pleas, to concentrate on being a wife and mother. I had to admit though that I missed teaching, so compromised by agreeing to do supply teaching from time to time.

I made half-hearted attempts to renew my interests in painting and sketching. I determined to spend more time on photography. But with so much time on my hands there was no urgency to anything I did. It was easy to make the excuse that for the first time I was really relaxing and not having to work to a full timetable.

There was more time of course to meet friends in the mornings but I could not see myself being seriously drawn into the coffee and bridge morning routines. The Hepworths, our old friends from Petauke, had moved into Lusaka. Johnnie was now working with African Farming Equipment and Aileen was enjoying living in a town for the first time since she had arrived in the country. It was great to able to get together - but that did not fill the days of course.

The Proctors had gone and we missed them sadly. The Redways

were leaving too. So many people were not renewing contracts now and most of the men pointed out that they felt that their jobs would be Zambianised in the foreseeable future and in which case they had to consider starting a new career elsewhere before they were any older, we felt a little deserted.

There were pessimists who pointed out that in a few years' time there would be very few, if any, white faces to be seen on Lusaka's streets. We laughed at this notion; there were so many settlers who had no intention of leaving Zambia. In fact a large number had been born there, where would they go? Would Zambia be able to produce all the trained personnel required in a matter of a few years?

The population was growing fast, the birth rate was increasing and the infant mortality was dropping - in spite of - to me - high figures. There could be room and work for everyone.

Even though the schools had been opened to all and more had been built, the demand for places could not be met. Nor could those who obtained a place in primary school be sure of entering secondary school; the drop out figures were a yearly headache and embarrassment to the Government and education was only one small sprocket on the cog.

As long standing friends began to disappear from Zambia it really came home to me that although I had made some Zambian friends they were not close friends. When I sat back and thought about it, it was painfully clear that although a Zambian friend would make me welcome in her home if I phoned or turned up on the doorstep, it was very rare indeed for one to call me or arrive at my house. True, many were holding down full time jobs like I had been doing and they too were busy ferrying offspring to and fro.

BUT I did not have a close Zambian friend.

When it actually came home to me I sat down and seriously thought about it. I had not gone out of my way to seek European friends but none of the friendships with Zambians had really developed. Was it because I had not learned the language? But if I had learned Bemba it would not have helped much with someone who was Tonga or Lozi or Nyanja.

It took me some time before I broached the subject with anyone else, so sure was I that I had failed miserably in my adopted country. What was even more alarming was to discover that I was not alone in my predicament. Both Stella Shamwana and Rosemary Chuula said they had Zambian friends - but - this was a very big BUT - they were not close. There was a gap in the relationship.

One was greeted and welcomed BUT where was the rapport? One could sit and try to analyse the whys and wherefores but it was not getting me very far. Whenever I met with Zambian friends now, I consciously analysed the tone and content of the conversation. I found I was keeping note of how many times I contacted someone before she contacted me - that was unutterably depressing! Andrew and I had a circle of friends both black and white. Andrew was on easy terms with all and sundry. Men of course talked work and politics ad infinitum. What about his close friends? I asked him whom he would regard as a confidant, a close friend to rely on ... he thought for a while and said,

'Goodie, I suppose.'

He had known Goodwin Mutale from school days at Munali, he was a sound fellow, he was (coincidentally) Bemba. In fact, all the other chaps were good friends but no more.

Was Andrew merely terribly self-sufficient, or are all men so self-reliant?

Returning to my own particular loneliness I knew that the rapport and friendship I required could not be forced but surely it was up to me to consciously develop and nurture whatever slim shoot I could discover. Perhaps I was too conscious about the whole thing now, perhaps I should put it all slightly to one side? I tried but it stayed very much on the perimeter of my thoughts.

So, old friends were departing gradually, so what? They were being replaced by people fresh out on contract and were to be met - oh, how they were to be met! - at each and every social function. Charming though many of them were, one big difference remained an obstacle. In no way were any of the newcomers considering staying in Zambia for long. One contract, maybe two; but they were here for the money, to see Africa, because there was a chance of some useful experience. But they had never set out with the intention of LIVING here. Unlike our departing friends, who had originally intended making their service in Northern Rhodesia their whole career.

So there I was with a very small nucleus of friends and acquaintances, beginning to admit we were merely linked by our presence in Zambia and – sometimes - similar interests.

And similar interests were not always enough - and commitment was not always enough. I had always admired Valentine Musakanya, Head of the Civil Service, thought he talked a lot of common sense. So it was a shock to hear he had been sacked. Sacked because he 'takes a stand on a wide range of issues contrary to policies of Party and Government'. Valentine of course denied the charges, stating, '*I never wanted the job in the first place but did it to the best of my ability and did not let personal stands interfere with work. I always took the line I thought to be in the national interest. I admit I have collected enemies because of my views on rural development and African capitalism. People in Government and the Party have been out to get me and I believe it's their pressure on President Kaunda. I feel no bitterness.*'

He talked a lot of sense, which wasn't always appreciated. He criticised '*the failure of the State to address the expectation of the population, adding that the money made in the very early days was ploughed back into development*', which confirmed my reading in the N Rhodesia Journal, for example, that the BSACo made an annual contribution of £10,000 for maintaining the police force between 1890-94. £75,000 was spent mainly on suppression of the slave trade – although there was still evidence of the slave trade in 1896 in the north east.

Possibly my restless feeling at that period stemmed partly from those causes. Whatever it was, I decided to return to teaching. Andrew said it was entirely up to me.

A change was necessary. I had to return to teaching but remembering the changes before I left Lusaka Infants I had to think twice. Large classes were no problem, the mixture of nationalities and language and cultures was stimulating ... but what about the new breed of fundis? The experts, who were producing the great breakthrough in Maths with their bits of spotted card? and the Inspector, who had called us all together for a meeting, to inform us that creative writing should no longer feature on the timetable. This was met with such blank incomprehension that even he realised that some explanation was necessary.

'Let's face the facts,' began this pompous individual. 'What use is this 'creative writing' going to be? How will it benefit these children? You are going to have more and more black Zambians in these schools as more and more expatriates leave. Most of the black Zambians will not be able to continue into secondary schools, so your job is to get them to read a form and be capable of basic arithmetic. Let's face it (he was very fond of facing things, our fundi from the Ministry), how many of these children are going to write a book?'

Such reasoning left our usually vocal staff totally speechless. But not for long of course. Surely we could not have been the only school to express complete revolt? He was amazed at our reaction. The most polite question being, did he think the purpose of creative writing was to produce a nation of authors? And was that the result in UK? However, he was totally unconvinced and departed saying we would have to follow the Ministry policy. We did not of course.

But did I want to return to those petty irritations?

Ceri had transferred from the Girls School to the Dominican Convent by this time and the more I saw of it, the more I liked the atmosphere and - AND - it was a private school - it would not have to follow the dictates of the Ministry to the letter.

So, let's have a complete change.

My mind made up, off I went to discover if there were likely to be any vacancies in the foreseeable future? Nobody was due to go on leave for some time in the primary but would I consider the secondary? No, Sister Cordula, I would not. There was no hurry, I left my name and phone number and continued my idle life.

Ceri had made a new friend at school, Nicole Bruce, who to a large extent replaced Suzanne and Fenella. They were in the same class and shared the same interest, including that of horses. Would Ceri like to ride with Nicole? As Nicole was the proud owner of two horses which were stabled at the showground and as the horses could be ridden round the racetrack and nearby open bush land, it was goodbye and thank you very much Mrs Cripps. Ceri was torn between her music lessons and the horses.

Sister Georgina was a fanatical teacher. A tiny person, barely five feet tall and as rumour had it, at least sixty years old, she was to be seen trotting along to the music room in the hostel to give a couple of lessons before school started at 7.30. She taught music to both primary and secondary pupils, having a full timetable until 12.30 when she was compelled to go for prayers and lunch. By 1.30 she could be found hurrying past the scarlet poinsettias by the chapel, round to the music house where all eleven pianos would shortly be in full use. This would continue until 4pm officially - but she was never known to stop before 5pm. Her enthusiasm, dedication and strict discipline were both feared and adored by her pupils, who strongly defended her against any criticism. Once a year the examiner from the London School of Music arrived; the results were always the same.

No pupil ever passed. They 'Passed With Distinction' or 'With Merit', but no one ever merely 'Passed'.

Ceri was soon scheduled for her Grade 1 examination. She was to be delivered to the Music House at 10am one Saturday morning, I should collect her at 11am. At that time I was not aware of Sister's reputation and I wondered if my daughter would pass, so I was interested in her reaction when I picked her up.

Sister Georgina at the Dominican Convent

Yes, the examiner was a very nice man. Yes, she had played the pieces well enough she thought. No, he had not asked any hard questions ... it all seemed to have gone well and all we could do now was to await the results. But Ceri had something on her mind.

At last she broke a long silence and said,

'It was all right really but Sister was so cross with me at the start that I nearly got it all wrong.'

'What on earth happened?'

'Well, you remember you dropped me off at the Music House? And we had to wait in the room at the end of the verandah until we were called and just as I was going in Sister Georgina came over and said, 'Where is your pocket?' and I haven't got a pocket in this dress, so I said I hadn't got a pocket and she was so cross and said, 'Stand still for a minute' and then she pushed something cold and hard up my knicker leg. Then she pushed me through the door and the examiner said, 'Sit down' and I had to sit on this thing and I didn't know what it was all the time I was playing. And when I came out she said, 'Quick, stand still' and she pulled it out and gave it to the next girl going in.'

What possible explanation could I offer Ceri?

Fortunately her friends soon enlightened us.

'Sister Georgina always puts her religious medals in your pocket when you go in for your exam.'

We live and learn.

Ceri was careful to wear something with pockets for her future exams and went on regularly to gain Passed With Distinction - religious medals or Sister Georgina's good teaching ?

Certainly in the first years it was not Ceri's hard work, her practising was a light and casual duty, which she appeared to perform effortlessly as she passed by the piano that I had managed to acquire from a departing American.

I was so relieved that this was so, I hate to see children practise hard to the exclusion of other activities in any sport or interest.

Ceri riding Blackie

She also enjoyed her riding and rode well but I did not encourage her to compete in gymkhanas. Nicole's mother thought me sadly lacking in ambition but if Ceri wished to compete, fine, if not, she could enjoy the riding and mucking out and grooming. Nicole was a good rider, winning many events in local shows. I waited to see how many rosettes Ceri would wish to festoon round her bedroom. Some did eventually appear but they were very incidental to the pleasure in the time spent with Nicole, Blackie and Gypsy.

Simon abandoned Mrs Cripps too and turned to football and

Cubs from which manly activities I was largely excluded. He enjoyed them and I could sew on his badges but he was not going to share any more with me. I suggested to Andrew that he should try to pick him up occasionally but had another male rebuff.

Simon had his close friends Michael Wallace and Bwembya Mutale - they were not into horses and gymkhanas, they liked messing about doing boys things in the house and garden - two acres gave them plenty of scope. Whatever it was, it usually involved lots of racing around at high speeds or quiet conversations in corners or following Banda on his many jobs.

Andrew read their school reports and if he were in the country could occasionally be persuaded to appear at a concert or Open Day - if this did not conflict with a 'Meeting' - hallowed words.

'Besides,' he reasoned, 'you are the teacher. You know how well they are doing - or not - and you know what to do about it'.

Being a teacher did not equip me for one meeting with Simon's class teacher at one Open Evening. Simon had, for him, waxed lyrical over Sir, an American who had a beard and played the 'geetar'.

Waiting to meet the hero I looked round the room and inspected my son's work, smiling at other parents self-consciously bent on the same mission. Simon's Maths seemed fine, he was certainly going to outstrip me if he maintained his present rate. His English was interesting albeit untidy. As I leafed through the book however, I found most pieces of work ended with the comment in red ink

'An exciting story! How about finishing it soon?

'Great description! Look forward to reading the end!'

'I sure enjoyed this! Are you going to finish it?'

And so on. None of the work was completed.

Mr Beard-With-Geetar was not all that perturbed.

'Why, no. I don't think it matters at all. Simon sure demonstrates he has ability. I don't see that completing an assignment is at all important if he has shown he can do it.'

We parted with our professional gap as wide as ever. What a

pity the Convent does not admit boys I thought, even while I recognised that uniformity and more than the slightest discipline seemed to have an adverse effect on my son.

I need not have worried however. The following year Simon moved up and entered Mrs McKeene's class. On the first day I collected the children as usual from school and we went home for lunch. The last mouthful was barely down when Simon stood up saying,

'I need some paper.'

'What kind?'

'Oh any kind, but it should be nice paper ... it's for covering my books.'

Stunned silence greeted this announcement but never query life when the gods smile upon you.

Hastily I produced a range of papers from sensible brown to plain colours to fancy wrapping. The latter was deemed worthy of MRS MCKEENE hereafter always referred to in tones of deepest respect. He shut himself up in his bedroom and a pile of books was later seen neatly covered, even unto mitred corners. 'MRS MCKEENE said this was the way to do them.'

Mrs McKeene also said that his writing would be copperplate and it was so. As for assignments being completed - anything else would have been unthinkable.

Thank God for the Mrs McKeenes of this world. Not only was his work better, he was even more enthusiastic!

As we drifted into 1972 it was sometimes difficult to reconcile Andrew's bouncy optimism - all was well with Indeco and therefore let us make merry - with Press reports and what one could see around one. The Times of Zambia continued to be fairly outspoken even after Vernon Mwanga replaced Dunstan Kamana as editor in chief. The Guardian in UK commented that Dunstan was replaced as he was too outspoken and critical of Government defects. But one could still read reports of mismanagement and mishandling - even if the bite were not quite so sharp.

Early in 1972 Defence Minister Grey Zulu met a delegation

of student leaders and informed them that all students who completed Form 5 would undergo two years National Service training in various fields including military. We had heard this before but now the advertisements appeared in the papers advising that the training would be in agriculture using modern implements and the hoe, domestic science would feature along with cookery, mother craft etc. building, plumbing, carpentry, bricklaying were not forgotten and ranked alongside military training.

Well, I was all for National Service if young people were to be taught useful skills and a little military training never did anyone any harm. I did wonder where all the instructors would be found as we seemed to be short of schools and teachers anyway. But the Government must know where it is going and must have its plans well organised to be so far into recruitment, I reasoned.

Of more serious concern was the news that Simon Kapwepwe had been beaten by a mob of more than 100 in the market only a few hours after taking his seat in Parliament as the sole representative of the UPP (United Progressive Party). Within a matter of two or three weeks the Government banned the UPP and detained 123 leading members, including Simon himself. The President announced that 'we had to do it, UPP were bent on violence and destruction'.

I seemed to have missed something - I had not heard of rampaging UPP mobs - but ... I could have missed it. Only three weeks later the President made yet another announcement - Zambia was to become a One Party State. A National Commission would work out a new Constitution to implement the change. The Cabinet had made this decision in response to demands by an overwhelming majority. (When? Where?) He hastened to add that he would never accept life Presidency.

Harry Nkumbula's ANC Party was quick to state that they would not sit on a One Party Democracy Commission; most emphatically they did not want a One Party State.

How long ago it seemed since I had walked into Shah's restaurant on Gower Street and seen Kaunda, Kapwepwe and Nkumbula lunching together in complete harmony and accord.

Power corrupts they say.

Certainly ideals seem to change.

I asked Andrew if he found developments worrying. Oh no! in fact a One Party State was actually TRUE democracy as there would be no party wrangling, we would all be one. Andrew could be very convincing and plausible, and usually left me without an argument but feeling only half satisfied.

Whatever thoughts I or anyone else had, we were heading towards a One Party State and that was that.

Perhaps Kaunda would have more time to concentrate on the problems of the State if he did not have to spend time on inter party bickering; there were enough problems in the country without that. In spite of all the talk of progress we were making it was still disturbing to see that the much vaunted University Teaching Hospital was not going to be used to its full potential. A letter in the times of Zambia from Abu Hassim, Consultant Gynaecologist, complained that *'before moving into the new maternity hospital my department had 39 qualified nurses for 9,000 deliveries. Now we have 35 nurses for 14,991 admissions during 1971... the premature and isolation wards and the Caesarean theatre will be ready for commissioning soon. However, the Deputy Nursing Officer for Zambia has ruled that the new wards will have to remain empty indefinitely because of the serious nursing shortage. For the Caesarean theatre the authorities have decided to run it with four daily paid workers and one non-existent Sister. This I refuse to accept. The Government has given the capital one of the finest and best equipped hospitals in Africa. They have failed miserably to run it safely and efficiently.'*

He had a point.

But what can a Government do when a large percentage of nurses in training did not complete their training due to pregnancies? The economy was not as healthy and we were beginning to see more drastic measures introduced, luxury imports were banned and extra import duties were slapped on items such as washing machines, vacuums, fridges, gramophones and cameras.

Yes, Kaunda had pressing problems and perhaps a One Party State would relax some of those pressures. We had become so used to seeing him waving his white handkerchief, it was a surprise to see him at the Cathedral of the Holy Cross at his mother's funeral minus the white hankie - but holding the hand of Bishop Makumba. On such a sad day for him he had also the anxiety of knowing that his State House secretary had been injured by an explosive device when opening the post.

DOMINICAN CONVENT PRIMARY SCHOOL

My leisure time for interest in politics was brought to halt by a call from the Convent - would I replace Mrs Higgins who had gone on leave?

The Dominican Convent was situated on Leopard's Hill Road. The school's correct name was Saint Mary's Dominican Convent School but it was always referred to as 'The Convent'. On the site was a primary school, a secondary school, a hostel for boarders, the convent itself, a large chapel and various workers houses and outbuildings. There was an extensive orchard, large playing fields and a swimming pool.

The primary Head, Sister Fausta, introduced me to my new class of forty little girls, aged five to six years dressed in blue or beige dresses. The classroom, at the end of a block of three, was large and airy. The class worked with a quiet hum and the morning proceeded smoothly. Mid-morning my colleagues walked me across to the staffroom in the secondary school and introduced me to the staff there. The atmosphere was friendly and cheerful and I thought I would like working in this larger and more varied group.

Back to the classroom, where we resumed lessons. Just before midday I looked round the room, the children were writing in their books, a few had finished and were drawing a picture. I could relax now, only half an hour to go.

Suddenly, as one, the entire class rose to its feet and burst into song

'Hail Mary, Mother of God,

Lady in blue, I love you.
Hail Mary, Mother of God,
Mary's my mother too.'

And as one, they sat down and carried on working. In the background I was vaguely aware of a bell tolling. It was all very well coming to work in a Convent school as a non-Catholic I reflected but I wished Sister Fausta had thought fit to fill me in with a little more detail about the day's routine. When I mentioned this to another teacher the next day, she laughed and said,

'Ah yes, the Angelus! The children are supposed to stop working and say a prayer. No one ever told me about it either and once when I was supervising Sister's class I didn't hear the bell at all but her girls seemed to have an inbuilt clock, they stood up, said a prayer and sat down again while I was still getting to my feet.'

I asked Sister whether there were any other religious observances I should be aware of but she smiled sweetly and said

'Oh no, I don't think so.'

'I just don't want to make any mistake or omit something. I'm not a Catholic remember,' I reminded her.

Again the sweet smile.

'Oh, Mrs Kashita! You love children and that is all that is necessary. We just say the usual prayers and have Scripture lesson to start the day, it is just the same as the schools where you were.'

Sister Fausta may have meant what she said but there was an enormous difference. There was a gentleness and a courtesy, a consideration and love which permeated the whole school in every activity and moment of the day.

Obviously this was the Sisters' influence and the lay Staff and children responded so that the working and living within a community so easily assumed its full meaning. Not that we did not have our differences of opinion and life did not have its ups and downs but there was an over-all feeling of permanent goodwill. It made such a difference to the working day. At that time we were four lay teachers and three Sisters in the primary school. In addition, Sister Georgina taught the music and we shared the PE teacher with the secondary school.

Sister Fausta Head of the Dominican Primary School with Rachel Jellis

And I grew used to the Angelus ... and seeing girls crossing the grounds, coming to a halt for a few moments, and either folding their hands or bowing their heads in prayer. It was just a pause in their day, almost automatic but nonetheless heartfelt.

The next hurdle was being told that the school would be making the usual procession to the statue of Our Lady in the grotto in the convent garden – and my class being the youngest was to lead the procession. I had no idea where the grotto was and Sister's directions were vague so I can only think divine guidance must have directed my feet as we sang

Immaculate Mary!
Our hearts are on fire!
That title so wondrous
Fills all with desire!
Ave, Ave, Ave Maria,
Ave, Ave, Ave Maria

We pray for God's glory
May His Kingdom come………
The girls voices carrying lightly on the sunlit air.
Arriving before the grotto at the close of the singing, my prayer
was heart felt.

Mrs Wallenstein of Grade 2

I was in Grade 1, next door with Grade 2 was Mrs Wallenstein, a
South African Coloured who taught with a rod of iron tempered
with a deep affection for her charges. Mrs Wallenstein was a
very well built middle aged lady, who insisted 'you can and you
will' with such conviction that every girl could and did to the
very best of her ability. Nor was she one for mincing her words;
straightforward home truths were delivered with a straight
smack on the chin. With my liking for the Yorkshire habit of
calling a spade a bloody shovel, we got on very well.
Mrs Wallenstein was gifted with a lovely voice and perfect pitch
so it was with great relief that I agreed our two classes would
sing together under her leadership. She would hum or la la la a
tune and then the girls would join in on the first line. I was willing
to join in but she very soon advised me just to 'smile along' after
I cheerfully began the words of a completely different song
'Couldn't you hear it was … ?' she asked in total disbelief.

She also advised that I should not stand next to her after turning suddenly one day and knocking me sideways with her rather ample bosom. I was scarlet with embarrassment but she roared with laughter and said her husband had had that problem a few times.

When Mr Wallenstein retired from the Roads Department they returned to South Africa.

'We are South Africans and we might as well retire to our home country, we don't really belong here. It will be different of course but we shall just have to make the best of it - and it's not all as bad as you hear.'

And I thought I should never see them again.

Lo and behold, the next time we went to England we spent the first few days in London and after lunch on Sunday we took a walk across Speakers Corner. There was a larger crowd than usual at one speaker and we approached it with curiosity. A couple of policemen were making soothing 'Let's move along now then shall we' gestures.

Suddenly there in front of me was Mrs Wallenstein! And Mr Wallenstein, standing quietly by, his usual position.

'Wally ... June ... what are you doing here?' we shrieked simultaneously as we flung our arms round each other.

The two policemen and the slowly dispersing crowd lingered and hovered, watching us with interest, which I found very disconcerting as Londoners take odd scenes in their stride – not that we were odd surely?

Mrs Wallenstein enlightened us about the crowd. Listening to a chap on a soap box defending Ian Smith and UDI she had been unable to resist correcting him and adding her bit on the subject of independent African countries and the benefit of living in South Africa, who could teach many independent African countries about the provision for 'the common man' and the feelings of a non-white living happily in an efficient police state ... having thus raised several controversial issues almost simultaneously she had abandoned the debate and turned away, coming face to face with us.

Our ecstatic reunion only served to confuse the crowd only further. But I leap ahead.

Not long after I joined the school the Grade 3 teacher left and a new teacher was appointed. She was a most attractive young woman who looked far too young to be the mother of three school age children, she looked more like their elder sister. Her name was clearly Italian and she talked of when they were back in Italy with great nostalgia so imagine my surprise when May Sharpe walked into my room one lunch time.

'Hi June, I'm collecting Susan but can I have a word? You've got a new teacher, what's her name?'

I told her adding, 'She seems very nice ...'

'Italian? are you sure? Who told you that?

It transpired that May and our new teacher had trained at the same teacher's training college in S Rhodesia – '... and you sure didn't go there if you weren't Coloured!'

She added, 'I thought I recognised her when we passed on the verandah and when she looked away and pretended not to know me, I wondered why. So, now she's passing for white!'

Why anyone should wish to do so in the enlightened days we were living in was completely beyond both of us. It was well known that people do so in South Africa, but WHY try to pass as white in an independent country where there was no colour problem and where in fact people now were being actively encouraged to be proud of what they were? She was an attractive intelligent woman in her own right, there was no need for her to pretend to be anything else.

However, I respected her wishes and when later she realised May and I were friends I never allowed her to know that May had mentioned recognising her. It was clearly on her mind for some time and she would raise the topic of our friendship occasionally and I felt sorry that her assumed life style was giving, and would always give, her cause for anxiety.

Chris Stone was in Grade 4, we had taught together at Lotus Primary and her dry humour was an asset in any staffroom. Sister Herlinde was in Grade 5 and Sister Edmunda in Grade 6, and Sister Fausta in Grade 7.

It was quite a change to be in an all-girls school but it was a very easy adjustment to make. Discipline was very easy - but then it always was in Zambia. Children and their parents so appreciated getting a place in a school that it was highly valued. The children were no more angels than their counterparts elsewhere, but once in school, education was taken seriously. This was coupled of course, with the tradition of respecting your elders, any elders. As a teacher you only had to walk into a classroom to warrant attention - you were older and you were a teacher.

At that time the class was not 100% Zambian but about half the children were and to have half your class giving you undivided attention meant that the other half fell into line. By this time I was used to Zambian children taking something from me with cupped hands and the occasional 'bob' or bended knee, which was the polite way of accepting something. I found that at the convent after the end of the day prayer the whole class would 'bob' or curtsey as they said

'Good afternoon Mrs Kashita and thank you.'

As usual with schools in Zambia, the basic three R's had priority and it says much for the teachers that in spite of the range of nationalities and languages and the size of the classes, the standard of achievement was gratifyingly comparable to UK. It could be argued that as all the children were not able to enter school, that we had only 'the cream' but this was not so. How does one 'cream' them off at the age of five? Many people were eager to enter their daughters at the school and would complete an application form well in advance, sometimes when the daughter was a mere babe in arms. But by the time five years had passed there was a natural wastage from people being transferred or leaving the country altogether, so that when Sister Fausta came to offering places to the first forty on the list, she would find that quite a number had gone. Even number sixty stood a chance in some years.

Waiting lists were eventually dispensed with in state schools and were replaced by Enrolment Day. A terrible day when queues formed outside schools during the night as anxious parents waited with their children clutching birth certificates or sworn affidavits to prove the child was five years old before the first of January - this was later changed to seven years. A valid smallpox certificate also used to be compulsory until the dreadful disease was eliminated.

Once the school gates were open and enrolment began there were many sad faces as the quota was reached. As it began to be suspected that parents were borrowing birth certificates and children were being admitted below the official age, a new rule was introduced. If the Head suspected the child was not five years of age, he would be asked to put his right arm over his head and touch his left ear, failure to do so meant the child was refused a place.

I well remember an occasion only a few years later when parents had queued all night outside Woodlands School and just as the gates were about to be opened at eight o'clock, up rolled some Army lorries. Out jumped soldiers with their sons and daughters, they marched to the front of the queue.

'We go first,' they said. And no one dare argue.

This pressure for school places was a constant headache for Heads (if you will pardon the pun) and Sister Fausta said she dreaded the afternoons when she was not teaching as her office was besieged by anxious parents, persuasive and pleading parents ... and even threatening parents.

'I know I can do no more,' she would say with her blue eyes full of tears. 'But imagine how I feel when a father sits in my office and weeps.'

Even more desperate were the parents who had come out on contract and been promised places at our schools and were faced with the prospect of two or three years of missed schooling - or sending the wife and children back home. Equally desperate were the parents who were transferred within the country by Ministries and Companies.

The idea of school attendance officers was a difficult one to explain to Zambians!

Not all our children were Catholics; I believe the Ministry ruling was that we could reserve no more than 30% of our places for Catholic pupils. Once admitted though all the children had to attend the same RE lessons and Mass which was held once or twice a term in the chapel. The chapel was a great asset in the school; its doors stood open all day and pupils from the little Grade 1's to the dignified Form 5's were free to enter at any time. A break or lunch time never passed without some girl popping in.

Saint Dominic's Day was an anniversary celebrated in a special way. It was officially a holiday but it was spent at school - probably the correct definition was for once - a holy day. The school day began with a Mass in the chapel for primary and secondary combined and the wonderful singing of

Dominique, nique, nique, over land he plods along
And sings a happy song, never asking for reward
He just talks about the Lord.
At a time when Johnny Lachland
Over England was the king
Dominic was in the background
Fighting sin like anything.....

Then there was a short break when children picnicked in the school grounds where they wished. After that we retired to the school hall. I asked one of the Sisters what the programme was to be in the hall and was told,

'We never have any idea, it is all left to the prefects,'

That explained the secretive groups I had noticed in the last week or two, but nothing prepared me for the standard of entertainment. Songs, plays, recitations, music (pop and other) all followed each other in quick and professional succession. Anyone could ask to take part from the five year olds to the eldest and there was a good cross section from both schools. After the Sisters, Staff and children had been well entertained there were more picnics and sports.

The school worked on the principle that everybody could so something and so events were arranged on Sports Days so that all could take part in at least one event and although the four Houses competed fiercely it was all in good spirit and the victors roundly cheered.

Minister of Education Lameck Goma presenting certificates on Sports Day – this one to Angela Mwanza

Sister Fausta had absolute faith. The rains were late ending one year and as we walked across to the pool just before the start of a swimming gala it was clear we were due a most unseasonal storm. I looked at the purple sky just above our heads and asked what the children were to do when the storm broke, there was only one small changing room, were they to run for the school verandahs?

'Oh no, Mrs Kashita, it won't rain. I went in the chapel after lunch and said a little prayer.'

Sad to say the heavens opened as the starting pistol went for the first race. But it was warm, most of the children were competing so were in swimming costumes and would get wet anyway, so Sister Fausta covered the recording table with a large umbrella she had brought to protect her from the sun (I said she had faith) and we battled on. It poured steadily until the last race when the sun broke through on to soaked competitors and spectators.

Sister's faith was unshaken as I was to discover when we purchased some new climbing frames and swings for the playground. I had designed them and had them made by Indeco Steel - there were some advantages in being married to the chairman, it speeded things up. But once they were installed I had slight misgivings - they looked much higher than I had imagined.

'Will the school insurance cover new equipment automatically?' I nervously enquired.

Sister Fausta looked surprised and said she would find out. I asked again the following week.

'It's quite all right. I had Father go down and bless them at the weekend.'

Perhaps Father's blessing was a little more effective than Sister's prayer for good weather, no one ever slipped from the bars.

It was Sister Fausta who introduced the Shrove Tuesday Fancy Dress Parade.

'I would like to introduce something for those who are not our best academically and who do not excel at sport and something where we can all have FUN - life should not be serious all the time. I want our girls to be HAPPY,' she said.

Grade 1 on two of the climbing frames

We all thought our girls were happy - but let's be happier still because once Sister got a bee under her bonnet, or under her veil, it was best to join in.

So on Shrove Tuesday - chosen for its links to Mardi Gras - the

401

entire primary school assembled near the boarding hostel, each child in a fancy dress. The only rule being that the costume must be entirely homemade, and in the case of the older girls, made by themselves. There were shrieks of laughter as they assembled but eventually they were lined up class by class and we walked down the path to stand on the lawn in front of the Convent. Then there was an expectant hush as all eyes were fixed on the balcony outside the bedroom windows. Before long a tiny figure appeared and there was a rustle of clapping as the girls called 'Sister Perpetua! Sister Perpetua, hello!'

Sister Perpetua was helped along the balcony by Sister de Angelis and they stood there together while the children were inspected. Now in her eighties Sister Perpetua had come out from Germany as a young nun, she had never been back home. She was nearly bedridden now and had not been downstairs for a very long time.

Once we had passed the inspection it was down to the Hall in a rowdy procession for the judging, prizes being awarded for novelty of idea and design and materials - it is remarkable what can be achieved with banana leaves to name but one unusual feature.

It was also Sister Fausta's idea that after the initial prizes were awarded every girl received a token prize for entering - as she beamed, 'We are all winners today'.

It was a lovely idea but became something of a minor nightmare in later years when goods became so sparse on the shop shelves. I shall never forget Sister de Angelis designing a flap over pencil case (zips were only available 20 inches long and at great expense) and together we sewed 280 cases each to hold a new pencil.

School concerts were held every two years and were produced with professional polish thanks to one of the parents, Thalia Barclay, who gave so unstintingly of her time. Like Sister Georgina, she accepted nothing less than perfect; the pair of them together were awe inspiring. One year it was the Mikado for the whole school followed by the Wizard of Oz, then we tried the first four Grades producing short individual items with the top three Grades in Joseph and the Technicoloured Dream Coat and later The Pied Piper - an original musical written by Father Redmond. Our school having the honour to first produce it.

The year of the Mikado was just before my time but I often heard what great fun it had been, enhanced by the sight and sound of tiny five year olds strolling round the grounds unconsciously humming various refrains and during quiet lessons it was not unusual for a class to spontaneously start singing while still carrying on working. When I first had to produce a solo item for my Grade Ones I decided to make use of the reading scheme we used - the Janet and John of dubious educational fame. Its sing song repetitive style was already a joke between the girls and so I decided to write a short skit in its style.

The curtains pulled back to reveal a very large Here We Go (first reader) centre stage and after a moment Janet and John stepped out from the 'book' to the calls of

'John.

John.

Come John come.'

At which there was a stunned silence in the Hall. As the little playlet progressed with Janet and John calling their kittens and breaking into 'I love little pussy' and later climbing into a boat to the refrain of 'Row, row, row your boat' over 400 parents collapsed into helpless laughter led by the President and his wife sitting in state on the front row. All those evenings listening to their offspring proudly reading their first Janet and John were rewarded.

That was the same year Ceri took part in Joseph's Technicoloured Dream Coat and I well remember the way the audience settled back for the final item on the programme, for what they clearly expected to be a quiet religious piece. The crashing lively introduction sat them bolt upright and they were riveted until the final song when the applause was thunderous. Thalia Barclay gave so much to the school and pupils over those years.

But we were not allowed much time for frivolities, there were exams to be passed and while expatriate girls sat entrance papers for overseas schools from time to time we were geared towards the Grade 7 selection at the end of the year. In addition to which we were not allowed to opt out of any activity in the educational field.

I vaguely remember some Science Competition being organised which was to culminate in the prize winners being invited to a two day demonstration at the University. This was too much for Sister Fausta - 'The chance to represent our school at THE UNIVERSITY ! what an honour!'

A mini competition was promptly planned within our two schools and science became our be all and end all.

Although my class were only five years old I thought we could still have a bit of fun and as the rainy season had recently ended, we were missing the fresh air the rains brought and water was very much on our minds. We made a model of rain falling and forming rivers and being used for human needs as it made its way to the sea, connected up to the classroom tap and a bit of cake colouring dropped in at the top of the plastic pipe - we had a lot of fun.

At home I was not so amused to find that Ceri and Nicole had planned a series of tests on seeds planted in pots of rabbit, chicken and horse manure laced soil, half of which were to be kept in light conditions and half in dark. Ceri had elected to be in charge of the dark section and was keeping them under her bed. 'You will have to sleep with your door open,' said Simon wrinkling his nose.

To my surprise my class were chosen to represent the primary school at the University after being grilled by the visiting judge. In all we had four entries from primary and secondary and Sister Fausta could find no words to express her happiness. Off we went on the great day with models and equipment and representative groups of girls. Very soon our models were set up and the girls prepared to demonstrate and explain to visitors. As it was a full day session, we had been given tokens for a lunch in the students dining hall. At which Sister Fausta positively bounced. So at midday we duly marshalled our pupils and made our way to lunch. It was served at a long low counter and as we held out our plates, huge masses of soggy rice and an unidentifiable 'relish' (a traditional Zambian form of stew) was dumped on top. Seeing what was happening ahead I managed to get one helping and four plates and divide it up for my group and settled them at a table. Within a matter of seconds we were joined by Sister Fausta managing to support her plate with two hands and already looking very pink in the face.

'Oh dear, oh dear,' she gasped. 'It is rather a large helping.'

We stolidly munched our way through the meal and once I thought the girls had had enough I allowed them to stand by a window and watch the world go by, discreetly finding a way of disposing of left overs. Looking at Sister's very pink face, I offered to take her plate when she was ready.

'Oh no, Mrs Kashita. I cannot do that. You see we Sisters take a vow of poverty and we cannot waste anything.'

It was in vain for me to assure her that it would not technically be wasted if a farmer's pigs or whatever benefitted - there must be some useful end to all this waste, I thought. But Sister believed she must never waste what she had been given and she ploughed valiantly on to the end, her plump face scarlet and her cheerful voice quite silent.

Mentioning waste for farmers' pigs has just reminded me of Gaynor Arnold, who gave me a day by day bulletin on the new piglets on her father's farm ... until the day I thoughtlessly agreed they sounded sweet and wished I could see them. The following morning saw Mr Arnold staggering in through my classroom door clutching a huge wooden crate. Had I really told Gaynor to bring the piglets to school? Looking at her beaming face I hadn't the heart to say no and smiling weakly, pointed to a corner. Fortunately he had only brought two and yes, they were sweet and the whole class were impressed and they made for an inspiring topic ... But two piglets in a classroom for five hours (7am to 12 noon) in the hot season was more than a little pungent. Sister Fausta paid a fleeting visit, praised Gaynor for her thoughtfulness and commended me for my bravery and vanished still holding her breath.

There were serious celebrations too. On Independence Day there was a flag raising ceremony when the whole school assembled round the flag pole; children read their own prayers for the wellbeing of the President Kenneth David Kaunda and for their country and its leaders. The National Anthem was solemnly sung as the flag was raised by the Head girl and the whole school saluted. Hearing girls spontaneously harmonising as they sang Stand And Sing Of Zambia to the tune of Sikeli Afrika was most moving.

I remember celebrating VE Day at my primary school long ago in 1946 but the Union Jack and the National Anthem seem to have largely disappeared from British schools, certainly I never heard mention of them when I was teaching, before and after my time in Zambia.

Zambia however was proud of its comparatively recently gained independence and was also consciously trying to weld together many different tribes. This was such a serious matter that the children of Jehovah Witnesses lost their school places if their parents forbade them to sing the National Anthem and salute the flag. The flag fluttered proudly outside every school daily but on the 24th October Head Teachers were even more aware of their responsibilities.

We were also very conscious of the fact that the children in our school were most fortunate in their homes and school. So in addition to the usual fundraising activities which go on in most schools - such as fetes and sponsored spelling bees to raise money for equipment - we were also very involved in fundraising for charities. I remember in particular money sent to villagers in the Tonga Valley after a prolonged drought, money to help build a church in Chelston, money for nappies and baby clothes and towards an incubator for the maternity wing in Lusaka Hospital. One day I had a visit from Sister Bernard who had taught for many years and been a popular Head in Broken Hill (now Kabwe). She had later gone to UK to do a film course with the idea of producing educational films for Zambian TV. Could she film my class at work?

Certainly, if it did not involve my being in front of the camera.

The girls were completely unselfconscious when acting on stage and with visitors in the classroom. In addition I told them that Sister Bernard was testing her equipment and there would not be an actual film in the camera. We had a wonderfully natural film, including watching Louise gently cheating on her friend Roberta in a dice game.

Some of my lessons could have happened in an English school with the same response. One day they all brought in a doll or a teddy bear and we proceeded to have a party. We spent most of the morning weighing on scales and measuring in pint jugs, we made small cakes and jellies. We counted the spaces in the cake tins and used our 'times tables' for quick calculations. We worked out the baking times with clocks - in short 90% of the morning was spent in some form of Maths and Language work.

The cakes and jellies were carried over to the Convent kitchens where Sister de Angelis, forewarned, had made preparations.

For the last half hour we sat, sweaty and exhausted, to sing Happy Birthday to our dolls and eat the goodies spread out on the carefully measured and decorated place mats. And wouldn't you know it? As soon as I said it was time for prayers before home time there was a cry of

'Already? But we haven't done any SUMS!'

Another lesson could not have happened in UK. Digging in a flower bed at home I unearthed some small white eggs, about a centimetre long. I had no idea what they could be but into a jar of damp earth they went and into school. We watched them for days for any signs of development, it may have been for two or three weeks in fact, but with no luck. On the last day of term before Easter I was tidying away the last items on top of the display cupboards and came across the jar - might as well throw it away. It was put on my desk until break time. Half an hour later we were enchanted by fifteen perfect lizards in miniature scampering over the books and among the pencils. There are no

Easter eggs like that in UK!

It was a wonderful school with a wonderful atmosphere. Thank you, Sisters and pupils and fellow teachers.

Was it 1972 or another year? ... I know I was teaching Grade 1 at the Convent ... Just another memory ... standing on a cupboard taking down some displays ... a knock at the door. One of the children opened the door - and a delivery of a huge bouquet of flowers. Amazing – thanked the young woman delivering and thought Andrew is so sweet – is it an anniversary? – remembered it was 14th February - looked for the card in the flowers and couldn't find one. At lunchtime my thanks met with complete consternation – Andrew had NOT sent me flowers. A phone call to the florist met with a blank - no record. But an atmosphere at home.

It was a little while before a phone conversation revealed it was a thank you from one of Andrew's secretaries ... I had forgotten I had lent a sympathetic ear to her tale of woe and persuaded Andrew to give her immediate leave to fly to S Africa in order to sort out a personal problem

The end of 1972 saw the announcement that the Government welcomed and generally accepted the recommendations of the Commission on the establishment of a One Party Democracy in Zambia. The President signed three vital Constitution Amendment Bills passed by Parliament and Zambia entered its second Republic. The ANC ceased to exist, MP's who were members of ANC were to sit as Independents until Parliament dissolved.

Whether one took an optimistic view of political developments or not, you could not feel very cheerful after reading the Auditor General's report in which he severely criticised the unauthorised spending of K6.1 million for the year.

Perhaps it washed over the heads of some of our leaders. After all, the President had announced that 'Zambia will be paradise in ten years ... important mineral finds ... discovery of gold, diamonds, nickel, iron ore and uranium ...'

Well, even I knew about Sesari gold mine. What an enjoyable

picnic we had had there with the Hepworths, little did we know what we were sitting on. Was it due to be reopened?

But even if important mineral finds were to be found ... there was still the problem of mismanagement ... Namboard had collected 4 million of the 6 million bag record maize crop but 200,000 more bags were needed and 1000 tarpaulins from W Germany to prevent the loss of much of the crop. The Ministry of Trade had only allowed half the import licences (this was in September with the rains due in November)

SO LIFE GOES ON 1973

Simon Kapwepwe was released from detention early in 1973; he said he was not bitter and after studying the One Party participatory democracy system would make up his mind on his future as a politician. Kaunda's quick response was that ex UPP members could not automatically join UNIP.

'That seems very unfair', I said to Andrew. 'If there is only one Party then surely everyone can join in together? I thought that's what it was all about. You said it would stop inter party bickering.'

'Not at all,' said Andrew. 'It's the same elsewhere. Russians can't automatically become Party members.'

I was lost. If you can only have one Party and you can't be a member, then do you criticise from the outside? And what are you then? Perhaps we should not have a Party at all?

Andrew was in America for a month at the beginning of 1973 trying to attract more foreign investors into Zambia. While he was away more trouble erupted between Zambia and Rhodesia. Rhodesia decided to close the border between the two countries until Zambia would give assurances that terrorists would no longer operate against Rhodesia from Zambian territory. Children going to school down south and international travellers would still be allowed to move across the border and copper - Zambia's foreign exchange earner - was exempt from the ban.

It did not take long for Kaunda to state that Zambia could find alternative routes for the copper and that Zambia would continue to support the freedom fighters. By the beginning of February Zambia sealed the border; only people leaving Zambia for good were allowed to cross. The whole border area became more tense as troops dug in on both sides and in May there was an international incident when two Canadians were killed and one American wounded on the Rhodesian side of the Victoria Falls. An official explanation was given that a Zambian sentry saw four people in swimming costumes, he claimed they appeared to be men with what appeared to be bandoleers or waterproof gear for protecting explosives going towards the bend opposite the power station. They got into the Silent Pool and as he thought they would attack the power station, he fired. A most unfortunate mistake. Zambia was rife with mistakes but fortunately most were not as tragic as this.

Most mistakes were expensive miscalculations. Zambia is a large country with a vast agricultural potential but sadly the human potential did not match up with requirements. It was common knowledge that when Kafue Textile Factory was first opened, insufficient cotton was available because the farmers could not get the manpower to pick the crop - even after the President himself gave a day's token labour to show that manual labour was not demeaning. And once production of cotton was better organised the public responded by wanting polyesters and home produced cottons stock piled up at Kafue.

It was found that tea would grow well at Kawambwa and a 600 acre project was launched in 1969. By 1973, 150 acres was under irrigation but 25 tons of tea was destined to go to waste because of lack of processing machinery and tea tasters.

Simpler exercises were also destined to suffer from the public's general lack of common sense and care. UBZ introduced Zamcabs and everyone was cheered by the prospect of a safe and reliable taxi service. Within a month we were treated to photos of 13 Zamcabs out of action because of accidents - only two were the fault of the drivers!

Vehicles in general, after all these years of being unavailable to the common man - were treated with a casualness of spirit which resulted in daily accidents of every degree of severity and none were safe from the depredations of the 'kabulala' (thief). We should not have laughed but we did, when we heard that thieves had lifted Kaunda's Land Rover used in the struggle for independence which stood outside his former home 394 Chilenje, put it on blocks and had stolen the wheels.

I had always had a soft spot for Land Rovers, recalling the days when we had first gone to Northern Rhodesia and Andrew was working as an agricultural officer. He had taken me on many field trips in a station Land Rover. They had been happy days and I looked back at that period with nostalgia, wishing I had taken more photographs, realising that the way of life was changing very rapidly.

Now his business trips were usually overseas and even if there had not been the children we could not have afforded the fare for me - nor were wives officially allowed to accompany husbands. As I have said earlier it was disappointing but a fact of life one accepted and, in my case, I made sure that my life was full with my work at school and the children's activities. Most wives hated the situation but accepted it and we often felt some pride in being able to run homes or businesses or small farms on our own.

As a chap got nearer the top of the ladder though, things began to take a turn for the better. Wives would be able to accompany husbands on an occasional trip - all expenses paid! Bearing in mind 'occasional' was the operative word.

But one does not look a gift horse in the mouth, even if they are very small ponies.

At long last in 1973 Andrew said I would be able to accompany him, what was lined up? Only a trip to Japan. And China. What more could one ask? It does no good whatsoever getting all excited of course, a small difficulty arose and for some reason was never resolved. According to Andrew, the Minister authorising the trip had to also authorise my going and for some reason I never found out, although there was no problem with my going to Japan, there was a hiccup over China.

411

To cut a long story short, permission and papers were never sorted out for the China part of the trip and in the end it was arranged we should go to Tokyo, Hong Kong and Bangkok. I kept my fingers crossed for Peking until the last moment, although with little hope of it materialising. Arrangements were made for Ceri and Simon to fly to London with us - at our expense of course - they were to have a holiday with the Redways.

Fenella and Veronica

Great excitement there! The Redways had been back in UK for some time and were comfortably settled in Hoddesdon. Fortunately the dates coincided very well with the school holidays both in UK and Zambia so the children would have a long time together and I was not upsetting my school routine.

With no more dates and plans to be arranged Simon promptly went down with the measles. Andrew's meetings could not be rearranged of course so once measles was diagnosed it was a case of how long before he was fit to travel, if there were no complications. It was a fairly mild attack and with some muti (medicine) courtesy of Dr Patterson I thought all would be well. But Simon was not a cooperative patient declining to drink at all, I could have whacked him over the head with a bottle as we offered him any drink he wished. Mazoe produced a wide range of fruit drinks which he normally consumed with gusto. Not this time. I offered Cokes and fizzy drinks - not usually permitted -

anything. But he turned his scarlet face away and shut his eyes. 'We could leave him with Aziz and Banda,' said Ceri callously. 'I want to see Fenella.'

In a final act of desperation I bought a bottle of Lucozade; I had been made to drink it when I had measles and hated it.

Simon loved it. And on a diet of Lucozade and Dr Patterson's muti he made a rapid recovery and on his next visit to the surgery was pronounced fit to travel.

We had a warm reunion with the Redways but in no time at all we were due to fly. We braced ourselves for the farewell with the children - why I don't know as they briefly tore their eyes away from the TV screen and bade us a most casual goodbye.

Japanese Airlines are to be highly recommended. It was a long flight with only one stop at Anchorage. What a depressing picture that was from the air, it was flat and bare and dull. Never mind, a chance to send the children the first of their postcards and buy another doll for Ceri's collection. We had plenty of time to talk as the flight took twenty hours and there is a limit to how long you can eat and sleep and watch Charlie Chaplin films. It was the first time for years that we had been able to talk like this I thought, without being interrupted by phone calls or other commitments. There was a companionable closeness we remembered from long ago.

We were booked into the Imperial Hotel in Tokyo, rather a plain building externally but more than comfortable and I loved the service. The little details one did not get in UK or Zambia. There was a woman seated at a small desk at the junction of the bedroom corridors and we were greeted by name each time we left and returned.

On the streets it was the same. Watching a man planting small flowers at the base of a street sign, I was impressed to see him produce a small dustpan and brush... no soil left on the pavement. Building sites were models of neat organisation of materials and equipment – no haphazard piles of this or that.

Andrew had a full schedule of meetings and I expected that I would be left to entertain myself. On our first evening we were taken to a Tempura restaurant and were introduced to the delights of Japanese cuisine. To those who have been to a good Tempura house I need say no more, to those who have not - try it.

Dinner at a tempura restaurant in Tokyo

The conversation of mine host was friendly and animated. At the end of the evening he explained that while he had invited us both to dinner in future I would not be invited. He hastened to add that this was the Japanese custom. Wives were not invited to business lunches and dinners. They were serious affairs and the men were not to be distracted by wives. Personally I thought it was a great idea and one which ought to be introduced in Zambia.

But, he added, we do not wish you to be lonely so we have arranged for a lady from the firm to accompany you daily and take you wherever you wish to go. Where would you like to go tomorrow? I had a list of tourist attractions and I asked his advice about which he thought should take priority, ending with the request that actually most of all I would like to see a primary school in Tokyo.

He looked rather taken aback at this but said he would see what could be done.

Andrew had not been long departed the following morning when a Miss Miyoko Koguchi presented herself at the hotel and introduced herself as my guide for the day.

We set off. Miyoko clutching a list which she kept checking rather nervously, and at last confessing that this was her first time to escort a foreign visitor. But by the second day she appeared to be enjoying it all as much as I was as we raced from one place to another. As we ate lunch on the third day I asked if she normally lunched there as it was not far from the office. She looked amused. People like her could not afford such places but as it was all on the expense account she was making the most of it. I was making the most of having someone who really knew the ropes, recommend what I should eat.

A visit to a primary school had been arranged and we spent most of one morning there looking at the classrooms and talking to staff and children. Each time I was introduced I found that while I was ' Mrs Kashita from Zambia', it was always added that I originally came from England. It seemed to be very important so eventually I asked Miyoko why she always added that I was English. She smiled and said,

'Otherwise they will think you are American. There are so many Americans still here and now we are trying to be proud to be Japanese again. For too long we were ashamed and tried to copy everything American. Now we young people are saying it is time to be Japanese again.'

Miyoko, like so many of her contemporaries, was having lessons in how to perform the tea ceremony and I was glad that there was a positive attitude towards their own culture and that this seemed to be a voluntary thing. Sometimes when I was introduced I would be greeted in Japanese until it was explained that my husband was a Zambian. The name Kashita is also a Japanese name so if ever I had to give it I would be expected to speak Japanese – and in fact was once rebuked for not having made the effort to learn at least some of the language.

In the evenings when Andrew was at his 'business dinners' I alternated between watching a little TV - and learning a bit about Noh dancers for instance - or walking around Tokyo. The shops were open till 9pm and I was not afraid of being alone in the city, merely taking the precaution of carrying a card with the name and phone number of the hotel. The underground was not packed solid with commuters in the evenings so I had time to work out where I was going without being jostled. Everyone was so friendly, finding someone who could speak English for me if they themselves could not, that I had no difficulties

By coincidence our time in Tokyo was known as the holiday week. There was the Emperor's birthday, May Day, and Children's Day. Three holidays so close together - the first two needed no explanation, but a Children's Day?

Visiting a temple in Tokyo on Children's Day

I was told that children are so highly regarded that one day was set aside for a special celebration. As carp fish are believed to be very strong and brave, kites in the form of carp fish are given to boys on this day and are tied to a pole outside the house. They ranged from a few inches long to many feet and were fascinating in their colours and designs; all over the city as the week approached Children's Day fish fluttered and flapped in the spring breeze.

'And the more popular the boy, the more carp you will see outside his house.'

Girls were given dolls and doll sized household items which were arranged on small stands and altars in the home. It was difficult to choose in all the variety of fish and dolls, one each for

416

Ceri and Simon, but a most enjoyable task.

On Children's Day itself Andrew and I toured a large temple and watched young couples taking their small children into the temple. Such a colourful sight I wished I had a cine camera.

On our last evening I was invited out to dinner again - I felt most flattered. TWO invitations to dine with the men! It was a very swish affair as we sat with our legs in the sunken part of the floor under a low table and were waited on by girls in traditional dress watched by a hawk eyed older woman, who knelt throughout.

I was thoroughly enjoying myself until our host leaned across and said,

'So, you have been causing problems for us?'

There was no answer to that one.

He smiled.

'Until now, wives have always wanted to know where to buy the best pearls or this and that and where to get the best discounts. We have NEVER had to find a SCHOOL before and Miss Noguchi says she has never seen so many temples and museums before. I understand you have not bought ANY pearls? Japan is famous for its pearls.'

I felt very embarrassed. He handed me a small neatly wrapped package. Inside was a dark blue velvet box from a Ginza store (the Ginza being the exclusive shopping precinct according to the hotel guide). Inside was a most beautiful gold and pearl brooch.

From the second man at the table was a dark red box containing two strands of creamy pearls.

The black velvet box from the third man held another brooch, silver and pearls.

After Tokyo we flew on to Hong Kong. Such a confusion of impressions in a very short space of time. I could have sat anywhere and watched and watched and listened for days at a time. I was again generously given a guide and was rushed from sight to sight until I was left with a blur of a myriad of impressions.

We drew breath again in Bangkok - that is, once we regained our breath. The driving from the airport was fast and furious, drivers relying on horns and accelerators to force a way through. Once more, there was the confusion of trying to absorb too much too quickly. My memory of Bangkok is crowded streets, attractive people, sticking gold leaf on the flanks of an enormous Buddha in a temple, yellow robed monks and fantastic food.

Temple in Bangkok

The food was my downfall. Andrew said later that he never ate fresh salad when he was travelling. I did. And spent the last day lying on the bed or making mad dashes to the bathroom. Andrew returned from a meeting and dropped a newspaper on the bed. A headline on the front page caught my eye
'Three dead from cholera'.
That was it. I had cholera. Would Andrew fly me home? I did not want to be buried in Bangkok. Andrew naturally laughed and callously went off to have his lunch before we left for the airport. I was determined to get on the plane - hoping if my body was halfway home, it would get there. Flying first class one is offered delicious snacks and meals and drinks. Such a waste. I turned my head to the window and wished to die.
But even tummy upsets come to an end and although I could not face any food, I thought I would be able to enjoy Tashkent. When we took off we knew there was to be a stop-over at Tashkent - what a romantic sounding name. I had no idea what to expect

but it sounded full of promise.

Shortly after we were airborne it was announced that Tashkent was cancelled. Pity, now I would never know. Later it was announced that we would be landing at Tashkent after all. Great. As we neared Tashkent it was intriguing to be told that all window blinds must be lowered until we had landed. It's quite useless to speculate about these things, the real explanation is always far duller. Some passengers guessed it was probably some troop movements.

Once landed and blinds up, Tashkent airport did not look much different from any other airport. It was the first time though, that we had to hand over our passports and papers to an official as we left the plane .

We were rapidly marshalled across the tarmac to the airport building, up a flight of stairs and into a lounge. There was a small shop at one end with a dull array of souvenirs. It would be far more interesting to look out of a window. Except that a long banner of some sort hung neatly outside obscuring the view of the street or square. There were busy feet going to and fro and an occasional sound, somewhat muted, of traffic. A well-built woman in uniform smiled, hovered with us but was unable to understand English - or any other language that frustrated passengers tried.

It was a very dull wait until we were escorted back onto the plane where the harassed looking crew returned our papers watched by Russian officials. There as a sigh of relief as we took off, blinds down.

I wonder what Tashkent really looks like?

The Redways welcomed us back - Ceri and Simon looked up from a game with Fenella and Veronica, said, 'Oh hello' and carried on.

Back in Zambia I felt restless. I was pleased to be back but could not settle down. Life resumed its routine of work and home and social events and every minute was accounted for, but still I had the urge to change, make a move of some kind.

That was it. We had been at Roma for some years now, the

garden was laid out and established, fruit trees bearing ... it was all 'done'. I wanted something fresh.

Andrew reacted with surprise at my idea of being restless. Was I not happy with Roma and him and my job? I wasn't Unhappy with them, I just wanted to DO something new. Give the man his due, his reaction was,

'Find out what you want and we'll talk about it.'

In the meantime Ceri and Simon were back in the thick of their activities. Simon went off on his first Cub Scout Camp weekend and returned with hero worship for the Cub master shining even brighter. Camp plus an eclipse of the sun! And Ceri was getting ready to get the competing bug now that the Agricultural Show was coming up.

Agricultural Shows are always good news. Katete held theirs in June and this year Wesley Nyirenda, Minister of Education and Culture, really captured people's attention when he said,

'The average Zambian is downright lazy and not used to regular work. Young men hang about the streets looking for white collar jobs. Villagers were habitually not used to regular work. They exert themselves for just one season to produce just enough to eat and for the rest of the year they just live it up. If Zambia was given to the Chinese or Japanese or Indians there would be miracles in food production.'

Ceri did not compete in the Show but did want to enter a mini gymkhana with Nicole, not that she was in the same class at all. If I had known it involved rising before 6am to be down at the stables to plait tails and manes and things, I would not have been quite so compliant. The staff at school laughed callously at my description of what was in store for me the coming weekend, said they would turn over in their beds and think of me. Sister Fausta looked concerned.

'I always worry about them being safe. They are so young and Nicole is such a thin little thing. But I suppose they are nice little ponies?'

I thought it best not to describe the huge beast with feet like dinner plates that Nicole rode. 'Why don't you come along?' I asked, little thinking she would consider the idea.

Her face brightened.

'It's very kind of you ... do you think I should? I do like to see what my girls do ... but it would be too much trouble for you ...'

Ceri on Blackie at the gymkhana

She was easily persuaded to agree to a time when Sister Herlinde said she had always wanted to see some of the girls in out-of-school events. I was to pick them up in the afternoon - by which time the horses would be plaited and polished and whatever else was in store for me.

I made sure we were right down by the rails with an excellent view and we relaxed on the benches. It was well into the dry season and the short grass was burnt yellow and puffs of red dust blew up with the slightest movement. I glanced at the Sisters white habits - perhaps we were too close to the ring? But Sister Fausta did not want to miss a moment now that she had ventured into new territories. I think she must have been expecting something along the lines of a little fluffy Thelwell and she gasped loudly as Nicole cantered into the ring on Gypsy. At first she flinched every time a horse galloped by the rails but as the pace hotted up she was cheering the Golliwog team on as loudly as any.

421

(Ceri, Nicole and their friends had chosen to name themselves the Golliwog team and it says much for people's lack of race awareness that no one there thought anything of the name - least of all Ceri. Today it would be unthinkable).

Describing the outing to Sister Georgina later, I said she should come along the next time. But large and smelly horses were not in her line at all.

'It's not that I'm not interested in what the girls do out of school, but horses ... they are so big ... and there is the dust you know. I would of course like to see what the girls do out of school. I often wonder what they do at home. Now that would be a treat!'

So would Sister Georgina care to come to tea? with a friend? She would!

This was even more difficult than rising at 6am to titivate horses, Sister Georgina was meticulous. In everything. I doubt she was ever aware of how the school appreciated her arrival at School Assembly. On Friday morning as soon as the bell rang at 7.30 the classes lined up outside the Hall and once Sister Fausta had arrived, they filed quietly in while one of the music pupils played the piano. As the last girl settled into place the music came to a final flourish and the girl carefully removed her music, dusted the piano keys and chair with a clean duster and withdrew.

All would be still and quiet. Sister Fausta would look patiently at the doors and on cue Sister Georgina would hasten in. As she scurried through the doors she would be furling the dark green umbrella which had protected her from the early morning sun, her white habit barely touched her in its laundered perfection. With a severe expression she would hover at the piano, remove sunglasses, place them neatly to the side with the umbrella, a white cloth appeared as if by magic and the piano keys were given a final whisk, the stool was dusted once more and she would be seated - but with such delicacy she barely rested on the seat. The cuffs were given a back flourish, fingers poised - and we could begin - and the school let go a collective sigh of relief.

Sister Georgina coming to tea was therefore an onerous task.

Aziz was warned this was a special occasion, he and Banda turned the house upside down all week. Everything had a daily polish and I swear the very tea leaves were dusted. On the actual day the cats were banned from the house and I waited with some trepidation for the Sister's car.

Tea went well and Sister Caratate was in fine form. Sister Georgina, perched on the edge of her chair, was somewhat absent minded. Ceri brought a couple of dolls from her collection to show her,

'I keep them in my bedroom,' she explained. 'Would you like to see the others?'

'Thank you dear, but your bedroom ... I don't think your mother ...'

'Not at all,' I said, 'I hope you ...'

But I spoke to an empty chair. Sister had disappeared down the corridor.

'You must excuse us.' smiled Sister Caratate. 'Living in a Convent, we miss our homes, and we are never in homes until we go to our families on leave every seven years.'

'Then would you ...?'

Well, that took care of the entertaining. Every item of furniture, every toy and book in Ceri's room was scrutinised and exclaimed over. After which Simon insisted he should not be left out and conducted them round his domain. They whisked the Sisters through our room and the bathrooms and back through the spare room and into the playroom via the sitting room where I raised an eyebrow and said,

'Do say if you are bored?' and went back to the newspaper and cup of tea.

I understood that afternoon better after a conversation with Sister Georgina when we were on even more friendly terms. An only child, her mother had died when she was very young and when her father remarried she was sent to board in a distant convent school in Germany. She was there until sixteen (? whenever the school leaving age was), never once going home for a holiday. When she was due to leave school her father came to collect her – and took her straight to another convent where she was to enter as a novice.

She looked at me and said, 'And this has been my life.'

Simon gets football fever

Apart from being a keen Cub Scout and footballer, Simon was more and more keen to spend his time at home, friends were welcome to join him but he was equally content and complete in his own company. He would spend the day out in the garden intent on his own adventures. It could start with him arriving in our bedroom as the day dawned with a small flower in a wine glass, this he would place carefully beside my bed and say, 'This is a nice one, isn't it?' and disappear again.

I would admire the tiny scarlet flower with the early morning freshness still on it and fall asleep again.

Just before breakfast he might reappear to recount what the dogs had done in the night and whether another litter of rabbits had been born. A huge breakfast would be consumed while he clearly had his mind on how he could assist Banda and off they would go to choose the vegetables for Aziz, feed the chickens and ducks and start the first water sprinkler going, a constant task in the dry season.

A grubby boy would appear at lunchtime to be banished to the bathroom. Afternoon siestas were a waste of time so the dogs were persuaded to follow his bike round the plot until even they would flop in the shade to follow him with their eyes. Ants nests were inspected, insects collected, stones overturned in his constant search to see what was going on. If Ceri could not be persuaded to swim perhaps she would help construct yet another chapter of their Lego world, this game had taken on a life of its own and, for a time, the characters became almost as real as themselves Of course, eggs had to be collected before sunset and the chickens locked up, a nightly ritual that the stupid birds still could not accept without much protesting.

Although Simon went out with us, he preferred being at home, but I had not realised how much until we were caught yet again in a Presidential motorcade one lunchtime.

Going anywhere when the President was expected was difficult as roads would be closed and one could sit in the car for a long time waiting for the motorcade to pass. At one time a policeman would be posted at each turnoff along the route to stop any traffic joining the road. The quantity of manpower involved was enormous and the delay to the public could be equally great as timing was not always well coordinated. Then it was changed, one or two powerful motorcycles would sweep along the road waving traffic to a standstill at the side of the road - where you had to sit in the sweltering sun - and wait.

This particular lunchtime we were within a few hundred yards of the Roma turn off when the first outriders swept around the bend waving we poor commuters off the road. Resignedly I pulled into the side of the road and we waited. I forget which particular dignitary was arriving or departing but he made a lengthy do out of it and we sat and sweated. I thought of inching my way along the hard shoulder towards the turn off but who knew when the motorcade might sweep around the bend and into sight?

We waited and we sweated. The children sighed and fidgeted. Half an hour later, a screaming of sirens and flashing of lights and it was all over and we could proceed home.

'And all that time,' said a small voice disgustedly from the back seat, 'we could have been doing something really useful.'

The same reasoning at long last trickled through to the powers that be and timing was better coordinated and fewer roads closed. Much later still the President took to using a helicopter which saved him and us a lot of time.

CHAPTER 7
LEOPARDS HILL ROAD

But Simon's words kept coming back to me, particularly as we lived in Roma on the Great East Road and were therefore prone to constant delays as motorcades blasted their way to the airport, to Parliament and Mulungushi Hall.

If only we had bought a plot on the other side of town ... Andrew, I think we should move house. Andrew was a remarkably patient man and listened to my idea.

'We should look for a plot that does not involve us in too many road closures, a quiet approach to town would be good - not the North Road it is so busy, not the west of town or we are driving into the sun both morning and evening, not in town, not too far out on a dirt road which would be a nuisance when you are late home in the rainy season, a bigger plot than this one perhaps so we could DO more ... '

'Where is this plot?' he asked.

'Oh, you agree?'

'You are so convincing I thought you must have a spot in mind already'

So we began to look around.

Goodie and Mabel Mutale liked the idea too, it was not long before we found a twenty acre plot out on Twin Palms Road in Kabulonga, only about a mile of dirt road, rich looking soil and TEN acres each. But Goodie and Andrew quibbled over the price and we lost the plot. It was infuriating. Goodie saw a plot actually in Kabulonga and decided to build on that. I scanned the papers in vain until Andrew came home looking triumphant.

'Cobbet Tribe estate agents have a plot for sale on Leopards Hill Road, if you are interested we could go and have a look at it this afternoon' and he went on to give me a brief description

'It's just bush, about ten miles out of town, nothing on it at all, it slopes to one side, the soil is not very good.'

'How many acres?'

'....er....two hundred.'

'What?'

'You said you wanted something to do!'

Leopards Hill Road wanders south east out of town from Kabulonga. Once we passed the cemetery on the town boundary there was bush on both sides of the road, which was dirt from there on. Bauleni compound was on the left just after the cemetery. From then on it was a flat open landscape with scattered scrubby trees and tall, tall grasses. A couple of houses well set back from the road on the right. The road turned left and down into a dip and up again, the trees were thicker here. After ten miles at the top of the next small rise Andrew slowed the car down and as we crested the rise he came to a halt.

'On your left is thirty acres and on your right is one hundred and seventy acres,' he said.

'Why on earth is it like that?'

'It's a sub division of a farm and the road went through later.'

He drove slowly down the longer steeper side of the hill as we gazed to the left and the right, at the bottom of the hill was a boundary - somewhere among the tall grasses -cutting across the road. Beyond that, going up the next hill was Nefdt chicken farm on the left and another house on the right.

We turned the car and made our way back, parked and got out. The hot sun beat down on our heads and the air was still in the heat. It seemed best to start with the smaller plot so we plunged into the grass, the ground sloped up from the road, there were scrubby trees and a few larger ones. There were several places where one could build a house but all the time the hundred and seventy acres across the road beckoned us. We turned to walk back to the road and then came upon a rough circle, where only a faint suggestion of grass showed. How strange I thought, that nothing at all should have grown all year and what had been there last year?

Andrew said it could have been a village hut, it takes longer than you would think for the bush to completely obliterate the site of a hut which has been there for a long time. We walked on. The ground continued to slope gently down and I found I was walking between two lines of mud bricks neatly edging what must have been a path, but we could trace no beginning or end. I shivered and caught myself weaving a fanciful tale of a settler whose wife tried to make a garden but the drought defeated all her efforts ... so they packed up the ox cart and moved on ... a villager who took his wife to live apart, but she pined for the village ... perhaps he had leprosy ...

'Are you coming to the other side?' demanded Andrew impatiently, 'or are you going to stand there day dreaming all day?'

Trying to get a firm impression of a hundred and seventy acres when you are walking through rough grass up to eye level and you cannot see from one end to the other because the land suddenly slopes up and over another rise away from the road is not easy. Once we found a little path, worn smooth by feet passing how often and for how many years, from where to where? It must enter from the road and cross diagonally we guessed but we did not follow it all the way that day. The soil was poor sandy laterite, here and there huge outcrops of large quartz boulders, which reminded us of Chelston and Andreucci. Walking back down the plot towards the road we stumbled on something which decided us. I walked towards a thick clump of trees and there, at the end of the dry season was a small pool. It was only about thirty yards across and was completely shaded by the trees, which accounted for it not completely drying out. We guessed it must be fed by a tiny spring and in the rains, fed by a higher water table and the run off from sloping land ... yes, there was the dry bed of a stream running eastwards.

There was a snare made of thin twigs carefully set near the water's edge, someone came to trap birds. That clinched it. Not only could we build our house at the top of the small hill but we could walk down to our own private pool where the birds would be safe to drink in future. As a sign, I broke the snare and threw it in to the bushes.

Two hundred acres for four thousand kwacha – roughly the equivalent of two thousand pounds.

How could we go wrong?

Quite easily if there is no water, said the ever practical Andrew. But there were two houses in sight on the skyline so there must be SOME water and we were not intending to go into full scale market gardening. We took the plunge and bought the plot.

Andrew called in the experts, in the shape of one water expert from the Ministry of Agriculture complete with an impressive array of gadgets and a box which clicked and whirred. We followed the man, while he stuck rods into the ground and measured the clicks, which were not as pleasing to him as I had thought; the clicks sounded quite chirpy to me. At last he came to the conclusion that there was water and X marked the most promising site. A concrete plug carefully marked the spot and off we went.

Over tea with May Hardie and May Sharpe I recounted our adventures. May Hardie sipped her tea slowly,

'And what about a water diviner?'

Her husband Leslie recommended a chap and somehow - not convinced, not persuaded - I had to admit I was curious. Recalling the clicks, I felt we should explore every possibility. Andrew did not exactly shriek with laughter but did the male equivalent. However, he had to admit it could do no harm and so there we were later in the week feeling extremely foolish watching another fundi (expert).

No impressive gadgets this time, our fundi pulled a twig out of his pocket and explained the principles of water divining; it seemed to boil down to walking to and fro until the twig bent down - or up ? and there you were. And there we were standing in the middle of the African bush gazing in fascination at a little itsy bitsy bit of twig.

He asked where we would like to site the house, all things being equal. We pointed to a spot near the clump of trees near the top of the rise. He frowned.

'Not much point in trying there ... you wouldn't consider it down in the dip itself? ... yes, it is near the road ... well, how about in between the two?'

He strolled off through the grasses and we followed at a respectful distance, should one not speak? He was passing the area where a cement plug marked site number one.

He walked on, turned at a right angle, back and forth, while we stood in the wings.

'There! You see? We're getting there! See that?'

Anxiously we peered at the twig, again he walked to and fro calling our attention but I could see no movement at all. Andrew said he could detect a twitch. And then, it moved. Or did it? Was he moving it himself? I could not make up my mind.

Now we had two sites to choose from and this one was further from where we wished to build. But here was a chap who was more positive about the amount of water we should get, a good steady supply, he said.

But a bit of twig against modern technology? We chickened out of a real decision and had both sites drilled! And then had to wait while both sites had tests run to determine which gave the best results.

It became one of the family jokes how we had gone out one day to check the water results. Andrew looked at the paper, shook his head looking rather crestfallen, saying, 'Oh, only 5,000 gallons an hour.' In such disappointed tones we were fooled, hearts sank, silence. And then, 'How much water do we need an hour for goodness' sake?'

Just another example of his sense of humour.

So both boreholes yielded water but the diviner had found the better spot. It warranted the electric motor. The first site had to be drilled much deeper and was then sealed to await the day we could find a windmill, it would be useful for the planned garden and orchard - and an emergency supply if there was a long power cut.

We took the precaution of having the water tested – it was fine although the copper level was higher than usual. Two huge storage tanks were installed on a stout platform behind where the house would be built, which were more than adequate for our needs. Near them we had Banda and White dig out a deep

431

rubbish pit as of course we were not on a refuse collection route. It looked as though it would last us for a very long time as there was very little actually thrown away. Any leftover food was taken home by Joseph to be shared. All clothes were passed on to be worn or sold by the servants. And anything we 'threw away' would first be examined for any possible use.

We had a plot and we had water, hurrah for progress! But we were not going to rush things, after all, two hundred acres was to keep us busy 'doing things'.

And we had discovered we had a neighbour – Don Fluck who had been our neighbour in Chelston. Sadly his wife Phyllis had died but he was still breeding Great Danes and Basset Hounds and content living out in the bush. He spotted us on the plot one day and drove in full of curiosity, telling us that his house was about half a mile further down the side road.

He told us that he and Phyllis had bought the house when no one else was keen and the owners needed to move. The owners had had a small daughter who became ill and died after an undiagnosed illness. It was discovered she had arsenic poisoning – because arsenic had been put near the house foundations to deter white ants. It was believed the little girl had nibbled leaves and grass as children will, and the plants had absorbed the arsenic. 'As we couldn't have children we decided to buy the house and let the couple move away,'

Ceri and Simon wanted a house with 'an upstairs and downstairs'. Andrew wanted a house that 'is just what you want, you have to run it'. Over to me. Upstairs and downstairs - it would be a change from all the bungalows we had had so far. That suggestion was accepted. 'Just as you want' - well, one could have a ball there. If there was the money, which there wasn't.

If you list what you need, add what you would like and then work out the most economical way of doing it, you can get there. And so I believe I did. The house was two storeys, large enough to be spacious and airy but still feel a family sort of house. It was painted white inside and outside the walls were to be covered with a rough cast plaster finish which would not require painting and the floors were pale grey cement; a feeling of quiet coolness everywhere. Large windows in all the rooms, so that wherever you looked was a wide view of one part of the plot or another. Downstairs was an L shaped sitting room with walls lined with built in bench seats, to hold bright splashes of cushions. Two large Chinese carpets lay like dark blue pools across the floor. Double doors opened into the dining room, which was merely functional. I remember it full of people and chatter or bare and dull. Ceri's piano was here and the sound of her music filled the house when she was home.

The kitchen was a cook's delight with ample space and cupboards and a walk in pantry and a good view of the drive so cook was always able to keep abreast of all comings and goings.

A small TV room opened off the kitchen - handy for snacks when watching the News. Toys were kept here, but they were largely abandoned now. And the children could eat here if we were entertaining.

Andrew had a small study tucked away near the foot of the stairs, which turned to the left as you went up and opened out into a large open plan study, which was my personal place. Here was the rich purple and dark blue wool rug I had bought many years ago at the Zambiri shop which had replaced Greatermans. One wall was lined with my books, a desk under the window, a white rocking chair. It was a room I used a lot.

To the left was our bedroom and bathroom, a door in the bedroom opened out onto the flat roof above the sitting room and we sat there often in the late afternoons or in the evenings listening to the frogs in the dam and night noises.

To the right of my study were two bedrooms and a bathroom for Ceri and Simon. The bathroom was often a cause for argument. Ceri said Simon spent too long in there. Simon said Ceri never cleaned the bath.

Once they both had to clean the bath together. Our friend Alan Drysdall, a dedicated philatelist, had given them a large bag of unwanted stamps in the hope of encouraging them. He gave them a few instructions on how to remove the stamps from envelope corners and how to mount them. Ceri and Simon ran half a bath of water, tipped in the bag of stamps and went off with the dogs. The bath very slowly drained and later, much later, the bath was found to be gaily decorated with stamps from all over the world firmly glued to its sides and bottom.

The courtyard leading off the dining room was popular with the dogs as they were not allowed into the house. They would lie there panting waiting for one of us, anyone would do, to emerge. At the side of the courtyard was a bedroom and bathroom for visitors - opposite a door to the kitchen and door to the separate ironing room. A dark red bougainvillea grew in the corner by the bedroom and eventually rioted all along the wall, giving a rich warm colour to the whole area.

I have jumped ahead. The house was a long time in building. But I make no apologies, whenever I think of the house, I walk through its cool rooms again and hear the ripple of piano keys, the sound of wind in the trees outside and the far off distant bark of a dog on the hot air. I slide my fingers down the smooth wood rail on the stairs as I turn the bend and hear the grandfather clock ticking below. Or I step out of my bedroom onto the roof and shade my eyes against the glare as I look back to the servant's quarters to hear the muted chatter of small children. The wind blows a faint smell of wood smoke from there as I turn to look down the plot towards the dam, a boy walks up followed by two dogs, tongues lolling.

I see it in the lush green of the rains and the bleached yellow brown at the height of the dry season. I smell the choking richness after a storm or the dry dusty heat when the air bounces back up at you. I see it in the brightest glare and in the soft blackness of night as it is swiftly spangled by brilliant stars so thickly crowded above. I can never mention the house without taking at least one swift passage through its rooms again. I planned it to hold what was most precious to me.

Now let's get back to its building.

Before you can build a house of course, plans must be passed by the Council planning authorities and my plans would not be accepted so off to an architect once more. I can see it must be very irritating for an architect to have a lay person come in and say this is exactly what I want and how. No scope for the professional at all. Poor Erhard could not change any of my ideas so he persuaded me to add one of his. A row of linked arches along the verandah at the front of the house, supported on wide pillars.

I was not so sure about these arches but agreed that perhaps my design was severe in its straight lines, rather bare and uncompromising, arches would soften the façade. And I had to agree to something he proposed - he had a habit of leaning closer in his enthusiasm and as he was an extremely heavy chain smoker - it was agree or choke.

While planning permission was being sought, the plot became the focal point for our weekends. We would walk for hours in the dry grass plotting and planning, the children exploring ever new corners. Once we came across a tiny grave, a child's grave. It could only have been there a year or two, nothing had grown on the rough mound but a shoot or two of grass. A small enamel bowl was upturned on the grave, its chipped bottom exposed to the elements. Andrew said it would have been a local worker, from a farm perhaps, who had buried his child there. We should perhaps have reported it but we both felt it should be left undisturbed. The child had clearly been buried with love and care and sadness; what use to open up old wounds even if the parents could have been traced?

Sometimes we arranged to picnic on the plot with friends, although it was only ten miles from town it felt as though we were miles out in the bush, so quiet and peaceful and undisturbed it was.

Once we had a picnic there with the Shamwanas, when we sat beneath the clump of trees where the house was to be built and cooked over a small fire. It was a long drawn out lunch when one over ate and over drank and talked until the silences came drifting through the conversation to bring their own contented peace. The smoke from the dying fire was thin and blue, the children had gone off to explore and we forced ourselves to get up and take a walk. Before leaving the two men beat down the remnants of the fire and scraped dry soil over it. Then, so typically in Zambia, the men walked one way and Stella and I the other.

Stella and I could talk for hours in those days and when there are acres and acres to walk on and talk on it is not surprising that it was a long time before we came back to the picnic site. A scene of devastation met our eyes. The surrounding grass and bushes were a charred mess and the children were sitting in subdued silence. Andrew was icily polite. The Shamwana boys were an adventurous four and aided and abetted by our two, had decided to have another picnic. Malcolm had initiated resurrecting the fire, one small smouldering ember being quite sufficient.

He had done his work only too well as a shift in the wind took it well out of control and if Andrew and Edward had not returned the whole plot might have burned off - not to mention adjacent farmland and bush. Andrew was furious which put an end to the day and we packed up and went home.

It was of course entirely our own fault for not making sure that the fire was completely obliterated but Andrew could only think about what could have happened. Bush fires were a constant annoyance - and worse - in the long dry season. They would start unaided or by design, which ever, the results were always the same. A black and charred landscape, dead animals and birds and possible damage to buildings. Only the previous year a fishing village near Monze had been wiped out by a bush fire, it was all over in five minutes leaving eleven dead and sixty homeless.

We not only went to see the plot in daylight. I once paid a visit very late at night. Andrew was away, the children were fast asleep and I started chatting on the phone to an old friend, Ruth Weiss. I mentioned that I had a case of the fidgets, thinking about the house we were moving to and things I had to decide.

'House? move?'

Ruth had been away and was out of date. I decided the best thing was to show her. Aziz was willing to babysit and off I went, picked up Ruth in Lusaka and - according to her -drove her out of town on an apparently endless dirt road. When I finally turned off on to a small side road and then pulled up to park in the bush, she thought I had taken leave of my senses. According to her, I then leapt out of the car and walked her to and fro pointing out where the house would be and which way it would face, the views etc . Stumbling over the rough grass and peering at shadowy sticks marking out where the foundations would be, only increased her bewilderment.

'You ... you ... have brought me out to see a house that isn't even built yet?'

The ridiculousness of the situation struck me and we were helpless with laughter. By now the stars had started to appear as rapidly as they do in Africa and we strolled back to the car.

'I'm sure it will be very nice,' said Ruth as I switched on the engine. I got the car back onto the side road and headed down towards the main road.

'Wouldn't it be a good idea to put the lights on?'

'I have.'

'Have you?'

Had I? I flicked them on and off. There was no difference. It couldn't be battery, the car was going quite nicely, so we kept on going. The moon and stars are very bright in Africa and you can drive very well by moonlight - although it is against the law. There was no traffic at all as we drove steadily into town, once there we crossed our fingers and hoped to reach Ruth's place with the help of street lights. It was a relief to park the car, but dare I drive on home and risk meeting a police car?

I decided to leave the car parked outside Ruth's flat and phoned the Hepworths, who lived nearby. Johnnie readily agreed to drive me home but teased me unmercifully.

'Thought you had more common sense than to go driving in the bush at this time of night,' being his kindest remark.

Nor was this the end of the teasing. Ruth said that Andrew's car parked outside her flat all night had caused some speculation among her neighbours, 'You know how distinctive his Citroen is!'

Ruth has been in and out of my life for so long that she seems to have been there for ever – she says we first met when she was invited to a party at our Roma house and viewing a non-existent house set the seal on our similar sense of humour. A well-known anti-apartheid journalist and activist one can read so much about her courtesy of the Net, I have found her ability to recall places, events, people absolutely daunting. She has a vast –possibly unrivalled – knowledge of African political history and yet has not lost her ability to empathise at all levels.

About that time we had an invitation to dinner at the Austins - Lily Austin of Milady dress shop fame - in addition to a most enjoyable meal we picked up a few house furnishing tips. We were seated at a magnificent black marble dining table, absolutely fantastic. Hearing me admire it, Lily explained that when the marble panels were being unloaded at Lusaka station, destined for the new Barclays bank, one was dropped and a corner broken off. It was left abandoned on one side, of no use. Hearing of it the Austins went and saw and were conquered (rather like Julius Caesar) and asked to buy it. Transport was arranged and - this was the best bit - their dining room had to be extended to allow the straightened off marble in, to be placed on supporting brick pillars. Result! Seated around the table we could only admire their inspiration. Lily then pointed out the Moorish decorative lamps hanging above the table, expensive to buy and transport, I thought. But no, they had seen such lamps in Morocco but thought them expensive so once home Lily set to and had her lamps cut from well cleaned tin cans. I began to think of asking Lily for more home making tips - she had plenty. One I did like, built in benches round a sitting room, piled up with bright cushions.

Once work actually began on the house we were constantly at the site. Until the borehole was drilled and functioning, water was carried out in drums so that work would not be delayed.

The foundation slab was laid before Christmas so that it could weather and settle over the holiday and then we would be able to carry on with the main building programme as the weather changed from the rains to dry season. At first we drove off the side road opposite the site of the house but early on the subject of a drive was raised.

'Do you want this to be the actual drive to the house?' asked Andrew, 'because it is time we got it properly levelled off.'

What a waste of space to have all this land and then just a short straight drive from the side road across to the house. We contacted Bill Barclay, husband of Thalia of school drama fame, who agreed to get one of his bulldozers out to the site for us. And one afternoon I walked from near the bottom of the plot up to the house site, weaving in and out of the scrubby trees so that the following bulldozer cleared a winding drive up to the house, with wide sweeping bends here and there.

The small pool as we originally found it.

Watching the bulldozers at work gave Andrew another idea, he cast an eye on the small spring and dry stream bed at the bottom of the hill.

'Once this pool fills, it overflows into a stream, you can see the old stream bed. If we put a dam across the stream bed, say about here, we could make the pool larger - into a small dam ! and stock it with fish!'

Off went the bulldozer and a small dam was built across the streambed and further down another dam. It had seemed like a good idea but once it was done it seemed like an outrage, the raw earth stood out against the green vegetation. The whole peace of the hollow under the trees was disturbed. I felt uneasy and avoided looking at that part of the plot.

However, once rains were well started the bare earth slowly turned green and we began to look for signs of the pool overflowing. Going out one weekend we found the small pool was gone forever in a large expanse of water, it was not yet enough to overflow down the spillway into a second hollow.

The rains had another effect. Going out one morning, Andrew called me over to see a mushroom - not being particularly excited by mushrooms I wandered across the garden to be confronted by the biggest mushroom one could imagine ... not the size of a dinner plate - considerably larger. What on earth would one do with a mushroom that size -invite a dozen people to share fried mushroom? Mushroom omelette? It certainly was enough for us and for Aziz and Banda and ...

Watching the walls rise and imagining how the rooms would look was fascinating enough but I was also keeping a close eye on the drainage and the septic tank and the soak away after hearing a horror story to end all horror stories. A friend of a friend had moved into a new house, all was well – for quite a while. And then one day the owners looked out and saw the septic tank inspection hatches lift off and float away across the garden. The septic tank had been dug. So had the soak away. But for some unfathomable reasons the two had not been connected! The result was indescribable as raw sewage overflowed on to the garden.

Our minds were abruptly concentrated in another direction at this point. Andrew came home from the office one day early in December with an abstracted air. He had been called to State

House during the morning.

'I am appointing you Minister of Mines and Industry.'

Andrew was taken aback and protested that while it was indeed a great honour, he was not, and never had been, a politician.

No matter. It had been decided. Andrew was a man of experience and integrity and

'Comrade, your country needs you.'

'I knew there was little point in arguing,' said Andrew and so he had reluctantly accepted. As it was already being announced on the eleven o'clock news it was a good job he did!

I was furious and protested bitterly

'You always promised you would not enter politics.'

'I haven't. It's not a political appointment ... I'm just ... well ... I'm just going to be a Minister.'

I never analysed my anger at this appointment, beyond thinking that one was not really FREE, but life is rarely fair. I associated Ministers with politicians, who had all too often had to follow and implement Party policy, damn it all, Ministers WERE politicians and Andrew had promised. I raged and sulked, all the while knowing it was a complete waste of time - besides which being most undignified.

All too often school was becoming a balm and once again I sought refuge. There is nothing like physical activity for restoring one's spirits and good humour so now was the perfect time to empty the cupboards down one side of the classroom and have a thorough spring clean. I had my own set of keys to the classroom, so after parking the car under the cassia trees, I let myself in and was soon lost in work and affairs of the State were long vanished.

Was there any point in keeping these work cards? They hadn't been used since I came ... but they might come in useful ... the usual infant teacher dilemma ... never throw anything away, it might come in useful.

I hardly heard the door open but Sister Fausta's voice brought me back to the present. Her face was quite pink and for a moment I wondered if she had caught the sun or been racing round the Convent grounds on some new enthusiasm. I sat back on my heels and waited while she caught her breath.

'Mrs Kashita! What are you doing? In the cupboards! Oh dear! Oh dear! And you the Minister's wife!'

She sat down on the nearest table, cheeks pinker than ever and blue eyes wide with worry and excitement.

The bloody Minister's wife! Was that what I was now? It had been bad enough being Mr Kashita's wife and not me, myself, but now I would be the 'Minister's wife'.

Damn, damn, bloody damn.

'One of the Sisters said she saw your car parked under the trees and I knew I must come down - you must congratulate Mr Kashita for me - for all of us! What an honour! Such a good man! The President is a wise man. It will be so good for the country! And now you are the Minister's wife! I could not believe my eyes when I saw you down on your knees in the cupboard ...'

And then she came to an abrupt halt, the flood of words stemmed mid flow. Her face grew sad.

'I suppose you have come to give me your notice?'

Now it was my turn to go red - with anger. Sister Fausta could not believe that I had not come to give my notice, that I was not cleaning cupboards preparatory to leaving.

'But can a Minister's wife work?'

'I don't see why not,' I answered shortly. 'Now, while you are here Sister Fausta, why is there all this white powder under the newspaper at the bottom of the cupboard? Is it to stop cockroaches? And should I put down some more?'

'Oh no, That's cyanide and it lasts a very long time, no need to put down more just yet.'

What a conversation stopper.

Cyanide for cockroaches was more than drastic. OK so you never got rid of them, but wasn't cyanide ... different?

But it was not for the cockroaches, it was to stop the white ants which came up through the concrete foundations and if not halted in their tracks would have munched their way through every stick of furniture and every book in sight. It was difficult to prise Sister Fausta away from the topic of Ministers - not that I could have enlightened her much at that stage. As for the cyanide, it was left under the newspaper and may yet be there, holding one of the scourges of Africa at bay.

It may all sound very far-fetched but we did return after one school holiday to find that the white ants had found their way through the concrete library floor and from the cement rose intricate stalagmites of red brown soil of tiny diameter. They rose straight up, twenty inches or so until they met the underside of a chair and then radiating arms ran under the chair as the ants set about consuming all that lovely wood.

Well, there we were. Andrew moving into the Minister's chair and me keeping a low profile at school. Although Andrew had always avoided direct involvement in the political scene he had always been keenly interested in developments and personalities. As who was not in those days? Zambia was a very small pool and we all felt pretty big tadpoles with a close eye on the frogs. Although he had been reluctant to accept the appointment, once he was presented with a fait accompli he put his heart and soul into his work. Business and affairs of State were one thing, some of the perks which accompanied the job were not so acceptable. The first difference of opinion came when Andrew refused to use a Ministerial car and chauffeur all the time.

'There's nothing wrong with my legs or my driving.'

And he took a perverse pleasure in driving himself to and fro. The car and driver were useful on long journeys within the country, he could read papers, but around Lusaka Andrew usually drove himself.

The next difference of opinion came when I refused to have a guard twenty four hours a day. The crime rate in Zambia had been steadily rising in the last few years - in some ways we could keep abreast of the rest of the world with the greatest of ease. And gradually one had become used to the change in life style.

When we had first arrived in Northern Rhodesia gardens were very open, one could leave cars and houses unlocked and there was a very relaxed and trusting life style. All too soon it was necessary to lock doors, plots were fenced and gated and before we knew what was happening, security guards outside homes were a common sight. At five o'clock every evening one could see among the 'rush hour' traffic, van loads of guards being dropped off outside homes, their only weapon being a stout truncheon. Your guard would sit or walk around your house until he was picked up again at about 6 or 7am.

More often he would sit outside the kitchen door having a chat with the servants, most people made sure he was provided with a drink and a meal. Once your lights were off, he would doze in the garage. I had agreed some time ago to have a guard when Andrew was away, I had not a lot of faith in the system if it came to the crunch but perhaps it was wiser to have one 'just in case,' Perhaps with robbers they had their uses but at other times they were more of a liability. One evening in Roma when the children had gone to bed and the servants back to their quarters, I was sitting reading a book when there was a knock at the front door.

'Madam! Madam!'

The worried looking guard stood as close to the open door as he could,

'Snake, Madam! Big snake!'

As it was a case of him leaping into my arms or my doing something about the snake, I went out onto the verandah. Sure enough there was a snake, leisurely making its way through some canna lilies.

'Yes, there is a snake,' I agreed. 'But I'm sure it's going away.'

'Ah no, madam, she big snake, she bite.'

There was no way I would get any peace with my book so rather reluctantly I asked for his truncheon, he handed it over with alacrity and retreated to the far end of the verandah. I have always felt guilty about killing that snake, it probably was not poisonous at all. The guard was very grateful and disappeared round the corner, dangling the four foot body at arm's length. I assumed he was off to dispose of the body and returned to my book.

Next morning as I was dressing I heard the firm's security lorry arrive at the gate, there was an unusual hubbub so I pulled back the curtains. My guard was holding out the snake and clearly expounding on his night's bravery, his fellow guards were exclaiming loudly over the dangers of the night work.

Of course, if one were a Minister one was allocated a guard twenty four hours a day, armed with a rifle to boot! I recalled Aaron Milner's witty description of how he and his wife Phyllis had returned from a late night dinner to find their guard fast asleep, rifle on the ground beside him. Aaron softly removed the rifle and took it indoors ... it was loaded. Next morning he and Phyllis watched with glee as the guard hunted around the garden in vain for his firearm.

I insisted I would prefer to continue as we were, a guard – unarmed - only at night when Andrew was away. I gathered much later that our 'low profile' was unpopular with some other dignitaries. Perhaps we were letting the side down! One could not entirely ignore the crime rate of course but I always felt that our best security lay with the dogs and geese and servants. Stories and rumours abounded and no gathering was complete without the latest 'have you heard?'

Guards, armed or otherwise, were here to stay.

One day Ceri and I went to town, we drove down Independence Avenue to the south end roundabout, turned right into Cairo Road, the main street, and immediately ran into a traffic jam - a great rarity and novelty for us. We came to a halt outside CBC stores, people were running down the side of the road, there was a wail of sirens. I was in the middle and completely hemmed in by traffic.

'Shooting ... robbers ...'

were distinguishable in the uproar in the street amid more sirens.

'Get down,' I said to Ceri, 'get down on the floor.'

It sounded melodramatic and I was angry with myself for finding my heart was pounding and I was sweating. Ceri crouched on the floor.

'I can't see! It's not fair!' she protested.

445

There was nothing to see except jammed traffic and people scurrying to and fro with a mixture of panic and excitement on their faces. It was not long before the traffic miraculously eased and I drove on. Nothing to see anywhere apart from a Police Land Rover parked hastily outside a bank and several officers chatting.

The story when it came out was worthy of the Keystone Cops.

At that time there was always a policeman armed with a rifle on guard just inside the doors of every bank. We always assumed the rifle was empty and he was there for 'show'. That day a bank teller, for reasons he was never able to explain clearly, had felt somewhat frivolous, and had tossed a small firework over to his companion.

The firework went Bang!

And the policeman turned 180 degrees, at the same time neatly spraying a row of bullet holes round the walls, just above the customer's heads.

No, we were never short of a story to top the latest 'have you heard?'

Every social get together was enlivened in this way. And other ways.

At Christmas we had the Maliks to dinner. Jalil and Barbara Malik had been friends since I taught their two daughters at Lusaka Infants. The Christmas dinner had its usual soporific effect so to waken us all up we decided to drive out to the plot and have a long walk in the bush.

It had rained heavily in the night and the countryside was wet and green as we drove out on to Leopards Hill Road, the air was rich with the smell of wet land steaming in the afternoon sun. The red laterite road was wet and sticky but not too bad to drive on. We turned off the side road and began the drive up the new winding drive to park by the house foundations.

Halfway up Ceri asked if they could be dropped off so she and Simon could show the Malik girls where the dam was. We drove on up to the 'house' - even foundations are fascinating and we were walking round pointing out what would be where, when muddy children came shrieking up the hill

'The dam! The dam! The dam is full'

In one night the water table must have reached its full height - or whatever water tables do - and the pool/dam had not only completely filled but had overflowed and the second dam was half full. I would never have thought so much water could have arrived in such a short time. By this time of course we were all down the hill and standing on the dam wall listening to the sound of water trickling round the spillway to the lower dam.

While the house was being built we thought we should make a start on the grounds. Fortunately some friends were at the end of their contract and were leaving Zambia for good, Alphonse and Meg Kumahor wanted to find employment for their servants before they left.

'We can really recommend White as a gardener,' said Alphonse. 'He has only one fault, he does not always understand what is being said. So you have to explain everything in the most basic English and show him, but after that he is a most hardworking and sensible fellow.'

We took White out to the plot and explained the situation. Once the job was complete there would be three servants houses, one for him, but in the meantime - would he be willing to live in a rondavel (metal round shed) on the site and start work on the grounds?

He would.

So we bought a workers metal rondavel and had it erected on the site and White and his family were duly installed. White hailed from Malawi and was, I suppose, somewhere between 35 and 45, he was not an impressive individual, being rather short and wiry, his teeth were crooked and his English was more than limited, it was almost non -existent. But what he lacked in looks he more than made up with energy and willingness. His wife was much younger and with an attractive shy smile. She spoke no English at all but would produce a wide enchanting smile and hitch one or other of her children higher on her hip and point in the direction of White's working area whenever I

447

spoke to her. There were three young children playing around the rondavel and I wondered about school provision but White had no qualms. When they were seven and old enough to start school, they would stay with his brother in town and come home for weekends and holidays.

Now, where should White begin? It was pointless to begin too close to the house with the workmen and all the building equipment so we embarked upon the orchard. Here we had our first encounter with White's lack of communication. The nursery in town was well stocked and we loaded up with ten orange trees, ten naajie (tangerine) trees, ten lemons, ten guava trees, ten mango trees, ten avocado trees, ten pawpaw trees - in fact ten of every variety of fruit tree in stock..

These we carted out to the plot and explained to White where and how we wanted the orchard. It would be this area east of the house where the land gradually sloped down to the dam. The trees would begin here and there would be a row of trees, so far apart, pacing out three metres. And we paced out and marked the places for the trees in the first row. And the second row, and the third row. White nodded his head and agreed it would be so. The holes would be of this depth and of this width - Andrew dug one hole as an example. Compost and fertiliser, so, would be placed in each hole. And so finally would the tree be planted. White nodded and smiled.

In the meantime, the one hundred or so small trees were carefully placed in a shady place where they could be kept watered. We emphasised that this was a big job, it would take a whole week or more.

All this we explained in simple basic English and demonstrated and repeated as simply as possible. White beamed and smiled and rubbed his hands together at the prospect of actually starting his new job. We would come out again at the weekend and bring him more provisions and see how he was progressing. In fact we had to go out in a couple of days to take some supplies to the workmen. White had made progress. Most efficient progress too. If we had wanted all one hundred trees planted about two feet apart.

This time we paced out and marked the place for each and every one hundred trees and insisted he could only plant so many trees per day. The prospect of digging one hundred fresh holes and replanting all those trees would have had me weeping but White beamed and set to work there and then. How could we be cross?

One day as we stood on the dam wall, I looked back up the hill and suggested,

'How about an avenue of cassia trees coming down from the house, so that when we walk down there will be shade and the smell of cassia flowers?'

So early in 1974 it was back to the nursery to collect a load of cassia trees, and White started on yet another row of holes.

The house was going up quickly and I went through the usual stage of walking in rooms where the walls were only a few feet high and being convinced that the rooms were ridiculously small and would never be big enough to hold anything. So then I went through the usual stage - for me - of lying down in each bedroom to convince myself that there was indeed room for a bed and more.

After that I began to have qualms about the pillars and arches. From the outside the house was beginning to take shape and look good but when I went inside I felt uneasy. I stood in the sitting room and looked out - to what should have been a wide expanse of bush. But there were huge pillars blocking the view and making me feel shut in. Perhaps we could have slimmer pillars? Lorenz agreed to have them thinned down. We stood in the sitting room again. It was better. But the pillars still blocked some of the view and the arches came down like frowning eyebrows. I did not like it at all. Andrew agreed and said it was my house and to do what I wanted.

So off to the architect. The arches had to go. I had to keep the slimmed down pillars to support the verandah roof but the arches went. So, coincidentally did he. Perhaps the house had reached the stage where his presence was no longer required, whatever the reason he did not visit the site again. Instead one of his assistants, Mrs Penn took over.

Who cared? Once the arches were gone, the whole house opened up and embraced the land.

Going into Lusaka one day I paused by the curio sellers on Cairo Road, there was something different. A five foot high carving of a Masai warrior complete with spear and shield, the owner was just finishing off the shield and only too pleased to have a quick sale and helped me heave him into the van. He was taken home to Roma, christened Matthew (?!) by the children and was destined to stand at the foot of the stairs in the Leopards Hill house. About the same time I bought Andrew a David Shepherd print of a steam locomotive which later hung near the front door. A smaller print also by David Shepherd of steam engine's wheels, a leaving gift from Indeco, was destined for the study.

The start of the cassia tree avenue down to the dam

The house was going on apace, the orchard and grounds were taking shape. The cassia trees were marching down the hill to the dam. Now that it was full and the water reflected the blue of the sky and the grasses had grown over the disturbed earth, the area no longer looked ravaged and raw. An expanse of water is always peaceful and full of interest as it catches the light and reflects the mood of the weather. Birds continually swooped and dipped around the dam and in the morning there were tracks of other visitors.

We planned to plant some trees on the banks, Andrew thought of planting bananas to one side where the soil was richer and moister. A house inspection now always included a dam inspection and the water level was watched with great interest. Until the day when the water actually overflowed the second dam and the tiny stream began to flow again across the bottom of the plot and under the road over to the piece of land we had on the other side.

I wonder now whether I was the only one who had some regrets for what we had done? I did like the dam but occasionally had some nostalgia for the tiny pool hidden under scrubby trees. It's very secret charm was lost for ever.

Now that the house was nearing completion Aziz who had followed our progress with interest asked to see the house, so one afternoon I took him and Banda out to Leopards Hill Road. We walked round the house and garden - as far as it had got! - then Banda went with White to inspect the progress of the fruit trees. Aziz and I walked back through the house and out onto the roof. He looked around at the space and the quietness of the afternoon, he looked back at the servants quarters which were nearing completion.

He sighed.

'It's very nice Madam, but it is too far.'

I could understand him not wanting to give up his own house at Mutendere but was this really further than Roma?

Then bit by bit the truth began to emerge.

It was not really the distance which was the problem but first of all one had to pass the cemetery at the beginning of Leopards Hill Road and then there was the wooded area where thieves and robbers had a hide out. Leopards Hill Road apparently enjoyed a dubious reputation for harbouring 'baddies' among some thick bush. I stared at Aziz in amazement. I could understand his reluctance to pass the cemetery at night - that was a well-known fear - but this was the first I had heard of there being a robbers' hide out in the bush off the road.

451

Not only was Aziz unhappy about travelling on the road, his wife had put her foot down and insisted he should not. And that was that. He agreed to continue with us until I could find another cook but that was all.

Banda was thoroughly pleased with the planned move and was beside himself with happiness at the prospect of a house of his own. He had looked at the servant' quarters and in comparison they were palatial. Each house had two large rooms, each had a bathroom with a shower and toilet, and then an open kitchen verandah complete with a small wood stove. There was electric light laid on and the windows were burglar barred and fitted with mosquito gauzes. And of course there was more than ample provision for their own gardens.

White and his family moved into the first house as soon as it was ready, relieved to be out of their rondavel, which had been dry and safe but very cramped. The other two houses waited for Banda and ... whoever would be our next cook?

Over the years there were many criticisms of people who paid their servants weekly 'ration money' in addition to the monthly wage - it was 'paternalistic' - it assumed the servant was incapable of budgeting and so on. We had always paid 'ration money' after giving servants the option - they always preferred it. And moving to Leopards Hill Road, ten miles out of town, I offered to collect a set amount of foodstuffs each month as transport would be a problem. No local bus service - just a bicycle or Shanks' pony. All the servants eagerly accepted the offer so the Hiace van I drove was useful each month as I loaded three huge bags of mealie meal in addition to an assortment of other commodities. Never forgetting Lifebuoy soap - still an essential for Banda and his artificial eye.

On all our frequent visits to the house Ceri and Simon had taken a keen interest in the progress and various developments. They had of course decided who should have which bedroom. Ceri wanted to have the one at the front so that she could see who would be coming up the drive and also be able to watch the birds in the trees. Simon wanted the room at the back so that he could put a bird bath on the flat roof of the kitchen outside his window. Relieved that they had agreed not to disagree as it were, I took them off to choose their new curtains. Ceri opted for blue with pink flowers, Simon choosing blue and green stripes. With all their discussion and participation we were totally unprepared for Simon's reaction when we moved. The great day came at last and Andrew was actually in the country and present for the move. We had been packing books and small things for the whole of the previous week and the move itself was arranged for the weekend.

Ceri at Leopards Hill Road

Early in the morning the lorry arrived and the first loading up began, we would drive to and fro seeing to the general supervision. Ceri and Simon were to stay at Roma with Aziz until the final load. The day proceeded smoothly and calmly, the cats were locked in a bedroom until the last trip. Ceri trotted to and fro helping and hindering. Simon walked round the garden with the dogs and I thought 'How helpful' until I caught sight of his face. Such misery.
'Never mind,' I called. 'We shall be going soon.'
And to my horror he said
'I don't want to go.'
Andrew thought it was just general miserableness but I was a bit

453

more apprehensive. By the afternoon we were down to the last trip, loading up the chickens, ducks and rabbits, peacocks and garden tools and left over odds and sods.

'Right,' said Andrew. 'That's the last load. I'll follow it in the car and could you see to the locking up and then come on with the dogs and cats and Ceri and Simon in the van?'

No problem

Getting the dogs and cats to agree to stay together in the van after all the upheavals of the day was not easy but Aziz and I finally managed it.

'Come on then,' I sighed. 'Let's get going.'

Ceri got into the van and sat in the middle of the seat. Simon stood in the middle of the garden with sheer misery all across his face.

'I'm not going. I'm not leaving my house.'

It was all in vain to reason and persuade, he would not move. He was so distressed that I felt like bursting into tears too. And all this, after all his visits to the plot and new house and our talks and plans for the new place.

'Look,' I reasoned. 'Everything has gone, the house is empty, we can't stay here now.'

'I can. I'll go and live with Aziz in his house.'

Aziz looked even more worried than me.

'No, no, Bwana Simon,' he said in his gentle voice. 'My house is empty too, when the Madam goes I lock up and go too.'

We looked at the little boy holding back his tears and then I nodded at Aziz. Together we picked him up and pushed the stiff body into the van. Aziz held the door shut while I got in the other side. He walked down the drive holding the door shut as I began to drive. He looked in through the open window

'It's all right Bwana Simon. It's a good house. You will like it and I will come tomorrow.'

I'll never forget that last drive from Roma to the house at Leopards Hill Road with the dogs pacing about in the back of the van and from time to time leaning over to pant in my face. The cats, as usual, escaping from their baskets and joining in the general melee at the back. Ceri wanting to talk but both of us only too aware of the stiff silent figure huddled at the far end of the seat, trying in vain to stem the tears silently pouring down.

Once at the house Andrew stared in shock at Simon. He would make no response to our remarks so we decided the best thing was to tell them both to see if they could fix their bedrooms as they wanted, the furniture and boxes had been just dumped on the floor. Ceri was keen and busy at once. Simon shut the door in our faces.

'Best leave him a while,' said Andrew. ' He'll come round soon. Who would have ever thought he would be so upset to leave a house?'

I went to call them for a meal some time later. Ceri had put most things where she wanted them and was busy with her collection of dolls and rosettes.

I opened Simon's door.

He had been busy too. He had arranged his furniture in a barricade around his bed and shut off access to the door.

Hunger made him agree to moving one bookcase slightly but it took over a week to get him to move the rest of his things into a more accessible arrangement. Aziz came out to the house to help us for some time but I knew he did not want to come for longer than necessary. So after several trips to the employment office at the Boma and scanning the newspaper ads I found another cook. I would much rather have had Aziz but the new chap appeared reasonably competent.

Banda and White worked together very well and we all seemed to be settling down, especially since Simon had come to terms with the move and was now as devoted to this house and plot of land as he had been at Roma.

Andrew made a point of consulting him on jobs that were to be done and they supervised the stocking of the dam together. Several hundred fingerlings - or so they assured me they were called - were delivered by a man from Game and Fisheries one weekend. Andrew and Simon tipped the drums of fish into the dam and took careful note of all the instructions. Ceri and I held off the dogs, who clearly wished to be in on the act and plunge in with the fish.

The next job they did together was the gravelling of the drive, the gravel was tipped in large heaps near the house and they spread and raked it across the open area nearest the house. It was hard work and Simon was soon in the house to organise refreshments. Andrew came in shortly afterwards, chuckling to himself.

'You know how those dogs bark at anything? Well, a man was cycling past on the road and the stupid dogs did one of their rushes in that direction barking their silly heads off and he fell off the bike.'

'Poor chap, they do look fierce,' I said.

'It's not that that's funny. He soon stood up and when he shouted they turned tail and fled back to me. I shouted 'They won't hurt you' and he ... he ... he got very angry and said that if I didn't hold the dogs in future he would come and complain. I said they never bite. And he shouted 'Don't you be cheeky or I will come and tell your Bwana'. I said, ' I AM the Bwana' and he got angrier and said, 'Don't be stupid. Bwanas don't work in the garden.' I didn't dare tell him that I am a Minister as well, he would probably have an apoplectic fit.'

It was all very well for Andrew to joke about being a Minister and working in the garden, we both knew he found it the most relaxing pastime. After a hectic week in the office and late nights he longed for the weekends when he could potter in the garden with the dogs at his heels. He would remove small trees, plant shrubs, another fish pond was made for the goldfish - this time deep enough to deter any dogs from fishing - what memories of Micky.

One of his earliest and most urgent jobs was to improve the rabbits' houses and runs. On our first morning at the house Banda greeted us with the news that all the rabbits had escaped in the night. There was little hope of finding and catching them and we went out into the garage to go to town, feeling saddened. Andrew started up the car and rabbits shot in all directions -

456

almost every one had spent the night under his car ... within sniffing distance of the dogs' blankets. Confused by the noise and the ever present dogs, who thought this was an ideal way to start the morning, they did a quick about turn and disappeared back under the car and van. Once they were caught, Andrew, Banda and White spent the rest of the weekend reinforcing the wire fence and foundations of the run.

Once moved in and settled into a routine a housewarming party was at the top of the agenda and by now we felt we could 'splash the cash' as the modern phrase has it. So to make life easier we booked the party with Eamon Xynias, the talented chef at Lusaka Hotel. It was exciting to watch the hotel vans roll up the drive and see the kitchen and dining room transformed as his men swung into action. Very soon guests and friends arrived in droves - some saying they had missed our gate and driven on for some time before realising their mistake - and a very merry evening was had. We discovered the following day that the candles we had thoughtfully placed in jam jars by the gate on the side road to guide in visitors had vanished. But how silly of us, not to realise that candles for the taking was too much of a temptation for passing villagers.

One Saturday morning Andrew returned from town saying we must go back immediately, he had a surprise for me. We drove down to Cairo Road, parking outside FredJoes – a second hand emporium owned by the local well-known wrestler. And there was A Grandfather Clock (not working). I had always joked that I would like one but of course in the middle of Africa it was the last thing I expected to see. We took it home and Monday morning found me on the doorstep of Klaus Rygaard, jewellers and watchmakers, with the clock mechanism and the pendulum, which weighed a ton, but thankfully the clock could be repaired and we stood it near the front door, its chimes marking our days. As I said, working and walking on the plot was Andrew's way of relaxing from the pressures at work but even so, as the weeks progressed I felt worried about his quiet sadness at times and his preoccupation. Then he began to sleep badly and my nights were disturbed by a tossing and thrashing Andrew, who could never recall what had disturbed him. At first he dismissed my concern but at last admitted he was sleeping badly and perhaps a holiday would be a good idea.

MAURITIUS

We had often talked about taking a 'local' holiday and Mauritius had been high on the list. Andrew admitting he could do with a break meant it was quite easy to persuade him that two weeks in Mauritius would be ideal. No sooner said than done, especially as the school holiday was coming up. The flight to Mauritius is short and we landed late afternoon in a heavy rainstorm.

Our first impressions were of acres upon acres of sugar cane and - after the vast empty expanses of Zambia - we were struck by the intense cultivation of every square yard. Mauritius is so small that all land is used and valued.

The hotel was set attractively among pine trees at the edge of the beach so as soon as we had dropped our baggage in the chalet we walked beside the sea with the children. The air was warm and moist, the waves lapped softly at our feet and I could feel some of the holiday relaxation creeping over Andrew.

We all had an early night; some of us would have had a late morning but for two children who naturally wanted to go on the beach. As they were surely old enough, Andrew said they could go on their own but there was to be no swimming or paddling until we were there.

Departure of offspring and we turned over.

Sleep, sleep, blissful sleep.

Only to be interrupted again by the news that Simon had 'just happened to trip up and fall into the sea - it was in the way.' Surveying our sodden son we bowed to the inevitable and got up.

Apart from a little token touristy sightseeing around the island we spent most of the time on the beach. It was possible to hire small glass bottomed boats and in these we paddled out on the coral reefs to watch the shoals of brightly coloured fish.

The beaches were long wide expanses of clean sand scattered

with a fascinating assortment of shells; more exotic ones could be bought anywhere on the island but we found the ones at our feet more than satisfying. Sitting on the beach one day and idly sifting sand through my fingers I was fascinated to suddenly see that amongst what I had thought was 'just sand' were the most exquisite miniature shells. Some, only a fraction of an inch in length, were complete to the smallest detail. I had never seen anything so detailed and microscopic, a teaspoon would have held a wide variety of perfect but minute shells.

The beach at Mauritius

Ceri and Simon were quite content to swim and mess about generally on the beach, Andrew and I were trying to have a relaxing holiday. I say 'trying' because I was very soon aware that Andrew found it impossible to really relax. After a while we would find ourselves walking and walking and walking. We walked for miles along that beach, we walked until we were exhausted and then we walked again. We would fall into bed tired from the sea and sun - and the amount of exercise. But then Andrew would begin to toss and turn and mutter in his sleep. One night he groaned and grumbled at last saying 'There are still more ... still more to do'

In the morning he admitted that he had been dreaming, dreaming of trees to be chopped down. He had chopped them down only to find there were more to be felled. It went on and on until the dream broke - probably when I had shaken him. Then he had slept again to dream again. This time he was signing the bottom of pages in a file but no sooner had he signed all the pages than there were more pages to be signed. His arm had ached but he could not stop signing and signing.

Recalling and talking about these dreams, Andrew had to admit that he was having disturbed nights and that perhaps - just perhaps - I was right and that a check-up at the doctor when we returned to Lusaka would not come amiss. The rest of the holiday passed fairly uneventfully, I just felt relieved that at least he admitted that he might be over working.

Uneventful if one did not mention the fact that I thoughtlessly walked to lunch in shorts soon after arriving and had the skin of my thighs burn so badly it peeled off in strips.

Once we were back in Lusaka of course it was a different story. See the doctor? Nonsense, he was perfectly fit, there was absolutely no need to go fussing off to a medic.

Undeterred I went to see Dr Patterson myself and explained my fears. He listened to the saga and said a check-up would be a good idea, if only to stop me worrying. Andrew accepted that idea and off he went 'for your peace of mind'. I cared little whose peace of mind. Unfortunately Dr Patterson could not even find a slightly faster pulse and although he thought the dreams were a clear indication of stress and that Andrew should ease up on his work load, he could not point to any other medical symptom. This Andrew interpreted as a clear bill of health and carried on as before, working all hours, convinced that he should cope with all the pressures and demands on his time and energies today, if not yesterday.

It was a time of intense pressures, the euphoria of independence was over and the harsh realities of the responsibilities of governing their own country placed a heavy burden on the many people, who gave so devotedly of their time and energies, but who had not had long enough or intense enough apprenticeships. Added to which, the strain of guiding Zambia through the hardships caused by Rhodesia's UDI and the unexpected rise in oil prices coupled with the fall in copper prices had placed an extra burden.

One effect this had on Andrew was to make him publicly critical of others and the Press delighted in headlines 'EAK slams armchair critics' when he castigated for example MP's who criticised para-statal organisations for making losses when they themselves were often on the board of directors.

Even the President was showing signs of stress and making more and more emotional statements to the extent of sometimes appearing to regard himself above the law.

There was a sad case of an expatriate Colin Brown, who had tragically run down and killed four cadet officers and injured seven others. He had rounded a bend on the road very early in the morning near Kabwe and run straight into a group of marching cadets. The newspapers carried photos of Kaunda in tears and quoted him as saying,

'I fail to understand what was in his mind when he killed these four young men' and went on to add that he did not wish to see him because if he did, he would hate him for the rest of his life.

I think we were all shocked to see the President making personal statements like that and in essence pre-judging a case. There was a quick attempt the following day to correct the statement but the damage was done.

I was particularly shocked at the turn of events - the niceties of the legal position had not occurred to me but I had recently driven on that stretch of road at an equally early hour in the morning. May Sharpe and I had driven to Ndola for a few days - I can't remember why now - but I can still remember we set off very early in the morning and were approaching Kabwe around sunrise when we ran into small pockets of mist without any warning at all. If we had met with a bunch of marching cadets - or anyone else - we could easily have mown them down too.

We fortunately had an uneventful journey and after experiencing the first pocket of mist, had driven very slowly until the sun had fully risen. I wonder now why we went to Ndola? We stayed in the Mines Rest House, as Andrew had arranged. We had dinner in the evening with several men who were in Ndola on Mine business and were heartily amused by one of our companions in particular. He had flown up from South Africa that morning and it was his first time to be 'up north'. He had had a stopover of several hours at Lusaka airport so I asked him what he thought of Lusaka. But he had not seen the town, only the airport from which he had not stirred at all. On your way back, we advised, get a taxi and have a look at the city. This was greeted by very doubtful looks, did we think it was safe enough? Quite safe we reassured him.

One heard such stories ... merely driving on the roads ...

'How do you think we got here?' we asked.

It took a long time to convince him that we had travelled on our own, really on our own and not even in a convoy. He obviously thought we were very rash to undertake such a journey.

As I say, it was a most entertaining meal, greatly enhanced by the fact that it was painfully clear that he had never sat down to a meal with a non-white before. May's sense of humour could hardly be restrained and she put herself out to be extra charming and ultra-sophisticated, being naturally very attractive and intelligent anyway, it was a most amusing meal.

What good we had done for racial harmony would have immediately been undone if he had seen us later walking round Ndola and me almost having to physically restrain May, who wanted to climb over a railing and take a few cuttings from some rose bushes outside the Ndola Municipal Offices.

'But June, they are YELLOW roses and I have been trying to buy some YELLOW roses for months ... just one or two cuttings from the bottom of a bush ...'

I think I only diverted her by having a brainwave for our South African friend. We hurried back to the rest house and phoned Andrew. He more than happily agreed to send his Ministerial car and driver to the airport in Lusaka and we said we would organise our end. The next morning I approached our new friend over breakfast and explained how concerned we were that he had not seen Lusaka and as gesture of hospitality my husband would arrange for him to see the sights on his stop-over on the return journey.

He was most impressed with the offer but rendered speechless when I wrote down my name and added Andrew's office phone number. He may have been on Mines business but he had never expected to be touristed around by the Minister's driver. And oh dear, oh dear, if I was the Minister's wife ... he was a ... oh, dear, had he had dinner with a white woman who was married to a ... oh dear, oh dear ...

I always believed in doing my bit for racial harmony.

OCTOBER 1974 TENTH ANNIVERSARY

We were of course into 1974 and the tenth anniversary of independence. This had to be marked in a special way. Each year the anniversary was marked by parades and processions but the tenth was clearly to be spectacular. Now we could show how we had developed and progressed in spite of the problems around us.

Lusaka sported many new buildings, the east side of Cairo Road was almost completely built up now, here and there multi storey blocks raised their heads. More children were being born, more were surviving, more were attending school, more Zambians owned businesses and property and so on. Oh yes, there was progress.

There was much yet to be done but over all there was a feeling of pride that we had come so far and the 24th October was planned with some satisfaction. For those who had some misgivings about the growing inefficiency in certain areas and the corruption revealed from time to time - well, it could be put down to growing pains of a young nation, and which nation is totally devoid of scandal?

One of the items planned for the great week was the March Past of the Independence Babies. All the children, who had been born in 1964 would take part in the Independence Parade. When I first heard of the idea I thought what a marvellous idea and what a good way to involve children in their country's great day. But as the details emerged more than a few of us had misgivings. The children were to parade as miniature soldiers; not only were they to be dressed in perfect army uniforms but they were also to be drilled by Army instructors, so that they would march in perfect military precision.

Most of us hoped - and perhaps believed - that the powers that be would soon realise that ten year old children were not exactly suited to this interpretation of what was essentially a good idea, and that the plans would be slightly modified.

But no. The children were marched on parade grounds for long hours in the hot sun and no allowance was made for their age. Teachers, who accompanied their charges, had to march with them. After the first practice Mrs Higgins protested to Sister that she would not be able to cope. We sat in the tiny staffroom and listened to her description with dismay. Sister Fausta was always sure she could find a way to cope with any difficulties so on the next practice she accompanied Mrs Higgins and the ten year olds. On their return her blue eyes were slightly troubled but there was still a hint of a twinkle.

'I said to the officer 'But officer, surely you don't expect an old lady like Mrs Higgins to march in the sun ... oh, yes she is over fifty ... I could not let her do it, officer ... but I know you have your job to do ... so I have come to take her place! '

The officer, faced with an elderly Sister declaring her teacher was over fifty, could not argue and offered a plump and elderly Sister already perspiring in the sun, knew he must capitulate.

We clapped as Sister smiled her sweet and gentle smile 'So he very kindly allowed us to sit and watch.'

Then she rose to her feet, looking slightly troubled,

'Please forgive me Mrs Higgins for telling such an untruth about your age. And now I must go to the chapel and make sure the good Lord understands. I am sure He will.'

So while Sister Fausta prayed for forgiveness from her Lord the ten year olds continued to march in the hot sun for the weeks preceding October. Their uniforms, correct to the smallest detail - and to the heaviest Army boots - were ordered from overseas and the children gradually began to march and respond with true military robot precision, which worried many teachers and parents. May Sharpe's daughter Jennifer was one of our Independence marchers, May said she could only hope that once it was all over the robotic response would disappear quickly.

It was about this time that Ceri stopped riding with Nicole at the Showgrounds. Nicole's father Don Bruce was a senior officer in the CID but apart from occasionally seeing him at a gymkhana when he was bursting with pride of his daughter, I had seen very little of him and knew far less about the work in which he was involved.

Great was our consternation therefore when we heard that his contract had been abruptly terminated and that they would be leaving the country in a very short time indeed. Rumours abounded that he had been involved in something slightly unsavoury; equally strong rumours abounded that in the course of his investigations he had come uncomfortably close to revealing which Very Important Person was concerned in a particularly large scale piece of corruption. One could believe either or neither. I knew nothing and therefore believed nothing. Debbie - Nicole's mother - asked if we would like to buy one or both of the horses but I felt that it was too great a commitment especially as Ceri said she would not be so interested in riding without Nicole's companionship.

Regretfully for the children's sakes I bade the Bruce's farewell and wished them every success in Australia whence they were heading. Regretfully also because my somewhat slow thought process had finally reached the conclusion that if Don Bruce were mixed up in something unsavoury, why had it not been made public? And if he were not, then WHO was involved in WHAT?

Andrew would only admit he had heard various speculations and would not commit himself to saying what he knew or believed, if anything. But I had not expected anything more. Sometimes he would talk about his work and his talk would range from optimism about plans and projects to voicing his disagreement and pessimism on other undertakings. Sometimes he would repeat gossip and rumour and speculation about people in responsible posts - and almost in the same breath dismiss them as being without foundation. It was almost as though he himself could not decide what or who he believed any more. I suspected that there was much more he did not tell me, quite rightly, and was aware that this was yet another pressure on him. Once more I was relieved we had bought the plot, its continuing demand upon both of us brought a welcome relief. There was more time to spend with friends again as we had settled down to some sort of routine.

Looking in the deep freezer one day I came across a turkey I had put there eighteen months earlier! It had been bought for Christmas in one of Andrew's helpful shopping moods but had proved far too big to fit in any tin which would go in the oven. In despair and amusement I had shoved it in the freezer and rushed out to buy another bird.

It could not sit there for ever so out it came - and whether it had shrunk, whether it was more 'adjustable' I will never know but fit a roasting tin it did. Hastily we phoned the Maliks and the Sharpes and Ruth Weiss, were they willing to try an elderly turkey? Friends will try anything in the cause of friendship and out they all trooped at the weekend. Andrew and Simon had got a fire going under the trees down by the dam while I loaded up the van at the kitchen door. Ruth arrived as we reached the last pile of boxes and plates and once again she queried my sanity,

'Not only do you preserve your food for nearly two years but then you make your friends consume it outdoors at a great distance from the house. Is it 'high' or something?'

But even she had to admit that it was a most peaceful afternoon. The younger generation lit their own fire some distance from ours, it was cold enough to be pleasant by a crackling wood fire and the dogs went to pant and beg by the children, leaving us in peace. The food and drink was plentiful, tasting better outdoors as food always does. And the turkey? It fell in tender succulent slices from the bones as the knife slipped in.

On the roof with Louise Williams, me, Barbara Malik, Andrew, May Sharpe, Ruth Weiss and Alfred Sharpe

There are times one would wish to preserve for ever and that afternoon was one of them. Good friends and good food and pleasant surroundings. We lolled back against the tree trunks as we sipped and picked at an odd bone, fish rose occasionally in the dam - proof that at least some of the fingerlings were surviving - dogs snuffled in the undergrowth in vague attempts at coming to grips with more than a smell.

The conversation rose and fell, very rarely touching on politics or serious topics for long. Who could really be bothered to get heated at such relaxed times?

'Marvellous way to enjoy oneself at home without the phone interrupting,' said Andrew. 'It's probably ringing its silly head off up there in the house but who knows and who cares?'

It was not easy to escape the phone; even when you thought you were safe at a distance it could wield an infuriating power over your life. After Mauritius Andrew did not let up on his workload but he was slightly more prepared to admit that he was working very hard and he would admit that we had less and less time together.

We both left the house at seven in the morning. I would lunch at home with the children; Andrew would come if he were not having a meeting or a working lunch. If he did come we knew better than to interrupt him while he ate with one ear cocked to the radio at his side and one eye on the newspaper. The usual routine - if it worked - was that I would take Ceri home with me, Andrew would pick up Simon from the International School. If there was an unexpected and late change, Andrew would send the driver to collect Simon and either take him to the office or, rarely, take him home. On one occasion Simon arrived home looking distinctly subdued. And later confessed that he had got to know the driver very well so when a total stranger appeared at the school 'to collect Mr Kashita's son', Simon climbed into the car, a little surprised. Surprise which turned to slight panic when the driver took a totally new, and unknown to Simon, route. He said, 'I thought I was being kidnapped ... but couldn't think why'. In the afternoons I took Ceri and Simon to their school activities and attended to my school clubs etc. we would be back at the house by four o'clock usually but Andrew would rarely appear before six o'clock and then he would be listening to the BBC News or local news until dinner at seven, after which he would work on files until late - that is if he didn't rush in to whisk us both off to some dinner or drinks party or other get together.

I have made a real effort to write down memories in fairly consecutive order but years and events and people do blur with the years. After independence in 1964 as Andrew rose in the ranks we began to receive invitations to the Queen's Birthday celebration at the British High Commissioner's home. As I remember it, it was on the official birthday in June which can be decidedly chilly in Lusaka and the High Commissioner's garden on Independence Avenue (at that time) would be rather bare and dusty where we would stand around making polite conversation, clutching the inevitable wine glass while watching for a passing tray of nibbles. With all due respect to Her Majesty, it did begin to pall after a few years and our attendance was not so faithful. At some point the High Commissioner moved to a house (on to Prince George Road? near the golf course). I don't remember attending any Queen's Birthday celebrations there but an evening dinner is ingrained in the memory. Proceedings had run smoothly and a party of twelve or more sat down at a long table, the food was good, company equally so and the conversations ran on.

Unfortunately I am somewhat shy and have a habit of fiddling - I will touch and turn a knife or fork for example. Not the thing to do, so being well aware of that I made a determined effort to sit with my hands below the table out of sight when not actually eating. But without thinking my fingers would pleat and fold the edge of the stiffly starched table cloth - but well out of sight so all well and good. While pleating and folding and keeping up with the conversation on my left (or right) my fingers suddenly hit upon a wire which seemed to be running the length of the table. Fairly firmly, because my fiddling fingers didn't detach anything. But ... I hadn't taken particular attention to the running of the proceedings. We ate the starter and as if by magic the waiters appeared at just the right moment to remove plates. And on to the main course after which two waiters appeared to offer the dishes once more, it had been delicious and several people helped themselves. Our hostess looked pleased and flattered. This was the moment my fingers met the wire. Which didn't fall down. But the waiters appeared to offer the dishes again. Third helpings were politely declined while the good lady at the head of the table looked a little surprised. No sooner had the door closed behind the waiters and conversations resumed - the waiters appeared yet again. No one took up the offer while head of the table looked a bit annoyed.

Light dawned - my fingers - wire – waiters ... I confess now I just could not resist one more time ... Was I right? This time the puzzled looking waiters were told very firmly no more was required, and told to return to clear the table.

I have wondered since, was the wire along the length of the table so that the bell could be rung from wherever a host was seated? Life was not always so entertaining. Andrew was extremely busy and preoccupied. We never seemed to have those leisurely times together when we could talk at length.

So we decided we would spend a weekend down at Livingstone and made a booking at the Intercontinental Hotel, the Musi-o-Tunya.

'We'll drive down,' said Andrew. 'And then we'll have the car for sight-seeing in the Game Park.'

Off we set on the Friday, looking forward to a family weekend relaxing by the Falls. The drive down to Livingstone is 475 kilometres and takes about four or five hours. It's quite a pleasant drive, the scenery becomes more interesting as you drop down into the Zambezi Valley.

Four or five hours even in a comfortable car is still a few hours too many and we were glad to turn into the hotel car park and get out, stretching our stiff legs. As we walked up to the main entrance the door opened and a hand was thrust forward,

'Good evening Mr Minister, welcome to the Musi o Tunya, could I please have a word?'

Andrew raised an eyebrow at me and went into a little huddle with the manager.

In a few minutes he came across with a scowl.

'There has been a phone call from State House. There is a plane waiting at the airport and I am to fly back at once for an urgent meeting.'

I contained my anger until we were in our room.

He had promised that there was no work or meeting outstanding and that he had made it clear that he would be away for the weekend - what was this matter of national emergency?

Andrew had no idea. Why didn't he phone State House and find out?

But apparently the plane was waiting and he would be late and he would be back on a flight in the morning. And off he went.

He was back early in the morning and I was even less appreciative of the call of national duty when he said that the meeting had not actually been urgent and could well have waited until the Monday. He indicated that Lishomwa Lishomwa, as Special

470

Adviser to the President, had only been exerting his powers for the sake of a whim.

It was only a few years ago that Lish had been one of our circle of friends, now I became aware of how rapidly we had all changed. Had it been a petty recall? I can't see why.

Naturally we made the most of what was left of our weekend but it left a nasty taste. I was ashamed of losing my temper but was still annoyed that we had no right to any private life or privacy. Andrew had not been able to refuse the post of Minister and once he had accepted, he had no control over his private life. I strongly resented the feeling of being under someone's control to such an extent.

The more I felt I was losing my individuality the more I clung to my work at school and old friends, reduced as they were. I was still asked occasionally whether I would be giving up teaching and I knew I would not be able to bear it. The classroom full of small girls with their trust and honesty was a benison after the rumour, counter rumour, scandal and revelations of the day.

It was not just the corruption in business which raised its head only too often but the discovery of more and more of one's friends being involved in one intimate dispute after another. One happy marriage after another went on the rocks, some floundered through, others went under completely. Most wives kept a proud silence for a long time and as I heard one sad story after another I wondered how they had managed for so long. Andrew said it was mostly exaggerated by women with nothing better to do than gossip, most of it was not true. But only a little while later he would be laughing and shaking his head with friends as someone recounted the latest peccadillo.

The CIPEC Conference in London was a welcome break, Minister's wives were invited, all expenses paid. Hurrah, a trip to London and a change of pressure.

The children took pride in the decision that they were old enough to stay at home. Louise Williams offered to come and stay at the house and we were able to depart with light hearts. Louise, married to Dick Williams of Water Affairs, had stayed

471

on in Zambia to complete her contract with Caledonian Airways after her husband had been posted elsewhere. She also worked as a volunteer Special Police Reservist in her spare time.

The Conference did not last long. Andrew spent most of his time at meetings of course and I was free to wander London. The Churchill Hotel was ideal, not far from the top of Oxford Street, but although my air fare and hotel expenses were free we had little spare cash for my excursions. Thank goodness art galleries and museums are free and my tastes ran in that direction!

All too soon we were on our way home and looking forward to hearing the children's news. They did not seem to have missed us much and were full of how they had coped in our absence. Louise was rather quiet. After the children had gone to bed, we had the real news.

I said earlier that the cook, although satisfactory in his work, had never really taken the place of Aziz. But this time he had more than justified my vague feeling of unease. While we were away Andrew had arranged for a security guard to be at the house every night and I had left the usual instructions that he should be given a meal before the cook went off duty.

One evening, said Louise, after the children had gone to bed, the cook went off duty and she was relaxing in front of the TV, she suddenly heard screams and shouts and the pounding of feet outside. She rushed outside to see the guard, in a state of near nudity, racing round the house closely pursued by the cook, who was brandishing an axe.

Without stopping to think, all her Police reserve training took over and she bawled,

'STO-O-O-OP!'

Both cook and guard stopped dead in their tracks.

'Give me that,' she ordered and the cook handed over the axe.

Averting her eyes from the guard's nether regions, she ordered the cook to go home and the guard to remain on the front verandah.

'We will talk tomorrow,' she said and went inside.

She locked the door, put the axe under the settee, sat down in front of the TV because her legs would no longer support her and then leapt to her feet at the sound of clapping.

'You're GOOD,' said Simon from the doorway. 'We didn't know you could shout like that!'

The cook said the guard had been pursuing his wife. The guard said he had merely taken the usual walk round the grounds and passed the time of day (or evening) with the wives as he patrolled by the servants quarters. As usual there was no way of discovering the truth, but whatever it was we did not want an axe brandishing cook, dressed or otherwise. We paid him off, discovering only too late that one of my watches and other small items had also left.

I could mark the changes in my life in cooks I reflected as I set off for the Boma once more. And wasn't it marvellous how everyone left the country extolling the virtues of their soon to be unemployed cooks when I was admirably suited. But as soon as I was 'in between help' nobody but nobody was prepared to part with one of their household gems.

It was a surprise to find Joseph Chambuluka so soon, and so promising - but then weren't they all? I engaged the man with some hope but also the knowledge that once again I could be let down. It made one wonder if one were totally unsuited as an employer.

However, nothing ventured, nothing gained, or whatever the saying is. I arranged to pick Joseph up with his katundu (luggage) the following day, he would work for a week and if we were both suited then his wife and family would follow. Promptly at three o'clock I parked the car near the Army barracks where he was staying with his brother and said to the children,

'There's the new chap.'

Joseph came up to the car with his katundu, I got out to put it in the boot and said,

'You had better get in the front with me, the children are taking up most of the space in the back.'

He smiled, nodded and got in, glancing into the back of the car and I was immediately aware that something was wrong. We drove out to Leopards Hill Road making polite conversation about the names and ages of his children and all the time I knew that his mind was very much elsewhere.

The servant's quarters obviously pleased him and then we went across to the house and I showed him the layout and discussed his routine. As we stood in the kitchen opening and shutting cupboards doors I suddenly stopped and said,

'Joseph, there is something you are thinking about, something you want to say?'

He hesitated for a moment.

'Madam, the Bwana is … is not European?'

'No, he is a Zambian.'

'A Zambian same like me?'

'Yes, why?'

'Ah, Madam, I did not know.'

'But does it matter?'

'It's not all right Madam. They say they are not good to work for.'

Well, what do you know?

There's discrimination and there's discrimination! Now we have a black saying a black will not be a good employer … let's bring the Colonials back?

'I suppose some of them are not,' I agreed. 'But then some of you are not good employees. I am taking a chance on you, how about you taking a chance on us? Anyway, when I told you my name you did not say anything about not wanting to work for a Zambian.'

'Ah, well, Madam, I did not think that YOU could have a Zambian name, I was not thinking.'

'You had better start thinking now,' I commented. 'Now, do you want to have this week's trial or not?'

Well, now he was here he would give it a try but he clearly was not impressed with the household he had found himself in and I had a feeling that I would be back at the Boma the following week.

Andrew arrived home shortly before dinner and passing through the kitchen he greeted Joseph, who responded politely but with

474

little enthusiasm. Dinner was delicious, a gastronomic delight. Over coffee we beamed at each other.

'A good chap, this.'

'You had better behave yourself then, I want to keep him.'

Andrew looked startled.

In between much laughter I repeated the conversation with Joseph. Andrew looked scandalised.

'But that's unfair,' he protested. 'The chap has probably never even worked for a Zambian before.'

'I'm sure he hasn't,' I laughed.

Thank goodness by the end of the week Joseph had decided that Andrew passed muster as an employer and off we went to collect his wife and children. We then embarked upon a most comfortable period, Joseph was an excellent cook and was extremely adaptable in every way. He had two weaknesses, the daily news and Green Buffalos - his favourite football team.

As far as the news went Joseph and Andrew had much in common, without their daily fix life was unbearable - for them and everyone else. Over the years I had grown used to Andrew switching on the radio for every available news bulletin and reading the paper from cover to cover. Now I had a cook with similar inclinations. If Andrew came home at lunchtime he brought the newspapers and after removing the first layer of newsprint he would leave them behind. I grew used to Joseph collecting the coffee cups after lunch and, with a deft sleight of hand, removing the newspapers at the same time. After a while I tired of pretending not to notice his subterfuge and said he was quite welcome to take the papers to read as long as he brought them back at four o'clock when he came to make the tea.

Joseph Chambuluka

This was the thin end of the wedge. At that time we could still obtain a weekly edition of the UK Guardian and he purloined that too. That I could cope with, what I did not particularly want was to discuss Margaret Thatcher's chances of becoming Leader of the Conservative Party. Joseph took a keen interest in her progress and was willing to make a bet - it was a good job I declined as I would have lost! Once Margaret Thatcher was safely installed we then had to compare her with Indira Ghandi and Mrs Bandaranaike - I forget which of the three earned his approval most but I can't forget the reprimand I earned

'You are a Madam from England, you should go to vote for her, now we have women Prime Ministers in many countries. They must be good if so many men vote for them!'

It was a great relief when the woman was elected, he could then concentrate on world matters in general - and wait for the day when Mrs Thatcher would be Prime Minister. Of that he had no doubts. About that time too I was able to persuade him that it would be more practical to borrow books from the shelves openly and be able to discuss them and cut out the long winded devious route he had been working, whereby books disappeared and then reappeared and then came into the conversation in

476

various roundabout ways.

In comparison his devotion to football was quite easy to cope with. If his team were playing in Lusaka at the weekend he would depart smartly after lunch on Sunday and breakfast on Monday would reflect his satisfaction with their performance.

If, as so often happened, we were entertaining on Sunday lunchtime we had a neat bit of organisation. Lunch would be served promptly at 1pm and looking at the marvellous meals he produced in such an unhurried atmosphere I am quite sure that no one ever guessed what was happening behind the scenes. Once we were served the main course, Banda would be elbow deep in the sink while Joseph had the sweet trolley all poised by the dining room door.

Once the sweet trolley was with us, coffee was laid out on trays and Joseph was giving his last orders to the willing Banda. Coffee trays came through and while I poured it out and smiled graciously at all and sundry I knew that Joseph was stripping off his uniform in the garage.

Andrew could be relied upon to keep the drinks flowing with the conversation and no one seemed to miss me during the twenty minutes when Joseph and I leaped into the van with his bicycle and roared off down the drive. I would drop him in Kabulonga with his bicycle and be back in time to find out who would like a second coffee. Perhaps friends and visitors thought we were sticklers about the one o'clock Sunday lunch times but it only happened when Joseph's team were playing at home.

Joseph's idea of bliss was for me to inform him that we had ten ... twelve ... many visitors for lunch. Initially he would beam and produce pen and paper for me ... wait politely for me to suggest a menu but all too soon we waived that formality and I would ask him what he wanted to cook and what I should buy - after all he knew the contents of freezer and cupboard better than me. I once asked why he hadn't opted for a job as a chef in one of the big hotels but he smiled sweetly,

'Ah, no! In hotel I must cook all same thing – all meat dishes or all sweets and puddings ... same thing all the time. Here' and he waved his hands wide, ' here, I cook everything, everything I want, different all the time.' I could see his point.

One of his highlights was a weekend lunch party which included the American Ambassador Jean Wilkoski, who was so impressed with his chocolate profiteroles she asked to go into the kitchen and congratulate him. And then, the icing on the cake, asked him if she could have his recipe. Once he had stopped levitating he managed to write down his recipe. I mentioned icing on the cake. I suppose one could say the candle on the cake was next day when his copy of the recipe was returned by the Ambassador's driver in the diplomatic limousine. Jean Wilkowski impressed us all with her dynamic personality, she was the first woman ambassador to an African country. A shining light in a Continent where women were rated rather low.

A card from Jean Wilkowski

I have written at some length on Joseph and his devotion to football – it was nearly matched by his interest in boxing for a while. For such a gentle man it was surprising to learn that he liked watching boxing on TV and was a devotee of Mohammed Ali, this we learned when he plucked up courage to ask if he could watch TV during the night ... The great Ali was due to make his famous Rumble in the Jungle fight. We slept through it all but then had an almost blow by blow account at breakfast. Driving up and down Leopards Hill Road at some speed had been made all the easier by the President buying a plot of land not far away and making full use of what became known as the Presidential Lodge. At first he travelled by road and so the road was tarmacked from Kabulonga out to the Lodge, which was down a left turn only a few hundred yards before our turning and which meant that we had only to drive a few hundred yards on a dirt road to our turn off on the right. I thought miserably that we would be inflicted with more occasions of being waved off the road to make way for his motorcade. Thankfully shortly after moving in, he took to travelling by helicopter.

At some point - and I can't for the life of me remember when, we had dinner with Louise Williams (of earlier cook and guard fame) and her daughter and friend out from UK. Somehow in the conversation Andrew said I regretted now our dams were full that we couldn't put swans there for a finishing touch. Daughter's friend said she would ask if it could be arranged. Of course, we laughed, the only swans we knew of were in UK courtesy of HM the Queen. Friend's father (or her friend's father) we now learnt was the Lord Chamberlain and as such was in some way responsible for / connected with HM's swans. Not what we expected to hear ... and we forgot all about it.

Andrew and a swan   *Geese and swans on the way to the dam*

Until there was a message to collect a large crate at the airport

- containing two large black swans - white swans belong to the Queen and were not available!

Another change was not quite so welcome. When we first bought the plot the small dirt side road continued past our plot, past Don Fluck's plot and on eventually past John Jellis's farm and to a small village. We occasionally saw or heard some villagers passing by and they in turn grew used to the dogs making noisy but totally ineffectual mad dashes to the boundary. We had not been living there long before we discovered that the Army had bought some land way down the road, including the village. Suddenly the village was gone, almost overnight it seemed. Every man, woman and child, together with their animals, had been picked up and transported to a new site, down near the Kafue river. How well the site was prepared I do not know but we did hear from a reliable source that many of the villagers were ill or died, they were not used to living by a river and had no immunity at all against the heavy mosquito infestation. Banda had found and married a young woman from the village just before they moved, and so we had occasional news of her family and friends.

I wonder now whether the army camp was sited there to be within reach of the Presidential Lodge but not on its doorstep. The army were not such quiet neighbours, instead of the odd passing bicycle or languidly chatting group we now had heavy Army lorries tearing to and fro occasionally in enormous clouds of dust. The only good thing to come out of it all was that the dogs took less and less interest in passing traffic.

I think it was about this time that we had to go to Livingstone for a few days and for various reasons thought it would be nice to have a few days to ourselves. Mentioning this to our friends the Hepworths all problems were solved, Aileen suggested the children stay there. Gillian by now had gone to UK to train as a nurse and Peter was in secondary school in UK. Both Ceri and Simon leapt at the idea - they loved visiting the Hepworths - there was a large pile of magazines, World of Wonder and Look And Learn, piled up on a bookshelf in the sitting room and they would spend every minute possible sprawled on the floor with the pile between them.

We had an interesting time in Livingstone - it involved some work of course, but as that included a flight instead of a long car trip we had more time to walk by the Falls, as one always did, and talk over some issues.

Ready to leave Livingstone

When we picked up the children they begged to go again, much to Aileen's delight. She whispered to me that she had worried that they might be a bit bored away from home and their beloved dogs. She need not have been at all concerned. On the way home and several times after that both Ceri and Simon emphasised how wonderful it was to wake up in a morning and smell the delightful aroma of freshly baking bread.

'And she does it every day!' added Simon.

As we had decided to keep the garden layout as simple and easy to run as possible it was not long before we could think of the plot boundaries. Two hundred acres was rather large so we sold the thirty acres on the other side of the road to Valentine and Flavia Musakanya and later, the far seventy acres to Dingiswayo Banda.

White and Banda then had the unenviable task of making the fire breaks along the boundaries. All round the one hundred acres we kept had to have a four foot wide fire break, once it was made it was fairly simple to keep cleared.

All through the dry season one kept an eye open for signs of a bush fire on the horizon. June to November - or whenever the rains came - was a particularly trying time, we would drive home watching the skyline for tell-tale smoke and try to estimate whether it was near enough to be of concern. Or we would go out onto the roof at night and see a red glow and watch its progress. During our first year we kept our fingers crossed until the firebreaks were made and then felt a bit safer although we knew a strong wind could soon blow sparks across if the fire came our way.

One day I had invited Sister Georgina - of the immaculate white habit - and Sister Caratate to tea. At lunchtime I checked with Joseph about tea and then did a hurried inspection for dust thinking of Sister Georgina. All was perfect.

Back down to the Convent at three o'clock to collect the good ladies and we drove home chatting of this and that, Ceri and Simon in the back of the van adding their bits. Halfway along Leopards Hill Road I looked ahead and saw smoke drifting above the trees and prayed it was further away than it looked. But it wasn't.

I drove up a winding drive between charred and blackened earth where faint wisps of smoke still lingered. Banda, White and Joseph were walking sadly and wearily back toward the house having failed to stop the fire from reaching the garden. This was all bad enough but then to go into the house where everything was covered with a fine layer of black ash was the last straw. Poor Sister Georgina tried to sit down but her heart was sorely troubled.

This particular fire had only come across part of the plot to the garden but a couple of years later we had a much worse fire. John Jellis and his wife farmed the land behind us and every year they had a big fire. I think they intended to burn a fire break round their farm but each time it seemed to get out of hand and spread - often in our direction. One day we saw the tell-tale signs of smoke and smelt it on the wind, which meant it was blowing nicely in our direction. Fortunately all the men were around and Andrew called them to get ready with spades and brooms and branches then they walked across the plot to see from which direction it was coming.

It came from behind and then it came from the side, it leapt the fire break in several places at once and the strong wind fanned the flames rapidly through the dry grass towards the house. Andrew and Banda and White and Joseph were here, there and everywhere trying to beat it back. The children and I had the hosepipes connected up hoping to get as much of the edge of the garden as wet as possible. There was no danger of the house being burnt of course but the garden would be spoilt, the orchard was at risk and the whole area would be a black waste until the rains - some two or three months hence.

It was impossible of course in that wind to hold it back and the flames reached right to the grass fences of the rabbits and chickens runs. The smoke was thick and pungent and as I beat the flames with a leafy branch I thought I would be smelling like a smoked kipper. We were all filthy and smelly by the time the last flames were out and in an angry mood with Jellis, who never seemed to organise his burning off properly.

Bush fires are a very sore point with many people in the dry season. Apart from the land being so disfigured until the rainy season, the damage to wild life is great. Farmers sometimes clear land by burning it off, this was known as the chitemene system and was being discouraged by the Ministry of Agriculture.

Ruth Weiss had departed some time ago from Zambia to work in England but reappeared from time to time to cover conferences etc and we were always happy to see her. In between we kept up an intermittent and casual correspondence.

One evening we went to a cocktail party and were pleased to see Andrew and Danae Sardanis but not as pleased as they were to see us.

'Are you collecting Sacha tomorrow morning?' asked Andrew Sardanis.

'Sacha?'

'Sacha Weiss. You did not pick him up from the airport and luckily we happened to be there and so we took him home. He is asleep with our two boys at the moment, he says he is to stay with you until Ruth arrives.'

'Arrives from where? and when?'

Andrew and Danae did not know any more than we. Sacha had arrived at Lusaka airport expecting to stay with us, Ruth was travelling and would be with us later. She was travelling by train and would reach Lusaka 'some time'. This was all Sacha could tell us. He said Ruth had written us and that he thought she was on a train in Angola - or on a train going to Angola - but when, or where, or why, or how he could not remember - and did not seem overly interested. A spare bed was fitted into Simon's room and the two boys got on together very well. Sacha was in boarding school in England and was a mine of information for Simon on the customs of English school boys. Ceri was not so impressed.

'Mum, will you stop those boys?' she demanded.

'Stop them doing what?'

'Sitting outside the bathroom door and singing.'

'Singing what?'

'Oo ah, she's lost her bra.

Doesn't know where her knickers are.'

Simon and Sacha took themselves off on their own excursions in the bush with the dogs and kept themselves out of our hair much of the time and we awaited news of Ruth. She appeared at last having trained through Zaire and Angola on the Bangweulu railway; she had travelled in some style in the General Manager's private coach and now prepared to closet herself in our spare room and knock out her report on her battered old portable. She and Sacha greeted each other with casual affection; I remarked that his arrival had been rather unexpected and as the days passed had passed into weeks we had wondered whether she had missed the train.

'I did write', said Ruth. 'Didn't I? I'm sure I did ... perhaps it's in the post somewhere ... I thought as you didn't reply it was quite all right. It is lovely to see you all!'

Ruth Weiss

Even in the short rainy season in Zambia one usually wakes to a bright and glowing sunrise, the world is born again, fresh and new. It is impossible to sleep on late; the clear fresh brightness beckons you outdoors. The air is fresh and cool with the promise of heat to come, birds call across the wide stillness, the heavens arch wide and high, you are living on top of the world, close to God and feeling great oneself - able to face the world and its problems with a sure confidence. All this before six o'clock!

Ceri and Simon also woke early at weekends and would be outdoors with the dogs long before breakfast. They would always walk down to the dam and then usually on to the east boundary, walking over the hill to the back of the plot. It was not long before they discovered that if they allowed the dogs to make enough disturbance Don Fluck's Great Danes and Basset Hounds would join in with gusto. From that it was a short step to a pre breakfast snack with Don and Phil Howard, who lived in a cottage on Don's plot, before returning home for another enormous breakfast with us.

Extra visitors at breakfast time were the peacocks who would wander into the courtyard and peer in through the dining room doors. Like much of our livestock, they had an insatiable curiosity.

Peacocks in the courtyard hoping to join in breakfast

About this time Alan Drysdall was told his contract would not be renewed. Alan was a geologist and had been working in Zambia for over twenty years. He and his wife Ciss (Cecile) were very depressed but managed to be fairly philosophical about the turn of the tide. We saw them more frequently as farewell parties and dinners were given. One in particular I remember at the Dutch Ambassador's, he was a keen philatelist like Alan and when we reached the coffee stage he made a short speech and presented Alan with a small box. Alan gasped when he opened it and stammered his thanks. It was a rare stamp he had long coveted. We laughed as we watched Alan, red faced, trying to find words to express his appreciation, although his face was expressive enough. At last Andrew and James Mapoma asked if he were going to sit there gazing in bliss for the rest of the evening or would we be allowed to see this magnificent gift? Reluctantly Alan nodded and passed the stamp, held delicately in his fingertips by the edges towards Andrew.

To my shock and embarrassment Andrew grasped the stamp firmly between his finger and thumb and held it towards James who likewise grasped it firmly. Talk about ham fisted! I glanced at Alan and the Ambassador, who were both holding their breaths with pained expressions watching the stamp's progress around the table. Fortunately it soon arrived back at the head of the table whereupon both men drew relieved breaths and the stamp was reverently placed back in its box.

Alan and Ciss owned a magnificent Great Dane - bred by our neighbour Don Fluck - and were worried about finding a good home for him, we already had two cross Great Danes, Peter and Paula, but as there was more than enough room on one hundred acres it did not take us more than a moment to consider before we offered Ben a home. The Drysdalls accepted but thought they should bring him out to meet our dogs, so one weekend they arrived and we stood around the car as the huge dog unfolded itself from the rear door. Peter and Paula, who had been offering a cautious welcome through the car window took a step back and gazed up. It was the first time they had met a larger dog and on their own territory, but there was no problem. Great Danes are renowned for their gentleness and it was not long before all three were amiably ambling down to the dam. But whereas our crossbred mongrels were sturdily bounding to and fro snuffling in the grasses, pouncing on unwary grasshoppers and digging furiously at the scent of mice, Ben high stepped daintily along, glancing down his nose at their activities.

This proved to be his attitude later when he moved in. He would accompany us on walks and took a tolerant view of their activities but he never dirtied his nose grubbing in the undergrowth and never once muddied his paws in the dam. On the hottest October days he would watch Peter and Paula plunge into the cool waters but we could never persuade him to even dabble his toes at the edge. He also had very strong views on how long a walk should be. Down to the dam was fine, a pleasant stroll. But then one returned straight back home, whenever we set off along the stream bed to walk along the boundary, Ben turned his back on us and set off back up the avenue. No matter how we called and whistled and cajoled, he would cast sad glances over his shoulder and turn his long nose even more firmly towards the house.

While Peter and Paula hunted vigorously among the grasses they never caught more than a smell of mice, lizards or mice. I think if they had actually closed a mouth about some small creature they would not have known what to do next. Probably they had copied the habits of their mother Candy, who had survived alone in the bush for a time.

Our closest contact with wild life on any notable scale was late one night when Andrew came home and found a hyena sitting in the garage. He braked hurriedly instead of driving straight in and stared at the hyena sitting unconcernedly in the head lights. He could see the three dogs gazing round the far corner of the house - they usually rushed up to greet the car. He called and he whistled but they showed an understandable reluctance to come forward. Or so I think. Andrew did not share this view, he opened the car door and stepped out onto the drive to insist they 'see off' the intruder. The dogs raced forwards and leaping past him they jumped into the car and from the back seat barked furiously.

The hyena yawned. It eventually trotted off into the night when Andrew threw handfuls of gravel. He drove into the garage and parked, whereupon the three dogs clambered out of the car and from the safety of the garage, barked loud and long.

The cats in comparison were mighty hunters. Simon's big grey cat, still known as Big Puss, and Wong competed as to who could carry home the most lizards and mice and voles. Usually they played callously with these in the courtyard and when Ceri and Simon rescued the small creatures neither cat appeared unduly perturbed but would sit nonchalantly washing a shoulder before stalking off to lie in the shade of the bougainvillea. Wong later developed grander ambitions and began leaping into the rabbit enclosure. Although we raised the height of the rabbit fence to six feet and although White endeavoured to make sure all the rabbits were locked in their house for the night, we continued to find the occasional rabbit in the courtyard. Sometimes they were half grown and one could only marvel at how she had not only killed it but also leapt a six foot fence with it in her mouth. Sadly it was all a precursor of what was to come. Wong went wild and would go missing for increasingly long periods.

Ceri with Wong   *Simon with Big Puss*

The rabbits and chickens gave us few problems, living contentedly in their well fenced runs. The ducks had been moved down the plot towards the dam. Andrew and Banda and White constructed two large ponds near the lower borehole and they splashed and dabbled throughout the day. At first we kept the geese there too but later began letting them out and shepherding them slowly towards the dam. There they would spend the day swimming and swearing until White or Banda would shepherd them back again to be locked up with the ducks for the night.

For the peacocks and guinea fowl we constructed an enormous aviary at the side of the drive in the shade of some trees and there they managed to coexist quite amicably. It must have proved a bit of a bore for the peacocks however as they took to escaping and wandering about the verandahs and courtyard, sweeping the ground with their magnificent tails and posing on the corners of the roof, their piercing shrieks continuing to unnerve first time visitors.

Unknowingly we must have built the house smack across the traditional mating route of scorpions. What other explanation was there for the fact that the beginning of every rainy season found processions of scorpions intent on crossing from A to B in a direct line. The appearance of a large and very solid house in no way deterred them and they would spend many hours trying to fight their way through the front door. And if ever they managed to scramble up and under the door they would head straight across the hall and dining room and scrabble against the door of the courtyard. One particular night when Andrew was away (isn't that a familiar phrase?) I had a guard who, finding he could not doze on the front verandah without a series of scorpions trying, as he thought, to establish a closer relationship, hammered on the door each time one appeared. It was kill the guard or the scorpion so I regretfully disposed of fifteen of these large and fascinating creatures. As each one would have been two or three inches long I suppose he did feel somewhat threatened.

More worrying was the large and hooded cobra we knew lived somewhere near the house. When we first moved into the house Simon had arrived in our bedroom early one Sunday morning with a large puff adder, which Banda had just killed near the chicken run. As puff adders are one of the deadliest snakes in Zambia, one tossed on the bed early in the morning was guaranteed to shake any sleep completely from the system. Puff adders have not only a strong venom, they are also one of the few snakes which will not move away at man's approach. And we saw no more puff adders on the plot. But we did know about the cobra.

Simon appeared in the dining room one afternoon - appeared being a very accurate description. One minute I was peacefully cutting out some material on the dining table and the next minute Simon had appeared at my side without apparently opening the door. He was wide eyed and clearly very shaken.

'I was just walking round the side of the fish pond,' he said, ' when a HUGE snake stood up in front of me - its head all wide and its mouth wide open, oh how it hisssssssed!'

Simon had fled across the grass and courtyard and into the dining room in one leap - or so it felt, he said. The snake had presumably fled in the opposite direction, although Simon said it had stayed reared up and hissing as he flew.

Banda and White searched the grounds but could find no trace, they thought it had been to the fish pond to drink.

'It will come back for eggs,' said White. 'Now we have maningi trouble with the chickens. These snakes, maningi trouble.'

From Simon's description we knew we were looking for a hooded cobra and all I could do was to warn the men to be on their guard. Probably unnecessarily, as they were more likely to be aware of the dangers than me.

It was a wily old snake though, giving us no more trouble for over a year. It must have returned to the hen run from time to time to take eggs until one evening when White went to shut the hens up for the night. In spite of a regular routine the dozy birds never got used to the idea and always had to be ushered into their shed. This particular evening they were more than usually recalcitrant, retreating from the shed door with squawks and flapping wings until White lost patience - and all caution.

He approached the shed door and bent down to peer inside to see which hen was causing the trouble.

The cobra, poised just inside the door, spat straight into his eyes. Fortunately both Andrew and I were both at home that evening when Joseph hurried in with the news. White was standing by the kitchen door as we ran through. I grabbed him by the shirt and pushed him, eyes still tight shut, on to a kitchen chair and pulled packets of milk from the fridge.

'Open your eyes,' I shouted and as he did so I poured the contents of the first packet into his eyes, praying I was doing the right thing. I was positive I had read that one should wash out the eyes with milk - was Long Life milk just as good? It was all we had in Zambia. As White spluttered and gasped, I cut open another packet and sticking my fingers in his eyes to wedge them open, I poured in another pint. Meanwhile Andrew was getting his keys and reversing the car out on to the drive. Joseph poured another pint of milk on to a clean tea towel and with this sopping compress over White's eyes Andrew drove him to the hospital where he was detained overnight. We picked him up the next day, he complaining bitterly over the treatment.

'The hospital, she no good,' he said shaking his head. 'They just give me water. No milk. Not like Madam. The Hospital she not have milk. It is no good. She wash eyes with water.'

Milk or no milk, Long Life or not, White's eyes were saved.

And the cobra was still at large.

With the animals and birds all properly housed and fenced we had time to reconsider the orchard. Until 1970 we had been able to buy fruit from South Africa and now that it was literally forbidden fruit I really missed apples. One also missed the peaches and plums and grapes, but it was the loss of apples which grieved me most. None of these fruits could be grown in Zambia of course, the altitude was a problem. Or so we had always been told. But then I found that one could order fruit trees from South Africa and acting upon a whim I persuaded Andrew to order some apple trees. They duly arrived and were carefully planted and if there were any truth in the tale that talked to plants flourish, our apple trees should have been the finest on the Continent. They were not. BUT they did produce apples. We watched with bated breath as the first fragile apple blossoms gave way to tiny fruit and we nipped off the extra small ones with great reluctance. And at last we were rewarded with apples, round and rosy and firm. We had almost as much pleasure from showing off these fruits as we had in eating them. Close upon the apples came peach and nectarine trees from Israel, these too flourished. I suppose the fruit did not compare with that in Israel and South Africa but for people who had no other supply, they were the most delicious fruits.

Life on Leopards Hill Road was more enjoyable than we had ever imagined. There was always something to do and the space to try out our new ideas and land to wander on for peace and privacy. No matter how trying the day, it was always possible to whistle the dogs and walk off in solitude, broken only by the whisper of wind in the grasses, the intermittent hum of insects, the snapping and cracking of seed pods underfoot and the pant of dogs as they foraged ahead.

In a matter of minutes one could be away from even the house and be as alone as the first man on earth. In the dry season tall sun bleached grasses rustled beside one and the sun beat down from a sky so blue and hot it seemed white and glowing. There would be silence all around as life suspended itself until the cool of the evening. In the rainy season one could walk between tall green grasses bursting with juice. The cloying rich smell of wet soil was overpowering.

Sometimes I would set off when the sky was dark and purple, then have to wait beneath a tree when the first heavy drops fell, slowly at first, loud in the stillness. Then faster they fell, leaves and grasses bending beneath the onslaught and the soil, unable to soak it all up fast enough, grew pools of muddy water. Then the storm would be over as fast as it had come and the sun would be hot on my back as I set off again. Showers of sparkling raindrops fell over the dogs backs as they brushed through the grass and shrubs and the birds would call again.

These solitary walks eased my mind. In spite of all the peace on the plot there was no getting away from the fact that Andrew was still a Minister and as such our lives were not as private as I would have liked. And there were interferences I just could not tolerate.

One day I had come home for lunch to find Joseph in a very grim mood. Lunch was served in an icy silence and unable to bear it I did not wait for coffee to be served in the lounge.

'What is on your mind?' I asked as I walked into the kitchen.

'It's not all right.'

'What isn't?'

'You know me Madam, when something is not all right, I say so.'

'Yes, you do,' I agreed. 'So how about telling me what is NOT all right?'

'You know me Madam, I come to work for you and I work for you and you pay me and that is right but this is not all right.'

I wondered if he thought he was due a rise and cast my mind back frantically trying to remember dates, surely he had not been with us a year?

'Yes, you work for me. And very nicely too.' I agreed. 'And I pay you, I pay you good money, so what is NOT all right?'

'This money, she is not all right!'

It must be a moment of deep concern for Joseph's English to desert him so.

'What is NOT all right with the money I pay you?' I asked as patiently as I could.

'This money, it is not all right.'

'What do you mean it is not all right? It's not even the end of the month yet and so I have not paid you for this month. So what is not ALL RIGHT?'

He put a long thin slip of paper down on the worktop and stood back, arm outstretched.

'This is not all right.'

I picked up the piece of paper but did not recognise it, nor did the figures mean anything at all.

'What is this all about?' I asked, feeling as though I were groping my way through a particularly dense maze.

Joseph stared at me as though I were witless.

'My money from the Government, she is not all right (dear God, if I heard the words 'she not all right' once more I would scream) I come to work for you Madam and you pay me and that is all right (silent scream) but now the Government she pay me and she is not all right (oh God !) Me, I am not happy.'

That makes two of us, I thought.

'What do you mean, the Government pays you? I PAY YOU.'

Joseph slapped his hand on the paper.

'The Government she pay me and it is not all right.'

I picked up the paper once more, feeling like a child just learning to read.

Joseph Chambuluka … cook … kwacha …

'Who gave you this?' I asked.

Joseph drew a deep breath.

'The Government,' he repeated. 'The Government she pay me now. The driver came this morning in Government car from the Ministry and he call me and Banda and say the Government pay servants for Ministers. And this, this is my money from the Government. It is not all right me, I am getting more money from you and I say No, the Madam pay me and he says No, the Government pays me. And he says the Government pay this much money for a cook and he says Banda is a garden boy and he is not happy because he work in the house in the morning and you pay him same as house servant. And White I call him but the man from the Government say they only pay me as cook and Banda as garden boy and White they do not pay at all and he is not happy . It is not all right.'

Dear God, it was not all right, I agreed. Not all right was an understatement.

Joseph was quite impressed with my rage and began to believe that I had not known what was going on. Banda and White were duly lined up in the kitchen and it was impressed upon them that they must not take money from anyone but me.

'There will be trouble,' warned Joseph. 'I had to sign the book.'

'You do not sign any books. You do not even let them come into the house. I will try to stop it all now but if they come again, say No.'

All three nodded but still looked worried.

Andrew was called upon to explain the situation before his foot was barely across the threshold. Apparently 'it had been decided' that Ministers would receive a 'servants allowance'. I suppose it was another of the perks of the position and one of the tax fiddles which abound in this world of ours.

I was not particularly interested. As far as I was concerned we employed the men, we had done so before the 'promotion' and we would continue to do so if the situation changed. The men worked for us and we would pay them - and certainly not the low wages the Government had deemed fit. Andrew seemed rather surprised at my anger but agreed that he would have the arrangement cancelled. The men accepted the news but it was not until the next pay day came and went normally that they relaxed. Apart from my objection I think they would have felt a personal bond would have been broken.

It may seem a trivial thing but somehow it typified the part of my life which I could not and would not accept.

Another, less vociferous disagreement, came when 'They' realised that there was no Ministerial flagpole outside our house, Andrew was told that the omission would be rectified as soon as possible. We turned it down and again caused something of a stir. It was in no way disrespect for the Zambian flag. It was merely that our home was our home and not an official residence and we resented any attempt to change that.

I also found it difficult to accept that we were talked about but had no way of answering back or justifying ourselves.

Alfred and May Sharpe came out one weekend for lunch and we chatted on in the usual relaxing way, ending up on the roof for coffee. As we sat there watching the wind blow through the proteas, Alfred chuckled,

'I was up on the Copperbelt earlier in the week,' he said. 'and one evening I was at a friend's house for meal, there were about ten of us and you know how you get talking about this and that? One particular chap started on about the extravagant living of those in high places. He said things were scandalous in Lusaka. He said, 'Look at that chap Kashita, one of the Ministers, he has a huge mansion, even has a swimming pool on the roof of his house! Talk about ostentation!!' I blinked and said, 'Hold on, you must have got the name wrong'. But he was insistent that Kashita had a swimming pool on the roof of his house and when I said he was wrong, that I knew you personally and had been to your house many times and you had no pool at all - let alone on the roof - he just laughed and said, 'These chaps are clever, man, and the ruin of the country.'

We all laughed but at the same time I felt sad that we could be talked about and so wrongly.

What else was being said? There was always gossip about the apamwamba (the elite), stories circulated about how much wealth or privilege they had. It was often exaggerated or even untrue but still the stories circulated.

It was useless to speculate. Again and again I was thankful for the classroom where I could work and forget outside pressures. I was glad we had a plot where we could walk and lose ourselves in the peace and tranquillity of the bush.

Recently I read an interesting article (Ben Crow, Mary Thorpe?) which explained that when the Zambian Government nationalised the copper mines in 1969 it did not possess the knowledge necessary to run the mines and so therefore negotiated a management contract with the TNCs (Transnational Corporation) – the previous owners Anglo American and Amax, whereby they continued to supply all managerial, financial, commercial, technical and other services needed to run the mines. In return they got 0.75% of sales proceeds and 2% of consolidated profits – before income tax but after mineral tax. They also continued to market the copper. But the contract contained NO legal obligations to train and employ Zambian personnel nor to use profits to diversify into other industries.

This kind of arrangement is often unsatisfactory since it's expensive and does not give control over most vital decisions. In Zambia the Government agreed to pay a total of US$296.5million in foreign currency for shares it nationalised. Payment was to be out of future profits on the Gov. 51% share. Therefore the Gov. ability to pay depended on the mines being run at a profit – which depended to a considerable extent on a management which it didn't control. After 5 years the Gov. concluded it didn't have enough say in the development of copper production and the management contract was terminated on 15 November 1974 at enormous cost, at a time when the industry was facing difficulties.

It could be asked why not total nationalisation and the answer may be antagonism and loss of markets.

Whatever ... it had a marked effect on Zambia.

I had now been in Zambia for more than twelve years, they had gone so quickly and life had been so full that I had no time to be homesick. True enough I did have nostalgia for an English Spring or a crisp frosty day. I often met people from Europe who sighed for Christmas 'back home' and while I understood their longing, I had no strong yearning to spend Christmas in UK.

Once in a while I thought it would be fun to give the children a taste of an English Christmas but as Andrew so practically pointed out, going to England just for Christmas would be an impossibly expensive exercise and who would want to spend a full 'leave' of two months in England in the winter?

I always had fun at school when the small children prepared for Christmas, it was also the end of the school year and so the festivities took on a special air of excitement. The end of the year drew to a close with an academic flourish of tests and then the grand round of parties and Carol Concerts began. Assembly in the last week was always a nativity play and later we would pull the Hall curtains across and sit in candlelight as we sang all the favourite carols. Small presents were made for parents and each classroom would be bright with trees and decorations. We would tour each other's classrooms to admire displays, all the girls in an increasing state of excitement.

On the last two days the rooms were stripped bare and we would clean and polish until everything was ready for the new school year in January.

Term ended in early December and then we were free to prepare for Christmas at home. I still had the childish enjoyment in shopping for Andrew and the children. In addition of course, I always prepared boxes for the servants and their families. It would begin with a practical collection of groceries and then I would search for shirts for the men, a length of citenge for their wives. I had to list their children and find each one a shirt or a dress and a small toy, packets of sweets and balloons.

Christmas is a time for spoiling children and I always enjoyed filling their boxes.

Ceri and Simon were full of excitement as they did their secret purchases and wrapped and rewrapped them in their rooms. Remembering my own childhood we never put up tree or decorations until Christmas Eve when Ceri and Simon would hover round the breakfast table asking if they could start blowing up the balloons. They would go out with Andrew to choose and supervise the digging up of a tree - what fun it was to choose a tree from one's own garden.

Digging up the first Christmas tree with Banda and White

Andrew would usually have some last minute jobs to do at the office and I usually tried to make an early trip to the market for last minute choices of fruit and veg.

I did feel at home in Zambia but each year it struck me afresh, how strange to be preparing it all in bright sunshine. Christmas carols and silver tinsel on the floor, brightly wrapped parcels piling up by the tree, huge mounds of food being prepared in the kitchen – and sunshine pouring through the windows. The rainy season had begun of course so sometimes we had a grey drizzly day - but it wouldn't last for long, the everlasting sun would break through.

In the early years we had the Proctors to share the day with, then the Hepworths came to live in Lusaka and we would have them out for the day. Don Fluck came from next door, sometimes bringing Phil Howard with him.

In addition to the Christmas festivities, the whole period abounded with parties given by and for and with Uncle Tom Cobleigh and all. In Zambia of course, the influence of the Scottish missionaries had been so strong that there was an even greater celebration for the New Year. This was one of Andrew's theories. New Year always seems to be such a sad time to me, the end of yet another year and I am full of regrets for all the things I have not achieved. Left alone, I would head for bed with a book. But Andrew was horrified when I voiced my thoughts and off we would go, to see another old year out and another new year in.

And I would stand among the cheering laughing crowd, feeling very much the odd one out.

A YEAR OF EVENTS 1975

Perhaps in January 1975 President Kaunda had had similar dismal thoughts for he did not mince his words at the Opening of Parliament; he lashed out at the people in key positions for having no sense of responsibility in their work.

A new year and we were off to a fine start. The Opening of Parliament was on 17 January and President Kaunda had strong words to say. According to a newspaper report he 'lashed those in key positions for having no sense of responsibility in their work'. I sometimes wished Andrew did not have such a sense of responsibility - wished he could leave Government and have an easier work load. I was to remember those thoughts before the month was out.

To me it was always a relief when the New Year was safely over and one could just get on with the year itself. Life would return to normal and I would begin to plan for my new academic year and new class. Quite often I would go into school a few days before term began to prepare my room and equipment. I would be expecting forty 5 year old girls, each year the number of white faces decreased. Not that it made much difference, I was beginning to forget what it had been like to have a majority of white faces. Most of the Zambian children arrived at school with at least a smattering of English, many were now attending nursery schools and settled in easily.

However, Christmas was over and so was New Year. I had been into school to prepare my work and term began.

The first day seemed to go very slowly. Mothers - and a very few fathers - arrived with their small daughters. Forty little girls with their faces scrubbed and shining, hair tightly braided or plaited. Forty new and crisp uniform dresses with neat white socks at the end of chubby pink or brown legs each little girl clutching a new small cardboard suitcase which held a biscuit or sandwich for playtime and a long new pencil. And, in the case of the Zambian girls in particular, each little girl stiff with pride at entering at last, 'The Convent School'. Although schools had been integrated now for some time, I remember the emotional feeling when African parents brought in their daughters on their first day.

There were no long farewells. Parents would disappear promptly and the day would begin. The day started at 7.30am and it seemed a long time until 9.30 when I would take my class out into the fenced 'infants playground' for a short break. On the first day they would walk soberly round the area and peep in the Wendy House, climb tentatively on the lowest bars of the climbing frames and stand clutching the fence, gazing across to the senior school.

Back into the classroom where we would continue working until the school break at 10am when both schools poured out and older sisters would come across to hang over the fence to chat to the little ones.

I always took the first week playtime duty so that none of my brood would feel nervous if I disappeared. I would sit on the verandah with a tray of tea and biscuits and relax. Back into the classroom at 10.30 and work on till 12 - always a slow day as the girls were finding their feet, not helped by some well-meaning parents instructing them they were not to talk in school!

But midday came at last and I took them out into their fenced playground clutching their small suitcases, where they waited to be collected. Some parents came early but many children had to wait until older classes finished. Again I would sit on the verandah watching as each girl was collected. At about 12.45 I was free to go home, Ceri would have finished too and we would go to collect Simon if Andrew were away.

This particular day I did not return to school in the afternoon but stayed on at home to prepare some work. Ceri and Simon had no afternoon activities on the first day.

To my complete astonishment Andrew walked into the house halfway through the afternoon.

He threw his briefcase across the study into his chair. I stared at him.

'I've been axed.'

I think the usual description is that there is a nightmare quality to the conversation. It is a very neat way of putting it.

Andrew had gone into work as usual. He had been axed. The President had fired him. He was out of office. The President had appointed him. The President could drop him.

It was as simple as that.

'But why?'

No official explanation had been or would be given.

Andrew told me why he believed the President had taken such a step.

But no official explanation had been - or would ever be given.

My reaction was a mixture of anger that a man's career and character could be tossed to and fro willy nilly - and also relief that Andrew was now out of office - but also frustration that we could not give any public statement. At least, Andrew would not. Therefore I did not repeat any of what he had told me. Suffice it to say that one's suspicions of corruption/bribery/petulance were more than confirmed.

We spent the afternoon walking round the house and round the plot. Andrew had no immediate plans or any coherent thoughts. Late afternoon a car rolled up the drive and out climbed a man I did not recognise. Andrew introduced him, a Member of Parliament. I thought I should withdraw. But before I could walk back into the house another car appeared at the bottom of the drive and as it was halfway up, another and then another.

The news of Andrew's dismissal had been announced in Parliament during the afternoon and as I watched more and more cars rolled up the drive with one after another solemn faced MP greeting Andrew and then joining the crowd in the sitting room. Joseph began serving tea and Banda was brought in to wash and rewash cups but time was getting on. I went in once or twice to walk round, bend the knee and shake hands in Zambian style.

Now I had more than thirty MP's sitting around, for how long?

I got the van out, squeezed through the ranks of cars and drove down to Kabulonga Supermarket where I hurriedly bought a large amount of steak and rushed back to Joseph.

'Some sort of stew with vegetables will be the quickest,' he said and set to work.

Andrew appeared at my elbow.

'I think that is the Nigerian Ambassador's car coming up the drive,' he said. 'I don't want him coming in the house and finding so many MP's here. He might think we are plotting something. Don't bring him into the sitting room' and he disappeared.

I went out onto the drive as the car drew to a halt and the Nigerian Ambassador climbed out. I had already unlocked the outside door into Andrew's study and, greeting the Ambassador with a bright smile, I ushered him through the parked cars and into the study.

Joseph appeared with refreshments and together we pressed the Ambassador into an arm chair.

'I have just heard the news ... how serious ... I see you have visitors ...' he began.

'Yes, yes,' I agreed vaguely. 'I'll call Andrew, I think he is just talking with an old friend.'

'Don't trouble yourself, I could find him,' said the Ambassador, trying to stand up.

Joseph pressed a glass in his hand and I kept talking - he would have known I was prevaricating - but I felt quite witless, events were moving rather fast. He clearly was not going to leave, so making an excuse I went to find Andrew in the crowd. He didn't want to see him - politically awkward, he said.

'He seems to have taken root in your chair. Just stick your head in and tell him you're busy, he won't take it from me.'

Another car braked outside and I went out to greet the newcomer, seeing Andrew go through towards the study. I don't remember all the people who came that evening but I think their appearance did much to both soothe and cheer Andrew. I went back to greet later arrivals while Andrew diverted the Ambassador, who soon realised he should leave and then went to check on Joseph's progress. He and Banda were producing vast quantities of stew and rice and nsima, seemingly too busy to comment on the turn of events, though I knew Joseph's eagle eyes were missing nothing and each time he served a drink he recognised another notable politician. In a low undertone he passed on information to Banda as they passed in the kitchen.

Andrew waved goodbye to the Ambassador and returned to the house. Ceri and Simon were watching TV in the TV room and trying to understand what was happening. As both Andrew and I treated it lightly in front of them, they seemed to take it as part of the adult world oddities and took more interest in their favourite programme.

Andrew sat with his friends and listened for a long time. But throughout he was adamant that he would make no public statement until the President had given a reason for his dismissal. The President never did.

He did manage to refer to sacking Andrew - but there was no specific explanation. 'He (KK) *did not like taking disciplinary measures against anybody but if the performance of an individual jeopardised the interests of the masses, he had no alternative. He described Kashita as a brilliant young man whose career had sadly been abruptly curtailed ... He did not like taking disciplinary measures but when somebody makes a mistake by default or delegation, which will make others suffer, his duty was clear'.*

Next morning it was strange to be going to work while Andrew was still at home; he said he would potter in the garden and think things over. Once at school I was back in another world, far away from politics. The morning started off feeling pretty much as usual until it came to the mid-morning break. The children were out at play, the other teachers had headed for the staffroom, - somehow they had all been very preoccupied and I had not really seen anyone to speak to. Now as I sat alone on the verandah I felt all the unhappiness from the previous night return. I wondered whether the other teachers were avoiding me or was I getting super sensitive? Normally someone managed to pass the time of day before now. Just then the door at the end of the verandah opened and Sister de Angelis appeared. She walked along and sat beside me on the bench.

'I just thought you might like a bit of company,' she said, staring straight ahead and looking pink and embarrassed. 'We heard some news on the radio and I don't know what it's all about but I thought you might feel a bit lonely just now.'

We watched the girls playing on the grass and listened to their shrill voices. We drank our tea and said how well the new children had settled down.

As the bell rang for the end of break she stood up and walking down the verandah said,

'I'll pop across tomorrow and have a cup of tea with you.'

The friendly thought helped me through the next session until midday. Then I had to brace myself to the idea of going out with my class and knowing that all the parents would have heard the news and would have been speculating all day, goodness knows what rumours were abounding in town.

I stood under the cassia trees watching the girls being collected one by one. No parent greeted me, but many stood around chatting together, no one glanced my way. A car drew up further along the parking area and out got May Sharpe. She was early to collect her daughters I reflected absentmindedly. May began to walk briskly in my direction, from several yards away she called out loudly.

'Hi there, June! How are you? And what's all this nonsense about Andrew being axed? What's going on?'

She flung her arms round me and continued in a loud voice.

'Alfred and I couldn't believe it when we heard the news! And as for what is in the papers! None of it is true is it? What does the President think he is doing?'

She rattled on, hardly pausing for breath, a few people were now staring openly at us and several gave me uneasy smiles and nods; they began to drift to their cars.

May stood there chatting cheerfully all the time and greeting anyone else she recognised in a bright way. Then lowering her voice she muttered,

'I am sorry. What a mess. Are you both all right? To hell with the lot of them!' and then back in her bright and breezy way she continued talking until the grounds were nearly clear of parents and girls and I was free to go home.

Real friends never change.

At that moment I had not seen the front pages of the newspaper 'KASHITA DROPPED

Mines and Industry Minister EA Kashita has been dropped from Cabinet and Parliament. A State House spokesman said last night that Mr Kashita ceased to be a nominated MP from yesterday. No reasons for the decision were given. Mr Kashita is the first Minister to be dropped since the One Party system was introduced ... Speaking from his home last night Mr Kashita confirmed he had received a letter asking him to relinquish his responsibilities as Minister of Mines and Industry and informing him that he would cease to be a Minister with immediate effect. He said reasons had been given 'but I am not prepared to discuss these...' then came a long description of his career.

The next day Wednesday 22nd January under

WHY KASHITA WAS AXED

President Kaunda said he *'did not like taking disciplinary measures against anybody but if the performance of an individual jeopardised the interests of the masses, he had no alternative. He was commenting on the dropping of former Minister EA Kashita during the swearing in ceremony of new Lands and Natural Resources and Tourism Minister James Mapoma. He described Kashita as a brilliant young man whose career had sadly been abruptly curtailed ... I do not like taking disciplinary measures but when somebody makes a mistake by default or delegation which will make others suffer, my duty is clear.'*

The President added he did not like pushing people around, but when the time came to take such necessary steps, they had to be taken for the interest of the nation. Mr Kashita was replaced by Minister of Power and transport and Works, Mr Axon Soko.

There were a few odd incidents after that.

We had sudden unannounced visits from the police, who insisted on looking round the house and interviewing our servants. We insisted on them being interviewed in the sitting room with us present. Although the questions seemed inoffensive they were delivered in a rather hectoring manner and it was all upsetting for the servants, who could not understand why they were being questioned - neither could we. Poor White had a little extra grilling when his identification papers were being scrutinised and showed he was from Malawi. Why was he here? An odd question, as so many workers in Zambia were from Malawi and always had been. It did not seem an appropriate moment to point out that the President himself had close family connections with Malawi - I seem to recall one or both of his parents originated there. Police and Army Land Rovers cruised up and down our road rather a lot in subsequent days - activity at the army camp down the road? or was someone keeping an eye on us?

It really did seem to be the latter case as we noticed helicopters were now flying over and round our plot daily. I got fed up with the noise and resented the fact that I was beginning to feel paranoid. But who could you phone and complain to? and if you complain about police and army helicopters flying around, would that sound like a guilty person? Guilty of what?

It was all so damn ridiculous.

I got fed up and every time I heard a helicopter I took to walking out on the flat roof from my bedroom and ostentatiously taking photos of the helicopters. The fact that there was no film in the camera did not matter - it gave me great satisfaction to make someone think I was taking as much interest in them as they in me.

Or were they? Why should anyone want to see what we were doing in the garden? Or did they think they might spot too many cars at the house, who was visiting a dropped Minister and why? Coincidentally the flights stopped shortly afterwards. Mission complete or were we merely boring?

Life after that was somewhat quiet. So many people avoided us for a long time. While it was understandable in the waves of rumour and counter rumour which swept the capital we also knew our real friends had not deserted us. For some time Andrew wanted to be at home while he thought things over. He had several ideas and there were approaches from several sources; he felt there was little point in making a hasty decision and while the period of non-employment had been forced upon him unexpectedly, he might as well take the opportunity to have a break.

I was very happy in Zambia but felt that it had served Andrew very badly - or at least the President had - and if he wished to leave for pastures new I would be in full agreement. However, he said that while he could take a position overseas it would then be interpreted by some as clear proof that he had been guilty of some serious fraud or piece of corruption.

'There is no way I shall let anyone think I am running away,' he declared, 'and I do not want to live anywhere else anyway.'

So it was quite clear that in Zambia we would stay. But doing what? At last he was offered a post with Pringles of Canada and we were then soon into a routine. Very shortly he formed Imbwili, a consultant engineers firm.

But things were never quite the same.

I for one never regretted the loss of a large section of social entertaining, although it was rapidly replaced by another one, nor did I miss the inevitable sycophants which surround prominent personalities. But Andrew's pride and self-esteem had taken a severe knock. I wondered how much he queried the standards and values and integrity of those he had believed in and trusted.

To my utter amazement he continued to defend Kaunda on most matters. I would have done my best to ignore the man's presence, and admitting it was not really practical, I would have done my best to look at him with as detached a viewpoint as possible. To Andrew the Government was the Government and the President was the President. While he might disagree with them, he still defended and supported them in a way I found difficult to understand. I puzzled over this from time to time and matters came to a head - for me - in August, some months later.

In August there was the Lusaka Agricultural Show which was very much the same year after year as these things usually are. Traditionally, on the day before the Show officially opened the President viewed the stands and admission to the showgrounds was by special invitation only. Andrew had some invitations and decided to go with Simon. Ceri and I had both lost interest in seeing the show every year. Andrew and Simon were back for lunch. Ceri and I listened to a description of one or two stands and then Andrew said,

'And this fellow! He didn't want to shake hands with the President! I had to say Come along now Simon, shake hands, don't be shy.'

'I wasn't shy,' muttered Simon.

'How come you wanted him to shake hands with the President?' I asked.

'We just happened to bump into the Presidential entourage as we were going round the show,' said Andrew. 'And KK greeted me! He shook my hand and we stood and talked about the show, and this chap turned all shy.'

'I wasn't shy,' repeated Simon.

I had listened with growing surprise. To this day I cannot visualise anyone walking round the showground and 'just happening to bump into the Presidential entourage'. The Presidential entourage was always of some considerable size and flap, an extremely EASY thing to avoid.

'I can't imagine why on earth you would WANT to shake hands with him,' I said, 'he would be the last person I would want to shake hands with after the way he treated you.'

But to my surprise Andrew insisted it had been an entirely accidental meeting and I had the impression he was both relieved and flattered that the President had both greeted him and chatted for a while. I was angered by what I felt was a lack of pride on Andrew's part. Years later I have wondered whether the President was acknowledging to Andrew that he appreciated Andrew not making any public statement. And Andrew was acknowledging he continued to accept the President's position of power.

This episode was most significant to me in a way I could not analyse satisfactorily. It was only years later when talking with an African man from South Africa and trying to explain to myself why Zambians could continue knowing so many details of the corruption within the country and Government and still not rise up in open anger and revolt of some form that I had some form of acceptable explanation.

The South African smiled and said,

'What you do not understand is that the African still has the village mentality. No matter how educated and developed he is, he is still a villager. In the village the elders decide and the younger men must accept. And they do so because they know that one day they will be the elders and make the decisions. Their turn will come.'

'But they are not living in a village any more,' I insisted.

'That is the point. They are not but they still do not understand that. They are so culturally indoctrinated to ACCEPT, that they can do no other.'

An interesting theory. And one which explains the position as well as most.

Well, life goes on, as they say.

And of course life went on for us.

Andrew rebuilt his career steadily and while he professed to be very happy out of Government he still followed events with a keen eye. He was in close contact with senior officials and Ministers and I wondered how much he missed being at the centre of things. I continued to smart a little on his behalf but on the whole I was happier with the new regime. And as always my mind was very preoccupied with school.

Serious changes were afoot there. The Dominican Sisters were now concerned that their numbers were dwindling and that they were thinly stretched over several Convent schools in Zambia and Rhodesia. Many of their Order had come out to Africa many years ago and most of the Sisters were now over forty years old, many were over sixty. In all the schools more and more lay staff were being employed and it was not always easy to find new teachers. This was of course, not unique to our part of the world. Convent schools in UK were experiencing the same problem.

It still came as a great shock however to learn that the closure of some schools completely was being considered. I had heard a vague rumour and then one day when chatting to the Mother Superior, Sister Amadea, I at last had some confirmation of what was to come.

We were walking across from the senior school towards the hostel where I was going to meet my class from Music. The sun was hot on our heads and I had to screw up my eyes as I looked sideways at Sister Amadea. I had been saying that Ceri no longer went riding and that she missed her friends Nicole Bruce and Paula Stone, so many people were not renewing their contracts and children's friendships were being as interrupted as ours.

Sister Amadea sighed heavily. 'It is true, Mrs Kashita, so many people are leaving. Life gets more difficult all the time. Tell me, is Ceri going away to school? Is she going to boarding school?'

'We have no plans,' I said slowly. I looked at her long face. 'Do you think we should consider it? So many people are sending their children away now.'

Sister plodded on, she always walked heavily as though burdened with many cares.

'I think you should think about it, Mrs Kashita, you should consider the possibility. I don't think we can carry on for much longer and who knows what will happen, things are changing so much and so fast.'

I stood still and stared at her.

'Do you really mean that you will not be here? Or any of the Sisters? What will happen to the school?'

Sister Amadea stood still too and looked at me with a sad smile, 'No, we shall not be here, the Sisters will have to go, we are so few now and the problems are so great. As for the school? Who knows? But I think you should consider sending Ceri and Simon to boarding school.'

She would not say any more but the little she had said made me think. I had heard rumours that the Convent might close, but why think of sending Simon away?

I began to look around me over the next few weeks and think about how many children had been sent away to boarding schools, mostly in the UK, some to South Africa and even some to Rhodesia. Some were sent because parents distrusted integrated education, some were sent because parents thought they would be returning to UK and it was better to stick to one educational system and some were sent because they had failed to obtain a secondary place. And others?

Whatever the reasons there was a gap in the seven to eighteen year olds. It was not only European children, more and more Zambian children were joining the 'educated overseas' group, again there were several reasons. Some did not get into secondary school, some had parents who were moved from diplomatic post to diplomatic post and some were sent because the parents thought 'it was better'.

While integration had gone smoothly I had to admit that parents were right to be concerned about the future of our schools. I had my first misgivings back at Jacaranda (Lusaka Infants) when the Inspector had instructed us to drop creative writing. It was quite correct for Zambia to take a long look at the education system and ask how much of this is colonial? And what is relevant to our society now?

But there had been too many hasty changes and it had been impossible to change from education for a few to education for all overnight. Primary schools had been opened and expanded without enough well trained teachers and the expansion of the secondary schools had in no way kept pace with the increase in primary schools. As it was officially admitted that it was impossible to offer secondary education to half, let alone all, the primary schools now had the task of cramming in as much as possible in seven years.

While this was a practical necessity for that particular time it was more than frustrating to see how much time was to be spent on the history of Zambia to the exclusion of the rest of the world, how much time was to be spent on Zambian culture when we also had a wealth of Indian and European culture on our doorstep. I did not want to see a continuation of a very English based curriculum but it was a pity to see it replaced by a totally Zambian one. As more and more emphasis was placed on the Zambian culture so the others retreated into themselves. I suppose it was an understandable reaction to the previous educational regime but what a pity we had lost such a chance to really consolidate a true multi-cultural society.

Looking at the schemes sent to us by the Ministry I was fascinated by the history of the Zambian tribes and the descriptions of their traditional way of life, no one could deny the wealth of fascinating wild life and natural history which surrounded us on all sides. But, what a pity that the Zambian child was to be denied even a basic general knowledge of the rest of the world. Was he not to wonder about the history and back ground of the other nationalities he would meet in his home land?

Of course rumour and counter rumour swept the country about the Governments plans for schools. One was used to this. Politics intruded in every walk of life in a way I had not been used to.

Then production units were to be introduced. Now production units as an idea were very good. It was a variation on the Young Farmers theme I suppose. Schools were to set up Production Units so that children could learn various skills and be self-supporting. As I said, in theory a very good idea.

To start off with of course, any production unit has to start somewhere and that takes money. Before one can even sow a field of maize, the tools and seed and fertiliser must come from somewhere - fortunately land was cheap and so therefore most schools were on large plots. Whether one was starting with crops or livestock, there is an initial expenditure, which had to come from school funds or special fundraising activities - all of which took time of course. The children then had to put in good amount of time and effort - as did their teachers too of course. At the end of the year or growing season there could be a worthwhile harvest which could then be used to reinvest the following year.

What happened in practice of course was that the field of maize could be stripped by thieves overnight and the whole crop lost. That is if pests, drought or floods had not accounted for it first. And who was to care for the production unit during the school vacation? Not all pupils lived near enough.

Youth Week intruded now too, for the whole of that week schools were supposed to spend their days in doing work for the community. Grand scale plans were made by the Ministry and whole schools would be sent to make bricks for a needy township - but there would not be enough brick moulds available or the water supply was inadequate ... and so the stories multiplied.

Whenever Heads of State visited Zambia or whenever the President arrived or departed on an official overseas trip, schools were sent out to line the route. It would not have been a bad idea from time to time but it became far too frequent. Nor were the times well planned, one would be directed to take one's school to line the route at X spot at 8am and there the children would be expected to stand perhaps for three or four hours, often in the hot sun at the hottest time of the year.

Then someone lent me a copy of

The Syllabus On Political Education For Pre School Children
Political education could take the following line
POLITICAL HISTORY
Singing Part A
Short political songs revealing the Africans before Independence
Listening to and learning by heart carefully chosen recorded
political songs sung during the struggle for Freedom and
Independence
Learning by heart the National Anthem
Story Telling
Short stories of how our fathers won their country from the
colonialists, songs urging for unity and hate for dissension,
songs portraying hate for foreign domination, songs in praise
of the Party and Dr KD Kaunda, songs in praise of the liberation
movement.
Singing Part B

514

.....traditional songs in praise of our armed forces for defending
Zambia against minority white regime in Southern Africa
Dancing and Plays
... mock political meetings ... short poems depicting the
supremacy of the Party ... anti imperialist themes
Look, Learn and Discuss
... guerrillas fighting white regimes in Africa ...

....
And then, incongruously
Road Safety!
How to cross roads ... how to find a pedestrian crossing ... (there
were two in the capital for example)
Humanism: quotations from President Kaunda
Listening
Specially recorded short political instructions for children ...
political instruction from various Party and Government ...

....

All this before the children entered primary school.

It appeared that Ceri and Simon could look forward to a narrowing of horizons. Tentatively I began to sound out Andrew's views. To my relief but also surprise, I found that he was very much of the same opinion. According to him, education was taking more than one retrograde step. He said that he had had a very rounded education and felt that he had a very broad based wide general knowledge.

We began to consider our children's future in a very different light. In one way we did not want to send them overseas but we were increasingly dissatisfied with the way things were going. Andrew was more in favour of boarding school than I. He had gone to board at Munali and felt that it made one very much more mature and able to cope with life. We listened to friends discussing their children's boarding schools with more interest and weighed up the pros and cons of this school and that - from a distance. I borrowed the Public Schools Year Book from the library and when we had to make a short trip to UK, we went to visit a few schools. They looked so very Spartan and my heart sank at the thought of Ceri and Simon being so very far from home. Actually visiting one or two schools was bringing it home to me what a step we were contemplating.

An added factor was the introduction of the Zambia National Youth Service. Again as an idea, it was good. But again, in the implementation things went sadly wrong. As the population of Zambia was increasing at so fast a pace, the number of school 'drop outs' was increasing at an alarming rate. More children were surviving, more were entering primary school and so consequently far more were being thrown out onto the streets with a mere smattering of education, which did not qualify them for a serious job of work but which made them dissatisfied with the prospect of living at subsistence level in the village - not to mention the fact that so many youngsters now had very little direct contact with village life.

In August Kaunda had yet another announcement to make on Youth Day - all form 5 school leavers were to go for National Service Training for twenty months as from the next year.

' ... *to make rural reconstruction programmes succeed, the Party and Government were going to create an orientation programme designed to fuse mental with physical energy as envisaged in the policy on the development of youth ... the youth must experience the practical problems of development and the general life in the countryside and create a well prepared security conscious group of young men and women to defend the Zambian nation ... national service would be a pre-requisite for admission to university ...'*

The jargon was quite catching.

At a Youth Day gathering by the Statue of Liberty, Grey Zulu announced '... *the youth movement is to be streamlined into an integrative force for social and economic development'.*

Zambia would be a much better place for us all if they could quit the jargon and speeches and get their act together, I thought, but did not say.

What point a rural programme if one knew that Kaunda had visited a rural reconstruction camp at Lukulu and found a heap of maize sent for famine relief in 1971 rotting on the ground

516

because it was not distributed by Namboard?

Perhaps it was with this in mind that we next heard that the Army was 'to spearhead the food drive'.

There was a lot of spearheading around.

I hoped it would not go the same way as the spearheading of the taxi service. At this time Zamcabs were ordered off the roads and all managers, supervisors and cashiers were sacked.

Rumours abounded. Aaron Milner was rumoured to have sent cash out of the country but, as he said, 'Where would I get all those millions?', like many people we ignored the rumours ... but they have a way of catching up with you ... even a year later.

What are we to do with the large numbers of teenagers wandering the streets of the cities and towns unfitted for one thing or another? Answer : Zambia Youth Service. A national service where all young people served two years learning technical skills as well as basic military service. After which they were older, mature and fitted for an occupation. Alas, once again the plans went sadly awry. A great deal of money went into setting up large camps and recruiting personnel and off went the first recruits.

In addition to the youngsters who had been unable to obtain a secondary school place it was announced that all students who were at school would commence their Youth Service as soon as they finished school. If they had a place at University later in the following year they could be released for the course and subsequently complete the Youth Service.

Although we received all this information it still came very much as a shock to learn that students would be collected from school on the Saturday after school closed. This meant that in the case of boarders they would not have time to return home to see their families before going off to camp. I went to school on the Saturday morning to see the girls collected. They were standing around the school grounds in groups with bags and cases beside them. To my surprise I could see only one parent. Turning to one of the Sisters standing nearby I asked why there were no parents.

'We were surprised too, but the girls told us that their parents did not want to see them go. It would be very upsetting and so they went away once they had dropped them off so as not to let the girls see their anxiety.'

At first I could not follow the reasoning but it slowly dawned that perhaps the parents feared for their daughters, and felt it better that the girls left in a calmer atmosphere.

Huge Army lorries turned in at the school gates and drew to a halt in front of the secondary school. Soldiers leaped down and began to organise the girls into groups. One of the Sisters greeted the officer in charge and after talking for a few moments asked which camp the girls were going to but of course had no luck. For some reason we could not discover, the students were not to be told which camp they would be in and left the school having no idea where they were heading. They could be sure of only one thing, that they would be as far from their home as possible. I heard the suggestion once that it was to make them as mature as possible far from parents, but as most Zambian students were mature, having had to cope with travelling long distances to school alone, it did not seem a very good argument.

We watched the girls scramble on board the lorries and before long the doors slammed and the trucks roared off. We were left standing under the trees with wet eyes wondering when and from where we would hear from the girls.

We tried not to think of the stories of girls being sexually assaulted, the stories of students being told 'you think you are educated and superior, now we will show you who is superior', of students whose fathers were well known, being picked out for special attention.

It was probably all rumour. It was not rumour of course that some young people on ZYS died or were killed. At one camp they were made to drink water from the river and refused permission to boil it 'you have to learn to live like the Army now'. Some died of dysentery. Some died when lorries overturned racing each other on the Great East Road - those students had not even reached their camp. Some died of malaria.

518

One girl came back to school after a long period, she had earned a leave. Carol walked into my classroom one day with her usual cheerful smile and after all the exchanges of news of old girls I asked if she would return the following day in her uniform to show my class.

It was a different Carol who appeared in my room in military uniform and the girls looked at her in awe. From their faces and reactions I sadly thought of what they must have already heard and learned of ZYS. It was not a reaction of impressed awe or being dazzled by the uniform, there was a tinge of,

'A-a-a-a, this is the Youth Service. This is for me.'

Carol showed them her uniform, its pockets for this and its pockets for that, she showed them how to march in her huge boots and how to salute. She described the long marches and the discipline. And she said,

'Learn to say nothing. No matter what is said and done, you say nothing.'

I wondered how many old girls revisited their old schools in this way.

Christmas was approaching, Ceri and Simon decided the shops weren't inspiring and took matters into their own hands. On the fence line as we drove down the bush road home they spotted a kaffir orange tree plentifully hung with fruit. They took themselves off down there with the dogs and picked a few gourds. Back home they persuaded Joseph to let them cut off the top third in the kitchen and scrape out the contents. After the shells dried they decorated them with their felt tip pens and wrapped them up as presents for Johnny and Aileen Hepworth. Useful pots, which survived the journey by sea back to UK and a few house moves and were still on a Hepworth bookshelf when I visited in 2016.

1976 A SAD YEAR

New Year, as I have often said, is not my favourite time of the year and 1976 was no exception. We got off to a particularly good start when Unia Mwila, Minister of Information and Technology, warned the nation of tight times to come. Copper prices continued to fall and oil prices to rise - and both had transport difficulties. Zambia's copper revenue had dropped to K56 million for January 1975 compared to K191miliion for the same period in 1974. The border closure with Rhodesia and the disruption on the Benguela railway line had all helped to hinder progress.

Farmers, who really had made an effort to make the country self - supporting in at least some commodities, complained that Namboard did not collect efficiently and the toilet roll factory closed because there was no tissue for Imco to make Satinex. While people, who had used detergents to wash themselves in the soap shortage, now found themselves suffering from dermatitis. Breakfast meal rocketed from K4.10 to K9.00 for a 50kg bag, which meant the average man's food bill was doubled in part.

Life is not meant to be a bed of roses, so to keep us on our toes and take our minds off minor problems we read next

STATE OF EMERGENCY

'We are at war,' declares Kaunda, *'with effect from last night.'*

The measure was in response to the grave security situation now developing and was designed to defend Nation and Constitution. 'There is a growing foreign interference in Zambia.' To help matters along it was reported that Prime Minister Vorster had told SA troops in future to cross any borders into countries believed to be harbouring freedom fighters.

The swift development in Lusaka next was armed police sealing off the University and arresting two lecturers. Education Minister, Mulikita, stated that *'UNZA was closed after student unrest ... over the past weeks a sad and regrettable situation had developed at the campus where provocation, intimidation and violence became common after student demonstrations. It resulted in a charged atmosphere not conducive to teaching and learning in the normal manner ... last Friday students boycotted lectures demanding to know why Cliffe, one of the arrested men, had been detained.'*

It was interesting to see that while Cliffe was later declared a prohibited immigrant he was never actually charged, which led us all to believe he was innocent of collaborating with other persons to organise political subversion against the State - a charge used at the time for the others.

It was bad enough the country being at odds but now we had a battle on our hands at school; the Dominican Sisters had decided to go ahead with closing it. A decision not helped by the knowledge that it was not a unanimous decision within the Order.

The PTA led by Andrew as Chairman, fought against this decision and eventually had the relief of seeing the Government declare that the school as such would not be allowed to close, but rather they would take it over. Faced with this, it was eventually decided after months of argument and negotiation that the school would remain open under the auspices of the Ministry and the Catholic Secretariat. In spite of the parents and public generally showing unanimous support for the Sisters and the school, quite a lot of ill feeling was generated and neither side appeared to fully understand the other.

The Ministry of Education had advised the Sisters a year earlier that *'the education at the Convent is in line with party policy except that it is better and more conscientiously administered than at most schools ... and it is surprising that a whole college of powerful Catholic bishops, the majority presumably Zambian, can settle with a clear conscience to trading 600 secondary school places for a super institution for 44 priests'.*

The plan for Lusaka Convent was to turn it into a seminary.

Many leading figures spoke out in support of the school -

Mainza Chona, Minister of Legal Affairs, said he nearly fainted when he heard of the decision to close the school because it was an indispensable institution.

IBM general manager Valentine Musakanya said it would be a misuse of a public resource if it were converted to a seminary... if the bishops wanted a seminary they would be given every assistance.

Namboard manager Dominic Mulaisho said since the voice of the people is the voice of God, the bishops should not go ahead because the people were against it '...*We will tighten our belts to help the bishops put up another building*'.

Standard Bank deputy chairman Elias Chipimo said the country had benefited greatly from the contribution made by the school and so it went on.

The Sisters were adamant however that they would be pulling out of the school altogether. The statement by the Mother General (who was based in Rhodesia) in which she said, '*Last year the Party appeared to frown on private institutions which could encourage elitism*' did not help matters.

Bombshells were being dropped in more senses than one.

In June a bomb shattered the High Court and main post office in Lusaka; damage was not as severe as it could have been but one stone lion outside the High Court lost its head and windows were blown out in both buildings.

A belief that the perpetrators were Rhodesian rebels was reinforced by Ian Smith warning Kaunda '*... if you allow freedom fighters to invade Rhodesia from Zambia, you will feel the consequences*.' This was shortly followed by a platoon of S African troops attacking and bombing a village on Western Province killing twenty two and injuring forty five.

Simon and Ceri on the roof at Leopards Hill

But elsewhere 1976 will be remembered in England as the year they had a long hot summer. One like the old people recall, and are sure they enjoyed every year in their youth.

I remember 1976 as the year our good friends Johnny and Aileen Hepworth left Zambia. They had arrived in May 1956, been our good friends in Petauke before finally coming to live in Lusaka, where the friendship continued. Their daughter Gillian had moved to UK to train as a nurse and Peter was in secondary school there. I was particularly sorry to see them go, Aileen had been a warm friend and supportive in many ways.

And I remember 1976 as the year we finally decided that Ceri and Simon should go to school in England and applications were made to Queen Margarets and Saint Peters in York. Ceri was thirteen and Simon was ten, they sat their Common Entrance exams early in the year and were accepted. I had had some misgivings over Ceri's acceptance. Sister Edmunda, her class teacher, had told me with much laughter that according to Ceri Queen Elizabeth the First was famous for inventing TV. I could only hope that Queen Margarets would feel a strong desire to educate this poor child from the backwoods of Africa. Simon had fared a little better but had done his graphs in miniature, mistaking the small squares of graph paper for the large squares. Ceri reread schoolgirl stories with perhaps some ideas of midnight feasts and lots of jolly hockey sticks, Simon declared himself uninterested in schools in England - and in England itself. But it was discovered that he had developed a marked liking for the Kings and Queens of England and would recite their names and dates of reign with an off handed casualness. I hoped he knew the main events of Elizabeth the First's reign.

We planned a long holiday in England in August, which would end when Ceri and Simon entered school. The following week Andrew arranged a business trip to Geneva for the September; I would accompany him.

Sister Fausta set about arranging for a relief teacher. She was very preoccupied that year, worrying about the future of the school. Whenever she was free from her Grade 7 class and meetings with parents, present and prospective, she talked endlessly about 'her girls'. She admitted there were pressures on the Sisters. It was difficult to recruit lay teachers and it was impossible to cope with the applications for places. And so on and so forth. She worried and she agonised and she lay awake at nights and she prayed.

'What is to be done, Mrs Kashita? We should be opening schools, we should be expanding. How can we close what we have? What is to become of my girls? And what is to become of the girls on the waiting lists? I have promised places to girls for the next four or five years. How can we close this school?'

But I had no answer.

And somehow I did not believe that the Sisters would actually pull out of the school, much less close it down.

Sister Fausta grew rather absent minded. Once she arrived in my classroom, we stood up and she gazed blankly at me. Her face went very pink.

'I am sorry Mrs Kashita. I have no idea why I came in here. I think I wanted to ask you something.'

It was almost as though she had no idea for a moment who I was, much less how she came to be in my room. I asked her to sit down, said I would get her a cool drink. But no, she must get on, there were so many things to be done. She walked out. I looked at her bowed shoulders and then decided to run across to the main building and find Sister de Angelis, who dealt with First Aid. My class were working quietly and could be safely left. Sister de Angelis came back and we searched for Sister Fausta. I blessed the spacious lay out of the school as we hurried from one set of classrooms and along the verandahs to another block and up to her office. No Sister Fausta.

'Perhaps she has gone to lie down in the Convent,' I suggested.

Sister de Angelis doubted she would have given in but said she would go to look, then we spotted Sister Fausta emerging from the chapel. I went back to my room. Sister de Angelis said later that Sister Fausta had smiled and said she had been to pray, there was so much work to be done and she insisted on returning to class.

We all realised as a staff that the proposed closure of the school weighed heavily on Sister Fausta's mind and as far as we could, we took on extra jobs, but she seemed unable to rest, or even sit for long, but would be seen at all times of the day walking round the school, up to her office and down to the chapel and back again. Perhaps the August break would give her some rest.

Ceri was looking forward to changing schools and seemed intent on excelling herself before leaving the Convent. She was elected House Captain and Yellow House won the coveted Sports Day trophy, we drove home in triumph with Ceri clutching the silver House cup and the individual trophy for Victrix Ludorem. Admittedly she had a distinct advantage in the hurdles with her long legs. For the last few weeks she threw herself into every activity with energy and enthusiasm as though she were saying, Remember me like this.

Ceri with one of her Sports trophies

Simon never mentioned going away to school and whenever the topic were broached he shrugged away his involvement. I recall his long walks with the dogs and the way he sought comfort in the quiet of the bush. Sometimes I watched the lonely figure far away and wondered if we were doing the right thing. For Simon, at this moment, probably not. But what about his future? In a country which seemed intent on narrowing one's horizons. If he had to complete his education overseas, was it not better to start now?

They had had a wonderful childhood in a land of space and light. They had been able to live a life of freedom which was not to be found everywhere. They had travelled long distances within the country and seen such wonders as the Victoria Falls and the vast expanse of the African bush. They had enjoyed friendships with different nationalities and known other customs. Now they had to begin to adjust to another way of life for some time, Africa would wait for them. And they would return to this open free life and appreciate it even more.

All too soon the time for departure came. Ceri and Simon packed a few favourite things and we left. Joseph and Banda and White could be safely left to care for the house and animals. They would have the presence of three Sisters who were going to stay in the house for a mini holiday but would be commuting to the Convent daily, we were grateful for their presence to keep an eye on things and they were happy to have a mini break. Sisters Bernard, Pia and de Angelis told us later that it had been a welcome change, once they had recovered from the piercing shrieks from Sister Pia the first night. She had gone into a bathroom and undressed before turning round to face herself in the full length mirror.

As always London was chill and grey in the early dawn and as we sped along the motorway into central London I looked out at the crowded houses where few were stirring.

I always looked forward to the fresh greenness of England especially after the dry dusty cold season left so far behind, but this year England was enjoying - or enduring? - an unexpected heatwave. The grass was parched in the London parks and the pigeons sat around panting, barely fluttering away as we walked by. The pavements of Oxford Street were gritty and filthy with spilt ice creams and sticky gobs of chewing gum. How we took the cleansing of the rain for granted I thought as I picked my way along the filthy pavements.

After a short spell in London we went up to Yorkshire to stay with Grannie Hodgson. The Dales were fresh and green even in a heatwave and especially in contrast to London. We revelled in the peaceful days there.

Ceri and Simon fishing in the stream at Lowlands

Andrew was enjoying his break from the office. It was his first real rest since the pressure of being axed and then setting up a new career. He relaxed with the children and had time to go fishing with them along the stream and then wander along the hillsides talking idly of this or that.

We had booked into the Viking Hotel in York for the last part of the holiday so that we could concentrate on buying the long, long lists of clothes with which Ceri and Simon would face their first English winter. Simon struggled into shirt and tie, grey jersey, navy blazer, duffle coat and long woolly scarf looking horrified. 'I'll never wear all this,' he protested, his face scarlet.

He regarded the short grey trousers with disfavour and muttered something about the good old International school back in Lusaka, which I hoped the patient school outfitter had not heard.

'What do I want a dressing gown for?' was his next complaint.

Buying his tuck box did lighten the mood as he insisted on sticking his precious puff adder skin inside the lid.

Ceri was an easier matter and regarded the rapidly growing pile of clothes with favour. We giggled over

12 pairs of knicker linings

But a pair of climbing trousers?

'Headmistress is very understanding,' puffed the good lady delving through the shelves of neatly folded garments, 'she knows some girls are little tomboys and DO like climbing trees and rather than forbid it, she allows them to wear climbing trousers.'

'Little tomboys ... climbing trousers ...' came a low rumble from the corner where Simon was seated.

(I never found out whether girls were sent out, prepared in climbing trousers, or whether they had to dash inside to change if overcome by a tree climbing urge).

The climax was a long heavy red wool cloak for wearing on the walk to church in the village.

Ceri and Simon in their school uniforms

Things cheered up once we had purchased the vast quantity of clothing. Andrew had to return to London for some meetings and I was inseparable from needle and thread and a slowly diminishing pile of name tapes.

Ceri and Simon set out on their own to explore York. And that was a huge success. Simon forgot all about school and set off early every morning with Ceri to discover more about the area. York is at all times for anyone, a most wonderful city. It has a long and detailed history but is also small and compact enough for anyone to explore it intimately on foot. And so throughout those long sunny days of August Ceri and Simon wandered around York. I remember on the very first occasion Ceri protested bitterly that Simon insisted on returning to the hotel for the toilet.

'He's just too mean to pay,' she complained.

Sometimes I put aside the pile of name tapes and accompanied them. We bought guide books and wandered from street to street and building to building, trying to absorb all the information and detail. The Castle Museum was as fascinating as I remembered from my childhood and we spent hours there, entranced by the exhibits, the reconstructed streets of long ago and the working mill. We walked the city walls which almost encircle the city and imagined what it had been like when soldiers were stationed on duty. We climbed to the top of York Minster to gaze - completely winded - at the surrounding flat Plain of York. The evenings were spent watching TV but I consoled myself that that was a treat they would not be able to enjoy for much longer.

Term loomed ever nearer.

Andrew returned from London and we checked lists and dates. The trip to Geneva was all organised. Then one night there was a phone call from Zambia for me. It was Mother Superior at the Convent.

Sister Fausta had been taken very ill and flown to Salisbury in Rhodesia. She would be in hospital for a very long time, as I was Deputy Head would I take over the running of the school as Acting Head and how soon could I return?

Ceri and Simon were due to start school the following week. I said I would fly out immediately afterwards. Andrew had heard half the conversation and now wanted the details.

'You can't go next week to take over,' he said 'you're going to Geneva with me.'

He was angered to find that I put the school first, that I was not only prepared but willing to forgo the trip to Geneva.

'But that's only a pleasure trip for me,' I protested. 'We have had this holiday together here. In Geneva you'll be busy at meetings all the time, you don't need me, school does.'

He did not understand me, that was clear. And I did not understand him.

'You put your work first,' I said angrily.

'That's different. I have to work, you don't.'

I was angered and humiliated that he did not take me or my work seriously and wondered why we could not understand each other. We did not mention it again.

When we took Ceri to school, the dormitories looked friendly enough with the soft toys beloved by young girls sitting on the beds. The old house echoed to the sound of laughing girls and the large grounds looked green and inviting. I thought Ceri would make friends easily and make the most of her time there. Simon's school was just outside the city walls and his House was on a street next to the main buildings. All parents of new boys had tea with the housemaster before we trooped off to say goodbye to our sons.

Simon was a stiff unfamiliar figure in his grey and navy uniform. He stood in the tiny dormitory at the top of the house and looked at me with what seemed a last mute appeal.

Andrew and I smiled and said something bright about Christmas holidays and I walked out of the room. I don't know how I managed not to fall down the stairs as my eyes were blind with tears. How could I have thought this was best for Simon? What would he do in this grey city when the cold days of winter came? how would he walk along the endless streets with no dogs at his heels?

As I stood in the school hall blowing my nose and reminding myself that I did not want him stuck with a narrow school curriculum and in a country where no one was completely free, another mother approached me. Joan Oldfield had just said goodbye to her son Christopher in the same dormitory.

'How did you manage to bring yourself to leave?' she sniffed.' If you had not walked out I would still be there. I just walked after you.'

Fathers did not appear to find it so hard we thought as they came cheerfully down the stairs after us. We adjourned to the hotel to comfort each other. Typically, while that was the beginning of a long friendship between the Oldfields and us, our sons did not hit it off so well.

All mothers I have talked to have found this first parting at boarding school one of the most difficult things in life. And for some of us the feeling of guilt lasts for what seems to be for ever. But no matter how hard some things are, it never helps to sit down and brood over the rights and wrongs. You make what seems to be the right decision at the time.

Now we had to pack our things in the Viking; Andrew was off to Geneva and I was returning home to take over the running of the school.

It seemed very strange and empty to be flying home knowing that the children would not be at the other end, nor would be for a very long time. I was quite used to Andrew being somewhere else and thought that he had probably forgotten all about our disagreement.

If it seemed strange to fly home alone it was even stranger to walk into the house and look at the tidy bedrooms. I sat and cried first in one bedroom and then the other. I told myself that I was being stupid and that they were probably so busy and interested in their new schools that they had hardly a thought for home. I did not know whether it was better to shut their doors or leave them open so I walked out onto the roof.

My plane had arrived in the early morning and it was now mid-morning. The sun was hot on my head, the weather was warming up, mid-September. The grass was parched and yellow brown. The smell of wood smoke drifted by for a moment from the servants quarters. Peter and Paula wandered round to the front of the house and flopped on their bellies looking down the drive, waiting for someone to come home.

I burst into tears and went back into my bedroom.

Joseph called softly up the stairs,

'Coffee, Madam.'

Splashing cold water on my face I forced myself to calm down. I would have an early lunch and drive down to the school. Joseph had put a coffee tray in the sitting room, a small vase of flowers beside it.

Flowers. Oh yes. Pulling myself together I walked quickly back up the stairs. Yes, there were some yellow flowers in the bedroom. Yellow flowers in the dining rom. White ones in the downstairs cloakroom. Red and yellow flowers in the sitting room.

I put my head through the kitchen door.

'The flowers are lovely, Joseph,' I said.

He smiled, 'Thank you, Madam.'

I sat drinking the coffee and thinking of the time we had come back from England to find flowers around the house and when Don dropped in to welcome us back, we discovered that Joseph and his servant had purloined his best blooms, which had been destined for the Agricultural Show.

I went back into the kitchen.

'Where did you get the flowers?' I asked.

Joseph smiled. 'Next door, Mr Fluck, but it is all right. I ask Braison and he tell Mr Fluck that I want flowers for the Dona and he says I can take this one.'

'This one looks like a whole flower bed,' I commented. 'Are you sure?'

'It is all right,' said Joseph firmly.

Well, if he said it was all right it would be all right.

After coffee I took a short walk around the house while Joseph explained what had happened in my absence but apart from asking if Ceri and Simon liked their new schools he wisely made no other comment, having taken one quick glance at my still red eyes.

It was now September and the third term of the school year. I got out the Hi-ace van and drove down to the Convent, the tall yellow grass rustled in the wide open stretches at the side of the road. The sun was hotting up now in readiness for the hot weather in October. I found Sister de Angelis in the boarder's hostel and we adjourned to the dispensary for a coffee and she was making it quite clear that I would be taking on most of the duties.

'I am so glad you are here,' she said. 'I really could not cope on my own, there is so much to do as it is.'

She did not need to remind me. I knew already that Sister de Angelis ran the hostel for eighty boarders almost single handed. She cared for Sister Perpetua who was confined to her room. She was in charge of the Convent kitchen and the domestic staff. She still taught needlework in the secondary school up to Cambridge level. She was responsible for First Aid in the Convent, hostel, both schools and the workmen. She played the organ for all their services in the Chapel. She was also Bursar, having taught herself book keeping and had the unenviable task of juggling the scanty fees to keep the place going ...

And now Sister de Angelis was to take Sister Fausta's place - no wonder she was pleased to see me back!

'I do feel guilty though,' she sighed, 'you should have had longer in UK.'

I comforted her by saying that probably Ceri and Simon would be too busy to think about whether I was in UK or Zambia. And as for me, it was certainly better to be back at work and occupied.

And the news of Sister Fausta? The news of Sister Fausta could not have been worse. While I had been in UK she had become even more absent minded and even when the school holiday began things did not improve. She looked ill and had a constant severe headache. At last she consented to see a doctor, who tragically wasted time having her attend Chainama hospital for the mentally ill. Fortunately this was not for long and she was then flown to Salisbury, Rhodesia, where she was admitted to hospital and the final news was that the cancer of the brain was too far gone to be treated in any way. It was a matter of weeks.

The school prayed and we sent letters and cards and messages which constantly flowed in from 'her girls'. I just prayed she could read or listen and understand how much she was loved and missed.

In the meantime of course, work had resumed with the pressure of end of term exams and the all-important Grade 7 selection exams. I was now teaching Grade 1 in the mornings from 7.30 to 12.30 and then after lunching at home, returned to school to work in the office. My morning work was fine but I was appalled at the work to be done in the office. Sister Fausta had been ill for far longer than we had realised. It took Sister de Angelis and I many hours to go through cupboards, discarding papers which had long outlived their usefulness. The admission file was a nightmare.

'How could she have allowed so many people to complete application forms?' I groaned.

But Sister de Angelis had the answer as usual.

'It was the only way she could get people to leave the office. And as you know, there are always a large 'drop out' of applications from people who double book places or leave the town or country.'

'Just as well,' I muttered. 'We could never admit half this number.' The whole file was made much worse by the fact that Sister Fausta had not removed any applications at all, even for children who would be too old by now to attend the school. We managed to thin out a good number of these.

If the office were bad enough, the store rooms were even worse. Working on the usual primary teachers' theory that 'it might come in useful' Sister Fausta had saved and hoarded and never thrown anything away.

'I distinctly remember having no use for these cardboard cones, nor had anyone else and we agreed to get rid of them at least two years ago,' I said as we gazed at hundreds of battered cardboard cones about eight inches long, piled and heaped and scattered in one storeroom.

The men, Saddy, Judah and Pelekani, were kept busy carrying away boxes and papers and rubbish and burning them. The tiny room we used as a staffroom was piled from floor to ceiling on three sides with files and boxes and now as we sorted, more than half was discarded. The teachers worked hard to keep up the children's spirits and the school carried on pretty much as usual. Once we had cleared the large amounts of 'stock', we felt we were able to cope with the normal school routine.

But it was not long before we had the sad news that Sister Fausta had died in Salisbury and while it was a merciful release, we mourned a very old and very dear friend. A Mass of Remembrance was arranged in the Chapel to which parents were also invited. The small white chapel was filled to overflowing with both primary and secondary pupils and staff, Sisters and parents. There were many wet eyes as the children's voices filled the small chapel and it seemed strange to be there without Sister Fausta's plump figure and gentle blue eyes watching over her girls. Perhaps we felt her loss there more than anywhere else.

After the service I took my class back down to the classroom and settled them down to some work. It was only a matter of minutes before three mothers appeared at my door. In between their sniffs and snuffles they explained that many parents had chatted on the chapel steps and were most upset at the thought of Sister Fausta dying far from home and now being buried in Rhodesia.

'This is where she worked and was most loved,' said Zeenie Mudenda, wife of Elijah who had first welcomed us at Mount Makulu and now Minister of Foreign Affairs. 'And we have all been talking. We would like to have a collection and bring Sister Fausta home to be buried.'

It seemed to be a thoughtful gesture so I suggested they should have a word with Sister Amadea and off they went. In a very short time they were back with cross and sad faces. There was clearly a communication gap involved. Sister Amadea had explained that the actual burial place was irrelevant to the Sisters but that if the parents had a collection she would see that the money was put to good use. The parents were annoyed that their wishes were not understood, that they wished to have Sister Fausta buried where they could visit the grave, they wanted her to rest here 'at home'. There was no reconciling the two view points and I reflected that it was a pity that they could not have worked together - perhaps Sister Fausta could have been brought back to Zambia and that the parents could have raised some money for a scholarship in her memory.

We had already had a collection in our usual weekly Assembly and made a donation to the Chelston Church Building Fund, for which Sister Fausta had already raised some money. This we had done in her memory knowing that she would have preferred it to flowers. Now the children missed her and had a feeling of loss which would not quickly go away. I had the idea of suggesting they show their appreciation of her work by writing to her family back in Germany. I had heard her talk of a brother there. I asked Sister de Angelis if the children wrote, could the Convent arrange to forward the letters?

When the idea was put to the school in assembly it was greeted with pleasure and before the end of the week the office was piled with letters and drawings and prayers and poems. As we looked through them we were touched by the thoughts and memories the children had of Sister Fausta. At last a large parcel was ready for collection and to my surprise Sister Amadea 's response was that perhaps it was waste of time, she didn't know if Sister Fausta's family could read English.

It did not take long to make contact with the German Ambassador, who arranged for the parcel to go to Germany and be delivered. I heard later that the family wrote to thank the school for their kind thoughts but that letter was never passed on to us.

Looking back at the apparent lack of feeling I have come to the conclusion that it was partly due to the fact that the good Sisters always tried not to let personal feelings and emotions be involved in their work - which seemed odd in view of the fact that their work always engendered a feeling of love and respect in their recipients! And that plus the fact that Sister Fausta had been campaigning for the school to be kept open while the official decision by the Mother Superior was that Lusaka Convent should be closed. Sister Fausta had not been popular with some of her Sisters.

However, writing to Sister Fausta's family had in some way helped the children to move on and close that particular chapter, although she was not forgotten.

The Staff at Primary School Dominican Convent
?, Dorothy Hearn, Joan Lusaka, Ursula ?, Sister de Angelis, Mrs Oomen, Mrs
Proietti, Mrs Wixted

There is always some new activity in school to preoccupy the mind and one of our next events was the Humanism Week in October. Sister de Angelis and I put our heads together and agreed that we would plan a week's activities so that if the Ministry summoned us on a brickmaking exercise we could show a plan of campaign and hope to be left in peace. Not that we would have minded making bricks - if we could be sure that the materials would be organised and that we would not have the girls twiddling their thumbs.

The staff thought this a very wise move and after a short meeting we sent off the following letter to the parents

15 October 1976

Dear Parents,

As it is Humanism Week next week, the Staff and children have decided to raise money for the Maternity wing at the UTH (University Teaching Hospital). The money will be used to buy nappies and matinee jackets.

To do this each class is having a mini project as follows
Monday   0830 – 0930 Grade 6 mini swimming gala
Tuesday   1200 – 1230 Grade 5 display of art
Wednesday   1130 – 1230   Grade 3 entertainment
Thursday 1130–1230   Grade 4 choral verse and results of story

competition and Grade 7 a debate

Friday   0745 – 0830 Grade 1 Assembly and Presentation to Matron

Please give your daughter 25 ngwee on Monday to cover the cost of daily entrance fee.

Grade 2 is collecting toys and games for the handicapped - as well as making some.

Donations will be most welcome.

Once again, thank you for your cooperation.

Sr de Angelis

Reading it through now I remember wondering if some official at the Ministry would object and tell us that we must participate in some Ministry organised activity. But no. Possibly they were only too relieved to have one less school to worry about, so many of their ideas were praiseworthy in their way but then left to overworked and unimaginative personnel to organise.

I do not recall what the official plan for schools were for Humanism week that year but we quietly went ahead and raised money for UTH in a way that kept our children safely within the school grounds and busy with useful activities. On Friday Matron came to our Assembly and was presented with piles of nappies and baby clothes.

Presentation to Matron of UTH for the maternity wing

I have a particular reason for remembering the Assembly. One

538

of Sister de Angelis's duties was to take the Assembly each Friday but from the very moment I arrived back at the school she confessed that the very idea of standing up in front of the assembled school filled her with horror.

'I am sure you would do it much better,' she added with a pleading look.

The idea filled me with horror too so we compromised. I would take Assembly if she were detained in the Convent – '... what with Sister Perpetua ... and then the men ... and there is always something in the kitchen...'

I should have known. Something detained Sister de Angelis every Friday morning! She would frequently appear, pink and breathless, at the door as we sang the last hymn and I would pretend to believe her vague excuses.

I had always thought the assemblies such a very important part of the school life that nothing would have allowed me to cancel one, even when it meant taking it myself. I said a silent Thank You to Miss Storr, my very first Headmistress at Selby Abbey so many years ago, who had insisted that each teacher must take a turn in taking an Assembly. And realising what a good piece of training it had been I offered the same chance to the rest of the Staff, they retreated in horror and with Sister de's example I could not insist.

It is strange how many teachers do such excellent jobs in the classroom but will not take an Assembly. Whether it is the school en masse or the presence of their fellow teachers I am not sure, perhaps more the latter.

However, I remember asking Sister de Angelis to make a special effort to take the Assembly in Humanism Week but some crisis in the kitchen intervened and there I was again standing in front of the stage where my class were all prepared, about to perform some little play they had practised all week. Matron had the seat of honour, the girls were seated on the dark parquet floor in their long rows with beaming smiles. Sister Georgina floated in light as breath of wind, umbrella folded under one arm.

Just as I was about to begin, another figure appeared in the doorway. Thalia Barclay, had been helping in the school and whispered, 'I would love to see the presentation.'

I could only smile and nod but my heart sank. Thalia took charge of all our school productions with a flair which would not have come amiss at Saddlers Wells or RADA (where she had been a student!).

Somehow I stumbled through the introductions and then my class performed with their usual unselfconscious charm. It never ceased to amaze me how unselfconscious these African girls were, performing in a language not their own. After which the school joined in the hymn with their melodious voices rising and filling the hall with the easy blend of harmony, which is heard nowhere outside Africa. This natural ability always made me feel small as I rose to speak afterwards. I explained to Matron how the children had worked to raise money and that it was perhaps a small token in view of the hospitals great need, we hoped it was of use and then I began the quotation

'Little drops of water

Little grains of sand ...'

And asked if anyone could complete it.

Silence greeted this departure from the norm and to my horror my mind went completely blank. There was an expectant hush as three hundred pairs of eyes waited.

'Little drops of water

Little grains of sand ...

I repeated meaningfully - but my mind was paralysed.

'Make a mighty ocean

And a pleasant land ' intoned Thalia's theatrical voice.

Filled with relief we smiled at each other and repeated the verse again, the whole school now joining in and the top juniors, turning with smiles at each other as the meaning came across.

We clapped each other in mutual self-congratulation as Matron rose to her feet.

One girl from each class came forward to present her with a parcel and soon the table at the front was piled high with baby clothes and nappies. Matron told us simply but movingly how so many mothers came into the hospital to have a baby with no baby clothes at all, either because they were too poor or because traditionally they did not prepare for a baby but waited first for its safe arrival.

'We always tell them that they cannot leave the hospital without some clothes for the baby,' she said, ' but now of course we shall be able to help those who are too poor.'

This time we had been able to use the official directive in our own way and - I believe - still achieve what was after all, the main intention, that of teaching children to think of and work for others in the community who were less fortunate.

Sometimes of course we had to follow directives literally to the letter. I recently came across the slip of paper from the Ministry which gave the school a list of posters and banners which the children were to wave as they lined the route for some 'spontaneous' demonstration.

POSTERS WITH THE FOLLOWING SLOGANS
The cause of the Party is the cause of the Youth
FORWARD WITH KK
We welcome the Agrarian revolution
The Youth always supports the Party
The Youth have confidence in K.K,'s Leadership
We pledge to follow our leaders so as to learn when our time comes
Youth in school welcome the idea to Reform the Education System

Lining routes for demonstrations - spontaneous or otherwise - waving banners would have been bearable if there had been some time control. But standing at a roadside in the heat for hours only made one reflect on the valuable lesson time lost. I could not have been the only one wishing to Reform the Education System.

All in all it was a difficult term. Sister Fausta's death saddened everyone. Sister de Angelis, with the best intentions on the world, did not have time to devote herself to the school as much as it needed. I was asked by Archbishop Milingo if I would take on the full Headship of the school, a most flattering request but I had to refuse as not only was I not a Roman Catholic, I very strongly believed that the school should have another Sister as Head.

This belief I am sure was shared by the vast majority of parents. We all hoped it could be another Dominican Sister but the Mother General, Sister de Pace, based in the Mother House in Salisbury, had quite made up her mind that the Lusaka school was to close. The PTA fought this decision very hard and with a sadness tinged with some bitterness. No one could understand why the Sisters apparently wished to turn their backs on what we regarded as a most popular and successful school. A rumour circulated that the lack of novices for the Order in our area was regarded with disfavour. But as is usual, rumour flew with counter rumour, often holding hands with fact and possibility.

It was rumoured that some of the Sisters thought the large buildings and private school status was incompatible with the Sisters mission and the philosophy of Humanism preached by the Party (this ignored the fact that the same Government had made some state schools fee paying). It was suggested that the number of Sisters was dwindling - fact - so some Convent would have to be sacrificed and that Sister de Pace was adamant it would not be Ibenga where she had been Mother Superior. It was hinted that some Sisters objected to teaching in a school for the wealthy and that they wished to go to work 'with the common man'.

All these rumours and stories dismayed the parents who had only two thoughts in their minds. One was that the Sisters and their work had been and was and would always be appreciated. The second was that the closure of the school would be a great loss to the community - and in the long run, to the country. They suggested it would be possible for the two schools to continue with any Sisters who wished and could be spared. And that all other Sisters who wished to do 'good works' elsewhere could

542

continue living in the Convent.

And, they argued, while the school only catered for a relatively small number of pupils, nevertheless it was an example and inspiration to other schools. The parents offered to raise enough money so that more lay staff could be employed. In fact, they would agree to any suggestion that the Sisters would put forward - except that of closing the school.

The whole situation was exacerbated by the fact that it very soon became clear that the Sisters themselves were divided on the subject. Sister Caratate left for home leave in Germany never to return, having said she could not continue in Zambia if they abdicated their responsibilities. Archbishop Milingo declared his sympathies lay with the parents. And finally the Ministry stepped in to insist the two schools be kept open, with or without the Sisters.

It should not be thought that the Ministry contemplated taking over the assets of the Convent. But it did mean that when the Sisters were faced with the loss of the two schools they had to reach an acceptable - to the parents - solution.

It all took some time of course but it was finally agreed that the secondary school would remain open as a Government assisted school. The primary school would remain open as a private school under the care of the Catholic Secretariat. And both schools would keep their grounds.

But the Convent and the boarding hostel would close as such. They were to be given to the Brothers to run a seminary. The Brothers would live in the Convent and the seminarians in the hostel; they would also take over the chapel, the orchards, the vegetable gardens and all other buildings.

It was an uneasy compromise and many parents were still disappointed even though the Secretariat promised to find a Sister to take over the Headship of the primary school.

I closed my ears to the ugly whispers about how the parents had raised the money to build the hostel etc. - no good would come now of recriminations. Perhaps in face of what the majority of most of the Sisters seemed to want, this would be a workable solution. But I was as appalled as anyone to discover later that a mere four Brothers replaced the twenty Sisters in the large Convent and that only ten seminarians replaced the eighty boarders in the hostel.

When a six foot wire fence topped with barbed wire was erected across the grounds separating the schools from the rest of the grounds - and worst of all, from the Chapel - we began to realise we would be two very separate units and we would no longer have the comfort, help and interest of the church close at hand.

All these changes at school took place over a long period of course. At the same time I was getting used to the idea of Ceri and Simon being so very far away from home. No, not getting used to, one never did that. One adjusted to the idea. That was all.

Andrew had long since returned from his trip to Geneva and I found that he still resented the fact that I had chosen to return to school in preference to accompanying him. We just did not understand each other so as far as possible I stopped talking to him about my work. He had never been very interested anyway. And when he expected me to attend evening functions I went along with as good a grace as I could muster and made no complaint about the frequent late nights. This sounds as though I never enjoyed our evenings out which is not really the case. There were many happy evenings and there were many entertaining people but, and it was a very big but, I did not enjoy cocktail parties and dinners which went on until the small hours in one hotel or another. Somehow they seemed more and more artificial, while I was more and more interested in what would become of the children in my school.

I had always enjoyed my work but now I had to admit that it was also becoming my refuge and solace. Once in the classroom I would forget my worries and preoccupations. No matter how bad the day was, the following morning I would wake with the first thought being 'Now, what are we going to do today?' and I would be anticipating how things would work.

Both Andrew and I woke easily about 6 a.m., the sunlight would already be flooding into the bedroom and the floor would be cool to my feet as I walked across into the bathroom. The bathroom window looked towards the servants' quarters and I would hear the sound of their conversations as the women tended their fires - there was always a fire burning on the open ground, even though they had a wood stove on each verandah. A child would wail briefly or there would be laughter and a shout if they had woken in a better mood.

I would dress in front of the long mirror which was on the wall between the double row of wardrobes. Andrew would talk about his plans for the day as he walked about, toothbrush sticking out of his mouth. I had long since given up hope that he would brush his teeth only in the bathroom. Faint sounds from Joseph in the kitchen would come up the stairs and Banda would call to White as they went about feeding the chickens and other livestock.

Breakfast was always eaten to the accompaniment of the radio, I doubt Andrew missed a news bulletin any day, anywhere. The cats would circle our feet briefly before sitting down to attend to their toilets and the dogs would hover outside in the courtyard, in the vain hope that it might be one of those wonderful days when we would not depart but would instead take them for long walks.

Joseph would be checking which of us would be home for lunch and White would be unrolling the long hosepipes ready for the daily task of watering vegetables. Banda would be giving the cars a last polish before going into the house to clean the bedrooms. Both Andrew and I would leave home shortly after 7am, he liked to get to the office early and start work before the phone began its incessant ringing. I had to be at school before 7.30.

I drove off down the curving drive as three dogs flopped on their bellies in the dusty grass with woebegone faces, knowing that as soon as I turned off the plot that Joseph probably went home for a lengthy tea break before releasing Banda and White for theirs. But why worry about all that I thought, it was well worth it to come home to a clean and shining house and know that they were completely trustworthy with our possessions. Well, if one did not include the small matter of sugar - and that was much easier once we had come to an agreement that I would not buy more than two pounds of sugar a week, especially as neither Andrew nor I took sugar in our tea and coffee and we didn't like sweet puddings. I heard so many people complain about their servants' sugar consumption but I found the matter resolved when I gave the servants a sugar ration and insisted I would buy a set amount for ourselves. I could ignore accusations of paternalism – we had an amicable arrangement.

No matter how often I drove along Leopards Hill Road it still filled me with pleasure. First down the winding drive then there was the short dirt road between tall grass and scrubby trees from our gate to the main road. Once on that, the bumpy dirt road eased into the smooth tarmac on its way to State Lodge on the right and down into town on the left. The road dipped and bent through thick bush where I had once seen a large bird swoop down and soar up with a long snake dangling and writhing in its claws. Then the trees and scrub gave way to open grassland where the tall grasses swayed in the wind. Lush and green in the rains and then bleached yellow by the sun in the dry season until a bush fire would pass through, leaving a black charred waste, to blow away in the wind. And small green shoots would make their appearance before the first rains looking so out of place in their black setting. Then again thicker bush until I was nearer town. All this beauty for several miles and on most days I had it completely to myself.

Just before I reached the town outskirts, there was Bauleni township on my right, where small houses built of mud bricks stood in brown and orange clusters, then the cemetery and I was at the crossroads and into Kabulonga proper.

Up the hill, past two enormous palm trees which could be seen for miles and then at the top of the hill, the large gates of the school on my left. Turning in, one drove between an avenue of flame trees up to the main parking area for both schools, where the statue of Mary stood in a welcoming place.

The secondary school on the right was an imposing two storey block but our primary school was two blocks of single storey classrooms and looked very much the poor relation.

The flagpole stood to the left of the statue of Mary and in front of the rose garden, so lovingly tended by Sister Ceslaus and a tall kapok tree stood at the corner of Grade 4, shedding its large pods and fine wool over the brick path.

I used to park my van under a cassia tree and walk along the verandah into my classroom at the end, knowing it would not be long before parents would be dropping off girls on their way to work. Most of them would bring their small cardboard suitcases into the classroom as they arrived, some would go out to play but there were always some who stayed to wander round the room reading display charts with their friends and chatting about their paintings. I would be busy with one job or another but would listen to their conversations, admiring their use of a second language. Some had started school earlier that year with very little English indeed.

Statue of Mary in front of the secondary school and some of my Grade 1's

Once the bell rang at 7.30 forty eager girls would be ready for the day and we had not time to think of anything else. We always worked hard at the more academic subjects first thing in the morning, knowing that by break time at 10.30 the hottest part of the day would soon be upon us. I used to let them eat their break before they went out to play so we would stop work ten minutes early and get out the small suitcases. How the contents had changed I thought, as I watched them munch their snacks. It had only been a few years ago that neat packets of dainty sandwiches, biscuits, some sweets and an apple had been a feature, they had been wrapped in cling film (Gladwrap was the trade name there). Now the sandwiches were made with thick hunks of bread which would not slice thinly no matter how you tried. Biscuits were only available of the homemade variety - and appeared and disappeared with the availability of flour and sugar. Apples, peaches and grapes no longer came from South Africa but there was a large range of bananas, guavas, naajies, mangoes and oranges. In a way this does not sound such a dramatic change. It wasn't of course - but it was a change. Things were no longer so neat and clean, wrapping papers were used and reused. Occasionally it was newspaper.

At some point a couple of mothers helped organise a tuck shop open at morning break. I would allow anyone to trot across if they wished and after an incident had to check how much money they were taking. One memorable morning one of the mothers appeared at my door to ask if I knew that several of my five year olds were shopping with twenty kwacha notes each (roughly equivalent to £10 at the time). Questioning revealed that one girl had a stash of K20 notes in her little case and she had been sharing them with her friends. Further questioning revealed that she had asked for some tuck shop money and her mother had said, 'Get some money from my bag'.

None of this bothered forty hungry little girls however and they opened their suitcases and sat cheerfully munching and talking until the bell rang and I shooed them out to play. I would walk along to join my colleagues for a most welcome cup of coffee. It was rare now that we joined the secondary staff, we had grown used to sharing the tiny store room with Sister Fausta for a while, then we moved to having coffee break in Grade 3, which was large enough to take a table for us . Joan Lusaka had joined us as an art teacher, her gentle humour was a great asset.

We roared with laughter at her explanation of a swollen and bandaged foot one morning. The previous evening she had gone to a little used outbuilding and on opening the door walked into a snake, which had predictably bitten her bare toes - or rather toe. The snake had fled one way as Joan fled indoors to her husband and told him she believed he should cut the wound open and suck out the venom. Paul had manged to slash her toe with a razor blade - very reluctantly - but then could not bring himself to suck her toe. There was a quick drive to hospital. We laughed even more when Joan said she couldn't blame the snake - she had walked into it.

And how we loved her when she arrived with a mid-morning snack surprise. Husband Paul had been Ambassador in Moscow and they still had friends who travelled there - all of which she reminded us as she revealed a large pot of caviar. A very swish accompaniment to morning tea.

(The only other time I remember eating caviar was at some dinner party where the Shamwanas were also guests. As we nibbled on the caviar starter both Andrew and Edward waxed lyrical, praising the hostess and asking why we (Stella and I) did not give them such treats. They really went over the top. Later when Stella and I complained that we only rarely saw caviar at exorbitant prices in the shops nor had they ever expressed an interest, both of them looked astonished, saying, ' Oh it was quite dull but we thought we should be polite').

After break one was very conscious of the growing heat and work proceeded more slowly. Cicadas shrieked in the trees outside and the men moved more slowly slashing the grass or slowly dragging hosepipes from one flower bed to another, the man standing with a faraway look as the water trickled across the dry earth.

I seem to remember it most in the dry hot days but of course there were dull cold days when the wind cut like a knife, days when the temperatures rose, the sky turned purple and we had torrential downpours with crashing thunder. Then we would sniff the choking smell as the earth tried to soak up the beating raindrops - and then the sun came out to raise clouds of rich cloying steam.

I remember a new teacher who replaced Mrs Wallenstein in Grade 2, newly arrived from UK in the dry season in May, and a very quiet reserved young person. And during our first heavy storm and downpour of the rainy season in December after she joined us, seeing her standing outside her classroom door on the verandah, leaning over the railing, arms outstretched into the rain, drenched to the skin, crying out when she saw me, 'Oh, isn't this wonderful? I thought it would never ever rain!'

At 12.30 parents would start to arrive, cars would come and go, chauffeur driven cars mingling with bicycles and trucks as the girls were collected.

I would climb up into the van and head back up Leopards Hill Road and to lunch. As I turned in the gates at the bottom of the drive, first one dog and then another would trot round the side of the house and welcome me with wagging tails and nudging noses. Joseph would be clattering things on and off the stove and after a brief greeting I would walk upstairs to wash, revelling in the cool quietness. Sometimes Andrew came home for lunch, in which case he would arrive shortly after me and we would sit down to eat with newspaper and radio news bulletin. But often I would lunch alone, always feeling that it was a case of dining in solitary state as I rang the bell for Joseph to bring the next course. But what bliss not to have to listen for the next news bulletin!

Now I had to return to school almost every afternoon, sometimes to deal with paper work but quite often to go out on what became more and more foraging expeditions. Once upon a time one had been able to find stock for school - such things as books, paper, paint, materials, card, wool, pencils, crayons - oh, the multitudinous basic things one uses in a primary school - in Nedcoz (National Educational Company Zambia).

Long gone were the days when one just bought equipment for practical work in school in primary schools. It was amazing how soon we had adjusted to the fact that such things were no longer to be seen on shelves in town. I frequently thanked God that Sister Fausta had asked me to order sets of reading books from England the year before she died. We had agreed to order large numbers because we thought the price would go up. Now it was no longer a case of higher prices, it was a case of not being able to get foreign exchange. We needed those books as the Zambian sets of Mulenga and Jelita were far from sufficient.

Quite often Sister de Angelis and I would go foraging together, it was far more profitable; I had the van, she had the veil.

On that we were agreed. We were not agreed on what constituted time! I would arrive as arranged, at say, two o'clock and park under the huge tree outside the hostel. I would wait a while. The grounds were quiet, the girls busy with afternoon activities were already on the field, in the pool or in their classrooms and in the distance Sister Georgina's Music House would be full of chords and discords. I would check my watch.

Then I would go into the hostel and call up the stairs, no response, I would trot up the grey stairs, knowing it was a fruitless exercise. The dispensary door would be open, back down the stairs to stand on the verandah feeling irritable that once again we had not made a prompt start. Five, ten, fifteen minutes later Sister de Angelis would come hurrying along her feet pattering softly on the verandah's grey cement. Her face would be pink - with haste or embarrassment I was never sure - and wisps of hair escaping from under her veil.

We would climb into the van and off we would go, sometimes being flagged down by Sister Pia, who would call plaintively, 'Are you going to Nedcoz? Get me something nice, anything! Just something nice!'

I was never sure whether it was just some materials for her Art room or ... just something nice ... and when she so sadly died far too early of breast cancer, I wished we could have just once found something really very nice for her.

Once in Lusaka we would head first for Nedcoz, intending to complete the most frustrating part of the expedition first. Nedcoz was established in a huge warehouse out in the industrial area of Lusaka, where all the educational supplies for all the schools in the country were stored and despatched.

When you first entered the building and your eyes adjusted to the cool darkness within, you felt a mood of anticipation. The building was crammed with goods, often stacked to the ceiling and overflowing into the aisles. We checked our list and set off, so many of those exercise books and so many of those. Boxes of pencils, gaily coloured from China. Packets of paint blocks and tins of powder paint and extra brushes.

After that things began to go rather flat. The huge piles of blotting paper were a pretty pink - but they would be no use at all. And the paper for art was dirty and creased, we had an alternative in mind so did not grieve too much over that. Card was likewise dusty and creased but again we had other ideas. One wondered who, if ever, bought those tatty sheets. Perhaps no one did, so as there was plenty of stock of that commodity, no more was ever ordered. Or was it eventually despatched to some luckless school far away on the bush? lengths of cotton material were needed but trying to match sewing threads was a frustrating task in that half-light and of course they were stored at a point furthest from the door.

Occasionally climbing up half forgotten ladders I found treasures at the top of shelf units and once the thick layers of dust were shaken off, we found ourselves the proud possessors of a packet of this or that. They were no great treasures really but when you have so little everything takes on an added value.

Back at the counter we would have our purchases totalled up and packaged and carried to the van. This was not as simple as it sounds. For example, take the day that we wanted to buy blocks of paint ... they were packaged in sets of 6 but were priced in tens, so we thoughtfully decided upon 10 packets. At the counter the assistant began the laborious job of opening all the plastic packets, when asked why he explained they were priced at 5 kwacha for 10 paint blocks. Smiling, I said we had made it easy for him, wanting 10 packets. Looking at me pityingly he repeated they had to be sold in tens. Patiently I pointed out 6 x

10 = 60 ... which was 6 lots of 10.

Just wasted my breath, he insisted on opening each packet, stacking the paint blocks in tens and then calculated 6 x 10. And so we waited.

Once the receipt was stamped - all five copies - we would sit in the van and have a wash with the wet cloths Sister had thoughtfully brought. I would manoeuvre the van round as many of the potholes as I could back to the gates, where a security guard would check our receipts and packages, this he would do in a perfunctory manner - Sister's veil being as good a pass as any, if not better.

Back into town and along Cairo Road to the post office where I would run upstairs to open the little green door of our post box hoping to see the thin blue air letters with news from Ceri and Simon. Back at the van I would give these a hasty first read while Sister fended off curio sellers or the odd beggar. Ceri's letters were always chatty with enough detail about her school life to reassure me. Simon's were more perfunctory apart from one of his first letters when he wrote about the steam engines from York's Railway Museum 'being exercised along the railway track at the end of the school playing fields'.

Over the bridge and into Church Road and left into Government printers. Here we had gradually built up a most cordial relationship with the manager and were always made very welcome. Through the printing room and over to the shelves and bins, where the 'off cuts' were stored and where we were always told to make ourselves at home. Faced with the piles of coloured card and paper we were filled with greed. All this paper and card! to be disposed of! And free!!

Each time we went we expected to be told it had all been a dreadful mistake. The manager would again assure us that we should take as much as we required and off he would go. Tentatively we took a small pile each from the shelves and placed them in the trolley. I added some pink and Sister added some green and blue. Some sheets of card, long narrow lengths of white card, just right for making into cards for Christmas and Easter and birthdays and ...

here were squares of striped card and there were sheets of red ... Each time we made a discovery we hesitated, found ourselves glancing round, feeling like thieves. All this wealth for free!

At last we stopped, the trolley was full. One of the workmen came to push it towards the exit and oh dear, here came the manager again.

'Ah Sister,' he beamed, 'have you got enough? Do come back, Sister. I know you will put it all to good use in your school. Thank you, Sister. Goodbye Sister.'

The van smelt deliciously of clean fresh paper and we drove back to school with a feeling of well-being. While Saddy and Judah unloaded the packages into the store room we adjourned to the dispensary in the hostel for a coffee. Alerted by some radar Sister Pia shortly appeared.

'Oh, is the kettle on?' she glanced around. 'Did you have a good time? At Nedcoz?'

We told her the sad and sorry tale of dusty and creased card and paper, she sighed.

But then we relented and produced some of the Government Printer's offerings.

'Would this be of any use in your Art department?'

Ah, Sister Pia and her, 'Bring me something nice'.

After all the stock was safely locked away I set off home more than ready for the fresh cup of tea Joseph would have waiting for me, there I would read and reread the letters from our children in England. Perhaps a short walk with the dogs and a quick look at what Banda and White had achieved in the garden. There was little for Joseph to do now except feed the dogs and cats, we were going out that evening.

But before I needed to get ready there would be time to sit at my desk upstairs and start letters to Ceri and Simon. I nearly always wrote a long duplicated letter with a personal bit at the end. I commented on their news, tales of school and kept them up to date with their pets' activities. I described events in the country and news of anyone they knew, writing every week meant that sometimes one felt there was very little news but it is surprising how describing how the guinea fowl and peacocks had managed to mix up their eggs and how the dogs had given their advice through the wire netting and so on, the pages filled week after week. I rambled on in this way for years and was most disconcerted eventually to hear Ceri and Simon compare their school fellows' reactions to my letters.

'WHAT?' I said.

Too late did I learn that they had repeated requests, which they granted, to read my letters aloud at breakfast.

'It's OK, Mum,' said Simon,' they really enjoy them.'

'Yes,' agreed Ceri, 'and I only got into trouble when you were too funny and everyone made a lot of noise laughing.'

But I could not sit and write all evening, Andrew was coming up the stairs and with a quick kiss, he reminded me that we were due at the Intercont at 7pm.

The Intercont, short for the Intercontinental Hotel, where we were due for dinner. I seem to remember we were hosting but I can't for the life of me remember why. There were so many functions, all so similar that one ran into another until they were indistinguishable.

Quick baths one after the other. I had to make it quick because the temptation to lie there in the hot water and postpone the moment of setting off for yet another dinner was always strong. Andrew would dress cheerfully, talking over the events of the day. I would make it as far as underwear and then hesitate in front of the long dresses at the end of my wardrobes. I disliked going out but as I had to make the best of a bad job I had gone to Milady and bought several long dresses with which to cheer the evenings. They were pretty, I suppose, but it seemed a dreadful lot of money to spend when so many other things were needed. I had had the vague idea once that if I splurged out on some clothes then I would be carried along to feel some kind of enjoyment. It didn't really work.

For a short time I had enjoyed going in to kiss the children goodnight and listen to their admiring comments, but that soon wore off. Anyway, they were gone.

Andrew would be downstairs waiting for me - giving last minute instructions to Joseph, who didn't really need them. Once we had gone he would sit in the TV room watching TV - I am quite sure he made himself a drink and that when the mood was on them, he was probably joined by Banda and White. He would sit there; half asleep until we came home, for which onerous duty he was of course, paid extra.

While Joseph dozed in front of the TV we were arriving at the Intercont, Andrew all eager to join the party and me trying to convince myself just once more that I would enjoy it. It was such a contrast, walking into the hotel with its clean sweeps of well furnished rooms, neatly uniformed waiters going about their duties and the hushed hum of people enjoying themselves. It did not seem like a real world at all, after the dusty streets and barefoot people. The well-groomed locals and overseas visitors were at odds with the rags of the beggars outside the post office earlier in the day. One could watch the waiters deftly piling steaks on the terrace barbecues and wonder how often their families got to eat meat.

But we were not eating on the terrace that night, we took the lift to the top floor and the Makumbi Room. About fourteen of us sat down to dinner that evening and the conversation was light hearted and quick. Mike O'Keefe from Ireland was seated opposite which was a blessing and a handicap. I liked the O'Keefes but found Mike's accent, so soft and Irish, hard to follow at the best of times. Now he was across the table and the band was doing its best to drown out conversation - I knew I would have to do my best at lip reading. I have often thought I am going deaf on such occasions as everyone else appears to talk away merrily, while I am straining to hear my nearest neighbour. Perhaps they are all having a whale of a time and the table is surrounded by a series of monologues - just think what would happen if the band came to a sudden halt!

The band did not come to a sudden halt that night, perhaps it would have been better if it had. In between numbers the bandleader announced that the next number was especially dedicated to a guest, Mrs Kashita, and with that, the band launched into some sentimental tune. I turned to smile at Andrew, only to be met with a frown. He had not made the request. Or so he said. But then who had?

'You should know,' he muttered.

The wretched tune went on apparently for ever while I tried to get Andrew to admit that he had requested it and he got more and more grumpy and eventually muttered,

'It must be your friend over there' glancing at poor Mike, who of course laughed and denied it. I wished the blessed band would play for someone else.

Not a perfect evening at all. Andrew was very cold to Mike, who was over from Ireland for a short time on business and who in the end looked very embarrassed. We drove home in silence, in the cool darkness, bright stars above us and frogs calling noisily from the dam as we turned up the drive. Mike's wife was not with him on this trip and as we were old friends, I would have liked to invite him to dinner the next day, but thought better of it.

Next day I forgot all about the previous night in the usual hubbub of the classroom and when at home time one of the parents asked if I had enjoyed the previous evening I had to think for a moment where I had been. Notuthelo's father had been the band leader; I tactfully did not say that I took very little notice of such things, being more than tone deaf, but complimented him on the pleasant music.

And then inspiration!

'Who made the request?' I asked.

Mr Tutani laughed,

'Well, actually it was me. I played it for you.'

As a change from the crowded dinner parties I once suggested to Andrew that we take ourselves off for a quiet dinner a deux, at one of the small restaurants. He thought it was an odd idea but eventually agreed and I looked forward to an evening on our own. It was a small restaurant in Longacres, Italian I think, and having been there before with friends we knew the food was good. It was only as the meal progressed I realised how far apart we had drifted. Conversation stopped and started. Looking round halfway through the meal I was struck by the animated conversations around us contrasting sadly with the long silences at our table.

Andrew did not travel as much and we no longer had a security guard if he did – there was only one night I wished we had. Andrew was away and I had retired to bed with a book late in the evening. Dozing off to sleep sometime later I was wakened by noises. It was difficult to identify them. Quiet, surreptitious noises – as though someone were moving about. I sat up and listened. All quiet and then just as I was about to lie down again the soft movements continued. There was a door at the top of the stairs - that would hold back intruders for a while. If I went out on the roof, who would hear me? The servants were doubtless all fast asleep.

I lifted the phone beside the bed and dialled Stella's number. And under the cover of the sheets, whispered that I had an intruder. She asked what exactly I could hear, said they would drive out, told me to lock the bedroom door. Stella always could be relied upon! I felt better already – at which point there was an almighty crash and flapping noise clearly audible down the phone line and she shouted, 'What's happening?'

We had a built in linen cupboard just inside the bedroom door. Both doors were flung back, there was a heap and a pile of sheets and blankets and Lord knows what else on the floor – on top of which was Big Puss.

Once over the hysterical reaction and Stella's caustic remarks, I carried the cat down and put her firmly out in the courtyard.

It may have been about this time that I took Banda's wife into Lusaka to the maternity ward. Banda and I left her there after being told firmly to return the next day to pick up mother and baby. We duly set off the next afternoon and I parked outside to wait for Banda – he was always quiet and had been even more so on the drive in. After a while I saw him walk out – alone, with downcast face. Appalled at what I thought must be bad news I jumped from the van and asked about his wife. He said he could not take his wife and baby home. 'Why?'

'Baby she have no clothes.'

And I remembered. Remembered hearing that women would not prepare for a baby's arrival in case something went wrong – the very opposite of a Western culture where the preceding 9 months are spent in buying and knitting all manner of baby essentials.

Blaming myself for not checking I made him jump into the van, drove down into town where I bought a range of baby clothes and nappies and we shot back up to the hospital. Banda went in again, looking despondent and apprehensive, not at all sure he would be able to collect his wife and child.

But eventually they emerged and I had to laugh. Banda was carrying his baby (properly dressed and dischargeable!) but at arms' length as though he were carrying a live bomb due to go off at any moment. A beautiful little baby but very quiet parents, I could hardly get a word out of Banda all the way back. He sat there holding on to the precious bundle as if he'd never let go.

It was easy to get wrapped up in one's personal life and only quickly glance at the daily papers or only half listen to Andrew's recounting the latest mishap or news.

So often you seemed to hear the same thing repeated - Choma farmers could not get sacks therefore they could not delivered the maize they had produced and therefore they had no money to repay their loans.

We were told again that experiments had shown that wheat could be grown in Zambia - this always irritated me. A local farmer had been growing wheat when we first arrived in Northern Rhodesia and were living at Mount Makulu in 1962.

One million bags of maize worth three million kwacha might go to waste if not collected within two weeks before the rains well and truly started.

Considering the emphasis the Government was putting on the agrarian revolution, especially now that copper was not the great financial support it had been, it was disappointing that they were still not getting their act together.

Kaunda watched a march past of six thousand Lusaka school children at the Statue of Freedom and a torch bearing Kabulonga school girl gave the message ...

'having accepted the programme of Party and Government the youth of Zambia have committed themselves to its implementation and declare their full support ... as the vanguard of the revolution the youth recognise the role of agrarian revolution which was the basis for the nations survival ...'

Kaunda responded with an inspiring list of advice and exhortation

'... youth must establish a high standard of self-discipline ...

Maintain higher standards of cleanliness...

Work hard in classroom production units and homes...

Strengthen the Party as vanguard of the revolution... make humanism the guiding light in the road to progress...

Be vigilant against the enemy...

Liberate themselves from foreign ideology...

Reaffirm their commitment to eradication of international capitalism, fascism, racism and exploitation of one man by another...'

(Was it only me who noticed the rhetoric had a marked resemblance to the ramblings in a certain Red Book circulating courtesy of our friend Chairman Mao? Or was it from our Korean friends who were active – doing what I can't remember).

If all the energy put into speeches and marches had been put to use on the land and at work there might have been a bit more progress. If only leaders in every sphere, no matter how lowly, had planned and organised efficiently and if only workers had responded to the best of their ability...

So many if onlys.

A few lone voices stood out in the wilderness.

Elias Chipimo spoke out about the proposed education reforms and on the political education which was incorporated at all stages and programmes of the reforms,

He said, *'... this could degenerate into sheer political indoctrination set either against other systems or directed at current leadership ...'*

John Mwanakatwe '... *I have been a very sad and depressed man since I was appointed Minister of Finance four months ago ... I would have expected top civil servants running our Ministries and departments would be front liners in enforcing financial discipline ... there is so much extravagance and disregard for financial stringency as was the case during 1973 – 1974, boom years for copper ...'*

We all knew what was possible, where was it all going wrong?

There were constant shortages - flour or butter or oil or soap or beef or ... any variation or combination of ... and there never seemed to be any sensible or satisfactory explanation.

The school year ended with the report that a UBZ bus taking students to a Zambia National Service camp was involved in an accident on the Great East Road and one student tragically lost his life.

Ceri and Simon had been at school for one whole term and now Andrew had the idea that I should go over to England to collect them from school. It seemed an expensive idea to me but I knew he would not suggest it if the firm were not doing well enough so I made arrangements with a light heart. Time was short and I found that I would have to fly the same evening that term ended, not an ideal day as the last day of term especially the end of year was always a tiring time. Somehow I got through all the jobs that had to be done and that night collapsed in my seat in the plane thinking that it was a good job I was a good traveller and had no problems sleeping on planes. We had barely taken off when I fell asleep.

There was stop scheduled for Kinshasa so when I was aware of the fasten seat belts routine, I merely complied and went back to sleep. We seemed to be on the ground for some time and take off assumed a faintly nightmarish quality as I seemed to wake up several times, each time on the point of take-off, with a rather strained pilots voice in the background.

I woke in the early light of dawn on the approach to London,

Heathrow. For once breakfast appealed as I had slept through dinner. My seat companion glanced at me tucking in to coffee and rolls.

'You sure have nerves of steel,' he remarked.

The coffee and rolls were no worse than usual ... I glanced at them and then back at him.

'I guess you were the only one to sleep through that take off,' he added.

I could not make out whether he had thought I was a little rude when we took off in Lusaka but at last discovered that once the plane had touched down at Kinshasa there had been a complete power failure. We had sat for some time in complete darkness on the runway until the power had been restored, taxied up for take-off, only to have the lights go out again. There were another two false starts and at last we had taken off with partial airport power and men standing along the edge of the runway holding paraffin lamps.

So that accounted for peering out of the window once and thinking there must be a high wind for lights to sway like that. I confessed my sleep had been sheer tiredness not bravery but the American looked unconvinced.

London was cold and grey but who cared? It was the end of term. Simon and Ceri would finish school that weekend. I went straight up to York, checking in at the familiar Viking Hotel. There was time for a little Christmas shopping and it was fun to walk along the festive streets, gazing into bursting shops. What a contrast to Lusaka's bare city centre and shelves. To my surprise I did not want to buy much - which was just as well as I hadn't much money - but it was bliss to walk and look and admire.

Sheila Wilson was coming over to meet me in York on Saturday morning and we were going to the Carol Service at Simon's school together. I went to bed that night feeling as excited as if I were a child anticipating Christmas morning. To my horror the exhaustion of the end of term and the flight must have still been there as I very much overslept and instead of waking early, I woke with barely ten minutes to spare before Sheila was due to arrive and we were due to set off for the school immediately. By missing breakfast I just made it.

The chapel is old and beautiful, we sat on the hard pews whispering what news we had not already exchanged on the walk across town. I spotted Christopher Oldfield's parents behind us and we exchanged smiles. Now the boys were filing in and by craning my neck I caught sight of Simon at last.

Carol Services are always emotional times with the sentimentality of Christmas and even with the commercialism there is today, I think most of us have a lump in our throats when boys' voices soar high in the rafters of the chapel. Too soon it was over and we crossed over to the House to collect our sons. Joan and Keith Oldfield had already offered to take home Simon's trunk and deal with the contents - a most noble offer as Joan discovered that neither of them had had their rugger kit washed for a term. After lunch Sheila left us and Simon and I went out to do some Christmas shopping for Ceri. I smiled at the thought of Simon admitting in school that he had never seen a Father Christmas and the Housemaster insisting three older boys had to take him into town and introduce him to one of the British customs.

'... and he even asked if I wanted to sit on his knee!'

in mixed tones of horror and amusement.

The streets were crowded with Christmas shoppers and from every shop entrance came the sound of carols. Simon and I were at last walking back up Lendal Street, our arms full of packages, when I glanced sideways and found him gazing at me as though he could hardly believe his eyes. The old thoughts about why we were doing this to our children all surfaced again, but now I was better at controlling them.

Once Ceri's term finished we hurried back down to London and boarded a flight home. What a relief to leave behind the grey chill days and land in the rosy dawn of Africa with the promise of a long hot day ahead. Andrew was there at the airport and the talk never stopped all the way home.

As we turned into the drive the dogs trotted round the side of the house and stood wagging their tails by the kitchen porch. As

Ceri and Simon stepped out of the car both Peter and Paula came forward and then went into ecstatic bounds and prances as they realised who they were sniffing.

Banda and White came hurrying round the corner and Joseph emerged beaming from the kitchen, taking charge of the situation. Hands were shaken and clasped again and again in the traditional welcome and the dogs fussed round the group, nosing first this one and then that one. We tried to get into the house while the servants collected the bags, all three intent on taking them upstairs and thus having an extra look at the two travellers.

Joseph, deciding at last, that he was most needed in the kitchen, where he had the trays already prepared. I stopped for a moment to thank him for taking care of the house and Bwana in my absence. He smiled his thanks and added,

'England is no good for them, Madam.'

'Why not? they have to go to school you know.'

'Ah yes, Dona, but England is no good, they are too white. They need to come back to Africa to live. Will they get brown again? Miss Ceri, she is too white!'

I went laughing to join the others and give them Joseph's opinion. Andrew and I were left with the coffee cups within a matter of a few minutes. Ceri and Simon were off down to the dam, dogs trotting and bounding at their heels. Once more the tears pricked.

Preparations for Christmas took on a more special feeling of thanksgiving that year and we valued each day. The house once again echoed to the sound of young voices all day, the piano sounded throughout the quiet of hot afternoons and no sooner had the dogs returned from one walk than there was the chance of another. Joseph excelled himself in the kitchen while Banda and White seemed to have more work to do near the house than ever before and were ready with beaming smiles for any job Ceri or Simon might request.

We made shopping expeditions with our usual humour and secrecy even though the shelves did not compare with those we had seen in York. The boxes for the men and their wives and children were soon filled and the children's bedrooms were out of bounds to others.

Andrew made a ceremony of choosing a tree with Simon. Two days before Christmas Day Banda and White dug it up and we had the usual uproar and mess getting it into a tub and into the house with Joseph clucking over the soil and bits of greenery trailing through the house. Even going to the usual spate of parties was not so bad when there was such overflowing happiness at home.

On Christmas morning there was the traditional early rising to drink coffee and exclaim over gifts. Joseph ushered in the children from the servants quarters, all scrubbed and shining, their eyes wide with surprise at being invited into the big house. White's children were sturdy, solemn but cheerfully expectant. Joseph's three were tall and thin and shy, one of them howling at finding himself in the unfamiliar surroundings. They stared wide eyed at the tree in the corner and clutched their boxes tightly, feet rooted to the spot. Later with their balloons they made their way slowly to the door. Then in came their mothers, left hand holding the right forearm while the right hand was extended ready to shake. They bobbed their heads and bent their knees, saying Happy Christmas again and again. Then the men came in, in a leisurely way to collect their boxes and they all departed across the garden to sit and open and compare and talk. It was not long before we heard the sound of children's voices as they chased their balls and ate the first of the goodies.

Joseph did not stay long, he was very conscious of his reputation and some of his favourite people were coming to dinner. The kitchen sent delicious smells over the house and he and Banda hurried to and fro as though a large scale West End production were in force. Don Fluck came from next door with his brother and mother, aged 92, both out from England. Phil Howard appeared in trousers not shorts so I did not recognise him at first. Then Paul and Joan Lusaka were not far behind with their three children and the day slipped into food and drink and conversation and laughter.

At one point in the afternoon I slipped away and stood on the flat roof and looked around.

The grass, the trees, the blue sky and the soft touch of the wind. The sound of voices from below in the house and behind where three other families murmured together.

'Come on! let's all walk down to the dam.'

'Come on, let's go together!.'

The end of 1976 had seen a slump in the price of copper, the devaluation of the kwacha, an all-round business slump, tight monetary restrictions, the list went on.

But we had our home and children and peace out of town.

LOOKING FORWARD 1977

Once Christmas was over of course, there was the downward spiral towards the day when Ceri and Simon would have to return to England. We tried not to mention it or even think of the day. But as we filled each day with activities or peace, I found myself clinging to each moment. Some of my friends had sent their children away to school long ago and I wondered how they faced the regular separation with such apparent calm.

One day I had to go into school to collect some papers and of course was delayed by queries from Sister de Angelis. For once Simon didn't complain, he had asked to accompany me so that he could use his skateboard on the smooth tarmac of the Convent drives and cement verandahs. Watching him swooping around I accepted the offer of a coffee - the skateboard was useless at home with dirt or gravel drives. Just as I was leaving, still talking to Sister de Angelis we saw Simon hurtle round the corner of a classroom block, narrowly missing a tall man walking the other way.

'Who's that?' I asked.

'Oh, one of the Brothers staying here for a while. Father Jesus.'

When Simon arrived at the van I couldn't resist asking if he had apologised to Jesus, enjoying the momentary look of panic on his face,

Close friend May Sharpe with Jennifer and Susan

The days flew by all too quickly but for now, we drove here and there, resuming old friendships with other friends home for holidays and the few, like Jenny and Susan Sharpe who had not gone away to school. Each day was packed with trips, picnics, parties and visits. All too soon of course they were due to fly and I spent an anxious night hoping the flight had gone according to schedule, that the friends had met them at the airport and that they had made the right rail connection to York.

After twenty four hours one was then convinced that all was well and sat back to wait for the first letter. Ceri used to write chatty and newsy letters, even so her lyrical one written after she had seen her first snow was an unexpected pleasure. Simon's letters were rather more perfunctory but still gave a picture of his life at Saint Peters.

This pattern continued over the years; Ceri continued writing newsy letters at regular intervals. Once Simon was not made to write the weekly letter home it deteriorated into an occasional note with the barest details and no reflection of his thoughts at all. All through the years of their schooling and later college and university I maintained my weekly letter knowing what the response would be. Then one year I went down with flu and did not write for a while, almost instantly a letter arrived from Simon with the indignant query, 'Where is your letter?'

Although I missed them terribly I was sure that we had made the right decision. We were looking forward to the day they returned to Zambia for good, in the meantime it appeared to be the best way to guarantee an uninterrupted education. They would of course have to fulfil the National Service requirements once they were finished at school or Uni. It had become acceptable that the occasional reports in the papers often went unnoticed. A plaintive letter form Chikwanda Mulenga in Kasama camp appeared to go unheeded ...

'We were made to run in rain which made our uniforms wet, then did PE in PE kit and it was wet. Our civilian clothing was confiscated so we stay in wet clothes. And we are beaten. Send a Commission of Inquiry.'

Wet clothes did not worry me unduly - although it did seem a bit unnecessary – but the beating and tone of the letter did make one wonder. I sincerely hoped that a copy of the newspaper was not read by any of the people in charge of Kasama camp.

Early in 1977 we received some very distressing news. Seven missionaries were taken from Musami Mission in Rhodesia during the night and were shot dead. Was it guerrillas or was it Selous Scouts? Does it matter? One of the missionaries was Sister Ceslaus Steigler, who had been with us at the Lusaka Convent for a very long time before the Mother Superior in Salisbury had her transferred south. An elderly nun of ample proportions she had made her mark with her brilliant work in the Maths department in the secondary school - and equally with her work and care for the rose bed in between the two schools near the flag pole. Woe betide the person who was tempted to cross the grass and bend over to inhale their fragrance. You would be within several inches of a rose and Sister Ceslaus would appear as if by magic. They were NOT to be picked or even handled. She had a reputation of a martinet but the girls adored her, recognising her devotion to her work and their welfare.

I have a particularly fond memory of her bluntness. She caught me once near her rose bed but I escaped with a short lecture on their care. Garlic planted by each bush prevented any depredations by white ants - a point worth remembering.

Then, as we stood chatting, she talked about Ceri's progress she said,

'... a good girl ... not so good with the maths but a good girl ... and so pretty! I did not approve of mixed marriages, I thought it was wrong, but now I know people like Ceri it is good if we have such beautiful children.'

Out of the blue I found myself saying,

'Well, Sister, you know what they say ...'

And we both recited together 'mixed breeds are always better' and then stared at each other appalled.

And then we laughed. She poked me in the ribs and said,

'I could only say it to you, but I thought it and it is so true. Such beautiful children are God's gifts and I have learned so much more now ...' she paused, looking round the garden. 'I thought I could not stay when independence was coming, but now I am happier and I love my work so much more. Thank God for your children - as I do.'

WHY shoot Sister Ceslaus in her seventies? she had come to Rhodesia in 1935 and all she had done was teach children and hope to instil in them some of her love for Maths. And roses.

Life goes on. Leave the grieving and worry about the shortages of feed for livestock. Bad enough for us with our small numbers of chickens and ducks and sheep and rabbits - but what about the farmers trying to feed the country and make a living?

The dairy, piggery and poultry industries were reported to be on the verge of collapse because of the shortage of feed and on Kafubu Dairy Farm near Ndola they experimented with feeding their cattle with chicken droppings to supplement their protein. Rogers Mumbi, who had a chicken farm, stood outside school one day and worried about whether he could continue to make a living and keep his daughter at school.

'And when you can get feed,' he added. 'It is under strength which is why the yolks are such a pale yellow and the shells break so easily.'

We had as usual chickens and ducks and geese, guinea fowl and peacocks, the rabbits and now Andrew had purchased a few sheep which we hoped to breed and augment our meat supply. The arrival of lambs reminded me of the fun we had had with the piglets in the classroom. It was a very short step to chatting up Sister James who drove the Convent bus and one morning off we went with thirty excited little girls in the bus and ten in my van. We had a lovely time looking at the lambs and the ducklings (they had risen to the occasion too), identifying the trees in the orchard and so on. Finally back to the house where Joseph had prepared orange juice and biscuits and an aside to me,

'Madam, Banda he say he very sad - he thought Miss Ceri come back' and looking at Kate Whittingham I could see why. So very like Ceri at the age of six.

Kate Whittingham on the left with friends in Grade 1

What also struck me then and more so now, when I planned it all I did was to send a note home asking parents' permission. All agreed. And off we went with three adults (Sister de went in the bus with Sister James) and no one, no one, ever queried the safety of the trip. But then of course, we knew a class of forty 5 year olds, mostly Zambian, would behave impeccably. One never thought otherwise.

The problem of shortages never went away completely. First it was one section of the economy and then another. The Government tried to keep the prices down but that aggravated the problem as profiteers could transport maize meal, soap powder, oil etc across the border into Zaire along the many bush paths completely undetected by Customs.

As usual when there is a food shortage the children are the first to suffer. Various voluntary groups grew up but as Joyce Watae reported

'The years between 1966 and 1971 saw a lot of activities all over the country. Nutrition groups sprang up with volunteers going into shanty compounds where malnutrition is common to sell cheap nutritious foods to mothers and teach them how to prepare the foods properly for their children. Secondary schools, especially girls' schools, had nutrition clubs and would meet nutrition group organisers, mostly expatriates, to go into shanty compounds teaching mothers what was best for their children. Now however the nutrition drive seems to have suddenly gone into oblivion. Nobody seems to have a good explanation as to what has happened. Could it be that because most of the expats have left we do not have enough Zambians willing to work as volunteers? This apathy among Zambians was also mentioned in the groups' annual report on 1974 as being one of the factors which were happening to nutrition groups in the country. The report expressed fears that several groups would collapse when expats left.'

In 1975 in an MP's debate on nutrition MP Fleefort Chirwa had said it was common for many leaders to condemn voluntary organisations on the flimsy excuse that they were expat dominated.

Food was not the only thing in erratic supply of course and reports that tonnes of imports were lying on the docks at Dar es Salaam for up to two years at a time because of importers negligence, unprocessed papers and other inefficiencies did little to cheer the lot of the common man.

It was very noticeable that when the President demanded

explanations, items appeared but when he was busy elsewhere shortages began again. Andrew was quoted as saying inefficient distribution of goods was largely to blame. For example, Nakambala Sugar Estate produced enough sugar - so where was it? Certainly not on the shelves in the shops all at the same time. If it was available in Ndola, it was missing in Lusaka and if it appeared in Lusaka it vanished in Choma. Coffee grown in Zambia was to be found in Botswana and Tanzania but not in Zambia.

In April it was reported that drugs were running out because Government institutions owed K2.2million to the Medical and Pharmaceutical Corporation and when the Government inquired into alleged shortages of drugs in some places Mepco Director Nalumango said some people over ordered to avoid criticism.

In the same month we were told that the country had 20,000 tonnes of wheat - enough to last 2 months. The US gave Zambia a K5million loan to buy emergency supplies ... 16,000 tonnes of wheat and 5,000 tonnes of edible oils.

Although at the same time Indeco announced there were no shortages.

However, we battled on at home and at work.

The first term of 1977 went more smoothly; we were in a more regular routine although we were still waiting to hear who would take over as headmistress. One day I took Sister de Angelis and Sister Lee Ann into Lusaka to shop. We had quite a long list and had planned out a route from the industrial area back to the town centre via the post office and thence to the Catholic Secretariat. All went smoothly as far as Sister de and I were concerned. Sister Lee Ann was still adjusting to life in Zambia having arrived from the States only a couple of weeks earlier and so found shopping expeditions somewhat disappointing. As we settled down in the van and set off, she produced a list saying,

'I have to get some herb tea. If we stop at that little store in Kabulonga I could get that there and then you will have to tell me where I can get the other things on my list.'

I looked at Sister de and she looked at me. True we had told Sister

Lee Ann that Kabulonga store was the nearest supermarket but we had also told her that there was a very limited range of goods available. Gently we tried to explain that herb tea was an unheard of luxury, finding tea itself was exciting enough. If we were lucky enough to find tea it would be one sort only, plain black Indian. Sister Lee Ann listened but clearly did not take it all in because as I parked outside the store in Kabulonga, she murmured,

'Just a packet of herb tea - camomile would do just fine, nothing special.

Sister de took it upon herself to escort Sister Lee Ann and I wandered off on the usual tour of the shelves - just in case something had come in that we had not seen for some time.

How things had changed I thought as I ambled along. Once I had made a monthly shopping list, gone into a store - often CBC (formerly Kees) - bought everything on the list and driven home. End of shopping for a month - except for fresh veg and fruit of course. Now we made regular trips round every store because we never knew what would be in stock when. It was not unusual to go several weeks without being able to get such mundane things as flour or sugar or soap or tea ... as for herb tea!!

We climbed back up into the van and I let in the clutch.

'There wasn't any tea AT ALL,' said a puzzled voice from the other end of the seat. 'No tea at all.'

As we progressed from shop to shop Sister Lee Ann began to understand some of what we had been trying to explain, even so she found it hard to grasp the fact that not only were some items unavailable, we had no idea if and when they would be. Apart from trying to come to grips with the shopping problems she thoroughly enjoyed the experiences and talked incessantly and enthusiastically about how she had come to Africa to work in the rural areas and was waiting impatiently to be assigned to a post in the bush.

In the meantime I was sure the quiet Dominicans were experiencing a very different kind of Sister in their midst. Her arrival had taken them all by surprise for a start. The Convent doorbell rang late one afternoon and when Sister Amadea opened the door she was confronted by the largest Sister she (or indeed any of us) had ever seen and a huge pile of suitcases. 'Hi there,' said this apparition, sticking out its hand. 'I'm Sister Lee Ann and I have just arrived.'

This in the broadest of American accents. And this was the first time that anyone knew that a Sister Lee Ann had been recruited in the States by the Catholic Secretariat and told to proceed to the Dominican Convent in Lusaka and await a posting. She had taken the quiet community by storm with her lively outspoken humour and her vivid American voice contrasted sharply with the quiet tones of the Sisters.

At last we were halfway round town and I stopped at the post office to collect our post. As usual I left the van and ran upstairs to the long double line of green metal boxes and put the key into 1528. There was a small bundle of mail and I sorted through it as I walked back to the van.

One was a telegram from England.

DOUG KILLED IN CAR ACCCIDENT. DENISE AND STEVE.

I suppose all such moments are unreal to those who experience them. One moment we had all been involved in shopping and showing Sister Lee Ann the highlights of Lusaka and now suddenly I was jolted out of the sunshine and was looking at a small boy with dark eyes standing at the front of the church as I walked up the aisle, a tall dark boy walking up and down outside Queens Hotel in Leeds, a boy whose smile always showed two very large front teeth.

I went home and phoned Denise and Steve and I phoned Andrew at the office and I phoned the airline and I booked a flight to UK. It was, for once, not easy to sleep on the plane. I sat through the long night hours thinking of the times I had seen Douglas and Denise, from the first time we met at the Children's Home. The times I had taken them out at weekends, either together or separately and the fun we had had. Riding on donkeys or rowing boats in Roundhay Park, picnics on the grass and meals out in small cafes.

My wedding when Denise had been so happy but Douglas had looked sad, being older he understood the coming separation. The letters and cards we had exchanged and the times we had seen them when we had come to UK. And the time we had met at Queens Hotel in Leeds. Denise, by this time married to Steve, turned up on time but we waited a long time for Douglas. At last I went outside to find him walking up and down unable to pluck up the courage to come in to Reception and ask for us. He said it was too posh and he was conscious of his colour. Oh Doug, with his slow wide grin and the two big teeth. I cried with my face turned to the shuttered window as the other passengers slept.

England was always cold and grey when you first arrived, even if the sun were producing an early morning watery sunshine - the first impression was always of cold greyness.

I made my way to Kings Cross station and joined a long queue snaking round the concourse, apparently one didn't just go and board a train anymore. I wondered vaguely when the change had first taken place.

A tall man behind me was intent on making conversation. He looked around him and nodded at this or that, made one or two general comments, glancing at me to see if I would respond. In my miserable state the last thing I wanted was to be drawn into conversation with a complete stranger but then, I thought, supposing he is in trouble and needs to talk? And it might take my mind off things for a time.

So at his next attempt I smiled vaguely and agreed that we were having a long wait, and that the station was chilly. So of course it was not long before I knew he was over from Australia, had in fact flown in that very morning, it was his first trip back to UK in more than twenty years, he was going north to see relatives.

'And it's nowhere near as bad as you're led to believe.'

'What isn't?' I was half listening.

'Why, there aren't the number of blacks about that you expect. Know what I mean? We keep hearing that the old country is over run with them. Blacks! I didn't want to come back if it was too bad and then I thought it is MY country too and why should a lot of black bastards stop me coming back? Mind you, they should all be shipped back to where they come from. That's what I say.'

'I quite agree,' I said loudly. 'But first of all of course, all the stupid bastards who have gone to Australia and New Zealand and America and Canada and Africa and so on would have to be shipped back to England, although I doubt there is room for all of the silly bastards. And now if you will excuse me, I will move to the end of the queue. You see, my husband is black and I should hate you to feel uncomfortable.'

I picked up my case and walked to the back of the queue; thank goodness it was not too far, I hate making gestures which cost me dear.

From the corner of my eye I could see a most red and uncomfortable looking Australian standing first on one leg and then the other, trying to look unconcerned but clearly conscious of the amused glances of those nearby.

Once on the train I slept most of the way. Steve and Denise met me at the station and we drove to their house in silence apart from Denise's occasional,

'I can't believe you're here ... none of this is really happening.'

Steve was a plump young man, usually rather quiet but now he could not stop talking about his worry for Denise and how she would cope with Douglas' death.

'He was her only family and they have always been so close, he used to come and see her every week you know.'

'But there is a mother somewhere ... ' I began.

'Don't mention her! She turned up all right. As soon as the news was in the newspapers she turned up and as Doug made no will, she is his next of kin and she is making a claim to the insurance money, which will be paid out. She has really upset Denise and I had to tell her we don't want her to come to the house.'

Poor Denise, her troubles did not come singly.

We sat over cups of tea as they told me how Douglas had died. He had gone out for the evening with friends, driving home they had gone round a corner and driven smack into a parked lorry. Douglas, who was sitting in the rear, had gone through a side window and was killed instantly. The other boys survived with remarkably few injuries. While Denise was in the kitchen, making yet another cup of tea, Steve whispered,

'I have told her he was not marked, you know? And that she should remember him alive. But he was badly messed about. I don't want her to know and I don't think you should see him either. If you do, please don't tell her.'

I agreed not to visit the funeral parlour either so that Denise would not wish to accompany me. All through the long evening friends dropped in and it was late before we got to bed.

The funeral was arranged for the next day, I had arranged to meet Sheila Wilson at the station. Charlie and June Mawson, who had lived near the Children's Home and taken an active interest in the children in those far off days, drove me to the station. Charlie was now a detective inspector in the police and was a great help and comfort to Denise and Steve at that time.

It was more than a poignant reunion for Denise and Sheila as they had not met since Sheila left the Home and her successor had requested no contacts - one assumes with the idea that their loyalties would not be divided. Naturally though, the children had felt doubly deserted.

We sat together in the small sitting room and talked, talked of Douglas and each other's news and Douglas again. And then the cars were at the door and the hushed voices of the undertakers and we were sitting in the too comfortable seats, following a car with a coffin. Douglas was in that coffin, we would not see him again and we wept. And we were now speeding along with the city's flow. Near the cemetery the cars slowed to a more respectful speed, we turned in at tall gates on to a long drive, which was lined on both sides with people. All along the sides of the drive were young people and a few older ones. The cars stopped and as we got out, I felt angry that funerals were planned so close together. Whispers and heads together.

'There isn't room for everyone inside the chapel,' said Steve. 'So they are going to stand outside and some in the doorway after we have gone in.

They were all friends of Douglas.

The coffin was going in now and we followed it, Sheila and I close behind Steve and Denise. We sat at the front, close enough even now to touch him and the Minister was asking people to crowd in as much as they could. They filled the aisle and the back and overflowed through the doorway outside still. The small chapel could not hold them all.

Steve was glancing about, he caught my eye.

'I am looking for the mother. I told her to keep out of sight.'

Services, like goodbyes, are always too short.

After the service as we climbed into the cars, Sheila said,

'I hadn't thought about afterwards - are all these people going to fit into the house?'

She had a surprise. The cars stopped outside a public house. Everyone began to climb out as I tried to explain to Sheila that the landlord had offered to have everyone there; Doug and his friends had spent so much time there, he felt it was one way to show his sympathy. The Mawsons, Sheila and I sat together feeling a bit uncomfortable as we watched the young people crowding in. There were expressions of quiet sympathy for Denise and Steve and then as plates of sandwiches appeared, they began to collect drinks from the bar.

'I suppose they did get together here, like a sort of club ... and he had no family,' said Sheila uncertainly, 'but it does seem strange ... oh dear, is he going to? ... he is ... '

I followed her glance and was just in time to see a chap drop a coin in the juke box.

Later that night Denise gave me some photos of Doug, they were all of him in the five a side football team, two shields and a cup and a ring he had worn. I read again the obituary in the local paper of the young star of the local team and then I left for London to catch a flight home.

BACK HOME

Andrew's mother was due to make another visit and this time she would be accompanied by a niece from the village. At first I thought of the two shrieking toddlers of 1964 but then Andrew explained that his mother was feeling her age and that it would be a teenager, who would be a help and company for her. They arrived at the station with their bundles as usual, mother in law looking much as I remembered, perhaps a little more wrinkled but with the same piercing bright eyes and deep voice.

'Eh heh, mwapoleni mukwai,' she laughed as I stumbled through the greeting which she knew was about the extent of my Bemba. And then she produced her one English phrase

'Mwapoleni mukwai OK?'

'OK,' I agreed laughing.

Sometimes I have regretted my laziness about learning Bemba but then most people in Lusaka spoke English and the local language was Nyanja so that was what was used on the street and in the markets. And Andrew himself was no encouragement at all, he had not even bothered to speak Bemba to our children. I know now that I missed a great opportunity to learn some genuine tribal history from my mother in law. And I would have liked to know more of her history and background and views on life. Like many people I thought there is always tomorrow, next time.

However, this time mother in law was with a niece who spoke English. Or did she? Officially she been to school and spoke English. So we should have been able to communicate but it was very difficult. First of all I could not break down the girl's traditional village shyness in the presence of elders. Add to that she was over awed being in a large town house and in close living contact with a musungu. At least she was past the stage of shrieking round the place I thought, as I battled to get her to meet my eyes and talk. Most of all it was disappointing to find that her English was very much learned by rote and when faced with a question or sentence she had not learned, she was completely at sea. I was sure she could not be as slow as she appeared and cursed the education system whereby poorly qualified and trained teachers were teaching in a second language. Nor had she the confidence to try to reach out and grasp the chance which was offered. In spite of all my attempts she remained quietly withdrawn, eyes cast down. I wondered if mother in law had ever been like this, it was hard to visualise.

Grandmother was noticeably older on this visit and was even more content to sit and muse away her time. She sat for long periods gazing across the garden into the bush, chewing on a tiny stick. From time to time she would rise and walk slowly across the garden for a while and take a turn along the edges where the grass was cut back, the dogs would follow hopefully but her days when she would have explored the plot in full were gone now. She sat and rethreaded tiny beads making simple bracelets. I have one still. She looked at the photos of Ceri and Simon taken since she had last visited and clearly made the typical grandmotherly remarks about how they had grown.

We went into town a few times and over to the Mwenyas, where she would relate the village news - and gather news to take home again. But throughout I felt this was rather a sad visit. Grandmother was old now and while her eyes shone as brightly as ever and I am sure her tongue was as sharp, she herself was tired.

Ceri and Simon were home for the summer holiday and the days were full of activity as they caught up with developments on the land and in the house and their friends and ... and ...

And Ceri was keen to play me a new piece of music on the piano which she had recently discovered and fallen in love with. As the notes of Beethoven's Moonlight Sonata filled the house I felt an unexpected tingle – the piece of music so many friends and relatives had talked about in my childhood, 'When your mother played that no one could talk for a long time afterwards' they said.

We did make a trip over to Munda Wanga where mother in law was scandalised to see Simon accept the invitation of the keeper to handle some of the snakes. She sat as far away as possible yet near enough to keep up a running commentary in Bemba.

*Ceri and Simon at Munda Wanga – could not get Grandmother
into the picture!*

Andrew seemed happy enough away from Government and the more his business grew the more cheerful he became. He had, of course, put on a good front but he had been very hurt and many another person would have been bitter. In public we had been cheerful and outwardly open, making it clear that Andrew had done nothing to be ashamed of, much less merit being axed. But the old proverb about there being no smoke without fire is well known and I am sure was used at this time to hint there really had been 'something'.

Some of the rumours eventually made their way back to us and sometimes we laughed at the sheer ludicrousness even while it hurt. I remember Andrew was reported to have a whole ship load of copper sailing somewhere on the high seas - even if he had, it would not have been worth much in those days. We had of course, so it was said, a villa in Italy and a house in London and a house - or was it a flat? - in Yugoslavia ... All one could do throughout all this period was to present a united and cheerful front. It was all past now but there was still a nasty taste left in the mouth. So the more Andrew worked and the more he achieved the more I was thankful he could rise above the situation.

It was a dubious comfort to see the President drop another

Minister from his Cabinet later in the year. Aaron Milner was dropped with the statement that *'he* (the President) *had constantly received reports which he could no longer ignore'.*

Milner stated, *'It includes a report that I exported two million kwacha out of the country'.* That rumour had been around for about a year.

This was followed by the President's statement that Milner was being investigated because he did not adhere to the Leadership Code. It was another seven days wonder when nothing concrete seemed to be produced and I never did know who or what to believe, except that there was an awful lot of pots calling kettles black.

The Milner publicity was soon overshadowed by Kaunda ordering a curfew on Lusaka, Kafue, Chilanga and Livingstone; we were to stay indoors and show no lights from 8pm to 5am. We were told that Rhodesia was planning air raids. Cinemas cancelled shows and hotels changed meal times. So from the 4th to 20th September the already quiet life of Lusaka became even quieter.

Simon Kapwepwe came out of retirement on his farm and with other ex UPP members went to State House to pledge loyalty to Kaunda because of the situation in the country.

But as far as we, the general public, were aware nothing much happened until we heard that the Zambian Air Force had shot down two Rhodesian aeroplanes in the Sesheke area for, I suppose, violating our air space. This did not cause any reprisals as far as I can recall. At the time I wondered why no statements by Rhodesia were quoted in our Press, did they make any? And if not, why not?

Meanwhile slow progress had been made at school. The Dominicans had made their final plans. Some Sisters were going to other Convents in Zambia, a few remaining in Lusaka. Three were going to live in a house in Bauleni compound alongside the 'common man'. There were some caustic comments as to whether they would also live in a house built of mud bricks and have no electricity and have only a bicycle for transport. They did not.

Three more were going to live in a house on Independence Avenue next to the Kenya High Commission, which would be known as the Convent in Lusaka. Obviously they all had their reasons for what they were doing but for the life of me I could not see that they were going to achieve more for the common man or for the general good of the country.

However, we were long since reconciled to their departure and soon we had the news for which we had long been waiting. The Catholic Secretariat, who were now responsible for the school, had found us a Sister to take over the Headship. Sister de Angelis and I went to a meeting with Brother Lemoyne,

'How did you find this Sister so soon?' we asked.

Brother Lemoyne smiled his wide lazy smile, a tall dark Canadian, he never seemed hurried or agitated.

'Sent by God. No, really, listen to this ...' rustling through some papers, '... Sister Paul from Ashford, Kent is arriving and is due to be posted to Ndola to teach English. But she has been, just listen to this, Headmistress of a primary school in Kent! I guess that means she was really meant for you. And to settle matters I have just heard that we are being sent another teacher who will be able to teach English in Ndola. So with a little bit of juggling here and a bit of manipulating there, we seem to be all fixed up.'

Now that we only had to await the arrival of our new Headmistress, Sister de Angelis and I could relax and enjoy the day to day running of the school.

In June of 1977 we had a second visit from the Bartovs. The Lusaka Musical Society brought international artistes out on a regular basis and on an earlier visit the Bartovs had been asked to play at the Convent School. They had agreed reluctantly, admitting they were used to teenagers in European schools generally being unappreciative of classical music. To their astonishment they were given a rapt and attentive audience of girls.

So, on this second visit they offered a repeat performance. Ignorant as I am of all things musical the names Inger Wikstrom, pianist, and her husband David Bartov, violinist, meant nothing at all to me but I joined in the preparations with a will. They were due to stay at one or other of the hotels but due to some mix up something went wrong with the booking and the next step on the agenda was that we provided accommodation for them. In the grounds next to the chapel was a small house which had been used by visiting priests but now stood empty. The Bartovs were offered this house and meals in the Sisters refectory.

The concerts in town took priority but after that they prepared to play for our two schools. The hall was swept and polished and dusted until the dark parquet floors shone like mirrors, the grand piano was likewise treated and an assortment of chairs and stools and small tables provided, enough for a small orchestra not a duet. And around it all floated Sister Georgina, her cheeks pink with excitement. The hall was filled with eager girls and the Bartovs received as enthusiastic response as previously. For two such talented people they were remarkably unassuming and stood for a long time chatting to the girls who crowded round and took a friendly interest in Sister Georgina's music pupils.

Afterwards we sat together over tea and biscuits and relaxed. David telling us that Inger would lose several pounds during a long concert. They had travelled widely with their work but regretted that their knowledge of a country was so often limited to hotels and city centres. Struck by the same idea Sister de and Sister Georgina and I exchanged glances.

'Come to tea tomorrow,' I said.

The next day I collected the Bartovs and Sisters and off we went for tea in the country, to my surprise the Bartovs had never been out of Lusaka itself on any of their previous visits - even going just the ten miles home made a big difference for them. We took a walk on the plot and they admired the view of the countryside from the roof and then we settled down to tea. All was going very well when David pointed to his jacket and asked if there was any way he could get it to two hour dry cleaner.

Recovering from our almost hysterical laughter we told him that a dry cleaner would take at least two days on the job - if he had the chemicals. He looked despondent saying,

'I shall just have to play tonight with these stains on my jacket.'

'Nonsense,' said Sister de, leaning forward and looking at the offending jacket. 'Just give that to me.'

He protested feebly but was no match and we watched as she left the room, he repeating that it was the only jacket he had brought, and he had to wear it that night, and that water would be fatal on an oil stain.

I kept the conversation going as well as I could, but there was a very worried looking man in one chair, who was making very little response. When she came back into the room he made a polite response - though I quailed at the sight of the huge dark patches across the jacket and thought his red face and deep breathing spoke wonders for his self-control.

Sister de had located Joseph and a bottle of Dettol, having sponged the jacket liberally she returned to explain that it always worked and as the jacket dried there would be no stains at all. Inger essayed a few soothing comments but her heart was clearly not in it. I poured Sister de another cup of tea and wished she were not quite so keen to take over everyone's problems. Sister Georgina essayed a few light remarks.

But true enough, as we watched the light weight jacket dried and the oily marks were gone. (Her other infallible remedy is - a teaspoon of sugar for the hiccups).

As we drove back to the Convent Sister de said with a sigh,

'Now for Sister Perpetua.'

'What about her?'

'I have to get her to Kabwe.'

I was surprised that Sister Perpetua was not going to return to Germany or move into the new convent on Independence Avenue. It 'had been decided' and I was not going to ask the reasons why. All this was beyond me. What was more to the point, how was she going to travel to Kabwe? The road was bad enough even though it was tarmac and the only polite thing to do was to offer the use of Andrew's car.

Andrew's pride and joy was his Citroen Pallas. He thought, like I did, that an old Sister who was more or less bedridden should have been flown back to Germany but he willingly offered the use of his car.

So there I was one Sunday morning, chauffeur–in-charge of Sister Perpetua. I arrived at the Convent very early in the morning and parked as close to the kitchen entrance as possible. Two of the men carried her down and she was settled on the back seat with numerous rugs and blankets and cushions. Sisters and men gathered round to bid her farewell.

I drove slowly out of the gates and said I was planning to take the main route down to town along Independence Avenue and then out on the Great North Road.

There was a hurried consultation in the back and Sister de's voice came over the seats, with a sound of suppressed laughter. 'She says she wants to see everything in Lusaka, she has not been out for so long and now she wants to see what has changed.'

There was very little traffic anywhere on a Sunday morning and certainly very little in Lusaka so we had a leisurely and detailed tour of the city centre, all three main roads, we had a minor detour round a suburb and then Sister Perpetua indicated she had seen enough.

Up to the North end roundabout and we set off up the Great North road. I drove slowly along thinking that Sister might appreciate the scenery after being confined upstairs for so many years and that I had better be careful of my precious cargo even in a well sprung car like a Pallas.

It is about ninety miles to Kabwe, we had not covered more than three when there was a rumble of discontent from the back.

'Sister says she is surprised that a big car like this has to go so slowly.'

Clearly I could do nothing right so I put my foot down and wondered how long before there would be another request from the back.

'Is this the fastest it will go?'

I said I never touched the top speeds myself and she would have to settle for eighty which matched her age, which witticism set her off into appreciative cackles and we had no further complaints.

Arriving at Kabwe we had barely come to rest in front of the Convent when a swarm of Sisters appeared all in a welcoming flutter and twitter. There were chairs to hand so that Sister could be carried in, there were suggestions of a crossed hands piggy and a general flap and flutter. In the midst of which Sister Perpetua settled the issue by grasping her stick firmly and heaving herself to her feet and setting off in the direction of the steps. I rather think she made her way up those steps herself with the flutter of hands as her only assistance. And they all disappeared.

I leaned back in the car in the ensuing peace and wondered if I would get a cup of tea.

It was quite a change to decide upon and accomplish a job so easily. As Sister de Angelis and I drove back to Lusaka we were once more involved in discussions about how to get what and where and if none were available, what we could use as an alternative. It was not only finding materials for school which was a constant headache, supplies of everything were so variable and unreliable that far too much time was spent searching around. Sister de Angelis of course, had far greater troubles than I as she had to cater for the Sisters and her eighty boarders. We once drove the ninety miles down to Mazabuka because we heard sugar was available there and we later took a trip to Ndola to do some shopping. Ndola being two hundred miles north on the Copperbelt. We stayed at the Convent there and took some paper and books with us, which they had requested and in return stocked up on sugar and tea.

The newspapers carried regular articles stating that there were no shortages or alternatively the shortages were due to stockpiling and those shopkeepers would be prosecuted. All in all, the general public did not care, all they wanted to do was to have at least the basic supplies to hand and be able to concentrate their time and energies on their own work. It was tough on the 'common man', who had little money to begin with, had less time than others and had as transport, his two feet - or perhaps a bicycle.

Andrew said it was more often a case of bad distribution ... who knew what? Least of all ordinary people who just wanted to get basic supplies regularly. At the other end of the scale were those who had friends who travelled overseas and could bring back such luxuries as spare parts for cars or clothes etc - if the foreign exchange could be found.

Ceri and Simon were coming home in the summer and as Andrew would be in UK when schools closed he proposed to spend some time with them in London and then put them on a plane. I met Simon at the airport early in the morning, he had broken up much earlier than Ceri. It would have been much easier if all the schools in UK had the same term dates, as we did in Zambia. It was the day after his birthday so I had planned a celebration for him and we set off to the Intercontinental with his friend Bwembya and had a terrific lunch.

In the middle of the night he appeared in my bedroom doorway, said in a puzzled voice, 'I don't feel very well.'

And was promptly sick all over the floor. After dealing with that and getting him back into bed and finding he had a temperature I mentally ticked off measles and chicken pox and wondered what he could be sickening for. Probably it was only the travelling. But in the morning his temperature was still high and he was decidedly unwell so off we went to the doctor.

It was only then that I heard Andrew had helped him to celebrate before the flight and had allowed him to drink wine. He had put him on the flight informing the crew that it was his birthday so a kindly hostess had plied him with extra portions of fried egg for breakfast, this on top of a sizeable portion of lobster and wine the night before.

I had completed the process.

On a diet of toast and water he was sobered up enough to meet Ceri and they set about making the most of their holiday, which included me teaching them to drive up and down the drive and on the open space at the side of the house.

Simon learning to drive in my van   *Bwembya, Simon and Ceri measure a*
snake killed near the house

ITEZHI TEZHI

We had planned another trip to Itezhi Tezhi when Andrew returned and this proved to be most relaxing. Itezhi Tezhi (otherwise known as Musungwa) was a safari Game Lodge set up by friends Cecil and Connie Evans in the Kafue Game Park west of Lusaka. The first time we drove out there the road was mainly tarmac and through country I had not seen before. Not that that made much difference, it was the same sort of open savannah country, with grass and shrubs and low trees which seemed to go on for ever.

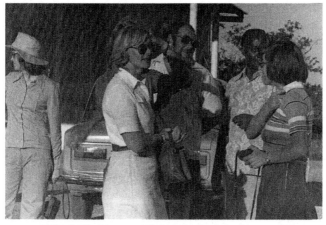

At Itezhi Tezhi - me with Connie, Cecil, Andrew and ?

Over the years we had got into a routine; Andrew liked to do the driving and I would be in charge of changing the tapes, Ceri and Simon would be organised in the back with books and fruit. Originally the tapes had been music of one sort or another but later we discovered story tapes and we would sail through the African bush absorbed in Treasure Island, Huckleberry Finn, Kidnapped and so on.

The first time we went to Itezhi Tezhi it was still very much in the early stages and building was very much in progress. However, it had changed remarkably from the first days when Cecil and Connie had lived in a couple of tents on the hillside above the lake.

Now we found that several chalets were ready for the tourists, the main dining room and bar were complete and they had begun work on a house for themselves. The dining room and bar were built in the shape of extra-large rondavels with thatched roofs. They were spacious, light and airy looking directly out on to the pool and then across the lake with breath taking views in all directions. The chalets were all en suite double rooms, they too looked out across the lake. A short distance away the walls of their own house were going up rapidly and joy of joys, it was to have a bathroom. Connie said, with great feeling, 'Such luxury after a year in a tent.'

Such luxury indeed that Cecil got carried away and decided to build a large quarter circle bath in the corner of the bathroom 'big enough for the wife and me.

And it was.

One takes the simple way in the bush, especially when you are short of money. The workmen had built a low wall in one corner of the bathroom, plastered and tiled it, installed the plumbing and hey presto ! a gigantic luxury bath, big enough to have a party in.

'I bet you both get in there at the end of the day with a couple of long cold drinks,' I said enviously.

Unfortunately Cecil had not taken into account how much water would be required for such a bath and the wood fired boiler was just not equal to the job. So it was cold baths or a few warm inches, which rapidly cooled in the cold brick and plaster.

At the side of the house was a large paved area with a lightly thatched roof where we sat for drinks and watched the lake ripple below us. The first time we sat there I was astonished to see a mongoose come bounding over the low wall and hurl itself on to Cecil's shoulder and start nibbling his ear. He had found it and raised it from a baby and although it was now free to come and go as it wished, it stayed very much a family pet. Ceri and Simon were green with envy, if another mongoose had been available I have to admit we would have adopted it on the spot.

The mongoose, Kimi, was quite sure of her welcome and dispensed her favours impartially. Ceri and Simon were thrilled to find she would settle on their shoulders for walk round the camp or scamper along at their heels. The swimming pool alone held no attractions, once they were in the water she would watch with a disapproving twitch of the nose and then trot off purposefully in the direction of the bar, in the hopes of being offered a nut or nibble by another admirer.

There were of course still piles of building materials and sand in various places, when Simon and Jamie, another boy on holiday, began to build bridges and tunnels the mongoose was right in there with them, adding spice to the work by disappearing down one tunnel and emerging from another, having completed her connection in no time at all.

Ceri with the mongoose Kimi

Simon and Kimi

Cecil took us on a few drives in the Land Rover to see game or out on the lake in his boat but most of the time was spent in the camp lazing the time away.

Andrew was particularly interested in how the camp was set up and was going to run, so spent a lot of time discussing the business with Cecil and later talking in the bar with whoever happened along. I wavered between talking with Connie and walking on my own. Connie was kept pretty busy supervising the kitchen, checking and training staff and I did not want to intrude. The trouble was that one could not walk very far from the camp without being out of sight in the bush and Cecil had made it very clear that this was not on; he had very caustic things to say about people who treated an African Game Park like Regents Park.

But when you are feeling depressed and angry you disregard the rules or think you know better - or just don't think. So off I went one day and walked down to the lake, knowing that I was in full sight of the camp - and that was sufficient as far as I was concerned. The ground ran steeply down to the water's edge and the grass was thick, coarse and dusty dry. In places it was short but in others as high as my waist or shoulders. Not far from the lake I came across a narrow path which ran parallel to the lake and seemed to head towards a rocky outcrop. I made my way there and sat for a time gazing into the distance, thinking, I know not what but feeling generally bloody minded.

After a while it was time to go back and put on the happy face. I set off along the path to where I could climb upwards again. It was hot and quiet and the only sounds were my feet, soft on the dusty earth and the wind in the grass. Then it dawned on me that I should not be listening to the wind in the grass - because there was no wind. I stopped and looked back, the path was empty, grass swayed gently on one side. There was a rustling noise. There was something in the grass.

How loud the silence was all around me. Just the grass moving and an occasional rustle. All the catch phrases about coming out in a sweat and the scalp prickling are very descriptive because that is exactly what happens. I came out in a sweat all over and my scalp prickled. Now, did I run? Or scream? Or what?

The only thing I could not do was remain rooted to the spot. And I certainly could not make a run for it because my feet were suddenly very stiff and heavy. So I did the only thing I could do, which was walk as softly and slowly as I could. The path seemed to go on for ever. The silence of the afternoon thudded in my ears and all the time there was a rustle of grass somewhere near me.

Once I reached the break where I had come down I set off upwards as fast as I could, my feet feeling lighter. Having one eye on the ground in front of me and one eye over my shoulder - I know it is possible, I did it! - I did not see Cecil until I bumped into him at the top of the rise.

'You are both stupid and lucky,' he said grimly, 'feeling better now?'

He told me that he had watched my descent and decided to keep an eye on me, which was no help at all when he saw a twelve foot crocodile making its way back to the water at right angles to me. I apologised for my stupidity and Cecil lowered the rifle, 'Could have hit you as well as the croc.'

And then. There was light at the end of the tunnel.

Sister Paul arrived from UK to take over the school, if she was at all disappointed at not going to teach English at a secondary school, living in a community, she certainly did not show it. What she did show was a remarkable spirit of independence and practicality. Arriving in the traditional white habit she lost no time in deciding that it was most impractical and not for her. 'I can't be doing with all this here white business,' she said with some asperity.' I shan't keep it clean for a minute, let alone for a day. Now where can I buy some material?'

I drove her down to town and introduced her to Limbadas.

Limbadas was the Indian store to end all Indian stores. It was a large warehouse with no pretensions whatsoever - rather like Sister Paul I reflected as we walked up and down the aisles. The walls were lined with shelves from floor to ceiling and filled with pots and pans, kitchen utensils, tools and gadgets, bric a brac such as china horses from China, kits for this and kits for that, long ago there had been toys, battery driven and otherwise. The list was endless.

But the chief attraction of Limbadas was the floor area filled with long stands covered in rolls of material of every conceivable design and hue, from warm woolly materials to light cottons and nylon, Java prints and - of late - rolls of Kafue Textiles (our locally produced material). I may have been surprised at Sister Paul turning down the idea of wearing a white habit but I was totally unprepared for her choosing blue denim.

'That made up into skirts will be just the job with white blouses,' she announced and began pulling the huge roll from the stand.

'Just a minute,' I said. 'You have to ask the man over there to take the roll to the measuring counter for you.'

We followed the man to another counter where another chap flipped the roll over and swiftly measured off the required amount, folded it into a square with several rapid flips and handed it to a third man whom we followed to the till at the door.

'What a performance,' muttered Sister Paul as she was given a receipt which I told her to hang on to as she would have to show it at the outer door, after another man had wrapped material in several loud slaps of brown paper.

'What a performance' was, I found, one of Sister Paul's favourite phrases and was used on many occasions over the next few months as she learned the routine in Zambia.

It was only a matter of a couple of days before Sister Paul appeared in her denim skirt and, with her sleeves metaphorically rolled up, was ready to take over the school. Tights were dispensed with 'except for high days and holy days I suppose' and Dr Scholl sandals were the daily footgear.

She was pleased with the school layout and the surroundings, the size of the classes did not daunt her nor the scarcity of supplies. But she did confess to being a little uneasy as to where she would be expected to lay her head in the near future, the Dominican Sisters were about to withdraw completely and there was no way Sister Paul could live with the Brothers or seminarians.

Sister Paul at Leopards Hill Road

The immediate solution was that she came to live with us at our house as we had plenty of room, and once established the situation was sufficiently unusual for the Catholic Secretariat to make an effort to reach another solution. She was offered the empty priests house next door to the chapel.

An ideal solution except that it had no kitchen. But we set about remedying that at once. A builder was found to install a small sink and cooker in one corner of the second bedroom. We ransacked the school for spare tables and cupboards, purloined a bed from the hostel - so few seminarians could not possibly use eighty beds. We found an ancient radiogram under the stage in the hall and after removing the defunct parts and stripping off all the varnish, we had a most attractive drinks cupboard. (At the time it did not strike me as strange that a nun would have much use for a drinks cupboard).

And in no time at all it seemed Sister Paul had a very pleasant home next to the chapel and opposite the school buildings. Once she was installed we had a celebratory drink - Fanta orange - from her drinks cupboard and then she confessed to her one real worry.

'It will be the first time in my life that I have lived alone!'

I must admit the thought had never crossed my mind but we agreed that as the whole school area was fenced and patrolled by dogs and a watchman at night and that the Brothers and seminarians were within earshot, well, really, she would be fine. Once she got used to it.

And if she did not, Sister Paul most certainly did not complain. She had arrived after the end of the UK school year and was plunged into the last term of our academic year with all the important Grade 7 selection exams. She taught the Grade 7's herself and then in the afternoons I continued to help in the office and of course my van was invaluable as she had no transport at all of her own.

The Dominican Sisters left and it was surprising how soon we settled into our new routine and more introverted life. There was less contact with the secondary school and no contact at all with the seminary. Gone were the days when I could take my class on an exploration of the grounds which included large orchards, and we could no longer use the kitchen facilities. Even the chapel seemed distant now that it was behind a six foot fence, which the Brothers had erected within the first few weeks.

But the school itself worked very much as before and the days were full of activities of one kind or another. Sister Paul had her coffee or tea with us at break times and we had lively informal meetings with everyone being up to date with all the school's events and plans. We all thought that Sister Paul had adapted to our school and situation very well but she had her doubts which at last were voiced.

'I don't really think I shall like teaching here after all. The children are very different - they don't really like me you know.'

'WHAT?'

And then she explained that after all these weeks she found

that the children were still quiet and shy and did not look her in the eye when they spoke to her. It took some time to explain and then convince her that the girls did not meet her eyes when they spoke to her as that was the height of bad manners. A polite Zambian child will look down when addressing an elder, especially a teacher.

'The more they look down when they speak to you, the politer they are,'

'Hmm, if you say so. But it won't do. I can't get used to it, although I suppose I shall have to, if you say so.'

The third term was busy but it all helped the days fly by to when I could expect Ceri and Simon home again.

CHRISTMAS 1977

Would I ever get used to the children being away? So many of my friends were in the same position and they all coped, although not happily. And of course, the women felt it far more keenly than the men. I began my preparations early, looking around shops for items for presents, the shops were drear. Goods were coming in but they were dull or shoddy or far too expensive. I thought it must be frustrating for parents of small children, trying to find toys. However, by going round and round from shop to shop and back again, I gradually found something to please everyone.

One afternoon I thought I had done remarkably well. I had bought quite a lot of groceries, found shirts and dresses for all the servants children and even found some balls and crayons and sweets. There were several boxes piled at the back of the van and I thought I would now be able to concentrate on preparations at home for the next few days.

I parked the van outside the butchers next to CBC (Kees) and went in to collect the order I had left earlier. Back at the van in three minutes I looked at the forced window and empty space and wondered whether it was the expense, or the thought of trailing all over town again which was the most disheartening.

But at last we were going out to the airport to meet the plane, the children were on their way home and who could be sad? We had invited Sister Paul for Christmas Day and the Flucks and Paul Lusaka - his family were away this year.

Christmas Day itself got off to a bad start. Long storms the night before meant that the electricity had been on and off most of the 24th but we went to bed on Christmas Eve with a working power supply and the turkey ready for the oven.

I woke early in the morning feeling that something was wrong. No smell of gently roasting turkey greeted our nostrils. Downstairs Joseph was muttering to himself.

'No power, Madam, it is not all right.'

'Never mind,' I said more cheerfully than I felt. 'The Bwana can phone Zesco and I am sure it will be on soon. And if dinner is late, then it is late.'

'It is no good Madam. You know me, I like to have Christmas dinner all ready and to start now. It is no good.'

I quite agreed but went back upstairs to stir Andrew into some forceful activity with the electricity board. Zesco were as polite as ever and promised wonders as usual.

Power came back with the arrival of breakfast, which had been produced with the help of the fire at the servants' quarters.

'Shall we take the turkey over there?' I joked.

But Joseph was not amused as he rattled doors and dishes. This was not the usual leisurely joyous start to the day. The servants children came in, looking as scrubbed and expectant as ever but Joseph did not linger with the men.

'Power is no good,' he said.

The clouds which had cast a gloom over the morning now opened at full throttle and it poured down. The children scampered back home clutching their parcels and the women hurried after calling to the men, who lingered in the courtyard to sympathise with Joseph.

And then power went.

The turkey was partly cooked.

Joseph was in despair.

At which point I had a moment of inspiration.

'Paul Lusaka is coming here. We will go and use his cooker - if they have power in town.'

Andrew could phone Paul and then try to get through to Zesco and get them to work another miracle. Joseph and I leapt into the van, Joseph nursing the turkey in its roasting tin with all the accoutrements he considered necessary. I drove to town through sheets of rain with a low steady mutter at my side,

'It's not all right ... dinner will be late ... me, I like to be early ...'

My idea was good but I had second thoughts as we hooted and shouted at the locked gates at Paul's house. At last a security guard appeared and reluctantly let us through and disappeared to find the cook.

He, when he appeared, had little idea of the kitchen and its workings. Probably the house servant I thought as Joseph tried to find out how the cooker worked and I tried to make the servant understand that he should wake the Bwana and tell him what we were doing.

Driving home we both wondered whether the turkey would make much headway.

'At least it will keep warm,' I joked.

Joseph gave me a withering look. Jokes about food he could not take. Back home he and Banda hurried on with their preparations and the kitchen was all poised for switch on - if Zesco managed a second time. Pans of vegetables gleamed beside bowls and jugs. Fruit glowed and silver was re polished as they tried to take their minds off the turkey, roasting in absentia.

Andrew poured drinks with a liberal hand and Sister Paul said she could exist on those and nuts quite happily. Electricity came back but before we could decide we could mount operation rescue it flickered and died. More drinks were poured and mince pies appeared.

The Flucks walked in and as they had no power either, took comfort in large drinks.

Late morning electricity returned once more and we had more drinks while we discussed whether it was here to stay. At last Joseph and I decided we would take a trip into town and off we went with a fresh onslaught of rain. The turkey had roasted quietly away on its own and was at a most promising stage. I could not be sure whether Joseph was pleased or annoyed that it had managed without his expert ministrations.

Carefully we loaded up the precious cargo and off we set again. The hot tin was balanced precariously between us on the seat and while I peered through the windscreen at the torrential downpour, Joseph hovered protectively over the bird as though he expected it to catch a chill.

The power was still with us and there were no further mishaps. The turkey completed its roasting under Joseph's protection and the vegetables and pudding were hurried along, as Paul arrived apologising for having overslept. He enjoyed the description of the morning's events as the servant had not woken him or told him of our visit in the morning and commandeering his kitchen. By the time it all appeared on the table of course I should think most of the company were so well inebriated they would have eaten fish and chips without remarking the difference.

SHADOWS IN 1978

Christmas 1977 seemed to foreshadow coming events in 1978. Life dragged its dreary way with constant shortages and frustrations. True we had had them for a long time but familiarity does not always breed contempt. Rather, in this case, there was an increasing frustration. We had been on a downward path for so long. There had been difficulties once Rhodesia declared UDI and the country had weathered those storms. But now we seemed to be on a constant downward spiral. Life continued to get more dreary and frustrating and monotonous with its shortages and cutbacks.

The first of January was made memorable by Police Inspector Fabiano Chela advising the public - to stay at home and minimise travelling because road accidents cost the nation a lot in foreign exchange to replace vehicles, it hindered development because there was a loss of productive personnel and the family suffered too. A jolly year to come.

One day I came home from work to be met by Banda telling me

that 'Peter is not all right madam'. He said he had noticed a little earlier that Peter, Simon's cross Great Dane, was just standing at the back of the house, not moving. We piled him into the back of the van and I drove as fast as I could to the Vets in town. There Chris Oporacha confirmed my fears, a spitting cobra had spat in Peters eyes. Chris did what he could, said I could wait and see for a day or two... it was horrible. The first day Peter responded to our voices and hands and Paula's nose but by the second day he lay on his blanket refusing to get up. A second trip to the vet, Chris came out to the van and gave Peter his injection while I held his head and told him it wouldn't hurt. And drove home blinded with tears.

Not a world shattering event but little things niggle away.

I had been a faithful user of Lusaka library but at the rate I read and the slow addition of new books meant after some years I had let my membership lapse. But then after some time Lusaka bookshop closed and Kingstons in no way replaced it. And so eventually I decided to make use of the library and not being able to find my ticket off I went to re-join. It didn't look any better, still the same dull rows of books but after a lapse perhaps some would be worth reading again.

Presenting myself at the desk I explained my situation and was told I would have to complete a form – a natural response and one I had expected and had actually remembered to carry means of identification – my driving licence and identity card. The chap produced the form and I got out my pen saying I'd get on with it ... a new book or two for the weekend...

'Ah no,' replied the chap. 'You must take it home – you need your husband's signature on the form.'

And that floored me. I was an adult resident and tax payer, had been a member before, had means of identification ... and I needed my husband's signature on the form to be able to borrow books! And he pointed out the bit at the bottom of the form. It was a mixture of anger and offence and frustration and God only knows what and I walked to the car speechless. There was no point in venting my frustration at the chap behind the desk who was merely carrying out instructions – made by ? why ? when ? Of course, there would be no problem getting Andrew to sign the form – he would also be willing to go in to protest the system on my behalf. But that was not the point! what kind of idiotic rules were slipping into place? And did we have to stage great protests to change a silly bit of bureaucracy? Was I not a person in my own right?

I did not bother to complete the form or complain anywhere. Just gave up.

I remember in January searching in vain for margarine, butter, sugar, milk, tea, cooking oil, chickens, and even vegetables and fruit were in short supply. The Times of Zambia office was bombed.

Schools fared no better ... there were not enough places - as usual. Uniforms were in short supply and there were shortages of text books and equipment. Katuba Primary School had only 3 teachers for 630 pupils and classes of 40 – 50 were common elsewhere as schools continued with their double shifts. Coupled with this, it was a wonder that teachers still stayed in the profession when they were under paid and badly housed. But as the Ministry of Education pointed out, rich nations could only have free schooling after they got rich - which may be true but was of little consolation to the education hungry masses.

We kept assuring ourselves that it could get no worse, that we would hit rock bottom and then bounce back up again - no one quite explained how. This theory and that were put forward. True no one had foreseen - how could they? – that the copper prices would fall so low. Or if they had, they had done nothing about it. The economy staggered on from one plight to another. There were cutbacks and shortages and yet there was always money for some new scheme, especially when it meant that large groups were off on fact finding missions overseas.

Aid was sought and granted in first one country and then another, but the concrete results were not so obvious to the common man - or woman. Like so many others I was thoroughly fed up with spending so much time trying to find common place supplies and if I did find them I felt guilty seeing the ever increasing prices and knowing that many things were becoming more and more out of reach of the ordinary man in the street. Everyday chores now took on a different aspect, if one looked around and took note of the apathetic queues, and the dull resigned faces walking the streets. I found it annoying that the average person accepted the increasing inefficiency and rudeness with a shrug. Where a smile and a cheerful greeting had been the order of the day, one now met with surly grunts, indifference or outright rudeness.

I wondered whether the Zambians felt the lowering of the standards embarrassing when dealing with msungus. And to them a white face was a white face, the average chap in the store or office would not know that I was an 'old' resident and one who was actually sympathetic and supportive of Zambia. To them I was just another white face who was possibly laughing at the growing inefficiency and corruption.

When I had first arrived in the country I had not approved of separate shops or queues for blacks and whites and now I was meeting with a reverse form of racialism. Listening to friends I heard the same sort of tales. Most of us accepted it and tried to show an indifference we did not feel. But occasionally one or other would lose tempers and then there would be a mini fracas, unsatisfactory all round. One felt as though one were being deliberately provoked, irritated in the hopes of provoking some scene of retaliation, which made one all the more determined not to do so.

Don Fluck dropped in for tea one day and told me how he had gone as usual to an office in the post office building. Arriving at the office he had knocked and entered to find the man behind the desk immersed in a book. Don had greeted the man only to be met with silence. He waited a moment and then spoke again. Once more he was ignored.

He looked again but the chap was only reading an ordinary book or novel so Don tried again but had no response. Don was not the most patient of men but being well aware of his failing and thinking that he was being provoked he waited - but to no avail. At last he lost all patience and forcefully said he would report this kind of reception to the man's superior. After which of course, he was accused of racialism.

Don had been in the habit of dropping in for a cup of tea and a chat on his way home. We would gossip about the news and who had said what ... but it came to an end. For whatever reason, we began to notice that when Andrew came home, he would nod curtly to Don and disappear upstairs. And so one day Don said he thought it would be better not to drop in unless he saw Andrew's car already in the garage.

One day I went to the Cold Storage Board to collect some meat, for a long time now we had been buying our meat in bulk. At first I had hated going into CSB feeling that Andrew had somehow managed preferential treatment, he assured me that many had the same agreement. So I had got used to buying a hindquarter of beef and half a pig, it saved so much time that I didn't mind. Later I hated going knowing that there were often shortages in the butcheries in town but Andrew insisted the manager at CSB had said it was perfectly OK.

However, one day early in 1978 I went as usual with the order and found the system had changed, this of course was nothing new. Almost every store or office changed its system with the moon or new management or to prevent pilfering - I shall never know.

On this particular day I worked my way through the system and at last reached the point of being able to pay for the meat and depart. Or so I thought. For once, I was the only person buying in bulk and arriving at the desk I thought I should soon be on the way home. The clerk behind the desk had other ideas. He continued writing and I waited. Then I cleared my throat and said,

'Good afternoon.'

Silence. He continued to write.

Later 'I am waiting to pay for my meat.'

Silence.

He continued to write.

I felt angry, thought that he would like me to say something rude so, thinking of Don, I very consciously told myself that I could wait it out longer than he. I stood by the desk for twenty five minutes while the clerk wrote and fidgeted with papers. By now he was also determined not to give in.

We could have been there till this day if the manager had not passed through to the office and came to a standstill. He had passed me half an hour earlier and after exchanging some pleasantries had bade me goodbye. There was an angry exchange between them which I did not bother to enter. Sometimes I repeated these tales to Andrew but sometimes it felt as though I were criticising HIS country, while really I had always felt it was OUR country.

I was appalled to find that I was losing this feeling of identity and belonging. Without a clear word or action I was being put outside.

School as usual was the solace and salvation.

Even with shortages and frustrations, school itself, was enjoyable and workable. Sister Paul was full of enthusiasm and energy and we battled on together to make the school as happy and exciting as we could. The Staff were good but all of them had young families to care for and their time was taken up with finding supplies or worrying about burglaries. So more and more, Sister Paul and I felt as though we should shoulder most of the responsibilities.

All work and no play of course makes Jack a dull boy so when Andrew was away on one of his trips overseas I said I would borrow his Citroen and take Sister Paul down to Livingstone and the Victoria Falls.

The drive down was as usual uneventful, just the long drive through bush and open savannah and we arrived feeling a bit tired and ready for cold drinks. We had booked into the Intercontinental and after a wash and drink, walked over to the Falls to stand and gaze, which is all one wants to do at first. Then we walked on to the bridge which had been built stretching in front of the Falls and got pleasantly wet and cooled by the spray. No matter how many times I went to the Falls I was always mesmerised by the sheer spectacular beauty of it all. And of course, it is an added pleasure to take someone there for their first visit and see their reaction. In the two or three days we walked by the Falls and the river, we drove round the Game Park and we went up the Lookout Tree.

We had decided one day to give me break from all the driving and went round the Game Park in the tourist Board bus. We were packed into a Land Rover - the bus being out of action - with three tourists from Germany, one of whom was a keen photographer. We did not mind waiting while he endlessly clicked and focussed and clicked, a new born baby giraffe all damp and wobbly on its legs is a wonderful sight. But his sessions became longer and longer and more frustrating as each time we were at a standstill the flies zoomed in through the windows. At last Sister Paul brought it all to a halt by slapping a large horse fly on the window and startling the buck on which he had focussed for ten minutes. Neither of us spoke German but the uncomplimentary remarks were clear enough.

Sister Paul produced her most winning smile, 'I am sorry! I thought you had taken the photo ages ago.'

Well, our little holiday was doing us both good, we cast not a thought to Lusaka or school. On the last night Sister Paul insisted that she would take me to dinner in the restaurant as a thank you gesture.

'No arguments mind,' she said, fixing me with her piercing blue eyes. 'This little treat is on me. And while we are on the subject, I want it to be a real treat so no ordering the cheapest dish. You are to enjoy yourself.'

So bathed and changed we made our way down to the restaurant where a band was thumping out some tune or other. We followed the waiter to a table in the furthest corner.

'Thank God for that,' muttered Sister Paul. 'I could not be doing with that noise all night. And I suppose he has got to put us here, it would not look right having a veil right up there in front.'

I laughed and we looked at our menus. Hers was lowered and once more I was fixed by those blue eyes

'You enjoy yourself mind. Wine?'

Now how could I say no?

We ordered a meal and a bottle of Blue Nun as it seemed most appropriate. When someone else has shopped, cooked and will wash up it can be most relaxing, add to that we could not be thinking about any jobs waiting to be done, they were many miles to the north. We sat and chatted idly of what we had seen and done and speculated about our fellow diners. It was a hot night.

'Another bottle, as you have downed that one pretty smartish?'

I was sure I hadn't but the bottle WAS empty. Before I could demur another bottle appeared and my glass refilled. The evening took on a rosy glow and I felt most relaxed. Sister Paul was an amusing companion, funny I hadn't noticed before how wide a grin she had. Like the Cheshire cat. I told her so.

The Cheshire Cat looked somewhat alarmed.

'Have you drunk too much?' it enquired.

Half a bottle of wine could not have had all that much effect, but now she was pointing out that I had drunk at least one and a half bottles.

'Nonsense, you drank some too.'

'That I did - but this is the third bottle.'

Food soaks up the wine - or so they say - so we ordered an extra-large dessert but then I found that I was expected to finish off the third bottle.

'Don't you go wasting my money.'

We lingered over coffee while I gauged the distance to the door.

'Do you realise we have to walk halfway round the dance floor?' I hissed.

'And don't you go falling all over the place,' was the comforting reply.

At last we could delay our departure no longer. Sister Paul elected to go first, having no desire to witness my fall from grace. I had an insane desire to giggle as I followed her. We kept our backs straight and faces composed until we had navigated the dance floor and the tricky bit by the door, once on the stairs we held on firmly for support. Never had a bedroom been more welcome.

The next morning I felt somewhat sheepish and was not helped by a graphic description of my attempts to emulate the bandleader with my toothbrush. We left Livingstone at an early hour intending to drive straight back to Lusaka without stopping; no sooner had we agreed that than I began slowing down.

'Now why will you be doing that? I thought you said you would not be stopping.'

I pointed ahead.

'Will you look at that now? The cheek of them! They are not going to move. Go on. Keep going. They will have to get out of your way.'

A troop of baboons were spread across the road, some sitting, some squatting, others walking on all fours and some standing up to take a better look at us. I drove very slowly, not wanting to stop completely. At last the ranks of baboons began to give way and we were able to edge gradually through. Most of them withdrew to the edge of the road gazing resentfully or curiously and a few males screamed abuse, bearing their teeth.

'Now what was that all about?' asked Sister Paul. 'And look back, they have taken over the whole road again.'

So then I had to tell her about how I had gone to Livingstone with Ceri and Simon a few years earlier and as Andrew had had to cancel his trip to go away on business at the last moment, we had offered his booking to Sister de Angelis.

We had had a very pleasant holiday and one day had decided it would be marvellous to get up very early to watch the sun rise over the Falls. When it came to the cold grey of dawn of course Ceri and Simon could not be prised from their beds so Sister de and I went alone. We found a bench near the Falls and sat there, peacefully thinking the wonderfully calm thoughts one has at that hour. Someone came and sat at the end of the bench, we were not the only ones out to view the dawn.

The new person sighed and fidgeted. I glanced sideways in irritation to find the most enormous male baboon I had ever seen sitting within a couple of feet on the bench.

I swear one eye remained riveted on him while the other swivelled to meet that of Sister de ,who mouthed, 'Don't move!' An entirely unnecessary remark as I was frozen to the spot. It is quite surprising how loud one's breathing seems to be at such times. We sat still, sweat trickling down my back. The baboon sighed again and scratched an armpit and inspected his nails. We were aware of other baboons wandering down to the water's edge, young and old, a few with babies on their backs. But none so large as our companion.

It was a small troop and they slowly passed on down the path which runs parallel to the Falls. As the last one disappeared among the trees our friend heaved yet another sigh and got down from the bench, presenting us with a close up of his enormous posterior and followed his family in a dignified way.

We slowly came back to normal.

'After seeing that little lot I can well believe it,' was Sister Paul's comment. 'And how about the sun rise? I suppose it was well and truly risen by that time?'

'Well, it had,' I answered. 'But it was only later that we discovered we would not have seen it anyway - we were facing the wrong way!'

And telling that story to staff back in the hotel we had heard that that particular troop of baboons came to the same spot every morning at the same time and after a brief contemplation of the spray and a drink, they would retrace their steps.

Once back in Lusaka it was not long before Sister Paul and I were planning another trip. Sugar had not been available in Lusaka for weeks and although Andrew and I had not a particularly sweet tooth, sugar did have its uses. More than that, the servants craved it. Sugar was to be found in abundance on the Copperbelt - or so we heard. Why goods could not be better distributed was a fact of life which no one ever explained satisfactorily to me. After waiting for some time for sugar to make its way south to us

I decided to go and get some. Andrew was as usual far too busy but was quite willing to lend his car as the trip would be rather bumpy in my van. Sister Paul phoned Ndola and we were offered accommodation at the Convent there and given a shopping list of things they could not obtain.

So one weekend off we went after school on Friday and were bowling along quite merrily up the Great North Road. Rounding a bend we came upon a long line of cars waiting at a road block. I drew in behind the last car and wondered how long we would be delayed. Sometimes the checks were quick but at other times the police or soldiers would be very thorough and ask for documents and search the car boot and any packages.

Sister Paul broke in on my reverie

'You had better hurry up - he looks impatient.'

At the head of the queue one of the policemen was beckoning us forward. Now what had I done? I glanced behind but he waved again so I inched the car out of the line and drove slowly forward all the time expecting an angry shout. As we reached him I stopped the car.

'Good afternoon Sister. And your name?' (looking at me)

'Mrs Kashita.'

He saluted smartly.

'Good afternoon Sister. Good afternoon Mrs Kashita.'

And he waved us through. As we passed all the other luckless drivers opening their boots and standing at the side of their vehicles we wondered whether it was the veil or the name Kashita.

'Who cares?' said Sister Paul. 'And I for one am not going back to ask. But perhaps we are just a combination he could not resist.'

'Or maybe just one of my old pupils,' I added.

'More likely a prospective parent', was Sister Paul's unkind thought.

Once in Ndola we made our way to the Convent where we and our packages were most welcome. We retired early to bed in the guest flat and early next morning went out on the search for sugar. Not only was it available, we were able to buy it in large ten kilo bags. More than enough for Sister Paul and us and our servants and the school messengers, we could even take some for friends.

'And if we meet our friendly policeman on the way back we can afford to give him some,' said Sister Paul.

That night we did not sleep so well. The Convent dogs barked loud and long but I did not even get out of bed as Sister Pieta had made it quite clear that we were not to venture outside after dark and the dogs had been let out. I wished someone would go out or even put a head out of the window but eventually went back to sleep.

When we walked across to breakfast the next morning we were met by a very cross Sister Bernosa, totally unlike the happy nun who had showed us round her school the day before. Yesterday she had showed us the staffroom she had nearly finished refurbishing. Today she showed us how the chairs and the new cushions and the kettle and the cups and saucers and the tins of sugar and tea had all been taken in the night.

While Sister Paul stood listening to the tale of woe as they waited for the police to arrive, Sister Pieta asked,

'Would you care to come for a walk with me?'

Off we went across the school playing field.

'Where are we going?'

'We might as well walk round till we find where they cut the wire, that is what they do and then we can get it mended till the next time.'

On we walked.

'I heard the dogs in the night.'

'Oh yes, that was when the thieves would have been breaking in ... Ah yes, there is a gap over there, let's go and check. I too heard the dogs and I knew it was another break in but what are we to do - go out and get hit on the head - or worse? if I had tried to phone the police it takes ages to get through on the phone - even when one can - and then IF they have transport and come, I still have to go outside and unlock the gates.'

'So you just lay awake and listened to the dogs?' I asked.

'Oh no, I got out of bed and took a couple of tranquilisers and then I went back to bed. I am not going to lose sleep over this sort of thing. One day they will have stolen everything we have and then we shall just pack our suitcases - if we still have a case - and then we shall leave. What is the point of worrying?'

I admired Sister Pieta's calmness but was saddened by the change in our lives. Crime was very much the order of the day. And increasingly it was robbery with violence.

In contrast to this changing way of life Andrew suddenly produced a thin book one evening and asked if I would read it and consider us joining.

It was a book about the Food And Wine Society.

Reading through it I could not believe he was serious. Not only serious, he thought it was a wonderful idea. He talked about who were members and how we could participate. I looked again at the book.

'Are you seriously asking me to be interested in something which is about culinary delights?' I asked. 'It is difficult enough getting basic supplies here without asking me to be interested in producing gourmet food. Neither of us has ever been terribly interested in food and I am not finding it a particularly enthralling topic right now.'

Andrew was very disappointed and pointed out that so and so was a member - aha, so that was the attraction! if he wanted to dine with so and so (or any other so and so's) he could take them out for a meal or invite them home for one of Joseph's excellent meals. But in no way did I want to get involved in what seemed to me to be a pretentious hobby at that time. How COULD people be interested in which wine suited this dish or enhanced that one, had one used the correct amount of spices or herbs (if they were available!) when on the other side of the wall, people were hungry?

One of us was out of place. Andrew made me feel it was me.

The great divide was growing ever wider and still the papers and politicians pontificated for and about the 'common man'. And all the while the common man's lot worsened. Jobs were few. There were still not enough places at schools and they were not producing good results. The medical services could not cope. Goods were in variable supply and their prices rose steadily.

The Leadership Code had been introduced to ensure that people at the top could not control businesses and have extra incomes but it was strongly rumoured that the President's own wife Betty, now owned Milady dress shop, City Radio, Curry's, Kingstons Stationers, a brickworks, a bottle store (or was it a bar?) and so on and so forth. (Or so it was claimed by some who should know). Even then perhaps we would not have minded so much if all the businesses had not gone so steadily downhill.

I had loved my family and my home but as I looked around me it seemed as though what I had loved and tried to build was somehow being eroded and washed away.

My children had had to go away to school. My husband treated most shabbily but had accepted it and even though he had worked hard to build a new career he had lost some of my respect when I saw he still slavishly followed the President. I realised we had drifted further and further apart. I could understand his commitment to his country but we no longer shared the same interests and values.

Friends had left the country. Friends and acquaintances whose skills and expertise had been dismissed without so much as a thank you – and the country was the poorer for their going. And after all these years I could not count one real true close Zambian friend. Not one.

And at last I wondered what the future really held for me and I did not like what I saw.

In 1978 I left Zambia.

And so it ended.

The life I had embraced so eagerly. I had not known what to expect of Africa but it had not disappointed. I loved the space, the light, the smells, the sounds, the variety of each day. Talk to anyone who has lived in Africa, no matter for how short a time, and you will get the same response. A silence, a faraway look as memories take hold.

'Can't forget … can't describe …' and another silence.

But the life I was living had changed as circumstances changed with the years and although the land - the space and smells - the stars so bright in the dark sky - and the land stretching away to such distant horizons - the unspoilt wildernesses of wild life - although they remained as heart pulling as ever, society and the way of life was changing.

I had had so many expectations of what independence would mean, like many people I suppose. We thought that all that had been wrong in society - the segregation and its effects would go and be replaced by something better. I believed that people who had experienced abuse or been frustrated by discrimination would be sure to avoid all repetitions. And as time went on, traditional customs I had admired were sometimes abandoned, the worst of some Western customs were admired and adopted … perhaps a natural development as a society finds its own way. But most foolishly of all, I had believed, truly believed, that overthrowing the Colonial Government and gaining independence would mean that the new politicians would whole heartedly work for the good of all. As the years passed I realised that the 'common man' (about whom we had heard so much during the fight for freedom) was no better off at all - except that his leaders were black not white. And I had believed that the ordinary worker when he had a job would put his all into it. But it seemed the order of the day was -

Get rid of the people who have lived and worked for many years, don't renew old contracts, don't value experience but look for yes men, who come on fat contracts but do not stay to remedy their mistakes. Turn your backs on the nations who opened you up to the world and welcome those who will rape your country of its minerals, natural resources and its' wild life.

It is fashionable now to heap blame and recriminations on the old Colonial system - easy to do if you ignore how short a time there was to make changes - to encourage differing and often warring tribes to join together into one nation, build roads

614

and railways without the present modern technology, open schools and hospitals .... Wealth created within the country was ploughed back in. And yes, there were mistakes but I look at the mistakes being made now by a people on their own people. And the world now is all too aware which nations are plundering Africa's wild life, its ivory, its mineral wealth, its timber ... but with whose connivance?

Sadly Zambia is not alone, one sees and hears a similar story east, west, north and south of the equator.

When I look back now and reflect on the past .... What do I think? I have never had any regrets about marrying Andrew, going to live in a completely unknown country and embarking upon a totally new life which angered and dismayed so many. I have often been asked if I regretted it - no, never.

It could be said - and no doubt was - that I was naïve and foolish, selfish and headstrong, misguided and provocative ... and probably more. I was young, I didn't think beyond the fact that I had met what I believed was the love of my life and, not to coin a phrase, we would sail off happily together into the sunset for ever. Beyond that? Nothing. That was it.

A mixed marriage at that time - and where we proposed to live - was going to upset and anger many people for a variety of reasons. So - selfish to some, misguided and provocative to others ... etc etc. but with the enthusiasm and a simple belief that we could please ourselves, we proceeded with some small heart searching - but never any doubts.

Difficulties and problems bound us closer together in many ways in the early years, confirmed us in our beliefs and love. But the years pass and we all change in different ways and sometimes we discover shared values begin to diverge. Interests become more varied ... Sometimes a natural progression when it becomes more difficult to maintain the unity. And then decisions are made, shaped to some degree by events and you understand what bound you so closely has loosened, is no longer worth preserving and so another decision is made.

As for Zambia – probably it would bounce back as the economic climate improved. The long made promises of education and jobs and opportunities would hopefully come to some fruition.

As for regrets - yes, I have. But regrets for not making more of my opportunities and time. I regret not making the effort to see more of the country - there was always tomorrow.

I regret not talking more with Banda, Joseph and White - and going further back Zulu, William, Benson, Lax and their wives. Wish I had made the effort to know more about them.

I regret not making the time to give their children some tuition in the school holidays - surely I could have made the time to give them a bit of coaching ... some practice in spoken English, instead of welcoming the school holidays and selfishly indulging in just the sheer enjoyment of time to spend with my own children and our friends.

I regret - sometimes - not being a more ambitious, encouraging (driving?) parent. Was I too content to let Ceri and Simon choose their interests and have as far as possible, a relaxed childish childhood?

I regret not taking more photos of scenery - places - events (Lord knows there were plenty, watching history change around us) - there was always 'next time ... when we can afford to buy a better camera...' And there is not to room here for the photos I do have.

I regret - always regretted – the fact that Andrew never had the time for us to visit his parents, see the village where he grew up. That I never persuaded Andrew to sit and translate so I could get to know more about his mother, what she thought of all the changes she had seen in her life time. 'There would be time next year ...'

Perhaps most of all, I regret not keeping a diary with notes and drawings. We were watching such rapid progress and changes where I often had a ring side seat - but in all honesty, I know my happiness was with my family, my friends, my pupils ... and who would want to know what I thought when I met some Important/ Influential people?

And that perhaps I regret not using my time more wisely. One is always wiser with hindsight.

CHAPTER 8
Back to Zambia, 2020

Many people have said, 'Enjoyed your book This Was My Africa – and then? What happened next?'

What happened next were years back in primary schools in England with great colleagues and many more children with engaging personalities. So I didn't retire until I was seventy. And time spent travelling around UK to places I loved and places I'd never seen before, a few trips to Europe and time for friends, learning to paint and more recently, some voluntary work.

It took time to adjust to life back in UK – the most surprising thing was that, generally speaking, people comfortably settled in their lives in UK are not over interested in the fact one has lived and worked elsewhere. When I first returned in 1978 my experience in teaching children of diverse nationalities and multiple languages seemed to count for little, despite it being acknowledged that schools in UK were increasingly multi-cultural.

In January 2020 I finally gave in to my daughter's oft repeated 'If you leave it too late, you'll always regret the fact that you never went back'.

Reminding her that I had been back in 1986 cut no ice.

'Going back to stay with Stella when Edward was in prison isn't the same.' Which was daughter being pernickety and I told her so.

(In 1980 Edward Shamwana, one of Zambia's first lawyers and a leading Lusaka figure, was arrested together with Valentine Musakanya and Elias Chipimo and charged with treason. Edward and his English wife Stella were close friends of many years standing – our children are still close friends. After his arrest I wrote to Stella every week, giving what support I could. In 1986 I decided to use my August school holiday to visit Stella and, hopefully, be able to visit Edward in Kabwe prison, where he had been after being convicted of plotting to over-throw President

Kaunda. It was an extraordinarily interesting month).

And so, we move on to January 2020.

We planned it carefully – this trip of mine back to the place where I had been so very happy and had not seen for so long. Daughter Ceri planned her regular visit to see her father and renew some old friendships. I was to stay with some friends and visit a few places – having been warned many times by many people 'It's all changed – you won't recognise it.' I had lost touch with most of the people I had known – others had left Zambia. We were booked to fly on 12th February.

On Monday 13th January Ceri had a phone call, Andrew had died in his sleep. The funeral would be on Friday 17th.

Then followed frantic rearrangements with me having last vaccination at Heathrow airport courtesy of Boots (highly recommended as emergency solution) just before we flew on Wednesday 15th. Changing planes in Dubai we met up with Ceri's stepsister Nonde and arrived in Lusaka early on Thursday morning. Ceri and Nonde were being met by cousin Fitz and I was to be met by Ann Wallace, a very old friend from the days when I taught her son Michael and she had had my son Simon in her nursery school.

Coming in, to land at Lusaka International Airport, I was inevitably reminded of the time when Andrew was Permanent Secretary in Transport and Works and we had gone out to check on the progress of the new airport every Sunday morning. It was all so familiar as I crossed the tarmac – seemed like yesterday – not a gap of forty two years. That was not the only similarity – the relaxed and friendly welcome as we queued for visas and the warm welcome of friends and family were unchanged.

Ceri and Nonde were to stay at the farm participating in the traditional Bemba mourning and I would be staying with Ann, although both Fitz and cousin Doris at the airport insisted as first wife I must be present for the funeral service.

And then began the New Experiences. Ann set off for Chamba Valley saying the familiar 'You'll find it's all very changed.' So, oh yes, I was prepared, had been prepared – but nothing does prepare you for the changes. Amazing, impressive, disappointing. The first one was a mixture of delight – delight at the space and light and heady quality of the unpolluted air and just being back in Africa – and shock – yes, it was a shock and continued to be a daily shock at the proliferation of hoardings ... billboards ... advertisements jostling for space along the roadside. Who had decided to insult the glorious Zambian countryside with such ugly intrusive things? And how were 'they' getting away with it? Everyone I appealed to over the next few weeks could only suggest that perhaps the City Council was making a fat profit from the rentals for these things.

I am hating myself for making this such an issue at the very beginning, but it coloured my visit enormously. Perhaps all of you who live there have grown used to having your eyes assaulted by endless repetitions to buy this or that, have forgotten how beautiful your garden city of Lusaka was and could still be. Or perhaps you even like this addition to your skyline – for some of these billboard monstrosities are of such heights they do blot the skyline. As for the danger to motorists and pedestrians alike, it is not for me to enquire about the safety aspect of blocked lines of vision - the police department must surely have a safety section?

I leave it there. Who am I to hope for a change in a country I may love but which is no longer mine?

It was disappointing that the long sweep of airport road and the Great East Road which I could recall in such detail were totally unfamiliar - even Chelston where we had bought our first house before independence. But I had been warned - and knew this must be the first of the many changes I would find. Nothing stays the same for ever. The Great East Road from the airport to town had still been flanked by wide expanses of open bush when I left in 1978. Now it is developed.

We had lived in Roma for a while, but I didn't recall anything about adjoining Chamba Valley – it too seems well spaced out, the roads vary from smooth tarmac to patches of potholes of varying depths and multitudes. The houses - when I saw them – were spacious and attractive but mostly hidden from view by walls and fences and huge metal security gates. Security had become a problem before I left in 1978 but had become a bigger issue later; high walls and fencing and gates and security guards had multiplied but even as peace returned and Lusaka became once more a relaxed and friendly place, no one it seemed could be bothered to go to the trouble or expense of removing them. Perhaps even thought it better to leave things as they were - for who knows what the future holds?

Ann and her husband Graham, who had worked at Evelyn Hone College and the Tobacco Board, had decided to retire in Zambia and had bought a plot in Chamba Valley, building a long low comfortable house set in five acres, much of which they had kept as unspoiled bush. Built traditionally with a long shady verandah, it is a haven of peace not too far from the centre of Lusaka. After Graham's death Ann cannot bear to move away, keeping busy with a variety of interests - chief of which is singing in the Cathedral choir – and welcoming all and sundry into her home. It was thanks to Ann that I made contact with people I'd lost touch with and others who remembered me when they heard I was back. The Lusaka bush telegraph continues to work overtime.

Mike and Gill, a farming couple from Choma, were staying with Ann for a few days and I felt as though I'd never been away as we sipped sundowners and then chatted about the weather and the slow start to the rainy season over dinner. Like all farmers, they were concerned the dry season had not broken reliably and so far, the rain had made little impression. I couldn't be sure but had a feeling that I remembered that way back in the early 1960's the rains would start in December, even perhaps in November, and by January the green lush growth would be well established. We were by now halfway through January. This may well be yet another result of global warming.

Friday morning and Ann insisted we set off at nine o'clock – an hour ahead of schedule but as Andrew was to have a State Funeral, Ann anticipated some delay in car parking. From Chamba Valley we joined the Great East Road, I remember the route from there to the Cathedral so very well – as it was in the 1970's! In that short journey with Ann, I completely lost my bearings – the entrance to the university was faintly familiar – the young saplings now sturdy trees. Addis Ababa Drive – which I had known initially as Cecil Rhodes Drive before independence in 1964 – had lost many of its trees and the neat grass verges were a scarred potholed mess. Huge impressive new buildings have replaced the old colonial civil service two storey houses set in spacious grounds at the end of Addis Ababa Drive, and we were nearing the Cathedral without my recognising how we got there. (The endless advertising hoardings had not helped but I am endeavouring not to mention them).

We had not anticipated the roads near the Cathedral being lined with so many military vehicles and buses bearing the names of various choirs. Ann calmly manoeuvred her way through into the smaller Cathedral car park, sure that her choir robes would give us clear passage. Once at the Cathedral, I was on familiar territory.

The Cathedral was filling up and there was a low hum of conversation; quickly spotting the marked and labelled Family, Friends of Family – centre, Diplomatic and Government to the right – I opted for Friends on the left and headed in that direction. Ann wanted to introduce me to Father Charles while we waited for an old friend Jane Kazunga, who had said she would sit with me, when who should we spot but David Thomson, who I last saw as a young schoolboy in shorts. His sister Dawn had been working in Maternity when Ceri was born in 1962 in the European hospital. Now here was David, tall, well-built and middle aged but so recognisable when Ann said his name. We embraced as I had a flashback of his parents Archie and Freda, who had welcomed us into their home in Emmasdale in 1962, Archie had had Scotch Bakery on Stanley Road, now Freedom Way.

Fitz introduced me to niece Dorcas, who in turn introduced me to the family who were seated at the front. I remembered sister-in-law Esther, who I had first met in 1962, and there were nephews, sons of Edward and Abner, Andrew's brothers who had stayed with us at different times.

After the service the coffin was open on the Cathedral steps. Andrew looked peaceful and so ended the sixty three years since we first met in 1957. I was glad the State had recognised his contribution to the development of Zambia with a fitting farewell.

After the service I met Andrew and Danae Sardanis – who have hardly aged over the years -and agreed we would go out to see them at Chaminuka. It was a strange feeling, meeting up with people after forty years - they look unchanged, and the conversation picked up as if we had met the previous day. But underneath, all the intervening years and events were there to be plucked forth ... perhaps.

After the internment at the farm Ann and I drove back down Leopards Hill Road. Driving out I hadn't paid much attention, now returning more slowly, it emphasised how great the changes. Forty years ago, I had left the ten miles of long quiet road, back to town flanked by tall grasses and bush with one or two houses to be seen in the distance ... the turn off to State Lodge ... the turn off to Golsons ... a turn off to Mudenda's (the house had belonged to Harry Franklin, leader of the Liberal Party pre independence) ... none of which could be seen from the road ... Bauleni compound ... I used to enjoy looking out across the land into the far distance in the rainy season as the tall grass swayed like waves in the sea. Now development is everywhere – as is to be expected of a rapidly growing capital – and we met with constant traffic.

Nearer town the small quiet cemetery I had left has spread far beyond the original boundaries and is running alongside the road and what was empty bush is now sprouting shops and buildings in all directions.

All this new-to-me development merged into Kabulonga where Ann suggested we stop to get something to eat. By now I was desperate for a halt to the proceedings – everyone had been at pains to tell me of the changes – but no one had attempted to explain this included a massive upsurge in traffic, which is often left to its own devices where crossroads and junctions are minus traffic lights or sometimes even indications of control. Ann approached these with a caution and confidence I could only admire as I held my breath. The modus operandi seems to be look every which way, assess others' speeds and intentions and slowly but surely ease forward with a casual but grateful hand gesture.

'It does help being both a mudala and a mzungu' commented Ann. 'There is enormous respect for the old in Zambia so it's one good thing about being old and white.'

Kabulonga shopping centre had been one store in my day – very well stocked initially it struggled on during the difficult times, which today's younger generation fortunately can- not remember. Now there is an assortment of shops and stores. We found a small restaurant and fell on to chairs in a corner as far from the music as possible and ordered chicken and chips. It is hardly surprising I was bewildered. Yes, I expected changes and was delighted with my first impressions of a bustling prosperous city – and I had only seen the edges. But I realised that I was still looking for what existed only in my memory.

Lusaka has changed and I must change, adapt. From now on I must accept I have two Zambias and particularly two Lusakas. And I find that works very well. Memories are unchanged, they can't be and have their value. And I can appreciate and enjoy the new Lusaka – and this entitles me to feel free to praise and comment – and criticise if and where I feel like it.

I do not and cannot join those who mourn the old Zambia. I would rather recall with happiness – and it wasn't all perfect to be honest - and accept the new with open arms. And it is easy, so very easy, because what makes Zambia the wonderful place it is ... is the people. The over whelming ambience of Zambia was always her people with their open faces and natural instinct to be friendly and welcoming and - accepting. And the people have not changed. The buildings and roads, the new shopping malls and the spanking new office blocks – all the new developments count for nothing beside the people who welcome you with the same cheerful smile and warm greetings.

Almost immediately I realised Ann wanted to tell everyone we met that I was her 'friend just out from UK who used to live here a long time ago'. The response was always the same – What did I think of the changes? Did I think it had changed? Was I glad to be back? How long was I staying? The shop assistants, the car park attendants, Ann's friends, her workers, the chap behind the counter at Fedex, waiters in the restaurants, the woman selling tomatoes on the roadside ... all and sundry were pleased to see me back, insisting on shaking hands, smiling when I slipped automatically into the double handshake.

We did get home to Chamba Valley after that and relaxed with a walk round the plot. As I said, Ann has left much of the original bush so it was a step back in time to walk through the scrubby grass between the trees following the narrow twisting footpath, which reminded me of doing the same long ago in a different bit of bush.

We were to keep a date for a reading and talk at the Alliance Francaise in the evening – a talk on publishing books by Ruth Hughes where I was amazed to find Malele Phiri, slipping into a seat just in front of us. Malele Chuula (as was of course), she has married, had children, been an MP, become a leading Lusaka figure since those far-off days. But the same Malele, who with her brother Mulilo, had had sleepovers with Ceri and Simon in our home in Roma.

Malele sat down, glanced around, beamed and said, 'Hello there' as if I'd never been away.

The talk and following diverse questions were interesting and it was just as good to talk with a few people. But all too soon we had to slip away, walking to our cars with Anne Phiri – who I'd first met at her wedding to David in Yorkshire when we were on leave in 1965 – once more there was the feeling of picking up quite seamlessly from where we had left off in 1978. It was early days for me to say what I thought of the changes we said, but agreed we were so hopeful back then in the early days. Not for us doubts about independence and the future of Zambia.

So ended my first full day back in Lusaka.

We set off early on Saturday morning to the East Park – Ann had shopping to do and was eager to introduce me to my first shopping mall. I wanted to change some money. Getting there meant braving the traffic and my! How that has changed! It is busy and it is fast and roundabouts are huge with speeding vehicles from all directions. The deep storm drains I remembered but they look deeper and closer after being away and roadworks in progress protected only by a casual tape or none at all made me flinch as Ann happily made her way through. There were endless fleets of minibuses parking on roadsides in the absence of designated bays and then pulling out from the roadsides with little warning. It took some getting used to, but I gradually accepted that the majority of drivers are amenable and cooperative. It all lent a feeling of vibrancy in the bright sunshine.

I had heard a lot about the shopping malls. I had left Lusaka with its centre of three main streets - Cairo Road, Chachacha Road and Freedom Way hardly changed since before independence – and the shops struggling to survive with endless shortages.

The new shopping malls are impressive, now I understand why

people talk about them so often. Enormous with ample parking, they are clean and spacious and a far cry from the one storey low shops with their shady verandahs on the main street Cairo Road, some dating back to the 1930's and 40's. But it wasn't just the size – it was how well stocked they are. Remembering the empty shelves or lack of variety of goods in the 1970's I stared in amazement at the loaded shelves offering whatever you could possibly require. No wonder returning friends had said 'You should see the shopping malls!'

But I'm not a keen shopper so - impressed and admiring. And instead of trailing about to compare exchange rates I headed for a bank to get my kwacha. This proved to be a fairly slow process when my passport disappeared into a back office somewhere. It was hinted to me later that photocopies would have been made. I couldn't think why. It was duly returned with smiles all round and a neat little gadget counted out my fat wad of kwacha notes. And after a few purchases we left. So far, so good. It was all quite different but acceptably so. Odd to go into a store, spend K229.50 and get no change from K230 – no one bothers with coins anymore, explained Ann, they are worth so little. True, I suppose, yet recalling how proud everyone had been of the new Zambian coins when they first appeared it is a little sad. Don't ask me why.

Ann then whipped me round on a mini tour which included other shopping malls and expanses of new roads in varying stages of completeness – totally bewildering and amazing to believe this was all part of Lusaka. As I said, the shopping malls are impressive and later sorties only served to confirm my impression. We always shopped in the early mornings and I appreciated the fact that there were never crowds or long queues although I'm told it's a different matter later in the day, which was a relief – otherwise I had wondered how the shops could make a profit.

Ann decided we should drive home via Kalingalinga which I remembered as an area of mud huts clustered at the end of the old airport runway, there used to be a useful gravel road shortcut from Kabulonga and round the end of the runway through Kalingalinga to the Munali turn off. All changed of course. Now the new wide tarmac road sweeps smoothly through a far more prosperous looking area with busy stores and samples of garden wares, baskets and furniture lining the roadside. There is even a new shopping mall in the process of being built.

Friends Alex and Steve came to tea in the afternoon and we sat out on the verandah for an entertaining talk on politics and economies – not merely an opinion on Zambia but on UK and the EU and looming Brexit and the Scottish independence aspirations. I wondered how many people back in UK would care to spend an afternoon thus – and whether some would have even known where Zambia is. But it has always been so – over the years I have grown used to explaining that I have not lived in South Africa - or even near there. The lack of knowledge and interest in Britain's colonial heritage astounded me back in the 1960's in UK – it is matched now by an ignorance supplemented by a hatred of a colonial system, which most have not actually experienced. There is a determination to reject colonialism out of hand without opening up to the possibility there were some benefits. And no, I am not saying the benefits outweighed the drawbacks and damage. I believe one must accept there were both.

History teaches us no system is ever completely perfect.

Alex and Steve left as the sky warned of coming rains. I watched as the sky darkened, a light breeze blew in and we heard the sound of approaching rain as it crossed the land towards us. Then it landed. This was why I had wanted to come back in the rainy season.

I had wanted to come back in the rainy season because I loved the drama of the heat building up, the sky darkening and the hush as if the land were holding its breath. And then you hear it, you hear the rain coming across the land as the first wave of cooler air sweeps by and then the rain is falling in sheets around you. And sometimes the far-off flash of lightning and low far-off rumbles of thunder – or the sharp crack overhead as purple skies are highlighted by frequent lightning flashes. My first storm since coming back so I just stood on the verandah inhaling deeply as the rain poured down off the roof in watery curtains on to the parched soil. The smell of Africa after rain.

There is even a name for it – the scent produced when rain falls on parched soil – petrichor. From, I believe, the Greek petra - rock or petros - stone and ichor - the fluid that flows in the veins of the gods in Greek mythology. I am quite sure if ever natural scents can be bottled, all the Africa exiles will be first in the queue for bottles of petrichor.

Sunday began with a service at the Cathedral; Ann in the choir and me sitting with her friend Val while the sermon drifted over my head as I began to assess my initial reactions to being back in Lusaka. I had purposely set off with no specific intentions or hopes or even expectations – or so I had thought = but now I was having to admit that unconsciously I had been looking for what I remembered. This could not be so, and I must concentrate on what I was experiencing. Open my eyes to being in a whole new place – and if a reminder of the old days popped up – all well and good.

That sorted and coinciding with the close of service we headed out for lunch at Lilayi Lodge; Ann then announced that she would give me a mini tour of places I would know. She said we would drive a circular route up to Kabulonga and Twin Palms Road then down Independence Avenue to the Kafue roundabout and then on to Kafue Road. This immediately was at variance with my most recent intentions as I found myself looking for what I could remember!

And yes, there were many recognisable features on this brief circular trip. Woodlands water tower , coming down Independence Avenue was familiar, past State House on the right and the Army barracks on the left, close by the very first British High Commission on the right (and lunchtime celebrations of the Queen's birthday on cold June days), past the former Legco and then The High Court on the twin roundabouts, through the traffic lights by the Cathedral, past the Civic Centre (attended state banquet there for President Tito), the traffic lights on Burma Road crossroads (had lived on parallel Elliot Road – now named?), had taught at Lotus Primary (somewhere just back there behind the mosque) ... and I should be seeing the edge of Kabwata market but was set adrift by the growth of new buildings and the overhead gantries with bewildering arrays of signs and advertisements and we were soaring over the flyover and down to the south end roundabout and on to Kafue Road.

So now I should be seeing empty land on the left where we had attended UNIP rallies in 1962 when Kenneth Kaunda and Mainza Chona and Simon Kapwepwe had spoken with such fervour – but now a mass of buildings with a very new Chinese shopping mall. And next should have been the Makeni turn off, petrol station to the left, turn off to the right. Now a massive flyover nearing completion - circumventing the temporary roundabout under it was a slow experience.

Turning off on the Lilayi road took us back to peace and calm once more. A smooth gravel road well soaked after last night's rain and vegetation already taking on a fresher greener hue. And I recalled our first visit there back in 1962 to have tea with Peter and Annette Miller, listening enthralled to his descriptions of his father's early days in Northern Rhodesia and travelling by ox cart – and hoping someone would record it all for future generations.

We sat on the terrace feeling refreshed and inspected the menu. It was a delicious meal in delightful surroundings, fully justifying Ann's lyrical description. I could have sat on much longer, but Ann was suggesting that as it was Sunday we could drive along Cairo Road once we were back in Lusaka. (I had admitted to several people that my only real desire was to go into Lusaka and walk along Cairo Road – everyone had told me that it was quite impossible. No one goes there anymore, they said. There's too much traffic, they said. You can't find a parking place they said and anyway the centre of town gets gridlocked). But here was Ann reminding me that it was Sunday, we should drive along Cairo Road and see it once more – and I should get it out of my head – although she kindly did not add that.

So, braving the underneath of the Kafue flyover we arrived at south end roundabout. Over the years I have mentally strolled along Cairo Road from south end to north end, always on the left-hand side, and then back down the other side past the Farming Equipment on the corner near the Post Office. I had written down the names of the side streets and names of shops, including those which had disappeared over the years. Even slipped through the Arcade, across the sanitary lane, the next bit of the Arcade, out by Guttmans toy shop and on to Livingstone/ Chachacha Road. And so on to the market ... perhaps over to Limbadas.

And now here I was. On Cairo Road again. There had been a garage on the left and a small butchery and Indian store selling fabrics before we reached Kees later CBC – and yes, there was CBC and over to our right Mwaiseni – great excitement when that was built on the site of the original small Boma (later it was a police museum) and we had a two storeys store with an escalator.

There had been Greatermans store, where I did my very first bit of shopping back in January 1962, and next Goodmans, rather too expensive for us then. The buildings are there but names change. And Lusaka Hotel – a dinner there with friends hosted by Andrew and Danae Sardanis, when Rev Papworth pulled the wiring of the sound system from the wall because he hated canned music.

I remembered Grills the jewellers with his own creations in Kabwe silver on the corner and on the side street Dels baby shop nearly opposite the useful three – Overseas Bakery with its wonderful cakes and pastries, the hairdresser and Miladys dress shop.

Barclays bank – the 'new' one is still there with Gabriel Ellison's colourful mosaic, which had replaced the small white colonial style building with steps leading up to the door. Holdsworths Chemist is still there and its name – but Kingstons had moved across the road next to OK Bazaars before I left. Royal Art

Studios – is still there and we were approaching the traffic lights with the Post Office on our right and Tarrys on our left. Lusaka Bookshop, long gone of course but fondly remembered, as was Lotus Chinese restaurant and so many others.

The central reservation with its double rows of flame trees was still there – but the curio sellers had been banished before I left. I hoped to go back another day ... to walk Cairo Road and climb the Post Office stairs to see if box 1358 is still there ... and stand on a street corner... and remember.

Then we reached the north end roundabout where I expected Ann to turn right up the Great East Road. But instead, she turned up the Great North Road saying she believed there was a connection across to Roma – none of this was familiar of course but we found it – more faith than knowledge I would say. Coming into Roma we searched for the nursery school which Ann had run and where my son Simon had had so many happy times. There was the hall next to the church and opposite must be where Mrs Cripps had run her riding school, where Ceri and Simon had had so many enjoyable mornings. Next turning on the right was Kakola Road (no sign to confirm we were right) where we had built our first house from scratch – yes, there it was.

This all sounds so very easy but it wasn't. High walls and fences coupled with very high security gates meant there were so few features to guide us and the absence of many road names was the final straw. There was a sign for the Botswana High Commission, we had been diagonally across the road to the right. Ann paused the car outside a high wall and we agreed that was the place but all I could see now was ... a high wall and a roof - which meant an extra house had been built on the front lawn near the road. The lawns Banda had planted and tended so carefully were probably all gone and I couldn't see the house we had built. I could have knocked on the gates and hoped someone was home, could have asked to look round – but I found that somehow, I didn't want to. Realized I wanted to remember it as it was when we built it and started the garden from virgin bush.

They say you should never go back.

We headed sadly home to tea and a torrential storm, which went some way to cheering me up. Power failed but the inverters kicked in and we had lights again. I don't understand how inverters work, all that matters is that they do. I tried to phone my old friends Goodwin and Mabel but the line was so bad it was difficult to understand Goodie when we did connect but had more luck speaking with Malele and her mother Rosemary. Proper power was restored by 9pm and we went to bed - me beginning to start working my way along the well-stocked bookshelf in my bedroom.

Early the next day we headed for Fedex – a whole new experience. Apparently, the postal system while not collapsed is far from efficient and so Ann, like others, was off to post two letters to UK courtesy of Fedex. I never had a satisfactory explanation; it was suggested by some that letters are not particularly necessary as everyone has cell phones, alternatively it was hinted that the postal workers are so poorly paid that they have lost all interest and pride in their work. A sorry state of affairs and all the more puzzling when I reflect that I have continued to be able to send letters to a friend near Harare Zimbabwe with nary a hiccup.

And then on to East Park shopping mall where I had a Zambian sim card put in my phone courtesy of Airtel - a very helpful chap advised me to invest K100 for four weeks worth of texts. It didn't seem very much to me but he seemed very confident and my passport disappeared yet again for a while. He said there are very stringent security checks but could not or would not explain why. Over the next few weeks, I heard vague comments about money laundering but who and why and how is all a mystery to me and how that would relate to sim cards is yet another mystery.

And that was how my holiday began.

I had set off with only a vague desire to walk Cairo Road once more (I know, I know, you've already heard that) and hopefully reconnect with a few old friends and a few familiar places. What I was not prepared for - was being swept along on a wave of

Welcome Back. I had taken a box of water colours and pads with the expectation of filling in time – apart from some pictures for my old friend Rosemary Chuula of some her favourite remembered English scenes and a couple of hasty Zambian pictures for John and Shupe Whittingham there was never time. The days were filled with invitations to tea and coffee, to lunch and dinner and there were constant meetings here and there, connecting up for shared reminiscences and discussions on the new-to-me developments in Lusaka and thoughts on Brexit, the EU, proposed Scottish independence, the Royal family, our own families – what are all the 'children' doing now? ... the list was endless. I felt a vibrancy in the air and was undecided whether it was a feeling of optimism mixed with contentment or just the warm bright light atmosphere of Africa I had remembered but not experienced for so long and the pleasure of renewed and new acquaintances.

So, it was from Lilayi Lodge to Prime Joint, from Bonanza Golf Club to the Showground, from The Marlin to Three Trees, from Ocean Basket to Fox and Hounds, from Pamodzi to Monkey Bean, from the Ridgeway (which still has crocodiles in its pool) to welcoming homes and my grateful thanks to all those who made it so possible.

The biggest change of course is Lusaka's expansion; from the neat, contained capital with its dated 1930's centre to a seemingly endless sprawl of buildings – from tall city blocks to miles of residential areas. And serving this expansion is the new road network like a bewildering plate of spaghetti. Even in the late 1970's the main tarmac roads soon gave way to the endless miles of gravelled roads. Now everywhere is connected by sweeps of smooth tarmac which will be even more wonderful one day. In the meantime, road signs and traffic controls have not kept pace with construction, roads may not connect fully - we found a new tarmac road ended in a gravelled potholed area which we slowly navigated across to the next stretch of tarmac, and once we found our side of the road was four inches above the adjoining lane. But I'm assuming all this will be rectified shortly.

What did disappoint though was the lack of provision for cyclists and pedestrians. The new roads are impressive but as space in Africa is never an issue and as the majority of the population are either relying on bicycles or 'footing it' why no cycle lanes? Why no space allocated to pedestrians? The latter particularly would not have to be tarmacked - though it would be very nice if it were so.

Add to the equation – minibuses. Public transport appears to be in a decline – I heard that UBZ and Zambia Rail no longer function as before. My parents in law used to travel down from near Lake Bangweulu to Lusaka by bus and rail with nary a problem. Tickets were bought, seats were booked and they travelled. Now I believe that people rely heavily on minibuses – so why not more provision for their parking to pick up and set down passengers? I may be wrong; it may all be in hand and will come to pass in due course.

The rains always trigger conversations about farming and as Andrew's early career was very tied up in farming, it has always been more than a passing interest for me. Farming is always a topic in conversations in Zambia; it has greatly expanded over recent years and much is being achieved by the arrival of commercial farmers from Zimbabwe and I believe South Africa. However, I heard the small-scale Zambia farmers face increasing competition from Chinese, who are coming to settle and farm in Zambia and reportedly undercutting the locals. The small-scale Zambian farmers have long had an ongoing struggle, trying to move beyond subsistence farming – cooperatives have not always been the solution and in the past the Grain Marketing Board was known to let them down. There have been reports over the years of late supplies of seed or collections of harvests. Fortunately, I believe, the Government is determined to make sure agriculture has a more prominent place and lessen the dependency on copper prices. I hope that while large scale commercial farming is both necessary and profitable, that the small scale Zambian farmers will be well protected.

I wonder why solar farms have not proved more popular in Zambia where there is so much more space and at least the sun is more reliable. Of course, I realise that we should not take for granted the immense spaces in Africa – though they are, as yet, largely undeveloped – but solar panels can also be used in towns to great advantage. For example, there are the examples of French car parks where the cars are parked beneath solar panels, thus providing two services, cool parking while electricity may be generated to power the supermarket. But I was informed that while solar farms are a great idea and are being attempted, Zesco won't sign a contract to buy electricity from them (since then I have heard rumours continue that Zesco is being taken over by the Chinese and whether that is true and has any bearings on the matter I have no idea). Hopefully, it should all be sorted out eventually and aspiring students may reap the benefits without resorting to building windmills for each village as one talented youngster in Malawi has done. (Do read the book and see the film – The Boy Who Harnessed The Wind).

Talking about farming and in my mind's eye seeing our recent trip out to Lilayi, made me realise what I missed when we were shopping. Green. Lusaka had always had so many trees and roads were bordered by wide grassy banks and, of course, one used to be able to see large well- tended gardens. Lusaka had truly been a garden city. Now it is a city of buildings, many impressive – but the overall impression is of concrete, glass and tarmac, high walls and security gates. It is exacerbated by residential areas having high walls and gates – no longer can we pass by well-tended gardens with flourishing colourful trees and flowers.

One day there was a phone call from Jay – he had contacted me some months previously having had my email address from a mutual friend. And he emailed me – a former pupil from Lotus Primary in the 1960's; now we were arranging to meet for lunch. While I may recall many former pupils from various schools, I had never expected to be contacted by one – until, that is, my book began to circulate and I'm hearing from pupils now scattered around the world.

A strange feeling – to think of lunching with someone who I last saw in short trousers and carrying the small cardboard suitcase all pupils had. We agreed we should revisit old haunts and headed off to Lotus Primary - spur of the moment decisions don't always work out as well as hoped. The school was quiet, no pupils and there was an air of neglect. We found the swimming pools were overgrown with bushes as we sadly recalled the cheerful cries of children splashing about. Perhaps funds do not keep pace with the great expansion of buildings and pupil numbers?

I mentioned earlier visiting Zambia way back in 1986; on that trip there was only a time for a hasty visit to Lusaka Infants (now Jacaranda) where I'd taught. It too had been a great disappointment; the classroom where I'd spent happy hours with 40 lively five years olds, was devoid of pupils (it was a holiday) - and furniture. The desks and tables and chairs had gone, replaced with a few cement blocks. No, tables and chairs do not last for ever – but I could not believe they had all crumbled away. Both experiences made me reluctant to attempt to revisit Thorn Park Primary, where I had begun my teaching career in Lusaka.

Ann Wallace and Grade 1 Classroom

Later another spur of the moment decision had Ann and I turn into the Dominican Convent School (now Saint Mary's) where I last taught. Here there was an amazing transformation; the long bare grounds I remembered are filled with flowering bushes and trees. An unplanned visit meant we could not meet with the Head, but we did make it into my 'old' classroom, grade 1 at the end of the block and met my successor - a cheerful young woman, who coped very well with a piece of history knocking on the door. And we met a few pupils who are still wearing the same style of uniform so that, for a moment, I felt as though forty years had completely rolled away. I heard that the school continues to have a highly successful academic record. And although a large section of the playing fields have been sold off for the building of yet another shopping mall, perhaps some of the money made its way into the school?

How the grounds have changed!

Being disappointed with the visits to Thorn Park and then Lotus Primary made me rethink my plans for visiting Munda Wanga, the botanical gardens near Chilanga and nearby Mount Makulu Research Station where we first lived. I heard that Munda Wanga is sadly neglected now and felt I could not bear to see it. I don't know whether it is mismanagement or lack of funds and Government support – whichever, it seems a sad loss. Munda Wanga could be such an asset for nearby schools and an extra tourist attraction for those who would like a quiet day, only ten miles from the city centre. I remember Munda Wanga when it belonged to a chap called Sanders, who loved gardening and collecting new species; he just kept extending his garden year after year, eventually opening it to the public at a minimal fee. It was a most popular weekend attraction for those who enjoyed a swim followed by a quiet picnic in beautiful grounds. As he aged, Sanders sold the place to the Government.

Ann agreed I could take her out for lunch again at the Marlin restaurant in East Park (or was it the Arcades? They are close together so I regularly mixed them up). Oh, but it was so good to have a Zambian steak again – that flavoursome melt in the mouth steak – the whole meal only costing K178 – about £8 for the two of us.

The restaurant and its terrace were impeccably clean as was the lower area where we watched in vain for a young woman have anyone take an interest in her table piled high with crafts. It meant we could take our time as I chose some souvenirs for friends back home in UK – warthogs and Guinea fowl fashioned from scrap metal, soap stone chunky elephants, beaded elephant keyrings, beads on leather bracelets and the like. There was a wide range of goods and I was sorry that the young woman was not attracting more custom. It was the same at the church fete we sampled one afternoon and the open air craft fair in the Arcades car park one Sunday morning. Stalls and tables were filled colourful souvenirs in a variety of materials and it was a joy to examine the range of crafts, but again, we were so much in a minority browsing was difficult when constantly accosted on all sides. I felt sorry for people being so creative and working so hard; hopefully increasing tourism will mean more time spent in the capital and more sales for local crafters.

One day I sampled Milton's driving – Milton, Ann's indispensable cook and general factotum. Ann has paid for him to have driving lessons and test, wanting him to have an extra asset for the future. Most days he takes Ann for a drive to maintain his skills. Could this investment in his future be considered a remnant of colonial paternalism? I would argue not. I know of many friends who paid and organised for one or other of their workers to attend cookery classes or night school classes; the employer -

employee arrangement often benefited both.

I was very keen to make contact with old friends Goodwin and Mabel Mutale, friends from before my marriage in 1961 and they were also Simon's godparents. They had moved to a new house but Ann and I had located it and mid-morning saw us outside the usual huge security gate ringing for a guard to open up. The years have treated them kindly, Goodie at 92 looks extremely well. The years fell away as we hugged and exclaimed how wonderful – old friends stay just that – old friends. And we picked up where we had left off, there was much to talk about. Son Christopher, who I remembered as a tall skinny schoolboy, is now a middle-aged chap of course and I could admire the pots he created for Moore Pottery before he settled down to build a successful career. Goodie looked at the copy of my book This Was My Africa with some envy. He has started writing his memoirs too but is having to do so longhand; he added that he had been the top civil service typist long long ago but now when he asked his grandson to get him a typewriter, the lad looked at him, puzzled, 'What's a typewriter?'

Sadly, Simon's close friend, their son Bwembya, died some years ago of cerebral malaria and I felt his loss from the family anew as we spoke of those far-off days. I had taught daughters Carol and Chisha in the 1970's and here was Chisha's daughter, on holiday from her university in South Africa, making us tea.

I always have a pang of guilt when talking with Goodie; he sent me a Bemba Grammar on my engagement to Andrew but as everyone knows, I never progressed beyond a smattering of Bemba and Nyanja. He seems to have forgiven me and has never uttered one word of reproach. It was wonderful to be together again and the time sped by.

John and Shupe Whittingham were over on holiday in their Kalundu home so I stayed there for a few days when we could talk about the changes over the years. And again, our past teaching years caught up with us – Jay having common ground with John talking about Kamwala Secondary and on another occasion when we lunched at the Marlin. No sooner had we all seated ourselves than we were accosted by two tall chaps who greeted John like a long lost brother – or as their long lost teacher, which he was. Reminiscences just had to include updates of their favourite football teams. Staying with John and Shupe meant we could meet up with old friends Kay and David with mutual memories going back to 1962 days in Eastern Province. Sadly, I couldn't stay with them long but had time to complete a couple of small Zambian water colours.

Ceri and I had agreed to visit old friends Andrew and Danae at their home at Chaminuka and I was looking forward to seeing what they had made of the expanse of bush Andrew and I had seen shortly after they initially purchased it. They had talked with such enthusiasm and I hoped they had achieved their dream.

More than.

This is what I've missed - space and light

Chaminuka is an interesting layout – planned initially, as I recall, to be their forever home on, I believe about 10,000 acres, and then moved into being a Lodge with their African art collection for all to visit. It is built on a hill overlooking Lake Chitoka in pristine miombo woodland. The architecture was inspired by African village design with separate huts for sleeping and then insakas, covered areas which have roofs but no walls.

The latter made me think of the Hawaiian villages where early missionaries shocked the locals by wanting walls in their churches, so hiding the views plus restricting air flow.

Apart from people from around the world staying for a few days, it is a popular destination for locals at the weekends. So perhaps it was hardly surprising to be loudly hailed across the terrace by another former pupil from long ago. Cindy Musakanya's 'Auntie June! My teacher!' had many heads turning.

It was satisfying to renew contact and be delighted to see what Andrew and Danae have achieved and are achieving. In addition to the peaceful ambience and being able to view game in natural surroundings, we learnt that they have accepted orphan elephants which are monitored by external wildlife associations.

All too soon the holiday was coming to a close – a few hasty get togethers, a last appreciation of the space and light and unpolluted sparkling air, a last stormy downpour and time to pack a case.

Typically, for me, this was an unorganised holiday with no schedule or pinpointed itinerary; it had only two clear objectives

To experience again the place where I had lived and loved for so long

And to walk along Cairo Road remembering how it was and to see how it had changed.

Nostalgia is a strong sense in most of us and certainly Africa casts a spell over those who have spent any time with her.

I had a wonderful time visiting places, renewing old friendships and making new ones. There were a few disappointments – and many pleasures. It left me with every intention of visiting again and with the realisation I had some unanswered questions.

How has life improved for the 'common man'?

How far has President Kaunda's ideal of humanism been

achieved?

Thinking of the trainee teachers and students we had in our schools, how far have schools and teacher training progressed?

Is the Postal service going to have a resurgence and resume its past efficiency?

Am I glad I went back? Yes, daughter - right again.

Glad to have experienced the new Lusaka – but it was limited. Having set off with no set plans or intentions it was rewarding to find I was impressed in so many ways (very disappointed with the billboards) and had the effect of making me want to visit again and experience more.

I had forgotten the amazingly open friendly society – UK can seem quite introverted in comparison. Perhaps climate has a great effect on lifestyle. Certainly, everyone I met agrees they have an amenable lifestyle in a peaceful country. To anyone who has left and never returned, carries unforgettable memories of life in N Rhodesia and - Zambia ... to those who think 'I'd like to see it again' ... Make the effort and go. Yes, so much has changed and yet, it is unchanged because what matters most are the people.

Sadly since my visit some friends have passed on and are no longer with us – so my decision to see Zambia again has meant even more.

So, in no particular order -

my grateful thanks to Ann for her wonderful hospitality
lunches and dinners, coffees and teas with...
Flavia Musakanya (MHSRIEP), Margaret Chisanga
and Chitalu Mwafulilwa
Goodwin and Mabel Mutale
Barry and Charles Coxe
Jane Kazunga and Wenda
John and Shupe Whittingham
Andrew (MHSRIEP) and Danae Sardanis
Malele Phiri and her mother Rosemary(MHSRIEP)

644

Jacob and Ilse Mwanza
Edna O'Donnell
David Chivers
Jay
Ann and Doreen
Mike and Jill Beckett
Mary Bourne, and Eileen Anderson and Father Michael and
Father Paddy
Fitz and Mercy Kaoma
David and Kay (MHSRIEP) Powell
Eileen Bender
Sally Dean
Alex and Steve
Anne Phiri and Doreen and Heather
Anne and Brigitte and Charlotte
Kelly and Doreen
Di Almond
Val...
Ann, Val, Sally, Mary, Penny, Thea, Jenny and their Book Club
Not forgetting – how could I?
Christopher Mutale
Clive Shamwana
Stelios Sardanis
Cindy Musakanya

(L-R)Margaret Chisanga,
Flavia Musakangya, Ann Wallace,
me and Chitalu Mwafulilwa

Ceri, Fitz Kaoma, and me

Barry Coxe and me

The Mutales, Christopher,
Goodwin, me, Mabel and Ceri

Stelios Sardanis and me

Ceri, me and Cindy Musakanya

Andrew Sardanis and me

Danae Sardanis and me

GLOSSARY OF WORDS IN GENERAL USE

(a mixture of Bemba, Nyanja, Chilapalapa, Afrikaans)

Apamwamba	the elite
Biltong	dried meat
Bonsela	gift (often used at Christmas)
Bundu	bush
Chibuku	maize beer
Chimbusi	latrine
Chitemene	burning off land to clear bush for planting
Chitimulukulu	Bemba funeral ceremony for a chief
Chongololo	giant centipede
Citenge	length traditional cotton print
Dambo	dam or small lake
Fani galor	like this
Fundi	expert
Gari motor	old car (jalopy)
Indaba	business / bother
Inswa	flying ants
Kaballala	thief
Kala pansi	sit down
Kala pansi lapa side	sit down here
	(used often at the beginning of term)
Kalimba	thumb piano
Kapenta	dried fish
Katundu	luggage
Kaya / kia	home (traditional village hut)
Lobola	bride price
Maningi	very much
Maningi shupa	too much trouble
Mbasela	extra
Mdala	old man – a term of respect
Msungu	white person
Mwapoleni mukwai	Bemba greeting
Muli bwanji	Nyanja greeting, used in Lusaka

Muti	medicine
Naajie	tangerine
Nsima	maize meal porridge
Putzi flies	a species of blow fly
Rondavel	round hut / building
Situpa	colonial identity card
Sousa	sixpence
Takkies	plimsolls
Ticky	silver threepenny
Voetsak	go away (rude version - Afrikaans)

ABBREVIATIONS

ANC   African National Congress
BHC   British High Commission
BSAC   British South Africa Company
CIPEC   Intergovernmental Council of Copper Exporting
           Countries
CSB   Cold Storage Board
DC   District Commissioner
DA   District Assistant
INDECO   Industrial Development Corporation
MINDECO   Mining Development Corporation
MSD   Mechanical Services Department
NEDCOZ   National Educational Company of Zambia
OPEC   Organisation of the Petroleum Exporting Countries
PA   Provincial Administration
PCMU   Petauke Cooperative Marketing Union
PWD   Public Works Department
UNIP   United National Independence Party

ACKNOWLEDGEMENTS

African Mail
Central African Post
Drum Magazine
Northern News

PHOTOGRAPHS COURTESY OF DENNIS PROCTOR

Page
63   1962 Cairo Road
65   Mount Makulu Admin Block
90   Thatched hut Eastern Province
99   Main shop in Fort Jameson (Chipata), main shopping
       centre Eastern Province
101   Lundazi Castle
104   Katete – katundu ox cart
106   Petauke rest house
285   Kariba Dam

PHOTOGRAPHS COURTESY OF AILEEN HEPWORTH

PHOTOGRAPHS COURTESY OF CERI KEENE

Printed in Great Britain
by Amazon

15008010R00376